THE OFFICIAL HISTORY OF
Nottingham Forest

First published in Great Britain 1998
by Polar Print Group Ltd., 2 Uxbridge Road, Leicester LE4 7ST, England

Text copyright © Philip Soar 1998
Design copyright Polar Print Group Ltd © 1998

The Official History of Nottingham Forest is by permission of
Nottingham Forest Football Club

ISBN 1 899538 08 9

Text preparation by Peter Arnold
Layout and design by Trevor Hartley
General Editing by Julian Baskcomb
Records based on research and authentication by Ken Smales and
prepared by Dave Smith
Secretarial co-ordination by Penny Lloyd
Public relations by Nina Gardiner
Picture research by Philip Soar

British Library Cataloguing in Publication Data. A catalogue record for this
book is available from the British Library.

Designed and Printed by Polar Print Group Ltd., 2 Uxbridge Road,
Leicester LE4 7ST. Tel: (0116) 261 0800

Photographs courtesy of Colorsport, Nottingham Evening Post, Popperfoto,
Ken Smales, John Sumpter (JMS Photography) and Nigel Wray.

Programmes and tickets used for illustration courtesy of Author's
Collection, Bob Fairhall, Ken Smales and Philip Wilkinson.

The publishers have been unable to trace the sources of all of the pictures
used in this book, but any photographer involved is cordially invited to
contact the publishers in writing providing proof of copyright.

Opposite page: The four badges used by Nottingham Forest in the club's 133 year history. The badge on the top left was the town of Nottingham's coat of arms in the late nineteenth century, although the club did not use it until early in the twentieth. The badge top right is the 'Forester' adopted by the club after the Second World War and used for approximately ten years, notably on the shirts of the 1950-51 Division Three South champions. Bottom left is the adaptation of the City coat of arms used from the mid-1950s until the mid-1970s and still familiar as a blazer badge. The tree on the banks of the Trent symbol (bottom right) was adopted in 1972 after a competition to design a new badge. The badges reflect the four themes that are invariably associated with Nottingham – Sherwood Forest, Robin Hood, the Trent and the Royal Castle. All are intimately linked with each other and the history of the City; more parliaments have been held at the Castle than at any place in the country other than Westminster, Kings John and Richard III spent most of their reigns at the Castle, hunting in the Forest, and Richard rode out from the Castle to his death at Bosworth, Edward III seized the crown from his mother, Isabella, in 1330 by using the secret cave networks underneath the town and Castle, and Charles I began the Civil War by raising his standard at the Royal Castle in 1642.

THE OFFICIAL HISTORY OF
Nottingham
Forest

PHILIP SOAR

POLAR PUBLISHING

Contents

DEDICATION

For my uncle, Ray Bonner, who, with my Father and Grandfather, took me to my first Forest game on Boxing Day 1954.

GARIBALDI, the Italian unifier, pictured on his farm at Caprera in 1865. He is wearing the red shirt and carrying the red cap that was the uniform of his "1000 Redshirts" and which was adopted in exactly this form by Forest in 1865.

Garibaldi had captured Sicily and Naples and proclaimed Victor Emmanuel II as King of Italy outside Rome in 1865. A.J.P. Taylor called Garibaldi "...the most wholly admirable man in modern history".

Apart from short-lived blue shorts in the 1890s, Forest have worn Garibaldi's uniform ever since, and for many years red was recognised solely as Forest's colour. Arsenal adopted red when given a set of Forest kit in 1887 but Manchester United (then Newton Heath) were then wearing yellow and green quarters and Liverpool did not adopt red until the 1890s, and then as a counter to Everton's blue.

INTRODUCTION

T HE true fan is born under a football star. Taken to a game by a father, a brother, a grandfather, he or she is sprinkled by that stardust. And, no matter where life's journey may take him, the real fan is tied for life. At five o'clock every Saturday there is only one name he really listens out for, just one result that quickens the pulse. The emotions that this commitment generates should not be demeaned or underestimated. For the supporters of a genuinely provincial club – and football is still about provincialism – the winning of the FA Cup or the European Cup will be among the three or four most emotional and memorable moments of our lives. How many of us were to shed tears in Munich and Madrid?

Mine was the lucky generation. As children we had the final of 1959, as teenagers we had that astonishing April afternoon when Forest beat Everton in the quarter-final, and the world seemed to be at our feet. At least one generation will attest that this was still the greatest of all games ever played at The City Ground. But then we paid our penance. We went and witnessed defeat at Hull and Carlisle and York and Peterborough.

And then came the fairy tale. At The City Ground in February and March and April 1977 we lost to Luton Town and Notts County and Cardiff City. Two years and a few days later, we were in Munich and John McGovern was carrying the European Cup around the Olympic Stadium. As one German writer said twenty years later: "There has never been a team like Nottingham Forest between 1977 and 1980, and there never will be again. They came literally from nothing and, overnight, became the best club side in the world. No one can explain how it happened. Perhaps the same God that gave the world Robin Hood smiled again on the poor of Nottingham. They must surely lay claim to the title of the most remarkable club team in football history."

And a year later, in Madrid, Forest were to do it again - this time totally against all the odds, with a squad so small that Brian Clough did not even fill the subs bench. And John Robertson, the wonderful John Robertson, scored the goal and left us with the best quote ever made about Nottingham Forest: "I saw it sail towards the corner. And then I thought; "It's going in. It's going in." And then I suddenly felt very tired. It had been a long run by my standards."

Nottingham is the smallest city ever to have won the European Cup. Forest are one of only eight clubs to have retained the European Cup – the names of the other seven are rather familiar. Forest have won the European Cup twice as often as Manchester United, as Barcelona. And infinitely more often than the likes of Arsenal, Spurs, Chelsea, Newcastle or Glasgow Rangers. That is the measure of Nottingham Forest as a football club.

The icons of a provincial city are likely to be a Town Hall, an ancient monument, a famous son, a football club, but we should not be overly blinkered about the latter. Football is a hard and occasionally unfair game played by tough men and run by those who are sometimes looking for their own personal route to fame. But there have been periods when the hopes and fears of whole communities have rested on the exploits of a small group of men who seem to have risen above the commonplace and have been able to carry far more than the prosaic on their shoulders. Forest have had their fair share of these days – the sides of the 1880s and 1890s which were, for a time, among the greatest in the land, the teams of 1959 and 1967 that gradually took Nottingham back to where it surely belonged. And the side of 1977-1980, which will

probably always be the one that the name Nottingham Forest evokes. This was perhaps the best moment, when football could still be a game of genuine loyalty, of flair, of honest commitment, of teamwork and of carrying all the hopes and fears of a city every Saturday afternoon. That was the era of a whole 42 game season without a League defeat, the era when virtually every undefeated and sequential record in the English game was to fall to Nottingham Forest. The trophies and the records seemed to tumble from the sky so fast that they could barely be appreciated then. But history appreciates them now.

A history has to be written in discreet moments. There are too many games to record them all. We must seek that 'one moment in time' which will define an era. With Forest there are perhaps a dozen such moments. The great Cup finals of 1898 and 1959 and 1979 and 1980. Ian Storey-Moore's hat-trick against Everton. Garry Birtles' goal against Liverpool in the first round of the European Cup. John Robertson's penalty at Old Trafford. Peter Shilton's save at Coventry.

But these were not perhaps the summits on which the hopes and fears of all the years rested. The expectation, the tensions, the fear and the fantasies that build up often focus on these very gateways – the moments which teams have to negotiate to have a chance of glory. So to start this history, I have chosen the moment and the goal which, I believe, defines Nottingham Forest. It was Ian Bowyer's goal in Cologne on 25 April 1979, the goal which took Forest to Munich and on to sporting immortality. Although our story has lasted 133 years, that was our moment of truth, our one moment in time.

I would like to thank Peter Arnold for preparing much of the text of this book. I would also like to thank Ken Smales, who helped throughout with pictures, facts and authentication and on whose research the records are based. Trevor Hartley designed the book superbly – despite being a Villa fan – John Sumpter strove to find the photographs and work out how to reproduce medals and Dave Smith spent many hours carefully keying in and cross-checking club records. I would like to thank Penny Lloyd, my devoted personal assistant, who remained cheerful in the face of constant torment and her colleagues Pippa Richards and Anita Alexander. I would particularly like to thank my wife, Lea, and my children, Olivia and Alexander, for their support during the past two, strange years and for their tolerance of my lasting belief in Nottingham Forest. Going to school in Reading, as they do, Olivia and Alexander had to withstand a great deal the day after the crucial match which sent Reading down in April 1998. I would like to thank Larry Lloyd, Garry Birtles, John Robertson, Frank Clark, Martin O'Neill, Ian Storey-Moore, Bob McKinlay, Bobby Houghton, Tony Woodcock, Paul Hart, Steve Wigley, Liam O'Kane and the many others who provided many of the new insights into the past 30 years. It has been my great good fortune to know so many of that wonderful European Cup team – perhaps the greatest club side ever to play the game. As a group, they are without peer. It is easy to see how they achieved what they achieved. How they held together as a group. How they understood their tasks, analysed their progress, survived their manager, laughed at the ridiculous and wrote their everlasting place in history.

Philip Soar
The City Ground
August 1998

Of all the moments, of all the moves, of all the matches, of all the memories this is the one that matters most in the history of Nottingham Forest. The time is 9:15pm. The place is the Mungersdorfer Stadium in Cologne. The date is Wednesday 25 April 1979. The game is the second leg of the European Cup semi-final between Forest and Cologne. The first leg ended 3-3. Forest must win the game to reach the European Cup final. In the whole 25-year history of the European Cup, no team had ever gone away for the second leg of a semi-final needing to win to reach the final and succeeded in doing so. John Robertson takes a corner from the left, Garry Birtles flicks the ball on, Ian Bowyer comes in behind the defender to head the ball home. Cologne 0 Nottingham Forest 1. There are no more goals. Forest are in the European Cup final and Nottingham will become the smallest city ever to win the world's premier club competition *(Colorsport)*.

One moment in time

COLOGNE, 25 APRIL 1979

THE tickets for the 1979 European Cup final were already printed. They had arrived in Cologne. 1FC Köln were ready to start selling them as soon as the final whistle of the semi-final sounded. The Germans had drawn 3-3 in Nottingham. In the 25-year history of the European Cup, no team that had needed to win an away semi-final to go through had ever done so. So why would Nottingham Forest? But the parade had already passed Cologne by – never again were they to confidently prepare for an appearance in a European Cup final. In the 65th minute of the game three young men took two seconds to write the history of Nottingham Forest. Those men were John Robertson, Garry Birtles and Ian Bowyer. The date was 25 April 1979. The time was 9:15 p.m.

Unheralded, unfashionable Nottingham Forest had reached the semi-finals of the European Cup. Two weeks earlier, they had played the first leg against Cologne in Nottingham and managed only to draw 3-3. The scorers were Robertson, Birtles and Bowyer. That meant, very simply, that to reach the final Forest had to win the second leg in Cologne.

A trademark 0-0 or 1-1 draw would not suffice. In their 114 years Nottingham Forest had won just one League Championship, one League Cup and two FA Cups. It was not a pedigree which suggested that they would succeed where so many had failed. They were surely not the stuff of which European champions were made. That was the size of the task facing Robertson, Birtles, Bowyer and colleagues. The Forest dream, surely the unlikeliest football story of all time, was about to end, and at the same semi-final stage where Brian Clough's Derby County had failed in 1973.

In the 65th minute of the game John Robertson took a corner from the left. Garry Birtles flicked it on at the near post. Ian Bowyer came through the ruck of players, stooped low and planted the ball past the formidable Cologne and national keeper Harald Schumacher. 1-0 to Forest. It is the goal that changed Forest's history. It was the most important goal ever scored in the history of Nottingham Forest. Everything that we now think or feel about Nottingham Forest was arguably defined in that single moment. There were to be no more goals that night. Forest went through to the European Cup final in Munich, beat Malmo 1-0 and, as holders, won the title

The scoreboard tells the story; Ian Bowyer, 65 minutes. There were no other goals that night. Exactly two years and 48 days earlier, on 8 March 1977, Forest had lost 2-1 at home to Notts County and were eighth in the Second Division. Now they were in the European Cup final. True Fantasy Football. The Forest team had arrived at their Cologne hotel on the Monday and had spent the evenings in the bar and trained very little. The hotel staff later told Tony Woodcock, after he joined Cologne, that they had been so amazed by this that they pooled all the money they had and bet the lot on Cologne winning, so sure were they that Forest did not stand a chance. The Cologne programme at the time was in the form of a newspaper and very few copies were bought by Forest fans. The Cologne symbol is a mountain goat called the Geissbock, hence the name of the programme. Köln is, of course, the German version of Cologne (*Author's Collection*).

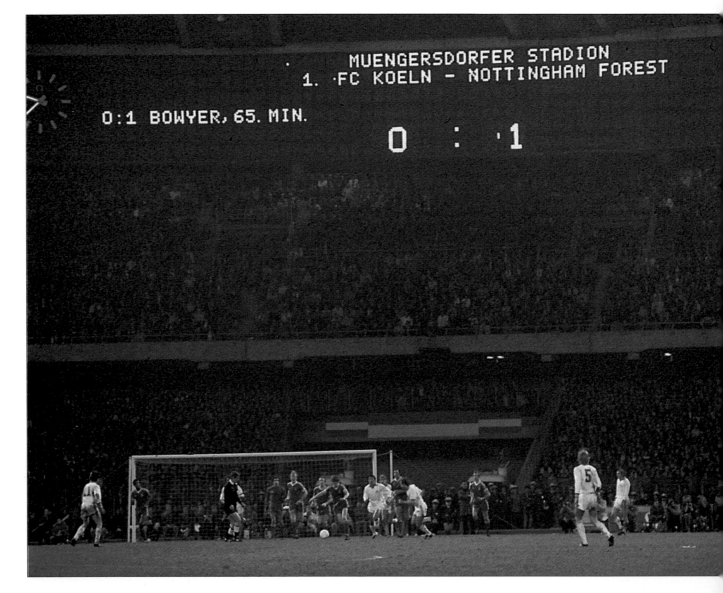

again in 1980. Only eight clubs have ever retained the European Cup. Those eight are the pantheon of the true greats. Read the names slowly. Real Madrid, Benfica, Inter-Milan, Ajax Amsterdam, Bayern Munich, Liverpool, AC Milan and … Nottingham Forest.

Today, let it never be forgotten, Nottingham Forest's name is twice recorded on the European Cup, the world's greatest club trophy. That is twice as often as the names of Manchester United or Barcelona. And infinitely more often than names such as Arsenal, Spurs, Newcastle, Everton or Glasgow Rangers, which do not appear at all. That is the measure of Forest's history, of those two historical seconds, and that trio – Robertson, Birtles and Bowyer.

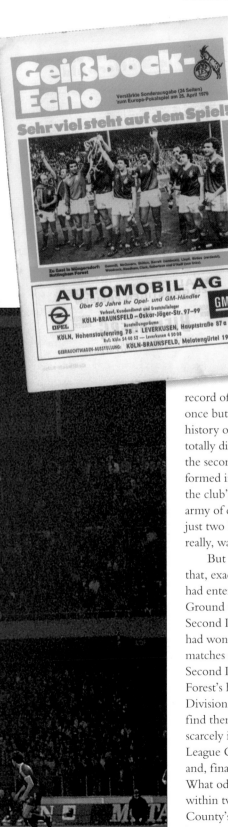

Without Ian Bowyer's goal Forest would have gone home to their prosaic history. They did not win the League Championship that season and they would not have qualified for the European Cup again. Forest still retain the unique, unlikely and surely unrepeatable record of having won their domestic League just once but the European Cup twice. And the history of the club would have no doubt been totally different. Although Nottingham Forest are the second oldest of all English League clubs, formed in 1865 three years after Notts County, the club's trophy cabinet had not exactly kept an army of cleaners occupied. Otherwise there were just two FA Cups – in 1898 and 1959 – and that, really, was that.

But far more remarkable is the knowledge that, exactly two years and 48 days earlier, Forest had entertained Notts County at The City Ground on 8 March 1977. The game was in the Second Division and County won 2-1. Forest had won just one out of their eight previous matches and, at that point, were eighth in the Second Division of the Football League. In Forest's history to that date, eighth in the Second Division is roughly where you would expect to find them. And, at that point, their fans could scarcely imagine the First Division, let alone a League Championship, Zurich, Athens, Cologne and, finally, the Olympic Stadium in Munich. What odds could a punter have obtained that, within two years and three months of Notts County's 2-1 away win, John McGovern would be carrying the European Cup around the Olympic Stadium in Munich, Germany?

A well-known German author has written: "In the whole history of football, there has never been a team that can compare with the Nottingham Forest of 1978, 1979 and 1980. They seemed to rise almost from nothing. They were football's equivalent of the Napoleon of 1797 or The Beatles of 1963. And they deserve those comparisons. For there will never be a story like the story of Nottingham Forest and Brian Clough. In just two years they rose from near obscurity to the greatest prize in the world of club football. No team, from any country, had ever achieved such a feat before. No team will ever achieve that feat again. The Nottingham Forest of the late 1970s are surely claimants for the title of the greatest club team in the history of association football."

Between 8 March 1977 and 7 May 1977, Forest crept up from eighth to third in the Second Division. They never went higher than third. By that date, Forest had just 52 points from 42 games (these were the days when there were just two points for a win) and their season was complete. But Bolton had 48 points and still had three games left to play, including two at home. Forest did not expect to go up and the team went off on holiday expecting the worst. It never came. In their last two games, Bolton lost at home to Wolves and drew away at Bristol Rovers. Forest were up with just 52 points.

Since the Leagues had been extended to 22 teams in 1919, nearly 60 years before, only five clubs had ever been promoted from the Second Division with fewer points. And this simple summary misses the vital, abandoned game against Southampton on 16 February. Forest were losing 1-0 at home after 47 minutes when this game was abandoned. Had they lost or drawn, they would not have been promoted. They won the replayed fixture 2-1 on 22 March. The fog that rolled in from the merciful Trent and led to that abandonment arguably gave Forest their European Cups and was the instrument that rewrote their history.

Of the many clubs which have been promoted from the Second Division in over 100 years, only four had ever won the Second Division and the First Division in consecutive seasons (Liverpool in 1906, Everton in 1932, Spurs in 1951 and Ipswich in 1962). No club had ever been promoted from the Second Division in second or third place and gone on to win the League Championship, and none has since. Welcome to the start of an astonishing three years which broke most of the long-standing records that then existed in first-class football.

Forest were everyone's favourites for relegation the next season 1977-78. Who was going to score the goals? Peter Withe, a much travelled, unrated forward? John O'Hare, surely now at the end of a career with Scotland, Derby

The first leg of the European Cup semi-final against Cologne was at The City Ground on Wednesday 11 April 1979. Peter Taylor had done the scouting and told the team in the dressing room before the match that Cologne were the slowest team they had faced all season. "Doncaster Pork Butchers - all that usual stuff," says John Robertson today. "They came out like lightning and were two up after 15 minutes," adds Martin O'Neill. "I remember, after the second one went in, all of us turning round to look at Peter on the bench. When we won in Cologne someone said to him 'Whatever you do, please don't go and see Malmo before the final'."

Top left: Martin O'Neill shoots wide after 20 minutes, when Forest were already two down.

Centre left: Garry Birtles heads the precious first goal after 27 minutes to make it 2-1.

Bottom left: John Robertson's famous diving header in the last few minutes seemingly to complete a glorious comeback at 3-2. "It is the only diving header I ever scored - apart from one at Grantham in non-League," says Robertson.

Top right: Martin O'Neill tries to dig the ball out of the appalling mud with just a minute remaining. As the old Bridgford scoreboard shows, Cologne substitute Okudera had added a late equaliser to make it 3-3. David Lacey's report in *The Guardian* carried the unforgettable headline: "Japanese sub sinks Forest".

O'Neill offers a particular insight into this match, which he regards as the most memorable and most intense of all the games he ever played for Forest. "What I remember, as if it were yesterday, is that Robbo's brother, Hughie, had been killed in a car crash a few days before. We all knew Hughie, a lovely man, and we had no idea whether John would be able to play until the last moment. We all felt terrible about it. And then John comes out and

pulls us back to 3-2 with that amazing diving header. Whatever the Cologne coach said about Robbo before the game it certainly wouldn't have been 'Watch out for his diving headers'. Of all the games, that's the one I remember most." Robertson doesn't agree: "Manchester United, when we went there and murdered them 4-0. That's when we knew we had arrived."

and Leeds? Tony Woodcock, literally an unknown? And how would the defenders cope with the likes of Liverpool and Arsenal? Larry Lloyd, surely past his best after Liverpool and Coventry? Kenny Burns, the archetypal bad-boy of the game? Frank Clark, a free-transfer from Newcastle? Viv Anderson, a very young, very inexperienced right-back from a Nottingham Council estate?

But, at the end of that season, Nottingham Forest were, for the first and only time in their history, Football League Champions, just one year after sneaking into the First Division almost by statistical fluke.

And the League Championship led to the European Cup, and a first round draw against the one team Forest could surely never beat home and away – Liverpool. Mighty Liverpool. Champions of Europe in both 1977 and 1978, looking for a hat-trick to match the feats of Real Madrid, Ajax and Bayern. It could not have been harder. But it happened, Forest won 2-0 at home and drew 0-0 away. And then eventually the road lead to Cologne and, gloriously, to Munich.

Ian Bowyer says of his goal in Cologne that rewrote Forest's history: "I remember it very well. It was a standard move. The perfectly placed corner from Robbo, Garry's flick, and surprisingly, a lot of space to knock it in. When I look at the pictures now, what strikes me is how young we all look. Look at Tony (Woodcock).

He's like a waif. Look how thin Garry is. Look at Kenny. But we always thought we'd win. I can't remember having many doubts. I can't think why! But it was really Peter's (Shilton) save on the near post at the end that got us to the final. I remember that as well as the goal."

Brian Clough remembered the interview he had given to Gary Newbon of Central Television after the first leg at Nottingham. "Well", said Gary, "that's that then, Brian." Clough's response was: "Absolute garbage. Let's see how valuable Cologne's three away goals turn out to be when we get there." Clough adds that he and Peter Taylor simply told the players that they were the better team and to get on with it.

The goal in Cologne came from a classic set-play, the flicked-on corner kick. Arsenal still use it as a standard ploy. "It was the only one we ever practised," say John and Garry, twenty years later. "We used to practise it in the mornings, but the gaffer and Peter never bothered with any other set plays. Clough and Taylor used to wander down to the training ground mid-morning, walk the dog round the pitch once or twice and head back to the warmth," says Garry. "Training wasn't too onerous. Perhaps three mornings a week. Often we'd arrive at 10:30 and be back in the dressing room by 11:30."

After the goal in Cologne, the defence held out easily. But Shilton, who had blamed himself for two of Cologne's three goals in the first leg,

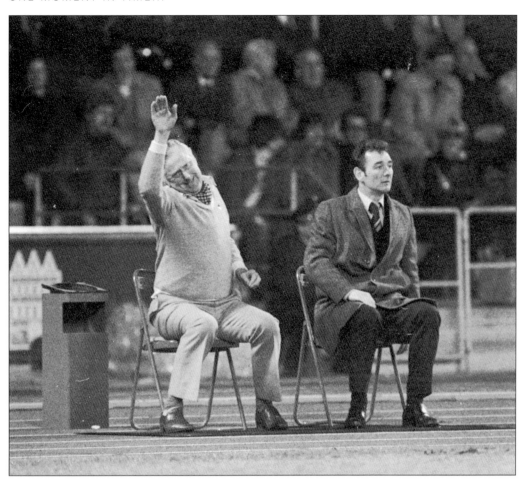

Left: There were no conventional dug-outs at the Mungersdorfer Stadium, so Brian Clough and Peter Taylor found a couple of chairs and took them down to the touchline, where they sat in splendid, if unconventional, isolation. They can also be seen conversing to the right of the goalpost (bottom right picture). After the first leg, Central TV's Gary Newbon had suggested to Clough that the tie might be over. Clough disagreed: "Garbage. Let's see how valuable Cologne's three goals are when we get over there."

Bottom left and right: Garry Birtles has flicked Robertson's cross on and Ian Bowyer stoops to conquer as Kenny Burns and Tony Woodcock look on. "We never had many doubts about winning," says Ian Bowyer today. "At that period, even if we were a goal down with three minutes to go, we always thought we could find one from somewhere."

Above: Goalscorer and goalkeeper celebrate at the end of the game in Cologne. Ian Bowyer says today: "It was really Peter's (Shilton) save on the near post at the end that got us to the final. I remember that as well as the goal." Says Shilton: "Although I say it myself, the shot from full-back Konopka was terrific. It swerved and did everything. I saved it going to my left and remember thinking I had balanced the scales for a poor display in the first leg." *(Nottingham Evening Post/Colorsport).*

still had to make his excellent near post save from Cologne's full-back Konopka in the last minute. Shilton remembered: "Although I say it myself, it was a terrific shot. It swerved and did everything. I saved it going to my left and I remember thinking then that I had balanced the scales after what had happened in the first leg." And that was that - Forest were the most unlikely side ever to reach a European Cup final.

Well, perhaps not the most unlikely. That probably went to the team who were to be their opponents in Munich on 30 May 1979 – Malmo FC. Forest's semi-final win was the defining moment because it made possible the overwhelming perception about Nottingham Forest. What does the club stand for? Simple.

Two European Cup wins, Robin Hood and Sherwood Forest. Had Ian Bowyer not scored his goal, then Forest would have been worthy losers on the away goals principle. But the distinction between winning and losing at this stage is utterly fundamental. Six years earlier, Derby County, also under Clough and Taylor (and, amazingly, also abroad when they learned of their Championship success through their rivals' unexpected failure, also at Wolves), had similarly won the League for the first time and had reached a European Cup semi-final. They drew with Juventus in Derby, without two key players, McFarland and Gemmill banned after being given yellow cards in the first leg in Turin, which Derby lost 3-1. That first result has ever since been regarded as highly suspect and the subject of numerous journalistic enquiries into refereeing morals. Nonetheless, Derby were out and, though they won the League again in 1975, who now instantly recalls their European record? Yet they came so close. The same would surely have been true of Forest. A great European run, memories …but nothing more. The club would be something else – not the astonishing team that had won its own League just once, but the European Cup twice.

The result in Cologne still seems remarkable

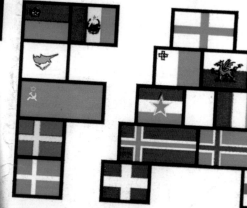

ENDSPIEL
Europapokal der Landesmeister
MALMÖ FF – NOTTINGHAM FOREST

Europäische

Fußball-Union

Offizielles
Programm
1,50 DM

Deutscher

Fußball-Bund

Mittwoch · 30. Mai 1979 · 20.15 Uhr

Olympia-Stadion München

Foto: In den letzten beiden Jahren gewann der FC Liverpool den Europapokal
...bun Hughes jubelt. Wer holt diesmal den Cup? (Foto: Sven Simon)

EST

LOGNE

lubs' Cup

11th APRIL, 1979

Vorkontrolle

Euro

SPIEL-NR.

24

KAU

WEDNESDAY, 7th MARCH, 1979
(or any re-arranged date)
KICK-OFF 7.30 p.m.
EUROPEAN CUP, 3rd ROUND, 1st LEG

FOREST
v.
GRASSHOPPERS ZURICH
THIS TICKET ADMITS BEARER TO THE
EAST STAND

£3.50

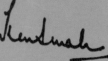

Secretary

This portion to be retained for inspection

ENTER
VIA B
CAR P
TURNS

BLOC

S

ROW

H

SEAT

7

WEDNESDAY, 11th APRIL, 1979
(or any re-arranged date)
KICK-OFF 7.30 p.m.
EUROPEAN CUP, SEMI-FINAL, 1st LEG

FOREST
v.
I.F.C. COLOGNE
THIS TICKET ADMITS BEARER TO THE
MAIN STAND ENCLOSURE

£6.00

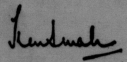

Secretary

This portion to be retained for inspection

ENTER
PA
RO

ROW

ZI

SEAT

199

Mementoes of a European Cup run from the collection of Forest director Bob Fairhall. The two tickets from the 1979 Cologne semi-final (bottom) and the Munich final (bottom right) have not, despite appearances, had their corners gnawed away during tense moments. The standard method at German stadia is to tear off corners of each ticket at various stages of entry. Tony Woodcock was transferred to 1FC Koln during the following season and discovered that the German club already had tickets ready for the final in Munich. They were so confident of going through that they intended to start selling them as soon as the second leg against Forest was finished. The Cologne club were completely distraught after the match. Only one German-speaking team had ever won the European Cup and it had been expected that Cologne would contest a Munich final with Vienna WAC. In the event Malmo beat Vienna 1-0 on aggregate and Cologne have never since challenged for the premier European title *(Courtesy of Bob Fairhall).*

after all these years. Surely the team could not have been so confident of the result? "Yes," says Birtles. "We were tremendously confident. The point was that we rarely conceded a goal. The game in Nottingham when we drew 3-3 was a pure aberration. No-one thought that we would lose the second leg. No-one. We didn't know how we were going to score – but we had so many options." Larry Lloyd is almost as certain: "Yes, we were confident. We had big Shilton at the back. Then if they got past Kenny (Burns) and me, they'd still got Shilts to beat. But it's a brilliant compliment to us defenders that Garry and the other forwards (Tony, Trevor, Martin and John) always had that confidence. What they always used to say – and they were certainly saying in Cologne – was that we only needed to score one goal. That's because they trusted the defence to keep a clean sheet. And we did."

"Actually," says Lloyd today, "we went into that Cologne game very relaxed. We knew we couldn't possibly play as badly as we had in the first leg and, as no-one expected anything, we couldn't really lose. We were in Cologne for a couple of days before the match and, although you couldn't speak the language, you could read the body language. The Germans thought it was all over. They really did. Kenny (Burns) and I used to think the same about a game. If we went in early and got it right first time – if I got the first header in against the centre-forward or Kenny got the ball away with the first sliding tackle, then we were confident we could do it that night. Robbo (John

Robertson) told me after the game that I'd done something after 15 minutes he'd never seen me do on the field before. I was running back towards our goal with a German forward. The ball was bouncing. My job was to pass it back to Shilts or to clear my lines – boot it clear. But I flicked it over my head, turned and pushed it upfield. I'd never done it before and I never did it in a game afterwards. Yes, we were confident."

Birtles says that he knew it would be OK after about 20 minutes. "Dieter Muller, their international centre-forward, had been spouting off about how they'd got it won before the match. We didn't like that. Larry said: 'He won't be spouting much longer.' After 30 minutes he was off. Larry and Kenny had sorted him out."

The club went to Munich for perhaps the least heralded of all European Cup finals up to that time. Nottingham and Malmo are the smallest cities ever to provide European Cup finalists and, by chance, they were to meet each other. For the Germans, it was a massive disappointment – they had been expecting a sell-out Cologne versus Vienna WAC final.

It wasn't only Garry Birtles who was confident of winning the final: "We were never going to lose the final. We knew it would all be

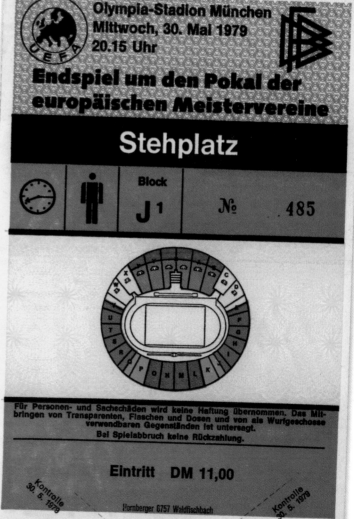

one way traffic. We knew they would just get ten men behind the ball. We knew it would be a slog, but we knew we would need only one goal." Philip Soar, chief executive 20 years later, drove all the way to Munich with his American wife Lea (her first ever game) and 30,000 Nottingham fans. "In 44 years of watching Forest, I can honestly say it is the only time I never considered the possibility that we could lose. After Cologne, it was our Cup."

Bobby Houghton was the young, English manager of Malmo and naturally saw it differently: "We knew we were the underdogs, but, having got there, anything was possible. After all, we had got to the final. My problem was that six of my best players were injured and we had to defend for that reason as much as any other." Malmo were unique in many ways – most notably because all 11 players came from that small southern Swedish city, another feat never repeated by any European Cup finalist.

"I saw Brian Clough before the game," says Houghton. "He was very friendly and we compared notes. He said he'd tell me the key to the game – but not until afterwards. The key was, of course, John Robertson. I knew that anyway. We tried to mark him man-for-man but he was very clever. Most players, when they are marked man-for-man, run around to try and lose their marker. He didn't bother. He stayed where he was, where his team-mates could find him. And he only needed four yards to get the killer cross in. That's what happened." There was only one goal. A cross from the left in the 45th minute by John Robertson. Trevor Francis – playing his first ever European game – met it beyond the far post and headed it just inside the post. Francis then rolled on to the shot-putt circle of the stadium (built for the 1972 Olympics) and looked as though he would injure himself. He didn't, and that was, to all intents, the end of the match.

It was perhaps inevitable that John Robertson should be the man who made the goal that won one European Cup and, a year later, scored the goal that won another. If one was forced to pick a single player from the great Forest team of 1977-1980, then it would be John Robertson. Arguably the most unlikely of heroes, Robertson joined Forest as an apprentice in 1970. When Clough arrived, Robertson was a fringe player – overweight, a smoker, a drinker. "A lazy slob" as Clough described him. But he was to provide Clough with what Alan Hinton had given the Derby of five years earlier – the outlet on the left. He could play the ball perfectly with both feet. He was never fast over ten yards, but dynamite over three or four. Larry Lloyd, who had played against Robertson and remains one of his closest friends, describes Robertson's technique: "Every

full-back thought they could get him. They thought they could pin him down, outrun him. They could outrun him, but it didn't matter. You'd see it time after time. His big fat arse would go to the right, and so would the full-back and 30,000 spectators. But John would go to the left, make a yard, and in would come the cross. I don't think he knew how good he was. He probably doesn't even now. He didn't realise the effect that he had on the whole team. He gave everyone confidence and he never missed a game. He was always there. The other thing that helped him was that we were a left-sided team – myself, Archie Gemmill, Frank Gray, Frank Clark, Peter Withe, Tony Woodcock. Our natural tendency was always to go to the left. It drove Martin (O'Neill) mad. He'd run up and down the right-hand side all day and never get a ball. No wonder he never got on with Cloughie."

The 1979 European Cup final was not a great game nor a glorious victory. But it put Nottingham Forest in the history books alongside Real Madrid, Benfica, AC Milan, Ajax, Bayern and Liverpool, only the third English club ever to win the European Cup and still the smallest city ever to produce the winner. It was still less than two years and three months since Forest had dropped to eighth place in the Second Division. Sometimes fairy tales do come true.

So how could it – did it – happen?

Bobby Houghton had been at Malmo for eight years when he took them to be the first Swedish club to reach a European Cup final. Over the previous three years Malmo had experienced a superb run of results – beating Bayern Munich, Inter Milan, Dynamo Kiev, Vienna WAC and knocking St Etienne out of the European Cup, the first game the French side had lost in 47 matches.

But his side had lost six of its best players before the 1979 final and both Houghton's central midfielders had to drop back to play centre-back. Bo Larsson, the club's best player, and later twice leading goal scorer in the Bundesliga, was one of the six missing, and, to compound matters, Stefan Tapper, a crucial component of the side, broke his toe with the last kick of the final training session before the match. Tapper played for the first 20 minutes after a pain-killing injection, but his substitution further disrupted the side.

"We had two 17-year-olds and two 18-year-olds," says Houghton today. "But if we had played Cologne in the final, we would still have won. Our style of play was perfectly suited to taking on German or French teams. In those days they still played it slowly from the back – a dozen passes to get forward. We were very organised and hard working. We made the space in which they could play very small. In that sense, we were very like the English teams of the time, which is why we would have preferred not to meet one in

Below right: After 45 minutes of the European Cup final against Malmo at Munich's Olympic Stadium, in comes John Robertson's cross, up goes Trevor Francis and it is 1-0 to Forest. There were no further goals. Garry Birtles, to the left of Francis, says: "The best decision I made that night was not to go for the ball. As it came across I thought 'I can get that' but I saw Trevor coming in and pulled back. Had I tried, it would probably have come off the top of my head and Trevor would

NOTTINGHAM FOREST

Peter SHILTON
Viv ANDERSON
Larry LLOYD
Kenny BURNS
Frank CLARK
Trevor FRANCIS
John McGOVERN
Ian BOWYER
John ROBERTSON
Tony WOODCOCK
Garry BIRTLES

MALMO

Jan MOLLER
Roland ANDERSSON
Kent JONSSON
Magnus ANDERSSON
Ingemar ERLANDSSON
Stefan TAPPER
Anders LJUNGBERG
Robert PRYTZ
Jan Olof KINNVALL
Tommy HANSSON
Tore CERVIN

Substitutes used:

Tommy ANDERSSON
Claes MALMBERG

One of the oddities of the game was that there were four Anderson/Anderssons on the pitch at the end and Malmo had a fifth who would have played if not injured.

have missed it." Francis's thoughts were more of self-preservation: "As I threw myself at the ball I saw the shot-putt circle coming at me and remember thinking 'This is going to hurt'. But it turned out to be made of rubber and I just bounced off it." Brian Clough said that John Robertson's cross was the single most satisfying moment in the manager's whole career: "When I sit in my garden and close my eyes I can still see that moment in Munich when Robertson made his move. Peter Taylor stiffened beside me and grabbed my arm. Robertson is not far from the corner flag. There are half a dozen Malmo players in the box. Trevor Francis is hurtling towards the far post, and Robbo sends over the perfect cross. One - nil. Pass me the European Cup. Thank you." *(Empics/Peter Robinson).*

the final. Forest, like most English teams, played a 4-4-2 which gave them balance and compressed the space and is still the best structured of all the formations. They moved the ball forward quickly and, with all the reserves in, we couldn't really counter them."

Nonetheless, Houghton does not feel that the result was a foregone conclusion: "I really thought we could win, as long as we worked hard enough and made it very difficult for Forest. The problem was that they had so many good players. If I had to pick just one who I would have liked in my team, I suppose I would have chosen John Robertson, but then they had Trevor, they had Woodcock and Birtles in the middle, the centre-backs were very strong and then there was Shilton in goal. We thought that Archie Gemmill, who had not played since the semi-final, being out would be a plus for us, but Ian Bowyer had an excellent match."

Houghton is interesting on why he and Malmo, with a team of local players from a small Swedish town, were so successful. "The same reason, as far as I can tell, that Brian Clough was so successful. You have to support the players. You have to create the right environment for the players. They have to feel confident. If they feel that they are respected and that you really believe in them, then they will respond. I know this doesn't appeal to the macho side of football – but it is a subtlety and with a Clough and Taylor transmitting their confidence, you saw it work in Nottingham."

So much has been written about Brian Clough that it is difficult either to add to it or to throw any new light on why he achieved what he did. There can be no doubt whatsoever that Brian Clough has only one challenger for the title of England's greatest ever club manager. That man is Herbert Chapman and he and Clough have a number of things in common. Both were Yorkshiremen and both took two totally unfancied and undistinguished teams to their first ever League Championships. In Chapman's case, it was Huddersfield and Arsenal. In Clough's it was Derby and Forest. Both Chapman's teams were to complete a hat-trick of Championships (though Chapman was with neither in the third year), whilst Clough's success was comparable in three times reaching the later stages of the European Cup. Kenny Dalglish – who has managed Liverpool and Blackburn to Championships – arguably has a right to be included among the notables, but in neither case did he build poor, undistinguished clubs from zero to the heights.

Twenty years later, the players can't really put their fingers on the key to Clough's success. Clough seems a remote figure, brimming with confidence but mysterious in his ways. Was it picking the right players, great players, or players who blended? Or a mixture of all of these? "Peter Taylor was equally important," says Garry Birtles. "He was very funny. We all used to look forward to his team talks on Fridays. They were

hilarious. He used to check all the doors and cupboards to see whether there was anyone listening. On one occasion, a couple of fans got in down the corridor. Peter couldn't believe it – he was completely paranoid. Assumed they'd been smuggled in. But he always calmed everyone down and played the perfect antidote to Clough. You couldn't over-estimate how important his humour and warmth were."

Larry Lloyd is equally complimentary about Taylor: "He always did his homework. He went to Perry Barr dog track to follow Kenny (Burns) around when he was thinking of signing him. Wore a flat cap to conceal who he was. Wanted to see what kind of guy he was. Eventually Kenny left and Peter found him trying to hot-wire his car (at least I think it was his car) outside the track. Kenny had lost his ignition key weeks before. Peter would come into the dressing room and have a great time. He'd throw Robbo's desert boots out of the window or door – horrible, brown things they were. Robbo never wore anything else. He'd grab *The Sporting Life* off Frank Gray or Peter Shilton or Martin, and berate them. When he was enquiring about players, he'd ask: 'Does he drink? Does he gamble? Does he smoke? Does he womanise?' No one did better than two out of four, but two out of four weren't bad, according to Peter. He'd sign you on that basis."

Larry Lloyd still muses on how Clough did it. "When I give speeches, people always ask the same questions. Was he a genius? Was he lucky? Well, maybe he was lucky – but twice? It's unlikely. But look what he did when he got to Forest. He inherited a couple of good players in John Robertson and Martin O'Neill, plus youngsters in Viv and Tony (Woodcock). Then he went and got John McGovern and John O'Hare and Archie (Gemmill) from his old Derby

squad. Then he signed Peter Withe – 'What a dopey signing' they all said. Been in South Africa, Southport and all that. But what happened? He went on to play for England and when Clough sold him before he could get a European Cup medal, he went and got one of his own with Villa. And off the post! Then he picked me up for £50,000 because I was so unhappy at Coventry that I'd go anywhere. I never really liked him and I took a drop in wages, but he had this sort of confidence. Then, in the summer, before we won the League, he went and bought this wild man, this neanderthal from Birmingham. We couldn't believe it. Peter Withe and Tony Woodcock immediately said they were out of business because Kenny had been playing up front for Birmingham. But we had a few training sessions and Brian suddenly said in the dressing room one day, 'Kenny, let's play you at the back with Larry.' It was a complete surprise. I don't know whether Cloughie had always had that in mind, or whether it was a hunch that just came off. But it did, and I'd still say we were the best back trio (with Shilts) that has played the game since the war. The run of 42 games without defeat was built on that trio and no-one will ever do that again.

"I remember very well," continues Lloyd, "that Clough never gave me a lot of direct advice. But he did, on one particular day, when I'd done something stupid, say one thing: 'Just head and kick the ball'. Bill Shankly had said exactly those words to me six years earlier at Liverpool. Admittedly, Cloughie added: 'And then give it to someone who can play.' But the interesting thing is that they used exactly the same words.

"There was never any key man for Cloughie. His key man was whoever was having a hard time with the crowd – John McGovern or Archie or

Martin O'Neill perhaps. Then he'd usually back them to the hilt. "They'll be my captain forever," he'd say the next day or something equally supportive. Well, maybe Martin was the exception. They never seemed to get on."

Garry Birtles puts much of the success down to the team spirit that was developed over that era: "They were a very intelligent group of players and we won everything with only around 15 of us. We were incredibly close - we still are really. We gelled perfectly. We'd come back from abroad, all pick our cars up and then all go off to have a drink and a meal together and we'd been in each other's pockets for days! It was an astonishing time. I suppose the truth is that all great teams gel - that's crucial to their success. But what the magic ingredient was - I just can't say."

Clough's tactics were certainly never revolutionary. He did nothing to compare with the development of the third back and three forward game that took Chapman's Arsenal on to glory, nor the tactical switch to 4-4-2 that won the World Cup for Alf Ramsey. Clough's formation was essentially the same with both Derby in the early 1970s and Forest in the late 1970s. He used a flat back four with his central defenders as the core (McFarland, Todd and Hennessey at Derby, Lloyd and Burns at Forest). He employed two central attackers who could roam as required (Hector and O'Hare at Derby and Withe/Birtles and Woodcock at Forest). He had one "spare" man who, in both cases, was the number 11. At Derby it was Alan Hinton for his speed and dead ball ability, while at Forest it was John Robertson. Clough then had a three-man core midfield. The two key members at both Derby and Forest were to be the same - John McGovern and Archie Gemmill, with Ian Bowyer and Martin O'Neill being the two extra men at Forest. It was always a counter-attacking formation and Forest generally looked as strong

Below: Brian Clough as football remembers him - shouting instructions from the Forest dug-out with Peter Taylor at his side. "He's probably telling us to hold-it and turn," says Garry Birtles today. "That was always the creed. Forwards had to be the first line of defence. When the ball came out you had to go deep to collect it, give the defenders time to get out of the penalty box. And you had to be prepared to turn and go at the defenders. Some managers just want you to lay it off, but Brian had been a centre-forward and he knew what defenders didn't like. 'It scares the s*** out of them if you turn and run at them,' he used to say." (*Colorsport*).

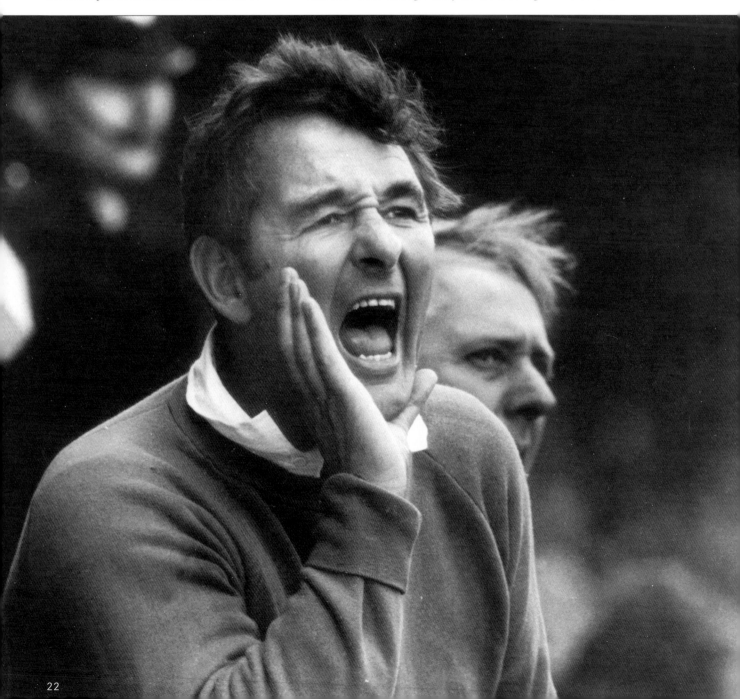

away as at home. The goals came from throughout the squads, with Derby's Kevin Hector being perhaps the one exceptional goal-scorer in Clough's two Championship winning teams.

The number of players who were to appear for both Forest and Derby over this period was remarkable – Henry Newton, Frank Wignall, Terry Hennessey, Colin Todd, John O'Hare, John McGovern, Archie Gemmill, Alan Hinton, John Robertson, Peter Shilton, John Middleton. Only in the case of the talismanic Ian Storey-Moore did either of the boards put their collective feet down over this peculiarly incestuous relationship, and that became the most celebrated non-transfer of all times.

It inevitably all comes back to the enigma that is Brian Clough. Only Herbert Chapman can rival Clough for the title of England's greatest soccer manager, but Chapman is a straightforward character in comparison.

Brian Clough was born on 21 March 1935 in a council house in Middlesbrough. He was the fifth of eight surviving children. His father, Joseph, worked at a local sweet factory. He joined his local club, Middlesbrough, in 1951 and played in their first team from 1955 to 1961, when he joined local rivals Sunderland. In October 1959 he won his only two caps – versus Wales and Sweden. In 274 Football League games, he scored 251 goals. This gives Clough an average of 0.916 goals per game, the highest goals per game average ever achieved by any major English footballer. On Boxing Day 1962, playing for Sunderland against Bury, Clough chased a long ball into the box and collided with the Bury keeper, Chris Harker. Clough had torn the cruciate ligaments in his knee. He had already scored 28 goals in 28 games that season, but did not play again until September 1964. By then, Sunderland had been promoted to the First Division and Clough managed to play just three games in the highest division (271 of his 274 appearances had been in the Second Division), before it became clear that his career was over. He was 29 and, after a short spell on the Sunderland youth staff, found himself unemployed. On the night of his testimonial game at Sunderland, Clough was approached by the Hartlepool chairman, Ernie Ord (on the advice of Len Shackleton) and offered the job as their manager. He thus became the youngest manager in the Football League.

As a diversion, it is perhaps a good moment to recall that Brian Clough managed five clubs (Hartlepool, Derby, Brighton, Leeds and Forest) over a period of 28 seasons. Under his management, these five played 1,140 League games, of which they won 505 and lost 344. They scored 1,678 goals and conceded 1,298. He won three Championships (the Second Division

with Derby in 1969 and the League Championship with Derby in 1972 and Forest in 1978). Of the 20 seasons he managed in the top division, only twice did he finish lower than ninth. Twice he was first, once second, and on four occasions third. But just how did he do what he did?

Clough himself has never offered any real explanations, apart from his occasional protestations of infallibility. He was, however, always proud of his ability to pick players. He has commented at various times about the key members of the Forest squad. Here is a small selection:

Clough on Frank Clark: "Frank was a symbol of ... our success. What a signing! What a team! What a manager I must have been! Frank joined us a year before the European Cup win. Doug Weatherall, the *Daily Mail's* man in the North East, rang me and said: 'Newcastle have dropped a clanger. They've let Frank Clark go on a free.' 'Where is he?' I said, 'Can I have a word with him?' Doug explained he was in Doncaster, talking to their manager, Stan Anderson. I couldn't have that. Stan had been a colleague of mine at Sunderland. Signing Frank to play in the Fourth Division! So I told Doug to get hold of Frank and tell him Cloughie wanted him. Frank turned up at The City Ground the next day and signed within half an hour."

Clark's most memorable game, according to Clough, was when he was put on as a sub for Peter Withe. "'Where do you want me to play, boss?' he said. 'Bloody well play at centre-forward.' I said. 'I've just pulled Withey off haven't I?' So he went up front, and scored his first League goal at the age of 32. Tony Woodcock, who was sitting next to me, said: 'The others will never get a bloody ball from him again you realise. Just look at him. One goal in a lifetime and he's after a hat-trick!'"

Clough on Kenny Burns: "It was Taylor's idea. 'Forget it,' I said. 'I don't want trouble-makers, I don't want s*** houses, and I don't want an ugly bastard like Kenny Burns littering up my club.' But Taylor was right. He persuaded me. That was his job."

Martin O'Neill, who rarely agreed with Clough, did agree with him on Burns. Asked at the 1997 Reunion Dinner who was the best player he had ever played with, O'Neill answered: "I don't know about the best, but I can tell you who was the ugliest. They wouldn't show Forest highlights before 9:00 p.m. in those days you know." Kenny, to his everlasting credit, seemed totally unfazed by this, proceeding to explain to Martin which of them really knew how to play the game and delicately asking him how often Martin had been voted "Footballer of the Year": Says John Robertson. "I still have a vivid picture of Burnsey in a match with Liverpool. He turned angrily on Kenny Dalglish and pointed a finger at him. That's all he did – pointed a finger. It was reminiscent of Dave Mackay."

Clough on Martin O'Neill: "I inherited him. I looked on O'Neill as a bit of a smart-arse, and I can't say I was altogether dismayed when he didn't take over from me following my retirement at Forest. I far preferred Frank Clark and I told the directors so." In fact, the directors didn't necessarily agree. Martin O'Neill was offered the Forest job and asked to be able to bring his own staff, particularly John Robertson as his deputy. The board wouldn't agree to the condition and Martin didn't take up their offer. As Forest were relegated in 1997, Martin and John were taking near neighbours Leicester City to the Coca-Cola Cup final and into Europe.

Clough on Archie Gemmill: "We nicked him for £25,000 from Derby. We threw in our goalkeeper John Middleton in part-exchange, and we should have let them have half our reserve side as well. Gemmill comes high on our list of 'best signings'. How we managed to get a player of such courage and talent for so small a price, I'll never know. He was a 'steal' – he was that good a player. I know he never forgave me for leaving him out of the 1979 European Cup final. Knowing him, he would have run and run all night whether he was fully fit or not. But you don't take risks in a match of that magnitude and, even though Archie and Martin (O'Neill) insisted they were fit, I left them out."

Clough on John Robertson: "Some people claim that he epitomises the method, style and secrets of my technique. That's for others to decide, but there has never been any mystique

Top left: Kenny Burns holds the League Championship trophy on the occasion of its first ever visit to Nottingham. The date was 29 April 1978, prior to a goalless draw with Birmingham in front of 37,625 spectators. It was back, without quite the same meaning, on 5 May 1998.

Above: Archie Gemmill, Martin O'Neill and John Robertson prepare a familiar wall in 1978. O'Neill and Robertson had been at the club since the early 1970s and had both put in transfer requests shortly before Clough arrived. Their's was a close

friendship, despite some ups and downs: "I fancied myself as a dribbler when I first arrived," says Martin today. "But after one youth or reserve team game I was sitting next to John in the dressing room and he said 'If I gave the ball away as often as you do, I'd give the game up now.' I don't think I was too pleased. John never worried much, but I always did. I didn't just worry about how I did, but about how the whole team played. That was because I always thought that if the team played badly, I'd be the one to be dropped."

about the way I have worked. Nevertheless, the tubby little Scotsman provides me with a memory that is still the most satisfying. When I sit in my garden and close my eyes I can still see that moment in Munich when Robertson suddenly made his move by the left touch-line. The anticipation, that something special, caused Taylor to stiffen and grab my arm. Robertson is not far from the corner flag. There are half a dozen Malmo players in the box, Trevor Francis is hurtling towards the far post, and Robbo sends in the perfect cross. One – nil. Pass me the European Cup. Thank you."

It still doesn't explain quite how Brian Clough did what he did. Michelle Gaunt, manager of the ticket office at Forest and a young part-timer during much of Clough's reign, describes how he appeared to the staff: "I enjoy

reading all the newspaper comments about how Brian Clough did this and that and why didn't the people stand up to him more often. I'd like to have seen some of these journalists in a room with him. They have no idea what it was like – the power of the personality, the pressure he was able to exert. I remember going to his office one day, walking in and suddenly he threw a cricket ball at me. I was a bit surprised but I caught it OK. Then he sat me down and asked me about my father (who was President of the Nottingham Panthers) and my family. I was only a teenager. No one ever knew what was coming next."

John Robertson, by common consent the core of the great European Cup team, remembers the Cologne game well. "I always took the corners. It was our only real set piece. We were known for it. I'd clip the ball to the near post and

Garry, Larry or Kenny would usually be there. I remember against Cologne that they brought someone to the near post to prevent the move, but Garry got the touch anyway. We didn't practise it much. In fact we didn't practise anything very much because we never had the time. We played so many games that we didn't seem to need to practise much. If it wasn't the League or the Cup, we'd be off on one of Cloughie's foreign tours. We didn't even have any other standard moves from the edge of the box. There was no free-kick specialist. We didn't get many free-kicks on the edge of the box anyway. We were a very honest team, so we rarely went down in a tackle. I really can't even remember a single goal from the edge of the area.

"We'd had that terrible first leg at home against Cologne of course. They'd caught us cold at the start. Peter had come into the dressing room before the match and told us they weren't up to much – 'Doncaster Pork Butchers' – you know, the usual stuff. Before you could blink, we were two down. So much for pork butchers. Then we got back to 2-2 and I scored with a diving header in the mud to make it 3-2. It's the only diving header I ever scored – well, I once got one for Grantham years later. Then Okudera, their Japanese winger, got an equaliser. 3-3." "Forest sunk by Japanese sub," adds Garry Birtles.

"I can only ever remember us conceding three goals like that in about two other games. Cologne was a complete one-off, but we never had any real doubts going there. We just needed the one chance – and we got it."

Despite reports to the contrary over the years Robertson never much concerned himself with Clough's criticisms. "My mother did though. She got very upset when he called me a tramp and a boozer. He'd ring me up and ask 'Is that bacon I can hear sizzling in the chip pan?' He was never convinced about my eating and drinking. He used to call me a wreck. I was always in trouble with the fags and the whisky. It was a bit cat and mouse. We were off to the Far East on one of his trips and were staying at one of the Heathrow hotels. I had a bet with him - £100 I think it was – that he'd have a drink before I had a fag. By about 10 o'clock, I couldn't stand it any more and slipped up to my room to have a cigarette. After a few minutes, someone knocked at the door. So I guessed what was coming, and put the fag out. It was Ronnie Fenton (Clough's deputy). He asked me some question or other and left. So I thought 'That's alright then,' and lit up again. Within four seconds, another knock at the door. I opened it, holding the cigarette, and there was Clough. He looked at me and said 'It's alright, if you don't tell

anyone I won't. I'm desperate for a drink.' When we got to wherever we were going, I had to hide behind a rubber plant in the hotel lobby for a smoke. Clough knew where I was and came and stood in front of the plant watching the smoke rise to the ceiling. I stayed behind the plant for five minutes and Garry and the boys distracted him somehow."

"Clough was very determined," says Robertson. "You could feel the energy when he came to the ground on the first day. He just walked into the dressing room, took off his coat, hung it up and set to work straight away. He'd walked through reception, called to the girls in the general office to put the journalists in the Trophy Room and said he'd be back by 5:00 p.m. Then he took us straight down to the training ground. Started right from the first minute."

"It was about a month before he introduced himself to everyone" says Lloyd now. "He used to come into the dressing room at 2:45, put his squash racket down (Birtles was his preferred partner) and immediately tell us just what to do.

The programme and match ticket from the 1980 European Cup final. While avoiding the dreaded 'Notts', Real have still managed to spell Nottingham wrong on the front of the programme.

Madrid, Wednesday 28 May 1980. Forest's second European Cup final and one they entered as underdogs. The time is 8:51 p.m. The game has been under way 21 minutes. John Robertson plays a one-two with Garry Birtles, who falls but gets the ball back. Robertson shrugs off a challenge from Keegan and hits the ball right-footed. "I could see the ball curling away towards the far corner and I thought 'It's got a chance. It's got a chance'. It just went in beside Rudi Kargus's right-hand post and I couldn't believe it. I held up my hands and thought 'I've scored. I've scored in a European Cup final.' That wasn't like me at all, that's why I remember it so clearly. And you have to remember that I was very tired. It was a long run by my standards."

NOTTINGHAM FOREST

Peter SHILTON

Viv ANDERSON

Larry LLOYD

Kenny BURNS

Frank GRAY

Martin O'NEILL

John McGOVERN

Ian BOWYER

John ROBERTSON

Gary MILLS

Garry BIRTLES

Substitutes used:

Bryn GUNN

John O'HARE

HAMBURG

Rudi KARGUS

Ivan BULJAN

Peter NOGLY

Manfred KALTZ

Dietmar JAKOBS

Holger HIERONYMUS

Felix MAGATH

Gaspar NEMERING

Wili REIMANN

Kevin KEEGAN

Klaus MILEWSKI

Substitute used:

Horst HRUBESCH

He had an elephant's memory for football. Could remember everything and everyone," says Robertson.

" 'It's a simple game made complicated by f***ing coaches,' he used to say, and that's how he played it", says Robertson. "The best moment? No doubt about it – it was our 4-0 win at Old Trafford in the Championship season, that was the moment we knew we'd really arrived. Personally I suppose the goal in Madrid was special. I played a great one-two with Garry, who was tripped but still got it back to me. Did brilliantly. My momentum carried me forward.

Keegan tried to come in from the side but I held him off, and hit it right-footed.

"I could see it curling away towards the far corner and thought 'It's got a chance, it's got a chance.' It went in just beside the post and I couldn't believe it. The feeling after I'd scored was astonishing, that sense of occasion. A European Cup final, the whole world watching. I held my hands up and thought 'I've scored.'

Above: Larry Lloyd's exquisite balance carries him away from a tackle by Hamburg's Kevin Keegan during the 1980 European Cup final. Keegan was grudging in his praise of Forest, commenting 20 years later: "After the final in Madrid, I didn't visit the Forest banquet. I am a bad loser and was too gutted by the defeat. Neither was I a lover of Forest. We lost to a poor shot from John Robertson. Rudi Kargus was normally unbeatable from that distance, and it was a soft goal to concede." Lloyd recounts a moment from the tunnel as the teams were waiting to come out: "We'd been at Liverpool together of course, so we knew each other. I said to Kevin: 'I don't want to mention this, but Burnsy isn't feeling very friendly towards you today.' We both turned round and there was Kenny staring at us just as he was taking his teeth out. It was a terrifying sight. Kevin started up front and gradually went backwards as the game went on."
(Colorsport)

Above: Bryn Gunn clears at The City Ground. Gunn, who had only played three games at full-back in the 1979-80 season, was one of Clough's four substitutes. Forest were entitled to five but Clough, uniquely in a major final, chose not to fill his quota. When Gunn came on for Frank Gray late in the game, Garry Birtles heard Peter Taylor remark, in perfect management style, "Christ, we are in trouble now!" Including his European medal-winning appearance, Gunn played 170 times for Forest in a ten-year career *(Author's Collection).*

Right: Martin O'Neill harasses Hamburg's German international full-back Manny Kaltz during the 1980 final. "The Hamburg game was enormously important to me because I had only been on the bench against Malmo and it had been my boyhood dream to do what Puskas and Di Stefano had done," says O'Neill. "It was vital to play well because Hamburg was one of the few games Brian ever thought he might lose. The side was not as strong as it had been in 1979, Trevor had done his Achilles and Stan Bowles had just gone missing." Larry Lloyd is more direct: "I think he picked that 4-5-1 line-up because he didn't want to get stuffed 4-0." *(Colorsport).*

Left: The front page of the Madrid sports daily on the day of the 1980 final and the morning after.

Not at all like me really, but I remember the feelings so well. I was also very tired, remember, it was a very long run by my standards. There were six magnificent players that night in Madrid – the back four, Garry and Martin. They ran their socks off."

Garry remembers the last few moments when he got clear, ran half the length of the pitch and then collapsed in the penalty area. "It seemed like I was on the end of a fishing line, being reeled in back to our own goal. I thought I was going to die."

The team had been banned from going out that night in Madrid by Clough and Taylor, but Robertson, O'Neill, Lloyd and Gray set off into town. "We got back at 6:30 a.m. and were sitting at the bar playing a fruit machine," says Lloyd.

"Peter Taylor suddenly materialised in the bar. 'You up all night playing that?' was all he said. He knew where we'd been." Robertson debates why they had been curfewed. "The only thing I can think of is that they thought we'd lose. Remember that Trevor (Francis) was out with a torn Achilles and Stan Bowles had simply gone missing. Clough didn't even pick the five subs he was entitled to – he only put four on the bench (a unique occurrence in any major football event). To start with, Peter (Taylor) had seemed thoroughly confident – 'We're going to pummel them down the left' he kept saying. 'That Manny Kaltz, he can't defend.' It didn't last. By kick-off they'd decided on a 4-5-1 with Garry alone up front." Lloyd is convinced that Clough expected to lose. "He picked a team to avoid a 4-0 embarrassment. It's the only time I think he ever went into a game really afraid to lose. It was a strange game. It all seemed to be about Keegan and Hamburg, even in the English papers. Forest, despite being European champions, were almost regarded as makeweights."

Lloyd recalls how he was on a coaching course at Lilleshall soon afterwards and the management there wanted to make Forest's tactics in Madrid a whole afternoon. "It was brilliant," recalls Lloyd, "They kept saying 'How did you do it? How did you plan it? Whose decision was it to remove the second striker and play five across the middle? That's what destroyed Hamburg.' Brilliant!"

"Well," says Lloyd now, "it was a bit embarrassing really. I tried to explain that Trevor was out, that Stan Bowles had refused to get on the plane and that we really weren't sure what would happen. Heavens above, Cloughie already had one youngster on the bench (Bryn Gunn) and apparently couldn't even think of anyone worth making fifth sub. And we were supposed to be European champions. I tried to explain that Brian and Peter thought it up in the dressing room and we had about an hour to talk about it. I don't think anyone believed me. Interesting that we still won the European Cup, isn't it?"

For Martin O'Neill, the Madrid final versus Hamburg was a moment of truth: "The Hamburg game was enormously important to me because I had only been on the bench against Malmo. It had been my boyhood dream to do what Puskas and Di Stefano had done and it was incredible that I could be involved and could do this thing.

It was doubly and trebly important because I had missed out on Malmo, although I did get a medal. It was very important to play well because Hamburg was one of the few games Brian ever thought he might lose. The side wasn't anything like as strong it had been in 1979 with Trevor (Francis) being injured and he'd had to throw in young Gary Mills. We arrived in Spain on the Monday and Peter Taylor was walking up and down the bus telling us how Hamburg couldn't play but by Wednesday he'd obviously changed his mind and ordered Kenny (Burns) and Ian (Bowyer) both to keep an eye on Keegan. The only other game I can think of that I remember him having real doubts about was when we drew Liverpool in the first round of the European Cup. I remember that 18 of the other 20 First Division managers said that Liverpool would win it. He always said he was very grateful to those other two managers for believing in him. It is possible

Below: Familiar place, unfamiliar angle. The 1980 European Cup-winning team hold the trophy aloft on the balcony of Nottingham's Council House.

Right: John O'Hare and Larry Lloyd (plus unlikely headgear) celebrate on the Council House balcony. Unlike the FA Cup, there is no single "real" European Cup. Real, AC Milan, Bayern and Ajax all retained the trophy they won and Forest have their own copy in the club's Trophy Room *(Nottingham Evening Post).*

that I was rather more paranoid than most of the team. John never used to worry too much, but then he was the key to the whole thing. I used to spend my time worrying not only about how I did, but also how the team did. That was because I always felt that if the team played badly, I would be the one they would drop. They say that only the paranoid survive but I suppose I couldn't have been that bad because I played 38 in the undefeated run of 42 games, and 38 in the championship season. Really I wanted to play central midfield because I always thought I could add running and strength to that position. I played there when we beat Barcelona 1-0 in the Super Cup and really played well, but when we got off the pitch Cloughie said: 'Don't worry, when McGovern's fit, you'll be back on the right again'.

"The Hamburg game was terribly important because I'd been injured three weeks before the Malmo final the year before and I was never really sure that the club tried that hard to get me fit. I went to a wonderful physiotherapist in Mapperley called Norman Collins. I owe my winner's medal from Munich entirely to him. He worked on me and worked on me to try to get me fit so I could play. I didn't play, but it was Norman who got me on the plane and on the Monday morning before that game, I ran round and round the track in Munich. Cloughie was amazed but my suspicious mind kept telling me that he really wanted to play Trevor (Francis) anyway. Trevor had not played in any of the previous games because of qualification rules but was available for the final. In the end, Cloughie called Archie (Gemmill), Frank (Clark) and myself over to one of the corners – actually the corner Robbo crossed from for the goal – and sat us down. 'Are you all fit?' We all said yes of course. He said, 'You're all lying and I can only risk one of you'. He chose to risk Frank and I don't think Archie ever forgave him. I have to say though that if it had been the day after we beat Cologne he would have picked us all, and if I had left the club the night after Munich, I don't think I would have ever forgiven him either. The sense of loss for me was immense because it was the one game I have ever been involved in that I was convinced we couldn't possibly lose and simply by not being selected, I was being denied a European Cup winners medal. If we'd thought about it at the time, we'd have all agreed that it was very unlikely to ever happen again and it really was a one off. So when we got to the final the following year not to play would have been heartbreaking. Against Malmo Trevor took my place and he was a very fine player. But it was very peculiar because we were a very tightly knit bunch of players and Trevor had to come in having not been involved in the gestation of our success."

"I still feel we didn't really get the

recognition," says Robertson today. "If we'd been wearing Arsenal or Tottenham shirts and done the same things we did you'd never have heard the last of those three years. The papers would still be full of it all today. I used to say to people: 'Terrible that European Cup. Made my arms ache something terrible. Really heavy you know. Dreadful to have to drag it round with us. Really heavy – and for two whole years dragging it about everywhere. It was so heavy that Cup. Terrible cross we had to bear'.

"When I left Forest, I thought it was time for a change," continues Robertson (who moved to Derby in June 1983). "My contract was up at the end of the season and I got a cartilage injury at Manchester United. Clough made some comment about it being bad timing for me, and when Peter Taylor suggested Derby, I thought I'd go there. It was a mistake, but I learned a lot. I certainly learned that all the talk about the play always going through me was nonsense. Not that I'd ever really believed it. I realised how much I needed the rest of the team. That I needed them to make me effective. That short time at Derby brought it home to me. Forest were a genuinely great team. Great players. Great people. Bright people. I hope that our principles at Leicester are the same now as Clough and Taylor had then. We try to play football. We try to make the players realise that we believe in them. We try to make them feel involved, though Martin (O'Neill) has to be a bit aloof."

Whole Brazilian rain forests have been cut down analysing Robertson's relationship with Brian Clough. "I always liked him actually. Martin didn't – he'd always argue. But I respected what he knew about football and that he knew how football should be played. He wanted it on the ground, to feet. He never talked about the opposition. I've played with managers who made you feel battered before you even went on the pitch – always going on and on about the opposition. Clough made you believe in yourself. 'If you get one, you'll get five,' he used to say to us. He knew how to make me feel good. If I'd done something well, he'd call me from the dugout and signal to me by putting two fingers together in a sort of O shape. Well done! it meant. It made me feel great. It's an overused word, but how do you define charisma? He was the sort of man who made a room go quiet when he walked in. You knew he was there, even if you couldn't see him."

"He was teacher's pet," says Garry Birtles, pointing, but Robertson just laughs. "Clough wasn't afraid of reputations," they both agree.

"He made everything very clear to me," says Robertson. 'Turn round,' he'd say. 'That's all you have to do.' Today you see players playing the ball off straight out. They don't turn. That's what I learned to do. Most important lesson ever. 'Hold the ball and turn …' he'd call out. And he was always shouting: 'Hold it.' It's a crucial part of the game. You have to have players who can hold the ball. Even for a few seconds. That gives the midfield and the defenders the time to come out and relieve the pressure. Garry (Birtles) was magnificent at it, so was John O'Hare. They'd hold the ball up front for long enough, and they'd stop the opposing centre-half from knocking it straight back in. At Leicester we drive it into them all the time – hold it, hold it, give the defenders time to get out. The principles don't change."

There is another side to Brian Clough, a more difficult side to write about and a more difficult side to analyse. But because of Clough's utterly central position to the history of Nottingham Forest, if should not be ignored. As a child, Clough was clearly the dominant personality in his family and his school class. He was a skinny, quick-witted patter merchant, who was afraid of no living authority. In an era of silent obedience, teachers had nothing but endless argument from Clough. He was always the boss. And this is the very personality that seemed to suffuse his whole managerial career, the very core of his success, and perhaps, his eventual decline.

Of the thousands of articles that were written about Clough and his methods, the best was probably by James Dalrymple. It is quoted at length, because it's doubtful if his words can be bettered. Dalrymple explains how Clough's treatment at Sunderland had led him to believe that there was no trust and loyalty in football and that money could dry up as quickly as it appeared. He vowed, as time went on, that he would not be short changed when it came to contracts, to sponsors, to media deals.

Dalrymple argues that: "The full flowering of this strategy came at Nottingham, where the board of directors were largely his servants, to be toyed with, insulted and manipulated at will. So powerful was he that he insisted on being club manager rather than team manager, with total control over everything from the gate receipts to the building of a £5 million stand and the selling and buying of players at will."

This analysis is broadly accurate. Clough totally dominated the club. With his success, it

Right top: The greatest of all Nottingham Forest teams, photographed in 1979.
Top row, left to right: Gary Mills, John Robertson, Ian Bowyer, Colin Barrett, David Needham, Viv Anderson, Kenny Burns;
Centre row: Martin O'Neill, John O'Hare, Jim Montgomery, Peter Shilton, Larry Lloyd, Jimmy Gordon;
Seated: Garry Birtles, Tony Woodcock, John McGovern, Peter Taylor, Brian Clough, Trevor Francis, Frank Gray.

Right bottom: Eighteen years later, most of the team reassembled for a reunion dinner in August 1997.
Top row, left to right: Gary Mills, John Robertson, Ian Bowyer, Frank Clark, Viv Anderson;
Centre: Martin O'Neill, John O'Hare, Peter Withe, Larry Lloyd, Kenny Burns;
Seated: Garry Birtles, Tony Woodcock, John McGovern, Trevor Francis, Archie Gemmill.

All of the players won European Cup winners medals, although Peter Withe did so with Villa in 1982 and Archie Gemmill did so as a substitute. The only medal winners who are not in either picture are Bryn Gunn and Chris Woods.

This page: Garry Birtles' European Cup winners' medals from 1979 and 1980.

became impossible for anyone to argue. Those that did were frozen out. Unlike at Derby or Leeds, at The City Ground there was no controlling shareholder or shareholders, just seven committee members or directors with, ultimately, just one vote each out of 209 votes in all. Together they controlled just three per cent of the club. In the face of a personality like Clough's, they were powerless. It was never in anyone's apparent interest to rock the boat. Forest already had the example of neighbours Derby to learn their lesson from. Derby had had Clough, they had their Championship but they had chosen to break the neck of the goose that laid the golden egg. The board of Nottingham Forest would not make the same mistake and it was Forest's very weakness which eventually proved to be its surprising strength. Because the club was still essentially an amateur set-up, it was not able to resist giving Clough complete control. Until 1982, Forest was literally just a club – no different from a team playing on the local park or a local golf club. And by then it had twice won the European Cup. It was only when the massive cost of the Executive Stand dawned on the 200 or so members, that one of those members, Brian Appleby, decided Forest must have the protection that a Limited Company brought. It was the weakness of the structure, with its seven non-executive committee members and no full-time executives at all, that allowed Clough to do as he wished. As he had seen at both Derby and Leeds, the more formal football structures of chairmen, owners and the like would inevitably eventually remove him. His abrogation of the powers of chairman and of senior players there ultimately became too much and, even though it was likely to be to their club's eventual detriment, they felt they would rather have respect and uncertainty than have Clough and success. Because of Forest's unique structure, this was never to happen in Nottingham.

According to Dalrymple: "It was at Hartlepool that Clough and Taylor developed a method of playing that was to take them right to the top in only a few years. They both regarded it as a simple game, in which stopping the other team from scoring was more important than getting goals themselves. You began building a good defence, then looked for that one spark that turned a workmanlike team into a successful one. The spark often came from just one key player, either a seasoned pro of undiscovered genius around whom the whole machine could flourish, or a couple of young talents who could be moulded according to their theories. By Derby, Clough was becoming a media superstar, appearing on football panels and chat shows, the master of the hilarious put-down and taunter of every football authority in the land. Everyone, regardless of age or status, was addressed as 'young

RECORD RUN OF 42 LEAGUE GAMES UNDEFEATED

Date	V	Opponents	Result	Scorers
26 Nov 77	H	West Bromwich Albion	D 0-0	
3 Dec 77	A	Birmingham City	W 2-0	O'Neill, Woodcock
10 Dec 77	H	Coventry City	W 2-1	O'Neill, McGovern
17 Dec 77	A	Manchester United	W 4-0	Woodcock 2, Robertson, B.Greenhoff (o.g.)
26 Dec 77	H	Liverpool	D 1-1	Gemmill
28 Dec 77	A	Newcastle United	W 2-0	Needham, McGovern
31 Dec 77	A	Bristol City	W 3-1	Needham, Woodcock, O'Neill
2 Jan 78	H	Everton	D 1-1	Robertson (Pen)
14 Jan 78	A	Derby County	D 0-0	
21 Jan 78	H	Arsenal	W 2-0	Needham, Gemmill
4 Feb 78	H	W'hampton Wanderers	W 2-0	Woodcock, McGovern
25 Feb 78	A	Norwich City	D 3-3	Withe, Barrett, O'Neill
4 Mar 78	H	West Ham United	W 2-0	Needham, Robertson (Pen)
14 Mar 78	H	Leicester City	W 1-0	Robertson (Pen)
25 Mar 78	H	Newcastle United	W 2-0	Robertson (Pen), Anderson
29 Mar 78	A	Middlesbrough	D 2-2	Woodcock, O'Neill
1 Apr 78	H	Chelsea	W 3-1	Burns, O'Neill, Robertson
5 Apr 78	A	Aston Villa	W 1-0	Woodcock
11 Apr 78	A	Manchester City	D 0-0	
15 Apr 78	H	Leeds United	D 1-1	Withe
18 Apr 78	H	Queen's Park Rangers	W 1-0	Robertson (Pen)
22 Apr 78	A	Coventry City	D 0-0	
25 Apr 78	A	Ipswich Town	W 2-0	Mariner (o.g.), Clark
29 Apr 78	H	Birmingham City	D 0-0	
2 May 78	A	West Bromwich Albion	D 2-2	Bowyer, Robertson (Pen)
4 May 78	A	Liverpool	D 0-0	
19 Aug 78	H	Tottenham Hotspur	D 1-1	O'Neill
22 Aug 78	A	Coventry City	D 0-0	
26 Aug 78	A	Queen's Park Rangers	D 0-0	
2 Sept 78	H	West Bromwich Albion	D 0-0	
9 Sept 78	H	Arsenal	W 2-1	Robertson (Pen), Bowyer
16 Sept 78	A	Manchester United	D 1-1	Bowyer
23 Sept 78	H	Middlesbrough	D 2-2	Birtles, O'Neill
30 Sept 78	A	Aston Villa	W 2-1	Woodcock, Robertson (Pen)
7 Oct 78	H	W'hampton Wanderers	W 3-1	Birtles 2, O'Neill
14 Oct 78	A	Bristol City	W 3-1	Birtles, Robertson 2
21 Oct 78	H	Ipswich Town	W 1-0	O'Neill
28 Oct 78	A	Southampton	D 0-0	
4 Nov 78	H	Everton	D 0-0	
11 Nov 78	A	Tottenham Hotspur	W 3-1	Anderson, Robertson, Birtles
18 Nov 78	H	Queen's Park Rangers	D 0-0	
25 Nov 78	A	Bolton Wanderers	W 1-0	Robertson

man'. The phrase became his signature. He had a taste for fame and gradually, according to those close to him, he began to believe that he could do no wrong. Players and fellow managers said they often felt they were taking part in some dramatic production acted out for the benefit of the Clough legend. 'I truly believe that, like many other media creations, Clough became trapped inside a comic performer that completely took him over,' said one leading football journalist who had known him both as a player and a manager. 'From the early 1970s he was not a comfortable man to be around. The laughter around him became uneasy and people in the game began to give him a wide berth. But his own players and

Left: Between 19 November 1977 and 9 December 1978 Nottingham Forest did not lose a League match. This easily surpassed previous records and set a new mark for the number of games without defeat (42 - a whole League season) and for the period of time (over a year) without a defeat.

Right: Far less recognised than the 42 League match run, is the fact that Forest also went 40 consecutive first-class matches undefeated in all recognised competitions between 14 March 1978 and 9 December 1978. There is no comparable achievement since the foundation of League football and this undefeated run of Forest's was so exceptional that there was no similarly celebrated run for Forest to exceed. Forest also broke all records for consecutive away matches without defeat and, in 1996, also set up a 25-game record of undefeated Premier League matches.

Below: The programme from Forest's last game in the two runs, a 1-0 win at Bolton on 25 November 1978. John Robertson scored the goal.

RECORD RUN OF 40 FIRST-CLASS GAMES UNDEFEATED

Date	Competition	V	Opponents	Result		Scorers
14 Mar 78	Division 1	H	Leicester City	W	1-0	Robertson (Pen)
18 Mar 78	LC-F	N	Liverpool	D	0-0	
22 Mar 78	LC-F replay	N	Liverpool	W	1-0	Robertson (Pen)
25 Mar 78	Division 1	H	Newcastle United	W	2-0	Robertson (Pen), Anderson
29 Mar 78	Division 1	A	Middlesbrough	D	2-2	Woodcock, O'Neill
1 Apr 78	Division 1	H	Chelsea	W	3-1	Burns, O'Neill, Robertson
5 Apr 78	Division 1	A	Aston Villa	W	1-0	Woodcock
11 Apr 78	Division 1	A	Manchester City	D	0-0	
15 Apr 78	Division 1	H	Leeds United	D	1-1	Withe
18 Apr 78	Division 1	H	Queen's Park Rangers	W	1-0	Robertson (Pen)
22 Apr 78	Division 1	A	Coventry City	D	0-0	
25 Apr 78	Division 1	A	Ipswich Town	W	2-0	Mariner (o.g.), Clark
29 Apr 78	Division 1	H	Birmingham City	D	0-0	
2 May 78	Division 1	A	West Bromwich Albion	D	2-2	Bowyer, Robertson (Pen)
4 May 78	Division 1	A	Liverpool	D	0-0	
12 Aug 78	Charity Shield	N	Ipswich Town	W	5-0	O'Neill 2, Withe, Lloyd, Robertson
19 Aug 78	Division 1	H	Tottenham Hotspur	D	1-1	O'Neill
22 Aug 78	Division 1	A	Coventry City	D	0-0	
26 Aug 78	Division 1	A	Queen's Park Rangers	D	0-0	
29 Aug 78	LC-2	A	Oldham Athletic	D	0-0	
2 Sept 78	Division 1	H	West Bromwich Albion	D	0-0	
6 Sept 78	LC-R	H	Oldham Athletic	W	4-2	Needham, Burns, Woodcock, Robertson (Pen)
9 Sept 78	Division 1	H	Arsenal	W	2-1	Robertson (Pen), Bowyer
13 Sept 78	EC-1/1	H	Liverpool	W	2-0	Birtles, Barrett
16 Sept 78	Division 1	A	Manchester United	D	1-1	Bowyer
23 Sept 78	Division 1	H	Middlesbrough	D	2-2	Birtles, O'Neill
27 Sept 78	EC-1/2	A	Liverpool	D	0-0	
30 Sept 78	Division 1	A	Aston Villa	W	2-1	Woodcock, Robertson (Pen)
4 Oct 78	LC-3	A	Oxford United	W	5-0	Birtles, McGovern, O'Neill, Robertson, Anderson
7 Oct 78	Division 1	H	W'hampton Wanderers	W	3-1	Birtles 2, O'Neill
14 Oct 78	Division 1	A	Bristol City	W	3-1	Birtles, Robertson 2
18 Oct 78	EC-2/1	A	AEK Athens	W	2-1	McGovern, Birtles
21 Oct 78	Division 1	H	Ipswich Town	W	1-0	O'Neill
28 Oct 78	Division 1	A	Southampton	D	0-0	
1 Nov 78	EC-2/2	H	AEK Athens	W	5-1	Needham, Woodcock, Anderson, Birtles 2
4 Nov 78	Division 1	H	Everton	D	0-0	
7 Nov 78	LC-4	A	Everton	W	3-2	Lloyd, Anderson, Woodcock
11 Nov 78	Division 1	A	Tottenham Hotspur	W	3-1	Anderson, Robertson, Birtles
18 Nov 78	Division 1	H	Queen's Park Rangers	D	0-0	
25 Nov 78	Division 1	A	Bolton Wanderers	W	1-0	Robertson

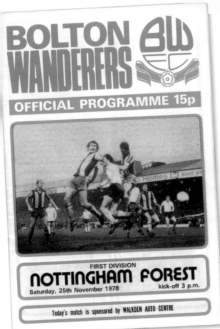

directors were stuck with him and from then on there was (certainly) fear and respect but (arguably) little affection.' "

Clough left Taylor behind in Brighton (where he had gone after being sacked from Derby), but his disastrous failure at Leeds made him think again. According to Taylor's wife, Clough eventually rang Taylor in Brighton at 2:00 a.m. sobbing that he had made the greatest mistake of his life. Taylor finally came to Forest (a year after Clough) and it was Taylor's arrival that provided the key to what happened later. They had been together since Middlesbrough, where Taylor had been the goalkeeper and Clough the goalscorer.

Thereafter, their names were to be forever linked like Romeo and Juliet, Laurel and Hardy or Alsace and Lorraine.

Much of Clough's success remains an enigma, clouded in the recognition of a simply remarkable personality, one of those rare freaks that emerges by genetic chance from the unlikeliest source. There is no doubt that Clough, in his way, was the Mozart or Newton of his age. But the relationship with Taylor was also at the core of his success and the final breach between the two was very surely the saddest moment of a career punctuated by occasional sad errors.

Taylor, who had always seemed to feel that Clough took perhaps too much of the praise, eventually had enough and decided to see if he could do it on his own back at Derby in 1983. This was bad enough, but the real crevasse was to be caused by Taylor's wooing of John Robertson, still a superb midfield creator. Taylor had, argues Dalrymple, given Clough 30 years of total commitment, of support, of brotherhood. He had been a second father to Clough's children and had helped turn Nigel into one of the great stars of the era. And now, Taylor had taken Robertson. Here were precisely the two men, Taylor and Robertson, whom, more than all the others, had been the instruments of Clough's wealth, success and reputation. Clough turned his back and never made it up with his partner. It was only at Taylor's funeral that he acknowledged his own loss. A friend said he looked bewildered and distraught – and now it was simply too late.

Brian Clough's relationship with Nottingham Forest shuddered to a sad and thoroughly unsatisfactory conclusion. In January 1998, he and Taylor's successor as his assistant, Ronnie Fenton, were charged with alleged misdemeanours relating to certain transfers. Allegations are not proof and the whole affair was publicly judged to be completely unsatisfactory. After his departure in May 1993 Clough returned to the club just once, to see Nigel play in a reserve match. The directors of Nottingham Forest plc, the new holding company, had been considering naming the Executive Stand after Clough, and putting his bust in the main entrance (a la Herbert Chapman at Arsenal) and preserving his name for ever at the club. The FA enquiry left the club and Brian Clough's family in a certain limbo, all hoping to make exactly those decisions in the future – perhaps after the trauma of the whole five-year enquiry had finally been concluded.

Of the great team of 1977-1980, it has been Martin O'Neill who has been the most successful as a manager himself and who is in some ways regarded as having inherited his mantle. This is doubly so because of O'Neill's partnership with John Robertson, probably the most popular man ever to play football for Nottingham Forest. Martin's view of Brian Clough is as measured and, given his current position, as thoughtful as perhaps that of anyone.

"I don't think I appreciated what Brian Clough achieved as a manager until afterwards, when I was able to make comparisons with other managers. It was only then that I could see that he was clearly a class apart. Obviously, like most players at any time, my thinking was subjective and not objective and my interests were my success, whether I was in the team and not so much what was good for the team. It's probably true to say that I argued with him rather more than any of the rest of the squad, although Larry weighed in with a pretty good second. When I

think about it now, all I ever really wanted from Brian was for him to say: 'You did really well out there…'. If we'd been playing in front of 40,000, and they all thought I was manure, it wouldn't have worried me at all if Brian had praised me afterwards. When I think about it now, I can only remember him praising me twice. The first time was after the terrible 2-0 defeat at West Bromwich in the FA Cup quarter-final in 1978. We were all depressed because we really thought we could do the treble that season. We were in the dressing room talking about the next week's game which was the League Cup final against Liverpool and, for some reason, we already had a special strip prepared for the final. He pointed at me and said: 'Let that young man try that shirt on. He was our best player today.' The other occasion was at half time in the Madrid final when he said to me 'I was thinking about moving you to a different position but I've changed my mind because you're playing too well'. Clough succeeded because of the sheer weight of his personality.

"I have never known a personality like his in football. Unlike our European Cup team, he was a one-off".

The answer lies, as O'Neill says, in a quite exceptional personality, a personality like that of a Napoleon or a Churchill, but one from a humbler background and dedicated to the elixir of that very background – football. But, at the back of the mind, one suspects, as both Martin O'Neill and Larry Lloyd confirm, there was an element of good luck. And if that luck existed, it was to be found in a tour of Ireland in 1975, when a fringe midfielder who had played just 17 games the previous season helped out by filling the left-wing spot and unexpectedly made six goals with that stunning pace over a couple of yards. That was when Clough suddenly saw that he had a potential match winner – a right-footed left winger who only went out there because all the normal wingers were injured or had stayed at home. Watch a video of the era. Count how many goals come from the left, from Robertson's crosses or Robertson's creativity. How many players have made the goal that won one European Cup and scored the goal that won another?

Say Larry Lloyd and Martin O'Neill today: "Brian Clough was a genius – but he had the stroke of luck which allowed his genius to flower, and that stroke of luck was John Robertson."

Brian Clough's career as a football manager finished at the end of the 1992-93 season, a year which also saw Nottingham Forest relegated from the Premiership to the Football League First Division. Clough's last game in Nottingham was on 26 April 1993 when Sheffield United won 2-0 and condemned Forest to the drop. Ironically, United's manager was Dave Bassett, who was to take Forest up in 1998. Season 1992-93 was only the second in Clough's 18-year reign that Forest had even been out of the top half of their division. The scenes were deeply emotional, rarely matched on an English football ground, and they were certainly unique from a full house of supporters who had come to see their team relegated. It was a celebration rather than a wake. James Dalrymple, in the *Sunday Times*, was an unemotional observer: "The 26,000 crowd, many of them hysterical and close to tears, bayed for a final performance from the man who had entertained them for 18 years and led them into a great sporting era that had brought international glory and fame to their pleasant backwater town. A great and joyous adventure was over, the people of Nottingham sensed, and they dreaded a return to footballing obscurity when this charismatic and unpredictable Pied Piper of a manager had gone. They wanted to show how much they had loved him." They need not have feared quite so much. Within two years, under Frank Clark, Forest finished third in the Premier League and were to be England's last survivors in Europe, reaching the last eight of the UEFA Cup.

Where it all began in 1865; The Forest, taken in the late 1870s, and the only photograph thought to show where Nottingham Forest originally played. Games were played on the pitch in the middle of the picture, where a pick-up game of football appears to be in progress. The area was still a racecourse at the time - the grandstand is on the left - and every manner of sport was to be seen here, even bear baiting. This is where Forest originally played shinney, a form of hockey, and where they played their very first "official" match, against Notts County on 22 March 1866. This was an historic game, as it is the first ever played between two teams which went on to become League members. Indeed, Forest and County were the only two League clubs which even existed at the time. Forest played their last game on the Forest on 21 October 1878. Note that the streets north of Gregory Boulevard are still under construction (*Author's Collection*).

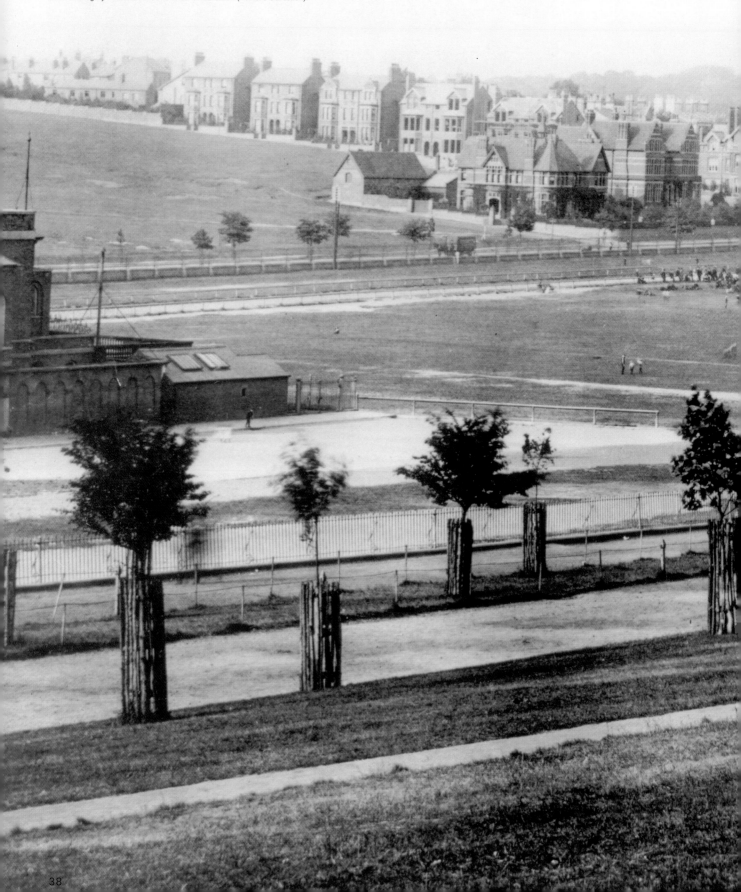

CHAPTER TWO

Early days and semi-finals

1865–1898

ANYONE who travels the world knows that the name Nottingham provokes two responses: Robin Hood plus the Sheriff and all that, and Nottingham Forest. It is naturally assumed that the great European Cup winners were named after Sherwood Forest and are part of the whole historical myth which defines Nottingham for so much of the world. It is perhaps Nottingham Forest's great good fortune that its name is so resonant of its home city and of one of the great English folk heroes. Robin Hood is, for instance, the only mythical character to have an entry in the National Dictionary of Biography. Fortunate, because as Nottingham folk know, The Forest is an open space which currently houses Goose Fair and, in the nineteenth century, housed Nottingham racecourse. It was originally named The Forest, apparently because it was a clearing in Sherwood Forest to the north of the city, but it is many centuries since bandits and thieves would have been able to hunt on its slopes.

In the mid-nineteenth century, there were two places in the city where young, relatively well-to-do men would gather to play the sports of the day. The first was on the banks of the Trent, in the open area around the cricket pitch at Trent Bridge. In 1862, several of these boys were to form Notts County Football Club, an offshoot of the cricket team and now the oldest of Britain's professional clubs. Stoke once claimed to be founded in 1863, but there is no evidence of their existence prior to 1867 and Forest thus preceded them in 1865. So Nottingham was to be one of the foundations of soccer in the midlands and the north and it was the adjacent clubs, Chesterfield and Sheffield Wednesday which were to become the third and fourth oldest.

In fact the area around Nottingham has been a centre of sporting excellence for hundreds of years, arguably from the 12th century when Robin Hood was the leading archer of the day, to the 20th when, among other sporting heroes, many on the football pitch, Torvill and Dean skated away with numerous ice-dancing championships and gold medals. In the 1860s, a famous Nottingham figure was "Bold Bendigo" who, years earlier, had become the first boxer to win the championship of England (and therefore the world) under the London Prize Ring Rules. He was so famous that a town was named after him in Australia. Bendigo was also a great angler, who fished on the Trent. He won nearly every major angling competition in England except the All-England Championship. In 1881 a huge memorial to him, which included the sculpture of a life-sized lion, was erected in Nottingham Cemetery.

For part of his life, Bendigo was engaged as a waiter on match days at Trent Bridge, the ground at times of both Nottingham Forest and Notts County, but principally of course the headquarters of Nottinghamshire County Cricket Club, cricket being another sport in which the city and the county have shone. In fact in the list of county champions published in the current Wisden, Nottinghamshire is only the second county (after Surrey) to hold that honour, the first time being in 1865. It was to be a great year for the city.

Nottingham in those days was quite unlike the major conurbation of today. Nottingham was the headquarters of the lace industry, and around the Lace Market were the narrow streets and alleyways in which toiled the workers who spent their lives in the lace and hosiery sweat shops. These lives were hard and often short. Drunken gangs roamed the streets (gin was 13 shillings, or 65p, a gallon, whisky 15 shillings a gallon). The most notorious gang was known as the Nottingham Lambs, of which the great boxer Bendigo (28 convictions for drunken offences) became leader after his retirement. Other gangs were the Yellow Lambs and Blue Innocents. Nottingham was a notoriously violent place.

Yet outside the built-up areas were fields where roses were grown to supply cut flowers to cities like Manchester and Liverpool. And 1865 saw the implementation of the Enclosure Act which allowed some of these areas to be enclosed and kept as healthy, open spaces as the town grew, but also allowed the town to expand outside its boundaries to the likes of Radford. Among these open spaces to the north of the city was The Forest, a huge natural amphitheatre surrounded by windmills. It was an obvious place for sports. Earlier in the century even bear-baiting had been practised there. In 1865 it was the site of the city's racecourse, and as well as horse racing other sports such as foot races, cricket, football and shinney took place. And it was a group of shinney players who were to form the Forest Football Club.

Shinney is a version of the word shinty, which is a hockey-like game which originated in the highlands of Scotland. By the 1860s shinney was losing its dominance while football was rapidly gaining in popularity. The Football Association was formed in 1863, and quickly issued a set of rules which, based on the first set of rules which had been drawn up at Cambridge University in 1848, differed significantly from the rules already in use by the Sheffield Association. Sheffield was really the home of organised football, the Sheffield club having been formed as early as 1857. This was an amateur club, not to be confused with United or Wednesday. The game was still very different to that played today. Handling was allowed to the extent that the ball could be stopped by the hands and placed on the ground to be kicked. The ball was not allowed to be kicked whilst in the air. Rule 3 stated that

Another view of The Forest, this time looking East, and taken when the land was still in use as a racecourse. In the background is the grandstand, built by John Carr of York in 1777. Racing ceased on The Forest in 1890, the sport transferring to the current racecourse at Colwick. The grandstand was pulled down in 1909 and the site has since become primarily associated with Goose Fair, held here since 1928. The Fair, dating back to at least the 13th century, is the second largest in the country, bettered for size only by Newcastle's Town Moor *(Author's Collection)*.

kicks must be aimed only at the ball, which would seem obvious to us today, but the Sheffield rules allowed "hacking", and the FA rules were seen by some as namby-pamby. (Imagine rules which allowed, even encouraged, Stuart Pearce to kick at opponents' ankles).

There is a popular legend, no doubt completely untrue, that during a game of shinney, a footballer threw a football to the players, who dropped their sticks and began kicking the ball about, enjoying it so much that some suggested they switch games and play football. At any rate a meeting was called to discuss this proposition, and was held one autumn evening in a hostelry called the Clinton Arms, in what is now Sherwood Street but was then little more than a country lane and some half a mile from the Forest recreation ground. At the time, the inn faced the Cattle Market, but in 1888 the whole area was redeveloped and the site became the Nottingham Guildhall. The original Clinton Arms was knocked down around the same time, and the site is now occupied by the Newton Building of Nottingham Trent University. The man who called the meeting, and can therefore be regarded as the first chairman of the football club, was J.S. Scrimshaw.

The main thrust of the meeting was to

change the main sport of the club from shinney to football, and this was passed. The 15 members present were all shinney players and all became footballers. They formed the football club's first committee. As well as Scrimshaw, they were: A. Barks, W. Brown, W.P. Brown, C. Daft, T. Gamble, R.P. Hawksley, T.G. Howitt, W.L. Hussey, W.R. Lymbery, J.S. Milford, J.H. Rastall, W.H. Revis, J.G. Richardson and J. Tomlinson. For two years shinney and football were played by various members of the club until, in 1867, the committee decided to give up the playing of shinney altogether. The club adopted the title of the "Nottingham Forest Football Club".

It seems that at the 1865 meeting to form the football club, the other main resolution passed was that W. Brown should purchase a dozen red caps, complete with tassels, for the players. In those days, players identified themselves as a team more by their headgear than their shirts, a custom which survives in part in the present day's awarding of caps to international players. Forest were the first club ever to "officially" wear red caps and the committee also specified that the colour be "Garibaldi Red". Garibaldi was, of course, the leader of the Italian freedom fighters known as the redshirts and organised a victorious

These pages: When those 15 young men formed Nottingham Forest at the Clinton Arms in 1865, the Nottingham that they knew was very different from the Nottingham of today. The town's population was only 80,000, compared with the 320,000 at its peak in the 1950s. The government had yet to approve the expansion of the town to incorporate areas like Radford and Lenton. Images from 1865 are few and far between, but these four give a flavour of that momentous year, in Nottingham at least.

Top left: The last time that the Riot Act was read in Nottingham was on 26 June 1865, when a political rally by Liberals Samuel Morley and Charles Paget led to these riots in the Market Square, the offices of the *Nottingham Daily Express* being burned out and the Mayor desperately sending for troops from Sheffield to quell the disturbances. Order was not restored until midnight and the election results were later overturned.

Centre: Trent Bridge in 1865. There has been a bridge on the site since A.D. 920, when Nottingham was the lowest bridging point on the Trent and the combination of the bridge and the castle rock made Nottingham a key defensible site. The bridge in the picture was demolished in 1871 when replaced by the existing Trent Bridge, which was further widened in 1926. The building is the Town Arms (now The Aviary), for many years the southern gateway to the town.

Bottom: The most notable new building of 1865 was definitely the Theatre Royal, imposingly built at the top of Market Street in that year. This picture probably dates from the late 1870s, before the tram lines were laid up Market Street.

Nottingham. Guildhall.

march through Italy in search of the unification of that country. At the time, Garibaldi was universally popular in England (hence the famous biscuit) and his goal was eventually achieved in 1870. The red caps were purchased by William Brown from another member of the committee, Charles Daft, who was a shopkeeper. Daft was a famous sporting name in Nottingham in the second half of the 19th century: Richard Daft was reckoned the country's best professional batsman around 1870, and four Dafts played for the Notts cricket club. A son of Richard, Harry Daft, played cricket for Notts and soccer for both Forest (in 1893) and Notts County, and while with County he won five caps for England as an outside-left. Charles Daft, the original committee man, was captain of Forest in their first known side, in 1866, but this was his only competitive appearance as a player.

Nottingham Forest played their first match as a football team on 22 March 1866 against, of course, Notts County, who had been formed in 1862 although it was 1864 before County were properly organised. That match, played on the Forest Racecourse, was originally planned to be between 13 of County and 15 of Forest, but two County players failed to turn up and Forest, who at those odds still expected to be defeated, decided to play with 17. Clearly elements of the handling game (which was to split from football completely around this time and become rugby), still existed, and the result has variously been reported as a 0-0 draw (according to the *Daily Guardian*) or a win for Forest by virtue of a touchdown, after Forest's W.H. Revis had raced County's H. Browne to score it and then "converted" by kicking through the posts from 15 yards out. Such efforts were not called goals in

Nottingham and Sheffield, but were termed "rouges", a notation which crops up frequently in match reports from the first half-dozen years or so of Forest's existence. In effect, a "rouge" was a converted try which was also called a "goal" in the rugby of the time.

The strong man in Forest's early history was one of the founders, Walter Roe Lymbery, who had captained the shinney club. He became captain, chairman of the football club and, from 1868 until 1886, was honorary secretary. He also became involved in the Notts FA, and was its representative at meetings of the Football Association. He was one of the men appointed to sort out the important question of professionalism which, in the 1880s, threatened to split football as it did rugby. In 1868 Lymbery took Forest into the Sheffield Association, and they added the Sheffield Norfolk club and Newark to Notts County as regular opponents. By the end of the 1860s Forest were playing ten matches or so a season, with Sawley, Derby Grammar School and Nottingham Manufacturing Company becoming regular names on the fixture list.

The 1871-72 and 1872-73 seasons were notable in the history of football – in the first the FA Cup was founded, and in the second England and Scotland played the first-ever international match (resulting in a 0-0 draw in Glasgow, a score not to be repeated in the fixture, outside of wartime, for 98 years). Forest were not one of the 15 teams to enter the FA Cup in its first year, in which Wanderers beat Royal Engineers 1-0. The Wanderers side was made up of ex-public school and university players and that team was to win the FA Cup in five of the first seven seasons (and never again).

However the losing Cup finalists, Royal Engineers, who were to win the Cup themselves in 1875, embarked on football's very first tour and played three matches in the Midlands, in Sheffield, Nottingham and Derby. Forest were chosen to meet the crack military side at Trent Bridge on 23 December 1873. The famous Major Marindin captained the Engineers, who had beaten Sheffield handsomely, in one of the most exciting games seen at Nottingham at the time. The Engineers scored first, after ten minutes, at which the players changed ends, the convention at the time being to change ends after each goal. C.J. Spencer equalised for the Forest, but just before the end the Engineers scored the winner. The spectators, who numbered not quite 3,000, enjoyed a stirring game, and Major Marindin said it was the best match his team had played in the north. Marindin was to appear in more FA Cup finals than any other figure – two as a player and eight as a referee.

One of Forest's most notable players was Sam Widdowson, the captain, who is credited with the introduction of the shin-guard into football. Sam played from 1869 to 1887, and first wore his revolutionary invention in 1874. And in those days he wore his shinguards outside the socks. Sam, from Hucknall, was something of an all-rounder, since he also played cricket for Nottinghamshire, and was a good hurdler and sprinter. He turned out for England against Scotland in 1879-80 in Glasgow when Scotland won 5-4, but he was not the first Forest player to win international honours. Arthur Goodyer beat him to it by a year, making his appearance on 5 April 1879 against Scotland at Kennington Oval. Strangely, England also won this match by 5-4, and Goodyer scored. In both cases, Goodyer and Widdowson, it was to be their only cap.

Forest were again at the cutting edge of technology in 1878 when a whistle was used by the referee for the first time. This occurred in a match with their old rivals Sheffield Norfolk. It was only in 1871 that a referee had been used for the first time – previously each side had provided an umpire, much as happens in club cricket these days. The referee was used to decide matters on which the umpires couldn't agree but he would

Forest had three other headquarters (as opposed to grounds - of which they have had seven) between their foundation in 1865 and a permanent office move to The City Ground in 1912. They were really just meeting places, the club secretary usually keeping the paperwork at his home. The three sites were all public houses - the Red Lion Hotel on Clumber Street (**top left**, now called The Lion), the Spread Eagle on Burton Street (**top right**) and the Maypole Hotel on Maypole Yard off Clumber Street (**centre left**). Maypole Yard was the rear entrance to the famous Black Boy Hotel, and much of the Yard (including the Maypole Hotel) was swept away in the development of Nottingham's ugliest building - Littlewood's on

only make judgements "if referred to" (hence the name referee). Football was beginning to look a little more like the game it is today. In the early 1870s goalkeepers were first mentioned as players being able to use their hands, and crossbars were replacing the tapes which had been used from the 1860s (before then there was no limit to the height of the goal). Corner-kicks were introduced. The style of play had changed from the free-for-all, all players chasing the ball, of the 1860s, to a more thoughtful formation, with the necessity of defensive play recognised. Again it was Sam Widdowson who has been given credit for inventing the "classical" formation of a goalkeeper, two full-backs, a three-man half-back line and five forwards. This formation was used on League club programmes until well after the Second World War, with the outfield players numbered from back to front and right to left, that is from 2 (right-back) to 11 (outside-left). The goalkeeper's jersey was rarely numbered. Of course regular numbering itself did not come into being until 1939, but Widdowson's formation had a remarkably long life, particularly as clubs

stopped using it as early as the 1920s, when Herbert Chapman invented the "third full-back" game.

More clubs with currently recognisable names began appearing on Forest's fixture list, like Chesterfield and Sheffield Wednesday, who beat Forest 5-0 in their first meeting on The Forest in January 1876 and won the return 9-1 at Bramall Lane. In January 1878, however, Forest won 4-1 on a pitch partially cleared of over an inch of snow and ice.

Season 1878-79 was a doubly important one in Forest's history. First, the Notts Castle Club was disbanded and the players decided en bloc to join Forest. They were a strong team and, while not all of the players could get into the Forest side, the influx of talent made Forest a very powerful team.

Secondly, with this improved side, Forest decided to enter the FA Challenge Cup for the first time. Notts County had made their first challenge the previous season, and now the two sides were forced to meet in the first round. The match was held at the Beeston Cricket Ground,

which Notts County were using at the time if they wanted a paying gate. The Forest team and officials made their way to the ground in a coach pulled by four horses, while many spectators made their way by train from Nottingham, some watching the match from the station platform at Beeston. Both sides were surprised at the size of the crowd, which was estimated to be around 500.

The match was played on a very heavy ground after recent rains, and the weather was very cold. According to a newspaper report the betting odds were 2-1 against the Forest, although when J.P. Turner opened the scoring for them from a corner-kick after five minutes the paper reported that the loud cheering confirmed that the Reds were the favourites with the spectators. A second after 15 minutes was followed by a goal for County (or Notts as they were then more popularly called) giving Forest a 2-1 lead at half-time, at which the players were reported to have refreshed themselves with sherry and ale. In the second half Forest had the advantage of the wind and scored again to finish 3-1 winners.

This was the eighth year of the FA Cup, and the 15 entrants of the first season had by now grown to 43, although six were to scratch. Forest's entry emphasized the growing interest of the "northern" clubs, with Notts County, Sheffield and Darwen and the Scottish club

Queen's Park having already taken part. Matches were not arranged by a draw but on a regional basis, so Forest found themselves facing Sheffield in the second round, winning 2-0 in a match played on three inches of snow. Forest's following match, a friendly against Edinburgh University, was played, according to weather-conscious Ken Smales in his admirable official statistical record of the club, *Forest - The First 125 Years* (Temple Printing Nottingham Ltd, 1991) on four inches of snow, before an astonishing number of 1,500 fans.

Forest beat Old Harrovians 2-0 at the Kennington Oval in the third round of the Cup, thus becoming the first provincial club to appear in London, and they returned to the Oval in the fourth round to beat Oxford University 2-1.

In the semi-final Forest met Old Etonians, while the third team left in the tournament, Clapham Rovers, had a bye! Old Etonians had received a scare in the previous round when Darwen scored four times in the last quarter of an hour to draw 5-5. The Old Boys refused to play extra time, forcing Darwen to raise funds by public subscription to travel down for a replay, which was also drawn. Not surprisingly Darwen caved in in the second replay. Old Etonians proved too good for Forest in the semi-final, winning 2-1 before 700 spectators at The Oval. Forest upset opponents Southwell Football Club by being unable to play them on the date of the

Above: The earliest picture that exists of any Forest team, taken the week before their FA Cup semi-final against Old Etonians on 22 March 1879. Forest are the only modern club to have reached the semi-final of the Cup at their first attempt and, but for the luck of the draw, would have definitely reached the final. There were only three clubs in the semi-final draw and Clapham Rovers received a bye to the final. The same thing happened again the next year, 1880, when Forest had to play Oxford University in the semi-final but Clapham Rovers again received a bye straight into the final. Forest lost 2-1 in 1879 and 1-0 in 1880, both games being played at Kennington Oval. The Forest team in 1879 was: top, left to right, Caborn, Sands, Edwin Luntley; middle, Bates, Smith, Holroyd, Turner, Walter Luntley; bottom, Goodyer, Widdowson, Earp. At the time, each club supplied one referee, who only gave decisions if "referred to" by the players (hence the name). (*Author's Collection*)

Above: In 1879 Forest moved from the Racecourse to the Castle Ground in the Meadows, an area also used by Notts County and for cricket (as in the sole existing illustration above). Forest moved so they could take a paying gate, playing their first game here on 8 March 1879 and their last on 27 February 1881 (*Nigel Wray*).

Below: Forest also used to play reasonably regularly at Trent Bridge, home of Notts CC and the local ground which could take the biggest paying gate. This picture was taken in 1886, after the opening of the new grandstand. Forest played their first home game at Trent Bridge on 23 December 1873 against Royal Engineers and their last on 17 February 1883 against Wolves, after which Notts County became the permanent occupants. Forest did play an "away" game at Trent Bridge as recently as 8 January 1910, as Notts County (founded by members of the cricket club, of course) did not move to Meadow Lane until that year. Forest lost the match 4-1 in front of 14,000 spectators (*Author's Collection*).

semi-final, although Old Etonians themselves then tried to alter the date on the grounds that two of their men were competing in the Cambridge University sports day. Forest agreed to this, only to find that by doing so they had upset the FA who, when they heard of the arrangement, insisted the match go ahead on the date planned. However Forest had the satisfaction of becoming the first club to reach the semi-final in its first year of entry in the Cup since the first days of the competition.

Before the end of the 1878-79 season Forest played a friendly in Glasgow against Glasgow Rangers. Although they lost 3-0, the reported crowd of 6,000 was probably the biggest in Forest's history at the time.

In 1879 Forest left their ground on the Forest Racecourse and played for a few months on a ground in the Meadows, a more defined ground than the Racecourse. It was a little south of Nottingham's Castle and was usually called the Castle Ground. The Racecourse was of course public ground on which Forest could not raise revenue by charging at a gate. Forest's finances were raised by membership subscriptions. At first, the players paid a shilling (5p) a week, which rose to five shillings (25p) a month, plus from 1875 an entrance fee to join the club of

ten shillings (50p). By 1880 the subscription had risen to seven shillings and sixpence (37p). A player who joined the club in 1878, Ernest Jardine, paid the entrance subscription of ten shillings. Later he became the business tycoon, Sir Ernest Jardine, and president of the club. Ordinary non-playing members of the club, as Sir Ernest became, paid from around 1877 an annual subscription of a guinea (£1.05). Although these sums sound small by today's standards, even a shilling (5p) a week for a game was far beyond what the working man could afford. So the players were the well-to-do, not surprising considering the game had begun its explosion into the most popular in the world only a few decades earlier in the English public schools and universities. Of course, as the game developed and clubs wished to enrol the best working-class players into their sides so professionalism began, particularly among the northern clubs. Indeed Darwen who, with Forest, reached the fourth round of the Cup in 1878-79, had in their side two Scots players who were reputedly the first two players to find money in their boots after a match - the way the "professionals" were surreptitiously rewarded for their efforts.

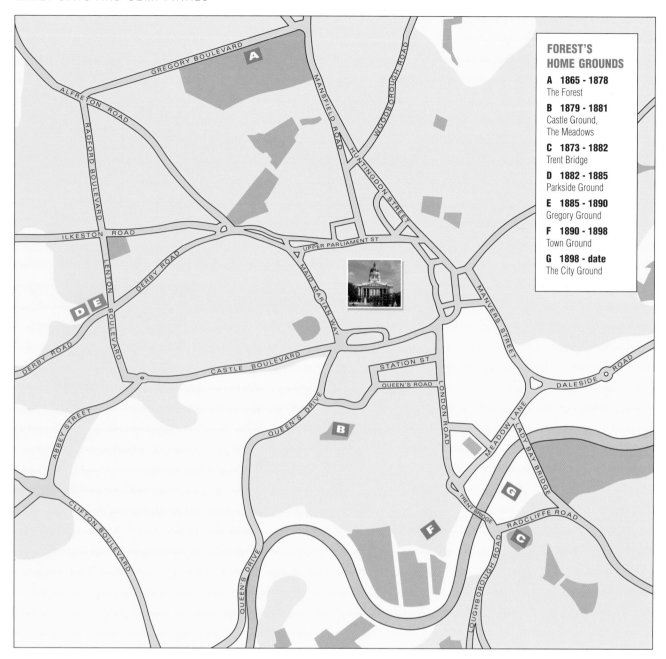

FOREST'S HOME GROUNDS

A 1865 - 1878
The Forest

B 1879 - 1881
Castle Ground,
The Meadows

C 1873 - 1882
Trent Bridge

D 1882 - 1885
Parkside Ground

E 1885 - 1890
Gregory Ground

F 1890 - 1898
Town Ground

G 1898 - date
The City Ground

The subscriptions were enough to pay the expenses of the club. A shirt might cost four shillings (20p), a cap one and sixpence (7p), while the club accounts detail what it cost to entertain both teams at a big match in 1872: 72 lunches, 28 dinners, plus sherry and punch (some of which would have been taken at half-time), came to a total of £6.17s (£6.85). In the light of problems football has suffered with hooliganism in recent years it is interesting to note that two incidents cost Forest money in the 1879-80 season: 12 shillings (60p) to the Midland Railway Company for damage to a saloon coach around Christmas and 27 shillings (£1.35) to a Mrs Bates for damage to a pram by visitors from Sheffield Wednesday.

Forest's three journeys to London to play matches in the FA Cup run of 1878-79 cost them a total of £36.9s (£36.45) in travelling costs - an average of £12 to take the whole team and officials on the return trip from Nottingham to London.

Although revenue from gate money was being seen as a necessity, it is unlikely that playing on the Meadows made much financial difference to Forest. The ground was in a natural enclosure of trees, and fields surrounding it were full of flowers - in spring thousands of crocuses, remembered later in the name of Nottingham's Crocus Street. Forest did not play many games on the Meadows and continued to play big games at the Trent Bridge Cricket Ground which, from 1880 to 1882, they made their home. They had played occasional matches there for ten years, and could charge an entrance fee. Forest made their first-ever three-figure sum at the gate on 10 February 1880, when they entertained a side called the Scottish Canadians. This was a team of Scots who were preparing to tour Canada and raising funds with matches in England. A crowd of 5,500 turned up to watch the match, and the gate receipts totalled £108 15s 7d. A half share of the net receipts, £51 2s 1d (£51.10), was given to

Above: Leaving Trent Bridge in 1882-83, Forest moved to the Parkside Ground in Lenton, which is now a recreation ground on Derby Road very close to the Savoy Cinema. The site can easily be identified by the "toothpeg" high rise blocks. Three years later the club moved just one hundred yards up the road to the next field and called it the Gregory Ground, which was located where the houses are in the centre of the picture. The only sign that there were once two adjacent football grounds here on Derby Road is the remnants of the cinder banking alongside the road in the distance. Forest's first game in Lenton was on 22 September 1883 and their last was on 27 September 1890. Their record crowd there was 12,000 against Notts County in a Cup tie on 1 December 1883.

Right: Forest moved from Lenton to the Town Ground in the Meadows, so named because it was adjacent to the Town Arms pub. Nothing remains of the ground because Nottingham Council, which owned the site, decided to use it to build their new tram sheds in 1898. As can be seen, the site, on Bunbury Street, is still used as a Corporation bus depot. Forest played here from 1890 to 1898, the record attendance for the ground being 15,000 for an FA Cup tie, also against Notts County, on 24 February 1894 (Author's Collection).

the Scots towards their Canadian tour expenses.

Season 1879-80 was another excellent one for Forest. It began when they entered a team at a grand five-a-side contest at the Castle Cricket Ground, Nottingham, which 13 teams entered, Forest winning the first prize of £10. Entering the FA Cup again, they disposed of Notts County 4-0 in the first round, Turton 6-0 in the second (on two inches of snow) and Blackburn Rovers 6-0 in the third. This brought them up against Sheffield in the quarter-final, the match resulting in a 2-2 draw, with Sam Widdowson dribbling the length of the field to score an equaliser two minutes from time. The disappointed Sheffield, like the Cup winners Old Etonians in a match the previous year, refused to play extra time and walked off the field. Widdowson, it was said, lined up his men, kicked off and dribbled the ball into the empty net for a "winner". In deciding the outcome the FA dealt with Sheffield much

more strictly than they had Old Etonians and disqualified them, thus putting Forest through to the semi-final for the second year in succession. Forest travelled to the Kennington Oval to play Oxford University, whom they had beaten 2-1 the year before, but this time the University won 1-0. Of Forest's 18 FA Cup goals that season Sam Widdowson netted seven and A.H. Smith six.

Forest's side in their first Cup tie against Notts at the beginning of their two-season run was described as J. Sands (goal), S.W. Widdowson (cover-goal), E. Luntley and C.J. Caborn (backs), A.J. Bates and A.M. Holroyd (three-quarters), A.H. Smith, A. Goodyer, J.P. Turner, F.W. Earp and W. Luntley (forwards). In their second semi-final at the end of the run L.O. Lindley and H. Billyeald had replaced Bates and Turner. Of these men Sands, Widdowson, Edwin Luntley and Goodyer were either already internationals or became internationals the following season.

These pages: Getting to the ground was something of a tradition from the late nineteenth century until perhaps the last two decades. Generations of Nottingham fans (both Forest and County) have caught hansom cabs, trams, trolleys ("tracklesses" as they were called when they replaced the trams) and buses from the Market Square to Trent Bridge for the match. The picture **top left** was taken prior to the introduction of the horse trams in 1878 and shows that the vehicle of choice in those days was the hansom or hackney cab. The old Exchange Building was superseded by the Council House in 1929. The view of St Peter's Square **bottom left** was taken in 1892 and shows that the trams to Trent Bridge (which started in 1878) were still horse drawn and some continued to be so until well into the Edwardian era. After a number of teething problems the new fangled electric trams (**bottom**) eventually started running to Trent Bridge in 1901, three years after the Corporation had taken over the adjacent Town Ground to build the depot *(All Author's Collection)*.

A new name appeared on Forest's fixture list in 1880-81: Aston Villa. Forest lost 2-0 in a friendly and three weeks later met them at home in the second round of the Cup. Lindley did not play - he was reported badly bitten by a rat. Villa won 2-1, and repeated the defeat the following year in the first round by 4-1, when Forest were hampered by one of the Luntleys spraining his ankle after 15 minutes. Later that season they lost 5-0 to Notts, when it "rained throughout the match", but they did achieve their biggest win to date when they beat Wednesbury Strollers 13-0, after Strollers arrived four men short and recruited four local lads.

In Forest's side that day was a famous double-international, William Gunn, who played two seasons with the club. Although best known as a Test match cricketer, he also played football for England at outside-left, although his caps came a couple of years later, when he'd moved to Notts County. From St Anne's, Nottingham, he was a co-founder of the flourishing sports equipment company of Gunn and Moore, still operating in Nottingham.

In 1882 Forest were forced to move from the Trent Bridge ground as Notts County took over there (possibly a reason for the switch of

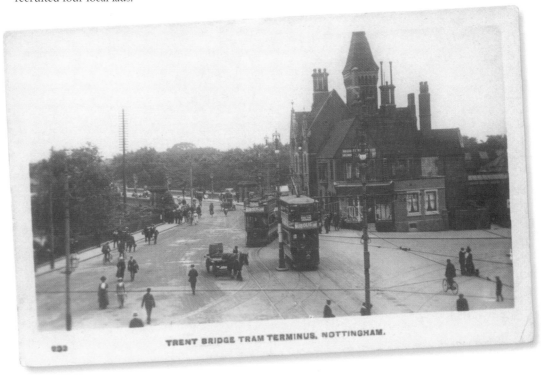

TRENT BRIDGE TRAM TERMINUS, NOTTINGHAM.

allegiance by Gunn). County were to play on the cricket ground for 27 years. Forest moved to Lenton, where they were to occupy two playing areas. First was a ground called the Parkside Ground which cost Forest £300 to construct, but had few facilities. It was on the north side of Derby Road, between the railway line and where Cottesmore School currently stands. Forest used the ground until 1885, and then moved to another in literally the next field called the Gregory Ground, which was used until 1890. This ground cost £500 to develop, including an enclosure for spectators. But the move to Lenton was a mistake as it was too far out from the centre of Nottingham, and crowds began to dwindle.

In truth, results also were not quite so good for a while in their new home. Although they beat Sheffield Heeley 7-2 in the FA Cup second round in 1882-83, they lost in the next after a replay with Sheffield Wednesday (strictly the Wednesday then, but usually accompanied by the "Sheffield" in reports). Notts knocked out Forest at an early stage in 1883-84, but Forest enjoyed another good run in 1884-85. First they beat Rotherham Town at the Parkside Ground 5-0, Rotherham having conceded ground advantage: 1,000 turned up. Then Sheffield Heeley were beaten 4-1, Sheffield Wednesday 2-1, Swifts 1-0 and Old Etonians 2-0, putting Forest into an FA Cup semi-final against Queen's Park, the Scottish

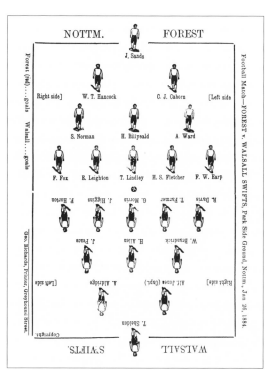

Left: The oldest known programme from any Nottingham Forest game, against Walsall Swifts on 26 January 1884 at the Parkside Ground, Lenton. Forest drew 1-1 with a goal from Frederick Fox in front of just 600 spectators (*Author's Collection*).

Below: The Forest team which contested the only FA Cup semi-final ever played outside England. Forest drew 1-1 with Glasgow's Queen's Park at Derby Racecourse and then travelled to Merchiston Castle School in Edinburgh to play the replay on 28 March 1885. Forest lost 3-0, yet another chapter in the astonishing Forest semi-final saga. Forest have (up to 1998) contested 26 FA Cup quarter-finals, winning 12 and losing 14. However, of the 12 semi-finals, Forest have won just three, by far the worst record of all major clubs. The 1885 team was: *Back row;* Danks, Caborn, Widdowson, Lindley; *Middle row;* Billyeald, Hancock, Fox, Ward; *Front row;* Norman, Leighton, Beardsley, Unwin. It was Fred Beardsley who later moved to Woolwich Arsenal and wrote back to Forest for Arsenal's very first set of red kit (*Author's Collection*).

Above: Forest were eventually to move across the Trent in 1898. It was still a rather remote spot, with the river not yet banked and prone to flooding. In 1895 the river froze solid for the first and last time in living memory; everyone walked across to West Bridgford and oxen were cooked in mid-river right next to the current location of the ground. The long-gone waterworks chimney alongside the Town Arms is from where the picture on pages 62/63 was taken *(Author's Collection).*

team. Ten thousand turned up to see a 1-1 draw at Derby, and a further ten thousand to see the replay at the Merchiston Castle School ground in Edinburgh. Queen's Park won 3-0 in the only FA Cup semi-final to be played north of the border.

In 1886 Forest players had a hand in the founding of Arsenal Football Club, then called Royal Arsenal. Two of Forest's former players, Fred Beardsley (who kept goal in the Cup semi-final against Queen's Park in 1885) and Morris Bates, played a part in founding the new club and, since they already owned red shirts (goalkeepers played in club colours in those days), suggested Arsenal play in red. Beardsley wrote to Forest to ask if Forest would help with some shirts, and Forest sent a complete set. Arsenal and Forest have always played in red.

The great Samuel Weller Widdowson (his parents were fans of Charles Dickens), who had served the club as honorary treasurer and was chairman from 1879 to 1884, played his last game for the club in 1887. Rules issued that year stated that the officers of the club consisted of a president, ten vice-presidents, a secretary, treasurer and ten committeemen, all elected by ballot annually. The committee picked the team and captain for each match.

The Football League was formed in 1888. Sam Widdowson attended the second meeting, at which it was decided that, as only 22 dates were available to be set aside for fixtures, the League could initially cater for only 12 members. The three whose applications were turned down were Forest, The Wednesday from Sheffield and the

now-defunct Halliwell. Possibly Forest's amateur leanings (they refused to embrace professionalism) told against them. Notts County succeeded in being elected, and thus were one of the 12 founder-members of the Football League, and for a short while enjoyed supremacy over Forest for this reason. At the end of the first Football League season Forest applied for admission again, but received only one vote, the four bottom clubs, who had to apply for re-election, all being re-elected. One of these was Notts County, who avoided last place only on goal average.

In 1888-89 Forest were drawn against Linfield Athletic, the Irish club, in the FA Cup first round. The match, at Forest, ended 2-2 after extra time and a week later Forest arrived in Belfast for the replay. Unfortunately Linfield had withdrawn from the Cup after Forest had departed on their trip, so the journey was wasted. However, so that their guests would not have travelled entirely in vain, Linfield arranged a friendly (which they won 3-1). Remarkably, 6,500 fans watched the English opposition. Bearing in mind that Forest had already played Queen's Park in Scotland in an FA Cup semi-final, and that they later played Cardiff at Ninian Park, they have the unique record of having travelled to all four home countries for FA Cup ties (although, as explained, it is not true, even if sometimes stated, that they actually played Cup-ties in all four countries).

In order to achieve competitive football, Forest joined the Football Alliance in 1889. There were 12 clubs in this league, of which the names Grimsby Town, Crewe Alexandra and

Sheffield Wednesday are well-known now. Two other clubs, Small Heath and Newton Heath, became Birmingham City and Manchester United respectively. Forest finished bottom in that first year, winning only six of their 22 matches. They lost 12-0 at Small Heath, their biggest ever defeat, and 9-0 at Darwen.

Another pioneering honour fell to Forest on 25 March 1889 when they played Notts Rangers in the first match played under electric lights. A battery of 14 Wells lamps, each of 4,000 candle power, lit the Gregory Ground. They cost £25, and 5,000 spectators saw Forest lose 2-0.

Forest did much better in their second season in the Alliance and finished sixth, after two points were deducted for playing an ineligible player. During this season they moved again – to the Town Ground, previously known as Woodward's Field. This was much their grandest ground so far. It was near the junction of the Embankment and Arkwright Street, the site of the present Meadows headquarters of the City Transport Department. It was but a few hundred yards from Notts County's ground at Trent Bridge. The club initially spent £1,000 to develop the site. A 50-yard stand with eight tiers of seats accommodated about 1,000 spectators and there was good terracing for several thousand more. The grand opening, at which the Mayor of Nottingham kicked off, was on 2 October 1890. Forest's intended opponents were Wolverhampton Wanderers of the Football League but the announcement of the match brought a big objection from Notts County, who were playing Bolton Wanderers in a League match

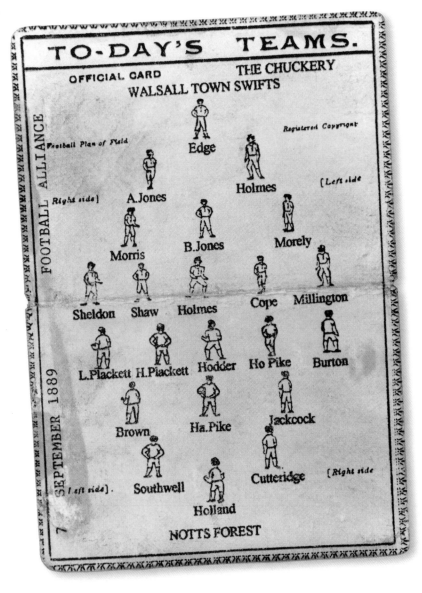

Left: The oldest programme for a Forest game in the club's possession is also the programme from Forest's first ever match in a recognised League. This was in the Football Alliance against Walsall Town Swifts on 7 September 1889 at the delightfully named "The Chuckery". Forest won the match 3-1 with two goals from William Hodder and an own goal from Edge. The attendance was a healthy 3,000 and this was, remarkably, the only game Hodder ever played for Forest. Note that the club already suffers from the title 'Notts' Forest - a problem to be regularly repeated in the illustrations that follow. This programme now hangs in the club's boardroom.

the same day. Notts protested to the Football League, who warned Forest that if they did not alter the date of the match they would ask all League clubs to cancel any fixtures they might have with the club. Wolves had to withdraw, of course, but Forest asked Queen's Park, their old Cup-fighting adversaries from Scotland, to stand in. According to a local report, Arkwright Street was thronged with Forest and County supporters who indulged in "a good deal of badinage". The rival gates were estimated at 6,000 for Notts County and 3,500 for Forest. Forest beat the Scots 4-2.

In these days of complaints about fixture congestion it is interesting to note that in that 1890 season Forest played 54 games between September and April. One of them was a visit to Woolwich Arsenal, to whom they had given the set of shirts. Forest's generosity ended with the shirts, as they beat the Gunners 5-0. Another match of that season has not been forgotten, since it remains the biggest away win ever recorded in any English first-class game. It was the defeat of Clapton in the FA Cup first round. On their opponents' ground, before 1,500 fans, Forest won 14-0. The team was W. Brown, M.J. Earp, A. Scott, Albert Smith, D.K. Russell, T. Jeacock, N. McCallum, W. "Tich" Smith, A. Higgins, T. Lindley, A.F. Shaw. Higgins scored five and Lindley four. Both were great servants of the club. Dr Tinsley Lindley's great forte was blistering pace as he was one of the fastest sprinters of his time, running for Cambridge University. He refused to wear the usual heavyweight football boots of the period in case

they slowed him up. In 1896 he was selected for the first Amateurs v Professionals match, a short-lived fixture, but he preferred to play for Forest instead. He was also the cause of one of the Football League's earliest attempts to break the rules - in fact he succeeded. The League was very aware of the danger of players being poached by one club from another. So, when Tinsley accepted an invitation and played a match for Notts County, the League were on to it immediately. Notts were fined £5 and the loss of a point. Notts appealed and at a meeting of the clubs had the punishment changed by a vote of six to five (the Preston representative being absent) to the restitution of the point but with an increased fine of £25. Alex "Sandy" Higgins, Forest's other main scorer in their record Cup win, was a Scot from Kilmarnock who joined the club from Derby and made his Forest debut in 1890. In his four seasons with them before retiring he scored 89 goals in 107 games.

Season 1891-92 saw possibly Forest's best achievement to date - they won the Football Alliance. Of their 22 Alliance matches they won 14, drew 5 and lost 3, winning by two points from Newton Heath (Manchester United), four from Small Heath (Birmingham City) and five from Sheffield Wednesday. A 3-0 defeat of Newton Heath late in the season was decisive. The attendance at that match was estimated at 9,000, of which 2,000 travelled from Manchester. However the biggest crowd in their history so far to watch Forest turned up at Wolverhampton for an FA Cup semi-final with West Bromwich Albion. Forest had beaten Newcastle East End,

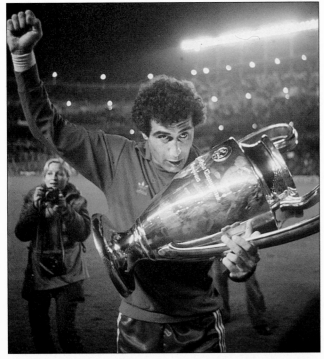 

Left to right: To date, just four players have captained England while being on Forest's books - Tinsley Lindley, Frank Forman, Peter Shilton and Stuart Pearce. Tinsley Lindley was a remarkable player who also represented Cambridge University. Between 13 March 1886 and 31 March 1888, he scored in no fewer than nine consecutive internationals, still a British record. He failed to score in just two of his 13 internationals, recording 15 goals in all.

Sunderland Albion and Preston North End to reach this stage, and 25,000 went to see the semi-final on neutral ground. The match was drawn 1-1, as was the replay a week later, also at Wolverhampton, when 14,000 attended. A second replay, at Derby (attendance 8,500), saw Forest thrashed 6-2 by the eventual Cup winners. It is interesting to note in passing that the Newcastle East End side, who visited Forest in the first round, changed their strip from their normal crimson, which would have clashed, to black and white. Next season they changed their name to Newcastle United.

A big change was afoot for Forest, too, largely brought about by their secretary, Harry Radford, a corporation official. He had been appointed secretary three years earlier, when he had been largely responsible for founding the Football Alliance to accommodate, among others, those clubs denied entry to the Football League. Later on he was to introduce professionalism to Forest. He was a far-sighted administrator who was to become eventually Forest's first representative to be a prominent member of the Football Association, representing midland clubs on the FA Council, and he also was elected to the League Management Committee and became League President. In 1892 he helped persuade the League to incorporate the Alliance, plus a few other clubs including Sheffield United and Burslem Port Vale, as a Second Division.

Fourteen new clubs obtained League status this season, three of them, Forest, Newton Heath and The Wednesday, going straight into the First Division, there being a new Second Division formed of 12 clubs.

Forest opened their Football League campaign with the hardest task possible, a visit to the previous season's Champions, Everton. Forest thus participated in yet another first by appearing in the first League match at Goodison Park, which had been opened little more than a week before. A turn-out of 14,000 watched the match and Forest acquitted themselves well by gaining a 2-2 draw. The first League team was: W. Brown, M.J. Earp, A Scott, K. Hamilton, Albert Smith, P. McCracken, N. McCallum, W. "Tich" Smith, A. Higgins, Horace Pike and T. McInnes.

The first League match at home, played a week later on 10 September 1892, resulted in a 4-3 defeat by Stoke, before a crowd of 7,000. The first League win came in the fifth game, on 10 October, away at Derby, by 3-2 and, exactly a week later, came the first League meeting with local rivals Notts County, which was lost 3-0 away. The highlight of the first season in the League was the return with Notts County, which saw Forest's biggest home gate of the season, 15,000, and a convincing 3-1 win, despite ace scorer Higgins dislocating a shoulder and missing the rest of the League programme. Forest

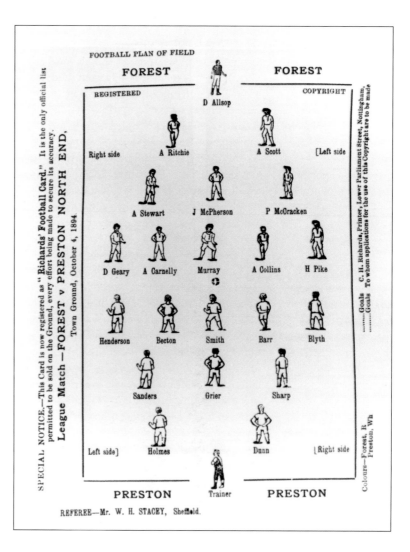

finished in a respectable 10th position, with 28 points (two for a win) from 30 games, four more points than Notts County who, as one of the bottom four, had to play off against the top four of the Second Division for promotion/relegation. County lost their match 3-2 to Darwen, and did not meet Forest in the League again for five years. Forest visited Goodison again that season, drawing 25,000 for an exciting second-round FA Cup tie that they lost 4-2.

Forest finished seventh in the League in the next two seasons, and in 1893-94 had to suffer being knocked out of the Cup by Notts County, who won 4-1 after a 1-1 draw at Forest. Notts County then went on to beat Blackburn Rovers in the semi-final and Bolton Wanderers in the final to be the first team to bring the FA Cup to Nottingham. Naturally, they were also the first Second Division club to win it. In the following two seasons Forest acquired a superstition concerning funerals. Travelling to Everton for the League game on 15 September 1894 the team passed a funeral cortege consisting of six carriages. They went on to lose the match 6-1. Almost exactly a year later, on 7 September 1895, they were on the way to Everton for a League match when again they passed a funeral cortege of six carriages. They feared the worst and it happened: they lost 6-2.

Above: By 1894 Forest had reached the heights of the First Division and were entertaining the likes of "Proud Preston", coincidentally the only other club ever to go through a whole season of First Division games without defeat. As an early sign of the problems of "pirate" programmes and merchandise "rip-offs", this was the first time Forest had issued an "official" programme. The game, at the Town Ground, was watched by 5,000 fans but Forest lost 2-0 (Author's Collection).

Below: Dennis Allsopp, the goalkeeper of the 1898 FA Cup winning team who had joined the club from rivals Derby. Allsopp is wearing the correct Forest strip of the era - Garibaldi Red shirts and dark blue shorts. The club has never worn anything other than red shirts but wore blue shorts between 1890 and 1900. All goalkeepers wore exactly the same strip as their teammates until 1910 and until 1912 they could handle the ball anywhere in their own half. It was not until 1890, in fact, that goalkeepers were prohibited from picking up the ball anywhere on the field. Note that the club wore no badge at the time *(Author's Collection)*.

Forest finished 13th in the League that year, and 11th the following year, when there was a dispute with Derby County. It was sparked off on 3 October 1896 which was the Saturday of Nottingham's famous Goose Fair. It is estimated there was an unruly crowd of 17,000 or so at the Town Ground which the police were unable to control, with the result that there were several stoppages of play. At last, with 20 minutes to go and the score 1-1, the referee abandoned the match. Derby promptly claimed half of the gate money of £357 but Forest wouldn't cough up. The League fined Forest £20, which Forest were happy to pay, being £337 to the good and with the replay to follow. This took place some six weeks later, witnessed by a more orderly 5,000 spectators. Derby County must have been very satisfied to win 2-1.

After two seasons in the bottom half of the table Forest just scraped into the top half at eighth in 1897-98, but this was to be easily their biggest season to date.

The 1897-98 season did not start at all well. They only drew their first League match 1-1 at home with newly promoted Notts County, despite Notts being down to ten men (no substitutes then) for most of the second half. They then lost 2-0 at West Brom, playing themselves with ten men in the second half. It was not until their sixth league match that they won - satisfyingly 3-1 at Notts County. Eventually they steadied and finished eighth in the table. But the FA Cup, the first round of which was in January, began with Forest enjoying a rich vein of form.

In the first and second rounds they had comfortable 4-0 home wins against Grimsby Town and Gainsborough Trinity respectively, both Second Division clubs, but in the third round were drawn away to West Bromwich Albion. It seemed their interest in the Cup was over when they were 2-0 down at half-time. But three goals between the 67th and 76th minutes from Frank Forman, Charlie Richards (his fifth in the Cup so far) and Alf Spouncer took them into the semi-final.

The semi-final opponents were Southampton, then a Southern League club, but by no means a weak side. In fact they were to take part in two of the next three finals, and in the one that they missed, another Southern League club, Tottenham Hotspur, became the only non-League club ever to win the FA Cup since the League was formed. There was considerable controversy over this semi-final. The first match, at the neutral ground of Bramall Lane, was drawn 1-1 before 30,000 fans, after a second-minute goal by Forest's centre-forward, Leonard Benbow, was equalised in the 22nd minute. The replay at Crystal Palace (no connection to the current club or Selhurst Park) caused the argument. Only 16,800 on a bitterly cold day saw a raging blizzard cause the game to be held up with no score and apparently little chance of resumption. However the match was restarted in much the same conditions as it was stopped and Tom McInnes and Charlie Richards scored goals in the 88th and 89th minutes to give Forest a 2-0 win. Southampton protested bitterly to the FA about the decision to restart the game, seeking to have it replayed, but the FA overruled them.

The final opponents were Derby County, who were a crack team boasting such all-time greats as the Goodalls, John and Archie, and the immortal Steve Bloomer, whose shot was said to be hard enough to knock goalkeepers over. Public sympathy was very much for Derby, partly because they had had a much harder road to the final, beating Villa, Wolves, Liverpool and Everton, but mainly because of the feeling of injustice, especially by southerners, on behalf of Southampton. *The Graphic* was very rude about Forest, stating that they "were to be accounted as one of the luckiest clubs which ever figured in a

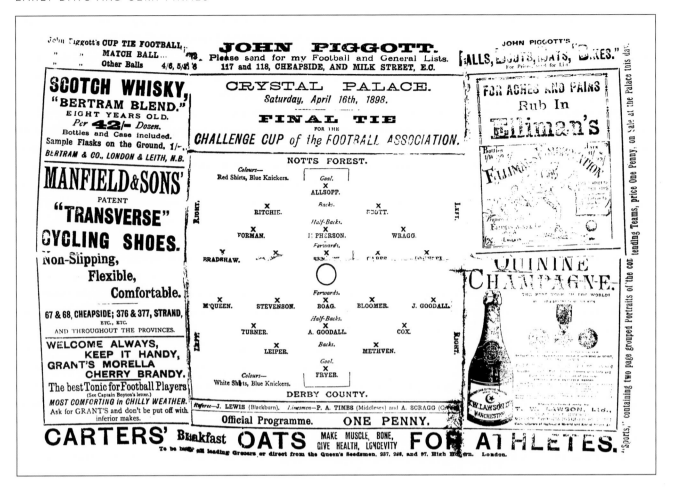

CRYSTAL PALACE.
Saturday, April 16th, 1898.
FINAL TIE
FOR THE
CHALLENGE CUP of the FOOTBALL ASSOCIATION.

NOTTS FOREST.

Colours—
Red Shirts, Blue Knickers.

Goal.
X
ALLSOPP.

Backs.
X   X
RITCHIE.   SCOTT.

Half-Backs.
X   X   X
FORMAN.   M'PHERSON.   WRAGG.

Forwards.
X   X   X   X   X
BRADSHAW.   BENBOW.   CAPES   SPOUNCER.

Forwards.
X   X   X   X
M'QUEEN.   STEVENSON.   BOAG.   BLOOMER.   J. GOODALL.

Half-Backs.
X   X   X
TURNER.   A. GOODALL.   COX.

Backs.
X   X
LEIPER.   METHVEN.

Goal.
X
FRYER.

Colours—
White Shirts, Blue Knickers.

DERBY COUNTY.

Referee—J. LEWIS (Blackburn).   Linesmen—P. A. TIMBS (Middlesex) and A. SCRAGG (Cheshire).

Official Programme.   ONE PENNY.

---

final tie." They went on to say that their luck didn't desert them: "With nothing to lose and everything to win, they played as many an inferior club has done before in such a match, with far more dash and vigour than their more talented opponents...".

Forest had played Derby County in a League match five days before the final, and lost 5-0, not a good omen. Bloomer scored three. They spent the intermediate time training at Matlock, a spa town in Derbyshire, where Derby County also prepared. Forest's party for this training period was without Alf Spouncer, their outside-left, who couldn't get the time off from work. In fact Spouncer had missed the League game with Derby, as did five other regulars. Forest's Cup final side was to have eight changes from the League side, only two positional, something the authorities might want explaining today. Derby had played their full Cup side in the League match.

There were 62,017 at the final, with gate receipts of £2,312. The guest of honour was Lord Rosebery, the former Liberal Prime Minister. Among the fans were around 5,000 from Nottingham, who had arrived on nine or ten special trains. John McPherson, the Forest captain, won the toss, and chose which end to defend. Boag kicked off for Derby at 3.30 p.m. Forest centre-forward Len Benbow was injured trying to reach a centre from Spouncer, but resumed. A foul on Spouncer near the line led to

a free-kick from William Wragg which allowed Arthur Capes to shoot along the ground through a ruck of players to put Forest ahead after 19 minutes. After 31 minutes Derby equalised, also from a free-kick, from which Steve Bloomer headed through, the ball beating Dennis Allsopp off the underside of the crossbar. Five minutes later Forest were in front again when Richards shot and Derby goalkeeper Fryer could only parry the ball for Capes, following up, to get his second. *The Graphic* carried an artist's impression of the goal, with the goalie tossing the ball to the attacker and the unfortunate caption, "Fryer throws the ball at Benbow's feet", not only getting the scorer wrong but the whole spirit of the incident.

In the second half Wragg, who had been injured in the first half, wrenched his knee again and went on the left wing, the usual place for the injured in those days, the double goalscorer Capes dropping to left-back and Spouncer moving inside. Derby had the better of the play, but luck and brave defending kept them out until, four minutes from time, McPherson made a strong tackle to win the ball near the Derby goal and while flat on the ground managed to get in a strong shot which found the net. So Forest ran out winners by 3-1 and received the Cup and their medals from Lord Rosebery in front of the pavilion. It was a particularly happy day for old stalwart Sam Widdowson, as it was his 50th birthday.

Above: A somewhat distressed example of the programme from the 1898 FA Cup final between Derby and (inevitably) "Notts" Forest. Despite a whole industry devoted to the subject, no programme from this final has come up for sale in the past 30 years. Good examples from finals in the 1890s currently sell for around £10,000 at Christies (*Author's Collection*).

Below: A rare contemporary illustration relating to the 1898 final - no photographs are known to have survived. The artist for this painting was a local cartoonist, Bob Jardine, who drew it for the newspapers of the time. Derby were hot favourites, having beaten Forest 5-0 in a League game five days before the final, and Jardine's original drawing showed Derby victorious and Forest being wheeled away. Jardine redrew the piece at the last minute by switching the locations of the Castle and Derby Cathedral and changing the shirt colours. The leading Derby player is clearly meant to be the balding John Goodall. It is fair to assume that Jardine had never seen a motor car, judging by the peculiar device he has drawn. The first motor car seen in Nottingham was probably driven over Trent Bridge by Councillor Atkey (later a well known motor dealer) in 1897.

Forest's winning team was given in a local paper as: D. Allsopp (goal); A. Ritchie, A. Scott (backs); Frank Forman, J. McPherson, W. Wragg (half-backs); T. McInnes, C.H. Richards (right-wing); L. Benbow (centre); A. Capes, A. Spouncer (left-wing). Forest had played the same team in all their FA Cup ties that season, except for James Iremonger replacing Frank Forman in the first semi-final and George Spencer replacing Len Benbow in the West Brom match.

The winning side stayed in London for the weekend and returned to Nottingham on Monday evening. According to the *Nottingham Evening Post*, crowds began to line the route they would take in the town long before the arrival of the train: "The whole community seemed to 'see red'. Flags, neckerchiefs, ties, sashes, ribbons, hat-bands - all manner of appendages flaunted the familiar colour..... Even the usually sober and sedate citizen appeared to have caught the infection and to be consumed with a desire to honour those who had done honour to the city." Four horses pulled the team and the Cup on a tour round the city, and the players were cheered all along the route.

A sax-tuba band played "See the conquering hero comes" as the players began their journey to the club headquarters at the Maypole Hotel, where chairman and former player William Hancock presided over a celebratory dinner. Notts County's chairman, H. Heath, filled the Cup to toast the club, just as Forest's chairman

George Seldon had done when County had won the Cup four years earlier. The County chairman suggested a special award for Frank Forman, not only for his play in the Cup final, but for a superb display against Bury a week before the Final, when he'd scored twice and ensured that Bury rather than County would be forced to play in the relegation play-offs which, in the event, were not required that season. Harry Radford, the Forest honorary secretary, declared the day the proudest of his life. Two days later the Cup was displayed on the stage at the Theatre Royal when the players went to see a play called "The Sporting Life". It was suggested by a newspaper that the Cup should be kept in the Castle Museum and not "hawked about indiscriminately which several previous holders have done" - no doubt a dig at Aston Villa, who had the Cup stolen from their care after winning it three years earlier.

So 33 years after turning to football, the former shinney players of Nottingham had achieved what more than one of the clubs that have graced the Premiership 100 years later had still failed to do - won the Cup. In that time they had many distinguished players and eleven of them had won international honours. Strangely of those 11 no fewer than seven were to win only one cap. Frank Forman, of the Cup-winning team, went on to win nine, but eight of these were still to come. Another of the Cup winners, inside-forward and ace goalscorer Charlie Richards, from Burton-on-Trent, won his only cap in 1889. As mentioned before, the first

Forest international was the centre-forward Arthur Goodyer, from Stamford, Lincolnshire, who played from 1876 to 1880 and made his lone appearance for England against Scotland at Kennington Oval on 5 April 1879, playing on the right wing. He scored in a 5-4 win. In actual fact he was beaten into the England team by Arthur Cursham, who played for Forest in 1872 and made six appearances for England from 1876 to 1883, but Cursham had by then moved on to Notts County.

Sam Widdowson of Forest played an attacking role for England against Scotland in Glasgow in March 1880 and was on the losing side 5-4. Edwin Luntley, from Croydon, Surrey, one of three brothers who played for Forest between 1878 and 1886, was a defender in that match in Glasgow, and he earned a second cap against Wales in Wrexham two days later when England won 3-2. With him in that victorious side was another Forest player winning a lone cap, John Sands, from Dudley, a goalkeeper who played for Forest from 1876 to 1883. In 1885 Tommy Danks, an attacker, played against Scotland at Kennington Oval in a 1-1 draw, his only cap. He came from Sherwood, in Nottingham, and had the amusement of playing in front of the Walters brothers, the full-backs with the humourous initials, A.M. and P.M. John Leighton, another Nottingham-born player, turned out on the right wing for England against Ireland at Belfast in 1886 and helped in a 6-1 victory.

Making his international debut in the same match as Leighton was the flying Dr Tinsley Lindley, who scored one of the goals. He was to

become one of Forest's most celebrated players but, at the time, he was only 20 and playing for Cambridge University, although his name appears frequently, if not regularly, in Forest line-ups from 1883. Born in Nottingham, he had attended Nottingham High School before going to the university. In all he won 13 caps up to 1891, his last appearance being against Ireland, when a regular Forest player. In only two of his 13 internationals did he fail to score, his best being a hat-trick in a 7-0 defeat of Ireland in 1887. He scored 15 goals in 13 games for England, a remarkable record. His four games as a Forest player produced three goals.

In 1889 Frank Burton, born in Nottingham, became yet another Forest player to win a lone international cap, a single appearance against Ireland in a 6-1 win, but Arthur Smith in the last decade of the century began to alter things by winning three caps between 1891 and 1893. Smith was also born in Nottingham, and joined Forest from Notts County. A defender, he was on the winning side in all of his internationals, which were against each of the three home countries.

When Forest won the Cup the new century was only two more years away. Forest were already raising funds for yet another splendid new ground. It would be open for the new season, complete with a proud banner fluttering in the wind "FA Cup Winners 1898". The energetic members of the private club that was Forest were not going to become complacent, and it seemed as if the football world was at their feet, inviting them to new heights. They reached them, but it took three-quarters of a century.

A remarkable photograph of The City Ground on the day it opened, 3 September 1898. The flag on the Main Stand reads "NFFC Cup Winners 1898". The new ground was named The City Ground because the old stadium was known as the Town Ground, after the adjacent Town Arms pub. Nottingham was granted its charter as a City in 1897 to commemorate Victoria's Diamond Jubilee and someone had the bright idea of making the link from Town to City. Hence The City Ground. This may have been civic, but it was singularly inappropriate as the new ground was actually in the County of Nottinghamshire and has remained so since. When Notts County moved from Trent Bridge to Meadow Lane in 1910, Nottingham was left with the "County" club playing in the City and the "City" club playing in the County at The City Ground *(Author's Collection)*.

CHAPTER THREE
A barren midlife
1899–1944

I N 1897, before their momentous Cup win, the officers of the Nottingham Forest Football Club decided to move to a new ground, which was to become The City Ground, the club's home for the next 100 years. The initial sum required to finance the move was £3,000, which the club decided to raise by subscription from members, supporters and businessmen in the town. The idea, which was called the "New Ground Scheme", was for them to buy bearer bonds in the sum of £5 each, which could be redeemed later. The conditions of the scheme were adopted at the December AGM, and over £2,000 was raised in this way. Many of the bonds were never redeemed, and indeed on the centenary of the founding of the club one was presented to the Nottingham Public Library for its archives. In effect, of course, the purchasers had made the club a donation towards the new ground.

The ground was only a few hundred yards from the Town Ground at the opposite end of Trent Bridge. When completed it was nothing like the fine stadium it is today, being wide open on three sides with no protection for spectators from the weather. But the playing surface was to be, and to remain, one of the finest in the country. The reason for this was the presence on the committee of J.W. Bardill, a nurseryman and landscape gardener. His company was given the task of preparing the pitch. The secret was the digging out of the playing area to a depth sufficient to take two feet of clinker, making sure that the pitch would drain perfectly for all time. The surface itself was then made up of top quality turf brought in by barge on the Trent from Radcliffe-on-Trent. Generations of footballers have reason to thank the workmanship of Mr Bardill, whose family firm flourished and still exists at Sandiacre.

Forest had one of their best players to date in the line-up for the first game at the new ground, half-back Frank Forman, who had made his debut for them aged just under 20 in 1895 (in a 6-2 Cup defeat by Villa) and had been more or less ever-present since. Frank had followed his brother Fred to Forest from Derby County. Fred was the older by 18 months and had made his Forest debut, aged just over 20, in February 1894. Fred was an attacking player, initially an inside-forward, later a winger, and also became an immediate regular, although unfortunately he missed much of the Cup-winning season and quite a bit of the next. A month before his efforts in the Cup final, Frank Forman made his debut for England in a 3-2 victory over Ireland in Belfast. It was the first of his nine caps, all won with Forest. When Fred Forman got his regular place back in the side, halfway through the 1898-99 season, he, too, was selected for the

season's internationals, in those days just the three matches with the home countries. They were his only caps, but neither Frank nor Fred was on the losing side for England. Fred scored three times in his three games. Both brothers scored in England's 13-2 defeat of Ireland at Sunderland in 1899. The Formans remained the only brothers from the same professional club to represent England together until Manchester United's Neville brothers nearly 100 years later. The Walters brothers, A.M. and P.M., had played for England together in 1889 and 1890 while playing for the amateur Old Carthusians, but were never "registered" players with that team as registrations were not required for all amateur sides.

The Formans were not the only members of their family to serve Forest and England, as their nephew, Harry Linacre, joined Forest in 1899 and kept goal for them for nearly ten years. He made two international appearances in 1905, and he too was not on a losing side. In fact a 2-2 draw with Scotland when Frank Forman was playing in 1901 was the only "international point" dropped by the whole family.

In that first season at The City Ground it took Forest until their eighth League game to win at home, a 2-1 victory over Stoke. They never got into the top half of the table, and finished 11th, but there were some milestones and big events to register this season. The most important, so far as the future performance of the club was concerned, was the debut on 3 December 1898 of Arthur Grenville Morris, a Welshman from Builth Wells, who joined the club from Swindon Town for the then huge fee of £200 ("can any player be worth it?"). He hardly missed a game for a number of seasons, making

Above: The club issued bonds as a means of funding the new stadium across the river in 1898. They were for £5 and this one was issued on 10 February 1898. £2,000 worth of bonds were sold and few were ever redeemed.

Right: Arthur Grenville Morris was the undisputed star of his era and among the greatest of all Forest players. He still holds the all-time club goalscoring record (with 199 in the League and 217 overall) a century after his debut in December 1898. He won 21 Welsh caps and the very first film ever made at The City Ground was a newsreel about him in 1904. This cartoon was by Amos Ramsbottom who was born in Auckland, New Zealand, in 1889 and later moved to Manchester where he became a well known caricaturist of sports personalities. Morris was the only Forest player he ever drew *(Author's Collection).*

Below: Harry Radford, the Forest secretary, became one of the leading lights in the Football League. Because of the unusual constitution of the League, the eight original subscribers, including Radford, continue to have their names on the bottom of the Articles of Association and recorded at every annual meeting of the League. Hence Radford's name is remembered today although, unlike four of the eight in Bentley, McGregor, McKenna and Sutcliffe, he never became president. This page is from the Annual General Meeting of 1998.

We, the several persons whose names and addresses are subscribed, are desirous of being formed into a League in pursuance of this Memorandum of Association, and we respectively agree to take the number of shares in the Capital of The League set opposite our respective names.

Names, Addresses and Description of Subscribers	No. of Shares taken by each Subscriber
JOHN J BENTLEY Acresfield, Bolton Journalist	One
T.H. SIDNEY North Road, Wolverhampton Gentleman	One
JOHN LEWIS Old Grammar School, Blackburn Carriage Builder	One
HARRY S. RADFORD Tavistock Chambers, Nottingham Agent	One
WILLIAM McGREGOR 306 Summer Lane, Birmingham Draper	One
JOHN McKENNA 28 Nuttall Street, Liverpool Vaccination Officer	One
GEO. H. LEAVEY 49 Highbury New Park, N. Hosier and Outfitter	One
CHAS. E. SUTCLIFFE Alder Grange, Rawtenstall Solicitor	One

Witness to the signatures of all the above named subscribers:

THOS. CHARNLEY 13 Winckley Street, Preston Secretary to The Football League

Dated the 4th day of March, 1904

The old Memorandum has 2,159 words as compared with this document with 1,096 words.

4

the number 10 shirt his own, in the position which would have been called in those days inside-left. In fact Morris was called "the prince of inside-lefts". He also occasionally led the line.

Grenville Morris was a brilliant all-round sportsman, being as good at tennis as football. Being a professional footballer prevented him playing tennis at Wimbledon and elsewhere, it being strictly amateur, so he became a coach and taught many of the leading players of the day. He was 21 when making his Forest debut, and already had five Welsh caps with Aberystwyth and Swindon Town. With Forest he went on to win 16 more, his last coming in 1912. Wales, of course, were not as strong as England or Scotland, but Morris netted nine goals, including both in a 2-2 draw with Scotland in 1911. Many of his games were in the same team as the immortal Billy Meredith, who said of him: "He was a great player, a brilliant schemer, a tricky dribbler and had a fine shot." In his illustrious career with Forest (during which time he also ran his own coal-merchant's

business, and had an agreement that he could train as he wished) he was captain for five of the 15 years and in 457 games scored 217 goals. On his retirement he held the appearance record for the club, and of his goals 199 came in the League, which figure remains the club record, and amazingly, is still not threatened 100 years after his debut.

When Forest's defence of the FA Cup began with a home tie with Aston Villa, the mighty "double" winners of the season before Forest's win, the crowd of 32,070 was a record for Nottingham, as were the gate receipts of £1,382. It was a stirring match in which goals from Arthur Capes and Fred Forman saw Forest home 2-1. The second round was away at Everton, and Forest, presumably taking care to avoid funeral processions on the way, won 1-0 with another Fred Forman goal. This was a good performance in front of 23,000, as many Forest players were said to be suffering from food poisoning. In the third round they were drawn to play Sheffield United, with their famous goalie, "Fatty" Foulkes, a match which broke the home attendance record again, with 33,500 present. This time gate receipts were not a record, being £14 short! Unfortunately Forest lost 1-0 to Sheffield United, who returned to The City Ground for the Cup semi-final with Liverpool.

This was drawn 2-2, but United won on the third replay and went on to win the Cup.

This year the man who had done so much for Forest, Harry Radford, was elected to the League Management Committee, and was to serve on it until he died ten years later. The minutes of the Football League still, one hundred years later, formally contain Harry Radford's name and address. Another Nottingham man chosen for the Committee this year was Charles E. Sutcliffe, a solicitor who would go on to serve the Football League for 50 years and to reach its highest office as president.

That Forest, at the turn of the century, were among the stronger teams in the League is apparent by their record for 1899-1900, when they finished eighth in the table and reached the FA Cup semi-final yet again. Grenville Morris described the semi-final defeat by Bury as the greatest disappointment in his footballing career. The first match was drawn 1-1 at Stoke, but in the replay at Bramall Lane Forest were cruising at two up with only ten minutes left. Bury scored and Forest defended until the last minute when the Forest centre-forward, Bob Beveridge, booted the ball 40 yards back over his own goal-line. The Bury captain, Pray, took the corner and waved up the whole team, goalkeeper included, to the Forest goal. The Bury centre-forward, McLuckie, scored, the final whistle blew immediately, and Bury scored again in extra time to win. As they went on to win the final easily (beating Southampton 4-0), Forest had obviously missed a great chance of a second Cup victory. Of all Forest's numerous semi-final defeats, this was perhaps the saddest and most avoidable. However, Nottingham Forest's baseball team, captained by Forest's goalie, Dennis Allsopp, earned consolation by winning the English Cup.

When Forest, with the Formans, Grenville Morris, Harry Linacre in goal and Jim Iremonger making his England debut at full-back late in the season, finished fourth in the League in 1900-01, their best so far, who could have guessed that this would remain the highest Forest would finish for the next 66 years? Forest finished only six points behind Champions Liverpool and, until they lost four of their last five matches in 19 days in April, including the last of all to Liverpool, they retained hopes until very late in the season of the Championship. A 3-0 win over Bolton Wanderers on Christmas Day must have seemed something like a seasonal present. Bolton goalie Sutcliffe broke a finger in the pre-match warm-up.

A reserve forward, Hanson, took his place. Had the match started, of course, Bolton would have had to play with ten men, as substitutes were unknown in those days.

In 1901-02, when Forest finished fifth, they yet again earned a semi-final place in the FA Cup with a game of penalties - Frank Forman scored two and Linacre saved one for Forest, resulting in a 2-0 win over Stoke. Unfortunately by the time of the semi-final with Southampton at White Hart Lane there was a smallpox epidemic in Nottingham and fewer than 200 fans took the train to London. With only 30,000 present, the Saints won 3-1. This period, 1897 to 1902, was

TRENT BRIDGE, NOTTINGHAM.

These pages: A series of postcards from the Edwardian era showing the startling structure that dominated Trent Bridge and The City Ground at that time. This was the Midlands Industrial Exhibition which opened in May 1903 and featured a funfair incorporating an Industrial Hall, an Ivory Palace, a Canadian Water Chute (100 feet high and 600 feet long), a Mexican toboggan and a Fairy River. Unfortunately on 4 July 1904 the Fairy River caught fire and most of the exhibition disappeared with it. The back of the Main Stand also caught fire (a portent of 1968) but there was little damage done, and, indeed, little to damage at the time. The picture above shows the crowd flocking away from a game. Some of the crowds were quite startlingly large for a ground which did not change from its opening until after the Second World War. As early as 1899, Forest were attracting 32,070 for a Cup tie against Aston Villa. The Victoria Embankment (shown centre right) was opened on 25 July 1901 *(Author's Collection)*.

Forest entertain Bury at The City Ground on 10 September 1904. The Forest players **(above)** are Spouncer and Niblo. Note that the Bury keeper wears the same strip as his teammates, the only distinguishing feature being his cap. Forest won 5-1, their best win of the season, with Grenville Morris getting a hat-trick. Of all the many distressing semi-final displays in Forest's history, the worst was definitely that against Bury in 1900. The teams initially drew 1-1 at Stoke but in the replay at Bramall Lane Forest were 2-0 up with ten minutes left. Bury scored one and then, in the 90th minute, centre-forward Bob Beveridge miskicked the ball 40 yards back over his own goalline and Bury brought everyone, including their keeper, up for the corner. McLuckie their centre-forward, headed the ball home to make it 2-2 as the referee's whistle went. Needless to say, Bury made it 3-2 in extra time and went on to beat non-League Southampton easily 4-0 in the final.

to be the best in Forest's history until the glorious first five years of Brian Clough. It was a period which could have been built on and used to create a greater club than the next seventy years were to foretell. But the chance was missed – for reasons that are lost in the mists of time – and we are left only to wonder at what might have been.

The next two seasons were disappointing for Forest as they settled into mid-table despite the goal scoring efforts of Grenville Morris. In 1902-03 he scored in eight successive League games, in three of them adding a second goal, yet Forest won only two of them. The second of these seasons saw the Formans retire from regular play. In 1904-05 Forest slipped to 16th place of 18, but there was no relegation this season as four newcomers to the League meant the two divisions were increased by two teams each (Notts County

finished bottom and also stayed up). The highlight of the season at The City Ground was the FA Cup semi-final between Everton and eventual Cup winners Aston Villa, where the receipts of £1,444. 4s. were a new record for Nottingham.

However 13 Forest players made a notable contribution to the spread of soccer's popularity by touring Argentina and Uruguay in the summer of 1905. The 13 who went, with secretary Harry Hallam and vice-president Harry Radford, were: goalkeeper Harry Linacre, full-backs Charles Craig and Walter Dudley, half-backs Sam Timmins, George Henderson, Bob Norris and C. Clifford, and forwards Tom Davies, Bill Shearman, George Lessons, Tom Niblo, Alf Spouncer and H. Holmes. They played Penarol of Uruguay and seven games in Argentina, one against a British residents team called Britanicos, whom they beat 13-1. They won all the other games with a goal tally of 44 against 3. There were some good attendances, ranging from 1,500 to 10,000. One of the spectators was a young boy who grew up to be the Argentine dictator Peron. The round trip took two months, the party arriving back on 2 August 1905, a month before the start of the new season.

Another famous Nottinghamshire and England cricketer turned out occasionally for Forest for a couple of seasons, Joe Hardstaff Senior. He was a centre or inside-forward, who disgraced himself on one occasion by missing the train for a visit to Stoke. Unfortunately for Hardstaff, most of his appearances were in the 1905-06 season, a disastrous one for Forest.

With Wolverhampton Wanderers finishing eight points adrift at the foot of the table, Forest were engaged in a struggle with Bury and Middlesbrough to avoid the second relegation place. Unfortunately Forest were away to Everton on the last day of the season and crashed 4-1, a result which saw them finish below Middlesbrough on goal average by five-hundredths of a goal and be doomed to relegation for the very first time in their history.

Forest were beginning to suffer by the fact that they remained a private club, and that therefore the money available to improve the side came only from receipts and members'

subscriptions. They clearly were at a disadvantage in this respect compared with the clubs which were limited liability companies. The members decided that they should adopt the provisions of the Company Act and become such a company themselves. It was decided at the annual meeting to issue 1,000 £1 shares and appoint five directors, but in the event nothing was done. This may be because in the 1906-07 season they bounced back to the top division at the first time of asking, and with a very impressive record.

Forest began badly with two defeats and a draw in the first three games, but they lost only four League games thereafter. They drew two big crowds with their matches against the new London glamour club Chelsea, who had been elected straight into the League on their formation the season before, when they finished third. Forest drew 22,000 to The City Ground and beat Chelsea 3-1 and at Stamford Bridge were watched by 25,000 with another 15,000 allegedly locked out. Forest won again, 2-0. Forest, in fact, won 15 and drew the other of their last 16 matches and ended with 60 points, three more than Chelsea and 12 more than the third club. Forest had two Welsh internationals this season. Edwin Hughes was born in Wrexham and joined Forest from Wrexham, who are the oldest Welsh club but who at the time were not a League club. Hughes, a right-half, had one cap with Wrexham, and won nine with Forest between 1906 and 1911

The Forest team visited Uruguay and Argentina in June and July 1905, the club's first ever foreign tour. Penarol were beaten 6-1 and Rosario 6-0. There was to be one forerunner of future Anglo-Argentinian conflicts when Belgrano were beaten 7-0 at the Sociedad Sportive (the Argentine Sporting Club) before 9,700 spectators. The journey took over three weeks in each direction.

before moving on and winning six more with Wrexham and Manchester City. A.W. Green, on the other hand, was at the end of his career. He had won six caps with Villa and Notts County before joining Forest in 1907. He won two more as a centre-forward before moving to Stockport County.

Forest did not flourish back in the top flight, finishing ninth in the first season back and then dropping to 14th for the next two, and without getting past the third round of the FA Cup. However in 1907-08 centre-forward Enoch "Nocker" West had the personal satisfaction of leading the League goal scorers with 27 goals. Moreover, four of these came in the same match, at home to Sunderland on 9 November 1907. He was the only Forest player to score four goals in the top division until Peter Withe did so against Ipswich Town just a month short of 70 years later. International full-back Jim Iremonger retired. He nearly followed William Gunn as a double international in 1911 when he toured Australia with MCC but he did not manage to oust the legendary Hobbs and Rhodes as an opening batsman in the Tests. Iremonger actually played in goal for Forest in his last two seasons and was keeping goal in one of the most remarkable matches in Forest's history.

On 21 April 1909 Forest were playing their second last League match with the threat of relegation still alive and it was essential that they win their last two games. Their opponents at The City Ground were local rivals, bottom of the table Leicester Fosse, the forerunners of Leicester City, who had been promoted the previous season and were playing their first season in the top flight. Leicester were so poor on this particular afternoon that Forest ran up what remains their record League victory: 12-0. This is also the record score for any game ever played in the top division of English football. For the record, the Forest side was: Jim Iremonger, Walter Dudley, George Maltby, Edwin Hughes, George Needham, Jack Armstrong, Bill Hooper, Tom Marrison, Enoch "Nocker" West, Grenville Morris and Alf Spouncer. Hooper, Spouncer and West each scored three, Morris two and Hughes one. This was the first instance of three players from the same team each scoring a hat-trick in a League match and it has only happened twice since. So bad were Leicester that there were rumours of collusion, and with Manchester City, Liverpool, Bury and Bradford City all in the relegation battle (City and Bury had both beaten Forest on successive days a week before), the League were forced to set up a Commission of Inquiry. The conclusion was that "the bulk of the Fosse players attended the wedding of R.F. Turner two days before the match and that the celebrations were kept up on the night before the contest. In the opinion of the Commission

these celebrations, at an inopportune time, accounted for the indifferent form of a number of the Fosse players...." The Commission had the grace to add: "All the witnesses agreed that the Forest team was in remarkably good form."

In their final match of the season, also at home against Middlesbrough, 8,000 fans saw Forest two up in two minutes. They won 4-1 and saved themselves from relegation, finishing two points clear of Manchester City, who were the unlucky ones to go down with Leicester Fosse.

An unusual event occurred in the local derby with Notts County that season. Jim Iremonger had a younger brother, Albert, who was to turn out for Forest in 1917, but for many years he played for Notts County. He was the tallest player of his day, standing 6ft 5in. In the match at The City Ground on 13 March 1909 the Iremonger brothers were in opposite goals. Forest won 1-0 through a "Nocker" West penalty.

Season 1910-11 was another traumatic one for Forest. It started in tremendous style with three wins and a draw in their first League games, three of them away. A total of 85,000 watched these games, including 28,000 for a win at Liverpool, 27,000 for a draw at Notts County and 20,000 for a home win over Manchester United. The match at Notts County signalled the opening of the Meadow Lane ground, and the attendance and receipts (£750) were both new records for County. So both Forest and County, after wanderings in and around Nottingham, were now in the grounds which they currently inhabit.

Forest's burst at the start of the season didn't last, and they settled down into their usual mid-table position. On Christmas Eve a famous name appeared in their colours for the first of many appearances over the next few years: it belonged to a 20-year-old centre-half born in Ellesmere Port and signed from Birrell Ironworks, Joe Mercer. He was the father of the Joe Mercer who later played with such distinction for Everton, Arsenal and England and who indeed, for a while, managed the England national team.

On 21 January Forest completed a double over Liverpool by winning 2-0 and fans were resigned to their usual end-of-season mid-table fare. However they endured what must be a record descent for any club in the top division. They lost seven matches in a row, scraped a 0-0 draw at home to Manchester City, then lost their

Harry Linacre, nephew of the Formans and the winner of two England caps in goal in 1905. He made 335 first-team appearances for Forest between 1899 and 1908 and has signed this photograph taken at the Bridgford End in front of the original scoreboard (*Author's Collection*).

final five matches. Thirteen matches, one point from a possible 26, eight goals scored, 29 conceded. Forest finished bottom, but even so only four points adrift from safety. Two wins in that horrendous run of 13 matches would have seen them safe. In fact, had they beaten Bury 1-0 instead of losing 1-0 at the start of that run they would have survived.

This season was disastrous all round for Forest. They went out in the first round of the FA Cup, 2-1 at West Ham in a match played in fog. Notts County, in their new ground, and in mid-table, had taken over the leadership of Nottingham while Forest dropped into the Second Division for the second time.

This time there was no immediate return for Forest and County were to join them in 1913-14.

The end of the 1913-14 season was the absolute nadir of Forest's history. Only 16 years after winning the Cup, they finished bottom of the Second Division and had to seek re-election. They finished top of the poll, but this was little consolation as the war clouds gathered.

The 1914-15 season began ten weeks after the assassination of Archduke Franz Ferdinand in Sarajevo which precipitated the First World War, so it was played in an unreal atmosphere. Forest were in severe financial straits, and used only 17 players this season, and four of those did not play often. William Fiske, a goalkeeper, and Robert Firth, right-winger, were reservists and had to rejoin the services - Firth didn't play that season at all. Joe Mercer, Tommy Gibson, Harold Iremonger (another goalkeeper - three different Iremongers played in goal for Forest) and Tim

Coleman joined the forces, although managing to play many games, and it was claimed that Forest supplied as many players to the "Footballers' Battalion" as any other club except Clapton Orient. Poor Fiske's four Football League matches and one FA Cup match were his last, for he was to be killed in action.

Bearing Fiske's sacrifice in mind, the fact that Forest avoided the need for re-election by one place might seem unimportant but, in the context of the history of Nottingham Forest, this was very important. Forest could very easily have gone out of business around this time.

Forest were still a private club (their position was to become more and more of an anachronism, until they finally became a limited company in 1982). Some influential men began to make their presence felt in the administration around this time. In 1912 R.G. Marsters, who had worked for former secretary Harry Radford, succeeded to the secretaryship after being assistant to Harry Hallam and F.W. Earp. Marsters wrote to Bob Cobbin asking him to join the committee. From 1920 to 1948 Cobbin was to be a dominant chairman, at first with Marsters as secretary. They were to be instrumental in keeping the club afloat after the First World War, and Cobbin again in the Second World War. Cobbin was to become Forest's longest serving Chairman and one of the most influential men in the whole history of the club. Meanwhile, even with players joining up and the small playing staff, as already mentioned, the 1914-15 season hadn't progressed far before Forest were forced to apply to the Football League for help in paying the players'

Below: The triumphant Forest team which won the 1906-07 Second Division championship. The team was: *Standing:* Needham, Hughes, Dudley, Wolfe, Linacre (goalkeeper), Maltby, Norris (trainer); *Seated:* Hooper, Marrison, Green, Morris

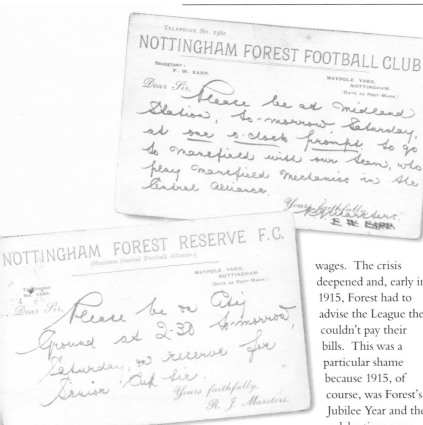

(captain), Nocker West and Armstrong. Enoch 'Nocker' West was among the most celebrated and notorious of all Nottingham Forest players, of any era. The following year, 1907-08, he scored 27 (some records say 28) of Forest's 59 goals and was the League's leading scorer, the only occasion a Forest player had ever led the goalscoring lists for the whole League until van Hooijdonk in 1998. Indeed, the only other occasions on which a Forest player has even led the lists for a single division are Duncan McKenzie with 26 in the Second Division in 1973-74 and Wally Ardron in the Third Division South with 36 in 1950-51. Ardron was just one goal away from leading the list for the whole League. Nocker West also holds the record for the longest ever suspension from the game - no less than 30 years between 1915 and 1945, and only lifted when he was 62 years old. This was for his part in fixing the result of the Manchester United versus Liverpool game on 2 April 1915, after he had been transferred to Old Trafford.

wages. The crisis deepened and, early in 1915, Forest had to advise the League they couldn't pay their bills. This was a particular shame because 1915, of course, was Forest's Jubilee Year and the celebrations were muted by the war, by financial reasons and because it seemed possible there might not be a 51st year! Forest kept going for the time being by means of a grant of £50 plus £10 per week to the end of the season from the League. Players took a 25 per cent reduction in pay. A public appeal raised £90, Forest's landlords returned a quarter's rent, £36 16s 6d (£36.82), local businesses were asked for donations and life memberships of the club were sold for a £10 subscription.

With all this, it was the war which was the main factor in Forest's survival as one of the country's most powerful League clubs. At the end of the 1914-15 season (Forest's last match resulted in a 7-0 defeat at Arsenal, who had just dropped the "Woolwich" from their name) the Football League was suspended for the duration of the war. Football itself continued, with leagues set up on a regional basis. Furthermore clubs could recruit "guest" players, who would turn out in many cases as war service permitted them to be available. And they did not need to be paid! It is not surprising that Forest, short of cash as they were, should be the club that possibly most used the system to advantage (in the Second World War, Aldershot, being near the well-known army barracks, did the same thing, and famously could field, week after week, the entire England half-back line of Cliff Britton, Stan Cullis and Joe Mercer - i.e. Joe Mercer "junior").

Forest began 1915-16 in the war-time Midland Section of the League, and secretary Marsters quickly rounded up one of the great goalkeepers of all time, Sam Hardy, who had won honours and caps with both Liverpool and Aston Villa, his club at the time. Hardy appeared for Forest in all 37 matches of the season, and Forest won both the Midland Section and a subsidiary League. Crowds averaged around 7,000 at the beginning of the war and dropped to around 4,000 by 1918, enough to get Forest back on a reasonable footing, and the 1918-19 season (the war ended in November 1918) was excellent for Forest. They again won the Midland Section (by a single point from Birmingham and Notts County) and after the armistice crowds grew to 24,000. Danny Shea, an international inside-right with Blackburn Rovers and the greatest playmaker of the day, had now joined Marsters' guests and proved a valuable goalscorer up front. Forest lost the last match of the Midland season 3-2 to Barnsley which drew the following unforgiving note from former Forest secretary Ken Smales 70 years later in his official statistical record *Forest, The First 125 Years*: "The winning goal was 'fisted' in."

At the end of the season Forest, as Midland Section champions, played Northern Section winners Everton for the Football League Victory Championship. It was a two-legged affair. The first match, at The City Ground before 20,000 fans, ended 0-0, with Everton's Gault shooting wide from a penalty. At Goodison, before 40,000, Forest won the second leg 1-0 with a goal from Noah Burton. Forest were awarded the League Championship, their first ever, and would perhaps have been surprised to hear that it was to be another 60 years before they would win the real thing.

After the war Hardy, after winning another Cup-winners medal with Villa and three more caps, joined Forest for the 1921-22 season and played just over three seasons for them before retiring aged 41.

On the resumption of the normal Football League programme in 1919-20, Forest took their place in the Second Division, both divisions being extended to 22 clubs. This allowed one piece of skulduggery to take place and another to go unpunished, at least so far as the club was concerned. First, politics managed to get Arsenal promoted to the top division, from which they've never since been relegated, despite their finishing only fifth in the Second Division of 1914-15, despite Barnsley, Wolves and particularly relegated Spurs having better claims to the place. Second, Manchester United avoided relegation despite having been found to have "fixed" their last match with Liverpool to escape the drop. One of the instigators of this was Forest's old player "Nocker" West, who was subsequently banned for life by the FA.

Forest had five players making their debuts in the first match of the post-war season and, in the first home match, they increased the entrance charge from 8d (about 3p) to a shilling (5p). It

was an undistinguished season for Forest, who finished 18th. One peculiarity of this season came when they were drawn at home to Newcastle United in the first round of the FA Cup. Forest sold the right to play at home to Newcastle for £500 plus an astonishing minimum of £1,500 as their half-share of the gate (this total of £2,000 would represent a big gate for Forest of around 30,000 spectators). Forest drew 1-1 before 47,652 at St James' Park, and replayed four days later (also at St James' Park) before another 30,728. So financially it might not have been a bad deal for both clubs. Greedy Forest also thought of seeking a sum from Notts County for removing the competition from their home tie with West Brom which would have been played at the same time.

The following season Forest were joined in the Second Division by Notts County, and in the League by 22 new clubs, who formed a Third Division. They were also joined by Sam Hardy and, whether or not they were inspired by the great goalkeeper, results improved dramatically after an initial 4-1 defeat at Crystal Palace. As Forest began to win regularly so the attendances improved, and gates of 15,000 or more became common.

It was a peculiarity of the post-war seasons up to 1923-24 that clubs would frequently play both matches against each of their rivals together, e.g. Forest would play Derby County on successive Saturdays, Leicester City on the next two, West Ham on the next two and so on. Thus on 8 October they drew 2-2 at Leicester before 25,000 fans (Forest scored twice in the last eight

minutes), then on 15 October played the return at The City Ground, where the attendance was even bigger, 30,000, thanks partly to five special trains running from Leicester. The result was another draw, 0-0.

Against Port Vale on 26 November 1921, it was noted that the ball "appeared to be painted white". Was this a forerunner of the white balls of decades later?

A very rare War League programme ("Official Card of the Match") from Forest's home game with Bradford Park Avenue in January 1919.

The squad which won the Second Division Championship and Shield in 1921-22. Forest finished four points clear of Stoke to regain the place lost in 1911. Despite Nottingham Forest's long history, it is surprising to recall that the club has won a Divisional title on only five occasions - the First Division in 1977-78, the Second Division in 1906-07 and 1921-22; the Third Division South in 1950-51 and the Football League in 1997-98 (Author's Collection).

Throughout the season the defence played so well that only 30 goals were conceded, the lowest ever in the Second Division. By 22 April 1922, in their third last game, Forest secured promotion by beating Stoke 3-1 before 15,000 at The City Ground ("rain fell throughout"), and they made themselves Champions with a match to spare with a 1-0 defeat of Leeds United a week later. Forest also had a good FA Cup run, reaching the fifth round, where they lost 4-1 away to Cardiff City before a crowd reported to be 50,470. The Forest regulars towards the end of the season were: Sam Hardy, Harold Bulling, Harry Jones, Jack Belton, Fred Parker, Jack Armstrong, Sid Harrold, Jack Spaven, Bob Parker, Walter Tinsley, Noah Burton and Paddy Nelis.

Of these players Jack Armstrong, the captain, was nearly at the end of a career that started in 1905. In 1922 he was transferred to Sutton Town, but by then he had broken Grenville Morris's appearance record. He turned out 461 times for Forest, a record which was to last for nearly 30 years until those stalwarts of the 1959 Cup-winning team, Jack Burkitt and Bob McKinlay, improved it in turn. Noah Burton was another long-server for Forest, who appeared from 1916 to 1931, apart from a season with Derby County in 1920-21. Jack Spaven was a goalscorer who was reckoned to be one of the hardest kickers of a ball the game has ever seen.

Centre-half Fred Parker and goalscorer Walter Tinsley were also very popular players.

If this season was seen as a renaissance for Forest, however, perspective was restored when, in the first season back in the top flight, they finished 20th, just outside the relegation places. They ensured their First Division status with a 2-0 win over Manchester City in the second last match of the season. Their accounts for that season are interesting, showing their biggest expense as wages at £11,151. Transfer fees cost £3,120, and match expenses (including reserve team) £4,015. In all their total expenses were £22,927. Their match receipts were £27,103 (gross) and £21,855 after tax. Of this £3,336 was due to visitors, slightly more than Forest received as visitors themselves, £2,905. Subscriptions (less tax) of £1,847 and ground receipts of £280 brought their revenue up to £23,551, a profit on the season of £624. As, however, Forest had carried over a debit balance of £1,143, the effect of their season was to reduce their debt to £519.

By now Bob Cobbin had taken over from former player Thomas Hancock as chairman of the club, Hancock having been chairman from 1897 to 1920. Another great player of the turn of the century, Frank Forman, had by now also joined the committee. Hancock, Cobbin and Forman were to be among the first six life members of Forest, the others being former

Below: Stony faces in the mud for five Forest stalwarts at the start of the 1927-28 season. From left to right: Sidney Gibson, Cyril Stocks, Noah Burton, Charlie Jones and Harold Wadsworth. Jones was by far the most celebrated. Already a Welsh international, he moved to Arsenal at the end of the season, won Championship medals in 1933 and 1934, and was a key part of Herbert Chapman's great Highbury team. In 1927-28 Forest were to finish a steady if unspectacular tenth in the Second Division, a position they were nonetheless to better only twice in the next quarter-century (*Ken Smales*).

players Joe Rawson, Dr Tinsley Lindley and Alf Parr. Cobbin had not been a player, but there can hardly have been a more committed Forest supporter. A campanologist, he had caused the bells of St Peters Church to be rung to welcome home the 1898 Cup winners, and his term as chairman was to last until after the Second World War. He served the FA well, eventually becoming vice-president, and in 1946 he joined the International Selection Committee. He was a bit eccentric, swimming in the Trent every Christmas Day, and was very autocratic, being one of those chairmen whose authority extended to every nook and corner of the club. He was almost the last of this once common breed, Bob Lord of Burnley hanging on till 1981.

On the field of play, Forest went to the penultimate match again before being safe from relegation in 1922-23 (they forced a home draw with Champions Huddersfield Town), but in 1924-25 their fate was sealed well before the end of the season. From 20 December to 2 April they played 15 League games without a win, and finished bottom, ten points adrift of safety. In the midst of their bad run, Forest secured a draw with Bolton on Boxing Day in strange circumstances. Forest had a penalty expert in left-winger Harry Martin. During the match with Bolton he received a bad injury to his leg, and retired to the dressing room. Forest went a goal down and were awarded a penalty. With Forest badly needing points, no Forest player on the pitch, realising the importance of it, was willing to take the kick. Finally, captain Bob Wallace went to the dressing

room and re-appeared supporting a semi-crippled Martin. Bolton's goalie was the England 'keeper Dick Pym, who played in three Wembley Cup finals in the 1920s without conceding a goal. The hobbling Martin beat him from the spot, salvaged a point and limped back to the dressing room.

Back in the Second Division again, Forest nearly slipped right through at the first time of asking, needing a run of wins in April to hoist them to 17th place. One peculiarity of the season was that in both the matches with Fulham, more than four months apart, referee T. Brown was booed off the pitch. Forest had their best Cup run for 17 seasons, however, reaching the quarter-final after disposing of Bradford City, Swindon Town and Sheffield United. Forest then came from behind twice to draw 2-2 with Bolton at home, drew again 0-0 after extra time at Bolton, but lost the second replay 1-0 at Old Trafford. Bolton (and Dick Pym) went on to win the Cup. A total of 87,004 watched the three quarter-final matches, with receipts of £6,628.

Forest had two internationals playing in these matches, their first since the lone caps won by Harry Jones for England in 1922 and Paddy Nelis for Northern Ireland in 1923. Francis Morgan had already been capped once for Northern Ireland when Forest bought him from Linfield Athletic in 1922, and he won six more caps with Forest up to 1929, when he moved on to Luton Town. He was a commanding centre-half. Charlie Jones was a tricky and intelligent outside-left who joined Forest in 1925 from Oldham and won four caps for Wales from 1926 to 1928 before

These pages: On 1 March 1930 Forest played Sheffield Wednesday in the quarter-finals of the FA Cup and the game drew a new record attendance of 44,166. This beat the previous record of 35,625 set up against Derby on 1 February 1928. Wednesday were a tremendous draw. Led by the great Jimmy Seed they were surprise League Champions in both 1929 and 1930 and their own fans expected the Double in 1930. Here a Forest attack comes to nought as Tommy Graham looks on, but the Reds still managed to come back from two goals down after 17 minutes to draw 2-2. Wednesday won the replay in front of 59,205 and the crowds were so great that the Forest bus could not get through and the team arrived late for the kick-off. As a result Forest were fined £50. Wednesday did not get their Double. They lost the semi-final 2-1 to Huddersfield when the referee disallowed a Wednesday shot which entered the net, claiming he had blown for full-time when the ball was in flight *(Nottingham Evening Post and Author's Collection)*.

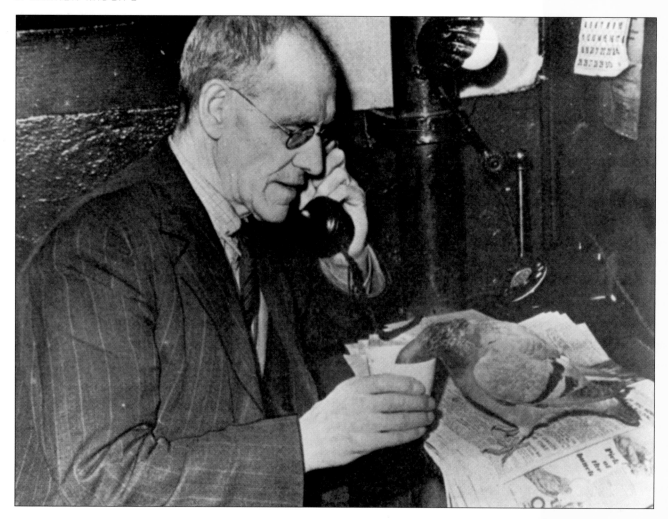

he was transferred to Arsenal, with whom he won four more caps in the 1930s and, of course, shared in their great Championship wins. Arsenal converted him to a right-half (they had Bastin on the left wing) but, unluckily for Jones, he missed the winning 1930 Cup final, despite playing in the earlier rounds, and his only Wembley appearance was in the controversial defeat by Newcastle in 1932. He returned to Nottingham as manager of Notts County for a short spell in 1934.

Forest could do little in the Second Division and, from their relegation in 1925 up to the Second World War, settled down mostly in the bottom half of the table. It must have been tough for the fans. A Second Division fixture at Grimsby on 1 January 1927 was chosen for the Supporters' Club annual outing! A 1-1 draw could not have made much of a day out. However, there must have been some fun at The City Ground for the Hull City Supporters' Club chose the match there in February 1928 for their outing. How those fans would have wondered at today's regular flights abroad by fans to watch European competition.

Despite their lack of League success Forest drew some good crowds - no fewer than 49,000 for a 1927 Second Division match at Manchester City - and had a good Cup run or two. In 1927-28 they beat Tranmere Rovers, Derby

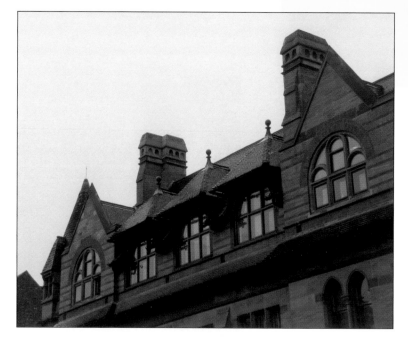

County (after a replay) and Cardiff City before losing 3-0 at Sheffield United before 52,640 in the quarter-final. In 1929-30 there was a similar run when Forest knocked out Rotherham, Fulham and Sunderland (after a replay) to reach the quarter-final again, this time against the other Sheffield club, Wednesday. The gates at The City Ground were closed half-an-hour before kick-off with 44,166 inside (receipts £3,822).

Right: In the inter-war period, season tickets were simple passes or, on occasions, discs which were shown at the turnstile by the holder each week. This is a typical pass for the centre of the Main Stand and was the most expensive in the ground at £3 3s (£3.15) in 1939. It is part of the collection of one of the club's most distinguished supporters, Philip Wilkinson.

Wednesday were two up in 17 minutes, but Forest got one back just before the interval and equalised in the second half amid "a pandemonium of cheering". Unfortunately Forest went out 3-1 in the replay when 59,205 spectators paid £4,100 at Hillsborough. Forest actually arrived late for the match and were fined £50.

In May 1931 Forest played a friendly at the Sparta Rotterdam ground against a Netherlands XI and won 3-1. Noah Burton's 15-year Forest career came to a close in December 1931, one of several to end that season. The names of two distinguished England cricketers appeared in the team line-ups: R.W.V. Robins, the Middlesex captain, both of whose League appearances were on Christmas Day, 1929 and 1930, and W.W. Keeton, the Nottinghamshire opener, who made five appearances in the 1932-33 season.

Forest's internationals weren't limited to cricketers: there were two footballing internationals as well in the 1930s. Tom Graham, a left-half, joined Forest from Consett Celtic in 1928 and appeared for England twice in 1931, against France in Paris, when France registered their first win ever over England, 5-2, and against Northern Ireland in Belfast. As an England international from the Second Division, he was a popular choice to represent Forest on the many cigarette card sets of footballers of the period. He played up to the Second World War, made a few appearances in war-time football and, after the war, became Forest's trainer. Jim Chambers, a winger, had won nine Northern Ireland caps with Distillery and Bury before joining Forest, for whom he played only nine games, from August to November 1931, before retiring. But he won three more caps (his last in December, after his last game for Forest). When he played against England (and Graham) in 1931, it was the second time Forest had supplied players to both sides in an international (Frank Forman and Grenville Morris had played against each other in 1903).

William Thompson, who played for Forest from 1922 to 1935, did not add a full cap to schoolboy caps he won in 1914, but he was described on a cigarette card as "one of the finest right full-backs that

Forest ever possessed". It is worth noting right-half Bill McKinlay, too, who played from 1927 to 1937, if only because his nephew Bobby, who Bill "discovered" for Forest when employed later as a scout, would play for the club for even longer and eventually hold the appearances record.

There were some nice coincidences in the 1934-35 season. A player called Ernest Smith joined early that season from Burnley and shortly departed for Rotherham. Meanwhile he made his debut at Bury on 15 September in a 1-0 defeat ("Blackpool illuminations blamed for low gate") and his only other appearance in the return match, which Forest lost 4-1 with Smith scoring. There was coincidence, too, in the two consecutive matches of 16 and 23 May, against Oldham and Burnley, both of which Forest won 5-0, the goalscorers in each case being, in this order: Dent, Peacock, Dent, Dent, Peacock. Although Tom Peacock was the junior partner on these two occasions, he was undoubtedly the club's best goal-getter of the era, and he had a purple patch in 1935-36. This came after he'd completely miskicked a penalty against Bradford PA, the ball trickling wide. But in a stretch of nine games between 9 November and 26 December he scored four goals in three separate matches: v Barnsley (6-0), v Port Vale (9-2) and v Doncaster Rovers (6-2). The quality of this performance can be judged by the fact that, in well over 100 years of competitive football, a Forest player has scored 4 goals in a first-class game on just 10 occasions (of which Peacock recorded 4 of the 10). Peacock was a schoolteacher, one of three who played for Forest in 1934-35, F. Saxton and W.C. Porter being the others, but only two (Peacock and Porter) ever appeared in the same side.

Forest still did better in the Cup than their League form warranted. The 1934-35 season, in which was reported variously fog "reporters could not see the play" and a thunderstorm, also saw a "regular blizzard" when Forest drew at home 0-0 with Manchester United in a fourth-round Cup-tie, but Forest then won splendidly at Old Trafford. They also forced a replay before losing to Burnley in the fifth round. All these matches brought excellent gates and receipts, and an away fourth-round tie with close rivals Derby County the following season was special, beating the Baseball Ground's records for both attendance (37,830) and receipts (£3,356).

An opportunity was missed in 1935 which could have made some of Forest's financial problems less onerous. It seems a price was agreed with the landlords of The City Ground, the Nottingham Corporation, to buy the ground, including car park and tennis courts for £7,000, but it was not proceeded with. Presumably the cash was not available and, 60 years later, the Council are still the landlords. The club name was commemorated for what must have seemed then to be for more or less all time, or at least for a lifetime, when the London and North Eastern Railway (LNER), gave one of their new locomotives, built at Darlington in 1937, the name "Nottingham Forest".

The Reds must have thought they'd been hit by a train on 10 April 1937, but it was only Blackburn Rovers. Rovers won 9-1 at Ewood Park and, as their centre-half Bob Pryde scored an own goal, Blackburn players were responsible for all ten goals. It remains Forest's biggest defeat in the League.

Forest were extremely lucky to avoid the ignominy of dropping into the Third Division in 1937-38. As it happened they visited Barnsley on the last day of the season with the two teams battling to avoid the relegation place - they were level on points but Forest's goal average was fractionally better - by less than two-thousandths of a goal. It meant Forest needed to draw to stay up. David "Boy" Martin, an Irish international when with Wolves, from whom he joined Forest in 1936, secured the lead, but Forest were in trouble after two goalkeeping errors put Barnsley ahead. First Percy Ashton allowed a long shot from 30 yards to bounce over him as he dived, and then gave away a bizarre goal when, after stopping a fierce shot, he turned round to bounce the ball and bounced it over the line. With 20 minutes to go, and Barnsley thoroughly in control, Forest right-half Bob Davies was crocked and went to limp on the wing. It seemed all over but, with five minutes left, centre-forward Martin followed up after the Barnsley keeper Binns saved a shot from full-back Reg Trim and barged the keeper so much he turned into goal to avoid him while still holding the ball. After long consultation with a linesman, and despite strong Barnsley protests and considerable activity and shouting from the terraces, the goal was given. Forest held out although, with the goalie beaten, Barnsley retaliated immediately by hitting the bar. Forest's goal average was 0.783, Barnsley's 0.781, so Barnsley went down by that two-thousandths of a goal. Forest's hero was always called "Boy" Martin because, in his young days, he was an Army band boy. In his first season with Forest, 1936-37, he had netted 31 goals (29 League, two FA Cup) to establish a record for the club, beating the 28 of "Nocker" West in 1907-08.

Incredibly, the following season, Forest travelled to Norwich on the last day of the campaign with the two sides again contesting second relegation place in an echo of the previous year. Here the issue was more in Forest's favour with Norwich, two points behind and with a worse goal average, needing to beat Forest by four goals to stay up. Norwich got one at the start of the second half and piled everything into attack, even knocking out goalkeeper Ashton on one

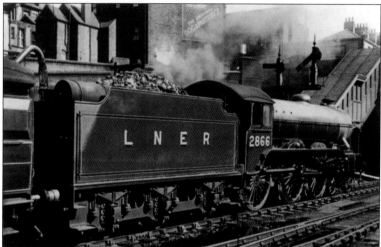

occasion, but they could not net again and Forest's status survived. In truth, it was Plymouth Argyle who sealed the Canaries' fate, as Argyle had lost to Forest 2-1 the previous Saturday before doing them the enormous favour of beating Norwich 1-0 in midweek.

In yet another of those coincidences which seemed to belong to Forest in the 1930s, the Norwich chairman, Mr J.F. Wright, had gone to school with Forest's chairman, Bob Cobbin, when they were boys back in the 19th century.

The 1920s and 1930s formed the period in professional football when the team manager began to assume the sort of mystical importance he enjoys today. Great figures like Herbert Chapman at Arsenal and Major Frank Buckley at Wolves showed that the manager could be more important to a club's success than even the greatest player. When Forest came into existence team selection was by committee and the nearest

"Nottingham Forest" was the name given to an engine built by the London and North Eastern Railway in 1937. It was originally numbered 2866 and renumbered 61666 in 1948. The engine spent its working life in East Anglia and visited Nottingham only rarely. The two pictures show it on separate dates in 1939 and are the only ones known to exist of "Nottingham Forest" in its home town. The two nameplates are now on display at the club, although one was badly damaged in the fire of 1968. For the record Derby County was 2851 and Leicester City 2865 but, strangely, Notts County was never honoured.

Three Forest programmes issued just before and during the Second World War.

Above: The red printed programme was for West Ham's visit in October 1938, whilst blue print was used for the England v Wales international at The City Ground in April 1941. Both were sized 19cm x 25cm.

Right: A smaller programme (12.5cm x 19cm) produced for the Forest v Chelsea game in September 1945.

the club had to a manager was the secretary. Harry Radford, who was secretary from 1889 to 1897, ran the club much like a modern manager might and is listed in current yearbooks as the first secretary-manager. Harry Haslam, his successor, was in the same mould. Fred Earp, a former player, was secretary-manager for three years and then Bob Marsters took the reins till 1925. John Baynes then came from Mansfield Town to take over the role, and he was followed by Stan Hardy and Noel Watson, an international referee, who was to remain secretary for 30 years from 1931 to 1961, and then to become club president. It was in 1936 that an additional post of team-manager was created, and the first occupant was a former Derby County centre-half, Harold Wightman. He had managed Luton Town successfully for four years in the Third Division (South), from where Luton eventually gained promotion in 1937.

Wightman left Forest early in March 1939 and, ten days later, Forest appointed the first man to be manager of the club as that term is understood today, Billy Walker. Walker had been an outstanding player with Aston Villa, whom he joined as an amateur in 1915, turning professional three years later. Walker was a clever inside-left who, in 1920, won a Cup-winners medal when Villa beat Huddersfield 1-0 after extra time at Stamford Bridge. In the Villa goal was Sam Hardy, who had guested for Forest during the war and who was to join them a year later. Walker also appeared in the second Cup final to be played at Wembley, in 1924, but was concussed after a collision and Villa lost to Newcastle 2-0 in the wettest of all Cup finals. Between times he had won his first cap as a centre-forward against Ireland in 1920, scoring in a 2-0 win. He went on to win 18 caps, and captained England, most notably in his last international in 1932, when the Austrian Wunderteam nearly became the first foreign side to defeat England at home, England holding on for a 4-3 win. An odd record he held is that in 1921 he became the first player

to score three times from the penalty spot in one match, a 7-1 defeat of Bradford City. The Bradford 'keeper refused to save the third as a protest against the referee's decision, and stood beside the goalpost instead. After retiring as a player, Walker was manager of Sheffield Wednesday for four years, leading them to a Cup win in 1935, and had been in the comparative wilderness of managing Chelmsford for a short spell before Forest engaged him. He was to be an influential manager for 21 years, and later committee man, but before he could do anything with Forest the Second World War broke out. Just before it did, Forest had again discussed the old question of becoming a limited liability company, but nothing was done and the war swallowed up any further action.

The 1939-40 season was started, with the declaration of war on 3 September 1939 seeming to catch the Football League by surprise. Forest, in common with most clubs, had completed three games, winning two, and were on the way to Swansea for a match when the announcement came, and they turned back at Oxford. The Football League programme was abandoned and regional leagues were rapidly arranged.

In an account of Forest's affairs during the war, Billy Walker revealed that at the end of the last full League season Forest were in debt to the tune of several thousand pounds, and were rescued from possible bankruptcy by the committee members digging into their own pockets, principally the chairman, Bob Cobbin. All players' contracts were cancelled with the war, and most, of course, were soon serving in the forces, civil defence, factories or in the pits. Forest recruited local and amateur players to fulfil their wartime fixtures and Walker immediately instituted a colts team, claiming later that during the war he tried out about 1,000 youngsters, of which he estimated 50 finally made the grade. The football authorities (Association and League) fixed a match fee for "guest" players of 30/- (£1.50) which again caused committee hands to be dipped into pockets, but Forest kept going through the war. Several illustrious players turned out for the club in those years, including Scottish international Andy Beattie, who would one day be Forest manager. A few of the other best known international guest players were: Ron Burgess, Raich Carter, Sammy Crooks, Eric Brook, Frank Broome, Eric Houghton (later to be chief scout), Wilf Copping and Ronnie Starling. There was also yet another Test cricketer, Nottinghamshire's Arthur Jepson, who was at the time Stoke City's goalkeeper.

Forest and Walker hoped that, when the war finally came to an end, Forest might be better equipped to regain their prominent place in the soccer hierarchy than they had been before it began.

Back from the summer break in 1949: from left to right; Billy Walker, Chairman J. Brentnall, Fred Scott, John Love, Geoff Thomas (the first, whose real name was Gerald), Bob Davies, John Linaker, Tommy Graham and Horace Gager. The Main Stand, on the right, had not changed since the ground was built in 1898. The smiles are not very convincing. The club was about to begin its very first season ever in the Third Division South *(Author's Collection)*.

CHAPTER FOUR

A return to the sun

1945–1958

WHEN the war finally ended with the surrender of the Japanese in August 1945, Forest visited Germany to play a BAOR team (consisting of men serving in the British army on the Rhine). They lost 4-1 at the Mungersdorf Stadium in Cologne where, 34 years later, the club would experience the turning point in its history, as described in Chapter 1. A year later they drew with a Combined Services team in Hamburg. The flight back in a hurricane (the weather, not the aeroplane) which threw the plane about scared the Forest party, who expected to be ditched into the sea any minute and were much relieved when they landed on the south coast. Two servicemen, a left-wing pair named Billy Steel and George Lee, impressed the Forest management so much that Billy Walker tried to sign them. He succeeded with George Lee, who arrived from York City in 1947, but Billy Steel went to Derby County from the Scottish club Morton for a British record transfer fee of £15,000. A brilliant player, he won 30 Scottish caps and played for Great Britain against the Rest of the World in 1947.

The war ended too late for the restoration of the Football League programme in 1945-46, but the FA Cup competition was revived on a unique home-and-away basis and Forest went out humiliatingly to Third Division Watford in the first round, losing 1-0 in a replay after both legs had been drawn 1-1. After years of war, the public was hungry for football, and the last season of the League South, in which Forest played, brought healthy gates with over 30,000 at The City Ground for the visit of Derby County and only a thousand fewer for the visit of Charlton Athletic. These two sides were to fight out the first post-war Cup final despite Charlton uniquely losing one of their two-legged games. Derby fielded such giants as inside-forwards Raich Carter and Peter Doherty. Charlton's best was inside-forward "Sailor" Brown, who played for England in wartime internationals, and a month after the Cup final Walker signed the 30-year-old for Forest. Although finances were still tight, Walker also spent a then record fee for the club of £4,500 to sign right-winger Freddie Scott from York City, a former schoolboy international who had flourished as a guest player for Charlton during the war.

With these men in the side Forest began the first post-war season of League football with optimism. The attendances were terrific, with nearly 33,000 turning up for the first home game - a 2-0 defeat by Newcastle United. Crowds over 30,000 became common - the gates were closed for the match with Burnley, although 31,484 was not the largest attendance. Receipts, which often topped £3,000, helped Forest's finances. For the visit of Manchester City (the eventual Second

Division Champions) in November, the match had to be played at Meadow Lane, as The City Ground was flooded, with the overflowing Trent almost reaching the crossbars. In the offices, many of the club's records were damaged, and some lost altogether. Over 32,000 watched the match. Forest's home gates couldn't compare with their biggest away League attendance, however, 56,827 at St James' Park - for a Second Division match!

The biggest crowd of all, and Forest's best performance for years, came in the FA Cup fourth round, away to Manchester United at Maine Road (Old Trafford was under repair because of wartime bombing). United were clear Cup favourites and the best side in the country at the time. They included four of the legendary forward line that scored 95 First Division goals that season: Delaney, Morris, Rowley and Pearson, but Forest won 2-0 in front of 58,641 fans. Newspaper headlines read "The Cruiser beat the Battleship" and "United Lost in a Forest", while United manager Matt Busby described the defeat in the next home programme as "a great shock to us all, none more so than the players themselves". The Forest keeper, Lawrie Platts, who had made his debut for Forest as an 18-year-old in 1940, and had played a number of wartime games, was the hero of the match, keeping out that star-studded forward line. He had made his League debut the week before in a 6-0 defeat of Southampton. Against United he was inspired, and his performance so lifted the rest of the team that the match ever hence has been called "Platts' match". Platts had an extraordinary career. Four days later, because of army duties, he failed to turn up for the away game with lowly Luton. Winger Tom Johnston had to keep goal and Forest lost 3-2. Then Platts was injured and so the two matches mentioned were his only appearances of the season. Manager Walker signed a new 'keeper, Harry Walker, from Portsmouth, who appeared in the last four games of the season and remained first choice, being virtually ever-present for the next seven seasons. With only six more League games to his name, Platts left Forest in 1951 for Chesterfield, finishing two years later at Stockport County. The soldier-hero 'keeper's League career, which had started so sensationally with an 8-0 aggregate in two games, totalled a mere 46 matches, most of them in the Third Division (North). Nonetheless, Forest's victory at Maine Road probably ranks as the greatest giant-killing act in the club's history.

Forest went out in the next round of the Cup in a replay at Middlesbrough. The teams drew 2-2 at The City Ground, where receipts were £3,842, and the great Wilf Mannion scored

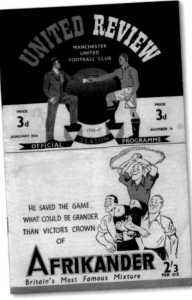

The programme from Forest's January 1947 FA Cup game with Manchester United, the famous "Platt's match" at Maine Road.

The winter of 1946-47 was the worst in living memory. Massive snowfalls led to numerous postponements, despite fans being drafted in to try to clear the pitch as here **(bottom)** before the FA Cup fifth round tie against Middlesbrough on 8 February 1947. When the snows melted (top) in March 1947 the River Trent overflowed its banks all the way from Derbyshire to Newark. The City Ground was flooded for days on end and Forest had so many postponements that their season did not end until 14 June, the latest in the club's history *(Author's Collection and Nottingham Evening Post).*

an own goal, but Middlesbrough won the replay 6-2, with Mannion putting three in the correct net. Mannion appeared twice at The City Ground that season, because in September 1946 the FA had staged a representative match between an FA XI and a Combined XI for the benefit of Willie Hall, a Spurs and England inside-forward who, eight years earlier, had scored five in 28 minutes (still a record) for England in a 7-0 defeat of Ireland. His career had recently ended with thrombosis in the legs (which ultimately led to amputation). Hall was born in Nottingham and was a former Notts County player. The selected FA XI was virtually England, including such as Frank Swift, Billy Wright and Tom Finney, as well as Mannion, while the Combined XI included three Forest players, Bob McCall (full-back), Bill Baxter (right-half) and Tom Johnston (outside-left). The result was 2-2.

That first post-war League season was remarkable for a big freeze-up in March, which created such a backlog of fixtures that the season was the longest ever, lasting into June. Forest's last match was on 14 June when, needless to say, it rained heavily.

Forest were not safe from relegation in 1947-48 until the third-last match of the season, after a bad beginning in which they lost nine of the first 12 games. Attendances were still good, particularly away, and over 60,000 saw them lose at Newcastle, and 38,000 saw them lose at Birmingham. These were the two promoted teams. Nearly 50,000 saw Liverpool score three in the last 12 minutes at Anfield to send Forest packing from the Cup 4-1 in the third round. Before that Notts County, who were in the Third Division and thus not exempt till the third round, had drawn 25,000 spectators to see them play non-League Horsham in the Cup while Forest drew only 18,000 for their Second Division match. This confirmed what everyone in the city instinctively knew, that County were still Nottingham's number one team.

The crash came for Forest in season 1948-49. Despite a spirited effort at the end, when they won six and drew one of their last nine games, they were relegated by one point in 21st position. The relegation battle held reminders of 1914, when Forest had to apply for re-election, and Leicester just avoided doing so on goal average over Lincoln. The same three clubs were engaged at the bottom again, with Lincoln doomed and Leicester and Forest fighting it out to avoid joining them. On the last day Leicester were two points to the good, but with Forest having a better goal average. Forest duly beat Bury, and then had to wait for the result of Leicester's match at Cardiff, which started a quarter of an hour later. Eventually news came through that Leicester had gained the point at Cardiff which sent Forest down. Liverpool again eliminated

Forest at the first hurdle from the Cup, but only after a replay with 87,000 watching the two games. The best event in the season from Forest's point of view, although they couldn't have known it then, was the debut of Jack Burkitt, who joined the club from Darlaston.

So in 1949-50 Forest found themselves in the Third Division (South) alongside Notts County and teams they'd never played before, such as Bournemouth, whose 50th anniversary was celebrated in November 1949 with a civic dinner and a League visit from Forest, who spoiled the jollity by winning 2-1.

Forest had started the campaign with a new centre-forward, Wally Ardron, a prolific scorer who had banged in almost a goal a game for Rotherham United. He scored on his debut and racked up 25 League goals in his first season for Forest. He was to be a great success with 123 League goals in 183 games up to the 1954-55 season.

Forest did much better in the lower division, but were overshadowed by Notts County. Forest's two biggest gates were against County: 38,000 at home and 46,000 at Meadow Lane (then a Third Division record). County won both matches. In the first round of the Cup both sides were at home, but Forest's gate of 15,567 for the visit of Bristol City was overshadowed by County's 28,584 for the visit of non-League Tilbury. Confirmation again of who was number one in Nottingham. At the end of the season County were promoted as Champions, seven points clear. Forest were fourth. The biggest humiliation of the season, for Forest, was to be knocked out of the Cup at The City Ground by middle-of-the-table Third Division (North) side Stockport County.

A turning point for Forest came in 1950-51. Jack Burkitt had completed a solid half-back line with skipper Horace Gager at centre-half and Bill Morley (who played from 1945 to 1959) at right-half. Harry Walker was "Mr Safety" in goal. Bill Whare at right-back and Geoff Thomas at left (a curious portent of another left-sided Geoff Thomas, forty years later), two other long-servers, formed a solid defence, and Wally Ardron, leading the line, had Tommy Capel and Colin Collindridge on his left and Tommy Johnson and Freddy Scott on his right. Roland Leverton played 22 games at inside-forward and, apart from these 12, only four other players, who totalled a mere 19 League games between them, were used all season. The side got off to a brilliant start, dropping only three points in the first 18 games, and coasted home to win the Championship by six points from Norwich. It was truly a record breaking season. Their total of 70 points was a record for the division and was never to be beaten, and they scored 110 goals, still the club record for a season. Wally Ardron scored 36 of

Below: After two seasons in the Third Division South, Forest finally regained the Second Division on 2 May 1951 when they defeated Newport County 2-1 with goals from the much loved pairing of Collindridge and Capel. The crowd invaded the pitch at the end of the game, the programme from which is also shown *(Author's Collection)*.

these, still the individual record for a season for the club. Tommy Capel, who played 35 games, got 23, Colin Collindridge 16 and Tommy Johnson 15 from 32 games. Freddy Scott scored a mere nine goals, but the typical Forest goal this season was a pinpoint cross from Scott headed in by Ardron. Ardron's scoring record is amazing, as he also holds the record for most in a season at Rotherham (38 in 1946-47). Three other players currently share the honour of being top scorer in a season at two clubs: Arthur Rowley at Shrewsbury and Leicester, Cliff Holton at Northampton and Watford, and Jimmy Greaves at Chelsea and Tottenham. Ardron's record has lasted longest.

Forest's two seasons in the old Third Division were the only two to date. Back in the Second Division in 1951-52 Forest immediately settled into regular promotion contenders. Several home gates topped 30,000, with 40,005 for the visit of Notts County and 39,530 ("thousands locked out") for that of Sheffield Wednesday on Boxing Day. As an amazing 61,062 saw Forest draw at Hillsborough on Christmas Day, over 100,000 saw the two matches between the clubs over Christmas. A 3-2 win over County began a run of six wins in seven games (the other a draw) which took Forest to the top of the table for six weeks. Only two wins

and three defeats in the last eight games, however, saw them finish fourth, four points behind Champions Wednesday and two points off a promotion place.

Bobby McKinlay made his League debut for Forest at centre-half aged 19 years 17 days on 5 October 1951, but made only one more appearance that season, Horace Gager keeping the position as his own for three more seasons yet. Ardron scored 29 more goals, with Forest netting 77 altogether. Forest's future secretary and official statistician, Ken Smales, found much to complain about in away pitches in this and the following seasons describing them as "a mud heap" (QPR), "of glue-like consistency" (Leicester), "a morass of black mud" (Luton), "ankle deep in mud" (Southampton), "a quagmire" (Swansea), "a quagmire" (Liverpool), and a "sticky, muddy morass" (Stoke).

Forest finished fourth, seventh and 15th in the next three seasons, the last of which saw Wally Ardron and Horace Gager retire and Bob McKinlay establish himself at centre-half. Tommy Capel and Colin Collindridge had moved on to Coventry City at the end of the previous season. Although Forest dropped to 15th in 1954-55 they reached the fifth round of the Cup after a prolonged tie with Newcastle United. They drew 1-1 at The City Ground when new outside-left Peter Small, bought from Leicester, was injured, taken to hospital for an x-ray, returned, and opened the scoring five minutes from time. Two minutes later Jackie Milburn equalised for Newcastle. At St James'

The promotion winning team of 1950-51. Forest won more League games than in any other season in their history (30), scored more goals than in any other season (110) and achieved more points than they have ever done before or since (70 under the two points for a win system, which would convert to exactly 100 under the three points system). Forest's record of 70 points remained the highest ever achieved by any club in the Third Division South, and their goal difference of plus 70 has only been bettered four times in the whole history of the Football League. Sitting to the left of manager Billy Walker is Wally Ardron, who scored 36 League goals, the highest ever scored by a Forest player in a single season. Ardron also remains Rotherham's leading scorer in a single season. He is one of only three players currently to lead the lists for two clubs. The 'Forester' badge was the first club variant on the city coat of arms *(Ken Smales)*.

Park, Forest were two down at half-time, but Jimmy Barrett and Freddy Scott equalised. It was still level after extra time, and Newcastle won the toss to host the second replay. After 22 minutes Tommy Wilson put Forest ahead, but Newcastle equalised and got the winner two minutes from the end of extra time. Newcastle, of course, went on to win the Cup for the third time in five years.

Forest improved to seventh in the table in 1955-56, a season in which the Supporters Club made the club a donation of £3,000 after a home win against Barnsley in October. Manager Walker made three shrewd signings in 15 months. In July 1955 he signed left-winger Stuart Imlach from Derby County. Imlach played 39 League games in his first season and was to become one of Forest's best players of the era. He won four caps for Scotland in 1958, and played in two of their three games in the 1958 World Cup finals in Sweden. His signing was quickly followed in 1956 by those of two veterans. In March Doug Lishman, an inside-forward, joined Forest from Arsenal, where he had scored 125 goals in 226 League matches and won a Championship medal. He turned out on 17 March against Middlesbrough and scored on his debut, netting six in 11 appearances to the end of the season. In October 1956, soon after the 1956-57 campaign began, Walker bought Eddie Baily from Port Vale, where he'd gone after 296 League games for Spurs. Baily was a brainy inside-forward worth more than his nine caps. It was around him that Spurs' great "push-and-run" Championship-winning side of 1951 had been built. The 31-year-old made his Forest debut on 6 October, wearing borrowed boots. Forest lost, as they did at The City Ground on 10 November 1956, when the visitors were Middlesbrough. One Peter Taylor was in goal for Middlesbrough, and kept a clean sheet. Brian Clough was at centre-forward and scored his first League hat-trick. Middlesbrough won 4-0. Taylor and Clough were, of course, to return to The City Ground in future years for even greater triumphs. But Forest didn't lose often that season and clinched promotion in second place behind Leicester with a game to spare.

The game in which promotion was secured was at Bramall Lane against Sheffield United. Baily dazzled and Lishman scored a hat-trick, with Tommy Wilson getting the other in a 4-0 win. The team which played in that match was the usual one for that season: Harold Nicholson, John Hutchinson, Geoff Thomas, Bill Morley, Bobby McKinlay, Jack Burkitt, Tommy Wilson, Eddie Baily, Jimmy Barrett, Doug Lishman and Stewart Imlach. That Forest lost their last game, at home 4-2 to Notts County, was regarded as an irrelevance. The Bramall Lane game has become one of the legendary matches in Forest history.

Forest had another excellent Cup run, too,

in 1956-57. In the third round they beat non-League Goole Town 6-0 (not surprising, as the reserves had beaten them the previous week), in the fourth they beat Portsmouth and in the fifth Barnsley. They were drawn away to Birmingham City, the previous season's finalists, in the quarter-final, and drew 0-0, but unfortunately they slipped up at home 1-0.

Lishman's hat-trick, which had taken Forest back to the top flight after an interval of 32 years, was his last scoring effort for the club, for he retired at the end of the season, in a way making it all the more significant.

Forest began their new life in the First Division with two newcomers, both ex-Chelsea players, making their debuts in the first match. They were Chic Thomson, goalkeeper, and Billy Gray, veteran winger, who had had a spell at Burnley after leaving Chelsea, and arrived with 284 League games already to his credit - yet he would play another 201 for Forest. Gray scored on his debut, a 2-1 win over Preston. The Reds got off to a terrific start, winning seven of their first nine games, the only defeat coming at Burnley, in those days among the top six sides in the country. But Forest promptly avenged this defeat with a 7-0 thrashing at The City Ground, which confirmed their entitlement to their new status. On 5 October inside-forward John Quigley followed Gray in also scoring on his debut, a 4-3 win at Tottenham, the first of his 236 Forest League games. This win, before a crowd of over 50,000 at White Hart Lane, brought particular pleasure to ex-Spur Eddie Baily, who was made captain for the day. The following match, on 12 October 1957, saw a new East Stand opened at The City Ground. Costing about £40,000, it had numbered bench seats to accommodate 2,500 fans. The visitors for the big opening were the fabulous "Busby Babes" of Manchester United, the runaway Champions of the previous two seasons, who had just been robbed of the first twentieth century "double" by

Right: One of the great rituals of the 1950s and 1960s was waiting for the FA Cup draw on the Home Service of the BBC on Monday lunchtimes. Having beaten Mansfield in the third round on 10 January 1953, captain Horace Gager (left), masseur Bob Davies and trainer Tommy Graham wait to hear that Forest have been drawn away at Everton in the fourth round. Forest lost 4-1, Tommy Capel scoring the only goal (*Nottingham Evening Post*).

Below: Forest clinched promotion to the First Division at Bramall Lane on 27 April 1957, returning to the top flight after a gap of 32 years. The goal is the third of Doug Lishman's hat-trick and the strange outgrowth on top of the stand is the Bramall Lane press box. Lishman retired a month later and his three goals were the last he ever scored for the club. Forest beat Sheffield United 4-0, with Tommy Wilson the other scorer (*Author's Collection*).

The Forest v Manchester United programme from 12 October 1957. This was then the club's record attendance of 47,804. Both teams later signed the matchball, which is still to be seen in the club's Trophy Room. United won 2-1. Of the United team that day, Byrne, Colman, Edwards, Taylor and Pegg died at Munich while Berry and Blanchflower never played again. Forest's return fixture at Old Trafford was on 22 February 1958, United's first League game after Munich. Only Bill Foulkes played for United in both games. The attendance at Old Trafford was also a record – 66,346 – still the largest ever to watch any Forest League fixture.

a cruel injury to their goalkeeper who was carried off after six minutes of the Cup final (no substitutes then).

A new record attendance of 47,804 saw a magnificent match, between the League's then leading sides, and summed up by the prince of football reporters, Don Davies of *The Guardian*, as "a great exhibition of football, of which skill was the final, the only, arbiter, and where the splendour of the performance was enriched by the grace of sportsmanlike behaviour". Forest played well that day, with Stewart Imlach equalising a goal by Liam "Billy" Whelan before Dennis Viollet scored the winner for United. Forest's terrific second-half efforts to equalise again were thwarted by a magnificent display from Duncan Edwards. It is worth recording both teams. Forest had Thomson in goal, Whare and Thomas at full-back, Morley, Watson and Burkitt at half-back and a forward line of Gray, Quigley, Wilson, Baily and Imlach. United had Wood, Foulkes, Byrne; Colman, Jackie Blanchflower, Edwards; Berry, Whelan, Tommy Taylor, Viollet and Pegg.

In the Cup, Forest proceeded to the fourth round, where they drew 3-3 at West Bromwich Albion, all six goals coming in a quarter-hour period from the 58th to 73rd minutes. But they lost the replay at The City Ground by 5-1, despite a record midweek attendance of 46,455 to cheer them on and Albion's Maurice Setters breaking a leg after 27 minutes. It was their most disappointing performance of the season.

In February 1958 came the tragic air crash at Munich which wiped out most of the great Manchester United side. A new side was hastily assembled by rapid transfers, and United won an emotional home fifth-round Cup-tie 3-0 against

Sheffield Wednesday with a makeshift team. Three days later Forest visited Old Trafford for United's first League match since the tragedy. Forest and Liverpool both contacted Old Trafford to offer players should they be needed – gestures long remembered in Manchester.

Only one United player remained from the team that had played at Forest four months earlier: Bill Foulkes. Of the rest, Wood, Blanchflower, Berry and Viollet survived the crash, but only Wood and Viollet played again. United's new team were being swept on in a wave of public passion and sympathy that saw them eventually reach the Cup final that season. Meanwhile, before 66,346 frenzied hyper-emotional fans Forest's men had to perform with resolution, dignity and absolute self-control. They succeeded admirably, playing calm, measured football, and came away with a 1-1 draw, Imlach's first-half goal being equalised after the interval by Alex Dawson. Forest's team had two changes from the first match, Bob McKinlay returning for Watson after missing the previous game through injury and Chris Joyce standing in for Eddie Baily. United had ten changes. Their team was: Gregg; Foulkes, Greaves; Goodwin, Cope, Crowther; Webster, Ernie Taylor, Dawson, Pearson, Brennan. Unfortunately Don Davies was not there to report the occasion with the skill it deserved - he had been one of the eight (out of nine travelling) sports writers who had died in the crash. The attendance was also significant - it is the largest which has ever watched Forest in any Football League game.

Forest, who played Fiorentina in Italy in a friendly during the season, and toured West Germany, Belgium and Holland afterwards, eventually took tenth place in the League. Mention of the season should not pass, however, without the odd story of Fay Coyle, one of the internationals on Forest's books. Born in Derry in 1924 he was an amateur international before winning three full caps with Coleraine in 1955 and 1956. In March 1958 he signed for Forest, made his debut that month on the trip to Fiorentina and, in the rest of the season, played centre-forward in just three League games, all of them away at Chelsea, Sunderland and Arsenal. He went with the Northern Ireland squad to the 1958 World Cup finals and played against Argentina, winning his fourth cap and thereby adding to the list of Forest internationals. However, the 34-year-old never returned to the English Football League, so Forest have an international, and a World Cup finalist at that, who never played a single game at The City Ground!

Never mind - Forest were quite happy with Bedlington lad Tommy Wilson at centre-forward, and his big moment was to come in the following season.

Tuesday 5 May, 1959, was the first time in the twentieth century that the FA Cup had been on view in Nottingham. Unless 1999 provides a re-run, it will also be the only time in the twentieth century that the Cup has been paraded through the Old Market Square. As captain Jack Burkitt carries the trophy, the crowds are massive in a city centre which still has a clear sense of austerity about it. Note the crowds on the roof tops.

A first tilt
at glory
1958 - 1974

ALTHOUGH Forest were now back in the First Division, no-one needed telling that they had won nothing in the twentieth century. It would not take much to send them back from whence they came, and Forest had a switchback start to the 1958-59 season. The first two matches, before 52,656 at Wolverhampton and 44,971 at The City Ground, were lost 5-1 and 3-0 (to Manchester United) respectively. But manager Walker's hopes for the season were resurrected by a 5-0 defeat of Portsmouth, a 1-1 draw before another 50,000 gate at Old Trafford and a 4-0 defeat of West Ham. Forest had climbed by the end of the year into a challenging position in the table.

Roy Dwight, an outside-right (famous in pub-quiz terms for being the uncle of singer Elton John a.k.a Reg Dwight) had joined the club from Fulham, where he had compiled the excellent scoring record for a winger of 54 goals in 72 League games. He netted on his debut in the first game of the season at Molineux, and by 31 December had 14 goals in 24 League games, including all three in a defeat of Leicester City. John Quigley had also got a hat-trick and Forest were scoring well. At right-half the tough-tackling Jeff Whitefoot made his debut along with Dwight on the first day of the season, taking over from Bill Morley, who later in the season would make the last of his 282 League appearances for his only club. Another great one-club career virtually ended when Joe McDonald, a Scottish international left-back bought from Sunderland, made his debut in the fourth match of the season and quickly made his own the position which Geoff Thomas had filled so well more or less since the end of the war. Thomas was to leave the following season after 404 League matches for Forest to join Bourne Town.

In the third round of the FA Cup, Forest were drawn against the amateurs of Tooting and Mitcham United, who had already put out two League sides in Bournemouth and Northampton. This was the first appearance of Tooting and Mitcham in the third round, and their programme notes pointed out that they'd already banked record receipts for the match, and that they hoped to be the first amateur team to beat a First Division side in the FA Cup competition "as we know it" (of course, sides like Oxford University had won the Cup in the old days).

The giant-killers' dreams nearly came true. Despite bitterly cold weather their small Sandy Lane ground was packed with a record 14,300 fans. The pitch was icy and covered in snow. In fact the weather conditions were so bad in January 1959 that four of the third-round ties (including Forest's) hadn't been completed by the date of the fourth round. Tooting and M (as they are usually abbreviated in the football results) initially mastered the conditions much better than

Forest, and took the lead after 20 minutes through outside-right Grainger. A quarter of an hour later wing-half Murphy netted again and Forest at the interval were two down.

Seven minutes into the second half, earlier hero Murphy had the misfortune to put through his own goal and, as the superior fitness of Forest's pros

Forest were drawn away at Tooting and Mitcham in the third round of the Cup on 10 January 1959. The amateurs went 2-0 up by half-time, then conceded a freak own goal when the ball hit an icy rut and bounced over the keeper's arms and a debatable penalty. Billy Gray scored from the penalty **(below)** to make it 2-2 and Forest won the replay 3-0.

Forest's fourth round draw was against Grimsby on 28 January 1959. Billy Gray scored a fourth minute penalty **(above)** and Tommy Wilson a 61st minute goal **(right)**. Gray scored a third and Whitefoot a fourth as Forest ran out 4-1 winners (*Nottingham Evening Post*).

began to tell, Tooting were forced on the defensive. A quarter of an hour from the end, Forest equalised with a disputed penalty. On the rutted pitch an awkward bounce of the ball caused it to strike a Tooting hand in a fairly innocuous position and Billy Gray sent the spot kick high to the right of a desperately stretching goalie. On such a small incident did Forest's fortunes change and most Cup winning teams seem to have such a moment.

Forest fans gave Tooting and Mitcham so much respect that 42,362 turned out for the replay, held on 24 January when most survivors were playing the fourth round. The kick-off was brought forward to 2 o'clock in case

extra time was needed. This time it was Forest who were two up at half-time, but it wasn't until the 89th minute that the amateur challenge was decidedly snuffed out with Imlach adding to the goals scored earlier by Dwight and Wilson. Four days later Forest played their fourth-round tie and, before 34,289 spectators, beat Grimsby Town comfortably 4-1, being three up at half-time. Gray (two), Whitefoot and Wilson got the goals.

The fifth round of the Cup was another cliff-hanger, in which Forest once more could easily have been eliminated. Forest were drawn at Birmingham City, the team which had put them out after a replay in the sixth round two years previously. Now City led for nearly an hour before Tommy Wilson headed in at the 89th minute for Forest to force a replay. Back at The

City Ground four days later, the teams were unable to score during the 90 minutes but, in the first period of extra time, John Gordon again put Birmingham ahead. Just five minutes from the end Roy Dwight lobbed the keeper to force a second replay. This took place at Filbert Street, Leicester, and Forest put up a dazzling performance, one which emphasised they actually had the ability to win the Cup. In a fluent display of teamwork they outclassed the side against which they'd already struggled for 210 minutes. The result was 5-0, with Dwight getting three and Gray the other two. The three matches had attracted nearly 130,000 spectators.

Forest's next match, just a week later, was the quarter-final tie with Bolton Wanderers, the Cup holders. This time, before a full house of 44,414 at The City Ground, Forest scored first, Tommy Wilson putting them ahead after only three minutes, and then adding a second two minutes after half-time. Brian Birch pulled one back for Bolton after 62 minutes, but Forest held on without too many alarms.

There was one League match

before the semi-final - against Birmingham City. So Forest ran out at The City Ground for the fourth time in six matches against the team that they had finally despatched from the Cup after five hours football. And in an odd echo of their matches with Derby County in their Cup-winning run 60 years before, they made four changes for the match, including two players making their debuts. One of them, Australian-born Scottish international goalie Bill Fraser, bought from Sunderland, would play only twice for Forest, while the other, 18-year-old Willie Younger, would make only 12 League appearances. Forest, with their

The fifth round tie with Birmingham City went to three games. In the first, Tommy Wilson headed an 89th minute goal to make it 1-1, in the second Roy Dwight also made it 1-1 with just five minutes of extra time left. The third game was very different. Played at Filbert Street, Dwight scored early on **(above)** and then completed a hat-trick. Billy Gray also scored two and Forest won easily 5-0. The game has an odd postscript. Twelve days later Forest played Birmingham in the League at The City Ground, their fourth meeting in three weeks. Birmingham won 7-1, still Forest's heaviest ever home defeat.

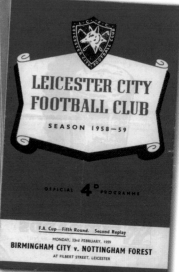

Five days after the defeat of Birmingham, Forest hosted Cup holders Bolton Wanderers in the quarter-final. Tommy Wilson scored the first goal after only three minutes (**right**) and then got the second (**below**) after Bolton keeper Eddie Hopkinson was only able to fist out Roy Dwight's 47th minute shot. Bolton's Brian Birch made it 2-1 after 62 minutes but Forest held on to reach their first semi-final for an astonishing 57 years *(Nottingham Evening Post).*

minds firmly elsewhere lost 7-1, still their heaviest home defeat in the League, but one which concerned them not at all.

Of course, the full Cup side was on parade for the semi-final with Aston Villa at Hillsborough, where over 65,000 paid £16,484 to watch. It was a match which coincidentally drew together the three main strands of Billy Walker's career. He had, in 1920, won the Cup as a player with Villa, and 15 years later he won it as a manager with Sheffield Wednesday. Now, a further 24 years

on, he was one step away from another final, with Villa standing in the way on Wednesday's pitch. It was not an outstanding game, with both sides edgy, but a 65th-minute goal from John Quigley proved enough to take Forest to Wembley. To get there, Forest had had to defeat the Cup winners of both 1957 and 1958. For many, it seemed that the hard part had been completed.

Before the Cup final, Forest followed what had now become an established practice with them before finals or semi-finals. Of the Cup side, which astonishingly remained exactly the same for all nine matches, only four, Whitefoot,

Dwight, Quigley and Wilson, played in both the League games before the final. Both matches were lost, the first 3-0 at home to Leeds United, against whom John Armstrong, Bernard Kelly and Jimmy Martin made their debuts. They were between them to play 23 League games altogether for Forest - in Martin's case it was his only Football League game ever! The other match was lost 2-0 to West Brom.

Forest's Cup final opponents were Luton Town, a club which had come up to the First Division four years earlier. Forest visited them in the League some three weeks before the final. True to form, Forest made wholesale changes to the team, and crashed 5-1, Allan Brown getting four for Luton. In this match goalie Bill Fraser made his second and last appearance for Forest, thus completing a record of conceding 12 goals in two matches.

With Forest 13th and Luton 17th in the table that year, the final was not regarded in the rest of the country as a glamour match. Luton's best-

known players were one-club goalie Ron Baynham, who had won three caps for England in 1955, Allan Brown, a Scottish inside-forward (14 caps) who as a Blackpool player had unluckily missed the "Matthews Final" in 1953 because he had broken a leg in the semi-final with Spurs, and much-capped outside-right Billy Bingham, who was in a two-year mid-career spell with Luton, with whom he won four of his eventual 56 caps for Northern Ireland. The sentimental favourite of the fans was Luton centre-half and captain Sid Owen, making his last appearance for the club. By coincidence he and Baynham both won three England caps and made 388 League appearances for Luton. This meant that, as in their previous final, Forest were not favoured by the impartial, who wanted Owen to end his long career with a medal. Luton had experienced a relatively easy run to the final – past Leeds (then a minor team), Leicester, Ipswich, Blackpool and then needing a replay to get past Third Division Norwich in the semi-final. Until Chesterfield's heroics against

Given Forest's dreadful history in semi-finals, the club could have been expected to approach the game at Hillsborough on 14 March 1959 with some trepidation. Their opponents were Aston Villa, Cup winners in 1957. This meant that Forest had faced Cup finalists from the past three finals in three consecutive rounds. However, given that no-one at the club could possibly remember the last time Forest were in a semi-final (1902), they had cause for confidence. Manager Billy Walker had won a Cup winners' medal with Villa in 1920 and brought the Cup back to Hillsborough as manager in 1935. Chic Thomson had a good game in goal, saving from (**top left**) Jackie Sewell and (**centre left**) Gerry Hitchens. The only goal (**above**) was scored in the 65th minute by Johnny

Quigley (on ground). The 1959 semi-final remains the only one of the six contested in Sheffield that Forest have won.

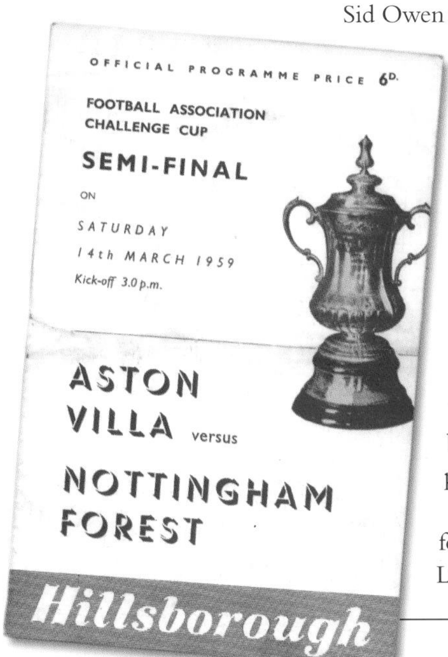

Middlesbrough in 1997, Norwich had come closer than any Third Division team to reaching the final of the FA Cup. Luton's place as sentimental favourites was further enhanced by Sid Owen receiving the Footballer of the Year trophy the night before the final. In the 1950s it was almost a tradition to favour a cup finalist – sadly Forest never seemed to have a player perfectly placed prior to one of their Wembley visits, Stuart Pearce in 1991 perhaps coming the closest.

A distinct oddity was that Luton were without a manager at the time, and chairman Thomas Hodgson led out the team at Wembley. The 100,000 fans comprised easily the biggest crowd that either club had played before in their histories.

The match was utterly one-sided for half-an-hour. Forest were brilliant, Luton poor, and it was one-way traffic. After nine minutes Roy Dwight was in the centre to meet a ball pulled back by his opposite wing man Stewart Imlach and blasted it into goal with Baynham watching hopelessly. Five minutes later a move started by Imlach in the left-back position ended with Billy Gray crossing diagonally towards the far post and Tommy Wilson heading home emphatically.

The tenor of the game changed, however, in the 33rd minute when scorer Dwight broke his leg in a tackle with Luton right-back Brendan McNally, and was carried off. It was the latest serious injury in a sequence that had dogged Wembley Cup finals in the 1950s - since 1952 this was the sixth of the eight finals to be marred by injury. This was to dominate the post-match discussions and, six years later, substitutes were allowed in football for the first time. Forest were the only one of the teams which lost a player to go on and win the Cup.

Forest kept their lead to the interval, and continued to play calm, polished football, with

Nottingham's first Cup final of the twentieth century generated unprecedented excitement. Standing tickets for the final on 2 May 1959 (**below**) cost 3/6 (which translates to 18 pence) but sold on the black market for £20, far more than the average weekly wage. At the time, each finalist received around 20,000 tickets. The staff at Nottingham Victoria Station (**above**) decorated the building with rosettes and giant cut-outs of Forest players - perhaps conscious that the last time Forest reached the final, in 1898, Victoria Station did not even exist (by the next time, in 1991, the station had been demolished). The club's special train (**right**) did, however, leave from Victoria rather than Nottingham Midland. The team had gone to see the semi-final replay between Luton and Norwich: "We were delighted Luton won," says Bob McKinlay. "Norwich looked by far the better team and, after the semis, we were always reasonably confident we'd win the final."

Opposite: Enthusiasm was as great then as it is today, if a little more dignified and innocent. This particular photograph became a great favourite in soccer anthologies in the decades that followed. Where are these lovely ladies today, we are bound to ask *(Popperfoto)*.

Forest's opponents in the 1959 final were Luton Town, appearing in their first final and led out by their chairman as they had no manager. After nine minutes Roy Dwight converted a centre from Stewart Imlach (**top left**) to make it 1-0. Five minutes later, Billy Gray crossed for Tommy Wilson to head home (**main picture**) and make it 2-0. Forest were dominating the game but, after 33 minutes, Roy Dwight broke his leg in a tackle with Luton's Brendan McNally and (**centre left**) was carried from the field. There were no substitutes in English football until 1965 and Forest had to play the last hour with ten men. They held out until the 62nd minute when David Pacey (**centre**) made it 2-1 with a close range shot past keeper Chic Thomson. There were to be no more goals. Bob McKinlay says that the team did not panic when Dwight was injured: "We were very worried for Roy, but it never occurred to me that we would lose the game because we were a man short. Luton came at us in the second half, but they had to anyway. The real heroes were Billy Gray and Stewart Imlach, who ran their socks off. Billy couldn't have run another five yards at the end."

THE FOOTBALL ASSOCIATION CHALLENGE CUP COMPETITION

FINAL TIE

LUTON TOWN
v
NOTTINGHAM FOREST

SATURDAY, MAY 2nd, 1959   KICK-OFF 3 pm

EMPIRE STADIUM

WEMBLEY

OFFICIAL PROGRAMME   ONE SHILLING

Left: A proud captain, Jack Burkitt, becomes the first Nottingham Forest player ever to hold the new FA Cup, which replaced the old in 1911. Burkitt was unlucky not to be elected Footballer of the Year, the honour going to Luton captain Sid Owen, who made his last appearance in the final. "Jack was the main man," says Bob McKinlay. "He was a tough bugger. If anyone on the opposition was being a bit rough, he'd tell us all to take it easy 'Leave it to me', he'd say. And a bit later he'd sort them out. He never came out of a one to one the loser as far as I can remember."

Top right: A youthful David Coleman tries to interview Jack Burkitt after the match. Behind Coleman is trainer Tommy Graham. Third from the right is masseur/physio Bob Davies and far right is a pensive manager Billy Walker. Bob McKinlay says of Walker that he was anything but a tactician: "He always held his team talks in the snooker room and, though the boys didn't play snooker during the talks, they might as well have done. He'd ask me if I knew the centre-forward, which foot he'd use and the like, then ask if anyone had any problems, and then say: 'Well, you all know your jobs. You wouldn't be here if you didn't.' I played under four managers – Walker, Johnny Carey, Andy Beattie, Matt Gillies – and they were all very similar. The players used to discuss tactics and planning in the café on Trent Bridge after training. The real thinkers were Eddie Baily in the 1950s and then John Barnwell in the 1960s. They would analyse things over cups of tea."

Bottom right: Traditional though champagne may have been, note that there is nothing coming out of the bottle. "No-one could get the cork out of the bottles. We were all beer drinkers, so it was a bit exotic for us. After about half an hour the photographer was getting exasperated and insisted that committee member Jim Willmer and Billy Gray pretend to be pouring the champagne. We were all killing ourselves laughing," says Bob McKinlay, looking at the picture today.

Left: Jack Burkitt and the stationmaster at St Pancras march the FA Cup to the special train which was to carry the team back to Nottingham Midland. Although the southern section of the M1 was opened in 1959, football teams still usually travelled by train.

Below: Don't worry if you miss the bus, there'll be another one along in a minute... crowds mob the team on Victoria Embankment on Tuesday 5 May 1959. Forty years later, Nottingham still awaits the next bus carrying an FA Cup winning team.

Opposite page: The victorious team marches down Processional Way in the packed Old Market Square. Billy Gray and Chic Thomson seem to have recognised familiar faces in the crowd, but Billy Walker (right) appears less than convinced while the crowds in the Square look up to the Council House balcony to see the team and the trophy. "Never in the world did we expect so many people," says Bob McKinlay, "When we got to Midland Station there were a few dozen to greet us, but the police had kept them off the platforms. Then we came out of the station there was an absolute sea of faces. I looked down and thought: 'What the hell is going on here!' We were all astounded."

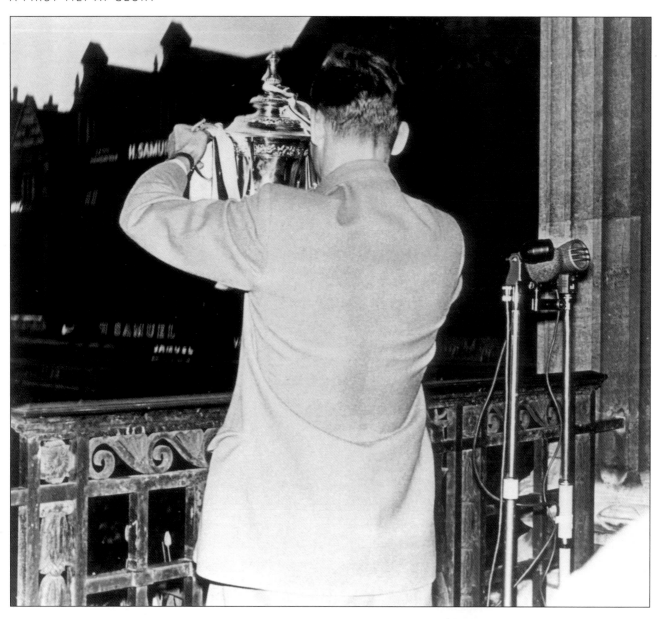

skipper Jack Burkitt and centre-half Bobby
McKinlay doing wonders at the back, blocking
the routes to goal. Early in the second half both
Burkitt and Bill Whare were laid out at different
times, but recovered to continue.

After 62 minutes Luton's full-back Ken
Hawkes passed to wing-half David Pacey who
scored. Luton pressed, but Forest continued to
defend capably. Five minutes from the end, with
Luton full-back McNally writhing on the ground
(he, too, momentarily left the pitch), Bingham
chased a ball to a corner flag, centred and Allan
Brown, hurtling forward, sent a header fizzing
past the post. Luton thus came so near to an
equaliser but, five minutes later, the whistle went
and the Cup was Forest's. Immediate celebrations
were delayed for half-an-hour - the management,
which had planned the triumphal procession
through Nottingham with every attention to
detail, had forgotten to lay on the champagne.

A nice touch connected with Forest's win
was that Frank Forman, hero of the 1898 final,
was able to watch the match on television at
home. How different it must have seemed to him

This page: The view the crowd outside
didn't see: Jack Burkitt holds up the FA Cup
from the Council House balcony on Tuesday
5 May, 1959 while Joe McDonald and
friends light up behind. "Joe even used to
have a fag at half-time," says McKinlay.
"The final was the highlight of our careers,"
he says today, "but the game which still
sticks in the memory was Old Trafford on
22 February 1958, the first league game after
Munich. The crowd noise was unbearable,
and it went on the whole match. The referee
came in before the match and told us how
important it was, no retaliation etc. I
remember Alex Dawson catching me chest
high with his studs early on – I've still got
the marks – but I didn't retaliate. The roar
was greater than Wembley and I had goose
pimples all night. The crowd was almost
insane with the emotion of it. After the game
the ref came in and thanked us – which was
unheard of – but he'd done a great job. We
drew 1-1. I was always a devout coward
where crowds were concerned – never went
over to take a throw-in if I could help it!"

Right: The City Council also invited the club back on Friday 8 May for a formal dinner attended by the team, the club's employees and the whole Council. At the time, as the dinner invitation indicates, Nottingham was both a City and a County in its own right, further confusing the parentage of Notts County.

Below: Roy Dwight was rushed straight to hospital with his broken leg. By Sunday breakfast, matters in hospital appeared to have improved somewhat and he returned to Nottingham with the team for the tour of the City on the Tuesday. Dwight makes regular appearances in quizzes because of being the uncle of Watford chairman and occasional singer Reg Dwight (alias Elton John). Dwight made a total of 53 appearances for Forest, scoring 27 goals between 1958 and 1959.

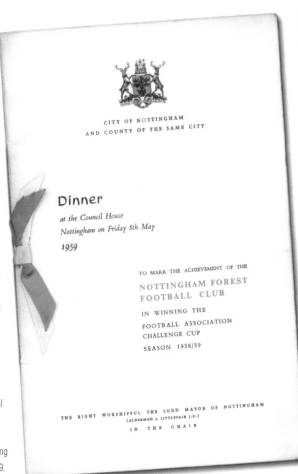

CITY OF NOTTINGHAM
AND COUNTY OF THE SAME CITY

Dinner

at the Council House
Nottingham on Friday 8th May
1959

TO MARK THE ACHIEVEMENT OF THE

NOTTINGHAM FOREST
FOOTBALL CLUB

IN WINNING THE

FOOTBALL ASSOCIATION
CHALLENGE CUP

SEASON 1958/59

THE RIGHT WORSHIPFUL THE LORD MAYOR OF NOTTINGHAM
(ALDERMAN J. LITTLEFAIR J.P.)
IN THE CHAIR

from the final of 61 years before! Another who had been forced to watch at least the last few minutes on television was Roy Dwight, but he was watching at Wembley Hospital, where Billy Walker and his team mates took the Cup to show him. On the Tuesday the team, including Dwight, returned home by rail to be met by a large crowd at the Midland Station. It is estimated that 200,000 fans saw the Cup and the players as their bedecked coach took them on a circuitous route to the Old Market Square. From there the players and officials strolled to the Council House where 300 guests were assembled in the Banqueting Hall to greet them.

Forest's Cup final team was Chic Thomson, Bill Whare, Joe McDonald, Jeff Whitefoot, Bobby McKinlay, Jack Burkitt, Roy Dwight, Johnny Quigley, Tommy Wilson, Billy Gray and Stewart Imlach. In the Cup run, Dwight and Wilson each scored six goals, Gray five.

In the summer, Forest toured Spain and Portugal. Their first match of the new season was the Charity Shield, played at the home of the Champions, Wolves, who beat Forest 3-1. Forest also played home and away games with St Mirren,

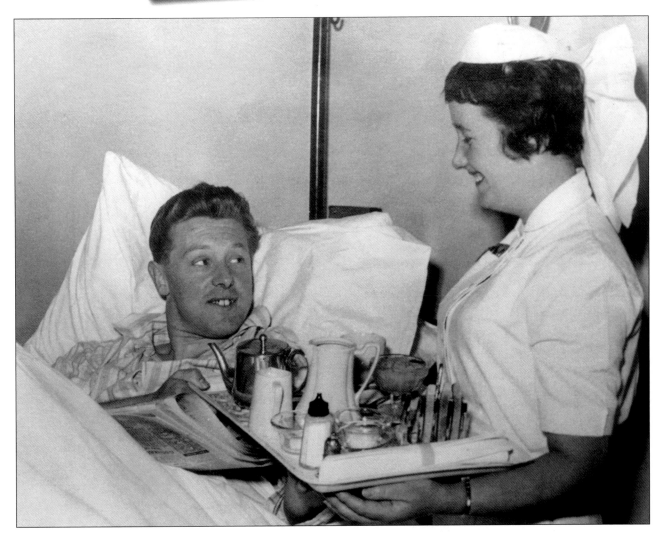

Left: The FA Cup winning team of 1959. *Top row, left to right:* Noel Watson (secretary), Bill Whare, Joe McDonald, Bobby McKinlay, Roy Dwight, Chic Thomson, Jeff Whitefoot, Tommy Graham (trainer).
Bottom Row, left to right: Johnny Quigley, Billy Gray, Jack Burkitt, Billy Walker (manager), Tommy Wilson, Stewart Imlach.
When asked how Billy Walker turned a Third Division team into the excellent outfit of the late 1950s, Bob McKinlay is thoughtful: " It wasn't tactical appreciation – we never discussed it and team talks lasted three minutes. The players were good, of course, and he made one or two excellent buys. Eddie Baily from Spurs was superb and Doug Lishman from Arsenal was strong and clever. Eddie Baily made Stewart Imlach's career with his balls inside the full-back – and Stewart got capped because of it. Eddie and Doug had gone by the time we won the Cup, but they had a great influence on building a side in which we were all pals. You have to be united to be a great team. Noel Watson, who's in this team picture, had a different view of things. Each season we were allowed to go to Redmayne and Todd to buy a new set of boots, but we could only spend so much. If we wanted a good set – around £4 or so – we had the extra deducted from our pay packet. I'm told it's a little different these days."

winners of the Scottish Cup. Only 8,000 saw them lose 3-2 at The City Ground, and a week later they could only draw 2-2 in the away leg. As Forest failed to win a League game until their fifth match, it was a very poor start. And the season failed to improve. In November, at Burnley, the Reds were beaten 8-0, their widest ever margin of defeat in the League, equalling the 9-1 against Blackburn Rovers in 1937. Jimmy Robson scored five for Burnley, inspired as always by Jimmy McIlroy. After scraping past Reading 1-0 at The City Ground in the third round of the defence of the Cup, Forest tamely lost 3-0 in the next round at Sheffield United. In March, with a battle against relegation going on, Roy Dwight returned but, two games later, both he and Stewart Imlach made their last appearances for the club, Dwight going to Gravesend before making a League comeback with Coventry, and Imlach moving to Luton. Imlach was, at the time, the only Forest player to have been capped by Scotland in the twentieth century.

Forest made significant buys in an effort to improve the playing staff, principally two under-23 internationals in wing-half Jim Iley from Spurs and inside-forward Colin Booth from Wolves, schoolboy international Tony Barton from Fulham, and Len Julians, a centre-forward from Arsenal. Geoff Vowden, a young Barnsley-born striker, was signed from Jersey. But it took a defeat of Newcastle in the second last match of the season to preserve Forest's First Division status, one point clear of relegation.

In the summer club secretary Noel Watson resigned after 30 years, and later became president. Ken Smales, the club's statistician, took over and was to hold the post for the next 27 years. He maintained the age-old link with Nottinghamshire County Cricket Club, as he had recently retired after 148 matches for the county, during which his off-spinners took 389 wickets, including all ten for 66 against Gloucestershire in 1956, the county's best-ever. Manager Billy Walker also resigned after a successful 21 years - he was at the time the longest-serving League manager. He joined the Forest committee.

Forest had won only two of the first nine League games in 1960-61 when Andy Beattie

assumed the role of manager. Beattie, a stylish full-back for Preston North End, won seven caps for Scotland in the seasons just before the war, which prevented him adding considerably to that number. Beattie had been manager of lowly Stockport when they knocked Forest out of the FA Cup at The City Ground in 1949. The first seven games under his control were all lost and Forest were already deep in trouble. Chic Thomson's last game for Forest coincided with the last of these defeats. Peter Grummitt took over in goal for the first of 313 League games he would play for Forest. In the first minute of his first match he was beaten - by an own goal from Jim Iley. Others to make their debuts for Forest included left-winger Richard Le Flem (always known as Flip), and 20-year-old centre-forward Colin Addison, signed from York City. Beattie turned the season round in time to avoid relegation with four matches to spare. The last match was at Stamford Bridge, where that scourge of Forest, Jimmy Greaves, netted all four in Chelsea's 4-3 win, Greaves's last match for Chelsea before his transfer to AC Milan.

Forest toured Czechoslovakia in the summer before resuming their annual relegation struggle in 1961-62, when they were one of three clubs representing England in the Inter-Cities Fairs Cup, the fore-runner of the UEFA Cup. Forest lost both legs of their first-round tie with Valencia, 2-0 away and 5-1 in Nottingham. Forest used floodlights at The City Ground for the first time this season, one of the last major clubs to install them. Jack Burkitt played the last of his 464 League games for Forest - according to one record book he would "surely have played for his country if with a more fashionable side". Burkitt stayed with the club as coach but, in April 1966, he moved to Notts County. With 18-year-old Trevor Hockey, 17-year-old David Pleat and 17-year-old John Winfield (who scored on his debut and was to prove the most influential of the three) making debuts this season, the average age of the side over the season (24 years 124 days) was more than four years younger than that of the Cup-winning season.

Forest started 1962-63 well, and a 9-2 defeat at Spurs (Greaves four) at the end of September was quite against their current form ("We scored first and last and they got nine lucky ones in-between," said Trevor Hockey). "Flip" Le Flem scored what was described as a "wonder" goal, beating five men on the way, against title-chasing Burnley. There was a good Cup run too,

Below: Peter Grummitt dives in vain as Jimmy Husband's shot skids towards the far corner to put Everton 1-0 up. The game was the FA Cup quarter-final on 9 April 1967, which Forest eventually won 3-2. Husband scored Everton's second goal to make it 2-2 and Ian Storey-Moore recalls that his most vivid memory that day was thinking: "Oh no, Wednesday at Goodison."

with Wolves, West Brom and Leeds being beaten before a quarter-final with Southampton, a mid-Second Division side. A 1-1 draw at home was followed by a replay at the Dell where Forest went 3-0 up, only for Southampton to score three times in the last 15 minutes. Saints completed an extraordinary turn-round in a second replay at White Hart Lane, winning 5-0, thus scoring a sequence of eight goals without reply. Forest's collapse in the last few minutes at The Dell was the cause of recriminations in the dressing room for some time afterwards – though scant consolation to Southampton for 1898.

During this season, with Forest hitting a sticky patch, Peter Hindley, a defender and the son of pre-war Forest player Frank, made his debut wearing the centre-forward's number 9 shirt, but played as an extra central defender alongside Bob McKinlay. Forest were booed off after losing 3-0 at Everton for what the fans saw as entirely negative football. In fact, Beattie was playing 4-3-3, and not unsuccessfully, but it was not appreciated by the home supporters either. Another notable debut this season was of 18-year-old winger Ian Storey-Moore, who made his only appearance on 10 May, two weeks before the end of the campaign. Forest finished ninth, their highest in the League since 1908, but the discontent over Beattie's tactics was such that he resigned in the summer.

So 1963-64 began with a new manager, Johnny Carey, one of those players credited with caps for both Northern Ireland (7) and the Republic (29). An outstanding wing-half or full-back, Carey had been captain of the great post-war Manchester United side that won the Cup in 1948 and the Championship in 1952. He captained the Rest of the World against England in 1948. As a manager, he had taken Blackburn Rovers and Leyton Orient into the First Division and between times managed Everton. So he came

to Forest with the highest credentials. It is notable that both Beattie and Carey were to manage their national sides.

Making his debut with Carey in the first match of the 1963-64 season was Frank Wignall, a centre-forward signed from Everton. He would have been glad, in his second match, to have gone to Anfield and score the winner as Forest won 2-1, as this match saw the opening of the new £350,000 cantilever stand, built to celebrate Liverpool's return to the top flight. Thirty five years later, Forest have still not won at Anfield since. Soon afterwards Forest won five matches running to go top of the table, but they only led for a week. They slipped to finish 13th and went out of the Cup at the first time of asking, so it was a poor season. Other notable players made debuts, however, in particular 19-year-old midfielder Henry Newton, 17-year-old forward and later midfielder Bob Chapman, 21-year-old Alan Hinton, a winger who had already attracted enough notice to be capped with Wolves, and John Barnwell, a midfielder with 138 League appearances for Arsenal. So the nucleus of a new young team was being assembled around veteran McKinlay at The City Ground.

After a summer tour of Germany and Switzerland, the youngsters did well in 1964-65. Chris Crowe, a midfielder, was signed from Wolves, and Peter Hindley, the subject of

City of Nottingham and County of the same City

Centenary Dinner

TO

THE NOTTINGHAM FOREST FOOTBALL CLUB

1865 — 1965

THE COUNCIL HOUSE, NOTTINGHAM
MONDAY, 9th AUGUST, 1965

The Right Worshipful The Lord Mayor of Nottingham
(ALDERMAN WILLIAM DERBYSHIRE, JP)
in the Chair

Above: The club celebrated its centenary in 1965, again with a dinner at the Council House.

Left: The Main Stand was also largely rebuilt in 1965; though it was to survive for just three years before being destroyed by fire. After flirting with an impressive main entrance for three years, fire allowed the club to revert to its "window in the wall" reception area, probably unique among European Cup winners. The Main Stand was still largely wood and the club chose to rebuild it within the same basic shell, missing an opportunity to add seats, restaurants and office facilities, an omission which was still greatly regretted 30 years later.

Above: The best supported team in the history of Nottingham Forest was the side which came second in the League and reached the FA Cup semi-final in 1967. Following on from a wonderful World Cup in 1966, the excitement spilled over to generate near hysterical enthusiasm for a team which finished higher than any Forest team had ever done before.

Top, left to right: John Barnwell, Peter Hindley, Bob McKinlay, Peter Grummitt, John Winfield, Henry Newton.

Bottom, left to right: Barry Lyons, Frank Wignall, Terry Hennessey, Joe Baker, Ian Storey-Moore.

The team eventually finished four points behind Manchester United in the League (the same United side going on to win the European Cup the next season) and lost 2-1 to Spurs in the heart-breaking Hillsborough semi-final.

Andy Beattie's disliked twin-stopper experiment, established a place at full-back. Addison, Wignall, Barnwell and Hinton each scored 12-14 League goals in the season. Forest set a new First Division record for themselves by getting 47 points (still two for a win). Their position of fifth was their highest since 1902. Amid the "youngsters", Bob McKinlay registered his 500th appearance, enjoyed a testimonial match in which Celtic were visitors, and completed a fifth consecutive League season of "ever-presents".

Forest's upward momentum received a check in 1965-66, the centenary year, the side dropping to 15th in the table. Team-building proceeded well, however, with players who were to be influential making their debuts. Wing-half Terry Hennessey arrived from Birmingham for £50,000 already having won 16 caps for Wales. He must have found life with his new club interesting if nothing else - in his first match Forest beat Blackpool 2-1 without any Forest player scoring, two Blackpool players getting own-goals. Later he was on the winning side in an FA Cup-tie for the first time in his five-year career. Towards the end of the season England centre-forward Joe Baker arrived from Arsenal at a record transfer fee for Forest of £62,500.

Forest invited Valencia, their Inter-Cities Fairs Cup opponents of four years before, to visit The City Ground for a club centenary match on 28 September 1965 and the "strolling senores"

played their part in an absorbing 1-1 draw. Before the match, Arsenal's chairman, Denis Hill-Wood, presented Forest with a set of shirts, a nice gesture recalling the help Forest gave to Arsenal by supplying their first shirts some 80 years previously. He also gave Forest a ceramic gun, which was replaced after it had been lost in the fire of 1968.

Forest's return to the First Division had increased their roster of international players by three in the 1960s. Terry Hennessey continued appearing for Wales and, with 15 caps between 1965 and 1969, almost equalled the total of Forest's most-capped player to date, Grenville Morris (16). In 1964 Alan Hinton and Frank Wignall both appeared twice for England, Hinton adding to the cap he had won with Wolves. In fact the two appeared together against Wales in a 2-1 win, with Wignall getting both goals. This was the first time Forest had supplied two players to the England team since the Forman brothers in 1898.

Apart from the 1959 Cup win, however, Forest's efforts at club level since reaching the top flight in 1957 had not been particularly fruitful. But 1966-67 was to be a magical season. It drew the largest crowds the club has ever had – before or since – and for a time it held out the outstanding possibility that Forest might, just might, win the "double". It is fair to say that the only other season in over 100 years of Premiership or League competition in which the "double" was a real possibility for Forest was 1977-78. But 1966-67 was special for a host of reasons, not least because England's World Cup win in 1966 had created a tremendously positive mood in the country, and everywhere the crowds to go with it. The team that Johnny Carey assembled had the virtue of being largely unchanged through the season. In goal was Peter Grummitt, then at the height of his powers. The back line was Peter Hindley, Terry Hennessey, Bob McKinlay (the only survivor of the 1959 Cup team) and John Winfield. Three of these were home-bred.

In mid-field, the creativity came from John Barnwell who, though not often recognised as such, was probably the crucial piece of the jigsaw. After he was injured in 1967, the team never again gelled, and his loss was to prove critical. The tackling midfielder was Henry Newton; a graduate of Bilborough's William Sharp School and very much the local flavour.

Johnny Carey tended to play a reasonably pure 4-2-4, in the manner of Brazil at their height rather than Alf Ramsey's 4-4-2 of the World Cup final. There were three candidates for the outside two forward roles – Alan Hinton, Barry Lyons, who joined the club from Rotherham in November and went straight into the first team, and Ian Storey-Moore, an Ipswich-born home grown talent. The central attacking pair were Frank Wignall, and the immortal "Zigger Zagger" Joe Baker. Of the five front men, all but Lyons were to receive England caps and he was to achieve under-21 recognition. Storey-Moore managed a single England cap against the Netherlands in 1970. He "scored" what would have been the only goal after six minutes, only to see it marginally disallowed for offside, and his injuries meant he was never to play for his country again. Forest had been a club eminently notable for having hardly any capped players in the twentieth century. Between 1905 and 1964 only two Forest players (Tommy Graham and Alf Spouncer) had represented England, and even then they had won just three caps between them. In the same period only Stewart Imlach had represented Scotland. To have simultaneously four forwards (Baker, Hinton, Wignall and Storey-Moore) who had (or soon would have) achieved England honours was quite remarkable for humble Nottingham Forest all of a sudden.

Although the heart of the team was solid defence and an excellent goalkeeper (as with all successful teams), in the hearts of the people of Nottingham the team was about Joe Baker and Ian Storey-Moore. They received an adulation certainly not seen in Nottingham since Tommy Lawton's days at Notts County, and surpassing that of the 1959 Cup-winning team. Joe Baker had been the first man to appear for England while playing for a non-English club (Hibernian).

After a brief spell at Torino he returned to join Arsenal at Highbury (then in a dull, unsuccessful period), and eventually left to join another ex-Arsenal man at Forest in John Barnwell.

In 1966-67, Storey-Moore scored 21 League goals, Baker 16 and Wignall, surprisingly, only five. Baker's party trick was to take the ball with his back to goal, turn past the centre-half and home straight in on the keeper. It brought him many of his Forest goals and the most exciting sight of the 1966-67 season was to see Baker running at full pelt 30 to 40 yards out from goal. His most memorable goal was, however, an astonishing mid-air volley against Bolton on 27 January 1968 (Forest won 4-2), which will always live in the memories of the 1960s generation who were lucky enough to witness it.

Ian Storey-Moore was altogether a different animal. Though mainly right-footed, he preferred to patrol the left-hand side of the field, initially sharing the position with Alan Hinton. Between 1966 and 1972, he was top scorer in all but one season, and his runs from the left, cutting inside the full-back or going outside to centre for Wignall or Baker were the team's hallmark.

Through the 1966-67 season, the excitement and crowds just seemed to grow and grow. Attendances that season were the best in Forest's history. In 1965-66, Forest had finished 18th, had no World Cup stars and could hardly expect that the season to come would be exceptional. But, somehow and in some way, it gelled.

Period piece: Brian Clough and Peter Taylor sign Terry Hennessey for Derby in a scene which could have come from the contemporary Ipcress File. Hennessey was one of numerous players who appeared for both clubs in this era.

Ian Storey-Moore's debut was on 10 May 1963 in a 2-1 defeat of Ipswich Town. The crowd was just 13,055. There were to be eerie echoes nine years later in March 1972. The visitors were again Ipswich Town. The crowd this time was just 9,872 (down from 20,000 for the previous home game). The fans stayed away because Ian Storey-Moore had gone and, on that day, played his first game for Manchester United. At half time, in a show of the public relations skills which were to dog the club for years, the fans were told that Storey-Moore had just scored for United. Forest lost 2-0, their eighth consecutive defeat. At the end of that 1971-72 season they were relegated – really the final sad chapter in the story of 1966-67.

But even that 1966-67 season started slowly – defeats by Stoke and Chelsea were unfortunately to cost dear, and the crowds were unimpressed. Little was understandably expected, and crowds of 21,000 were at first the norm. But three things had changed – Hennessey, Baker and Storey-Moore. Terry Hennessey joined Forest from Birmingham in November 1965 and had gradually settled in as Bob McKinlay's partner. Joe Baker came from Arsenal in March 1966 and scored twice in his second game against Burnley. And Ian Storey-Moore finally established himself as a regular in March 1966, at exactly the same time as his partner Baker.

The highlight of Forest's unexceptional start to the 1966-67 was a superb display by Chris Crowe in getting a hat-trick against Manchester United on 1 October. He scored after only 15 seconds and gave a virtuoso performance to lead Forest to a 4-1 win. Amazingly, they were the only League goals Crowe scored all season. The campaign progressed otherwise unexcitingly until 12 November, incidentally Barry Lyons' debut, when a 3-1 win against Sunderland was the start of a 14-game unbeaten spell, then the best Forest First Division sequence in history. At the end of it, on 11 February, Forest were contesting the leadership of the division with Manchester United and went to Old Trafford for what would prove to be the decisive game of the season. Before a crowd of 62,727 Forest played well but couldn't score. With a few minutes left, Peter Grummitt made a quite superb save from a close range shot by Denis Law. The corner came over, Law converted and Manchester United went top. Forest won ten and drew three of their next 13 League and Cup matches, but could not displace United. The excitement was palpable, the crowds over 40,000 every week. 47,188 turned out to see Leicester, the largest crowd ever for that fixture. Similarly, 41,468 was the largest crowd ever for a Forest v Villa game. The rest of the League season was almost perfect, with just two glitches – unexpected away defeats by Sunderland and by Southampton. In the end, the game on

11 February proved to be the "four pointer" everyone had guessed it would be. United won the League by those four points. And, looking back, the two defeats in the first two games against Stoke and Chelsea were to be just as important. But the raw facts cannot possibly conjure up the mood of the season, the excitement in the city and the way the team built up a following unprecedented in Nottingham history.

It is often the case that a team plays well, builds up the excitement and then flatters to deceive without ever living that defining moment which remains forever in the memory. That was not the case with the Forest of 1966-67. Although they were eventually to win nothing, there was a day when all of that pent-up longing, that yearning for deeds only dreamed of, that deeply provincial commitment to the one identifying force in the City, was to reach a crescendo. The date was 8 April 1967, the venue was The City Ground, the opponents were the FA Cup holders, Everton, and the event was the quarter-final of the FA Cup. Philip Soar, later deputy chairman of Nottingham Forest, said at the packed Extraordinary General Meeting the club called to determine its future in 1997 and surrounded by cameras and microphones, that if he could live just 100 minutes of his life again, he would choose that afternoon, that Saturday, that season.

Authors Martin Tyler (later of Sky Sports) and Richard Widdows chose this game as one of the 60 most memorable ever played in the British Isles in a book of that name. It was the only game chosen which involved Forest. This is how they saw those 90 minutes, under the title: "Some Game, Some Goal, Some Finish"...

REALLY great matches are not easily compounded. They can emerge in a great context, when the crowd is packed and expectant, when the players are tense and utterly committed, when there is some great prize to be gained.

After the sixth-round draw for the FA Cup was made in 1967 it was clear that such a game was in prospect, for Nottingham Forest had been drawn to play the Cup holders Everton at The City Ground. But few could have anticipated just how memorable the encounter would be. In 1967 Nottingham were being managed with gentle Irish charm by Johnny Carey, who had been captain of Manchester United in 1948, and moulded by Tommy Cavanagh, a silver-haired sergeant-major of a Liverpudlian, who was their trainer-coach. Carey had inherited a predominantly pretty side, playing the neat football which had destroyed Luton Town in the early stages of the 1959 Cup final, but vulnerable to the pressures of the long English season. To counteract this Carey had bought Terry

Hennessey, a stooping, spindly player from Birmingham City, and seldom can one signing have had such a major effect on a side. Hennessey, with his acute positional sense, hard but eminently fair tackle, and his natural inclination to attack whenever the opportunity presented itself, had given Forest a broad and solid foundation on which to build a successful team.

The speed of their transformation proved yet again that although the ingredients of a good side can be bought or developed locally the blend which is essential to success will come and go of its own accord.

Most of the club's players were not outstanding individually. Never the wealthiest of clubs, Forest had to buy men below their best and coax something extra out of them or develop whatever talent they could find on their own doorstep. Cavanagh took much of the credit for this. The players worked for him willingly and with success came new assurance; their skills were blended so successfully that their shortcomings did not matter. John Barnwell, a former Arsenal forward, was the key figure in midfield, finding his men with chips, lobs and deflections; Frank Wignall was a mobile, easily-found target for the long, high passes of Winfield and Newton. Playing off Wignall, Forest had Joe Baker, another former Arsenal player, supposedly slowing down but still capable of upsetting a defence with sudden bursts of acceleration through the middle. Most important of all, as it turned out, they had Ian Storey-Moore, a young forward whose penchant for scoring goals had begun to give the side a taste of greatness.

While chasing Manchester United in the League, Forest's Cup campaign had gone well. Defeats of Plymouth in the third round and Newcastle in the fourth were simple enough. In the fifth round, Second Division Swindon provided tougher opposition with a goalless draw at The City Ground and a 1-1 draw at the complementary County Ground. The second replay was at Villa Park on Monday 20 March 1967 and it produced an unprecedented 50-mile traffic jam on the A453 between Nottingham and Birmingham (no motorways in those days). Some idea of the interest generated in the team in that magical season can be gauged from the attendances for these Cup matches. The Newcastle game at The City Ground drew 47,500, as did the Swindon game (this was technically the stadium limit at the time and the games then were never all-ticket, so we must assume that the figure was exceeded and the published figure was diplomatic). The replay at Villa Park, which Forest won 3-0, was eventually watched by 52,596, half of whom missed at least the first half-hour. These are the sort of attendances that have never been associated with Forest before or since, and it is hard, 30 years

later, to capture the sheer magic of a season in which the team won the heart of the city but, in the end, was to win nothing else.

The Everton team to meet Forest in the quarter-final bore little resemblance to the side that had won the Cup the previous year. Only Wright, Wilson, Labone, Harvey and Young had played at Wembley; the most important addition had been that of Alan Ball, signed from Blackpool for a British record of £110,000. With Ball in the side, Everton's wealth of talent had at last begun to have some meaning. Previously the team had had much individual skill but lacked purpose; Ball, working with Colin Harvey, had given the side a backbone and it was obvious that if both or either could dominate the midfield against Forest then the game would be half won. More vital to the result, however, was the blow suffered by Everton at White Hart Lane on Easter Monday when Gordon West, their goalkeeper, broke a bone in his right hand. This left Andy Rankin, a willing but inexperienced understudy, to face the bustling Nottingham attack.

April 8 1967 was a typical Nottingham day. The air was damp, the little shops in Arkwright Street glowed mistily in the gloom and the Trent flowed darkly past The City Ground. Inside, the keenest Nottingham supporters were packed into the Trent End, a narrow strip of terracing tucked between the goal and the river; the followers of Everton were massed, in a broad band of blue and white, opposite the Main Stand.

Yet no sooner had the game started than there was a threat of anti-climax. After only two minutes, Baker set out on a typical sprint straight at the heart of the Everton defence. He was approaching the penalty area and was in the act of shooting when Labone, flinging himself feet first in a slithering tackle, blocked him. Baker rolled over and over in acute pain. He could hardly bend his left leg. Every kick, every tackle was agony yet he carried on for another half-hour before Alan Hinton, whose form that season had been erratic, took his place. Baker never truly recovered from that tackle, seemingly losing his most valuable asset – the courage for the telling sprint past the centre-back.

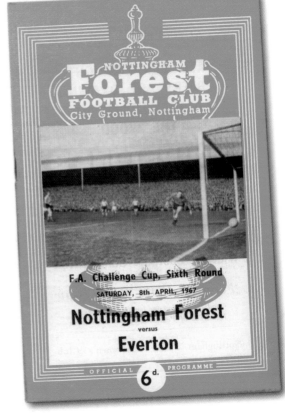

Forest's ebullient confidence was draining away with Baker's injury. Ball and Harvey were controlling the pace of the game to Everton's choosing and, while Nottingham were reorganising themselves to accommodate Hinton, the Cup holders struck. Jimmy Husband ran on to a glorious lob from Ball to flick the ball wide of Grummitt's left hand. The sense of disappointment lasted into the second half. It was not so much the fact that Nottingham were losing or, indeed, that the quality of football was poor, for Everton were displaying a cool mastery of the situation that looked likely to take them into the semi-finals. But Baker's injury appeared to have deprived the encounter of its classical context.

But by half-time Forest were over the shock of the loss of their inspiration Baker and Frank Wignall, who had moved to Forest from Everton for a give-away £20,000, chose the next 45 minutes to give perhaps his most memorable display.

The second half saw Labone increasingly pulled out of position. The Everton captain was suddenly unable to reach crosses he had cleared majestically before the teams changed ends. And, as Labone shrank, so Wignall grew. To his right, Hinton – never a brave player, occasionally retiring to the point of vapidity – was gaining confidence against another World Cup star, Ray Wilson, and all over the Everton half was a hyphenated star in the making as Storey-Moore rushed round trying to pick up the crumbs from Wignall's forehead.

Suddenly, the spirit of the Cup was alive again. As if by a signal, Nottingham were moving forward to a greater purpose. As Everton, taken unawares, reeled back, Rankin faced his first test of the match – and failed. West would probably have held Wignall's shot but Rankin could only block it and Storey-Moore pounced on the rebound to bring the scores level after 66 minutes. Two minutes later, everybody was on their feet. Again the Everton cover was swept aside, again Wignall played an essential part, nodding Hinton's cross down to the onrushing feet of Storey-Moore who gave Forest the lead with a superb shot squeezed through the narrowest of gaps.

It says much for Everton that they remained unshaken. They had made no attempt to close the game up after their first-half goal, continuing to come forward in a wave of blue that had occasionally threatened to swamp the Trent End and flow into the grey that was the wide river beyond. Husband and Morrissey were the vanguard, reacting like marionettes as Alan Ball pulled their strings with those lightning through passes that are always inconceivable until he seemed to make them inevitable.

After Forest went ahead, the pace actually quickened. Neither side seemed to want a replay.

But the momentum was now with Forest. In midfield Newton was tackling like a dumper truck, Barnwell was as delicate as ever – dropping balls for Hinton and Storey-Moore to run on to – and Hennessey and his forthright full-backs were content to pump long balls up front where Wignall, with all the grace of a runaway threshing machine, was forcing Everton's back four to struggle for everything that came into their path.

But, as if at the whim of a playful deity, the game suddenly swung again and it was Everton who found the net next. Ball conjured a pass out of nothing to send Brown away on the right – where the ungainly Winfield had long been a chink in Forest's armour. Hennessey moved to cover, a body swerve, and Brown was gone. A second later, so was the ball and there was Husband to turn it past the despairing Grummitt with a coolness that turned Forest's sunny spring into icy mid-winter.

In a moment, the wheel had turned full circle. Everton were now like a pack of hounds after the scent of Wembley turf. Grummitt tipped a marvellous shot from Morrissey over the bar, but Everton could not capitalise on the mood of the moment and, inexorably, Forest re-established their foothold. A rare excursion into the penalty area saw Bobby McKinlay put the ball past Rankin – only for Harvey to head off the line – and as the game crept to its fitting finale, the crowd nervously consulted their watches. The climax came with less than 60 seconds left.

Winfield sent a long, high centre into the penalty area and the omnipotent head of Wignall deflected the ball down to Storey-Moore, who proceeded to win the game for Forest in astonishing fashion. He kicked the ball against Hurst, hammered the rebound at Rankin, nodded Rankin's weak clearance against the bar and finally, at the fourth attempt, headed the ball over the goal-line.

Seldom can the dramatic course of a game have been plotted so perfectly. It was a fitting climax to a great game, to Forest's season and, in a sense, to their 100-year history. But that was not clear at the time – the climax was yet to come according to the 100,000 who queued all night for Forest's allocation of semi-final tickets. It would have taken a brave man to suggest to anyone in Nottingham that Forest would not win the "double".

But the lace city was to be disappointed. At Hillsborough, an imp who had long figured in Forest nightmares – one Jimmy Greaves – swayed a semi-final Forest should have won with a marvellous opportunist goal, and Terry Hennessey gave away a second to a voracious Frank Saul. In the League, Forest could never catch Manchester United.

Forest had simply not been good enough. Perhaps like a surfer overreaching himself, they had been carried along on top of a wave of enthusiasm and a temporary blend which had reached its zenith on that April Saturday. Sadly, it left them in the seasons to come. Bobby McKinlay had grown too old, John Barnwell suffered an injury which was finally to put him out of the game, the enthusiasm of the full-backs never again compensated for their shortcomings in ability. Cavanagh and Carey were unable to find the right men to fill the holes and the club wasted £100,000 in a moment of sheer madness – trying to replace Barnwell with a Jim Baxter patently past his best.

Just five seasons later only one – full-back Peter Hindley – of the twelve men who had represented Forest that wonderful day was still in the first team. Eight of the other eleven had been sold, fetching an astonishing (for the time) £600,000. And all Forest had to show for it was a place in the Second Division.

––––––––––

That was how Tyler and Widdows saw the game, and, as a commentary, it surely stands the test of time.

Ian Storey-Moore, chief scout at the club in 1998, remembers the game as if it were yesterday, despite the lapse of 30 years: "I thought Frank Wignall was the star that day. I got the accolades because I scored the goals, but that was wrong really. Frank was marvellous. He set up all the goals and I think it was the best game he ever played for the club. It could have had something to do with the fact that he had joined us from Everton." Storey-Moore also remembers the atmosphere. "Everyone felt so close. I loved that. The crowd were almost on the pitch – but still very well behaved. Towards the end, the tension must have been overwhelming. My mum was at the game – but she just had to leave before the end. She said she just couldn't stand the excitement. I remember after the final whistle went I looked around and no-one else had left. The crowd were all still there. Standing and singing and shouting. Amazing. Funnily enough, the moment I remember most was when Jimmy Husband scored to make it 2-2. I distinctly remember thinking: 'Oh no, Goodison Park on Wednesday.' The final goal still has a slightly dreamlike quality. It all happened very quickly for me, though people watching tell me it seemed to go on for ever. What struck me afterwards was that, despite my having four goes at it, no Everton defender tackled me. I think they must have been just as bemused as I was that it just kept coming back to me."

The semi-final was the greatest disappointment of Ian's career: "I remember coming out at Hillsborough and looking towards the Kop. It was just a sea of red. The emotional pressure from our supporters was impossible to underestimate. I felt terrible for them afterwards.

Right: Ian Storey-Moore leaves the field after the game which secured his place in the Pantheon of Forest greats. "My mother was at the game," he says now, "but she just had to leave before the end. She said she couldn't stand the excitement. I remember after the final whistle when I looked round and no-one else had left. They were all still there – singing and shouting." Bobby McKinlay remembers it for a different reason: "I'd been marking Husband and he scored twice. I knew I was going to be for it in the dressing room from Tommy Cavanagh, so Ian saved my bacon." This was the greatest of moments for the baby-boom generation of football fans. Somehow it released a generation of suppressed dreams and fantasies. 47,510 stood screaming and shouting – and 100,000 were to queue overnight for semi-final tickets. Not even during the great European Cup triumphs were there to be such scenes. Storey-Moore was to lead Forest's scorers for five seasons out of six until his transfer to Manchester United spelt the very end of a great Forest side. He won just one England cap – against the Netherlands – in 1970. It was said that Alf Ramsey would have picked him far more often, but for the problem of his name. Ramsey already had a Storey (Peter) and a Moore (Bobby), and to add a Storey-Moore would have been far too confusing for everyone! As it is, Ian remains the only player with a double-barrelled name to play for England. Ian Moore was famous for the transfer that never was – when Brian Clough paraded him around the Baseball Ground only for Forest to refuse to sign the transfer forms. "Clough never forgave me – he literally threw the forms at me," says Ian, Chief Scout at The City Ground in 1998, "but that's nothing compared with what David Nish had to put up with. Cloughie stormed into a Leicester City board meeting to tell them he intended to sign David. They asked him to leave. Politely, I think."

We never got going and Jimmy Greaves' goal was an absolute body blow. Would we have won with Joe Baker? Well, who can say. Perhaps. It was sad because we had played so well that season. The really important difference from the year before was that Terry Hennessey had dropped back to be a second centre-back. Before that he had played as a midfielder, but he was never a penalty-box-to-penalty-box player. With Terry at the back, we started playing 4-4-2, or 4-2-2-2 really, with me and Barry Lyons playing as the 'middle two'. Harry Newton was a large part of our success – great in the tackle and the steel that any successful side needed. We didn't really have a weakness except that wingers like Willie Morgan used to give John Winfield a hard time."

Management in the 1960s was very different from today. "Johnny Carey was a nice man," says Ian, "but he didn't exactly teach us a lot. He used to come into the dressing room and say 'Fizz it

about today lads', which wasn't exactly the most informative of team talks. It was Tommy Cavanagh, the coach, who used to run things. He gave me a terrible time – always on at me, on at me, on at me ... all the time. In retrospect, it probably did me good. But after Joe Baker and John Barnwell were injured, it all fell apart. Johnny Carey was replaced by Matt Gillies – whose Leicester were actually the only team below us in the League at the time – and we just kept selling: Alan Hinton, Terry Hennessey, Joe Baker, Harry Newton. I was the last of the team to go really. The transfer deadline was coming up in 1972 and I was just told that Derby and Manchester United had shown an interest. I went to the Edwalton Hotel down the road from the ground with Matt Gillies, Bill Anderson and Ken Smales to meet Frank O'Farrell (then the United manager). I talked to O'Farrell but his terms weren't good enough. With Forest in 1967 we earned £40 a week with £4 for a win and £2 for a draw. I never earned more than £100 a week the whole time I was in the game. So I turned United down. As a result Matt Gillies rang Brian Clough from the hotel and Cloughie said he'd be there in 20 minutes. He was as well, but Gillies, Anderson and Smales all shot off, leaving me alone when Clough and Taylor arrived. Well – they were straight in, coats off – terrifying really. I could understand then why the others had decided to leave. I signed there and then and Taylor took me back to the Midland Hotel in Derby, where the Derby players always met the night before a game. The following day they paraded me on the pitch for the crowd and I thought it was all decided.

"I woke up the next morning, and switched the radio on. But, instead of the usual news about middle east wars or strikes, the lead story was all about my transfer falling through. I knew nothing about it. Tony Wood, a Forest director, called my wife Carol, and told her the board wouldn't let me go to Derby under any circumstances. They were afraid of what the fans would do after so many Forest players had gone there. So Matt Busby came round to my house and I signed for United. End of story. Forest were relegated at the end of the season and the rest is history."

So how were relations with Clough? "Terrible. He never forgave me – even though the one person who was blameless was me. I still wanted to sign for Derby. When I went to see him after Tony Wood had called Carol, he stood up and threw the forms at me. Literally threw them. I was virtually banned from the Forest ground when Clough was manager. Not formally you understand, but he would never speak to me."

The Everton game has become Forest's equivalent of the 1966 World Cup final, still repeated on television round-ups, with the goal scoring finale and even Kenneth Wolstenholme's ("The crowd have gone bonkers") final memorable line. Through all the glory years of Brian Clough, there was never a game which generated quite such emotion and this was, perhaps, because so many great Forest displays were away from home – Munich, Cologne, Madrid, Berlin, Old Trafford. If there are two that come close, they are probably the 2-0 European Cup defeat of Liverpool and the 3-3 semi-final draw with Cologne.

But back in 1967, as Tyler and Widdows said, over 100,000 queued all night to obtain tickets for Hillsborough and the semi-final against mighty Spurs. Although Forest won their semi-final at Hillsborough in 1959, it is a ground which had so often seen dreams end – notably in the 1980s.

FA Cup semi-finals are hardly Forest's forte. Their record remains by far the worst of all the major clubs. The 1967 game was the ninth time Forest had reached the semi-final stage, and the club had still won only two of them. Forest were to lose the next two drawn to be played at Hillsborough (1988 and 1989) and it was not until 1991, in their first appearance at Villa Park, that they were to see another success. The 1898 semi-final had initially been drawn at Bramall Lane and Forest had won the replay at Crystal Palace. The 1959 game is, therefore, the only one of Forest's six semi-finals played in Sheffield that they have ever won. Including replays, Forest have taken the field for an FA Cup semi-final on no fewer than 18 occasions and of those 18 they have won just three. By contrast, Forest have won all six of their League Cup semi-finals.

The 1967 semi-final, before an absolutely packed Hillsborough of 55,000 with Forest occupying the Kop, really turned on one moment of magic from Jimmy Greaves. He scored one of his most memorable goals, a killing psychological blow as much as a single score because of his strange affinity for Forest. During his career Greaves scored far more goals (29) against Forest than any other club – including four on three separate occasions. Clearly he terrified the Nottingham club and his 30th-minute goal demoralised them so much they lost a game that really should have been won. As a goal it was probably not as classic a moment as some others that will always live in the memory – his volley of a ball dropping over his shoulder as one of five scored for Chelsea against Wolves in his second season, 1958-59; his bicycle kick against Blackpool in his first game for Spurs; his turn and dribble past four Manchester United defenders at White Hart Lane on 16 October 1965; and his run and shot past three Forest defenders when he never touched the ball but beat them simply by letting it run, dipping his shoulders and dummying left and right. But the semi-final goal was a great goal because of its context, because it got Spurs to a Cup final, because it was one of those goals that only Greaves seemed to be able to score, and because it was proof, if it was needed, that a single player can occasionally win for a team trophies that they would not otherwise have won. In recent domestic years only Jimmy Greaves, George Best and Eric Cantona fall unquestionably into this category.

Greaves' goal came out of the blue at a time when Forest were clearly on top. A long clearance from Mike England was headed sideways by Gilzean. As the ball bounced at Greaves' feet, he suddenly twisted and hit it left-footed on the half-volley from about 25 yards. The ball shot along the ground, snicked Grummitt's right-hand post and settled in the far

If the 1967 Everton quarter-final was to be the zenith, then the Hillsborough semi-final on 29 April against Spurs was to be the nadir. No Forest game in history has ever generated such disappointment and despair. Forest were already two down after goals by Jimmy Greaves and Frank Saul when (**right**) Terry Hennessey (out of picture) scored with a header which struck the bar and bounced onto the line. The referee (standing to the left of Ian Storey-Moore) gave the goal but Forest could not add a second and went out 2-1. Greaves' 30th minute goal, a sudden volley from 25 yards, was one of the greatest he ever scored and it cut the heart out of Forest. Greaves scored more first-class goals against Forest (29, including four on three occasions) than any other player in history. "Would we have won if Joe Baker had been fit?" asks Ian today. "Well, who knows. But it changed the way we had to play and he was such an inspiration."

Bottom right: Bob McKinlay holds off Alan Gilzean in the Hillsborough semi-final. Bob McKinlay says: "I blame myself for the first goal. Terry had gone upfield and I needed to get close to Greaves, encourage him to hold the ball and try to pass me. But I was much closer to the goal than I thought and he got the shot in before I could tackle him."

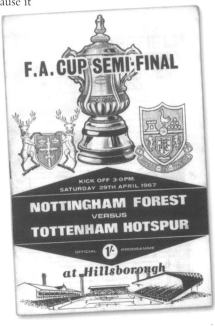

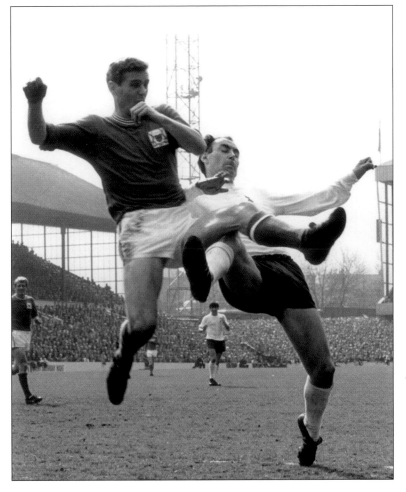

corner of the net. The Forest defence never moved. With a quarter of an hour left Frank Saul robbed Terry Hennessey in the defender's half, set off for goal and whacked a magnificent shot into the net. Forest attacked frantically but could reply only once, from Hennessey himself, and Spurs were through.

For Forest's travelling support, the gloom was as great as any they had ever experienced. On the bright side, the club finished second in the League, its highest ever in over 100 years of football. Although the next season was to start brightly, injuries to Ian Storey-Moore and John Barnwell removed the creative core and Forest were to finish just 11th. Strangely, the crucial game was to be a 1-0 defeat at Sunderland on 4 November 1967. Barnwell had been injured earlier in the season and, although he was back briefly, Sunderland's dominance was due to an outstanding performance by Jim Baxter. On 2 December John Barnwell was injured again against Everton and, as important, the game was a fourth consecutive defeat. Storey-Moore played, but this was to be his last game for two months. The board met and, in all probability, rushed to judgement. On 31 October, Forest had been eliminated from the Fairs Cup by FC Zurich. Although they won 2-1 at The City Ground, Forest lost 1-0 in Zurich. Unfortunately, the

On 24 August 1968, the Main Stand at The City Ground caught fire just before half-time during a game with Leeds United. Much of the stand was made of wood and the fire, which probably started in the dressing rooms, quickly took hold. Despite there being a crowd of 31,126, there was no panic and the occupants of the stand all came onto the pitch as the whole stand eventually went up in flames. Given what was to happen later at Bradford, it is remarkable that there were no injuries. The following day Bob McKinlay stood in the wreckage of the stand: "You should see what the Leeds players put on their insurance claims," he says, "I never knew footballers owned so many Rolexes." Forest moved to Meadow Lane for their next six home games, including (left) the 3-3 draw with Stoke on 5 October 1968. They won none of the six – drawing three and losing three. This was particularly frustrating for the unstoppable Ian Storey-Moore, who scored no fewer than 13 goals in the 13 games (home and away) Forest played while homeless – and saw his team win just one of the 13, albeit a 5-2 away success at The Hawthorns. For the record, Forest were drawing 1-1 with Leeds when the fire took hold. Storey-Moore was immensely popular, once coming second only to Garry Birtles in a poll for the club's most attractive player.

NOTTINGHAM FOREST
FOOTBALL CLUB

Football League
DIVISION
ONE

SEASON
1968-69

PRICE
ONE SHILLING

Volume 4
Number 3

SATURDAY
24th AUGUST
kick-off - 3 p.m.

FOREST
REVIEW

CITY GROUND
TRENT BRIDGE
NOTTINGHAM

THE OFFICIAL PROGRAMME OF NOTTINGHAM FOREST FOOTBALL CLUB

NOTTINGHAM FOREST
versus
LEEDS UNITED

123

Forest management did not appear to understand the rules and the team remained on the pitch after the final whistle waiting for extra time that never came. The result thus became a double humiliation.

Faced with the loss of both Barnwell and Storey-Moore, the board decided to invest £100,000 in purchasing "Slim Jim" Baxter from Sunderland, largely on the evidence of his performance against the club on 4 November. Baxter became only the fifth player to be transferred for £100,000. It was to prove a disastrous decision. Baxter was patently past his glorious best with Glasgow Rangers, and was to play only 51 times, scoring three goals. The most memorable was an astonishing 35-yard bullet directly from a goalkeeping clearance at Stoke on 30 December 1967.

Baxter departed on a free transfer, the financial loss therefore being the greatest ever at that time suffered by any English club on the purchase and sale price of a player. From this moment on, Forest were chasing their tails. The creativity was gone with Barnwell's injury and the club was struggling after writing off the £100,000 on Baxter. With nothing more to spend the club tried to balance the books with major sales and minor purchases. As the club was still genuinely a club run by a committee, there was no source of funding and the committee members proved incapable of dealing with the consequences of their success in 1967. The sale of the better players accelerated and the team's 11th place in 1968 was the last top-half position until the Championship was won in 1978.

The fragility of Forest's success in 1967 was ultimately clear to see. It was dependent on two or three players and a temporary gelling. It could easily have been built upon - crowds of 40,000 were virtually guaranteed at the time - but it was not. The reasons were twofold. The first was poor football management which bet the whole bank on one truly dreadful signing. The other was the very nature of the club – its unique committee structure and its proud amateurism almost inevitably led to its inability to sustain the success of 1967 and that wondrous display against Everton.

After Matt Gillies left in October 1972, there were two short managerial reigns by Dave Mackay and Allan Brown. Looking back now, there is a "Waiting for Godot" feel about their managerships – but that is because we know what was to come next.

For a time there was dull Second Division fare – 14th, 7th, 16th and 8th places – the last two under Clough. The period is remembered solely for Duncan McKenzie's magnificent season of 1973-74 and that year's Cup run. McKenzie scored 26 League goals and two in the Cup, with only one other player (George Lyall) getting into double figures. The Cup led to two of the most memorable games ever played by Forest occurring in the fourth and sixth rounds. In the fourth (forever McKenzie's game), Forest beat Manchester City 4-1 in front of 41,472 with McKenzie tearing City apart, scoring one himself and making two for Ian Bowyer and one for George Lyall. After beating Portsmouth in the fifth round (another McKenzie goal) Forest went to St James' Park for the quarter-final. Bowyer, O'Kane and Lyall scored for Forest and Pat Howard was sent off for United. With the score at 3-1, the Newcastle crowd invaded the pitch to try to get the game stopped. A belief had built up in Newcastle that this was to be "their season" and the anthem they followed that year was Alan Price's hit "Follow the Geordie Boys". They could not bear what they were seeing. This was to be the very first crowd invasion of an era that was about to descend into violence. Forest player David Serella was assaulted but, when the crowd finally left the field, referee Gordon Kew debatably allowed the game to continue. Despite their 10 men, Newcastle came back to win 4-3, although the final goal by Bobby Moncur was so patently off-side as to be almost comical. Forest protested and, today, would surely be awarded the match. The FA deliberated and, perhaps inevitably, reached a thoroughly unsatisfactory compromise. They declared the game void, thus acknowledging that Forest had been deprived of a fair chance, but would not let the replay be played at The City Ground. Instead, 12 days later, it went to Goodison, where the teams drew 0-0. Now, surely, the third match would come to Nottingham. "No," said the FA, in a decision entirely lacking in sense or logic, unless they believed that Forest fans would invade the pitch if Newcastle were winning (unlikely given Forest's record, and surely an unfair prejudgment). The third leg was at Goodison three days later. Forest had a well constructed free-kick "goal" by George Lyall disallowed because of a decoy by Paul Richardson, then Malcolm Macdonald scored for Newcastle in extra time. It was clearly a tie which Forest were destined to be denied by fans, the football authorities, referees and the fates. It remains the only occasion when a team has had to play three games in a single round and been denied a home tie. Duncan McKenzie – the man who could leap over Minis and throw a golf ball the length of the pitch – proceeded to score in all five of the season's last games and was then promptly transferred to Leeds. It was so typical a tale of post-war Nottingham Forest, but just around the corner lurked a force that was to change everything, forever.

Above: On 6 January 1974, The City Ground hosted its first ever Sunday game. Forest beat Bristol Rovers 4-3 in the third round of the FA Cup. There was no programme, just a teamsheet as, at the time, the rules on what could be sold on Sunday were peculiarly severe.

Forest's quarter final tie against Newcastle on 6 March 1974 was unique in the annals of football. Forest had experienced an exciting League season courtesy of leading scorer Duncan McKenzie, seen outpacing Newcastle captain Bobby Moncur (**top left**). McKenzie scored 26 League goals in 1973-74 and became only the third Forest player ever to lead any divisional scoring list. Forest had gone 3-1 ahead in their quarter-final at St James' Park courtesy of goals from Bowyer, O'Kane and Lyall and Newcastle's Pat Howard had been sent off. Unfortunately, a belief had built up in Newcastle that this was to be "their" season and, faced with the near certainty of losing the tie, large numbers of Newcastle supporters (**above and below**) invaded the pitch. At least one Forest player, David Serella, was struck by fans and, in later years, the game would certainly have been abandoned and the match awarded to Forest. Referee Gordon Kew decided to play on after the pitch had been cleared and, in an appalling and unprecedented atmosphere, Newcastle came back to win 4-3, their last goal being clearly offside. The FA refused to award the game to Forest and ordered a replay at Goodison. When it ended 0-0, a further replay was ordered, also at Goodison, which Newcastle won with a Malcolm Macdonald goal. It is the only time in the history of the FA Cup (excluding semi-finals) that a team has been forced to play three games in a single round and not been allowed to contest a single one at home. Newcastle, depressingly for football, went on to the final, where they were well beaten by Liverpool. While there can be no provable cause and effect, the conclusion that had to be drawn was that the Newcastle fans had succeeded in disrupting a game they were almost certain to lose and had been rewarded for their actions. This was not a precedent the game needed as it headed towards the agonies of the 1980s. Note that even in 1974, Newcastle were unable to spell the name of Nottingham Forest correctly.

CHAPTER SIX

Clough, Europe and the glory game

1975 - 1993

I T was Clough's very first day. You couldn't move for journalists. The car park was packed. Clough walked straight through them, right into the general office. It was the first time he'd ever been in there. He hadn't spoken to a single soul at the club before. He said: 'Get this f★★★ing rabble into the Guest Room or whatever you have here, give them a cup of tea and I'll speak to them after training.' Then he was off to the training ground. End of discussion. And it was a week before he sat down with anyone and discussed anything."

And so it went on from there. The whole history of Nottingham Forest changed at that moment. The speaker was Paul White, once a player and assistant secretary at the club, and who was to live through the whole Clough era.

That era had begun on 6 January 1975. After Allan Brown was sacked on 2 January, committee member Stuart Dryden was asked to approach Clough. The manager had been out of work for four months having left Leeds after just 44 infamous days. Clough had told the Leeds team that he didn't respect their success under Don Revie and he thought that they had achieved it dishonestly, or worse. The Leeds players told their board that they wouldn't play for this man and won only one of their first eight games of that season. Clough had departed after the 44 days, albeit leaving with a massive pay off. Almost his last significant act was the signing of Duncan McKenzie for £240,000. Now he was back.

At first Clough's influence was limited by budget. He appointed Jimmy Gordon, who had been with him at Derby and Leeds, as first-team coach. Gordon had been in charge of Middlesbrough's youngsters when Clough started playing, and had made a lasting impression. In February Clough bought John O'Hare and John McGovern from Leeds United for £60,000. The pair had played for him at Derby, and Clough had brought them to Leeds in August 1974 for £150,000. The £90,000 difference represented just 10 League games for Leeds between them, but they were Clough's men and, in consequence, were never going to fit in at Elland Road.

Clough also began a campaign to improve the behaviour of a section of notoriously yobbish fans, requesting them not to swear, told players that he wanted only those who wanted to play for Forest, and that discontents could go (remarks largely aimed at Robertson and O'Neill, who had made transfer requests while Allan Brown was still manager) and tried to instil a sense of unified purpose in the club. His first match in charge was a 1-0 FA Cup win away at Spurs in a third round replay, with the only goal a header by Neil Martin. The fourth round tie with Fulham went to three replays, Forest losing 2-1 at The City Ground in the fourth match. Relegation

threatened Forest before they rallied to finish 16th in the table, still a poor performance and all of nine places lower than the previous season.

At the end of the season free transfers were granted to Neil Martin and Tommy Jackson (who went on to get ten more Northern Ireland caps with Manchester United), while Clough astutely acquired full-back Frank Clark on a free transfer from Newcastle, where he had played 389 League games over 12 seasons and enjoyed European success. Clark was to make 117 League appearances for Forest and was eventually to succeed Clough as manager.

After a successful summer tour of West Germany and Ireland, during which John Robertson's abilities on the left were unexpectedly discovered, Clough began the 1975-76 season with this team: John Middleton, Viv Anderson, Frank Clark, Liam O'Kane, Sammy Chapman (captain), Paul Richardson, John Robertson, John McGovern, John O'Hare, Ian Bowyer and George Lyall. Tony Woodcock and Martin O'Neill were awaiting their chance. Season ticket prices had increased (Main Stand £22, terraces £10) and backroom staff trimmed in an effort to improve the club's finances. In the summer of 1976, Jim Willmer who, the year before, had been succeeded as club chairman by Brian Appleby, lost his place on the committee after 27 years with the club. He had been an outspoken opponent of Clough's appointment, warning Appleby against it, but already the reality of Brian's reign was taking shape. Many directors and shareholders were to voice negative opinions on Clough in the next two decades but the outcome was always the same. The 209 shareholders, each with just one share and one vote, understandably valued the success Clough brought to their club. Doubts they might have, but the majority invariably lined up behind Clough's supporters and would give no truck to his detractors. They wanted success, and Brian was usually able to help influence them to vote with those that would support him. In July 1976, Clough was re-united with Peter Taylor, who resigned from Brighton and finally joined Forest as assistant manager. It was from here that the real success began.

Taylor had been born in Nottingham and supported both local teams as a boy. He had joined Forest as an amateur goalkeeper. However, it was Coventry City who signed him as a professional in 1946. He made his League debut in 1950 and, in 1955, after 86 League games, was transferred to Middlesbrough, where Brian Clough, seven years younger, was beginning his

On 11 August 1975 Forest played a friendly at Coleraine and received this pennant from the Irish club. Forest won 3-2 with Ian Bowyer scoring all three goals, but the significance was that John Robertson played on the left and made all three. Previously Robertson had been a central midfield player but a sudden lack of wingers led Clough to put him out there as a stopgap. Robertson's performance in two Irish games (the other one was at Ballymena) surprised his manager and the Scot moved to the left wing for much of the next season. Martin O'Neill says now: "It was that tour which made John the unlikeliest left-winger ever and, in the long run, was probably the single main reason we won two European Cups."

career. The two became friends, with Taylor very much the senior partner - he spotted Clough's talent as a player early and did all he could to foster it, almost acting as an unofficial PR man for Clough. Clough was transferred to Sunderland, then in 1961 came the dreadful injury which caused his early retirement. Sunderland's manager George Hardwick made use of Clough as a youth coach, but this didn't please the board and, in 1965, when the insurance money on Clough's injury was received, both Hardwick and Clough were sacked. Taylor, meanwhile, whose playing career ended in 1965, was managing Burton Albion in the Southern League. Three months after Clough's sacking, he was offered the job of managing Hartlepools United, a no-hope side which held the record for applications for re-election to the League. Clough accepted on condition Taylor could join him. Taylor took a cut in salary to do so. It was still more a case of Clough needing Taylor than the opposite.

Taylor later said that in the four years since they'd parted at Middlesbrough, Clough had lost his zest, and in his three months of unemployment had been boozing heavily and was going nowhere in football. The two men, joint managers at Hartlepools, so lifted the club that in 1968 Hartlepools United was promoted to the Third Division for the first time. Clough and Taylor had already left, however, to weave their magic at Derby, lifting the club from the lower regions of the Second Division to the Championship and into the European Cup semi-final. They had parted only when Clough left Brighton to briefly manage Leeds, and now they were re-united again at Forest. In 1998 Martin O'Neill analysed Peter Taylor: "He was the spotter. He spotted the players, but his greatest spot was Brian Clough. He saw very early that Clough was different and, in a way, he attached himself to Clough's coat tails and tried to steer his man through the stormy seas that followed."

Clough made a good decision in a negative way in the summer of 1976, in not allowing Graham Taylor to sign Tony Woodcock for Lincoln. Woodcock had made four appearances for Lincoln while on loan. Woodcock, however, was allowed to make another six appearances on loan to Doncaster Rovers in 1976-77 before he won a regular place in Forest's attack.

Forest lost their third League game of the new 1976-77 season, 3-1 at The City Ground to Wolves, and there were more ugly demonstrations on the terraces. However Forest began to perform quite well in the League, with Terry Curran, who had joined the club the previous season, doing well on the wing. In September an important signing was made when the much travelled Peter Withe was obtained for £44,000 from Birmingham City. He soon made the centre-forward shirt his own. A week later and

Larry Lloyd, a centre-half who had won three England caps and a Championship medal in the early 1970s with Liverpool, appeared for Forest on loan from Coventry. Later he signed for £60,000 and became the regular centre-half. Lloyd remains the most bemedalled Forest player of all time, but any other sort of riches were not to be forthcoming: "I'm amused by much of the talk of brown envelopes and the like. In my day, there was nothing. Well, I suppose I did get a secret bung. Cloughie asked me if I was settling in OK, if I needed anything. So I said my wife could do with a washer-drier. The following day one arrived – twin-tub too! That's as far as it ever went in those days." "And he was lucky at that," says a listening John Robertson, "I got nothing."

A setback was a severe knee injury to Curran in October. Clough was quoted as saying: "Promotion has just limped out of the door." However, Woodcock was brought back and immediately struck form at inside-forward, being voted Forest's Player of the Year by the supporters at the end of the season and getting selected for the England Under-21 summer tour. In March another notable debutant was Garry Birtles, a 20-year-old Nottingham-born forward, better known as Cloughie's squash partner, but he was to make only two appearances in his first season.

A diversion this season was an Anglo-Scottish Cup, which Forest went on to win, beating Orient 5-1 in a two-legged final. On the way Forest played their youngest-ever player in Steve Burke, a local schoolboy of 16 years 22 days, against Ayr United in a second-leg tie at Ayr. Burke didn't make a League appearance for Forest, but later played League football with Queen's Park Rangers and Millwall. Clough was delighted with the Anglo-Scottish Cup. "It may not mean much to you lot," he said to the press, "but we've been starved of success here and once they get their hands on a bit of silverware, they'll want more."

It would not be an exaggeration to say that the events of February 1977 could have altered the whole subsequent history of Nottingham Forest - and possibly of Derby County as well. The departure of Clough and Taylor from Derby had been acrimonious, fuelled by a clash of obdurate personalities: those of Clough and autocratic chairman Sam Longson. The row had flickered on long after Clough had gone, with Clough himself stoking the fires by inspiring protest meetings among fans and players aimed at his reinstatement. After one Clough-inspired meeting, the players (with the exception of John O'Hare) had given manager Dave Mackay a note in which they refused to report to the ground for training until Clough and Taylor were back. Now, in February 1977, a new chairman at Derby, George Hardy, sacked Mackay and invited Clough and Taylor to return. There were long

discussions, terms were apparently agreed and, on 22 February 1977, the media were assembled at the Baseball Ground and The City Ground to hear the announcement. But overnight Clough changed his mind. Why has never been made clear. Hardy later telephoned an improved offer to Clough, who turned it down without consulting Taylor. The whole affair was reminiscent of the non-transfer of Storey-Moore from Forest to Derby five years before. What a strange relationship these two clubs have dating right back to 1898. Clough returned from the announcement at the Baseball Ground (Taylor had declined to accompany him) and the two men settled down to devote their efforts to getting Forest into the First Division.

It had been an astonishing week. One that defined Forest forever. On 16 February, six days before, Forest had played Southampton at home. The Saints went one up in the first half and were well on top when a merciful fog rolled in from the Trent and the game was abandoned after 47 minutes. When the game was replayed on 22 March, Forest won 2-1. Had the first score

stood, or had Forest managed to pull just one goal back, they would not have been promoted and then would probably never have even contested the European Cup. In the space of just six traumatic days, Forest nearly lost Clough, promotion, the following year's championship and two European Cups. Larry Lloyd says of that first abandoned game: "We were terrible that night. We wouldn't have scored if we'd played till midnight. Peter Osgood was giving me a terrible time, but the fog turned out to be a blessing in more ways than one. The referee couldn't see a thing and I sorted Peter out in the fog. I bet he still remembers it."

In a long season which, with pre-season friendlies, amounted to 68 games, Forest finished third in the table, one point ahead of Bolton and Blackpool, and were promoted. In an extraordinary way, which seemed a recurrent motif in Clough's career, Forest finished their programme before Bolton, who needed five

Opposite page: Of all the crucial games that determined what was to come in the dramatic three years between 1977 and 1980, the least recognised is the abandoned match of Wednesday 16 February 1977. The game was a Second Division fixture against Southampton and Forest finished the week seventh. Forest had gone one down in the first half before, in the 47th minute, the fog suddenly rolled in from the Trent and referee Roy Capey had to abandon the game. "We were terrible that night," says Larry Lloyd, "We wouldn't have scored if we'd played until midnight. There was no way we were ever going to get a point out of the game, never mind two. Peter Osgood gave me a roasting - pulled me all over the place. The other good thing about the fog was that the referee couldn't see a thing and I was able to sort Peter out." The game was replayed on 22 March and this time Forest won 2-1 with goals from Woodcock and O'Neill. Only 12,000 bothered to turn up to see the replay, a reflection of the fact that Forest had won only two of their previous ten fixtures. If the fog had not rolled in and Forest had either lost or drawn the original game against Southampton, then Forest would not have been promoted at the end of the season and history may have been completely different. On such random events do great tales depend.

Right: Forest's final game in the 1976-77 promotion season was at home against Millwall. They just squeaked a 1-0 win via a Millwall own goal in front of 23,529 spectators, none of whom could possibly have imagined what was to come in the next two years. At the time, Forest expected to finish fourth as Bolton still had three games to play and needed five points to take the third and final promotion place.

points from three outstanding games to pip Forest for promotion. Bolton had won the first when Forest flew off to Majorca for a holiday. In mid-air the pilot gave them the result they wanted: Bolton 0 Wolves 1. A controversial goal for Wolves sent Forest up - or perhaps it was a Millwall own goal which was the only score in Forest's last League game of the season. The Forest side for that match, the side which clinched promotion, was John Middleton, Viv Anderson, Frank Clark, Sammy Chapman, Larry Lloyd, Ian Bowyer, John McGovern, Martin O'Neill, Peter Withe, Tony Woodcock, John Robertson.

By coincidence, the 1977-78 season was also to consist of 68 games for Forest, although this time it was long runs in FA Cup and League Cup that boosted the total. Meantime, in the summer, Clough and Taylor had their original four-year contracts extended by three years, and set about reinforcing their squad for the First Division. On 11 July Kenny Burns, aged 23 and with eight Scottish caps, was signed for £150,000 from Birmingham City. His was the only new face in the team as it kicked off in the first match of the season. He was a player who could play almost anywhere, and had scored 20 goals for Birmingham the previous season, but he felt his best position was alongside the centre-half in defence, and that was where Clough played him in what had been Sammy Chapman's position.

Despite early success, no journalist, commentator or bookmaker gave Forest a chance of winning the title. With the benefit of hindsight this seems silly but, at the time, it was surely perfectly reasonable. Since the Second Division was founded 85 years before, only four promoted clubs had ever won the League Championship

and every one of the four had come up as champions of the Second Division. Forest had sneaked up third, with a 42-game points total (52) that was the fifth lowest of any promoted club in history.

It was fitting that this first match of a momentous season should be at Goodison Park. Forest played their first-ever League match there in 1892, coincidentally the first League match ever played at Goodison, and also played their last First Division game there in 1972. This time Forest did better than the 2-2 draw of 85 years earlier with a 3-1 win. They won their next three matches at home, against Bristol City, Derby County and West Ham United (a League Cup match) without conceding a goal, 1-0, 3-0 and 5-0 respectively. But then there was a setback at Highbury with a 3-0 defeat by Arsenal, after which Burns and Lloyd found themselves fined by Clough for ugly behaviour on the field. Burns had come to Forest with a big "bad boy" image and his signing was seen as a gamble, which critics were now happy to say Clough had lost. But Clough said: "Burns can play the rest of the season for nothing or he can become one of the best and highest-paid players in the game. It's up to him." Burns became a reformed character and absolutely essential to Forest's successes. He and Lloyd, the Highbury culprits, formed a superb defensive partnership, with Shilton arguably the best back three to play in the post-War English game. "We were the core of that 42-game unbeaten run," says Lloyd. "We just didn't concede any goals. The understanding was near perfect." Even today the best way to rile Larry Lloyd is simply to say what a great player Kenny Burns was.

Four wins and two draws later, including a 4-0 defeat of Ipswich in which Peter Withe scored all four to make his total nine goals in nine League games, saw Forest top of the First Division, a position they were never to lose during the season. Withe's four, incidentally, came all of 70 years after "Nocker" West had last achieved four in any First Division match for Forest.

By now the team had changed again. Two other players Taylor had long coveted arrived at the club. Peter Shilton, who Taylor regarded as the best goalkeeper in the world, was bought from Stoke for £270,000. This allowed Forest's England Under-21 goalie, John Middleton, plus £20,000, to go to Derby in exchange for Archie Gemmill. The 30-year-old Scottish international got into the side at the expense of Bowyer, who nevertheless made 29 League appearances as an outstanding utility man during the season. There had been an enforced change, too, after Frank Clark pulled a hamstring in the defeat at Highbury. Colin Barrett, who had been signed by Clough from Manchester City at the end of the 1975-76 season, but had lost his left-back place to Clark, now took over again and was a regular to the end of the season.

November and December brought stumbles in Forest's advance to the Championship on two fronts. First of all, the FA were in the process of appointing a new England manager, following the resignation of Don Revie four months earlier. The Forest chairman, Brian Appleby, admitted that Clough, with his permission, was about to be interviewed for the post. The fans pleaded with him to stay, most humorously by adapting his earlier poster which had read: "Gentlemen, No Swearing Please, Brian". Now a new poster greeted Clough as he went to and from the dugout: "Brian, No Leaving Please, The Gentlemen". Clough complained that, although fans were pleading with him not to go, they weren't buying season tickets. It was reported that £10,000 worth were bought in three days. A lot of money in those days.

While the uncertainty existed, Forest lost to Chelsea at Stamford Bridge. A fortnight later they lost at Leeds. They weren't to lose again, except in the FA Cup, for the rest of the season.

Clough desperately wanted the England job, and newspaper polls suggested the vast majority of fans (outside Nottingham) wanted him to have it. According to Tony Francis, who interviewed Peter Swales, of the FA Selection Committee, for his biography "Clough", Brian Clough was so impressive before the committee that he almost got the job. But the prejudice against him, in particular his perceived arrogance, which was held most strongly by the chairman of the committee, Sir Harold Thompson, prevailed, and the vote went to the safe candidate and caretaker manager, Ron Greenwood.

Just as Forest discovered they had survived the possible loss of their management team, they were hit by the second threat. On 10 December Larry Lloyd broke his toe in a match with Coventry City. Clough immediately paid £140,000 to obtain David Needham from Queen's Park Rangers. Needham had played 429 League games in 12 years for Notts County before, in 1977, moving up a division to join QPR. He played only 18 games for them before Clough brought him back to Nottingham. Needham went straight into the side for a clash with Manchester United at Old Trafford on 17 December. Forest won 4-0 and United manager Dave Sexton said: "Forest showed us up..... they could have doubled the score." John Robertson regards this game as the best of all the performances by the great Forest team. Six points out of eight after a difficult Christmas and New Year which saw Forest draw at home with both their main rivals, Liverpool and Everton, left Forest five points clear of these two clubs at the top of the table.

Three weeks later the Forest players made a record with a Nottingham group called Paper Lace. It was a march, a version of "We've Got the Whole World in our Hands", amended to "We've Got the Best Team in the Land". It was not one of the better club songs, and remains Nottingham's only contribution to the genre.

Until 11 March Forest were in contention for a unique treble - Championship, FA Cup and League Cup - but on that day they suffered their fourth and final defeat in the 68 game season. It came in the quarter-final of the FA Cup, away to West Bromwich Albion. Goals by Mick Martin and Cyrille Regis earned Albion a 2-0 win. This was a massive disappointment after it had taken three matches to get past Queen's Park Rangers in the previous round. As Martin O'Neill said 20 years later: "We really thought we could win all three. We really did. We got in the dressing room afterwards and couldn't believe that we had lost." Forest were not to lose any of their next 40 first class games in all competitions – the longest pure undefeated run in the history of English football and unlikely ever to be approached again.

On 22 April, Forest drew 0-0 at Coventry and clinched the First Division title. The game is remembered for Shilton's stunning save from a Ferguson header. There were still four games to go. The next match, at Ipswich, was the one in which a recovered Frank Clark came on as a substitute for Peter Withe and scored his first League goal in his 486th match. He then wouldn't give the ball away. "Thinks he's Pele," said Tony Woodcock. The next game, at home to Birmingham, was when the Championship trophy was presented to the club for the first time in its 114-year history. The enigmatic Clough invited the local police force, who were on duty, to carry the trophy, with the League and County Cups, round the ground. At the end of the season the title was won by seven points from

A flying Peter Withe celebrates his goal against Leeds United on 15 April 1978. Forest were just two games away from the Championship but could only draw this match 1-1 in front of 38,662 expectant fans. It was a great surprise when Withe left the club at the end of the season, and he did not figure in the two European Cup triumphs. To everyone's delight, Withe was still to win a European Cup winners' medal when he scored the only goal in Aston Villa's defeat of Bayern Munich in the 1982 final (the famous in off the post shot) (Colorsport).

Liverpool. Forest's total of 64 points had been bettered only four times since the war, and the strength of the defence was indicated by the fact that the 24 goals conceded equalled the record low set by Liverpool in 1969 and 1971 (in neither year were Liverpool Champions). Larry Lloyd delighted in pointing out to his colleagues that he had been the centre-half on the second occasion, and thus held the League defensive record with two separate teams – a genuinely impressive statistic. (As an aside, the year after Forest's title, Liverpool conceded only 16 goals in the League.) The 24 goals conceded and three defeats were both record lows for Forest in any division, and they created new First Division records for the club with 25 wins, 10 away wins, and 64 points (two for a win). And Brian Clough joined Herbert Chapman as the man who had managed two clubs to the Championship.

This superb performance by Forest was only part of the story of the season. They also progressed steadily through the League Cup, now being taken seriously by the clubs after a half-cock beginning in 1960-61.

They had begun in the second round with a 5-0 home defeat of West Ham, already mentioned, and in the next round beat Notts County 4-0 at home, County's first defeat at The City Ground for six years. Because Shilton was Cup-tied (alongside Gemmill and Needham) 17-year-old Chris Woods made his debut in goal. Woods was to remain in goal throughout Forest's run. Aston Villa, the holders, were beaten 4-2, also at home, and then Third Division Bury, who'd got to the fifth round, were beaten 3-0 at Gigg Lane. Leeds United were the two-leg semi-final opponents and were beaten 3-1 at Elland Road and 4-2 at The City Ground (much satisfaction for sacked manager Clough). This year was really the coming-of-age of the League Cup, because for the first time the two best clubs in the country reached the final, Forest and Liverpool. Liverpool were, of course, European Champions.

Clough and Taylor were so much a management team that there were plans for the two to lead Forest out together at Wembley, but the Football League wouldn't allow it. A full house of 100,000 at Wembley saw Liverpool completely dominate the game but Forest, with O'Hare coming on as a substitute when Frank Clark was injured, escaped with a 0-0 draw, thanks to a superb display from Chris Woods who, at 18 years 125 days, was the youngest goalie to play in a Wembley final. He also created a more significant record in winning a major medal (or tankard as it then was) having never played a single League match in his career. His only appearances had been deputising for Shilton in

Forest's very first trophy of the Brian Clough era was the League Cup, won at Old Trafford on 22 March 1978 after a goalless draw at Wembley. The game turned on a clear foul by Phil Thompson on John O'Hare (top), which Liverpool claimed was outside the penalty area. Television replays (top) confirmed their view but by then it was too late as referee Pat Partridge saw it differently and gave the penalty to Forest. The inevitable John Robertson stepped up and put the ball (centre) to the right of Ray Clemence. It was the only goal in 210 minutes of football and Kenny Burns, captain in John McGovern's absence, claimed the trophy with the help of John Robertson and Tony Woodcock. Chris Woods was in goal for Forest because Peter Shilton was cup-tied and he established the unique record of winning a major medal without ever having played a single League game.

Above: Kenny Burns holds his Sportswriters' Footballer of the Year Award in 1978. He remains the only Forest player to have won the trophy. Forest made a unique clean sweep of all the awards in 1978, with the four trophies being won by four different people. Peter Shilton was the PFA Player of the Year, Tony Woodcock was PFA Young Player of the Year and Brian Clough was Manager of the Year (**below**). Les Bradd, Commercial Manager at Forest in 1998, says that Burns and Lloyd were terrible to play against: "You knew it was going to be tough. One game I recall Larry came up to me at the start and said 'If you score today, I'll have you.' I did score, he did whack me and I did go off injured. We get on rather well these days."

the League Cup. Four days later 54,375 were at Old Trafford for the replay, where O'Hare replaced an injured McGovern. Once again Woods played magnificently. In the second half John O'Hare was through the Liverpool defence and approaching the penalty area with only goalkeeper Ray Clemence to beat, when a tackle from behind by Phil Thompson brought him down. The referee, Pat Partridge, awarded a penalty, though television replays showed the offence was just outside the area. The controversy about the award lasted for days, with Liverpool, backed by the TV pundits, making the case for Liverpool having been robbed. Nowadays, of course, Thompson would have been sent off for the tackle. In the event John Robertson netted the penalty, Forest kept Liverpool out, and Forest won the Cup. Robertson netted no fewer than ten penalties during the season, and, like that in the League Cup final, six were vital in that they affected the outcome of the match. The aftermath was memorable for a televised scene with Peter Taylor. Taylor was holding the Cup and was told by the commentator that replays showed the foul was outside the box. Asked to comment, Taylor said: "Really? So who's got the Cup then?" With which he turned and headed off down the corridor.

The season was remarkable for what Forest had achieved in so short a time. Two seasons before nobody would have been surprised to be told that Forest would remain a mid-table Second Division club for the next 50 years, so neatly did that niche seem to fit them. Clough summed up his satisfaction at the achievement: "I saw Frank Clark, a free transfer man, and Peter Withe, bought for only £44,000, finish the season with two medals. There was the same reward for John McGovern, who has been everywhere with me. Tony Woodcock, Viv Anderson, Ian Bowyer, Martin O'Neill and John Robertson, who were all at the club when I arrived, saw the results of a lot of hard work. Then there were the signings I made last season - Peter Shilton, Archie Gemmill, Kenny Burns, and David Needham. People talk of fairy tales, but what about

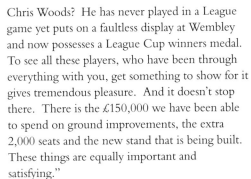

Chris Woods? He has never played in a League game yet puts on a faultless display at Wembley and now possesses a League Cup winners medal. To see all these players, who have been through everything with you, get something to show for it gives tremendous pleasure. And it doesn't stop there. There is the £150,000 we have been able to spend on ground improvements, the extra 2,000 seats and the new stand that is being built. These things are equally important and satisfying."

Forest players made a clean sweep of the end of season awards. Kenny Burns was voted by the Football Writers Association the Footballer of the Year, the only Forest player ever to win it. The PFA chose Peter Shilton as their Player of the Year, and as Young Player of the Year, Tony Woodcock. Clough was, of course, Manager of the Year.

Says Paul White: "It was a combination of genius and, let's face it, a little madness. But, after working with him for 15 years, I'd have to say he was not the man the world thought he was. He was cantankerous, difficult, terrifying. The players both feared him and respected him. They wanted to succeed for him, to impress him. After he'd taken Derby and Forest to their Championships, he was untouchable really. He'd done what no living manager had done. No-one could really dispute what he said or question him. But how did he do it? I don't know. He saw things in players – like John Robertson – that no-one else could see. When he wanted to buy a player, he'd wear them down till they couldn't say no. And when he wanted to get rid of someone, he was the same. He'd make life so miserable for them that they just had to leave, no matter what they were earning. I've never met anyone like him. He really didn't care what anyone else thought. His brothers said he was the same as a lad. I remember one brother telling a story about Brian, aged about 11, on a bus in Middlesbrough. There were seats upstairs but people standing downstairs. So he went down and yelled to people to come upstairs. The sort of thing we'd all like to do, but always seem too embarrassed."

Neil Webb, a star of the late 1980s: "If you go to the training ground, there's a line of poplars. Mine is fourth from the left. It was very windy and cold when we were training one day. Suddenly the gaffer disappeared and came back with a car load of saplings. He'd been to the local garden centre. He made all the players pay £2 each for their tree and then we had to plant them – in a line. They're quite big now – ten years on it probably is a bit warmer. Like I said, mine's the fourth from the left." Liam O'Kane, player and coach at Forest for 25 years, is explicit: "He never believed in training. After one hard game on a Sunday he suggested giving the players Monday off. I said I'd been thinking of having them in

Monday and giving them a break on Tuesday. He thought about it a bit and then looked at me. 'You're right,' he said. 'I agree. Let them have Monday *and* Tuesday off.' And we did."

Clough's remark about Chris Woods never yet having played a League game makes an interesting footnote to the season, reminiscent of the goalie Lawrie Platts who, after that famous Cup display at Manchester United in 1947, played only seven League matches for Forest. This turned out to be seven more than Woods played in three seasons at The City Ground. Woods did not disappear into obscurity, however, later playing for QPR, Norwich, Glasgow Rangers and Sheffield Wednesday and winning 43 caps for England.

Forest began the 1978-79 season with four major trophies in their sights: Championship, League Cup, FA Cup and European Cup, the first two of which they were defending. Their pre-season tours took in Yugoslavia and Greece and then, after returning to play Ipswich for the Charity Shield, they took part in a four-club tournament in Spain. They drew four and lost two in Europe without winning but hammered Ipswich 5-0 in the Charity Shield at Wembley. Martin O'Neill scored two of the five, then Clough pulled him off. O'Neill was annoyed, sensing a rare hat-trick. "Why did you do that?" he asked his manager. "Because you're crap and you always will be crap," said Clough. Twenty years on, Martin was able to muse about the incident: "I wouldn't exactly describe it as man management …"

Before the League campaign started, Clough struck a strange deal with his squad which he came to regret. They all agreed that 60 points should be enough to retain the Championship (as it was in five of the six seasons before Forest's win). So Clough offered the players a £1,000 bonus for each point they scored over 53, the first 53 to carry the usual £25 bonus.

The opening League match was an interesting one, a visit of Spurs, with their new signings in Argentinian World Cup stars Ossie Ardiles and Ricky Villa. A crowd of 41,223 packed into The City Ground and saw a draw, O'Neill's effort being cancelled out by Villa. This match marked Peter Withe's last game for Forest. Dissatisfied with the terms offered him, he put in a transfer request. Newcastle offered £250,000 and Clough accepted. He claimed later that Withe changed his mind at the last minute, but Clough was adamant he went. "We got excellent service from him, and sold him at a £200,000 profit. That's good business," he said.

However, goals dried up. Steve Elliott, who had been an apprentice at the club, assumed the number 9 shirt, but made only four League appearances before joining Preston North End, where he made over 200 appearances before moving on. But Forest had four successive 0-0 scores in League and League Cup before they started scoring again. In the following League match, at home to Arsenal, Garry Birtles came into the side for the first time that season, and Gary Mills made his debut. At 16 years 203 days Mills was Forest's youngest player in the League.

Arsenal were beaten 2-1 but the next match was the European Cup first round first leg match against …Liverpool. Liverpool had begun their League programme with five straight wins. They were the team in form. Reg Drury wrote a famous article in the *News of the World*. In it he said: "I don't think Forest have the know how to win the European Cup. That's why Liverpool must (beat them) if the trophy is to stay in England. Forest are European novices and do not

Left: The only time Forest have ever won the Charity Shield was in 1978, when they defeated FA Cup winners Ipswich 5-0 at Wembley. Here Martin O'Neill scores his second goal. Clough substituted him soon afterwards and Martin, having sensed a hat-trick, was furious: "Why did you pull me off?" he demanded to know when he got to the bench. "Because you're crap and you always will be crap," is how Martin records Clough's reply today. "I'm not sure he always knew how to get the best out of me," says O'Neill.

Garry Birtles scores his most celebrated goal - the first in Forest's 2-0 defeat of Liverpool in the European Cup first round tie at The City Ground on 13 September 1978. Birtles remembers the tie vividly: "The Liverpool side were very tense, very aggressive, angry that they had drawn us rather than any of the foreign sides. After I scored Phil Thompson said to me 'One won't be enough'. When Colin (Barrett) got the second with three minutes left I ran past Thompson and said 'Will two be enough then ?' I must have been mad doing that, what with Souness in their team. Afterwards they were unlike any team I've known since - not shaking hands, banging the walls of the dressing room, shouting about what would happen when we got to their place. It really was a baptism of fire for me. I'd played in a couple of friendlies the season before, but nothing significant. Suddenly Cloughie threw me in taking Steve Elliott's place. My first three games were Arsenal, Liverpool and Manchester United, all in the space of a week."

inspire the same awe as Liverpool." Ken Smales was so incensed by Drury's article that he kept it – it is the source of this quotation. But this was to prove to be the match in which Garry Birtles came of age. He had scored a brilliant goal in a previous match against Middlesbrough, and now he prodded in a Woodcock pass to give Forest a first-half lead and, three minutes from the end, made a second goal scored by Barrett, who volleyed in when Woodcock nodded down Birtles' cross. "With five minutes to go Phil Thompson ran past me," says Birtles twenty years later. 'One goal won't be enough,' he said. Well, he sort of spat it out really. Colin scored the second about 30 seconds later. As I went back upfield, I said to Thompson 'Will two be enough then?' I can't think why I said it. I'd only played about two serious games in my life. Thought Souness would kill me if he heard. After that, they hated us at Liverpool. So much for the loveable scousers. My dad always used to go to the games at Anfield – coins, darts, bricks, they'd throw everything at our supporters. Never forgave us. Added to which Clough threw me in for three games back to back - Arsenal, Liverpool and Manchester United. Talk about a baptism of fire!"

The consensus was still that Liverpool, going for a hat-trick of European Cup victories, would be easily capable of making up the deficit at Anfield. But Forest, who had drawn both League games between the two legs, were, as John Motson and John Rowlinson put it in their history of the European Cup, "chillingly competent". The 52,000 packed into Anfield built up an electric atmosphere. Dalglish had two great efforts, the first cleared off the line by Anderson, the second magnificently stopped by

Shilton. Neither side scored and Forest won on aggregate 2-0. Taylor, who had insisted beforehand Forest would get through, said quietly: "We came to do a job, and we did a job."

Tony Woodcock remembers the tie from the distance of 1998: "I suppose the game I still remember best is the first leg against Liverpool when we won 2-0 and Garry scored. God, he was good. After the game, Liverpool were furious, battering the walls and shouting at us that we weren't through yet and just wait until we got to Anfield for the second leg. There were no congratulations from the Liverpool team, not a word of praise, few handshakes. They were absolutely livid. They couldn't believe the position they were in. Clough was superb with us when we went to Liverpool for the second leg. We were waiting in the hotel and Clough and Taylor had just disappeared. Time went on and we got on the bus and still they weren't around. We all kept looking at our watches and it got to half past six before they turned up, which was only an hour before kick off. Peter said: 'Just stop worrying. Everybody's at Anfield. The streets are going to be completely deserted. It will take us ten minutes to get to the ground and we don't want you hanging about worrying.' They were also very rigid about behaviour that night. They made it very clear: Absolutely no gloating – Straight off the pitch – Changed immediately – Straight on the coach – Straight back to Nottingham. And that's what happened. We drew 0-0 and that was probably still the greatest of our victories. There were repercussions though. It was only ten weeks later that we went there in the League having gone those 42 games without defeat. Kenny, Martin and myself were all suspended or injured and we went out to a club in Liverpool the Friday night before the League game. When we got inside, the manager came running up to us and asked us if we were trying to start a riot. He said the place would erupt as soon as people realised we were there, so intense was the dislike of Forest after the European Cup result. We couldn't believe it, but he literally grabbed us and forced us out of the back entrance. It wasn't friendly, it was very aggressive. He didn't apologise or anything. He was terrified. I've never experienced anything like it before or since. For us the tie was a highlight, a moment of glory. But for Liverpool, it was the end of their European hat-trick."

Barrett missed the second leg against Liverpool because of injury, and Frank Clark came into the side again. He and Bowyer were to share the number 3 shirt for most of the rest of the season. Forest won their League Cup third round match with Oxford United and won both League games before the second round first leg tie of the European Cup in Athens, against AEK Athens. By coincidence they were returning to a stadium they'd visited on their summer tour, when they drew 1-1. The AEK manager was the great Hungarian former player Ferenc Puskas, who dropped his 36-year-old midfield general, Mimis Domazos, after a blazing argument just before the tie. A 35-year-old was the hero of the match: Frank Clark. The first goal was scrambled in by John McGovern after Clark's quick free-kick was moved on by Robertson and Woodcock. After 21 minutes, the replacement for Domazos, a tough Uruguayan, Milton Viera, was involved in an incident with Kenny Burns, punched him and was sent off. Burns was booked. Just before half-time Clark beat the off-side trap by taking the ball half the length of the field and then squared to Birtles: 2-0. AEK retrieved a goal from a penalty in the second half after a Burns foul, but 2-1 away was extremely satisfactory. In the second leg, AEK were soundly thumped 5-1. David Needham replaced the suspended Burns, and young Gary Mills came on as substitute for the injured Clark. Puskas's only consolation was a meeting with his old 1953 adversary and opposing captain at Wembley, Billy Wright, then with Central Television.

Burns sustained a torn cartilage during the fifth round of the League Cup, Mills again being the substitute. The result was a superb 3-2 win at Goodison, the two sides having drawn in a League match at The City Ground three days before.

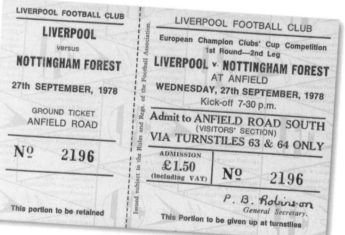

Viv Anderson robs Kenny Dalglish during the second leg of the European Cup first round tie at Anfield on 27 September 1978. This was the famous game when Clough and Taylor disappeared and didn't turn up for the bus until 60 minutes before the match. They wanted the team to arrive late so as not to get tense. The game ended 0-0, Forest were through and the atmosphere was, in Garry Birtles words: "As bad as I have experienced at an English ground. They were watching their European hat-trick walk out the door." It was the end of a run of 16 victorious European ties for Liverpool.

Two matches more and a 0-0 draw at The City Ground with Queen's Park Rangers on 18 November ensured that Forest would go a full calendar year without defeat in the League, their previous League defeat having come on 19 November 1977 against Leeds at Elland Road. This was only the second time in history that a side had gone a full 365 days without a First Division defeat – the first having been Preston in 1888-89, but they played only 22 matches. Forest were to surpass Preston's record by eventually extending their period without a defeat to 1 year and 13 days, just seven days longer than Preston. In addition, on 25 November 1978, Forest went to Bolton for what was to be their 42nd League game without defeat. This was truly a moment of football history – the first and only time a club had ever gone a "full season" of 42 League games without losing a single one. The result at Burnden Park was to be 1-0, with John Robertson scoring. The run comprised 21 wins and 21 draws. Two weeks later, at Anfield on 9 December, Forest lost 2-0 and the run was

The League Cup final of 1979, against Southampton, has a special place in the memories of the Forest players. "Cloughie kept us up drinking until 1:30 a.m. the night before. Heaven knows what he was thinking about," says Martin O'Neill. "Robbo and I ended up carrying Tony upstairs and we were absolute garbage for the first half against Southampton. We went into the dressing room 1-0 down and Cloughie just looked at us. 'Don't any of you dare suggest that performance had anything to do with last night,' was all he said. So we all just sat there for ten minutes and no-one said a word. We just sat in total silence. We eventually won 3-2 and, when I was managing at Wycombe, I tried the same thing myself at Runcorn. All I got for it was a splitting headache and a six-goal thrashing." Garry Birtles had an outstanding game to bring Forest back. He got the ball in the net four times - two were goals, one was a good goal wrongly disallowed for offside and the other was marginal.

broken. Nonetheless, no fewer than four all time records were broken and still stand. In addition to the 42 League games and 378 days without defeat, Forest also established a run of 22 away games (in all competitions) without defeat, and often overlooked, a run of 40 first class games *in all competitions* without defeat. The previous comparable record was always given as 35 first class games, established by Blackburn Rovers during their Cup runs of 1880-1882, but that was clearly a run of a different quality.

In the New Year Arsenal proved a problem to Forest with two wins. First they beat Forest in the League 2-1 at Highbury, to drop Forest back to sixth. Then in February, after Forest had progressed to the fifth round of the FA Cup with wins over Aston Villa and York City, Arsenal knocked Forest out 1-0 at The City Ground with a second-half Frank Stapleton header. Stapleton was one of those rare players who always constituted a threat to Forest at this time. By then Watford had been beaten in the League Cup semi-final over two legs, 3-1 at home and 0-0 away.

Grasshoppers Zurich were the third round opponents of Forest in the European Cup in March. Four days before the first leg at The City Ground, Forest paraded Trevor Francis, their latest signing, in a League match at Ipswich.

Francis was signed on 8 February 1979 against competition from many clubs, principally Coventry. The deal has gone down in football folklore as being the first £1 million transfer between British clubs, but Tony Francis' biography of Clough claims it wasn't. According to him, Clough's "final" offer was £950,000, but Birmingham City manager Jim Smith, who was selling, told his directors the deal was £1 million. Smith and his directors were desperate to appease City fans for the loss of local legend Francis by appearing to get the £1 million for him. The existing record, it should be remembered, was only £512,000 for David Mills. Finally Smith proposed a deal, which Peter Taylor agreed to: they would split the difference at

£975,000, but Birmingham would be allowed without contradiction to claim the fee was £1 million. Francis remembers that his first game was for the youth team in front of 20 people. "I ran out without shin-pads. Clough chucked me a pair, saying: 'Young man, I've paid a lot of money for those legs!'" By any standards, it was an extraordinary buy for Forest, the only club in the land who were not a limited company. Money was being rapidly made with their Championship and League Cup runs, but was being spent out of proportion to their average gates. The 200 members who had a stake in Forest must have worried about where their committee and Mr Clough were leading them. It is difficult to recall now just how peculiar Forest were at that time. They were literally a club with around 200 members, each of whom was equally responsible for any debts and losses the club might incur. In effect, each of them was personally responsible for £5,000 of the Trevor Francis transfer fee. It was astonishing that such a situation had continued for so long.

Francis was Cup-tied so far as the League Cup was concerned, and Cup-tied until the final so far as the European Cup was concerned. So he was not in the team which met Grasshoppers Zurich at The City Ground. Clough banned live radio commentary on the match in an effort to get more through the turnstiles, but 31,949 was not the sort of gate that Liverpool, for example, would expect for a European Cup quarter-final. It was a harder game than the final score suggests. Grasshoppers went ahead through their star striker Sulser, and although subsequently Forest took the lead with goals scored each side of half time from Birtles and Robertson (penalty), Sulser nearly levelled the score 15 minutes from time, Shilton making a great save. Two goals in the last three minutes from Archie Gemmill and Larry Lloyd got a 4-1 result and practically assured Forest's progress.

Before the second leg, Forest defended their League Cup in the Wembley final against Southampton. This time Peter Taylor led the side out. It was almost as if it were a deliberate riposte to the Football League ban of the year before. How dare they interfere with Clough and Taylor! Viv Anderson had picked up an injury and, with Burns still out, Colin Barrett and David Needham were in the side. At half-time Southampton led, but in the second half Birtles crashed home an equaliser and with 13 minutes left added another from Woodcock's pass. Woodcock himself scored a third before Southampton made the final score 3-2. Forest were the first side in the 19-year history of the competition to retain the Cup. Birtles was unlucky – he had a third disallowed for offside when he clearly wasn't and thus missed out on becoming only the third man to score a hat-trick

THE FOOTBALL LEAGUE CUP FINAL

NOTTINGHAM FOREST v SOUTHAMPTON

Saturday 17 March 1979 - Official Souvenir Programme 40p

Wembley Stadium

in a major Wembley final (the two who did being Stan Mortensen in 1953 and Geoff Hurst in the World Cup final of 1966). Martin O'Neill recalls other, less public, aspects of the game: "The night before Cloughie was trying to relax us. He insisted we went down to the bar for a drink, then wouldn't let us go to bed. By around midnight, Archie (Gemmill) was getting jumpy – asking the boss to let us go. He always liked his sleep. Cloughie wouldn't. We finally left the bar at 1:30 a.m., Robbo and I literally carrying Woody (Tony Woodcock) upstairs. We all felt terrible the following morning and the first half was garbage. At half time we trooped into the dressing room, 1-0, down and Cloughie just looked at us. 'Don't any one of you dare say that was anything to do with last night,' was all he said, challenging us to speak. And no one said another word for the next 10 minutes – not a word! And we won. 'Team Psychology' I thought, so I tried the same thing ten years later when I took Wycombe to Runcorn for a Cup tie. All I got for it was a splitting headache and a 6-0 thrashing."

In the second-leg European Cup match with Grasshoppers, Forest again went one down, to a Sulser penalty, but Martin O'Neill equalised and that ended the scoring.

Forest continued to do well in the League and had climbed to third before the semi-final of the European Cup, with Cologne as the opponents. The first leg, at The City Ground on 11 April 1979 before 40,804 fans, was most unlike a Forest Cup performance. Barrett and Needham were still in the side, a fit Anderson now being

suspended because of two yellow cards. Cologne were ahead in six minutes with a low shot which eluded Shilton and hit both posts before going in. After 19 minutes a tap-in goal after the Forest defence had been opened made it 2-0. Gemmill was injured and Clark came on at the back with Bowyer going into midfield. Forest looked as good as out with two away goals against them, but fought back splendidly. Birtles headed a goal, Bowyer levelled with a low shot through a crowded penalty box and John Robertson, with his only diving header, put Forest ahead. With 27 minutes left, they seemed set to clinch a useful first-leg lead. But a Cologne substitute in the form of a little Japanese forward, Yasuhiko Okudera, tried a 25-yard shot with his second touch and the ball squirmed under Shilton. "Japanese sub sinks Forest" was the inevitable headline, especially on a mudbath of a pitch. The final score was 3-3.

How Forest gloriously retrieved the situation in Cologne on 25 April and how two seconds led on to greatness when Forest, in their 76th match of the season, won the European Cup, joining Celtic, Manchester United and Liverpool as the only British clubs to do so, is described in Chapter One of this book.

Tony Woodcock said in 1998 of that game in Cologne: "I was eventually transferred to Cologne, of course, in 1979. I stayed at the same hotel that we'd stayed at before the semi-final. All the staff there came up and complained that

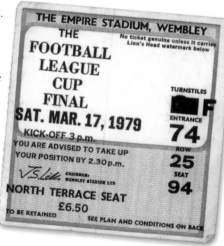

Above: Garry Birtles pushes the ball past Southampton 'keeper Terry Gennoe for his second goal to give Forest a 2-1 lead in the 1979 League Cup Final against the Saints at Wembley.

they had lost a fortune betting on the semi-final. We'd arrived on the Monday, and all we had done was played cards, had a few drinks in the bar, and even on the Tuesday night, the lads had a few beers. The staff had seen all this and were convinced we didn't stand a chance. 'What kind of football team is this?' they kept asking themselves. So they all bet a fortune against us. Lost the lot.

"What was interesting was that it never crossed our minds that we were a very good side. We were probably the best team in the world for a time but no-one ever thought it for a second and certainly no one ever said it. It never crossed anyone's mind that John Robertson might well be the most effective player in the world during our great period either. We were just a group of friends, enjoying life.

"Of course, Clough was a great manager, but you still can't do it without the players. He was particularly good on making the game simple and straightforward. He would always tell us at team talks: 'Look, Larry's there to head the ball out. Tony's there to run at defenders …'

"Clough and Taylor seemed to have a sixth sense on how to gee players up. Martin was the one they always used to drive mad. I remember before one game, Peter complaining that Martin just wasn't up to it. That he'd rather play the groundsman than Martin, he kept saying. Then Cloughie would chip in and say: 'Come on Pete, he's not that bad…'

"Cologne was very typical for us. We were effectively 1-0 down of course – but we never used to worry about being 1-0 down or even 2-0 down. Even if there were just three minutes to go and we were a goal behind, we never used to panic. We always used to feel that we could get a goal from somewhere. Cologne were convinced they were through but we really didn't worry about it. We always felt we could fashion a goal from somewhere. When I joined them later in 1979, they told me that they'd actually printed all the tickets for the final and they were going to put them on sale immediately after the match. They were all going to Munich. They were that confident. They didn't understand just what they were up against.

"The Malmo game was a terrible anticlimax," continues Woodcock. "The dressing room was really down afterwards – though that can happen after any big success. It had not been a great game, but Brian worked hard to lift us. He kept telling us we had to judge ourselves on the whole competition and what we had done since the very first round against Liverpool. The final was only one game out of many and we'd completely dominated it anyway. It cheered everyone up, but it was still an odd feeling because the team was so down. I didn't play against Hamburg but I imagine the feeling

was the exact opposite because no-one had expected us to win."

So Forest, for the second season running, won two of the major competitions. Nor did they do badly in the League. In the end they finished second. In fact they achieved exactly the 60 points they'd decided at the start of the season were necessary to win. Unfortunately Liverpool achieved 68. Clough's bonuses were worth £7,000 to each player involved. It cost the club around £100,000 for being second, and Brian Clough was not entirely overjoyed about it. And although being second was, in some ways, regarded as a disappointment, it should not be forgotten that this was the second best League performance in the club's history, then encompassing 86 years of League football.

The new status of Forest was reflected in the number of internationals on the books. Until well after the Second World War, any internationals at The City Ground were worthy of note, as the side rarely had more than one or two at a time. At the end of the 1978-79 season, with Viv Anderson having made his pioneering debut for England, Forest had eight current internationals on their books, plus two former internationals. Anderson, Woodcock and Shilton had all played in the same match for England against Czechoslovakia, and Trevor Francis was a fourth England player. Burns, Gemmill and Robertson were all Scottish internationals and Martin O'Neill a regular Northern Ireland international. The former caps were Larry Lloyd of England, who was later recalled for another game against Wales, and John O'Hare of Scotland.

The men who had brought about the transformation from mid-Second Division side to European Champions in three seasons, Messrs Clough and Taylor, had thoroughly differing personalities. It would not be true to say that they were like the classic police-state interrogation pair: one a sadistic bully and the other an apparently sympathetic softer type who gets the results on the rebound. This is because Clough combined these elements in himself. He could be incredibly cruel in a gratuitous manner to all his staff and at other times kind, always when least expected. The result was that nobody could feel entirely comfortable with him. He reckoned to get the best from people by keeping them guessing. He accepted the greatest performances by his team in a down-beat manner, making much more fuss about routine matches. Taylor was the friendlier, much-more-liked partner. Taylor was much the better at spotting players who had the talent to succeed, and had been since his first championing of Clough himself. He was the man who chose Burns and Shilton for the club, and supported Robertson when Clough argued that he was a waste of time.

Clough brought men who had performed for him before, such as McGovern, Gemmill and O'Hare. One of his longest associations was with Jimmy Gordon, who was training the Middlesbrough juniors when Clough arrived as a 16-year-old amateur. Even in those days Gordon warned his superior, Harold Shepherdson, the England coach, about the overbearing arrogance of the youngster, but nobody could do anything about it. Nevertheless Clough forged such a bond with Gordon that he employed him as a trainer at both Derby and Forest. But even Gordon was not immune from Clough's autocracy. Arranging a benefit match for him against Derby County, Clough stunned Gordon by telling him half the money would go to Forest. In fact concern about money was a factor which many resented about Clough. Players wondered sometimes if they got all they might have done from Clough's managership and even Taylor was kept in the dark about salary affairs if it suited Clough. As Garry Birtles said: "We were always on tour. Just look at the records – was it six overseas trips in 1981? Something amazing. Anyway, we just did as we were told. We got on the planes, got a daily expense allowance, came back jet lagged and exhausted and didn't complain. I don't think it would happen today."

There were changes in the summer of 1979 as Forest prepared to mount another Championship challenge and defend their two Cups. Chris Woods, not content to be in Shilton's shadow, went to Queen's Park Rangers for £250,000. Sunderland's veteran Cup final hero of 1973, Jim Montgomery, joined Forest as goalkeeping cover and is the trick answer when Forest fans are asked to name every player who won a European Cup winners' medal with the club. Frank Clark retired with his European Cup medal and took an assistant manager's job at Sunderland. Taylor signed Frank Gray from Leeds for £500,000 as replacement left-back. Gray already had seven Scottish caps. In an effort to get the average age of the Forest side down, Clough transferred Archie Gemmill, who had been disappointed not to be selected for the Munich European Cup final (he had lost his place to Bowyer) to Birmingham City for £150,000. Gemmill was the only key member of the great sides not to get a European Cup winners' medal on the field (he got one as a substitute) and Peter Withe got his with Villa. Asa Hartford was bought from Manchester City for £500,000 as replacement but, after the first three League games of the season, was promptly sold to Everton for £400,000. Although Forest had won all three games, scoring six goals against one, Clough decided that he didn't fit into Forest's style of play, and he couldn't alter the team's style to suit one man. Taylor said that they made a mistake and corrected it. It was either bad

management or good, and he saw it as good.

So the usual side for the early matches was: Shilton, Anderson, Gray, McGovern, Lloyd, Burns, O'Neill, Bowyer, Birtles, Woodcock, Robertson. A new £2 million stand was being built at The City Ground (at Clough's insistence), so for the first half of the season capacity was limited to about 30,000. The new stand, peculiarly and unimaginatively to be named the Executive Stand was only the fourth major new cantilever stand in the country – after those at Hillsborough, Chelsea and Wolves – and it seated 10,000. It was also notable for being the first ever to have a club's name picked out by different coloured seats.

Blackburn were beaten over two legs in the League Cup, 1-1 away and 6-1 at home, and Middlesbrough followed 3-1 in the next round, and when Forest beat Bolton Wanderers 5-2 on 20 October in their 12th League match, they moved to the top of the League table. It was an impressive start and achieved without Trevor Francis until 6 October. Francis had signed on the understanding that he could continue playing for Detroit Express in the American season, which overlapped the English. On his return he displaced Martin O'Neill, much to the fraying of the Irishman's nerves, but there were to be many midfield and attacking changes before the end of the season.

The 1979-80 season marked the Silver Jubilee of the European Cup, and two English clubs were eligible: Forest, as holders, and Liverpool, as Champions. These two had won the Cup for the previous three years, and a period of English ascendancy was in progress. Despite Forest's outstanding two seasons, Liverpool were still regarded as the English giants and it was a great surprise when they went out in the first round to Dynamo Tblisi. Forest adequately negotiated their first hurdle, beating the Swedish champions Oesters Vaxjo 2-0 at home, with goals in the last half-hour by Ian Bowyer, but for a time being in danger in the return leg until Tony Woodcock's equaliser to make it 1-1 more or less settled it. The cross for Woodcock to head in to an empty net was made by 17-year-old Gary Mills, who played as well as anybody on the day. There were no more goals.

The concern of the Forest committee about the amount of money Clough and Taylor were spending on players and ground improvement became banner headlines after a Clough outburst when the team arrived in Sweden. He was quoted as saying of the committee: "If they have the slightest doubt that Peter Taylor and I are handling their affairs to the best of our ability, I suggest they get someone else. Some football directors are a bunch of nobodies trying to be somebody through football. They are welcome to do so, but not off my back. Let them earn their

The astonishing new Executive Stand rises over the humble Trent End in 1980. It was to hold almost exactly 10,000 with 36 boxes and was only the fourth new cantilever stand to be built in the country. Because of its sheer size and its visibility from Trent Bridge, it was the first stand in the country ever to have the name of the club picked out in different coloured seats. The idea caught on elsewhere rather quickly. It was also the reason that Forest ceased to be a simple club with around 200 members and turned itself into a limited company. The stand required the club to fund a seven-figure overdraft and it occurred to one or two members that, should anything go wrong, bankruptcy was not an option. The members were literally responsible for the club's debts but it still took until 1982 for the articles of a new company to be accepted.

own corn." The committee were naturally incensed and Clough later apologised, but it was a kind of blackmail he was practising, virtually saying the club must do what he wanted or he would depart and it would sink. Just like Derby before, he might have added.

Four days after going to the top of the First Division, Forest played the first leg of the second round European Cup tie with the Romanian side Arges Pitesti, a side with a reputation for robust play. Forest were two up at The City Ground in 15 minutes through Woodcock and Birtles, but couldn't score again despite the Romanians losing defender Mihar Zamfir for persistent fouling. Three days after this match, however, Forest lost the First Division leadership after losing 1-0 at Tottenham to a well-remembered and still often replayed Glenn Hoddle volley, and could never recover it.

However, things progressed well enough in the Cups. A 1-1 draw at Bristol City in the League Cup fourth round was followed by a comfortable 3-0 win in the replay at The City Ground and between times two more early goals from Bowyer and Birtles ensured European Cup progress at Arges Pitesti, who could manage only one in reply and so lost 4-1 on aggregate.

Forest's League form and famed consistency dipped badly in November and December. Between two 4-1 away defeats at Southampton and Derby, Forest lost 1-0 at home to the League's bottom club, Brighton. Thus ended a

run of 51 home League games without defeat. Brighton's season was turned round and they finished 16th. Forest, meanwhile dropped to eighth by the end of the year, and never got higher than their finishing position of fifth.

In November, Forest lost Tony Woodcock, against their will. Woodcock wanted to play on the continent and, after seeking advice from England colleague Kevin Keegan, who had joined Hamburg, and England manager Ron Greenwood, who assured him his England place would not be threatened, held out for a move. On the day of the defeat by Brighton, Woodcock told Clough that, despite a good offer from Forest, he was determined to leave. That proved to be his last match. Bowyer was substituted for him during the game. The German club Cologne paid £650,000 for him, a bargain price, and entertained Forest to a friendly as part of the fee. The £650,000 was the maximum that a player could be transferred to Europe for at the time. Such moves were still very rare – how times change.

Forest fielded a surprise new signing in that friendly in Cologne. To try to fill a gap caused by Woodcock's departure and the difficulty encountered by Bowyer, Mills and O'Hare in attempts to fill the role vacated by Gemmill, Clough and Taylor turned to the mercurial but suspect temperament of Stan Bowles, who had been on the transfer list at Queen's Park Rangers without takers. Bowles had five England caps but was a self-confessed gambling addict with a reputation of not always being fully fit for games. Clough said he was ignoring warnings that he was signing a problem player: "We've had so-called bad boys in the past but haven't had any trouble with them." Bowles was not an inspired buy at £250,000 and, after 19 League appearances, he departed for Orient the following summer. Bowyer, however, remained a Clough favourite. On one memorable occasion, when Bowyer was a substitute, he was still picked as captain. So he went out to the middle, tossed the coin and retreated to the bench. This is not thought to have happened at any other League match, ever!

Bowles was the only signing during the season but Clough and Taylor almost signed three others. Peter Ward, who had played under Taylor at Brighton, was set to move for £500,000 but at the last minute Clough changed his mind, believing he could have been bought for less than the fee Taylor had agreed. It was an early sign of disagreement between Clough and Taylor (who had usually been responsible for finding the players) that was to widen to a rift later. Then Mick Ferguson of Coventry was set to move to Forest with Martin O'Neill in part exchange (Clough consistently undervalued O'Neill), but Ferguson dithered and Clough and Taylor pulled out, affronted. But in a First Division match with Leeds in January another strange face appeared above a Forest shirt: Charlie George. Clough and

Taylor had admired George for years and had tried to obtain him from Derby a year earlier, but the Derby board vetoed the move. George, another of the game's inspirational but unpredictable players, had won honours with Arsenal and a single cap for England in 1976, but injuries had hindered his career and he was now with Southampton. He came to Forest on a month's loan but played only four matches, two in the League. Forest would not commit themselves to a £500,000 fee without seeing more of him. George at first disagreed to extend the loan period, which was enough for Clough and Taylor to lose interest. George and Bowles did, however, both win a European Super Cup medal in the victory over Barcelona.

Meanwhile, West Ham had been removed from the League Cup, again after a replay, a 0-0 draw at Upton Park being followed by a 3-0 win at The City Ground, after extra time. Leeds were beaten in the FA Cup third round and then, in the space of four weeks, came four games with Liverpool, three of them Cup games. Forest's only victory was in the first, the League Cup semi-final first leg. Shilton played a blinder at The City Ground and a last-minute penalty, yet again converted by the ice-cool John Robertson ("I never remember worrying too much about them") after Garry Birtles had been brought down, gave Forest a vital lead. Four days later the teams met again at The City Ground in the

Below: The incomparable John Robertson slots away another penalty, this time against Southampton on 22 March 1980. Forest won 2-0. Charlie George and Dave Watson look on, George presumably thinking about what might have been. He had played four games for Forest on loan earlier in 1980 and had even managed to pick up a major medal by playing in the European Super Cup games against Barcelona. George scored the goal in Nottingham that gave Forest a lead to take to Barcelona and hence allowed Forest a 2-1 aggregate victory. After the four games Clough decided that George was not for him and an interesting chapter was to remain unwritten (*Nottingham Evening Post*).

Below: On 15 March 1980 Forest became the first team ever to appear in three consecutive Wembley finals in the same competition when they played Wolves in the League Cup final (Arsenal were to match this feat with three consecutive FA Cup finals just two months later). Forest were clear favourites but were out of sorts up front. Larry Lloyd was suspended so David Needham played instead. In the 67th minute a simple long ball out of the Wolves defence led to a misunderstanding between Needham and Shilton. The two collided and saw the loose ball run to a grateful Andy Gray, who put it away to give the game to Wolves, 1-0. It was the first time Forest had ever lost a major Cup final - at the sixth time of asking (Author's Collection).

THE EMPIRE STADIUM, WEMBLEY
THE
FOOTBALL
LEAGUE
CUP
FINAL
No ticket genuine unless it carries a Lion's Head watermark below
SAT., MAR 15, 1980
KICK-OFF 3.00 p.m.
YOU ARE ADVISED TO TAKE UP YOUR POSITION BY 2.30p.m.
TURNSTILES
H
ENTRANCE
43
ROW
5
SEAT
46
J.S. Lill CHAIRMAN WEMBLEY STADIUM LTD
SOUTH STAND SEAT
£11.00
TO BE RETAINED
SEE PLAN AND CONDITIONS ON BACK

fourth round of the FA Cup, before Forest's biggest crowd of the season, 33,277. This time Liverpool at last loosened Forest's stranglehold on them by winning 2-0, goals coming from a Shilton error and a penalty. But in the League Cup semi-final second leg, Forest again went ahead with yet another Robertson penalty after O'Neill was brought down. Shilton again played well, but Forest were denied a rare outright win at Anfield when supersub David Fairclough equalised in the last minute. Forest have still not won there since, but Forest were through to their third successive League Cup final.

Meanwhile they beat Barcelona, the holders of the European Cup Winners Cup, over two legs in the European Super Cup. Charlie George played in these games, and scored the only goal in the home leg. Before 90,000 fans in the Nou Camp a week later, Forest went behind to a penalty but equalised before half-time when Kenny Burns headed home after a corner. Robertson missed a penalty (a memorable moment!) but there were no further goals so Forest won on a 2-1 aggregate. The 90,000 crowd is the largest Forest have ever played before in any normal club game – the only larger crowds being at Wembley Cup finals.

The next continental club to play Forest were Dynamo Berlin, an East German side, their next European Cup opponents. Forest's plan was to rely on the midfield flair of Stan Bowles in the home leg and the more dogged qualities of Ian Bowyer in the away leg. In the event Forest's attack was weak at The City Ground and, in the 73rd minute, the Germans broke away and Hans-Jurgen Riediger scored the only goal. With Burns collecting his second yellow card and therefore unavailable for the return, Forest faced a situation far worse than that they'd faced against Cologne in the previous year's semi-final.

David Needham took Burns' place for the second leg. Before a 27,000 crowd, Dynamo, in the competition for the first time, were clearly uncertain how to approach the match with their lead and their away goal. They didn't know whether to act as the usual home team, or try to sit back and defend the lead. They had a clearer picture after a quarter of an hour when Trevor Francis levelled the tie, but were unable to prevent Forest getting a grip before half-time. In the 35th minute Francis turned quickly to ram home a right-foot shot, and three minutes later Robertson was brought down in the box and scored from the penalty. A second-half penalty by Dynamo spurred them to go for an aggregate equaliser, but Forest's defence held out and they were through to the next round. It was probably Trevor Francis's best performance for Forest and certainly the most crucial. It was also the first time a club had ever lost the home leg of a European Cup tie and then won away to win on aggregate.

Between these two legs, however, Forest had been to Wembley to face Wolves in the Football League Cup final. It was the first time any club had ever appeared in three successive Wembley finals of a major competition. David Needham played in place of Larry Lloyd who picked up a suspension of one match on the principle of accumulating yellow cards. Unfortunately for him he had no opportunity to serve the

suspension before the final, unlike the man he would have marked, Andy Gray, who had a similar suspension but was able to miss a match five days beforehand and turn out at Wembley. Lloyd says of the suspension and his replacement by David Needham that Clough always knew his best side: "He told David he would play, but that, whatever happened, I'd be back as soon as I was available. We always knew the best side, though "Bomber" (Ian Bowyer) was in and out a lot and Martin was always expecting the worst – Cloughie never let him think the right side midfield slot was secure. Talk about paranoia!"

After Clough and then Taylor had led out Forest in the previous two years, the honour this time was given to coach Jimmy Gordon, who was told 20 minutes before kick-off, when dressed in his tracksuit. It was typical of Clough to grant this honour in such an off-hand way.

Forest went into the game unbeaten in 25 League Cup games over three seasons (still a record for consecutive games in any English Cup competition) but, on this occasion, despite having much the better of the game, their forwards couldn't beat Paul Bradshaw, and in the 67th minute Shilton and Needham collided when going for an innocuous cross and the ball dropped to Andy Gray to tap into an empty net. Forest had become the first club even to appear in three successive Wembley finals of the same tournament (Arsenal were to match the feat in the FA Cup the following May) but, sadly, failed to become the first club to win all three.

Ajax Amsterdam were the semi-final opponents in the European Cup, with the home leg first. After 33 minutes of Forest pressure, Francis drove in a Robertson corner, and in the 61st minute Francis hooked the ball over the keeper and defender Cees Zwamborn handled. Robertson slotted home the penalty and Forest had a two-goal lead to take to Amsterdam. Forest went on a three-match tour of the Middle East before the second leg, an arguably extremely odd decision by the management. Ajax had only one defeat in 46 European games at home, so the task was hardly over yet. Bowyer, as before, replaced Bowles. After an early effort by Francis, Ajax pressed constantly, but Shilton, Lloyd and Burns stood firm until the 63rd minute when Soren Lerby headed in a corner. A good chance for the aggregate equaliser was missed in the last minutes and Forest were in the final. A measure of Forest's away-leg organisation was that this was the first away leg they'd lost in the European Cup. Forest's 1979 European Cup success had been notable for the fact that they weren't defeated – a record shared by Celtic and Inter-Milan.

Five weeks later Forest played SV Hamburg in the final. But meantime misfortune struck Forest in a home match with Crystal Palace. Trevor Francis scored twice in a 4-0 win, but a ruptured Achilles tendon put him out of the game for months. Then Stan Bowles, annoyed at not getting a regular place in the side, told Clough he was dissatisfied, and when Forest flew to Majorca

Above: Trevor Francis scores his and Forest's second goal in the 35th minute of the away leg of the European Cup third round tie at Dynamo Berlin on 19 March 1980. Dynamo had stunned the European Cup holders by winning 1-0 at Forest with a goal from Hans-Jurgen Riediger. But Francis was to score twice in the first half of the return and then John Robertson scored from a penalty. Forest ran out 3-1 winners and 3-2 on aggregate. It was the first time in the history of the European Cup that a team had lost the first leg at home but won away to go through to the next round *(Author's Collection).*

for a holiday before the final, he didn't turn up. He wasn't to play for Forest again and in the summer went to Orient. Gary Mills came in to replace Francis and, with Bowles having walked out, Bowyer was in the side, too. Kevin Keegan was playing for Hamburg. Forest were allowed five substitutes, but Clough picked only four – uniquely for a club in any major final. There were no remaining players in the first team squad and Clough took his chances. It was tight – he needed all his outfield players.

Hamburg attacked from the start, with Forest soaking up pressure with only Birtles up and Clough playing a makeshift, worried 4-5-1. Shilton had to make a number of good saves, but in the 21st minute Robertson picked up a loose ball just outside the area and put a right-foot shot across goalkeeper Rudi Kargus and in off the far post. This was the moment of Robertson's immortal: "Of course, I was very tired as well. It had been a long run by my standards." Hamburg attacked with renewed vigour. Shilton pushed out a shot diverted by Keegan, and Willie Reimann shot the loose ball home only for the effort to be disallowed because Keegan was offside. Thereafter Burns and Shilton in particular played magnificently as Hamburg attacked. In the second half a tired Mills was replaced by John O'Hare and seven minutes from time Frank Gray had to go off injured, Bryn Gunn replacing him, in only his fifth senior appearance outside friendlies in three seasons. As Gunn stood up to get changed, Peter Taylor greeted him with what will surely remain the most remarkable words of encouragement ever given to a player in a European Cup final: "Oh Christ, we are in the shit now." Forest held on to the end, and the European Cup was retained. Forest's fortunes had reached their peak. This was also the zenith of Brian Clough's career. This small, undistinguished club had come from literally nothing to the humbling of Europe's giants and to two European Cups. And it was not as if Forest had been so successful in a period of weak competition. It was the period when English clubs dominated Europe – Liverpool winning the European Cup in 1977, 1978, 1981 and 1984; Aston Villa doing so in 1982. And teams such as Arsenal, Manchester United, Everton and Spurs were all contenders and yet Forest were to play 184 competitive games in six major competitions in the period 1977-1980 and lost only 26.

"It all happened too quickly," says John Robertson today. "No one had the time to savour it. Unlike Manchester United or Liverpool, there was not that long, slow build up to the ultimate success that gradually heated up the temperature of their fans or of their club. We were totally different – one minute we were playing Luton, Orient and Hull, the next we were in the Olympic Stadium in Munich winning the European Cup or at the Nou Camp in front of 90,000 winning the Super Cup. It was wonderful, but it was unreal. I've heard it said, and I think it's probably true, that Nottingham Forest has the only group of supporters for whom all their dreams have come true. And, in some ways, that may be a little sad. There have to be dreams in football – and perhaps it did have some of the elements of a dream. How did we go from the middle of the Second Division to the European Cup in just over two years? How could such a thing ever happen? One very good consequence I can tell you – it gives everyone hope."

Forest began the 1980s as European Champions, a status which would see them challenge for the European Cup again, the European Super Cup and the World Club Championship, as well as the two main domestic cups and the League Championship. They say

Right: Kevin Keegan struggles to keep his balance when tackled by Ian Bowyer during the 1980 European Cup final in Madrid on 28 May. Bowyer went into the history books after Brian Clough named him as captain for a game in which he was selected only as a sub. Bowyer went out to the centre circle, chose which way to kick and headed back to the bench.

that great sides last for just three seasons, and so it was to be for Forest.

It could be a busy season, and Forest improved their squad with two big close-season signings, the first being Scottish international centre-forward Ian Wallace who had been scoring well for Coventry, to whom Forest paid £1,250,000. Trevor Francis's injury would keep him out until December and Clough next signed Swiss international Raimondo Ponte, who had played against Forest for Grasshoppers Zurich in the European Cup quarter-final two seasons previously. Forest paid £230,000 for him, but he was not to be a great success, making 17 League appearances during the season and then departing for Bastia in the French League. Ponte was to return in 1996 as the front man for one of the bidders for the club.

The first match of the season was at White Hart Lane, where 43,398 spectators, which would prove to be the biggest crowd of the season to watch Forest outside the World Club Championship and one European Cup match, saw the Reds get off to a bad start with a 2-0 defeat. It was to be a portent of the season, at the end of which Forest finished seventh in the League and, for the first time since 1977, had no silverware to add to the trophy cabinet.

The season was to be summed up in just two matches – home and away against CSKA Sofia. Yonchev scored the only goal in Sofia on 17 September, and this was rightly regarded as a good result for Forest. But, two weeks later, CSKA repeated the scoreline and Forest were out of the European Cup in the dullest, most down

beat manner possible. Their hopes of a European Cup treble had disappeared on an autumn night in Nottingham, just as had Liverpool's exactly two years earlier. Amazingly, despite twice winning the European Cup, the crowd was only 25,813. It was a sign of what we were to hear so often in the next two decades – that the Nottingham public were fickle, that Nottingham was not a football town. Certainly there were not the Baker and the Storey-Moore followers of 1967 and on that night, 1 October 1980, the glory, glory years were laid to rest.

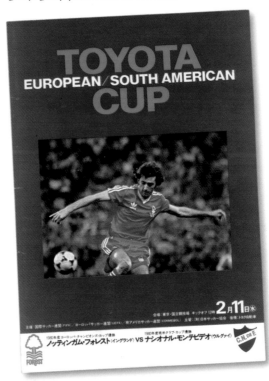

On 11 February 1981 Forest travelled to Tokyo to play Nacional of Montevideo in the World Club Championship (handily renamed The Toyota European South American Cup for Japanese audiences). The FA and UEFA were keen to revive a trophy which had fallen into disrepute and which had not been contested by the winning clubs since 1976. Forest had to play Manchester City on the Saturday (they would not rearrange the date), Nacional in Tokyo on the Wednesday, and then Bristol City in the FA Cup three days later. Forest tried to stay on English time, despite the eight-hour difference, and lost 1-0 to Nacional via a Victorino goal. Martin O'Neill **(below)** had one of Forest's few good chances in the game. By 1998, no British club had ever won this trophy *(Author's Collection)*.

Viv Anderson gets the better of a
tussle against Notts County on
12 April 1982. Forest won 2-1
with goals from Ian Bowyer and
Calvin Plummer. Anderson was
the first coloured player to be
chosen for the full England
international team.

Garry Birtles, a player described by Viv
Anderson as: "The best centre-forward I have
ever seen," played only one more game for Forest
that season, the next home match with
Manchester United. Manager Dave Sexton then
broke the United transfer record to take Birtles to
Old Trafford for £1,250,000. "He was then the
best centre-forward in the country by far," said
Anderson. Birtles had cost Forest £2,000 when
signed from Long Eaton in March 1977. Always,
and rightly, one of the club's most popular
players, he was to return to Forest soon enough –
but not after filling many magazine pages with his
'unusual' sartorial preferences. Clough had
thought he was over-priced at £2,000. A week or
so later Peter Ward made his debut in Birtles'
number 9 shirt. Ward, signed for £400,000, failed
to command a regular place in the side, and in
March 1982 he returned to Brighton.

Before Trevor Francis had recovered from
injury, Forest had also lost interest in the League
Cup, losing 4-1 at Watford in the fourth round.
A slump in League form followed, with successive
defeats by Birmingham, Spurs and Ipswich, the
last two at home, but the home leg in the
European Super Cup was won 2-1 when
Valencia, who had won the European Cup
Winners Cup on penalties from Arsenal, were
beaten by two goals from Ian Bowyer. Francis
was back for his first competitive game since
injury for the second leg in Valencia, but Forest
lost 1-0, and so lost the tie on the away goals rule.

During a promising FA Cup run which ended
disappointingly in a 1-0 sixth-round replay defeat
at Ipswich, Forest snatched time for an excursion
to Tokyo for a revived World Club
Championship but lost 1-0 to the Uruguayan
club Nacional.

There now began a change of personnel
among the playing staff that echoed to some
extent the rapid changes which followed the great
1966-67 season. And most of the buying and
selling that took place seemed in retrospect to be
equally ill-judged. Just as in 1967, a great team
(this time a European Cup winning team) was
broken up with indecent haste. To a man, the
great team will say now that the squad was broken
up far too quickly. Many say the purchase of
Francis did not ultimately add to the whole jigsaw
puzzle, but, to be fair to Clough, he knew that he
was likely to lose Woodcock and needed a
replacement of pace and scoring power up front.
Nonetheless, he had been prepared to let Withe
go and now Birtles, Withe's replacement, was also
gone. There was a sense that Clough felt he
could conjure up the magic whatever happened,
but he was caught now in a downward spiral
which was not really to be reversed until the end
of the decade.

The departure of Birtles has already been
mentioned. In January 1981, old faithful Ian
Bowyer was transferred to Sunderland for
£250,000 (although, like Birtles, he would one
day be back). In the following month Martin
O'Neill went to Norwich for another £250,000
(and he almost returned as well, though as
manager). O'Neill was later to move to Notts
County and, at one point, was the most capped
player at all three clubs – far more remarkably
because they are alphabetically in sequence. In
March, Larry Lloyd was allowed to move on a free
transfer to Wigan Athletic. In June Frank Gray
returned to Leeds United for £300,000. Trevor
Francis was transferred (controversially, it has to
be said), to Manchester City for £1,200,000 in
September 1981 and, the following month,
Kenny Burns went to Leeds United for £400,000.
In the summer of 1982, John McGovern was
transferred to Bolton on a free transfer and in
August Peter Shilton went to Southampton for
£325,000. In October 1982 even Gary Mills, the
replacement for Woodcock in the European Cup
final, was transferred to Derby County, although
he was yet another who would return.

So, two years after their second European
Cup win, the only two players left at Forest of the
fourteen who had started in one or other of the
European Cup finals were Viv Anderson and
John Robertson, and both of those had gone by
1984. It was an astonishingly rapid disposal of a
glorious history.

Some of the players themselves expressed
surprise at the break-up. Martin O'Neill said:

"I think we could have gone on and won a few more things with the basis of that side." Ian Bowyer thought that the team could have been changed more gradually, in the manner that Liverpool managed for so many years. Liverpool, incidentally, after Forest's brief challenge to their supremacy, won the League Cup four years in succession from 1981, the Championship three years in succession from 1982, and the European Cup in 1981 and 1984. Bowyer said: "A lot of people get disillusioned very quickly when you start letting players of the calibre of Withe, Woodcock, Francis and Birtles go." Bowyer argued that expensive signings like Wallace, Ward and Fashanu were nowhere near the class of those that went.

Wallace and Ward have already been mentioned. Justin Fashanu, a centre-forward, was bought from Norwich City in October 1981 for £1 million but failed completely to fit into the side. "It was bad judgement on my part," said Peter Taylor, "I thought he could improve with age but I'd read him wrong. Justin didn't want to play football." Clough wasn't keen on Fashanu, whom he perceived as a barrack-room lawyer.

After one year, 31 League matches in the number 9 shirt and three League goals, he was transferred to Notts County, via a loan period at Southampton, for £150,000. One could say each League goal cost Forest nearly £280,000 and Fashanu's purchase was almost on a par with Baxter's and later, Silenzi's as an error. Rightly or wrongly, the world believed Taylor had bought him on the strength of that one famous, televised goal for Norwich against Liverpool, which won the Goal of the Season Award. Fashanu was to die in sad circumstances in 1998.

Other purchases around this time turned out to be well short of inspirational. The touch that had brought the likes of Lloyd and Burns to The City Ground seemed to have deserted Taylor and Clough. Mark Proctor, an England Under-21 midfielder from Middlesbrough, cost £425,000 in August 1981, but stayed less than two years before moving to Sunderland, and Norwegian international defender Einar Aas was purchased from Bayern Munich for £250,000 in March 1981 and made the last of his 20 League appearances eight months later. Jurgen Rober, a West German midfielder, was bought from Chicago

Below: Peter Taylor and Brian Clough celebrate European success in Munich. Martin O'Neill says of Peter Taylor: "He was the one who spotted the players. But his greatest spot was Brian Clough. He saw what Brian could become, he encouraged him and he nurtured him. And he lived the whirlwind."

Kenny Burns in full flight against West Brom with John Wile, Cyrille Regis and Bryan Robson in attendance. Burns was regarded as a risky buy when purchased from Birmingham City because of his fiery and combative temperament but he settled down to become, with Lloyd and Shilton, part of the best central defence in the country.

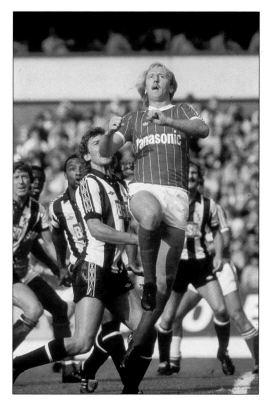

Sting in December 1981, but at the season's end moved on to Bayer Leverkusen. The same month that Rober arrived, Willie Young, an abrasive centre-half, was bought from Arsenal for £150,000 to fill some of the gaps left by the departure of Lloyd and Burns. Young, too, was to be a Forest player for less than two years, but before he went the biggest departure of all took place when, towards the end of the 1982 season, Peter Taylor announced to Clough his intention to resign.

The relationship between the two men had for some time been almost entirely a professional one. There was little socialising any more and on Taylor's part much mistrust. The occasion when Clough declined an offer to return with Taylor to Derby without mentioning it to Taylor has been mentioned already. Taylor later discovered what had happened and was furious.

Even back in their Derby days, after Taylor had suffered a heart murmur which kept him out of action for six weeks (one visit from Clough), Taylor seriously considered his position when Clough accepted a large pay increase which was apparently kept secret from Taylor, who was not given a rise and who apparently discovered the details accidentally.

In 1980 Forest had played in Dublin to help a testimonial for Paddy Mulligan, an international full-back, and *The Sunday Times* had alleged that Clough and Taylor had accepted what later came to be called in football "a bung". The two discussed what action they should take, and a threat to sue by Clough elicited a correction and an apology from the newspaper, clearing Clough but making no separate mention of Taylor, who was understandably appalled at any inference that

Clough had seemingly demanded the apology for himself alone.

Taylor seemed to feel that Clough, despite his passionate admissions at times that he needed Taylor, was apparently rather more concerned with his own ambitions and financial rewards. In 1980 Taylor published a book, "With Clough by Taylor" (Sidgwick and Jackson), which was not cleared with Clough, who boycotted the launch and made public his dissatisfaction with Taylor.

It all came to a head after a home defeat by Manchester United. Taylor told Clough he couldn't carry on any more. Although he didn't say so, Taylor had come to feel that he actively disliked Clough, and his partner's apparent need to be the centre of attention. When Taylor was not to be persuaded to stay, Clough was forceful in his criticisms of him. Sadly, he was to say that because of Taylor's judgement Forest (and by inference Clough) had been landed with £3 million worth of bad players.

Relations deteriorated even further when in 1982 Derby County persuaded Taylor to return to manage the club, by then struggling in the Second Division. In January 1983, by extraordinary coincidence, Forest were drawn at Derby in the FA Cup third round. Clough was understandably desperate to win, but Derby took the game 2-0 and Clough was inclined to blame Willie Young, who till then had been playing well, even accusing him, in an over-the-top dressing-room outburst, of being in Taylor's camp and suggesting he push off to see his friend. It so happened that Young did talk to Taylor before Forest left the ground and shook his hand, an act that did not improve Clough's temper. Young was transferred to Norwich during the close season.

June 1983 marked the final depth of the Clough/Taylor relationship, and it involved the talismanic John Robertson. Robertson was out of contract with Forest, having been unable to negotiate an acceptable new one with Clough. Robbo had been injured at Old Trafford with a cartilage and Clough had been reluctant to support him. When Clough went off on a charity walk, Robertson accepted an offer from Taylor and signed for Derby, an act of discourtesy by Taylor and Robertson which Clough regarded as absolute treachery. His reaction was to produce at the transfer tribunal evidence of offers for Robertson from Luton and Southampton which persuaded the tribunal to set a transfer fee of £135,000, higher than Derby expected or could comfortably afford. Robertson's transfer was not a success (his subtle rather than energetic style not being suited to the Second Division) and Derby were relegated and Taylor sacked. Clough, having at one time banned Robertson from The City Ground, then bought him back in August 1985. He then let him go again to Corby Town after a mere ten League appearances, complaining of Robertson's apparent preference for beer to football. Robertson remained humorous and phlegmatic and, fifteen years later, is a regular and very welcome visitor to The City Ground.

Skipper John McGovern had been a victim of the Clough/Taylor split. Taylor thought he was finished and put him on the transfer list without the knowledge of Clough, who wanted McGovern to stay as a squad player, filling in gaps during the season. McGovern went after the 1981-82 season. This was a season which, among the expensive comings and goings, saw some important new young players make competitive debuts. Chris Fairclough, a Nottingham-born central defender who had signed as an apprentice, was well short of 18 years old when he appeared in a League Cup fourth round win over Tranmere Rovers. Peter Davenport, a centre-forward, came from Birkenhead and made his League debut at Anfield aged 21. And Steve Hodge, another Nottingham-born apprentice, made his debut in the last League match of the season, a 3-1 win at Ipswich Town, where Davenport scored his first hat-trick. Forest finished 12th in this traumatic season, but Davenport and Hodge both went on to win England caps.

In the summer of 1982 Colin Todd arrived at The City Ground from Birmingham. An England international, he had been one of Clough's big buys and main players in his success at Derby. Clough had also wanted him at Leeds. Todd was now a veteran with over 600 League games to his name. He cost £70,000 and was to play 36 more League games for Forest. Kenny Swain, full-back, was another established newcomer who had over 260 League appearances for Chelsea and Aston Villa to his name. He cost £25,000, and made 112 League appearances for Forest before moving on to Portsmouth. Ian Bowyer also returned to The City Ground from Sunderland for £50,000.

Forest had a strange season in the League in 1982-83. A superb run lifted them from 13th in mid-October to second after the Christmas holiday games. But after that defeat to Taylor's Derby in the FA Cup, as described, they plummeted, and a nine-match run of six defeats and three draws from 22 January to 26 March, dropped Forest to tenth. From then to the end of the season, another nine matches resulted in seven wins and two draws, and lifted Forest to fifth, and won a place in the following season's UEFA Cup. It was a heartening end to an odd campaign.

When the 1983-84 season began, Birtles and Davenport became the preferred strikers while Ian Wallace was the stand-in. In November Wallace rejected a £100,000 move to Glasgow Rangers, but in May he moved to Brest in the French League for £60,000. This was to cut Forest's wage bill, as he was being paid £1,000 per week.

In 1985, Brest wanted to sell him back but he went to Sunderland instead for £50,000. Forest began with Paul Hart, bought from Leeds United, at centre-back, and with Colin Walsh assuming the place of John Robertson, who'd gone to Derby. Around November Chris Fairclough took over Colin Todd's role on the right of midfield. Frans Thijssen, the cultured Dutch international midfielder who had been a big influence on Ipswich Town's FA and UEFA Cup successes of the previous seasons, was signed from Vancouver Whitecaps, but didn't see the season out before leaving for Fortuna Sittard. According to Viv Anderson's biography Thijssen read in a newspaper after his first training session that Clough had said he made a mistake buying Thijssen. Although starting not too well, and losing at the first time of asking in both domestic Cups, Forest improved steadily throughout the season and enjoyed a good run in the UEFA Cup. Moreover Forest assumed their old innovative ways on 2 October 1983 at White Hart Lane, when their match with Spurs was the first League match to be televised live.

Forest's first leg UEFA Cup tie was with the East German club Vorwaerts, and they won 2-0 away and 1-0 at home. In the second round PSV Eindhoven were the opponents and again Forest won the away leg first, 2-1, giving them a cushion for the home tie, which they won 1-0. Glasgow Celtic formed the next hurdle, and Forest were at home in the first leg, and could only draw 0-0. By far their biggest crowd of the season, 66,938 (the largest British crowd Forest have ever played before in their history – excluding Wembley), saw the return at Celtic Park, when second half goals by Hodge and Walsh earned Forest a 2-1 win and a quarter-final tie with Sturm Graz of Austria. Forest won that 1-0 at home with a rare goal from Paul Hart, and drew 1-1 in Austria in a match of two converted penalties, Forest's scored by Walsh with six minutes of extra time remaining. Belgium's Anderlecht were the semi-final opponents (Forest had lost 4-2 in Anderlecht on their pre-season tour), and Forest began convincingly with a 2-0 win at The City Ground, with Steve Hodge netting both.

The away leg was to be one of the most controversial games Forest have ever played. Anderlecht won 3-0 after the referee gave an absurd penalty against Kenny Swain, who was nowhere near the relevant forward, and then disallowed a last minute headed goal by Paul Hart for no reason that anyone, including the Anderlecht players, could determine. Ian Bowyer said years later: "The ref wouldn't even shake our hands. Cloughie came in and effectively told us

These pages: Perhaps the most controversial game ever played by Nottingham Forest was the away semi-final leg of the UEFA Cup against Anderlecht on 25 April 1984. Forest had won the first leg 2-0 with both goals coming from Steve Hodge and were favourites to reach the final, where they would have played Spurs. What happened in Brussels that night was that Anderlecht gave the Spanish referee Guruceta Muro £18,000 and Anderlecht won the game 3-0. The picture (right) shows Muro asking Ian Bowyer to call before the game begins and the pictures (centre and bottom) show Paul Hart's headed goal from a corner in the last minute. The goal would have taken Forest through on away goals but, to the mystification of both sides, the referee disallowed it without giving any reason. The referee had also given a comical penalty against Kenny Swain when the Forest defender was nowhere near a diving Belgian forward and, after the game, Clough made it clear to his players that he felt the game had not been

U.E.F.A CUP

RSC ANDERLECHT

WEDNESDAY
MERCREDI
WOENSDAG
25.4.1984

1/2

SEMI
FINAL
SECOND LEG
Retour · Terug

NOTTINGHAM FOREST

STADE · STADION
C. VANDEN STOCK

Programme(s) 30 F.

above board. Over the next ten years, several hundred thousand pounds were allegedly paid to individuals who threatened to reveal the story until, in 1997, the whole affair came to light when the alleged blackmailers were arrested. Anderlecht admitted the payment to the referee but argued that it was a "loan" which was never repaid and which was never recorded in writing. They were unable to explain why, therefore, they paid off the alleged blackmailers. UEFA were not fooled, but let Anderlecht off lightly with a year's ban for bribing officials. At the time of writing both Forest and the players that night are suing Anderlecht in the Belgian courts. The programme for the game (**below left**) makes amusing reading. On one page it congratulates the 'remarkable' Anderlecht President (Constant Vanden Stock) from the hearts of all Anderlecht supporters on his elevation to the post of first Vice-President of the Belgian FA (**top right**). On the centre page, between the team line-ups, the programme cynically declares "THAT THE BEST BE THE WINNER!" (**far right**). The same Constant Vanden Stock had renamed the Anderlecht stadium after himself. *(Nottingham Evening Post and Author's Collection)*

that the referee was bent and we should just get out of there. It was the only time I never knew Brian to believe that an official had been fixed." In 1997, Anderlecht confessed to having paid the referee £18,000 after the game, supposedly as a 'loan' which he never repaid. UEFA found Anderlecht guilty of bribing the referee and banned them from Europe for a year. The case had become public because it emerged that Anderlecht had allegedly paid two individuals a six-figure sum over a period of years to keep quiet about the matter.

At the time of writing, Forest and the players are suing Anderlecht in the Belgian courts. It left a sense of dullness around Forest. As Paul Hart says: "How can you put a price on a European medal? I never won a medal, ever. This was my opportunity. What's the point in bothering if clubs can pay referees and get away with it? We deserve justice, not for ourselves, but for the game. What Anderlecht allegedly did undermines the whole moral and competitive basis of football. It's that serious."

Forest spent the second half of the season in the top five in the Championship and finished third, so European football was guaranteed for another season. On 22 January Brian Clough signed a new contract with Forest which would keep him at the club till 1986. Forest's end of season tour was to Australia.

Season 1984-85 was a disappointing one for Forest, the first of three in which they finished either eighth or ninth in the First Division and failed to make any impression in the Cups. It began with a turn-round of personnel. Viv Anderson left when Arsenal, seeking a replacement for Pat Rice, enquired about him. Clough, needing to save money on salaries and thinking (wrongly) he'd seen the best of Anderson, promptly sold him for £200,000. Soon he had bought three new players for £400,000: Dutch-born Johnny Metgod, a central defender with a powerful free-kick, from Real Madrid, Gary Megson, from Sheffield Wednesday, and Franz Carr, a flying winger from Blackburn Rovers. Less than a month after these purchases Clough was publicly criticising Megson, and three months later Megson was transferred to Newcastle at a loss to Forest of £15,000 on the fee plus his wages. He did not make a League appearance for Forest.

After six League matches Forest led the Championship and entertained Brugge in the UEFA Cup at The City Ground, but neither side could score. In the second leg a fortnight later Brugge scored a last-minute goal, the only one of the match, and Forest's European adventures had ended for 11 years, though no-one in Nottingham could have believed that it would be that long. This was not their fault, of course, being largely due to the tragedy that season at the Heysel

Stadium in Brussels during the European Cup final, when the behaviour of the Liverpool fans led to British clubs rightly being banned from European competition for six seasons. Nonetheless, it condemned Forest to a dull fare of domestic competition and crowds which meandered unenthusiastically around the upper teens. These were dog days for English football.

Brian Clough himself found it impossible not to make news in the oddest ways. In January the Midland Sports Writers Association arranged a dinner at which to present him with £200 worth of crystal glass to mark his ten years as Forest manager in thanks for the years of reputation making copy he had provided for them. At the last minute Clough went to Tenerife instead and the dinner, with its proposed VIP guests, had to be cancelled. The following month Clough took Forest off to Iraq, to play two matches with an Iraq Select XI, ignoring the fact that Iraq was engaged in a war with Iran.

The first League match of the 1985-86 season saw notable Forest debutants. Stuart Pearce, a left-back, and defender Ian Butterworth were bought from Coventry City for £450,000. Butterworth was to play 27 League games for Forest before departing for Norwich less than two seasons later, but Pearce would become a long-serving player and for a short while manager of Forest, and he still holds the record for the number of international caps won by a Forest player, 76 for England in eleven seasons from 1986-87 to 1996-97.

Also making his debut was Neil Webb, a clever goal-scoring midfielder, who had built a reputation with Portsmouth and who, the previous season, had rejected a move to QPR and been in abortive talks with Aston Villa. Clough paid £250,000 for him. Webb was to win 19 England caps with Forest before moving to Manchester United in 1989. Another player who established himself in the first match this season was Des Walker, a fast centre-half who also made

Above: One of Forest's earliest imports was the superb Dutchman Johnny Metgod, seen here shooting from distance against Manchester City. Metgod is perhaps best remembered for his astonishing goal against West Ham on 2 April 1986. It was a free-kick taken from 30 yards out which was later judged to be the fastest moving free-kick ever analysed. The ball was hit directly above keeper Phil Parkes, who sensibly ducked rather than try to stop it. It is one of only two Forest goals ever judged to be "Goal of the Year" in the various competitions of that name - the other was Archie Gemmill's against Arsenal in the Championship season.

himself a regular with England, winning 36 of his England caps with Forest before in 1992 he went to play for Sampdoria in Italy. Walker, from Hackney, London, had made seven League appearances for Forest in the previous two seasons, having joined Forest as an apprentice in 1983. He displaced Chris Fairclough, for whom Clough declined an offer of £500,000 from Spurs in the summer of 1985, although he eventually went to Tottenham two years later at a price of £387,500, fixed by the transfer tribunal.

Brian Clough's relationship with his directors became more and more abrasive this season, with reported demands in March that seven of them should resign. He was instrumental in the resignation of director Frank Allcock in February, after Clough had heard about some betting on the result of a match with Manchester United, which took place on the directors' coach on the way to Old Trafford. It seems *The Sporting Life* had quoted odds of 7-1 against Forest winning and, with a passenger anxious to back Forest at this price, Allcock had accepted a £10 bet - in effect betting against Forest. Clough made much of this in his programme notes a fortnight later and Allcock, a director for four years and a Forest member for 30 years before that, resigned. As it happened, Nigel Clough scored a late goal for Forest to earn a 3-2 win, so Allcock lost £70 as well. Clough's relationship with the board at the time is well illustrated by a story told by Ian St John, who arrived at The City Ground to interview Clough for his programme "Saint and Greavsie": "Clough was late as usual," said St John, "but when he arrived he headed off towards the board room. 'We'll do it in here' he told me. We were just about to start when the Forest chairman came in. 'Hello, chairman,' yelled

Cloughie. 'Have a drink, sit down and keep quiet – we're talking football.' We did the interview, the chairman went out and Cloughie got up to go, giving me the keys and telling us to have a drink. With that he walked out, leaving me holding the keys to the Forest boardroom and carte blanche to help myself to the drinks cabinet."

Forest, who recovered to eighth in 1985-86, finished in the same position in 1986-87, but this time their descent was downwards, as they led the table to November, and as late as February were still in the top four. They had a run in the League Cup, getting to the fifth round before losing 2-0 at Highbury, although for the fifth time out of six they departed the FA Cup at the first hurdle, losing at Second Division Crystal Palace. In fact Forest had now won only one FA Cup tie in six seasons.

A highlight of the season was the goalscoring run of Neil Webb, who scored eight goals in four League matches in September. In fact Webb and Birtles scored five apiece in two matches, defeats of Aston Villa 6-0 and of Chelsea away 6-2, probably Forest's best performance of the whole decade. Birtles, in particular, was probably playing the best football of his career, subtlety as well as quality.

In 1988, Forest at last had a decent run in the FA Cup, despite not being drawn at home in any round. Halifax Town were beaten 4-0, Leyton Orient 2-1 and Birmingham City 1-0 before Forest registered an outstanding 2-1 win at Highbury in the quarter-final before over 50,000 fans, their best Cup performance for a decade. Paul Wilkinson, with a glorious 30-yard volley, and Brian Rice scored to set up a semi-final at Hillsborough with Liverpool. Forest put up an

Below: Nigel Clough attacks the Bristol City goal during Forest's League Cup semi-final at Ashton Gate on 26 February 1989. Forest won 1-0 after extra time via a Garry Parker goal. Up to 1998, Forest had contested six League Cup semi-finals and won them all - a remarkable record in total contrast to the dreadful FA Cup semi-final record *(Popperfoto)*.

excellent show but, despite a goal from Nigel Clough, they were beaten 2-1. Liverpool that season were a class above the rest and, four days later beat Forest 5-0 at Anfield in the League, which they went on to win by nine points, only to be deprived of a "certain" double by losing 1-0 to Wimbledon at Wembley. Dave Beasant, later a Forest star, became the first keeper ever to save a penalty in a Cup final when Liverpool's John Aldridge failed.

Forest's 1988-89 season, good as it was, could have been one of tremendous triumph. It is true that they maintained their top three League status, and won two Cups as well, their first major trophies for nine years, but the FA Cup dream ended in circumstances of real tragedy.

The side was strengthened for the big kick-off by the welcome return of Steve Hodge from Tottenham. Having won 15 England caps in his three seasons away, he was to win nine more in

his second spell with the Reds. The strike force was also strengthened with the signing for £378,000 from the French club Niort of Lee Chapman, the former Sheffield Wednesday striker who, at 29, immediately became the oldest member of the squad. The defence had a boost, too, when full-back Brian Laws, who had helped Middlesbrough in their advance from Third Division to First in three seasons, was signed for £120,000. He proved particularly useful from December, taking over at right back, when injury kept Steve Chettle out for a while.

The side began pretty poorly in the League, with five draws and a defeat in their first six matches, and indeed Forest did not win a home League game until January, an astonishing record for a side that would finish third. Their form from the turn of the year, however, was excellent, especially in the Cups where, until 7 May, they were in line for a glorious treble.

These pages: The 1989 League Cup final was against Luton Town, almost exactly 30 years to the day after the same two sides had met in the 1959 FA Cup final. Although Luton went into half-time 1-0 up, second half goals from a Nigel Clough penalty (**top right**), Neil Webb (**centre left**) and another from Man of the Match Nigel Clough (**bottom left**) ensured a comfortable 3-1 victory. Forest were to win the Simod Cup (4-3 against Everton) at Wembley on 30 April and had already won the Mercantile Credit Trophy the year before at the same stadium to celebrate 100 years of League football.

It began with the League Cup (at that time the Littlewoods Cup) in September, where second round opponents Chester City were beaten 6-0 at The City Ground and 4-0 at Chester, with six Forest players getting on the scoresheets. In the one-legged third round Forest eased past visitors Coventry, who twice led but went down 3-2 when Nigel Clough netted 20 minutes from time. Away at Leicester in the fourth round captain Stuart Pearce was sent off after a second yellow card in the first half, and Forest did well to hold on for a scoreless draw. In the replay, Lee Chapman got the winner eight minutes from the end in a 2-1 win.

Queen's Park Rangers were fifth round opponents, and the occasion was marked by the return to The City Ground of QPR player-manager Trevor Francis. But Rangers were hit by injuries - Ossie Ardiles broke a leg - and the match was a personal triumph for Lee Chapman, who scored four in a 5-2 victory. The semi-final against Bristol City was a two-legged affair, and at The City Ground the Third Division side shocked Forest by taking the lead just past the hour. It needed an own-goal four minutes from time to earn Forest the draw and allow them to start the second leg on equal terms. In a rain-sodden match, there were no goals in 90 minutes but, six minutes from the end of extra time, a crashing shot by Garry Parker from the edge of the area sent Forest to Wembley.

Luton Town, the holders of the trophy, were Forest's final opponents, bringing back memories of Forest's FA Cup win of 30 years earlier. Luton went ahead in the first half by way of a Mick Harford header, a lead they held to the interval. But Forest were back in it when Luton keeper Les Sealey unnecessarily brought down Steve Hodge and Nigel Clough scored the penalty. A revived Forest went ahead through Neil Webb, despite off-side claims from Luton, and Nigel Clough added another to ensure his father could claim his first trophy for the club since the European Cup nine years earlier, when Nigel was just 14. Brian Clough gave his own personal trophy (a replica of the actual Cup) to his assistant manager Ron Fenton.

Brian Clough had been in trouble during the Cup run. When Forest beat QPR 5-2, Forest fans invaded the pitch, and millions watching on TV saw Clough react violently by striking a couple of fans. Clough admitted that his reactions, while prompted by correct motives, were wrong, and within two days the fans had been identified and they and Clough had mutually apologised to each other. Nevertheless Clough was charged by the FA with bringing the game into disrepute, fined £5,000 and banned from the touchline. The majority of fans' reaction to his behaviour was shown by the ovations he received in the succeeding home

games. It was inevitably headlined, by Jimmy Greaves: "The day the s*** hit the fan." This event came, incidentally, during a purple patch for Forest. When they drew with QPR in a League match on 11 February it put an end to a run of ten straight wins in Cup and League, eight of them by margins of two or more goals.

While progressing in the League Cup, Forest were also doing well in the Simod Cup, a curious competition which succeeded one called the Full Members Cup, originally designed as an extra competition for all First and Second Division clubs not engaged in European competition. This year there were 40 entrants, with Liverpool, Manchester United, Arsenal and Spurs being the four clubs from the top divisions not taking part. The top eight of the previous year's First Division, which included Forest, had byes to the third round.

Forest's campaign started at Stamford Bridge, where three goals in extra time got them past Chelsea 4-1. At Ipswich in the quarter-final, the home side scored first, but Forest were in front by half-time and won 3-1. The semi-final was at The City Ground, and Forest entertained Crystal Palace. Forest led after 14 minutes but in the 66th minute Palace equalised. It wasn't until Palace defender David Burke was sent off six minutes from time that Forest added two more goals to win 3-1.

So for the second time that season Forest were in a Wembley Cup final, their opponents this time Everton.

Brian Clough was to find himself in trouble on one or two occasions for taking the law into his own hands when fans ran onto the pitch. This clown incident was relatively light-hearted, but the FA fined him £5,000 for striking two supporters during Forest's 5-2 defeat of QPR in a League Cup game in 1989. This was, incidentally, the time Lee Chapman scored four goals, the last occasion a Forest player performed this feat. Inevitably, Clough's intervention was headlined: "The day the s*** hit the fan."

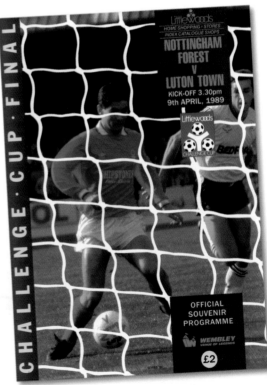

Again Forest were forced to come from behind. A Tony Cottee goal for Everton was equalised by Garry Parker to make the half-time score 1-1. Graeme Sharp put Everton ahead again, and in a thrilling match Parker again levelled matters after a 60-yard run to convert a through ball from Nigel Clough. The match went to extra time, and Lee Chapman put Forest ahead for the first time only for Cottee to haul Everton level again. The match was decided in Forest's favour when Chapman took a pass from substitute Franz Carr to chip the winner. So Forest set a record by becoming the first side in history to win two Wembley Cup finals in the same season.

It could easily have been three. Forest were only two wins away from winning the FA Cup as well, as they were in a semi-final with Liverpool. Their run started with a 3-0 defeat of Ipswich Town at The City Ground, and continued with another home win, 2-0 over Leeds. A visit to Watford in the fifth round, televised live on a Sunday, resulted in another comfortable 3-0 win. The quarter-final was a difficult proposition - away to Manchester United.

Forest played superbly in a manner they had perfected - careful defence in depth when required, interspersed with concerted attacks when the ball would be played with accurate passing from one end of the pitch to the other. Two minutes before the break, one such move allowed Garry Parker to side-foot home after some brilliant wing play by Franz Carr. Thereafter Forest's defence held out, though United claimed a shot from Brian McClair crossed the line before Steve Hodge cleared, a view not shared by the referee. Forest were through to the semi-finals and were again drawn against Liverpool.

The seeds of what then happened at Hillsborough lay in the peculiarly interesting

season of 1988-89. In January Arsenal had led Liverpool by no less than 19 points and the Championship was on its way to Highbury.

But a remarkable decline on Arsenal's part was matched by an equally impressive, unbeaten run of 17 games (the last 11 victories) by Liverpool. By the morning of 15 April, the date of the Football Association Cup semi-final at Hillsborough, Liverpool actually led the League and, due to entertain Arsenal in a League fixture at Anfield a week later, were now almost odds-on for the "double". Liverpool's sudden, dramatic and almost unprecedented surge had understandably generated massive enthusiasm on Merseyside, even a Merseyside which ought to have been sated by their two teams having won no fewer than 15 of the last 25 League Championships.

Paralleling Liverpool's late surge was that by Forest. Between Christmas and the semi-final, these two sides had played 42 matches and lost just two. A win at Hillsborough for Forest would make them the first club ever to contest three Wembley finals in the same season. The two clubs had met at Hillsborough in the previous year's semi-final in 1987-88 of course and Liverpool had won 2-1. It had been the game of the season.

In 1989, only the third time this century that the same two sides had contested consecutive semis, it seemed certain that the winner would also win the Cup. In Liverpool's case, their fans also assumed that would inevitably mean the "double". The 1989 semi-final was not just to be the match of the season, its build-up justified the title Match of the Decade. How right that build-up was to prove to be. Outside the ground it was impossible to buy a ticket. Though semi-finals are always all-ticket, for the previous 20 years it had always been possible, usually even easy, to buy a ticket if you were prepared to pay three or four times its face value. In 1988, for the very same game, the author had a ticket to literally give away and found no takers. But 1989 was different. There just weren't any tickets. Thousands, probably tens of thousands, of Liverpool and Forest fans wandered around the ground asking "Got any spares?" There weren't any. The Liverpool dispossessed gravitated to the Leppings Lane end of the ground, where they mingled with thousands who did have tickets, but many of whom had arrived later than usual because of delays on the M62.

Liverpool had fewer tickets than Forest, despite their bigger support, because the police wanted each club to inhabit the ends of the grounds nearest to their arrival points. This was logical, as for at least ten years the police had been much more concerned to keep fans apart outside grounds – the problems inside having largely been solved. To have switched ends would have meant

Below: Ronnie Moran, Kenny Dalglish, Brian Clough and Alan Hill leave the field at Hillsborough after the enormity of the disaster, on 15 April 1989, had become apparent. The Leppings Lane Stand is in the background *(Popperfoto)*.

the two sets of fans having to cross in the crowded terraced streets. The police, with unassailable logic, pointed out that the arrangements had been identical the year before and there was no discernible trouble then. The seeds of hope for the ticketless had really been sown before the FA Cup final of 1986, when a number of ticketless Liverpool and Everton fans had apparently been allowed into Wembley in similar circumstances. No doubt, many had hoped for a repeat of this experience, whether mythical or not.

At the Leppings Lane (Liverpool) end, the crush outside the ticket barriers became impossible at around kick-off time, with thousands still outside. How many didn't have tickets will never be known. The police, fearing that someone would be killed outside, understandably opened a gate and let in thousands. A roar as Peter Beardsley hit the Forest bar after four minutes compounded the impatience of those who couldn't see. They rushed for the nearest, central entrance to the terraces, although (they didn't and couldn't know) to the left and right were entrances to the side terraces still with lots of space available.

The centre was already packed. The new arrivals simply pushed those already there forward, and then the mass collapsed on itself in the tunnel. Those at the front were crushed, unable to get out because of the absurd oxymoronic "safety" barrier. For the people on the terraces there was no way out – impassable barriers at the front, fences at the side and a tunnel at the back blocked by bodies. It took over an hour for the police to empty the terrace. By then 95 were dead and a 96th death came later. Hours later, the "safety barriers" were still mutely standing there, having resisted all the attempts to pull them, push them and even cut them. By then, football as it had been known, and certainly as it had been when Forest began the decade by winning the European Cup in 1980 and when Liverpool succeeded them in 1981, was surely no more.

It was the third and the worst of the three disasters which blighted English football in the 1980s. In May 1985 came Bradford; a discarded cigarette in a pile of rubbish eventually set fire to a packed stand. Live television was to observe 56 deaths – and it was that chance presence in the country's living rooms which perhaps made the event so stunning. Three weeks later, Europe was treated to another live disaster when rampaging Liverpool fans caused the deaths of 39 Juventus supporters, a wall collapsing at the European Cup final. English clubs were rightly banned from Europe and, until July 1990, remained isolated and alone.

But Hillsborough was definitely even more emotional. The victims were again completely

innocent. They were not hooligans. They had not been drinking or misbehaving. Again, the scene was relayed live to the world in all its gruesome details. For those who were there, like the author, the most striking memory is of how slowly it all happened. It took 90 minutes for the scene to unfold. For at least 45 minutes no one seemed to know what had happened or what to do. The police lined up on the half-way line, apparently to keep Liverpool and Forest fans apart. In retrospect there was no danger that they would clash - but here the victims were suffering from the reputation Liverpool and other football supporters had garnered over the previous two decades.

The police were eventually to be blamed for Hillsborough, but semi-finals had been held there for eight decades and no one had ever died. Nor had they at numerous other packed semi-finals at Villa Park, Old Trafford, Highbury and White Hart Lane. The same teams had contested the semi-final a year earlier – and there had been no trouble.

So why was this day so different from all the others that had come before? The fences played a major part – how many would have died at Bradford if that ground had had fences? – but the behaviour of many fans outside the ground was relevant. The crush was terrible; many were pushing and hoping to get in without a ticket. The tragedy was that the victims were all entirely innocent, just as they had been in Brussels. They were the people who arrived early, who were at the front, who just wanted to support their team.

After the disaster football stopped. The League tried to order teams to continue with the next week's fixtures but many – notably Arsenal – refused. Anfield became a shrine, covered in flowers and scarves.

It was a strange time, a deeply emotional one, yes, but something unlikely to have been seen in any other British city, even a Newcastle or a Glasgow. It was an ultimate expression of the truth that football in England is about provincialism.

After much debate about whether the Cup should go on at all that season, the semi-final was replayed at Old Trafford. Only Manchester United's return to the same ground after Munich in 1958 could ever be comparable. Liverpool beat Forest 3-1 and went on to defeat

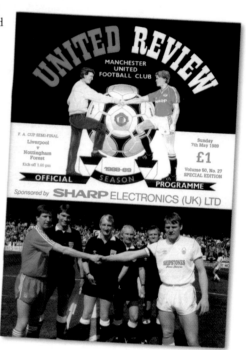

Everton 3-2 in the final. Forest had in truth become bit players in this whole drama, and it is hard to imagine the team being able to treat the replay as just another game.

Despite the unprecedented end to this season, this was an outstanding Forest side which practised a measured style of play that came to be recognised over several seasons as distinctly belonging to Forest. It had nothing to do with tactical innovations or individual flair, although many Forest players had their distinctive skills, such as Clough's awareness and ability to split defences with subtle passes, Pearce's aggression in the tackle and ferocious free-kicks, Walker's speed, especially in recovery ("You'll never beat Des Walker" was the fans' chant), Hodge's industry and the rest, but basically all Forest did was to perfect the basic, traditional arts – accurate, purposeful passing, everybody supporting and backing up everybody else, each player making himself available and all working as a unit. There were no distractions with feuds, fouls, arguing or whatever.

Brian Clough expressed it well with his view of the season: "I don't think I have ever been involved with a side who have been applauded so much having won away from home. Supporters have appreciated us, referees are glowing in their praise about our discipline and my fellow managers have been unstinting in their praise for the manner in which we go about our work. We've always tried to play the game in the way it was intended. We don't argue, we don't moan, we don't spoil.... in fact there's not a negative thought running through the whole club. It's a collector's item if we catch the opposition offside..."

In 1990 the Football League (Littlewoods) Cup was again to produce the main interest for Forest fans. Drawn, as in the previous year, against a Third Division side in the second round, this time Huddersfield Town, Forest's experience was quite different from the 10-0 aggregate of before. At The City Ground, where John Sheridan played his only senior competitive game for the club, Huddersfield drew 1-1. In the second leg, Forest eased 3-1 ahead after the interval, but were pulled back to 3-3, and went through only on the away-goals rule. In the next round, which was not two-legged, Forest managed to survive 0-0 at Crystal Palace, but it all came good for Forest in a 5-0 home win in the replay. Geoff Thomas recalls that Clough took the mickey by taking two men off and finishing the game with nine men. After Thomas complained to the press, Clough came into the Palace dressing room at a subsequent League match and pinned Thomas up against a wall. "I didn't know what to do," says Thomas today, "nor did Steve Coppell." Forest beat Everton 1-0 in the next round, but very controversially. Near the end, a free-kick was given against Everton goalie Neville Southall for time-wasting and, from Nigel Clough's free-kick, Lee Chapman forced the ball home.

Forest were 2-0 up in the second half against Spurs, again at The City Ground, in the next round, but were pulled back to 2-2 in the last half-hour. But the replay was a triumph for Steve Hodge, returning to White Hart Lane after his transfer 18 months before. He scored twice, including the winner, in a 3-2 victory. The semi-final was a two-legged affair, and in the first leg at The City Ground Forest again found a player to score the winner against his former club. This time it was Stuart Pearce, who gave Forest a 2-1 win over Coventry City to take to the second leg. Forest achieved a goal-less draw at Highfield Road, and so for the third time in two seasons took the pitch for a Wembley final.

Forest's opponents were Second Division Oldham Athletic, who had enjoyed a fantastic Cup season, narrowly failing to reach Wembley in the FA Cup, too, when just edged out in a semi-final replay with eventual winners Manchester United, having been leading 1-0 in the initial game at Wembley with one minute to go.

Forest and Oldham put on an exciting display for the fans both at Wembley (it was now an all-seater stadium for the first time) and watching on television. The match was won by an early second-half goal from Nigel Jemson, who converted a chance created by Nigel Clough. Near the end Steve Sutton produced a superb save to make sure Jemson's goal remained the winner. Jemson, a 21-year-old, had been bought from Preston near the end of the 1987-88 season for £150,000. He had had periods on loan to Bolton and Preston, making his Forest debut against Luton on Boxing Day 1989, and keeping his place to the end of the season. Forest's winning League Cup final team was: Sutton, Laws, Pearce, Walker, Chettle, Hodge, Crosby, Parker, Clough, Jemson, Carr.

At long last, in 1991, Brian Clough was to get his Football Association Cup final and for Forest the main excitement this season came in the FA Cup. Their first opponents were Crystal Palace, who were enjoying their best-ever League season (they were third, which is the position they finished), so a visit to Selhurst Park was a tricky assignment. Forest got a 0-0 draw. The replay at The City Ground was again evenly fought, but Forest looked safe as Stuart Pearce put them 2-1 ahead in extra time. However in the last minute a bad back pass by Keane forced Crossley to rush out and clear hurriedly. The ball went to John Salako, who was near both the half-way line and the touch line, and Salako curled a 50-yard ball back over Crossley's head for one of the goals of the season. Forest won choice of ground for the second replay, and finally put paid to Palace 3-0.

Forest had another tough draw at Newcastle in the next round, and after 13 minutes were two down. Pearce got one back, and Newcastle missed a sitter before Clough equalised with two minutes left. Forest again won at The City Ground 3-0. Another away draw at Southampton saw the home side lead for 78 minutes after a second-minute goal. Ten minutes from time Steve Hodge equalised, and Forest were again lucky when Rodney Wallace's hard shot cracked against the crossbar. Nigel Jemson, troubled this season by injuries, was the hero of the replay at The City Ground with his first hat-trick in a 3-1 win. Forest were away yet again in the sixth round but this time didn't need a replay as Roy Keane's goal at Norwich proved the only one. The semi-final was at Villa Park, at long last a respite from the unlucky Hillsborough. It was the third semi-final in four years and the eighteenth time in all (including replays) that Forest had taken the field for an FA Cup semi-final. Forest fans did not need to be told that, in all those matches, their club had won just two.

The semi-final was spoiled somewhat when West Ham's defender Tony Gale was sent off for a professional foul on Gary Crosby after only 25 minutes. It was the first time a referee had applied the recent edict of dismissing the last defender. Forest's poised football eventually wore out the Hammers and four goals in the second half gave a rather false impression of the match, West Ham having hit the woodwork before Forest scored. The goals went to Crosby, Keane,

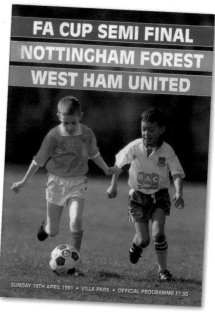

Above: The programme from Forest's third semi-final in four years. It was the first semi-final Forest had contested at Villa Park and Forest were the only non-London club in the last four.

Left: West Ham's Tony Gale was sent off for bringing down Gary Crosby after just 25 minutes with the game goalless. It was the first application of the new 'last defender' rule in a major game and seemed harsh as Crosby was heading diagonally crossfield rather than straight in on goal. The referee is Keith Hackett (Colorsport).

Right: The semi-final was scoreless at half-time, though ten-man West Ham had struck the woodwork. In the second half Forest took over, scoring four goals from (**top to bottom**) Gary Crosby, Roy Keane, Stuart Pearce and Gary Charles. Note that Pearce's goal is a collectors' piece - he scored it with his right foot *(John Sumpter)*.

These pages: The 1991 FA Cup final was preceded by unprecedented hype about Paul Gascoigne and was followed by unprecedented post-mortems about Paul Gascoigne. Yet he was on the field for just 15 minutes and did absolutely nothing worthwhile while on it. Forest entered the game as favourites, after an outstanding run of seven games without defeat, and there was a sentimental desire for Brian Clough to win the one prize that had eluded him.

Top left: After 90 seconds Gascoigne lunged at Garry Parker at chest height with the ball nowhere near. Terry Venables, Spurs' manager, said later: "I thought straight away, Christ, that's him booked - or worse. That day he looked as if his mind was somewhere else." Referee Roger Milford just chuckled and gave Forest a free-kick, although Parker was clearly very shaken by the incident. Gascoigne's tackle is arguably the worst ever seen in a Cup final.

Left centre: Just ten minutes later Gascoigne was at it again. This time he simply kicked Gary Charles on the knee as the Forest player ran the ball along the edge of the area. The ball was again nowhere near the incident. Milford again declined to even book the player, a decision he admitted later was an error. The reality was that Gascoigne should have been sent off without further ado and Forest should have played the last 75 minutes against 10 men. It has been mooted many times since that, had Milford

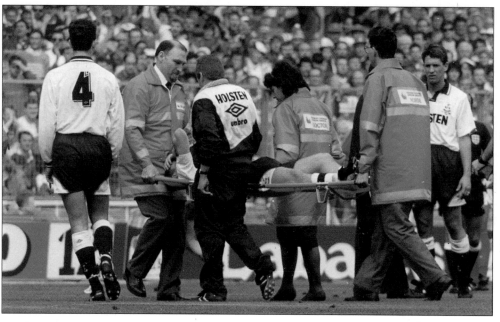

acted correctly, then Gascoigne's later career might well have been very different.

Bottom left: Gascoigne had damaged his cruciate ligaments and was not to play again for nearly a year. Within two minutes he was to be carried off to Wembley Hospital. Unfortunately for Forest, they still faced 11 men and, with Nayim on as substitute, Spurs looked a better balanced side.

Bottom right: The free-kick resulting from Gascoigne's tackle on Charles was in the perfect place for Stuart Pearce. The Forest routine at free-kicks was well rehearsed and predictable. Lee Glover pulled men out of the wall, Pearce put it top left corner. Erik Thorstvedt, in the Spurs' goal, knew exactly where it was going but still could not stop it. 1-0 to Forest and a record for Pearce - it was his 16th goal of the season, a record for a full-back, and none of them from a penalty *(JMS Photography)*.

Pearce and Charles. It was not a great game and, even for Forest fans delirious at a long awaited third FA Cup final, it could not be described as memorable. The Spurs-Arsenal game at Wembley took the headlines, with Spurs depriving Arsenal of an odds-on double and Gascoigne scoring the goal of the season with a 30 yard free-kick.

So Forest were to meet Spurs again, 24 years after that 1967 Hillsborough semi-final had broken so many hearts. The North London club were in a rare old state, facing a host of difficult financial issues and manager Terry Venables trying to buy Irving Scholar's large stake. Some of the following description of the match appears in current author Phil Soar's *Tottenham Hotspur: the Official Illustrated History*.

The night before the Cup final has its own mythology. On one celebrated occasion Arsenal's Alex James disappeared completely from the Regent Palace Hotel, but there could have been few eves to compare with 17 May, the night before the 1991 final. The Tottenham players had been booked into the Royal Lancaster Hotel, a football favourite because of its close proximity to Football Association headquarters at Lancaster Gate.

But the day was to be taken up by negotiations on two fronts – firstly the efforts by Terry Venables to acquire the club, and secondly by the continuing saga of where Gascoigne would play in the future. With the players resting upstairs, it seemed almost certain that the Saturday would see Gascoigne play his last game for Spurs, and with their ownership uncertainties, the future was anything but clear. Gascoigne complicated the issue – Scholar wanted to accept a lower price if Gascoigne could be kept at the club. By 10:00 p.m. it was clear that there were no deals to be struck. And though both Venables and Scholar sought any means possible to keep

Gascoigne at White Hart Lane, he had already committed himself to Lazio. So, with just 17 hours to go to kick-off, the talks were called off and the fate of Tottenham Hotspur remained in the balance. Venables returned to his players and, in particular, Gascoigne.

In an interesting paragraph in his own book *Venables: The Autobiography*, the former manager notes that: '… for once the team doctor was not required to fire his usual 'tranquilliser dart' into Gazza to put him to sleep." Venables goes on to say that Gazza never needed anyone to hype him up, and all of the efforts before the Cup final, in particular, were designed to calm him down, not wind him up. But, as Venables also says about Gascoigne that day: " … it looked like his mind was somewhere else … the transfer might have been on his mind … in any event he was not as hyped up as normal and certainly nothing like he had been before his semi-final." That was the night before – what happened on the day was rather different.

Wembley that day was to be a breeding ground for memories that few finals provide. Most FA Cup finals are anti-climaxes; few provide talking points that will outlive their participants. Since the Second World War there have been only a handful that truly met everyone's hopes – 1948, 1953, perhaps the first game in 1970, 1973, Ricky Villa's game in 1981. But 1991 was to be as dramatic as any. It may well have contained the worst foul ever seen in a Cup final, it saw only the second ever penalty save, it saw an indisputably good goal disallowed, it had the emotion of Brian Clough's failure, and, of course, it had Gascoigne's self-destruction.

Forest were favourites. It was the third time in four years they had reached the semi-final stage and this time they finally had made Wembley. Historically Forest have a record almost as good as that of Spurs in Cup finals – this was their tenth

major final and they had previously lost just one (the League Cup to Wolves in 1980).

Forest were also the emotional favourites – Brian Clough never having won the FA Cup and still being enormously popular. But Clough, unlike Venables, had crucial selection decisions to make and history was to suggest he probably made the wrong ones. Unlike many Cup finalists, Forest had finished their League season in fine style with five wins out of six games. This sequence included a 7-0 defeat of Chelsea, 5-0 against Norwich, 2-1 against Liverpool and 4-3 against Leeds. Perhaps unsurprisingly Clough chose to stick with his winning team – including

youngsters Ian Woan and Lee Glover. Current England midfielder Steve Hodge and Nigel Jemson, who had scored the fifth round hat-trick against Southampton and had won the League Cup with a goal against Oldham at Wembley two seasons earlier, were left out. The consequent lack of experience in the team showed.

The game was to engender rare emotions and the experience and calm of Hodge, in particular, would arguably have been invaluable. The fact that Hodge had, of course, been a Spurs player should also have counted in his favour – the law of the football returnee.

As the teams took to the field the Forest manager grabbed Venables' hand and held onto it. As Venables said later: "He wouldn't let go, so I made him laugh, which at least made it look as if we were joking and not a couple of lovers." Just as they reached the edge of the playing area, Venables brought his hand up as if to wave at someone and Clough was forced to let go.

It remains very difficult to think of any other important English football match which had become, in advance, the story of one player. There may be international comparisons – Maradona and the 1986 World Cup final, Puskas and the 1954 final perhaps – but no FA Cup final had been previewed this way; even 1953 became the Matthews final after the event.

But Gascoigne had become a football celebrity the like of which had not been seen since the peak of George Best's career 20 years before. Since the famous tears in Turin and Lineker's frantic finger pointing gestures to Bobby Robson, Gazza had become public property. The run to the Cup final had reached an almost dreamlike quality, capped by that

Above: Stuart Pearce turns away after scoring from the 13th minute free-kick in the 1991 FA Cup final *(Popperfoto)*.

Below right: After 30 minutes Forest keeper Mark Crossley brought Gary Lineker down in the area, Lineker took the penalty himself, but Crossley, an accomplished penalty expert, saved well going to his left. It was only the second penalty ever saved in an FA Cup final – the first was by Dave Beasant in 1988 from John Aldridge of Liverpool. The only other penalty missed in an FA Cup final had been by Charlie Wallace in 1913 – he shot wide. At this point Forest had to be odds-on to win the trophy. Both teams which had missed Cup final penalties had lost the game, while the team that scored first had failed to win the FA Cup in only three of the previous 20 finals. History says it was not to be – goals from Paul Stewart and Des Walker (an own goal) left the final score 2-1 to Spurs. And although he was to stay with Forest for another two years, this game was really the end of Brian Clough's glorious career.

astonishing free-kick in the semi-final. "Many players can bend a ball from 30 yards – take Ronald Koeman. Many players can hit a ball hard from 30 yards – look at Stuart Pearce. But to hit the ball that hard with that curl, from that distance is very rare indeed …" said one writer afterwards.

So the game had become Gascoigne's final even before it kicked off. The fact that it was almost certainly his last game in England, at least for a while, and no-one knew for sure when anyone might play in a Tottenham shirt again, added piquancy to an already over-tense build up. The Prince of Wales meets the Prince of Wails, as John Motson's well rehearsed (and impossible not to repeat here) line went as Gascoigne cheerfully shook hands with the Prince and Princess of Wales and the Duke and Duchess of Kent.

The game was just 90 seconds old when Gascoigne confirmed with his studs what everyone in the ground suspected – that he was hyped up to a level that was beyond anyone's control. Out on Spurs' right, Gascoigne tackled Forest's Garry Parker. In truth, to call it a tackle is to flatter Gascoigne's behaviour. As Parker moved towards him, Gascoigne lifted his leg to the horizontal and simply kicked Parker at chest height. The ball was nowhere near. It was an astonishing act – totally out of keeping with the setting, the mood and the excellent reputation of the two clubs. Parker went down in a heap. The reaction of everyone watching was identical: "He'll be very lucky to stay on the field". Terry

Venables said afterwards that the tackle was vicious and his first thought was: "Christ, that's him booked." As Venables said: "Gazza was still looking wild. I don't know whether he was anxious or what the reason was, but he did himself no favours."

In the short database of memorable Cup final fouls it is impossible to find anything comparable. The only man sent off in an FA Cup final was Kevin Moran for a tackle on Peter Reid in 1986, but that was genuinely mild, by comparison. Many will remember Willie Young's trip on Paul Allen after 87 minutes of the 1980 final, for which Young received a yellow card. That was a "professional" foul par excellence, for which today Young would be immediately sent off. Peter McParland's tackle on Manchester United goalkeeper Ray Wood in the 1957 final, which broke Wood's cheekbone, left United with ten operating players and helped McParland score two goals later in the game, looked nasty, though McParland was not booked. Looking at replays today, one believes the referee was correct – that McParland was challenging hard rather than unfairly, that Wood stood his ground and that both expected to bounce off the other.

It was the post-match consensus, and one which has grown with time, that not only was Gascoigne's tackle on Parker the worst ever seen in a Cup final, but also that Roger Milford's decision not even to book him has few competitors as possibly one of the worst

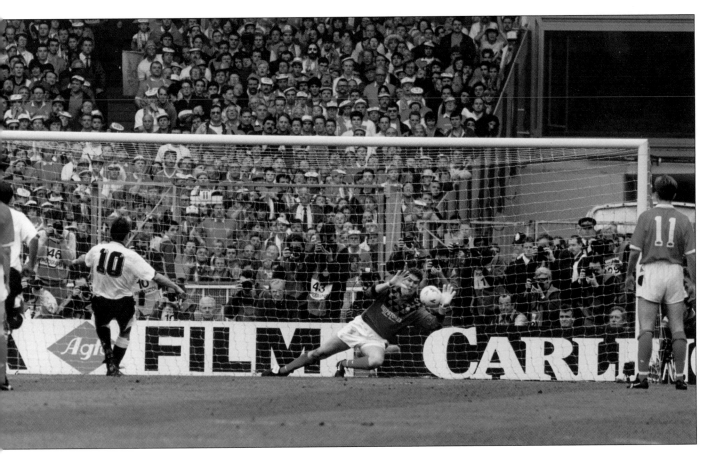

refereeing decisions ever seen in the showpiece of the English game. The closest comparison is probably Dutch referee Charles Corver's decision not to send off German keeper Schumacher after he had knocked out Battiston in the 1982 World Cup semi-final. What remained astonishing back at Wembley was that Milford never even showed Gascoigne the yellow card. Perhaps the referee had also been carried away on the wave of sentiment about Gascoigne's last game. Seven years later, Milford admitted his mistake. Gascoigne should have been sent off, but it was seven years too late for Forest. Gascoigne was to cross Forest's path again in March 1998, when Bryan Robson signed him for Middlesbrough in the hope of overtaking Forest and gaining promotion to the Premier League. The football world was sceptical about the transfer in 1998, referring constantly, in italic type to *that tackle*, no other explanation being required. Chris Lightbown in *The Sunday Times* extended the debate to the long term psychological effect on Gascoigne: "Gascoigne should (have been

dismissed) before he unleashed the second horrendous lunge on Charles. After just seconds, he had fouled Garry Parker. The referee, Roger Milford, a man with a reputation for wanting to be one of the lads and relishing contact with star names, did not seriously admonish Gascoigne, let alone book him. Had Milford done his duty on the Parker foul, the shape of Gascoigne's career and English football might well have been significantly better."

Gascoigne's rashness was to strike again after just after 12 minutes of the match. Forest's young right-back Gary Charles ran right to left across the edge of the penalty area and was tackled by Gascoigne, who simply kicked him on the right knee long after the ball had gone. Charles got up without a murmur, Roger Milford chuckled and Gascoigne was treated for an apparent injury to his own knee. Again, he wasn't even booked. As one commentator said the following day: "Gascoigne would probably have had to pull out a revolver and shoot Stuart Pearce before he was shown even a yellow card."

Above: Roy Keane has a typically quiet word with Justin Edinburgh during the 1991 FA Cup final. Keane had come from Cobh Ramblers for a mere £25,000 and when he left Forest for Manchester United in 1993 his £3,750,000 fee was the largest Forest had then ever received. *(Popperfoto)*

Stuart Pearce took his trademark free-kick, left-footed into the top left-hand corner. Thorstvedt was even standing at that side of the goal knowing exactly where the ball would go, but could barely move as Pearce's shot rocketed past. It was Pearce's 16th goal of the season, all from left-back, and none of them a penalty. That was an English record for a defender. As Forest celebrated, Gascoigne collapsed in the middle of the field clearly unable to play on. The players gathered around him. Venables came onto the pitch. Suddenly, everything was in the balance – Gascoigne's future, Spurs' future, the fee for Gascoigne, Venable's future at White Hart Lane – even whether there was a future at White Hart Lane at all.

Nayim came on as substitute, but the reality was that Spurs should have been down to ten men. Roger Milford said later that he didn't feel it was necessary to take any action with Gascoigne because the Spurs player was clearly not able to continue. But that was hardly fair to Forest.

Venables did not appear particularly panicked. There were still 75 minutes to go and, as he commented afterwards, until Gascoigne went off the balance of the side was not quite right. As Venables said: "Forest normally played wingers so wide it drew the full-backs out with them and left large spaces through the middle for Nigel Clough to exploit. So I took David Howells from the left to play in front of the two centre-halves." Venables had had a problem about whom to leave out of the centre, having too many midfield players who were playing well. Samways had been in good form and Venables eventually preferred him on the left side to Nayim. But, as Venables said: "My difficulty was that Samways did not really like playing on the left and he soon began to follow the ball and vacate his position. It could have cost us the game, because Gary Crosby got through where Samways had gone into midfeld a few minutes later and Crosby was one-on-one with the keeper. If Crosby had scored (as he should have done) I don't think we would have been able to come back and, apart from the goal, it was the only real chance they had." Thorstvedt competently made the save that was required from him.

When Gascoigne came off Nayim took over on the left and Samways occupied Gascoigne's more central role. With Stewart moving to the right side of midfield, this gave Spurs a considerably better balance and helped to reduce the threat from Crosby and Charles on the Forest right. The game settled down to a more even contest and, after 25 minutes, Paul Allen put Gary Lineker through to score a classically sharp Lineker goal. Lineker was clearly onside, but the linesman made the most public mistake of his career, and it was disallowed. Five minutes later,

Lineker was through again, this time from Paul Stewart.

Mark Crossley, in the Forest goal, brought Lineker down and was arguably lucky not to be sent off himself. The penalty was indisputable and Lineker took it well, putting it in the corner to Crossley's left. Unfortunately for Lineker, Crossley guessed correctly and turned the ball away. It was only the second time in the 120-year history of FA Cup finals that a goalkeeper had saved a penalty – the other being Dave Beasant for Wimbledon from John Aldridge of Liverpool in 1988. It was also only the third time in an FA Cup final that a penalty had been missed – Charlie Wallace of Villa had shot just past the post in 1913 and cost his side the game.

So at half-time Forest were 1-0 ahead and the 80,000 crowd had surely seen one of the most dramatic 45 minutes of football in the history of the competition. It would not have been possible for the next 45 to be so exciting, but they were no less interesting as Spurs gradually clawed their way back into a match which seemed to have stored up a season's misfortunes in a single afternoon.

Venables spoke to Gascoigne, by now in a hospital bed, at half-time. The medical team already knew that Gascoigne had torn his cruciate ligaments. He certainly wouldn't play for at least six months, Lazio would presumably not now pay for him, and it was quite possible he would never wear a football shirt again. It was the very same injury that had ended Brian Clough's magnificent playing career.

But it took Spurs just seven minutes of the second half to equalise. Nayim put Stewart through and the midfielder capped what was surely his best ever performance for Spurs with a beautiful cross-shot goal. Forest, with Spurs keeping Nigel Clough well under control, did not have a clear-cut chance in the second half and, by the end of 90 minutes, the pendulum had firmly swung towards Tottenham.

Venables talked to his players before extra time. "We're back in the game and it's got WIN written all over it. The only thing that can stop us is if we stop ourselves. They're on their heels, they don't know if they have got anything left in them." Venables' assessment was correct, and Brian Clough sat on the bench chatting to a policeman while Archie Gemmill and Alan Hill tried to inspire a flagging Forest in the five-minute break.

There was just the one goal in extra time. Nayim put in a corner from the right, Paul Stewart flicked it on and Mabbutt came charging in on the far post. In attempting to head the ball out for another corner, Des Walker managed to put it just inside the post, for an own goal. Mabbutt, the loser via his own o.g. in 1987, went up to collect the trophy. Spurs thus became the first club to win the FA Cup eight times and no one had missed the fact that the year ended in a one. It was the first domestic trophy that Venables had ever won as a manager.

Venables says: "It was the most action-packed, incident-filled final that I can remember. It seemed as if it needed something to go wrong – Gazza's injury – to bring it to the boil."

The pre-match had all been about Gazza and the game lives in the memory of even Forest fans as his match, despite his positive contribution being zero. The memory, or course, can become blurred. Because the semi-final was also held at Wembley, the images of Gascoigne's free-kick against Arsenal, the fouls on Garry Parker and Gary Charles, Gascoigne being carried off and his winning shot past Arsenal's David Seaman all became jumbled – as if it were a single game. The team and their wives got on to the club coach and took the Cup to the hospital for Gascoigne to see. Gascoigne, whom Venables says was crying, received his medal in his hospital bed. That was the end of his Tottenham career. It was also Irving Scholar's last game as Tottenham chairman (his next as a director of a football club was, remarkably, at Tottenham with Forest) and, if the truth be told, the 1991 FA Cup final was really the end of Brian Clough's career.

Clough hung on for two more seasons –

getting Forest to a dreadfully dull and forgettable sixth League Cup final in 1992 (Manchester United won 1-0 amid allegations of mis-selling of tickets and Forest never looking like scoring) and eventually succumbing to relegation a year later. His troubles have been well documented and, after selling Sheringham in the decade's most controversial deal in 1992 (and one that still reverberates for the club), he had no-one to score goals.

Gary Bannister, a veteran who had been on loan to Second Division Oxford United from West Brom, came to fill the gap left by Sheringham, and did well in his only season at The City Ground, getting eight goals in 31 League appearances, plus two more in six Cup games. In November, Neil Webb returned to the side from Manchester United, who released him for £800,000. Webb's international career had been interrupted soon after he joined United by an injury received when playing for England against Sweden and, although he eventually regained his club place, his England career had already ended. He played only nine League games for Forest during the season.

The 1992-93 season had begun well, with Sheringham getting the only goal in a 1-0 defeat of Liverpool, the first Premiership match shown live by Sky after their multi-million pound deal with the Premier League. Forest looked

Below: Archie Gemmill, Liam O'Kane, and Alan Clarke try to rouse Des Walker, Steve Chettle and the rest of the Forest team after 90 minutes of the 1991 F A Cup final. Brian Clough stayed on the bench talking to a policeman. Clough had famously done the same during the 1978 League Cup final, but this time, Terry Venables' psychology was superior and Spurs went on to win 2-1.

impressive. But then six successive defeats, the longest run without a point since Brian Clough became manager, put Forest on the bottom of the table. By the end of December, Forest had added only two more wins to that first day victory, and remained at the foot. It was 30 January when Forest managed to get off the bottom with a 2-0 win over fellow-strugglers Oldham. Throughout the season conventional football wisdom was that "Forest were too good to go down," a phrase that still fills newspaper columns today ("I remember when they said Forest were too good to go down…") They were playing the thoughtful, passing football that had been their trademark since their European Cup days, but without results because of no-one to score the goals. However, with two wins and a draw at Liverpool to follow the Oldham win enabling the club to climb to 19th, their highest since the first month of the season, it seemed perhaps that Forest were too good to go down. But it was a temporary reprieve. Forest finished where they had been for all but seven weeks of the season – last. Clough sold Sheringham because he was relatively slow and too much like Nigel, but the club was then frozen into inactivity while Clough did not seek a replacement.

Discontent had been mounting during the season, of course, and on 1 March 1993 the club was forced to hold its first extraordinary meeting for 23 years. A group of shareholders wanted to know more details about Brian Clough's day-to-day running of the club, but they were eventually heavily outvoted. Three weeks later Clough was given the freedom of the City of Nottingham in a ceremony at the Council House.

On 26 April, with relegation almost certain, Brian Clough announced his intention to retire at the end of the season. His last home game, on 1 May, was against Dave Bassett's Sheffield United, also in danger of relegation. United won 2-0, the first of three wins in their last three games, which saw them to safety. The match also condemned Forest to relegation for certain. Clough was given a tremendous and emotional ovation by the fans at the match. He had been manager of the club for just over 18 years, during which this was only the second time (12th in 1981-82) that Forest had been out of the top half of the table. He (and Peter Taylor, who had died in retirement in Majorca in 1990) had transformed Nottingham Forest Football Club from a run-of-the-mill Second Division side to one of the leading clubs in the land.

The end was pure tragedy, with a packed ground, weeping supporters and near hysteria. James Dalrymple, observing with a more jaundiced eye than most, was cruel: "The 26,000 crowd, many of them hysterical and close to tears, bayed for a final performance from the man who had entertained them for 18 years and led them

into a great sporting era that had brought international glory and fame to their pleasant backwater town. A great and joyous adventure was over, the people of Nottingham sensed, and they dreaded a return to footballing obscurity when this charismatic and unpredictable Pied Piper of a manager had gone. They wanted to show how much they loved him. But what might – and should – have been a dignified farewell had a downside. Clough, perhaps prompted by years of playing his role of the garrulous clown touched with genius, did his best for them on that May Day. But by then he was playing only from memory. There was no more fight left in the body and mind of a tough Yorkshireman who had always relished a fight. He had committed the only capital offence in an industry that could routinely accommodate corruption and violence: he was no longer a winner and he had just seen his team relegated. The nation, which had adored him and relished his antics for more than three decades, followed every new revelation (of his life) with that horrified fascination – almost a British characteristic – that seems to demand the final downfall of its heroes."

The final game was at Ipswich – happily a friendly place. The ground was packed with Forest fans. Clough took dignified bows. Forest finished the season as they had conducted it throughout – losing 2-1. The final goal of the Clough era was scored by his son, Nigel. It was to be the last goal that this lovely, intelligent, personable young man was ever to score for his father. It was fitting that this one young man should end the reign of the father who called the whole world by that phrase.

Right: The end of a glorious era – Brian Clough's final home game against Sheffield United on 1 May 1993. Dave Bassett's team won 2-0 and Forest were relegated. Nigel Clough scored his father's last first-class goal at Ipswich a week later.

On Sunday 3 May 1998, Forest played their last game of the Championship winning season at West Bromwich. They had already won the trophy and the game was a friendly 1-1 draw before a packed crowd. The end of the game saw the traditional champagne fight between Andy Johnson (left) and Pierre van Hooijdonk. Van Hooijdonk's 29 League goals made him the country's leading goalscorer. Not since Enoch West, in 1908, had Forest had the country's leading scorer. Kevin Phillips of Sunderland scored 30 in all but, after some debate at Rothmans, the two that Phillips scored in the play-offs were discounted and he finished one behind van Hooijdonk. It was only the fifth time in Forest's history that the club had won any championship – after 1906-07, 1921-22, 1950-51 and 1977-78.

THERE were just two real options to replace Clough – and both retained a link with the European Cup winning teams. Favourite was Martin O'Neill, then with Wycombe. He was tentatively offered the job but, knowing only too well the club and its recent history, insisted on the freedom to remove any staff he wished and to appoint anyone he wished, in particular the legendary John Robertson as his number two. The board, for reasons that remain debatable, would not agree and then asked Martin if he could work with Frank Clark. Nothing came of that proposal leaving Frank Clark, Clough's original choice, as the only credible contender. Clark was appointed in May 1993. He had managed Leyton Orient from 1982 to 1991, when he became managing director, and Orient were in the Second Division when Forest tempted him to manage them. Although Alan Hill (promoted to assistant manager from chief scout) and Liam O'Kane (first team coach) were to remain, changes in the rest of the support staff meant the departure of reserve team coach Archie Gemmill, who had been seven years behind the scenes at Forest after his days as a player.

Clark had soon engineered a big turn-round in players. The main ones to go were Nigel Clough, for whom Liverpool paid £2,275,000, Roy Keane, who fetched £3,750,000 from Manchester United (a new Forest record for fee received), and Gary Charles, for whom Derby paid £750,000. Nigel Clough had made it clear that he would not remain with the club after the way the announcement of his father's departure was handled.

Sadly, Clough's career was never to take off at Anfield. At Forest he had been the core of the team, always available to take the ball with his back to the goal and instantly swing it out wide to Webb or Pearce or Carr. Graham Taylor kept Clough in the England squad for his whole tenure, but never found the moment to build his team around this remarkable talent. Rather like a Malcolm Macdonald or a Johnny Haynes, either you built the team around Clough or you didn't play him. Recalling this dilemma in 1998, Taylor said: "I took Nigel to the USA for a three match tour in 1993. I told him in advance that I would try him in all three games and, if it worked, I would try to build things around him. He did well, but perhaps not quite well enough. We were always concerned about that slight lack of pace at international level."

Nigel returned to Forest briefly during Stuart Pearce's temporary management and Pearce, had he stayed permanently, would have liked to install Clough in a senior position. It was not to be and this immensely likeable and presentable young man was to return to Manchester City reserves. Perhaps the greatest tribute to him is that no-one ever thought for a single second that he owed his place in the Forest team to the coincidence that his father was the manager.

The newcomers were many. Stan Collymore, a goal-scoring centre-forward, was signed from Southend United for £2,100,000 to set a new club record fee for a player, just a week after central defender Colin Cooper was bought from Millwall for £1,500,000. In rapid order followed right-back Des Lyttle, from Swansea City for £375,000, versatile midfielder David Phillips, a Welsh international, who signed from Norwich for £500,000, and Gary Bull on a free transfer from financially troubled Barnet. In September Northern Ireland international goalkeeper Tommy Wright arrived from Newcastle United for £400,000 and in November Norwegian international midfielder Lars Bohinen joined the club after long transfer negotiations from Lillestroem for a fee of £450,000. Just as important as the signings was Frank Clark's persuasion of Stuart Pearce to continue in the new First Division rather than to seek a move to a Premiership club. It has to be said that Clark got every single paid transfer in that period absolutely spot-on.

The star signing Collymore was to miss the first three League games of the season with tonsillitis - the first match was against his old club Southend and was chosen for a live Sunday television broadcast. The team for the first match was: Crossley, Lyttle, Pearce, Cooper, Chettle, Stone, Black, Webb, Rosario, Glover, Woan. Interestingly, six of the team were to be part of the challenge to return yet again to the Premier in 1998. Steve Stone was a player signed from school as long ago as 1987, most of his few senior appearances having been in central midfield. Clark played him on the right and he was so successful he missed only one game all season. "I played for Gateshead Boys, but no one ever came to see me. They were all watching the lads at Roker or St James's. So I sat down and wrote to all the big clubs and asked if they would look at me. Forest replied, watched a couple of games, then offered me a place. All of a sudden, Newcastle, Sunderland and the rest were interested, but it was too late. I will always be grateful to Forest for giving me the chance, and for sticking by me through all the injuries," said Stone, ten years later.

The side drew their first two matches 1-1, and the £10 million plus worth of transfer dealings seemed irrelevant as hopes of a quick return to the Premiership began to look like dreamland. All three League matches in September were lost and the club were standing 19th in the table, with apparently more chance of going down again than up. Dog days indeed. New keeper Wright came into the side but was injured after ten games and Crossley resumed to

the end of the season (Wright eventually left for £450,000 to Manchester City in 1997 without another chance to establish himself in the side, but after performing absolutely brilliantly in his very last game for the club, at White Hart Lane in a 1-0 win). But by the time Forest lost 2-1 to Notts County at Meadow Lane on 12 February, the defeat ended a run of 13 unbeaten League games and Forest had moved into sixth place. A little blip followed with a home draw with Palace and defeat at Oxford, but from 2 March Forest were to lose only once more in their last 16 League matches - a run good enough to carry them into a clear second place seven points behind Palace but nine ahead of third-placed Millwall. So the Reds were back in the Premiership at the first time of asking, and 75 points would have been enough to take them up. In 1998, they were to achieve that mark with nine games to go and were still nowhere near the promised land.

Many had contributed to the success. David Phillips, who had left Norwich just as they were about to appear in Europe for the first time (and famously eliminate Bayern Munich with an away win in the UEFA Cup), was voted Forest's Player of the Season. Collymore played inspirationally and netted 19 goals, despite missing 18 matches

with illness or injury. Black, Cooper, Chettle, Crossley, Gemmill and Phillips all played over 30 games. Bohinen was smooth in midfield after his late arrival and Jason Lee, a long-haired striker from Southend United, who was bought for £200,000 in March, came in for 13 of the last 15 League games and was on the losing side only once.

Forest were in the Premiership again, where their fans believed they belonged, for 1994-95, after only one season out of the top flight. The squad was strengthened in the summer by yet another record signing - Forest's highest fee had increased three seasons running. Bryan Roy, a striker, who had starred in Holland's World Cup campaign in the USA, was signed from the Italian club Foggia for £2,900,000. Forest began in magnificent style, remaining unbeaten until their 15th match, twelve in the League, by which time they had established themselves in second position behind Newcastle. Collymore and Roy had immediately struck up an understanding and had already netted 14 goals between them, 11 in the League. After a bad run of six League games without scoring, which dropped them to fifth, Forest got their season in gear again in December. Their best performance of the campaign was probably the 2-1 win at Old Trafford on

17 December. Manchester United had won all nine home League games so far, scoring 23 goals without reply. But Collymore spoiled the defensive record with a superb first-half goal, and Pearce, scoring for the third match running, had a free-kick deflected into goal just past the hour. United could get only one in reply from Cantona.

A bad run of ten games to 4 March which included five defeats and three draws, saw several points dropped to late goals, but Forest kept in fifth position and from then on ended the League season in magnificent style with nine wins and two draws in their final 11 games. This included an extraordinary game at Hillsborough, where Sheffield Wednesday, managed by Forest's European Cup hero Trevor Francis, were overwhelmed 7-1, Forest setting a new Premiership away-win record. It was also incidentally Wednesday's biggest ever home defeat in any competition. Collymore and Roy each scored twice in this match, Roy for the third match in succession, while Collymore was in a sequence which saw him get ten goals in ten games. Forest finished third in the Premiership and, if the season had lasted another month, they would have won it. The tactics were surprisingly simple. Collymore was so inspired and enthusiastic, and Roy such a talented, left-footed ball player, that Forest tended to get their men behind the ball and knock it forward for Collymore and Roy to collect and cause havoc. Clark was a defender himself and built a defence first and foremost. Colin Cooper, winner of two England caps, and Stuart Pearce were the keys to the back field, both having a series of superb seasons. Colin Cooper feels that the Forest team which came up did not make any dramatic changes between divisions. "Frank Clark brought some very good players in – Stan, Des Lyttle, Lars Bohinen. We all fitted into the system very well and Frank did not need to adapt the team he inherited that much. Stan was an amazing player. He would just pick the ball up and run at them. He had this unique effect on the crowd – I've never seen or heard it with any other player. As soon as he got the ball, even in our penalty area, there was this sudden buzz, the noise level suddenly went up. They were all willing him to go on one of those runs. I don't think he's played that way since at Liverpool or Villa – except when he plays against us of course! The only overall difference was probably in our fitness levels. Peter Edwards came in as fitness coach and, though he took a lot of criticism, really did make us a lot fitter. We carried on the same way, Bryan Roy came here and fitted in for a season, and we were a very good side, playing to a very simple system."

In all matches Stan Collymore scored 25 goals and Bryan Roy 14. Stuart Pearce netted ten from full-back. One of the most heartening

stories of the season concerned Steve Stone, who was voted by the fans Forest's Player of the Year, recognition for a man who had three times overcome breaking a leg on his progress which would lead in the forthcoming season to caps for England.

The new season would also see the return of Forest to European competition. However this was to take place without Stan Collymore who, after two highly successful seasons, insisted on moving on to Liverpool for £8,500,000, which remains the highest fee received by Forest for a player. It was also the British transfer record, exceeded up to 1998 only by Alan Shearer's move to Newcastle. £5 million of this money was spent equally on two new players, one of whom, Kevin Campbell, from Arsenal, took over the number 10 shirt worn by Collymore. The other was versatile midfielder Chris Bart-Williams from Sheffield Wednesday, like Campbell an England Under-21 international, although he was born in Sierra Leone. Forest's third big signing of the summer was the first Italian international to play for an English club, the tall 29-year-old striker Andrea Silenzi, who cost £1,800,000 on signature from Torino, where had had been the leading scorer in Italian Serie A football in 1993. He had also played for Roma, Internazionale and Napoli, where he partnered Maradona. This first Forest season was marred by injury and illness and he made only seven appearances and scored two goals before Forest cut their losses and released him for free in 1997. Silenzi was arguably Forest's worst buy ever, with the sole exception of the disastrous Jim Baxter.

Only Campbell of the new trio appeared in the first League match of the season at Southampton, where Matt Le Tissier scored a hat-trick for the home team but Bryan Roy scored two and Forest won 4-3. Four successive League draws followed, including a 1-1 draw at Highbury where Campbell scored his first Forest goal against his old team. Bart-Williams came into the side for the following match, Forest

Above: Heroes a generation apart: John Robertson, Martin O'Neill's assistant manager at Leicester, and Steve Stone share a joke in the Robin Hood Lounge at The City Ground, where both are regular speakers at club dinners (*John Sumpter*).

beating Everton 3-2. Forest went undefeated for the first twelve games of the season, thus setting up the record undefeated run for *all* Premier League clubs of 25 games (to be added to their existing 40 and 42 game record runs of 1977-1978). Forest were developing a monopoly of unbeaten run records.

During this run Forest had transferred their Norwegian international Lars Bohinen to Premiership Champions Blackburn Rovers for £700,000 in acrimonious circumstances when Bohinen invoked a clause allowing him to leave unless Forest paid a pre-arranged sum. Bohinen inevitably appeared against them in Forest's next match at Ewood Park. Bohinen played brilliantly and scored twice and, with Alan Shearer getting a hat-trick, Forest were crushed 7-0. So their 25-game run came to an end with their biggest defeat for 33 years - that being the 9-2 defeat by Spurs in September 1962 with Greaves netting four. Forest's record Premier League undefeated run came to an end with the Premier League's record win. Remarkable – but certainly not boring.

Another old boy to do the Reds a bad turn was Stan Collymore, on New Year's Day at Anfield. With Stone and Woan giving Forest a two–goal lead in 17 minutes, all looked fine for the visitors, but Collymore responded by scoring for Liverpool and playing a part in three more goals to give Liverpool a 4-2 win. For the return match in March at The City Ground, it was reported there had been death threats to Collymore. He failed to shine in the face of unprecedented hostile abuse from the Forest crowd and was taken off as Forest won 1-0. There was no such revenge for Forest in the return with Blackburn, however. Blackburn took their season's tally against Forest to twelve with a 5-1 win. As Manchester United beat Forest 5-0 a fortnight later, 17 goals of the total of 54 Forest conceded in the League that season - nearly a third - had come in only three matches.

Forest had a strange run in the FA Cup, getting through to the sixth round by virtue of replay victories against Stoke, Oxford and Spurs. The tie with Spurs was remarkable. Televised live at The City Ground, the first match kicked off in reasonable conditions but within minutes a blizzard developed which, despite

the change to an orange ball, got so bad that after 15 minutes the match had to be abandoned. Nine days later the match was drawn 2-2 with Ian Woan scoring two literally staggering free-kicks "I only get a chance when Pearcy's out," he said afterwards. "I don't argue with him much when he plays. In fact, I'm a bit worried about saying this much." A year later he found he had the same problem with Pierre van Hooijdonk. The replay at White Hart Lane ended 1-1, necessitating penalties. Crossley brilliantly saved three (enjoying penalties against Spurs) and Forest won the shoot-out 3-1. Forest were unlucky to lose in the quarter-final when Crossley was beaten by his old friend Franz Carr, returning to The City Ground for his first full match with Aston Villa, his sixth team since leaving Forest.

Forest's UEFA Cup campaign, up to the quarter-final, was a triumph of calm, organised defence, in both home and away legs. Malmo were beaten by virtue of the away goals rule. Forest lost 2-1 in Malmo but won 1-0 at The City Ground, with the defence manfully preventing all Malmo's efforts to score and Bryan Roy scoring with a stunning left-footed drive. In the second round Forest won 1-0 in Auxerre, despite Auxerre's almost complete dominance, as the statistic of their 20 goal attempts indicates. The second leg at The City Ground was little different - Forest could hardly get out of their own half - but held on to a 0-0 draw.

Another French side, Lyon, suffered a similar fate to Auxerre. With the first leg in Nottingham, Forest won 1-0, despite Lyon having most of the play. A young player, Paul McGregor, signed from school in 1991 but not yet having made a full senior appearance, came on as a substitute 18 minutes from time with another youngster with limited experience, Bobby Howe. A Howe shot was handled, Pearce's spot-kick saved and McGregor scored on the rebound. In the return, all Lyon's pressure could not produce a goal.

By now Forest were the last English team left in Europe, and met star-studded Bayern Munich in the quarter-finals. Another impressive defensive display in Munich kept the deficit for the home leg down to 2-1, with Steve Chettle getting a potentially valuable away goal. Forest were optimistic for the home leg, but this time the previously reliable defence strangely cracked. Having conceded only four goals in the seven previous UEFA Cup matches, they now conceded five in one match, with Jurgen Klinsmann getting two. Bayern won 5-1.

The City Ground was one of those used for Euro 96, the European Championship, and staged three matches in which Croatia, Portugal and Turkey took part. The Trent End had been rebuilt to seat 7,500 and the ground just managed to reach the 30,000 minimum capacity required

Below: Forest's 1995-96 UEFA Cup campaign kicked off with a first round pairing with 1979 European Cup final opponents Malmo. The Swedes were beaten on away goals and the Reds went on to eliminate French sides Auxerre and Lyon before going out to Bayern Munich at the quarter-final stage.

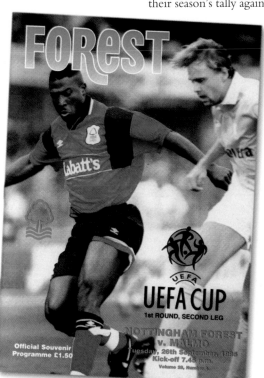

for Euro 96 – the official capacity now being 30,587, all seated. Because of the need to separate away fans, the ground can never be entirely filled. By the end of 1998, the record all seated attendance was the 29,302 who paid to watch the crucial promotion game against Reading at the end of the 1997-98 season.

Frank Clark's optimistic view of the 1996-97 season was that, without a European adventure, Forest could concentrate all their efforts into finishing as high in the Premiership as possible and going as far as possible in the domestic Cup competitions. Alas it was to turn sour for Clark, and before Christmas he would have left The City Ground. Clark's biggest purchase in the summer was Dean Saunders, the Welsh international striker, who was signed from the Turkish club Galatasaray for £1,500,000. Another seven-figure purchase was the Croatian international defender Nikola Jerkan, who was to make only 14 appearances during the season.

The first match of the 1996-97 season looked so promising for Forest, who fielded Saunders and Jerkan at Coventry. The game was a triumph for Kevin Campbell who scored a hat-trick, all with assistance from Saunders, as Forest won 3-0. Campbell, troubled by back problems, scored only three more goals in the League all season. But in the second game at The City Ground, Forest crashed 4-1 to newly promoted Sunderland. Forest were not to win their second League match of the season until the run-up to Christmas. On 17 December, when Forest lost 4-2 to Liverpool at Anfield, it was their 16th game without a win, the longest in the Premiership, passing the record previously held by Swindon.

So Forest, a season after setting a Premiership record with the longest *unbeaten* sequence since its inception, now set a record for the longest sequence *without* a win. There seemed no overwhelming reason for this extraordinarily rapid change round in fortunes. The main one might be the loss of the charisma of the Collymore-Roy partnership of two seasons before. Without Collymore, Roy had lost much of his spark, and the whole team as a consequence played with less certainty, the midfield not pressing forward to support the front runners and thus inviting the ball to come back to their penalty area.

The immediate effect of the loss at Liverpool was that Forest now trailed by three points at the foot of the League table. Frank Clark felt he had no choice but to resign. Chairman Irving Korn immediately asked Stuart Pearce to take over as caretaker manager and, after 24 hours thinking it over, Pearce accepted, although it would clearly be a strain, combining this role with that of a player, and one who was still involved at international level at that. Pearce became the first player-manager ever to play for England, and he captained the team against South Africa, another first to add to Forest's catalogue of many.

By this stage, the club had become the focus of constant media attention, but for events off the field rather than on it. 1996 was the height of a financial frenzy which was to eventually lead to 20 clubs floating on the Stock Exchange. Of all those flotations and take-overs, Forest's was to become the most contentious, the most high profile and, by far, the most drawn out.

By the summer of 1996 it had become clear to any perceptive observer that the club was facing a major crisis. The financial stakes for Premier

Below: Bryan Roy powers a left-footed shot past the Bayern Munich post during the UEFA Cup quarter-final second leg at The City Ground on 19 March 1996. Forest were England's last representatives in Europe but were to lose the game 5-1 and 7-2 on aggregate *(John Sumpter)*.

Right: Steve Chettle guards Jurgen Klinsmann in the same game. Chettle had scored Forest's away goal in Munich, but that lifeline was to prove irrelevant *(John Sumpter)*.

clubs had been raised dramatically with the new BSkyB contract, by the enormous sums being invested by Blackburn, Chelsea and Newcastle, and also being generated off the field by Manchester United. At the time, many other clubs were raising significant sums by way of stock market flotations or by acquisition, while underfunded Forest were clearly slipping further into debt. They remained (as they had for over 100 years), the *only* club in the country which had no means of raising capital. Although Forest had finished ninth the season before, it was now not clear where the goals were coming from and the £8.5 million received for Collymore had been spent. Collymore had provided a cash lifeline but the honest assessment has to be that Frank Clark and the board had not spent it well.

By September, it was apparent that the board needed to do something, though what was unclear. The club was sliding rapidly into uncontrollable debt – the total deficit reached £11.3 million by February 1997 – and individual members of the board began to speak with prospective interested

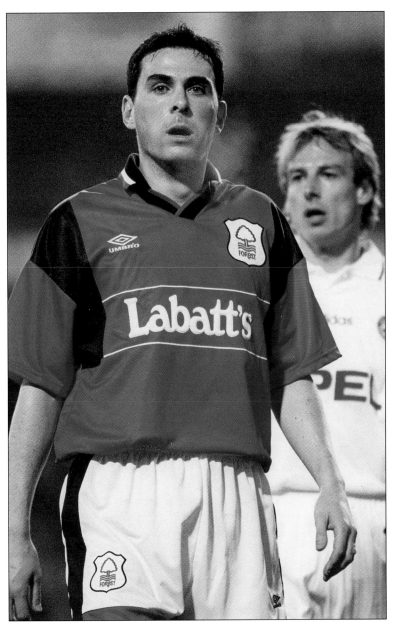

parties. Although Forest did receive approaches from several merchant banks experienced in take-overs, the board eventually decided to place the future of the club in the hands of its auditors, Price Waterhouse. This was in some ways an unusual decision. Granted, the board and Price Waterhouse provided independently assessed figures but never, however, allowed bidders to conduct their own separate investigations into Forest's finances and the process of achieving the best possible deal became arguably far more drawn out than was beneficial for the club.

It is no secret that individual board members had their own preferences throughout the process. Even literally hours before the final decision on 24 February 1997, there were open debates and newspaper reports about the board and a group of shareholders going it alone and rejecting all outside offers. The composition of the club and its shareholdings remained a unique one and was, in itself, an immense complication. Right to the very end there were those who felt that the club might never be sold and would, if necessary, have to simply lapse into bankruptcy. Certainly this was a technical likelihood – if 75 per cent of the (by then) 203 members were not prepared to support a single solution, then bankruptcy would probably have been the consequence.

The crucial figure in the drama was to be Chris Wootton, a director of the club for many years, but who was to be voted out of office on 31 October 1996. He had been Clough's bête noir and had been at least partially responsible for the revelations about Clough's problems in the later stages of the manager's career. This was arguably one reason why he was to be voted out as a director on the crucial date of 31 October 1996, crucial because this was the very moment when the takeover battle was hotting up. Wootton provided a vital link between the members of the board who wanted to see the best solution possible and the rest of the shareholders (then numbering 196 plus the 7 directors).

Working with a group of close friends and long term Forest shareholders, notably Peter Blackbourn and Mel Cox, and often in contact with impartial but influential shareholders such as Cathy Coupe, Tim McCarthy, Graham Davidson and Pete Atkins, Wootton pulled many of the strings behind the scenes. Many of the newspaper articles ran widely distributed quotations which were attributed to a whole cast of characters, but were actually generated through the auspices of Wootton and a small group of activists. Larry Lloyd, a Forest hero, a shareholder and an influential radio broadcaster, was one of the few people who always knew what was happening. The problem everyone faced, particularly the seven man board, was that the club then had 203 shareholders (there had originally been 209, but six had died and their shares had not been reissued), each with one share.

Bidders were not able to offer to buy the shares, only to reconstruct the company so that the existing shareholders kept a percentage of the "new" Nottingham Forest. Shareholders were not able to sell or pledge their shares to any buyer – their only option was to return them to the club. Unfortunately or fortunately, it needed at least 75 per cent of the shareholders to vote in favour of any reconstruction.

It was the group organised by Nina Gardiner, Irving Scholar and Philip Soar who realised what this really meant. It wasn't so much that 75 per cent of votes were needed to win the club, it was that 25 per cent of the votes would always stop anyone else winning it. As a result, this group,

known as the Bridgford Group after the end of the ground at which Philip Soar had first stood as a seven year-old, worked hard to develop a solid block of support which would be large enough to wear down other bidders. "We recognised that 150 votes weren't really vital. If we had more than 50, we could always prevent anyone else winning and gradually wear the opposition down," said Nina Gardiner. The takeover battle lasted six months, during which time the club declined palpably. As the author of this book was a participant, although hopefully unbiased, it is better to relate the story in the words of Emily Bell, Business Editor of *The Observer*, who wrote this story for her newspaper in February 1997, a week before the take-over finally went through.

DEEP IN THE FOREST SOMETHING STIRRED

"How dare you try and give me your money, how dare you – it's a disgrace!" The grey-haired lady in the Nottingham Forest tracksuit berated a bemused Irving Scholar in the shareholder's lounge at the football club's City Ground stadium.

"I'm not offering you cash," replied Scholar, coolly. "I'm offering you *shares*." It was a subtlety lost on the angry stockholder. Scholar is possibly more famous than any other football executive. He became the first man to take a football club to the City when he floated Tottenham Hotspur in 1983.

But even in the darkest days of Tottenham's financial crisis Scholar cannot have witnessed anything as bizarre as this – a shareholder upbraiding him for daring to make an offer for her shares.

But this was no ordinary takeover; it was part of the five-month ongoing battle for control of Nottingham Forest Football Club.

It is a saga that would not disgrace the best television soap opera; its main participants, many of them experienced business people, say they have seen nothing like it before.

A revolving carousel of bidders – characters as colourful as the language in the manager's dugout – have fought a dirty war. A war that, back at the beginning of October, the Forest board promised "would be resolved in three or four days".

Forest might be the favourite club of Chancellor Kenneth Clarke, but even he would have been hard-pressed to sort out the antiquated economy of The City Ground.

The background of this gripping but damaging saga is one of traditional football club values meeting the new financial realities of the modern game. Every week another football club announces that it is seeking a stock market listing, transfer fees are smashing all previous records, and even mediocre players are entering the realms of the super-rich on the promise of that great cash cow – pay-TV – yielding billions of pounds for the game.

But Forest, now in its 132nd year, remained touchingly unchanged. The club by the Trent was still proud of its status as a "club", run by a seven-man unpaid board, all of whom have jobs which take up the majority of their working

day. The real power in the club lies with its 209 shareholders – though only 203 votes are currently in use.

This almost masonic clique is made up of some former directors, one or two former players and a wide selection of Nottingham citizens who share a passion for Forest. Issued at £1 each, the 209 shares are not transferable and cannot be sold or inherited – there is a waiting list for new shareholders.

So in its 132 years of existence, Nottingham Forest Football Club has received just £209 of capital investment.

This amateurish set-up may have a charming whiff of Roy of the Rovers about it, but it does not fit with the stringent financial demands of a Premier League club. As one potential investor put it: "I have seen better run gardening clubs." Another added that this was "a very scurrilous thing to say about gardening clubs".

These charming amateurs found themselves at the beginning of the 1996-97 season in dire need of new finance – a £5 million facility with NatWest Bank would not be sufficient to see them through the season.

Forest needed debt relief, they needed money for players and they needed the kind of cash that would stop the medium-sized club from falling out of the Premier League into the financial abyss that is Division One.

Investors had to be brought in and the club floated on the stock market – or even sold. But for this to happen the Articles of Association must be changed, and changing the Articles of Association required the approval of 75 per cent of the shareholders.

Accountant Price Waterhouse was brought in to advise on finding Forest financial salvation.

It was a Sunday in September, remembers Phil Soar, former Chief Executive of Blenheim Exhibitions. He and his wife were entertaining friends for lunch when the phone rang.

"Have you ever thought about buying Nottingham Forest?" said a voice at the end of the line. It was Lawrie Lewis, a Monaco-domiciled multi-millionaire with whom Soar shared a business past. They had worked together at Blenheim and, although Lewis's departure from the company was not a happy one, he had since rebuilt bridges with Soar.

The flamboyant Lewis, whose £55m fortune does not stop him flying in from the principality on a bargain basement Easyjet flight, had become intrigued by the financial opportunities in football. Encouraged by his old friend Chris Akers, now chief executive of Leeds United, Lewis had been sizing up the market.

He had also been chewing over the possibility of becoming a football entrepreneur with his near neighbour on the Côte d'Azur, Irving Scholar, a man whose own tax exile and difficult experiences with Tottenham has not dimmed his enthusiasm for the beautiful game.

When Lewis heard that Forest were looking for a white knight, Soar was the obvious man to call. Alongside his career as a publishing executive, Soar fitted in a hectic life as a football writer – compiling the official histories of Arsenal and Tottenham and the Illustrated Encyclopaedia of British Football, reputedly Britain's best-selling football book.

More importantly, Soar was born and raised in Nottingham and is an avid Forest fan. He also had the advantage of being in England rather than Monaco.

Scholar, Soar and Lewis may have quietly succeeded in winning round the Nottingham Forest board away from the rude gaze of the press if lottery lovely Anthea Turner had not intervened.

Turner had agreed to make a corporate video for Grant Bovey, the Midlands born video entrepreneur whose Watershed Pictures holds, among other things, the rights to the FA's image library. (Bovey was later to leave his wife for Turner in a highly public but short-lived romance).

More importantly, Bovey's brother was the next-door neighbour of the Forest chairman Fred Reacher. Through him Bovey had learned that the club was looking for outside investment. Bovey formulated a plan to present to the board: he would structure a flotation deal, extending the club's debt in the short term for a hopefully greater long-term pay-out.

To make the presentation an all-singing, all-dancing affair, Bovey booked a private room at Claridges in London to which he ferried all seven members of the Forest board. Over lunch they were treated to Bovey's corporate video – complete with Anthea Turner. It likened the flotation of a football club with winning the lottery. The board were impressed; one member went so far as to pass the video over to the *News of the World*, who splashed it on their back page that Sunday.

"My company makes hundreds of programmes and videos a year," muses an affable Bovey with the benefit of hindsight, "I now know that there, sitting under my nose, was my first and probably last chance to make a truly unbelievable TV documentary."

When Soar spotted Anthea wooing the Forest board with promises of untold riches, he alerted Scholar and Lewis to the fact that others seemed to be getting in on the act. In early October Soar travelled to Nottingham to set up a meeting for his consortium and the board. When the triumvirate eventually travelled to Nottingham, they were so nervous of the press blowing their cover, that the trip turned into something more like an episode from a Len Deighton novel than a business meeting.

The Forest board members had to meet at three separate locations an hour before the meeting; they were then phoned and given a fourth venue where they were to meet the consortium. But the element of surprise did not end there. "When the board were introduced to Scholar, their jaws literally dropped. They all recognised him and they were all amazed," says Soar.

The proposals, which involved Lewis putting some £10m into the club, with further plans to float at a later date, were well received, though one or two directors harboured some reservations about a Tottenham chairman as a new figurehead for Forest.

On 30 October, the club's board met a day ahead of its annual general meeting to discuss the bids. By this time a third and fourth party were emerging. One was a shadowy Indonesian group; the other was the appropriately named Nottingham Consortium, led by Sandy Anderson, boss of Derby-based Porterbrook Group, which made millions from rail leasing at the time of privatisation.

Forest fan Anderson's interest was ignited by an ad Price Waterhouse ran in the *Financial Times* looking for investors in the club. Anderson was on holiday abroad at the time, but one of his colleagues had cut it out for him. If Anderson had known at the time how many sleepless nights lay ahead of him – the phone ringing constantly as anxious Forest fans turned to him as something of a saviour – he might have been inclined to drop the cutting straight in the bin.

Instead he found himself at the centre of the "local consortium" along with Nottingham venture capitalist Nigel Doughty and the chief executive of the Cordiant (previously Saatchi) advertising group, Charlie Scott. Financially powerful, the group had the backing of most of Forest's supporters, who, as one close to the Nottingham Consortium put it, "could not bear to think of fans of other clubs running their club".

The Forest board agreed to meet and recommend a bid to table to the next shareholders meeting. The fateful date was 25 November – when Forest were at home to Blackburn Rovers. At 2:00 p.m. that day, Phil Soar was told that his consortium had the board's backing; by 5.15 p.m. it was Sandy Anderson's Nottingham Consortium that had snatched the recommendation.

What happened in the intervening two-and-three quarter hours was that Lewis, the money man in Soar's consortium, had taken exception to "golden share" clauses. These made certain guarantees, including the onerous proviso that 80 per cent of all transfer fees be ploughed back into the club. Lewis's outraged reaction was: "Who do they think they are – Margaret Thatcher?"

Scholar was away in the US and had been told the bid was in the bag. So when he tore off the fax a few hours later and learnt that Anderson had been recommended by the board, he paled with incredulity.

Meanwhile, Soar watched Forest draw 2-2 with Blackburn and went home sorrowfully to file his Nottingham Forest cuttings – which took him until 4:00 a.m. But by 7.30 a.m. the next day he had already received the first call of the day from a Forest director, suggesting that perhaps the board had been too hasty. By midday, four more directors had called expressing similar uncertainty.

Soar pointed out that his consortium had been counted out because of its refusal to accept the 'golden share' clauses.

'What clauses?' asked the directors. It turned out the board had not even seen the conditions of the deal they were recommending.

This offered Soar, Scholar and Lewis a way back. So did the structure of the Anderson bid, which would refinance the club but took the view that the shareholders, instead of being paid upfront, should only share in its success when the club was successfully floated or went into the black.

"The joke in Nottingham was that the Anderson bid had 97 per cent local support, but the 3 per cent it didn't have were the Nottingham Forest shareholders," says a rival bidder.

One of the Anderson consortium was even heard arguing in the shareholders' lounge with a club member – presumably not the track-suited old lady. "You paid a pound for your share and that, for the moment, is all it's worth," boomed the heated potential investor.

On 10 December the Scholar consortium was engaged in a presidential-style campaign on the streets of Nottingham. The bid still did not have official board backing, but it was raising the interest level of the shareholders and waging a more successful publicity campaign. Then disaster struck. On 18 December, one day before the official offer document to shareholders was to be finalised, Lewis had second thoughts. He didn't like the irrevocable nature of the £10m bid – and his dithering prompted a row with Scholar. Lewis could not commit. Soar 'phoned Lewis at 8.30 a.m. on 19 December. Was he in or out? 'Out.' Soar remembers: 'It was a very short phone conversation.'

It looked as though Anderson would go to shareholders at their extraordinary general meeting on 6 January unopposed and with the official backing of the board. To add spice, Lewis, having fallen out with Scholar, joined the Anderson bid. What could possibly go wrong now for the Nottingham Consortium?

Plenty, it seemed. In between 20 December and 6 January, Scholar and Soar scoured the country for potential new backers. By the morning of 6 January, they still had no extra money to take to shareholders but had set up a meeting at the Westbury Hotel with a promising prospect. By 1.30 p.m. they had secured the signatures of property tycoon and Saracens Rugby club owner Nigel Wray and another backer, successful and highly respected businessman Julian Markham.

At 3:00 p.m. Soar, Scholar and Wray caught the train to Nottingham and three hours later Soar was able to address the shareholders' meeting via a proxy share while Anderson and his partners waited meekly outside.

Vote down Anderson, hang on, we will get you a better deal, was the message. And even though Soar had nothing on paper and no money committed, the meeting swung against Anderson.

Anderson received 111 votes – 40 votes short of the necessary 75 per cent. He was beaten, and though the angry supporters railed at subsequent matches about the greed of shareholders who wouldn't back him, there was nothing to be done.

A new year, a new bidding round for Forest.

Re-enter Bovey, with his new backer – Lewis, who this time is pledging £25 million to the cause.

Enter also a man very much in the news, Albert Scardino, American Pulitzer Prize-winning journalist and husband of new Pearson chief executive Marjorie Scardino. On Scardino's team is Jonathan Barnett, agent to cricketer Brian Lara. Scardino's and Barnett's sons attend the same school; the two boys practise their fencing as the two fathers talk sports investments.

Barnett had links with Mercury Asset Management, which is backing the Scardino bid. Scardino himself is amused by the suggestion that he has garnered the backing of MAM, one of the most powerful venture capitalists in the country, only because of his wife's position: 'If I am meant to be a beard for my wife's company, it is the most ridiculous thing I have ever heard – if they are using this to pitch for business at Pearson, it's a fairly odd way of going about it. What sort of business do they think they are going to get?'

In the meantime Bovey was feeling optimistic about *his* bid. "On 29 January, when Forest were playing Coventry, Lewis and I went to meet the board. Lawrie spoke about putting up all the money for the bid and told the board 'that's one of the benefits of being very wealthy'. I'm glad the board heard it from him."

Twenty-four hours later, Bovey was sitting with Lewis and their lawyers going through the deal. But, says Bovey, when it came to signing on the dotted line, "Lawrie's hand actually began to shake". Lewis, not for the first, or even the second time, was out of the bid, taking Bovey with him.

At the end of four months, what is left is Scholar, Soar and Wray versus Scardino.

In an attempt to shake off the 'yank and the bank' label, Scardino, MAM and further investor Electra are trying to add local flavour to their venture capital deal. Sir David White, successful businessman, chairman of the Area Health Authority and Forest shareholder is now signed as chairman. Another local businessman, David Mansfield, has been signed up as a non-executive director.

He argues that he has remained in the background thus far because backing any bid which did not remove the current board "would be like turkeys voting for Christmas". But he is on the record as far back as two years ago warning that poor management was spelling disaster for the club.

Today both remaining consortia address the supporters club. Next Saturday, before the Aston Villa game, they will address the shareholders, and on Monday, 24 February, the shareholders will vote on the future of Nottingham Forest Football Club. So will that be it? "Don't bank on it," warns a weary observer.

There is already a move afoot from some shareholders to try to raise funds themselves to float the club. If this happens, and neither consortium gets 75 per cent of votes it needs, all parties go back to square one, except this time the bank will start insisting that players are sold to reduce the £7.5m overdraft.

And where will the extra cash come from to tide the club over? What about Bovey, or maybe Anderson? Stranger things have happened.

On 24 February, the shareholders voted 189 votes to seven in favour of the Bridgford bid. Albert Scardino's group, backed by financial giants Mercury Asset Management and Electra, had pulled out of the bidding two days earlier.

After 132 years of gentle change there was suddenly a completely new culture at the club. Things did not always go smoothly – when Linda Wray, wife of the new chairman of Nottingham Forest plc, came to her first game with Nina Gardiner, they were refused admittance to the board room. The previous board had maintained a strict 'men only' rule. This was just one of many outdated attitudes that was going to have to change if Nottingham Forest was to have any future at all. Interestingly, the combatants for the club have always maintained very good personal relations – Nigel Doughty, Sandy Anderson, Tim Farr (a director from 1997) and Grant Bovey being regular and welcome visitors.

On the field, the club was having perhaps its least memorable season ever. As related, after that superb 3-0 win at Coventry on the opening day of the season, Forest went another 16 games before winning again. Frank Clark departed just before Christmas, when Forest's cause seemed hopeless. Stuart Pearce took over as caretaker manager, and inspired five wins on the trot in January. Inevitably, Pearce won the Manager of the Month Award (in his first full month as a manager), and just as inevitably, it was the kiss of death. Forest – still with 16 League games to go – won only one more game all season. The crucial moment was on 5 April 1997 when Southampton, then bottom of the League and still four points behind Forest, came to The City Ground and won 3-1. It ultimately saved Southampton and spelled the death knell for Forest. In the end, Forest finished bottom with just six wins and 34 points. The problems appeared to be up front where Saunders, Campbell, Woan, Lee and Roy could only summon up 13 League goals among all five.

But, as Dave Bassett said in the summer, the real problem was in midfield. "It was like a knife through butter. We couldn't hold the ball in midfield, so we always started playing too deep. The forwards didn't have the midfield carry through to support them, so the ball kept going straight back to the defenders. And because the midfield didn't have the confidence that the forwards would hold the ball up, they hung back and invited the opposition to play in our half."

Stuart Pearce remained as caretaker until the end of the season's final game at Newcastle on May 11th, a game Forest lost 5-0. Pearce had said earlier that he would probably not take up the option of becoming a full time player manager and Dave Bassett, who had come in from Crystal Palace as general manager in February 1997, took over as manager at exactly 6:00 p.m. on the evening of that Newcastle game. It was not exactly an appealing prospect for Bassett.

Colin Cooper says that the Clough era really ended at this moment: "Frank and Stuart had both developed under Clough. They employed his methods. Dave Bassett is a very different manager. There is a lot more on tactics, a lot more on specifics and a lot more hard work. Particularly in defence. The Boss is a perfectionist in defensive situations. He'll repeat it time and time again until he's sure we've got it right. We're not really spectacular in defence – but we've got the second best record in the League in 1997-98. It makes a big difference – like all the goalkeeping work under Mike Kelly." Stuart Pearce's next game as a player was also to be at Newcastle – but this time as a Newcastle player. During the close season, Pearce asked whether Forest would release him if a Premiership club made him an offer. Forest, in recognition of his years of outstanding service, said they would and Pearce went to St James' Park on a free transfer. He is easily Forest's most capped player

The two most significant original organisers of the Bridgford Group, which eventually took over the club, were Irving Scholar (**right**) and Nina Gardiner (on the right of the left hand picture, celebrating on the day of the takeover with shareholder May Townsend).

– having appeared for England 76 times while a Forest player – and is one of only four Forest men ever to captain England.

In addition to Pearce, Jason Lee of pineapple hair fame, Bryan Roy, partner to Collymore, and Alf Inge Haaland were also to leave in the close season, and in came Andy Johnson from Norwich, Alan Rogers from Tranmere, Geoff Thomas from Wolves, Thierry Bonalair from Neuchatel, Marco Pascolo (the Swiss international) from Cagliari and, after the season began, the majestic and immensely popular Dave Beasant, at the time only the third choice keeper at Southampton.

Dave Bassett chose his training staff carefully. Bobby Houghton joined as assistant manager and rekindled an association with Forest which had begun when he had managed Malmo in the European Cup final of 1979. Mike Kelly arrived from Middlesbrough and was to take over the number two job when Bobby Houghton was offered the chance of managing the Chinese National team to the 2000 Olympics and the 2002 World Cup.

And the 1997-98 season was to be an outstanding one, kicking off with six consecutive competitive wins (four in the League and two in the League Cup), which was the first time Forest had ever managed this feat in the club's 120 years of competitive football.

Steve Stone, with a few fits and starts, gradually came back to fitness and the long League programme ensured that Bassett had to perm any selection from a high quality squad. Full-backs Des Lyttle and Alan Rogers were regulars, but the centre-backs were a permutation of Jon Olav Hjelde, Colin Cooper, Steve Chettle and Craig Armstrong. The midfield saw a mixing of Ian Woan, Thierry Bonalair, Steve Stone and Chris Bart-Williams as wing-backs, and Scot Gemmill, Andy Johnson, Geoff Thomas and Colin Cooper in the centre. Up front, Pierre van Hooijdonk and Kevin

Above: Des Lyttle and Graham Bolton, Marketing Director of Pinnacle Insurance, show off the new Forest shirt in 1997. Pinnacle became Forest's new sponsors that year, the first time for many years that the club's sponsor had not been a brewer. Pinnacle formed a very close relationship with the club, supporting it in numerous areas.

Left: Scot Gemmill shoots against Leeds United in 1997. Gemmill, son of Forest's League Championship hero Archie, was to go to the 1998 World Cup with Scotland and was the core of the midfield during the 1997-98 Championship winning season (John Sumpter).

Right: Pierre van Hooijdonk's "wrong side" free-kick against Port Vale in 1997-98, one of eight he scored during the season. Van Hooijdonk's 29 League goals made him the leading scorer in the country, the first time for 90 years that Forest had provided the country's top scorer (John Sumpter).

Above: Ian Woan takes a break from warming up to enter into debate with a linesman on the subtleties of the offside law *(John Sumpter)*.

Campbell established themselves early on and Dean Saunders, at 33 desperate for first team football, was allowed to go to Sheffield United without a fee. Steve Guinan and Ian Moore filled in whenever the front two were missing. Although it was the forwards that got the headlines, Scot Gemmill was the crucial pivot. He played deep, always making himself available for the short pass from the full-backs or centre-back.

Gemmill could carry the ball forward or pass it out to the backs or push it through accurately to Campbell and van Hooijdonk. He performed the vital roles of patrolling the edge of the area at corners and always being behind the play to pick up the loose balls. It is no coincidence that Forest's worst spell came after Gemmill had been injured at QPR. Van Hooijdonk, the club's record signing from Celtic at £3.5 million plus another £1 million depending on goals scored, was a revelation to the English leagues. Having taken some time to settle, he was soon leading the country's goal scoring lists and, by February, the club was willing him to stay there and become the first Forest player since Enoch West in 1908 to lead the whole country's goalscorers. In the end, he was to achieve exactly this with 29 League goals.

Van Hooijdonk is quite unlike any other player in the English game. He takes up positions all over the pitch, he is a tall man who far prefers the ball to feet, he plays behind the front man (making Campbell's role doubly important) and he runs with a stooping gait "reminiscent of a moose" as Neil Custis of *The Sun* described it. By mid season, Forest had taken on some of the characteristics of a rugby team, with free-kicks anything up to 45 yards out being seen as potential goalscoring opportunities. Van Hooijdonk's ability to hit free kicks from anywhere round and over the wall was starting to cause chaos in First Division defences and his free kick duel, in particular, with Andy Dibble of Middlesbrough was remarkable to behold. Perhaps the best of the lot was a "wrong side" free kick round the right hand side of the wall against Port Vale – an impossible goal. The turning points for the team were against Stockport on 20 December 1997, when Forest scored twice in the last ten minutes to win 2-1, and on 1 March 1998 against Middlesbrough in front of television and a 26,000 crowd when we saw the best game of the season. Doubts had been growing: van Hooijdonk had missed the previous two games, Sunderland had come through strongly with a statistically improbable run, and all of a sudden, third place looked a real possibility. Middlesbrough were top and had just beaten Liverpool 2-0 to reach the Coca Cola Cup final. They came to Nottingham confident of protecting their lead, but they were to be demolished in Forest's best performance of the season. Van Hooijdonk got two, Campbell and Cooper one apiece and Forest went back to the top with a 4-0 win.

Three days later, Sunderland came to The City Ground needing to win to stay in touch – and did so 3-0 by out-fighting Forest, legally and illegally, in midfield. Forest bounced back to the top with a 4-1 win at Crewe and a 3-0 defeat of Bury, both very encouraging because they were the sort of games Forest had been struggling with earlier in the season. Forest had now achieved as many points as they had needed to achieve promotion in 1994 and with nine games to go. At Birmingham the following week, Pierre van

Left: Alan Rogers at speed against QPR on 30 August 1997. Arriving from Tranmere in the summer, Rogers was the only member of the Forest squad to play in every game in 1997-98. He won England 'B' caps during the season and achieved the seemingly impossible by replacing Stuart Pearce in the affections of the fans. Chris Bart-Williams, who played ahead of him at number 11, says: "He's certainly ambitious. He'd knock the ball up to me and, before I could even control it, he'd be round the back and haring off up the wing for the return. I kept saying to him: 'I wish I was as confident as you are that my control is that good'." *(John Sumpter).*

Hooijdonk was at his sensational best. Forest were 1-0 down with six minutes to go. Then van Hooijdonk was fouled twenty yards out. He took the free kick himself. Ian Woan stood over the ball and offered a left-foot option around the side of the wall. "I thought it was a sensible move as the keeper couldn't be expecting it. Pierre gets a bit confident in situations like this and didn't even reply. It's a good job I'm not the sensitive sort." The ball whipped over the wall and into the far left-hand corner. It was Pierre's eighth goal from a free kick of the season. Three minutes later a short pass from Woan left Pierre free 25 yards out on the left. A curled shot found the far corner. From 0-1 to 2-1 in the last few minutes of an absolutely crucial game. Trevor Francis, the Birmingham manager, was philosophical. Speaking to Larry Lloyd after the game, Francis confessed that his team had spent the whole of the Friday morning working on how to defend against van Hooijdonk free-kicks. "And then he goes and does that. Makes you weep. If we had him, we'd be top of the League." Forest were. Karren Brady was less demonstrative. "I don't know why I watch sometimes. Where did you find him?" said the most notable of all football icons.

Ian Woan, as ever the club's wit, was rarely anything other than amusing about van Hooijdonk. "Pierre never gets told off," he commented after a training ground rollicking, "It's always 'Well done Pierre, great cross, good shot.' Even when he's substituted, it's 'Great Pierre, you sat down on the bench really well then!'" Woan, a quantity surveyor until the age of 22, has a rather more worldly view of life than many in the game.

Dave Bassett, always highly entertained by the Dutchman's unconventional approach to the game, his peers and the world in general, comments: "Pierre is certainly unusual. In the end, we told Bart (who takes all the corners) to stop aiming for him. If he was supposed to be at the near post, he'd be on the far post, if he was supposed to be on the far post he'd end up at right-back or somewhere. Bobby (Houghton) stopped telling him where to stand because he'd only go and stand somewhere else. You'd find Alan Rogers haring down the wing, knocking the ball across the six-yard box and you'd say 'Where's Pierre?' and he'd be in his own half. Great shot though – I'd say the best dead ball kicker in the country in 1998. Better than Beckham, certainly better than Bergkamp. Quite astonishing. Most players who score 30 or more goals get most of them from close range – but Pierre hardly scores any from close range. If he gets a free-kick, he waits until the ref's not looking and then moves the ball further away from the goal."

Kevin Campbell was, after a difficult 18

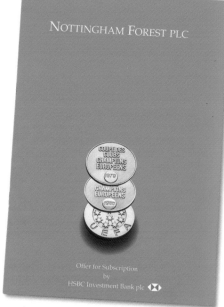

NOTTINGHAM FOREST PLC

Offer for Subscription by HSBC Investment Bank plc

Nottingham Forest plc floated on the Alternative Investment Market of the London Stock Exchange in October 1997 – the twentieth football club to float. By mid-1998, the company had approximately 4,500 separate shareholders.

Above: Colin Cooper's superb first goal against Bradford City on 6 December 1997 *(John Sumpter).*

months, an equal revelation. He had worked hard on a back problem, building up the muscles to the point where it no longer bothered him. With van Hooijdonk, they were the most prolific front duo in the country, Campbell scoring over 20 goals for the first time in his career. "When I first arrived, I don't think Kevin had many friends – only me, his wife and Chris Bart-Williams," says Dave Bassett. "But he worked hard, did well in pre-season and he's never looked back. In his Arsenal days I used to call him the Rottweiller, because of the way he used to frighten defenders."

Most of the seasoned observers around The City Ground rated Campbell's contribution as vital as van Hooijdonk's – their League goals being broadly equal at 23 to 29. "Kevin leads the line," says Larry Lloyd. "He's always there, he takes the knocks, he makes it possible for Pierre or Andy Johnson to get those balls on the edge of the area. He can run on to a long ball with his speed and strength, or play the target man and lay it back. He was always there – the outlet all season. And remember, between them they played 84 games out of 92 – a vital fact. You need continuity at this level. You need to stay free of injuries." An oddity was that Chris Bart-Williams was asked to play up front just twice – against Crewe and in the second half against Reading. He scored in both games.

The most important game in a season of consistently important games was probably the away match at Birmingham, won with Pierre van Hooijdonk's two strikes.

But the moment of truth was at home against

Reading on 26 April. It was Forest's penultimate game. Defeat would definitely send Reading down and Sunderland and Middlesbrough had put the pressure on by winning game after game, if only by the odd goal. Forest had to win, but Reading were the team which had contrived an impossible 3-3 draw earlier in the season after Dave Beasant was sent off (the referee later admitted he was wrong and the sending off was deleted from the records, but it still cost Forest two valuable points). The crowd of 29,302 was the largest Forest had seen since the ground was converted to an all-seater stadium. The atmosphere was committed but tense. So were the team. Steve Stone said he was exhausted at half-time, but couldn't understand why. Reading, needing to win, didn't yield. Kevin Campbell went off with a hamstring, Steve Chettle went off with a recurrent back injury. With seven minutes to go, Reading substitute Paul Brayson hit the post. The ball bounced lazily back across the goal and Dave Beasant did well not to deflect it into his own net. There were no Reading players following up and the ball bounced away to safety. "Well left," yelled Ian Woan, as the ball bounced over Beasant's prostrate body. Everyone sat and thought "How can we cope with another seven days". The referee signalled the end of normal time with four minutes of injury time to play. Ian Woan ran to him and argued: "There's at least 10 minutes left ref." Then, seconds later, Chris Bart-Williams picked up a loose ball in the area, pulled to his left, neutralised two defenders and then suddenly whipped the ball left footed into the far corner.

Ian Woan ran to the referee again: "How long ref? It can't be more than two minutes!" The referee played seven nail-biting minutes after Bart-William's goal, but the score stayed 1-0. Forest had 93 points. To all intents and purposes they were there. It had been a one-off season, never seen before and never to be repeated. Previously, the most points *ever* scored by a team which had not been automatically promoted in any division of the League, ever, had been 88 by Portsmouth in 1991-92. This was also a record under the two points system, and was also the all-time record for a non-promoted club. And yet the First Division in 1997-98 was to see *four* clubs exceed this number. It was an appalling Division to be trapped within – the hardest to get out of in the whole history of English football.

After the Reading game, Forest had 93 points but, as Dave Bassett said, "We still don't know whether we're promoted – it's ridiculous!" Both Sunderland and Middlesbrough could theoretically have overhauled Forest, and both had mid-week games. Two days after Reading, Sunderland went to Ipswich for the game which they knew would define their season. Colin Cooper was at home watching it on television: "Ipswich scored and the 'phone went straight away. Ian Woan – he was running around his house screaming. Then Ipswich missed a penalty. I told Ian not to call me again and slumped down, convinced it was all going to go wrong. But then, three minutes later, Alex Mathie got Ipswich's second, and the 'phone went again. I couldn't get him off the line." 2-0 to Ipswich and Forest were promoted. The following night, Middlesbrough were at home to Wolves, who had not scored away from home since the beginning of January. After six minutes, Wolves broke their duck and Middlesbrough could only get one in reply. 1-1 and two points dropped. After four impossibly tense days and three impossibly tense games involving not only themselves but also Middlesbrough and Sunderland, Forest were confirmed as champions. The following Sunday's 1-1 draw at West Brom was simply a celebration. A few days later, Colin Cooper finally got his hands on the Championship trophy. "I had always wanted this – I'd remembered going up with Stuart when we were promoted and wanting to do this for Nottingham. Being vice-captain to Stuart was always a double-edged sword. As the crowd saw me leading the team out they would always groan – knowing Stuart was injured. A bit hard to take sometimes."

The performance of the defence was also to prove vital. Only once did they concede more than one goal in consecutive games, and there were no fewer than 22 League clean-sheets. Marco Pascolo had been injured in the 3-1 defeat by Manchester City on 3 September, and Dave Bassett went straight to Southampton for his old

Wimbledon keeper, Dave Beasant. Beasant played for the rest of the season and hardly conceded a goal that the club thought was preventable. Dave Beasant said as the season ended: "Football never ceases to amaze me. There I was in Southampton reserves – then all of a sudden Forest come along and I've got a Championship medal. The most annoying thing was that people always remember my two televised mistakes for Chelsea and Southampton – but not all the good things. The errors were shown live – but all the games over 20 years haven't been." Nowadays, Dave Beasant's most memorable moment is being shown dozens of times a week. In 1988 he became the first goalkeeper to save a penalty in an FA Cup final and BT have featured the moment in a famous advertisement. "John Aldridge had scored 11 penalties that season and I got them all on video. I knew he preferred to go right – and he did. The problem is that my sons don't take it

seriously. They don't remember the game and the only thing they seem to believe worth commenting on is that my haircut was terrible."

Forest's only defensive weak link was Charlton who scored eight goals in two games at The Valley in League and Cup. The final run-in was to be crucial – of the final 17 games, Forest won 11 and drew four – 37 points from 17 games. Middlesbrough and Sunderland both had superb runs but, in the end, they couldn't keep up. The whole division set statistical records. Forest got 94 points, Middlesbrough 91, Sunderland 90 and Charlton 88. Sunderland were to record the highest number of points ever achieved by a club not promoted, were to score four goals in the play-off final, were to score six consecutive penalties in the shoot out – and still not be promoted. It had been a statistical freak as well as the most competitive division in the history of League football. And Forest had won it.

For Dave Bassett, it was also a record, as he became the first manager ever to win promotion on seven different occasions. He had started his managerial career under Alan Batsford at Wimbledon in 1980 (Batsford is now a scout at Forest, also reunited with keeper Dave Beasant) and had taken them from Fourth to First with an extra relegation and promotion on the way, and had also taken

Sheffield United from the old Third Division to the top. "Well, it was a little different with Wimbledon. I once told a player I'd stab him if he didn't get out there and play. I doubt if I could do that with Pierre today. I know I'm not a fashionable manager. I'm not one of those who's regarded as a whizz-kid or someone who can handle the big stuff. I'm the sort of guy who they call for when they're in the mire. When I came here, the fans weren't convinced – they still thought 'long ball', though that was ten years ago and the team had just laid down and accepted relegation. That was dreadful. But we're a better team now and who knows what next season will bring? When my wife, Christine, watched Manchester United and Leeds the day after we finished the season, she suddenly turned round to me and said:

Bartman and Reading: 26 April 1998 was to see perhaps the tensest game ever played at The City Ground. Forest needed to win to be virtually sure of promotion, defeat for Reading would send them down to Division Two. The crowd was 29,302, the largest the club had ever seen since going all-seater. This was a far cry from 70 years earlier when a Second Division game against Reading on 29 March 1928 set a record *low* attendance of just 2,572. After 88 minutes, with nails bitten down to the quick, Chris Bart-Williams slipped the defence and shot left-footed into the corner. Reading were relegated, Forest had 93 points but, as manager Dave Bassett (**top right**) said: "It's amazing – we still don't know whether we are promoted!" For Bassett, it was eventually to be a record breaking seventh promotion (four with Wimbledon, two with Sheffield United). No one has ever managed more promoted sides. The players, nonetheless, felt justified in celebrating in the dressing room afterwards. Thierry Bonalair, captain Colin Cooper and Andy Johnson share a quiet moment. "It's surprising to see Andy with a drink in his hands" said Dave Beasant afterwards, "he's usually among the more sober and reflective members of the squad." Sunderland were defeated by Ipswich two days later and Middlesbrough drew with Wolves the following night. Forest were champions.

"Oh dear me, we've got to play them next season." Nigel Wray, Chairman of Nottingham Forest plc, didn't have any doubts. "Dave Bassett has been absolutely right for Nottingham Forest. An excellent manager and an excellent man. I don't know what we'll do in the Premier League, but the last two occasions Forest were promoted, everyone said we'd come straight back down. We finished first and third." Football is nothing if not an unpredictable business.

One hundred and thirty three years is a long time. The 15 young men that formed Nottingham Forest in 1865 would probably have been grandfathers before they saw a motor car. Few of them could have lived even to know of the First World War. Their Nottingham was a small town – the size of a Mansfield or a Chesterfield today. They could not have possibly imagined their offspring playing for such great prizes in Munich, Madrid or Tokyo. The

German state did not even exist in 1865. Munich was the capital of Bavaria. Tokyo was called Edo, and Kyoto was the capital of Japan. The process by which this small group of men created such a progeny, while hundreds of similar groups in Nottingham did not, is a mystery. Certain names stand out – Walter Lymbery, Harry Radford, Grenville Morris, Billy Walker, Jack Burkitt, John Robertson, but, above all others, Brian Clough. A genius appearing down the A52, surely the greatest football manager of all time. And the men who, in two years and three months, turned a team which was eighth in the Second Division into European Champions. A story so incredible we still don't really believe it today.

When they reached their first semi-final of the Football Association Cup in 1879 they didn't even have a ground. When they finished third in the Second Division in 1977 only five clubs had ever been promoted with fewer points. When they won a second European Cup, they had won their own League only once. And when they went to Bolton on 25 November 1978, they had not lost a game for a whole year. They won the European Cup undefeated. How marvellous to say that, for at least one moment in time, Nottingham Forest could rightly claim to be the greatest football team in the world.

Left: The Captain and his Championship Trophy, on the Council House Balcony on 7 May 1998.

Below: The Championship winning squad of 1998. Back row: Des Lyttle, Paul McGregor, Kevin Campbell, Geoff Thomas, Jon Hjelde, Andy Johnson, Steve Stone. Centre: John Haselden, Craig Armstrong, Steve Chettle, Marco Pascolo, Dave Beasant, Mark Crossley, Steve Guinan, Ian Moore, Liam O'Kane, Mike Kelly. Seated: Scot Gemmill, Thierry Bonalair, Pierre van Hooijdonk, Colin Cooper, Dave Bassett, Chris Bart-Williams, Ian Woan, Alan Rogers. The rather unusual bend in the League Championship Trophy can be explained by it having been dropped by a certain forward **(inset)** at a celebration the night before *(John Sumpter).*

The Complete Forest Record

1865 - 1998

The largest crowd ever to watch Forest in a League match was at Old Trafford for Manchester United's first League game after the Munich air crash.

ATTENDANCE RECORDS FOR NOTTINGHAM FOREST

Date	Ground	Opponents	Competition	Score	Crowd
28 Feb 1868	The Forest	Sheffield Norfolk	Friendly	0-1	1,000
23 Dec 1873	Trent Bridge	Royal Engineers	Friendly	1-2	2,500
10 Feb 1880	Trent Bridge	Scottish Canadians	Friendly	0-2	5,500
1 Dec 1883	Parkside Ground	Notts County	FA Cup 2	0-3	12,000
13 Feb 1892	Town Ground	Preston North End	FA Cup 3	2-0	14,500
24 Feb 1894	Town Ground	Notts County	FA Cup 3	1-1	15,000
28 Jan 1899	The City Ground	Aston Villa	FA Cup 1	2-1	32,070
25 Feb 1899	The City Ground	Sheffield United	FA Cup 3	0-1	33,500
26 Dec 1911	The City Ground	Derby County	Division 2	1-3	35,000
1 Feb 1928	The City Ground	Derby County	FA Cup 4	2-0	35,625
1 Mar 1930	The City Ground	Sheffield Wednesday	FA Cup 6	2-2	44,166
12 Oct 1957	The City Ground	Manchester United	Division 1	1-2	47,804
28 Oct 1967	The City Ground	Manchester United	Division 1	3-1	49,946

Largest attendance for any Forest game

2 May 1959	Wembley	Luton Town	FA Cup final	2-1	100,000
18 Mar 1978	Wembley	Liverpool	League Cup final	0-0	100,000
17 Mar 1979	Wembley	Southampton	League Cup final	3-2	100,000
15 Mar 1980	Wembley	Wolverhampton Wanderers	League Cup final	0-1	100,000

Largest away ground attendance for any Forest game

22 Feb 1958	Old Trafford	Manchester United*	Division 1	1-1	66,346
5 Feb 1980	Nou Camp	Barcelona	European Super Cup	1-1	90,000
7 Dec 1983	Celtic Park	Glasgow Celtic	UEFA Cup	2-1	66,938

* first League game after Munich air crash

FULL INTERNATIONAL CAPS WHILST WITH NOTTINGHAM FOREST

Player	Country	Era	Caps	Player	Country	Era	Caps
Arthur Goodyer	England	1879	1	Miah Dennehy	R. Ireland	1973-74	6
Samuel Widdowson	England	1880	1	Viv Anderson	England	1978-84	11
John Sands	England	1880	1	Kenny Burns	Scotland	1978-81	12
Ernest Luntley	England	1880	2	Archie Gemmill	Scotland	1978-79	11
Tommy Danks	England	1885	1	John Robertson	Scotland	1978-82	26
John Leighton	England	1886	1	Peter Shilton	England	1978-82	19
Frank Burton	England	1889	1	Tony Woodcock	England	1978-79	6
Tinsley Lindley	England	1889-91	4	Trevor Francis	England	1979-81	10
Albert Smith	England	1891-93	3	Frank Gray	Scotland	1979-81	7
Chas Richards	England	1898	1	Garry Birtles	England	1980	3
Frank Forman	England	1898-1903	9	Larry Lloyd	England	1980	1
Fred Forman	England	1899	3	Alan Davidson	Australia	1985	5
Grenville Morris	Wales	1899-1912	16	Peter Davenport	England	1985	1
James Iremonger	England	1901-02	2	David Campbell	N. Ireland	1986-87	7
John Calvey	England	1902	1	Gary Fleming	N. Ireland	1986-89	9
Albert Jones	Wales	1905	1	Kjetyl Osvold	Norway	1987	7
Harry Linacre	England	1905	2	Stuart Pearce	England	1987-97	76
Ernest Hughes	Wales	1906-11	9	Neil Webb	England	1987-89	18
Arthur Green	Wales	1907-08	2	Stephen Hodge	England	1988-91	9
John Hanna	Ireland	1912	2	Des Walker	England	1989-94	40
Paddy Nelis	N. Ireland	1922	1	Nigel Clough	England	1989-93	11
Harold Jones	England	1923	1	Thorvaldur Orlygsson	Iceland	1989-93	16
Fred Morgan	N. Ireland	1924-28	6	Gary Charles	England	1991	2
Charlie Jones	Wales	1926-28	4	Roy Keane	R. Ireland	1991-93	16
Alf Spouncer	England	1926	1	Kingsley Black	N. Ireland	1991-94	12
Jimmy Chambers	N. Ireland	1931	3	Scott Gemmill	Scotland	1991-	13
Thomas Graham	England	1931	2	Alfie Haaland	Norway	1993-97	21
David Martin	N. Ireland	1936-38	4	Lars Bohinen	Norway	1993-95	19
Noel Kelly	R. Ireland	1954	1	David Phillips	Wales	1994-97	15
Stuart Imlach	Scotland	1958	4	Tommy Wright	N. Ireland	1994-97	8
Fay Coyle	N. Ireland	1958	1	Bryan Roy	Netherlands	1994-95	7
Alan Hinton	England	1964	2	Stan Collymore	England	1995	2
Frank Wignall	England	1964	2	Colin Cooper	England	1995-	2
Terry Hennessey	Wales	1965-69	15	Dean Saunders	Wales	1996-97	9
Ronnie Rees	Wales	1969-71	16	Steve Stone	England	1996-	8
Ian Storey-Moore	England	1970	1	Alan Fettis	N. Ireland	1996-97	5
Peter Cormack	Scotland	1970-71	5	Mark Crossley	Wales	1997-	1
Tommy Jackson	N. Ireland	1970-75	19	Nikola Jerkan	Croatia	1997-	8
Liam O'Kane	N. Ireland	1970-75	20	Pierre van Hooijdonk	Netherlands	1997-	14
Martin O'Neill	N. Ireland	1972-80	36	*Caps correct to 1 August 1998*			

FA CUP SEMI-FINALS HOSTED BY NOTTINGHAM FOREST

26 March 1896 (replay)
Sheffield Wed. 3 Bolton 1

18 March 1899
Sheffield Utd. 2 Liverpool 2

6 April 1901
Sheffield Utd. 2 A. Villa 2

27 March 1902
Sheffield Utd. 1 Derby 0

29 March 1905
A. Villa 2 Everton 1

23 March 1961 (replay)
Leicester 0 Sheffield Utd. 0

31 March 1965 (replay)
Leeds 1 Man. United 0

Below: Action from the 1905 FA Cup semi-final between Aston Villa and Everton at The City Ground.

FA CUP QUARTER-FINALS CONTESTED BY NOTTINGHAM FOREST

Date	Result	Home Team	Score	Away Team	Score	Notes
1879	W	Nottingham Forest	2	Oxford University	1	(At The Oval)
1880	D/W	Nottingham Forest	2	Sheffield	2	(Last 10/Sheffield disqualified)
1885	W	Nottingham Forest	2	Old Etonians	0	(At The Oval)
1891	L	Sunderland	4	Nottingham Forest	0	
1892	W	Nottingham Forest	2	Preston North End	0	
1894	L	Nottingham Forest	1:1	Notts County	1:4	
1895	L	Aston Villa	6	Nottingham Forest	2	
1897	L	Nottingham Forest	1:0	Liverpool	1:1	
1898	W	WBA	2	Nottingham Forest	3	
1899	L	Nottingham Forest	0	Sheffield United	1	
1900	W	Preston North End	0:0	Nottingham Forest	0:1	
1902	W	Nottingham Forest	2	Stoke	0	
1909	L	Derby County	3	Nottingham Forest	0	
1926	L	Nottingham Forest	2:0:0	Bolton Wanderers	2:0:1	(Third game at Old Trafford)
1928	L	Sheffield United	3	Nottingham Forest	0	
1930	L	Nottingham Forest	2:1	Sheffield Wednesday	2:3	
1957	L	Birmingham City	0:1	Nottingham Forest	0:0	
1959	W	Nottingham Forest	2	Bolton Wanderers	1	
1963	L	Nottingham Forest	1:3:0	Southampton	1:3:5	(Third game at White Hart Lane)
1967	W	Nottingham Forest	3	Everton	2	
1974	L	Newcastle United	4:0:1	Nottingham Forest	3:0:0	(Second & third games at Goodison)
1978	L	WBA	2	Nottingham Forest	0	
1981	L	Nottingham Forest	3:0	Ipswich Town	3:1	
1988	W	Arsenal	1	Nottingham Forest	2	
1989	W	Manchester United	0	Nottingham Forest	1	
1991	W	Norwich City	0	Nottingham Forest	1	
1996	L	Nottingham Forest	0	Aston Villa	1	

Record: Ties contested 27, Ties Won 12, Ties Lost 15

Above: Bob McKinlay's FA Cup winners medal from 1959 and a runners-up medal from Forest's 1991 final with Tottenham.

Below: A medal presented to Forest's directors *before* the 1989 FA Cup semi-final with Liverpool. While such medals are not uncommon, very few were retained after the Hillsborough disaster.

FA CUP SEMI-FINALS CONTESTED BY NOTTINGHAM FOREST

Date	Result	Score				Notes
22 March 1879	L	Nottingham Forest	1	Old Etonians	2	The Oval
27 March 1880	L	Nottingham Forest	0	Oxford University	1	The Oval
21 Feb 1885	D	Nottingham Forest	1	Queen's Park	1	Derby Racecourse
24 March 1885	L	Nottingham Forest	0	Queen's Park	3	Merchiston Castle School, Edinburgh
27 Feb 1892	D	Nottingham Forest	1	WBA	1	Molineux
5 March 1892	D	Nottingham Forest	0	WBA	0	Molineux
9 March 1892	L	Nottingham Forest	2	WBA	6	Derby Cricket Ground
19 March 1898	D	Nottingham Forest	1	Southampton	1	Bramall Lane
24 March 1898	W	Nottingham Forest	2	Southampton	0	Crystal Palace
24 March 1900	D	Nottingham Forest	1	Bury	1	Stoke
28 March 1900	L	Nottingham Forest	2	Bury	3	Bramall Lane
15 March 1902	L	Nottingham Forest	1	Southampton	3	White Hart Lane
14 March 1959	W	Nottingham Forest	1	Aston Villa	0	Hillsborough
29 April 1967	L	Nottingham Forest	1	Tottenham Hotspur	2	Hillsborough
9 April 1988	L	Nottingham Forest	1	Liverpool	2	Hillsborough
15 April 1989	A	Nottingham Forest	0	Liverpool	0	Hillsborough Disaster
7 May 1989	L	Nottingham Forest	1	Liverpool	3	Old Trafford
14 April 1991	W	Nottingham Forest	4	West Ham United	0	Villa Park

Record: Games 18, Won 3, Drawn 5, Lost 9, Abandoned 1, For 20, Against 29
Locations: Sheffield 6, London 4, Derby 2, Wolverhampton 2, Birmingham 1, Edinburgh 1, Manchester 1, Stoke 1

The greatest Nottingham Forest team ever?

Peter Shilton 97%

Viv Anderson 96%

Des Walker 83%

Kenny Burns 79%

Stuart Pearce 95%

Martin O'Neill 41%

Roy Keane 52%

Archie Gemmill 71%

Ian Storey-Moore 54%

Trevor Francis 58%

John Robertson 99%

SUBSTITUTES
(based on five men on the bench)

Goalkeeper:	**Peter Grummitt (2%)**
Defender:	**Larry Lloyd (51%)**
Midfield:	**Steve Stone (37%)**
Forwards:	**Tony Woodcock (46%)**
	Stan Collymore (38%)

In 1997 and 1998 we asked the supporters of Nottingham Forest to name their greatest ever team.

We received hundreds of replies and this page is a summary of all their opinions. The number after the name shows the percentage of the responses that mentioned the particular player (in other words, 58 out of every 100 replies included Trevor Francis in their greatest team). Four players – Shilton, Anderson, Pearce and Robertson – were selected by almost every one of the hundreds of responses. Only three people did not name John Robertson in their greatest ever team!

In all, only 30 players were mentioned by more than 10% of supporters. Apart from the players mentioned here, the favoured defenders were Terry Hennessey (25%), Bobby McKinlay (17%) and Colin Cooper (15%). In midfield, the other favoured players were Nigel Clough (29%), Steve Hodge (25%), John McGovern (21%), Henry Newton (20%), Johnny Metgod (18%), Ian Bowyer (18%) and Neil Webb (12%). The other forwards were Joe Baker (30%), Garry Birtles (24%), Peter Withe (17%), Duncan McKenzie (14%) and Pierre van Hooijdonk (12%).

It is perhaps no surprise that no fewer than nine of the European Cup winning teams are included in the first team squad of 16. Nonetheless, it is interesting that only one (Bobby McKinlay) of the 30 players who achieved more than 10% of the votes played for Forest before the 1960s. This is obviously a reflection of the average age of the respondents – you would need to be nearly 50 to remember the Cup winning team of 1959. Nonetheless, it is essential to add that any observer who could have bridged the generations would surely have considered players such as Frank Forman, Tinsley Lindley, Grenville Morris, Charlie Jones and Wally Ardron as members of this select band.

Each respondent was also asked to name their three favourite matches. The percentage of votes shows the number who mentioned that game as one of their three favourites (in other words 38 out of every 100 voters included Forest versus Everton).

The list of favourite matches is remarkable for a club which has won two European Cups, in that the two European Cup finals rank only second and fourth. Even more surprising is that two of the top seven matches are the same tie - the home and away legs against Cologne in the semi-final of 1979. If they were treated as a single game, they would come first, and the dramatic 3-3 draw at The City Ground is the only one of the top 10 that Forest did not win. There are some surprising omissions – Forest's FA Cup final win against Luton features only at 16th in the final lists and no other game prior to 1967 received any worthwhile numbers of votes. This is obviously a reflection (in part) of the age profile of supporters and the obvious point that a voter would need to be nearly 50 to have any memory of Luton in 1959. Indeed 8 of the top 10 fall between 17 December 1977 and 28 May 1980. All the more remarkable, then, that the most memorable game in the history of Nottingham Forest should date from 1967 and should win this contest by such a clear margin as to be beyond dispute. The quarter-final of 1967 is covered at great length in the book.

Top ten favourite Nottingham Forest matches

1 Forest 3 Everton 2

FA Cup quarter final, 8 April 1967

38%

2 Forest 1 Malmo 0

European Cup final, 30 May 1979

29%

3 Forest 2 Liverpool 0

European Cup first round, 13 Sept 1978

28%

4 Forest 1 Hamburg 0

European Cup final, 28 May 1980

27%

5 Forest 3 1FC Cologne 3

European Cup semi final, 11 April 1979

24%

6 Manchester United 0 Forest 4

First Division, 17 Dec 1977

22%

7 1FC Cologne 0 Forest 1

European Cup semi final, 25 April 1979

15%

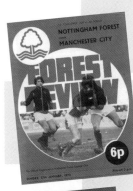

8 Forest 4 Manchester City 1

FA Cup fourth round, 27 Jan 1974

15%

9 Forest 1 Liverpool 0

League Cup final replay, 22 March 1978

14%

10 Forest 3 Southampton 2

League Cup final, 17 March 1979

9%

Notes on Forest's Season-by-Season Records

Nottingham Forest are one of the oldest clubs in the country and, when they were founded in 1865, there was no such thing as a fixture list because there was no-one to play against. In the early days, most games were just between teams from within the club and friends (Singles versus Married, Red versus Blue etc) but it was inevitable that Forest's first official game would be against Notts County.

Forest had no real fixture list for their first six or seven seasons, but by the 1870s there was a decent group of teams from Nottingham, Sheffield and Derby who were able to play each other regularly. The results included here have all been verified with reference to the various Nottingham newspapers of the time. There are one or two occasions when the final score is either not known or is disputed, and these are noted in these records. We have included all the games for which Forest are known to have put out a first class team, although many friendlies and games in leagues other than the Football League and Football Alliance would have included at least some reserve players.

Goalscorers are a source of inevitable discrepancies, particularly in what constitutes an own goal. Before 1939, goalscorers were sometimes not recorded at all by newspapers and most of the official Forest records were destroyed in the fire of 1968. We have tried to be as accurate as is now possible but there are occasions where, for instance, appearances or goals do not add up to the required totals and there is no way of correcting the figures. Own goals are taken to be occasions when, without the intervention of the defending player, the shot would not have entered the goal.

In recent seasons, substitutes have added a further complication. Our rule has been to include a substitute as having made an appearance only if he came onto the field. The appearances and goals figures at the end of each season apply only to Football League fixtures, unless otherwise stated. Since 1994, Premier League players have worn squad rather than positional numbers on their backs and the player number given is solely to assist the reader in judging where the players performed on the field.

For the record, Forest's All Time Football/Premier League record, solely on a 2-point basis, up until the end of the 1997-98 season is as follows:

	P	W	D	L	F	A	Pts
Home	1906	975	466	465	3366	2139	2416
Away	1906	467	487	952	2259	3395	1421
Total	3812	1442	953	1417	5625	5534	3837

The 2 point / 3 point system makes an analysis of average points a little meaningless, but on purely a 2 points basis, Forest have achieved 1.0066 points per game, a little better than average. They have scored an average of 1.4756 goals per game and have conceded an average 1.4517 goals per game.

In terms of total points scored solely in the First/Premier Division since 1888, Forest rank sixteenth of all English clubs (Everton are first). In terms of total points scored in all Divisions of the Leagues since 1888, Forest currently rank 20th. This is not necessarily very meaningful as 60 points in the First Division is clearly superior to 70 points in the Second (Liverpool rank first in terms of total points recorded). In terms of goals scored in all League games, Forest currently rank 22nd of all clubs (Aston Villa are first).

ABBREVIATIONS USED IN SEASON-BY-SEASON RECORDS

AIC	Anglo Italian Cup
All	Football Alliance
ASC	Anglo Scottish Cup
BasC	Bass Charity Cup
BCC	Birmingham Challenge Cup
BnkC	Bank Charity Cup
BurC	Burford Cup
CHC	Chesterfield Hospital Cup
CS	FA Charity Shield
EC	European Cup
ESC	European Super Cup
F	Friendly (inc. testimonials)
f	Final
FAC	FA Cup
FL	Football League
FLC	Football League Cup
FMC	Full Members Cup
ICFC	Inter Cities Fairs Cup
JTF	Jubilee Trust Fund
KCC	Kettering Challenge Cup
KHC	Kettering Hospital Cup
LHC	Lincoln Hospital Cup
MC	Midland Cup
MCT	Mercantile Credit Trophy
NCC	Nottinghamshire County Cup
Nf	Northern Final
NHC	Northampton Hospital Cup
NNHC	Norfolk & Norwich Hospital Cup
NSC	Notts Senior Cup
p	Preliminary Group
PHC	Peterborough Hospital Cup
PL	Premier League
q	Qualifying Round
r	Replay
r2	Second Replay
Sf	Southern Final
sf	Semi Final
TC	Texaco Cup
THC	Trowbridge Hospital Cup
UC	UEFA Cup
UCL	United Counties League
WC	War Cup
WCC	Wednesbury Challenge Cup (pre World War One)
WCC	World Club Championship (post World War Two)
WL	War League
WLC	War League Championship
WLP	War League Principal Tournament
WLS	War League Subsidiary Tournament
/1	First Leg
/2	Second Leg

1865-66

22 Mar	F	H	Notts Co	D 0-0
19 Apr	F	A	Notts Co	D 0-0

Final Record

	P	W	D	L	F	A
- Forest	2	0	2	0	0	0

1866-67

13 Dec	F	H	Notts Co	D 1-1
28 Feb	F	H	Notts Co	L 0-1

Final Record

	P	W	D	L	F	A
- Forest	2	0	1	1	1	2

1867-68

26 Dec	F	H	Sheffield Norfolk	D 0-0
28 Feb	F	A	Sheffield Norfolk	L 0-1

Final Record

	P	W	D	L	F	A
- Forest	2	0	1	1	0	1

1868-69

19 Dec	F	*	All comers	W
26 Dec	F	H	Sheffield Norfolk	D 0-0
16 Jan	F	A	Newark	D 0-0
13 Feb	F	A	Sheffield Norfolk	L
13 Mar	F	H	Sawley	W 2-0
20 Mar	F	A	Sawley	W 1-0

Final Record

	P	W	D	L	F	A	NR
- Forest	6	2	2	0	3	0	2

* at Meadows Ground

1869-70

6 Nov	F	H	Notts Co	D 0-0
13 Nov	F	H	Notts Co	L
18 Dec	F	A	Sawley	D 1-1
15 Jan	F	H	Sheffield Norfolk	L 0-3
5 Mar	F	H	Derby GS	W 5-0
12 Mar	F	A	Sheffield Norfolk	L 2-3
19 Mar	F	A	Derby GS	W 1-0
26 Mar	F	H	South Derbyshire	D 0-0

Final Record

	P	W	D	L	F	A	NR
- Forest	8	2	3	2	9	7	1

1870-71

5 Nov	F	H	Nottm Manufacturing	L 0-2
19 Nov	F	A	Ockbrook/Borrowash	*
26 Nov	F	A	Derby GS	W
3 Dec	F	H	St Andrews	W 2-0
17 Dec	F	H	Derby GS	W 2-0
11 Feb	F	A	Sheffield Norfolk	L 2-4
4 Mar	F	H	Sheffield Norfolk	Abnd
11 Mar	F	H	Notts Co	D 1-1

Final Record

	P	W	D	L	F	A	NR
- Forest	7	2	1	2	7	7	2

* played under different rules, no information available

1871-72

7 Nov	F	A	Ockbrook/Borrowash	D 1-1
20 Nov	F	H	Mansfield	W 1-0
4 Dec	F	H	Chesterfield	D 0-0
18 Dec	F	H	Derby GS	W 1-0
30 Dec	F	A	Combined Team*	L 1-2
13 Jan	F	A	Sheffield Norfolk	L 1-5
27 Jan	F	H	Ockbrook/Borrowash	W 3-0
10 Feb	F	A	Chesterfield	D 1-1
14 Feb	F	A	Notts Co	W 1-0
26 Feb	F	H	Notts Co	W 2-1
11 Mar	F	H	Sheffield Norfolk	W 1-0
18 Mar	F	A	Derby GS	L 0-5

Final Record

	P	W	D	L	F	A
- Forest	12	6	3	3	13	15

* Combined team from Town Club, Public Schools and Law Club

1872-73

2 Nov	F	H	Mansfield	D 0-0
16 Nov	F	H	Derby GS	D 1-1
23 Nov	F	H	Spondon School	D 0-0
30 Nov	F	A	Law Society	D 0-0
7 Dec	F	H	Notts Co	W 1-0
14 Dec	F	A	Stoke-on-Trent	D 0-0
4 Jan	F	A	Notts Co	D 0-0
18 Jan	F	A	Burton-on-Trent	D 1-1
1 Feb	F	'H	Stoke-on-Trent	W 3-0
8 Feb	F	A	Derby GS	D 0-0
15 Mar	F	H	Spondon School	L 0-1

Final Record

	P	W	D	L	F	A
- Forest	11	2	8	1	6	3

1873-74

1 Nov	F	A	Derby School	L 1-6
23 Dec	F	H	Royal Engineers	L 1-2
27 Dec	F	H	Notts Co	D 1-1
7 Feb	F	A	Notts Co	D 0-0
17 Jan	F	A	Sheffield Norfolk	L 1-7
28 Feb	F	H	Mansfield	W 3-1

Final Record

	P	W	D	L	F	A
- Forest	6	1	2	3	7	17

1874-75

31 Oct	F	A	Trent College	L 1-3
7 Nov	F	A	Derby Derwent	L 1-3
14 Nov	F	A	Notts Co	D 0-0
21 Nov	F	H	Trent College	W 1-0
5 Dec	F	A	Mr Cursham's Team*	D 0-0
21 Dec	F		Royal Engineers**	
16 Jan	F	A	Duffield	W 2-0
30 Jan	F	H	Mansfield	W 3-1
9 Feb	F	H	Notts Co	W 5-1
13 Feb	F	H	Derby Derwent	W 2-0
6 Mar	F	H	Duffield	W 4-0
20 Mar	F	H	Derby GS	W 1-0

Final Record

	P	W	D	L	F	A
- Forest	11	7	2	2	20	8

* consisted mainly of Notts Co players
** no match report found, possibly cancelled due to inclement weather

1875-76

13 Nov	F	H	Notts Co	W 2-1
18 Dec	F	H	Derby Derwent	W 3-0
8 Jan	F	H	Sheff Wed	L 0-5
5 Feb	F	A	Derby Derwent	W 2-0
12 Feb	F	A	Birmingham	*
29 Feb	F	A	Notts Co	L 0-1
11 Mar	F	H	Birmingham	D 0-0
18 Mar	F	A	Sheff Wed	L 1-9

Final Record

	P	W	D	L	F	A
- Forest	7	3	1	3	8	16

* no match report found, possibly cancelled due to inclement weather

1876-77

4 Nov	F	H	Birmingham	L 0-2
18 Nov	F	H	Notts Co	L 0-2
23 Dec	F	A	Coventry	W 3-0
26 Dec	F	H	Coventry	W 2-0
13 Jan	F	H	Sheff Wed	W 2-1
27 Jan	F	A	Sheff Wed	W 1-0
8 Feb	F	A	Notts Co	D 1-1
13 Feb	F	H	Sheff Wed	L 0-1
24 Feb	F	A	Birmingham	W 2-0

Final Record

	P	W	D	L	F	A
- Forest	9	5	1	3	11	7

1877-78

17 Nov	F	H	Birmingham	D 1-1
15 Dec	F	H	Herts Rangers	L 0-1
26 Jan	F	H	Sheff Wed	W 4-1
16 Feb	F	H	Glasgow Rangers	L 2-4
23 Feb	F	A	Birmingham	D 1-1
5 Mar	F	H	Sheff Wed	L 0-1
9 Mar	F	A	Birmingham	W 3-0
16 Mar	F	H	Stoke	W 2-1
6 Apr	F	H	Derby	W 1-0
20 Apr	F	A	Glasgow Rangers	L 0-2
22 Apr	F	A	Ayr Thistle	W 3-0

Final Record

	P	W	D	L	F	A
- Forest	11	5	2	4	17	12

1878-79

14 Oct	F	H	Stoke	W 2-1
21 Oct	F	H	Derby	D 0-0
26 Oct	F	H	Glasgow Rangers	L 0-2
7 Nov	F	A	Birmingham	W 3-1
16 Nov	FAC1	A	Notts Co	W 3-1
30 Nov	F	H	Chesterfield	W 4-0
7 Dec	F	A	Sheff Wed	L 0-1
21 Dec	FAC2	H	Sheffield	W 2-0
18 Jan	F	H	Edinburgh Univ	W 4-1
28 Jan	FAC3	A	Old Harrovians	W 2-0
8 Feb	F	A	Chesterfield	W 6-0
15 Feb	F	H	Birmingham	W 6-1
22 Feb	F	A	Derby	L 0-3
25 Feb	FAC4	A	Oxford Univ	W 2-1
8 Mar	F	H	Chesterfield	W 5-1
22 Mar	FACsf	*	Old Etonians	L 1-2
29 Mar	F	H	Chesterfield	W 2-1
12 Apr	F	A	Glasgow Rangers	L 0-3
19 Apr	F	A	Stoke	D 0-0

Final Record

	P	W	D	L	F	A
- Forest	19	12	2	5	42	19

* at Kennington Oval

1879-80

27 Sep	F	A	Local Clubs Team	W 6-0
4 Oct	F	H	Stoke	W 4-0
18 Oct	F	A	Darwen	W 3-1
25 Oct	F	H	Birmingham	W 6-0
1 Nov	F	H	Edinburgh Univ	W 6-1
8 Nov	FAC1	H	Notts Co	W 4-0
15 Nov	F	A	Birmingham	W 6-0
13 Dec	FAC2	A	Turton	W 6-0
27 Dec	F	H	Blackburn R	D 1-1
10 Jan	F	H	Wednesbury Strollers	W 4-0
17 Jan	F	H	Notts Co	W 7-1
24 Jan	F	H	Sheffield	W 3-2
31 Jan	FAC3	H	Blackburn R	W 6-0
7 Feb	F	H	Sheff Wed	W 2-0
10 Feb	F	H	Scottish Canadians	L 0-2
18 Feb	FAC4	H	Sheffield	D*2-2
21 Feb	F	A	Sheff Wed	L 0-1
28 Feb	F	H	Darwen	W 5-0
13 Mar	F	A	Stoke	L 1-3
27 Mar	FACsf	**	Oxford Univ	L 0-1
30 Mar	F	A	Edinburgh Univ	L 1-2
31 Mar	F	A	Blackburn R	L 1-5

Final Record

	P	W	D	L	F	A
- Forest	22	14	2	6	74	22

* Sheffield disqualified, refused to play extra time
** at Kennington Oval

1880-81

2 Oct	F	A	Aston Villa	L 0-4
9 Oct	F	A	Wednesbury Strollers	W 3-0
16 Oct	F	H	Notts Co	W 4-0
23 Oct	F	A	Darwen	D 4-4
30 Oct	F	H	Glasgow Rangers	W 2-1
13 Nov	F	H	Aston Villa	L 0-2
20 Nov	F	H	14 of Second Team	L 2-4
27 Nov	F	H	Second XI	unknown
4 Dec	FAC2	H	Aston Villa	L 1-2
9 Dec	F	H	Cambridge Univ	W 3-1
11 Dec	F	A	Glasgow Rangers	D 2-2
27 Dec	F	H	Blackburn R	L 0-4
1 Jan	F	A	Sheffield	L 1-2
8 Jan	F	H	Leics Rangers	W12-0
29 Jan	F	H	Darwen	W 3-0
12 Feb	F	H	South Derbyshire	W 2-0
19 Feb	F	H	Vale of Leven	W 2-0
27 Feb	F	H	Clapham Rovers	W 3-0
1 Mar	F	H	Sheffield	W 1-0
5 Mar	F	A	Notts Co	L 0-1
12 Mar	F	A	Blackburn R	D 3-3
19 Mar	F	A	South Derbyshire	D 2-2
2 Apr	WCC2	A	Elwells	W 4-0

Final Record

	P	W	D	L	F	A	NR
- Forest	22	11	4	7	54	32	1

Forest received a walkover in FAC1 after Caius College scratched

1881-82

29 Aug	F	A	Wollaton	W 10-1
3 Sep	F	A	Southwell	W 9-1
17 Sep	F	H	Brigg Britannia	W 6-0
24 Sep	F	A	Small Heath	W 2-1
1 Oct	F	H	Small Heath	W 3-2
7 Oct	F	A	Local Combined XI	W 4-1
15 Oct	F	H	Blackburn Olympic	W 3-0
22 Oct	F	A	Darwen	W 1-0
29 Oct	F	H	Glasgow Rangers	D 0-0
5 Nov	FAC1	A	Aston Villa	L 1-4
12 Nov	F	H	Walsall	W 8-3
3 Dec	F	H	Accrington	D 3-3
15 Dec	F	H	Camb Univ Wand	W 4-2
17 Dec	F	H	Notts Co	L 0-5
24 Dec	F	H	Blackburn R	L 0-2
31 Dec	F	H	Alexandra Athletic	W 1-0
21 Jan	F	H	Darwen	L 4-5
4 Feb	F	H	Wednesbury Strollers	W 13-0
11 Feb	F	A	Notts Co	W 2-1
4 Mar	F	H	Bolton W	W 2-1
11 Mar	F	H	Derby Town	W 4-0
22 Mar	F	A	Trent/Wand'rs comb	W 4-0
8 Apr	F	A	Accrington	W 5-3
10 Apr	F	A	Blackburn Olympic	W 4-1

Final Record

	P	W	D	L	F	A
- Forest	24	18	2	4	93	36

1882-83

23 Sep	F	A	Small Heath Alliance	W 4-0
30 Sep	F	A	Halliwell	L 1-3
7 Oct	F	H	Stoke	L 2-4
14 Oct	F	H	Blackburn Olympic	W 1-0
21 Oct	F	A	Blackburn R	L 0-6
11 Nov	F	A	Bolton W	L 1-9
18 Nov	F	A	Sheffield	W 5-1
25 Nov	WCC1	H	Wednesbury Old Ath	D 4-4
2 Dec	FAC2	H	Sheffield Heeley	W 7-2
26 Dec	F	H	Bolton W	W 3-1
27 Dec	F	H	Sheffield	L 0-5
6 Jan	FAC3	H	Sheff Wed	D 2-2
13 Jan	FAC3r	A	Sheff Wed	L 2-3
20 Jan	F	H	Notts Co	D 1-1
27 Jan	F	A	Clapham Rovers	W 2-1
3 Feb	F	H	Darwen	W 2-1
5 Feb	F	H	Blackburn R	D 0-0
17 Feb	F	H	Woverhampton	W 6-1
24 Feb	F	A	Stoke	W 7-2
10 Mar	WCC1r	*	Wednesbury Old Ath	W 3-1
24 Mar	F	A	Darwen	L 2-4
26 Mar	F	A	Stoke	W 8-2
7 Apr	F	A	Small Heath Alliance	W 2-0
14 Apr	WCC2	A	B'ham St George	W 2-0
19 May	WCCf	**	WBA	W 5-3

Final Record

	P	W	D	L	F	A
- Forest	25	14	4	7	72	56

* at Castle Ground ** at Perry Barr
Forest received a walkover in FAC1 after Brigg Britannia scratched

THE COMPLETE FOREST RECORD

1883-84

Date	Comp	Venue	Opponent	Result
22 Sep	F	H	Small Heath Alliance	W 3-2
13 Oct	F	H	Sheffield	W 9-1
20 Oct	F	H	Notts Co	D 0-0
25 Oct	WCC1	H	Wednesbury Strollers	W 9-2
27 Oct	F	H	Stoke	W 2-1
3 Nov	F	H	Nottingham Swifts	W 6-1
17 Nov	F	H	Sheffield Attercliffe	W 5-0
24 Nov	F	H	Dumbarton	L 2-3
1 Dec	FAC2	H	Sheffield Attercliffe	L 0-3
8 Dec	F	A	Darwen	W 8-0
15 Dec	NCC2	A	Notts Rangers	W 6-0
22 Dec	F	H	Blackburn R	D 2-2
26 Dec	F	A	Notts Co	L 1-5
7 Jan	F	A	Cambridge Univ	L 1-2
19 Jan	F	A	Sheffield Attercliffe	W 8-1
26 Jan	F	H	Walsall Swifts	D 1-1
2 Feb	F	A	Dumbarton	L 1-3
9 Feb	WCCsf	A	Wolves	W 2-0
16 Feb	NCCsf	A	Notts Olympic	W 4-0
23 Feb	F	A	Small Heath Alliance	L 2-3
8 Mar	F	H	Sheff Wed	L 0-2
22 Mar	NCCf	*	Notts Trent	D 1-1
29 Mar	F	A	Aston Villa	L 0-2
5 Apr	NCCfr	*	Notts Trent	W 5-0
- Apr	F	A	Wolves	W 1-0
- Apr	F	H	Lincoln	W 1-0
4 May	WCCf	**	Wednesbury Town	D 2-2
- May	WCCfr	**	Wednesbury Town	L 0-3

Final Record

	P	W	D	L	F	A
- Forest	28	14	5	9	82	40

* at Castle Ground ** at The Oval, Wednesbury

1884-85

Date	Comp	Venue	Opponent	Result
27 Sep	F	A	Stoke	L 4-6
4 Oct	F	H	Bolton Association	W 5-1
11 Oct	F	A	Lincoln C	W 4-2
18 Oct	F	A	Walsall Swifts	L 1-3
25 Oct	F	A	Blackburn R	L 1-3
8 Nov	FAC1	A*	Rotherham T	W 5-0
15 Nov	F	H	Sheff Wed	W 6-1
22 Nov	F	H	Sheffield	W 5-0
29 Nov	F	H	Walsall Swifts	W 6-0
6 Dec	FAC2	H	Sheffield Heeley	W 4-1
13 Dec	NCC1	H	United Amateurs	W 4-0
20 Dec	F	H	Walsall Town	D 1-1
26 Dec	F	A	Notts Co	W 3-0
3 Jan	FAC3	H	Sheff Wed	W 2-1
8 Jan	F	H	London Casuals	L 1-2
10 Jan	F	H	Small Heath Alliance	W 3-0
24 Jan	FAC4	A	Nottingham Swifts	W 1-0
31 Jan	F	H	Derby Co	L 0-6
7 Feb	NCCsf	A	Notts Olympic	W 2-0
14 Feb	F	A	Sheff Wed	W 5-0
17 Feb	F	H	Great Lever	W 3-2
21 Feb	FAC6	A	Old Etonians	L 0-1
28 Feb	F	H	Blackburn R	W 3-0
14 Mar	FACsf	**	Queens Park	D 1-1
21 Mar	NCCf	***	Queens Park	W 6-1
28 Mar	FACsfr	****	Queens Park	L 0-3
11 Apr	F	A	Small Heath Alliance	L †
18 Apr		***	Notts Co	L 2-3

Final Record

	P	W	D	L	F	A
- Forest	28	17	4	7	71	39

* at Parkside Ground, Lenton - Rotherham conceded ground advantage
** at Derby Cricket Ground
*** at Castle Ground
**** at Merchiston Castle School, Edinburgh
† Newspapers only reported a "drawn game"

Forest received a bye in FAC5

1885-86

Date	Comp	Venue	Opponent	Result
26 Sep	F	H	Stoke	W 4-1
3 Oct	F	H	Walsall Swifts	W 3-1
10 Oct	F	H	Wednesbury Old Ath	D 2-2
17 Oct	NCC1	H	Eastwood	W 4-0
24 Oct	F	H	Aston Villa	D 0-0
31 Oct	FAC1	H	Mellors Ltd	W 6-2
7 Nov	F	A	Cambridge Univ	L 1-5
14 Nov	F	H	Blackburn R	W 4-0
21 Nov	FAC2	H	Notts Olympic	W 4-1
28 Nov	F	H	Notts Co	L 1-4
5 Dec	F	H	Derby Co	W 2-1
12 Dec	FAC3	A	Staveley	L 1-2
19 Dec	F	H	Sheff Wed	D 1-1
31 Dec	F	H	London Casuals	W 2-0
2 Jan	F	H	Walsall Swifts	W 4-1
9 Jan	F	A	Derby Co	L 0-1
16 Jan	F	A	Notts Co	L 0-5
23 Jan	F	H	Bolton W	L 0-7
30 Jan	F	H	Preston NE	L 1-4
6 Feb	F	H	Halliwell	L 0-2
13 Feb	NCC2	A	Jardines	W 3-2
20 Feb	F	A	WBA	L 0-1
27 Feb	F	H	Glasgow Rangers	D 2-2
13 Mar*	F	H	Small Heath Alliance	L 1-2
13 Mar*	F	A	Stoke	W 1-0
20 Mar*	NCCsf	A	Sneinton Institute	W 6-0
27 Mar	NCCf	H	Sheffield	W 6-0
10 Apr	F	A	Preston NE	L 0-7
23 Apr	F	H	Burnley	W 4-2
24 Apr	F	A	Glasgow Rangers	L 1-2
26 Apr	F	A	Newcastle & Dist	W 5-1

Final Record

	P	W	D	L	F	A
- Forest	32	16	4	12	70	59

* two fixtures played on same day, both classed as first team

1886-87

Date	Comp	Venue	Opponent	Result
18 Sep	F	A	Small Heath Alliance	W 2-0
25 Sep	F	A	Wednesbury Old Ath	W 10-0
2 Oct	F	H	Walsall Swifts	W 3-0
9 Oct	F	H	Sheff Wed	W 4-1
16 Oct	F	A	Staveley	W 2-1
23 Oct	F	A	Stoke	L 0-2
30 Oct	FAC1	H	Notts Olympic	W 3-0
6 Nov	F	H	Cambridge Univ	W 3-0
13 Nov	FAC2	H	Grimsby T	D 2-2
20 Nov	FAC2r	A	Grimsby T	W 1-0
4 Dec	NCC2	H	Kimberley T	W 7-0
11 Dec	FAC3	A	Lockwood Bros	L 1-2
18 Dec	NCC3	H	Notts Rangers	W 2-0
27 Dec	F	A	Notts Co	W 4-1
28 Dec	F	H	Stoke	L 0-5
1 Jan	F	A	Accrington	L 2-4
22 Jan	F	H	Birmingham Excelsior	W 6-3
29 Jan	F	A	Cambridge Univ	L 0-2
12 Feb	F	H	Notts Co	L 1-2
19 Feb	F	A	Derby Co	L 0-2
22 Feb	F	H	Burnley	W 3-2
5 Mar	F	H	Glasgow Rangers	L 0-1
12 Mar	F	A	Birmingham Excelsior	D 2-2
19 Mar	NCCsf	A	Notts Co	D 1-1
26 Mar	F	H	Wolves	W 1-0
8 Apr	F	A	Burnley	L 0-4
9 Apr	NCCsf	A	Glasgow Rangers	D 0-0
11 Apr	F	A	Bootle	L 0-1
16 Apr	NCCsfr	H	Notts Co	W 2-1
23 Apr	NCCf	H	Notts Olympic	W 3-0

Final Record

	P	W	D	L	F	A
- Forest	30	16	5	9	66	38

1887-88

Date	Comp	Venue	Opponent	Result
17 Sep	F	A	Preston NE	L 2-5
24 Sep	F	H	Wednesbury Old Ath	W 3-2
1 Oct	F	H	Long Eaton Rangers	W 1-0
6 Oct	F	H	Sheff Wed	W 2-1
8 Oct	F	H	Stoke	W 2-1
15 Oct	FAC1	H	Nottingham Swifts	D 1-1
22 Oct	F	H	Burslem PV	L 1-2
29 Oct	BCC	A	Stoke	W 2-0
5 Nov	FAC2	H	Mellors Ltd	D 1-1
12 Nov	F	A	Lincoln C	D 1-1
17 Nov	F	H	Corinthians	W 2-1
26 Nov	FAC3	H	Notts Co	L 0-1
3 Dec	F	H	Notts Co	W 2-0
10 Dec	F	A	Accrington	W 2-0
17 Dec	FAC4	H	Old Etonians	W 6-0
26 Dec	F	A	Notts Co	D 0-0
27 Dec	F	H	Bolton W	W 3-2
7 Jan	FAC5	H	Sheff Wed	L 2-4
14 Jan	F	H	Preston NE	W 2-1
21 Jan	F	H	Grimsby T	W 1-0
28 Jan	F	A	Cambridge Univ	L 1-5
4 Feb	F	H	Lincoln C	W 2-0
14 Feb	F	H	Burnley	L 1-2
18 Feb	F	H	Cambridge Univ	L 0-3
3 Mar	F	A	Aston Unity	L 1-3
10 Mar	F	H	Burnley	W 4-3
30 Mar	F	A	Bolton W	L 1-3
31 Mar	F	A	Bootle	L 1-3
21 Apr	F	A	Burslem PV	L 2-7

Final Record

	P	W	D	L	F	A
- Forest	30	15	3	12	51	57

1888-89

Date	Comp	Venue	Opponent	Result
8 Sep	F	A	Sheff Wed	D 2-2
15 Sep	F	A	Mitchell St George	L 1-7
22 Sep	F	H	Warwick County	W 5-0
29 Sep	F	H	Sheffield	W 8-1
4 Oct	F	H	Aston Villa	L 1-2
6 Oct	F	H	Long Eaton Rangers	L 0-2
20 Oct	F	H	Sheff Wed	L 1-3
25 Oct	F	H	Preston NE	L 0-2
27 Oct	F	H	Mitchell St George	W 1-0
3 Nov	F	A	Clapton	D 2-2
10 Nov	F	A	Derby Co	L 0-3
17 Nov	F	H	Blackburn Olympic	L 1-3
24 Nov	F	H	Notts Co	W 3-0
1 Dec	F	H	Walsall Town Swifts	L 1-2
8 Dec	F	H	Sheffield Heeley	W 4-1
15 Dec	F	H	Derby Junction	W 3-0
26 Dec	F	A	Notts Co	L 1-4
29 Dec	F	H	Casuals	L 1-4
5 Jan	F	A	Derby Junction	W 2-1
12 Jan	F	H	Sheffield	W 1-0
19 Jan	F	H	Glasgow Rangers	W 2-1
26 Jan	F	A	Corinthians	L 1-2
2 Feb	FAC1	H	Linfield Ath	D*2-2
9 Feb	FAC1r	A	Linfield Ath	L 1-3
16 Feb	FAC2	A	Chatham	D 1-1
23 Feb	FAC2r	H	Chatham	D 2-2
28 Feb	FAC2c2	**	Chatham	L 2-3
4 Mar	F	H	Stoke	D 2-2
9 Mar	F	H	Newton Heath	D 1-1
16 Mar	F	A	Small Heath	L 1-3
23 Mar	F	A	Newton Heath	W 1-0
25 Mar	F	H	Notts Rangers	L 1-4
30 Mar	F	H	Notts Co	L 2-5
6 Apr	F	H	Clapton	W 3-0
19 Apr	F	A	Sunderland Albion	L 0-2
20 Apr	F	A	Glasgow Rangers	L 0-2
22 Apr	F	A	Bootle	L 0-5

Final Record

	P	W	D	L	F	A
- Forest	37	10	6	21	59	84

* Linfield subsequently scratched from FA Cup, after Forest had already left for replay in Belfast
** at The Oval

1889-90 Football Alliance

Date	Comp		Opponent	Result
7 Sep	All	A	Walsall Town Swifts	W 3-1
14 Sep	F	H	Halliwell	L 2-3
21 Sep	All	A	Grimsby T	L 0-4
28 Sep	All	H	Bootle	D 2-2
5 Oct	All	H	Grimsby T	L 1-2
12 Oct	All	A	Birmingham St George	W 3-1
19 Oct	All	A	Crewe Alex	D 1-1
24 Oct	F	H	Preston NE	W 2-1
2 Nov	All	H	Small Heath	D 0-0
9 Nov	All	A	Sunderland Albion	L 0-4
16 Nov	F	H	London Casuals	W 3-1
23 Nov	All	A	Long Eaton Rangers	L 3-5
25 Nov	F	A	Sheff Utd	L 0-2
30 Nov	F	H	Notts Co	L 2-4
7 Dec	All	H	Sunderland Albion	W 3-1
14 Dec	All	H	Crewe Alex	L 2-5
21 Dec	F	A	Clapton	L 0-1
26 Dec	F	A	Notts Co	D 1-1
28 Dec	All	A	Sheff Wed	L 1-3
4 Jan	All	H	Sheff Wed	L 1-3
11 Jan	BCC	H	Walsall Town Swifts	L 0-1
18 Jan	FAC1	A	Derby Midland	L 0-3
25 Jan	F	A	Everton	L 0-7
1 Feb	All	H	Darwen	W 3-1
8 Feb	F	A	Chatham	D 1-1
15 Feb	All	H	Newton Heath	L 1-3
22 Feb	All	H	Long Eaton Rangers	D 1-1
1 Mar	F	A	Sheff Utd	W 2-1
8 Mar	All	A	Small Heath	L0-12
15 Mar	F	H	Chatham	W 2-0
20 Mar	All	H	Birmingham St George	D 2-2
22 Mar	All	A	Darwen	L 0-9
29 Mar	All	H	Walsall Town Swifts	W 3-0
5 Apr	All	A	Newton Heath	W 1-0
7 Apr	All	A	Bootle	L 0-2
17 Apr	F	A	Notts Rangers	L 1-4

Position in Alliance Table

		P	W	D	L	F	A	Pts
1st	Sheff W	22	15	2	5	73	36	32
11th	Forest	22	6	5	11	31	62	17

Election to Football League

1891 (6 places) Aston Villa 8, Accrington 8 (both re-elected), Darwen 7, Stoke 7 (both elected), Derby Co 6, WBA 6 (both re-elected), Ardwick 4, Forest 1, Sunderland Albion 1, Newton Heath 0 (all not elected).

1892 (6 places) WBA re-elected as FA Cup winners without going to the vote, Sheff Wed 10 votes, Forest 9 (both elected), Accrington 7, Stoke 6 (both re-elected), Newton Heath 6 (elected), Sheff Utd 5, Burton Swifts 1, Newcastle East End 1, Middlesbrough Ironopolis 1 (all not elected).

Subsequently, Football League Division 2 formed largely from remainder of Alliance.

1890-91 Football Alliance

Date	Comp		Opponent	Result
1 Sep	F	A	Wolves	L 0-1
3 Sep	F	H	Notts Olympic	W 4-0
6 Sep	All	A	Bootle	W 5-1
13 Sep	All	H	Darwen	W 5-2
15 Sep	F	A	Hearts	L 0-1
20 Sep	All	A	Newton Heath	D 1-1
27 Sep	All	H	Crewe Alex	W 5-2
29 Sep	F	A	Sheff Utd	W 2-1
2 Oct	F	H	Queens Park	W 4-2
3 Oct	All	H	Stoke	D 2-2
11 Oct	All	A	Sunderland Albion	D 0-0
18 Oct	All	H	Bootle	W 7-0
23 Oct	F	H	Aston Villa	W 3-0
25 Oct	F	A	Clapton	W 4-0
1 Nov	All	A	Sheff Wed	W 2-0
8 Nov	All	H	Birmingham St George	W 4-0
13 Nov	F	H	Wolves	W 5-0
15 Nov	F	A	WBA	D 2-2
22 Nov	All	H	Newton Heath	W 8-2
27 Nov	F	H	Bolton W	W 7-1
29 Nov	All	A	Stoke	L 1-2
6 Dec	F	A	Clyde	W 5-2
13 Dec	All	A	Darwen	D 4-4
18 Dec	F	H	Burnley	L 3-4
26 Dec	F	A	Notts Co	D 0-0
27 Dec	All	H	Grimsby T	D 1-1
1 Jan	F	A	Bolton W	L 0-3
3 Jan	F	H	Hearts	W 8-2
10 Jan	F	A	Glasgow Rangers	W 2-1
17 Jan	FAC1	A	Clapton	W14-0
24 Jan	All	H	Sunderland Albion	D 1-1
31 Jan	FAC2	A	Sunderland Albion	D 1-1
2 Feb	All	A	Birmingham St George	L 3-6
7 Feb	FAC2r	H	Sunderland Albion	D 3-3
11 Feb	FAC2r2 *		Sunderland Albion	W 5-0
14 Feb	FAC3	A	Sunderland	L 0-4
21 Feb	All	A	Crewe Alex	W 7-0
26 Feb	All	H	Small Heath	L 4-5
28 Feb	All	A	Small Heath	L 2-4
2 Mar	F	A	Sheff Utd	W 4-1
12 Mar	F	H	WBA	L 2-3
14 Mar	All	H	Walsall Town Swifts	W 2-0
16 Mar	F	A	Aston Villa	L 2-3
21 Mar	All	H	Sheff Wed	D 0-0
27 Mar	F	A	Middlesbrough Iron.	D 2-2
28 Mar	F	A	Newcastle East End	W 2-1
30 Mar	F	A	Chatham	W 2-0
31 Mar	F	A	Woolwich Arsenal	W 5-0
2 Apr	F	H	Blackburn R	W 4-0
4 Apr	All	A	Walsall Town Swifts	L 2-3
9 Apr	All	A	Grimsby T	L 0-3
11 Apr	F	H	Glasgow Rangers	W 3-0
18 Apr	F	H	Notts Co	L 2-4
20 Apr	F	A	Everton	D 1-1

Position in Alliance Table

		P	W	D	L	F	A	Pts
1st	Stoke	22	13	7	2	57	39	33
5th	Forest**	22	9	7	6	66	39	23

* at Bramall Lane
** Two points deducted for playing unregistered player (Widdowson) on 6 Sep

1891-92 Football Alliance

Date	Comp		Opponent	Result
3 Sep	All	H	Burton Swifts	W 7-0
5 Sep	All	A	Bootle	W 4-1
9 Sep	F	A	Mansfield Town	W 4-0
12 Sep	All	H	Walsall Town Swifts	W 5-1
19 Sep	F	A	Sunderland Albion	W 1-0
21 Sep	F	A	Everton	L 0-2
24 Sep	All	H	Birmingham St George	W 3-0
25 Sep	F	A	Queens Park	W 3-1
1 Oct	F	H	Canadians	W 5-0
3 Oct	F	H	Notts Co	W 3-1
8 Oct	All	H	Small Heath	W 2-0
10 Oct	F	H	Sunderland Albion	W 5-3
14 Oct	F	A	Mansfield Green.	W 6-0
17 Oct	All	H	Crewe Alex	W 5-0
24 Oct	F	A	Kettering Town	W 5-1
26 Oct	F	A	Stoke	W 3-0
31 Oct	All	A	Birmingham St George	W 2-1
7 Nov	All	H	Sheff Wed	D 1-1
12 Nov	F	H	Bolton W	W 5-0
14 Nov	All	A	Ardwick	W 3-1
19 Nov	All	H	Ardwick	W 4-0
21 Nov	All	H	Grimsby T	D 3-3
28 Nov	All	A	Sheff Wed	L 1-3
3 Dec	F	H	Stoke	W 2-0
12 Dec	All	H	Bootle	W 5-1
19 Dec	F	A	Everton	D 0-0
26 Dec	F	A	Notts Co	W 1-0
28 Dec	F	A	Derby Co	L 0-3
1 Jan	All	A	Newton Heath	D 1-1
2 Jan	F	A	Darwen	D 2-2
9 Jan	All	A	Burton Swifts	W 3-1
16 Jan	FAC1	H	Newcastle East End	W 2-1
23 Jan	F	A	Aston Villa	L 2-3
30 Jan	FAC2	A	Sunderland Albion	W 1-0
6 Feb	All	H	Lincoln C	D 0-0
13 Feb	FAC3	H	Preston NE	W 2-0
20 Feb	All	A	Lincoln C	W 4-1
27 Feb	FACsf	*	WBA	D 1-1
1 Mar	F	A	Rotherham T	D 2-2
5 Mar	FACsfr	*	WBA	D 1-1
9 Mar	FACsfr2	**	WBA	L 2-6
12 Mar	F	A	Wolves	L 0-5
19 Mar	All	H	Newton Heath	W 3-0
24 Mar	F	H	Everton	L 1-2
26 Mar	F	H	Darwen	W 3-0
2 Apr	All	A	Walsall Town Swifts	L 0-3
4 Apr	F	A	Glasgow Celtic	L 1-4
9 Apr	F	A	Grimsby T	W 3-2
15 Apr	F	A	Bolton W	L 0-1
16 Apr	All	A	Small Heath	W 2-1
23 Apr	All	A	Crewe Alex	L 0-2
28 Apr	All	A	Grimsby T	D 1-1

Position in Alliance Table

		P	W	D	L	F	A	Pts
1st	Forest	22	14	5	3	59	22	33

* at Molineux
** at The Racecourse, Derby

1892-93 Division One

Date	Comp		Opponent	Result
1 Sep	F	A	Ardwick	D 2-2
3 Sep	FL	A	Everton	D 2-2
8 Sep	F	H	Lincoln C	W 3-1
10 Sep	FL	H	Stoke	L 3-4
14 Sep	F	A	Lincoln C	W 3-2
17 Sep	FL	A	Preston NE	L 0-1
24 Sep	FL	H	Preston NE	L 1-2
1 Oct	FL	A	Derby Co	W 3-2
3 Oct	FL	A	Sheff Wed	D 2-2
8 Oct	FL	A	Notts Co	L 0-3
15 Oct	FL	A	Aston Villa	L 0-1
20 Oct	FL	H	Bolton W	W 2-0
22 Oct	FL	A	Stoke	L 0-3
29 Oct	FL	H	Newton Heath	D 1-1
3 Nov	F	H	Sheff Utd	L 0-1
5 Nov	FL	A	Wolves	D 2-2
12 Nov	FL	H	Aston Villa	L 4-5
19 Nov	FL	A	Sunderland	L 0-1
26 Nov	FL	A	Burnley	D 1-1
1 Dec	FL	H	Sheff Wed	W 2-0
3 Dec	FL	H	Sunderland	L 0-5
10 Dec	FL	H	Burnley	D 2-2
17 Dec	F	A	Royal Arsenal	W 3-2
24 Dec	FL	H	Wolves	W 3-1
26 Dec	F	A	Notts Co	W 1-0
31 Dec	FL	A	Blackburn R	W 1-0
7 Jan	FL	H	Accrington	W 3-0
12 Jan	FL	H	Everton	W 2-1
14 Jan	FL	A	Newton Heath	W 3-1
21 Jan	FAC1	H	Casuals	W 4-0
28 Jan	FL	H	Derby Co	W 1-0
4 Feb	FAC2	A	Everton	L 2-4
11 Feb	F	A	Sheff Utd	L 3-4
16 Feb	F	A	Grimsby T	W 2-0
18 Feb	F	H	Derby Co	W 3-2
25 Feb	FL	H	Notts Co	W 3-1
2 Mar	FL	H	WBA	L 3-4
4 Mar	F	A	Small Heath	W 3-2
11 Mar	FL	H	Blackburn R	L 0-1
18 Mar	FL	A	Accrington	D 1-1
21 Mar	F	A	Grantham Rovers	D 0-0
25 Mar	F	A	Newcastle U	L 1-4
29 Mar	F	A	Loughborough	D 0-0
31 Mar	FL	A	Bolton W	L 1-3
3 Apr	FL	A	WBA	D 2-2
8 Apr	F	A	Sheff Wed	L 1-2
15 Apr	F	A	Leicester Fosse	W 5-1
20 Apr	F	H	Derby Co	W 4-1
22 Apr	F	A	Burton Swifts	W 3-1
26 Apr	F	A	Chesterfield T	W 5-0

Position in League Table

		P	W	D	L	F	A	Pts
1st	Sund'ld	30	22	4	4	100	36	48
10th	Forest	30	10	8	12	48	52	28

1893-94 Division One

Date	Comp		Opponent	Result
2 Sep	FL	H	Wolves	W 7-1
4 Sep	FL	A	Everton	L 0-4
9 Sep	FL	A	Stoke	L 1-2
13 Sep	F	A	Mansfield	W 6-0
16 Sep	FL	H	Burnley	W 5-0
23 Sep	FL	A	Newton Heath	D 1-1
30 Sep	FL	H	WBA	L 2-3
5 Oct	FL	H	Bolton W	W 1-0
7 Oct	FL	H	Aston Villa	L 1-2
14 Oct	FL	A	Wolves	L 1-3
21 Oct	FL	H	Stoke	W 2-0
28 Oct	FL	H	Sheff Wed	W 1-0
4 Nov	FL	A	Burnley	L 1-3
11 Nov	F	H	Notts Co	L 1-2
18 Nov	FL	H	Sheff Utd	D 1-1
25 Nov	FL	H	Blackburn R	D 0-0
2 Dec	FL	A	Preston NE	W 2-0
9 Dec	FL	A	Derby Co	W 4-3
14 Dec	F	H	Sheff Wed	W 3-1
16 Dec	F	A	Liverpool	L 0-3
23 Dec	FL	A	Darwen	W 4-0
26 Dec	F	A	Notts Co	D 1-1
30 Dec	FL	H	Derby Co	W 4-2
1 Jan	FL	A	Sheff Utd	W 2-0
6 Jan	UCL	H	Notts Co	W 1-0
13 Jan	FL	H	Sunderland	L 1-2
18 Jan	FL	H	Everton	W 3-2
20 Jan	UCL	A	Sheff Wed	D 2-2
27 Jan	FAC1	H	Heanor T	W 1-0
3 Feb	FL	A	Blackburn R	L 1-6
10 Feb	FAC2	H	Middlesbrough Iron.	W 2-0
15 Feb	UCL	H	Sheff Utd	W 3-1
24 Feb	FAC3	H	Notts Co	D 1-1
3 Mar	FAC3r	A	Notts Co	L 1-4
5 Mar	FL	A	Sheff Wed	L 0-1
10 Mar	F	A	Small Heath	D 2-2
15 Mar	FL	H	Darwen	W 4-1
17 Mar	FL	A	Sunderland	L 0-2
23 Mar	FL	A	Bolton W	D 1-1
24 Mar	FL	H	Preston NE	W 4-2
26 Mar	FL	A	WBA	L 0-3
31 Mar	UCL	A	Sheff Utd	D 0-0
2 Apr	F	A	Woolwich Arsenal	W 3-1
4 Apr	F	A	Mansfield Greenhalghs	W 3-2
7 Apr	FL	H	Newton Heath	W 2-0
11 Apr	F	A	Burton Swifts	D 2-2
12 Apr	UCL	H	Derby Co	L 0-3
14 Apr	FL	A	Aston Villa	L 1-3
19 Apr	UCL	A	Notts Co	W 4-3
21 Apr	UCL	H	Sheff Wed	W 5-1
25 Apr	UCL	A	Derby Co	D 0-0
26 Apr	F	A	Grimsby T	D 2-2
27 Apr	F	A	Bulwell U	W 2-0
30 Apr	F	A	Kettering	W 2-1

Position in League Table

		P	W	D	L	F	A	Pts
1st	A Villa	30	19	6	5	84	42	44
7th	Forest	30	14	4	12	57	48	32

Position in United Counties League Table (East Midlands)

		P	W	D	L	F	A	Pts
1st	Derby	8	5	2	1	22	7	12
2nd	Forest	8	4	3	1	15	10	11

1889-90 Alliance Appearances (Goals)
Brown G 7; Burton F 10 (3); Coleman J 13; Earp M 9; Fox F 1; Grant 1; Gutteridge F 19 (2); Hazeldine 1; Hodder W 1 (2); Holland J 20; Howell 1; Jackson H 1; Jardine R 6; Jeacock T 21; Lindley T 2; Mabbott C 1; McUrich 1; Palmer A 2; Pike A 1; Pike, Harry 19; Pike, Horace 20 (11); Plackett H 15 (2); Plackett L 10 (1); Radford 1 (2); Shaw A 5 (2); Shepperson G 1; Smith A 13 (1); Smith G 14; Southward J 7; Tolley O 10 (1); Turner G 1; Tutin G 3 (2); Weightman F 4; Widdowson T 1; Uncredited goals 1; Own goals 1.

1890-91 Alliance Appearances (Goals)
Brown W 10; Bullock J 1; Cox J 4; Duncan J 3; Earp M 21; Higgins A 19 (10); Holland J 3; Jeacock T 22; Lindley T 1 (1); McCallum N 20 (8); May E 7 (6); Pike, Harry 3; Pike, Horace 20 (12); Rorke 2 (1); Rowan M 3 (1); Russell D 20 (1); Scott A 21; Shaw A 15 (6); Smith A 20; Smith W 21 (4); Widdowson T 5; Uncredited goals 2; Own goals 1.

1891-92 Alliance Appearances (Goals)
Brown W 21; Bullock J 1; Burton F 1; Bywater 1; Earp M 7; Hamilton K 17 (1); Higgins A 19 (26); Lindley T 4 (1); McPherson J 19 (4); Mason F 19 (5); Oscroft P 1 (1); Pike, Horace 21 (8); Ritchie A 17; Russell D 13 (4); Scott A 19 (1); Shaw A 19 (2); Smith A 8 (1); Smith W 18 (4); Thompson F 16; Williamson A 1; Own goals 1

1892-93 League Appearances (Goals)
Allsopp D 10; Barker A 1; Brown W 17; Bullock J 1; Daft H 4 (1); Earp M 13; Hamilton K 7; Higgins A 25 (12); McCallum N 19 (5); McCracken P 29; McInnes T 30 (10); McPherson J 21 (3); Mason W 5; Pike, Horace 27 (4); Ritchie A 21; Robertson T 1; Scott A 28 (1); Shaw A 24 (6); Smith A 19 (1); Smith C 1; Smith W 23 (4); Thompson F 1; Thornhill S 3

1893-94 League Appearances (Goals)
Allsopp D 25; Brodie J 9 (6); Brown W 5; Collins J 29 (13); Connor J 5; Cross J 1; Geary G 1; Higgins A 22 (4); McCallum N 17 (5); McCracken P 16; McInnes T 28 (14); McPherson J 29 (7); Pike, Horace 17 (5); Ritchie A 30; Rose T 2; Scott A 30; Shaw A 15 (1); Smith A 7; Smith W 13 (1); Stewart A 29.

1894-95 Division One

Date	Comp	Venue	Opponent	Result
1 Sep	FL	H	Burnley	W 2-1
3 Sep	F	A	Woolwich Arsenal	L 2-3
6 Sep	F	H	Notts Olympic	W 9-0
8 Sep	FL	A	Derby Co	L 2-4
10 Sep	F	A	Kettering	W 2-0
13 Sep	F	H	Jardines	W 7-0
15 Sep	FL	A	Everton	L 1-6
17 Sep	F	A	Heanor T	W 1-0
22 Sep	FL	H	Everton	L 2-3
29 Sep	FL	A	Sheff Utd	L 2-3
4 Oct	FL	H	Preston NE	L 0-2
6 Oct	FL	H	Aston Villa	W 2-1
10 Oct	F	A	Sussex Martlets	W 8-2
11 Oct	F	A	Casuals	W 4-3
13 Oct	FL	A	Stoke	W 3-0
20 Oct	F	H	Notts Co	W 2-0
27 Oct	FL	A	Burnley	W 1-0
3 Nov	FL	H	Derby Co	W 2-1
9 Nov	F	A	Loughborough	L 1-2
10 Nov	FL	A	Wolves	D 1-1
17 Nov	FL	H	Sheff Utd	W 3-0
24 Nov	FL	A	Aston Villa	L 1-4
8 Dec	FL	H	WBA	W 5-3
15 Dec	FL	A	Sheff Wed	D 0-0
22 Dec	FL	A	Small Heath	W 2-1
26 Dec	F	A	Notts Co	D 1-1
27 Dec	FL	H	Sunderland	W 2-1
29 Dec	FL	H	Blackburn R	L 2-3
1 Jan	FL	A	Blackburn R	D 0-0
5 Jan	FL	A	Sunderland	D 2-2
12 Jan	FL	A	Liverpool	L 0-5
19 Jan	FL	H	Sheff Wed	W 2-1
26 Jan	FL	H	Small Heath	W 2-0
2 Feb	FAC1	A	Southampton St Marys	W 4-1
16 Feb	FAC2	A	Liverpool	W 2-0
23 Feb	FL	H	Stoke	W 3-1
2 Mar	FAC3	A	Aston Villa	L 2-6
9 Mar	UCL	H	Derby Co	W 2-0
11 Mar	UCL	A	Sheff Utd	W 6-2
16 Mar	FL	H	Bolton W	D 3-3
23 Mar	FL	A	Preston NE	L 1-3
30 Mar	UCL	H	Notts Co	W 3-0
4 Apr	UCL	H	Leicester Fosse	W 3-0
6 Apr	FL	H	Liverpool	W 3-0
12 Apr	FL	A	Bolton W	L 1-4
13 Apr	FL	H	Wolves	L 0-2
15 Apr	FL	A	WBA	L 0-1
16 Apr	UCL	A	Derby Co	L 0-3
18 Apr	UCL	H	Sheff Utd	L 0-1
22 Apr	UCL	A	Leicester Fosse	D 1-1
24 Apr	F	A	Mansfield T	W 3-1
25 Apr	F	A	Hucknall Portland	W 8-1
29 Apr	UCL	H	Notts Co	W 1-0

Position in League Table

	P	W	D	L	F	A	Pts
1st S'land	30	21	5	4	80	37	47
7th Forest	30	13	5	12	50	56	31

Position in United Counties League Table (East Midlands)

	P	W	D	L	F	A	Pts
1st Forest	8	5	1	2	16	7	11*

* fixtures not completed, competition defunct

1895-96 Division One

Date	Comp	Venue	Opponent	Result
2 Sep	F	A	Leicester Fosse	W 1-0
5 Sep	FL	H	Bury	W 5-0
7 Sep	FL	A	Everton	L 2-6
10 Sep	F	A	Langley Mill Rangers	W 6-1
14 Sep	FL	A	Blackburn R	L 0-2
21 Sep	FL	H	Small Heath	W 3-0
28 Sep	FL	A	WBA	L 1-3
5 Oct	FL	H	Derby Co	L 2-5
12 Oct	FL	H	Everton	W 2-1
19 Oct	FL	A	Bolton W	L 1-2
26 Oct	FL	H	Preston NE	L 0-1
31 Oct	F	H	Leicester Fosse	W 5-2
2 Nov	F	A	Corinthians	W 2-0
9 Nov	FL	A	Small Heath	L 0-1
16 Nov	FL	H	WBA	W 2-0
23 Nov	FL	A	Sheff Utd	L 1-2
28 Nov	FL	H	Stoke	W 4-0
30 Nov	FL	A	Sheff Wed	L 0-3
7 Dec	FL	A	Derby Co	L 0-4
14 Dec	FL	H	Sheff Utd	W 3-1
21 Dec	FL	A	Burnley	D 0-0
26 Dec	F	A	Notts Co	D 1-1
28 Dec	FL	H	Blackburn R	W 4-2
4 Jan	F	H	Corinthians	W 5-1
11 Jan	FL	H	Bolton W	D 0-0
18 Jan	FL	H	Sunderland	W 3-1
25 Jan	FL	A	Aston Villa	L 1-3
1 Feb	FAC1	H	Everton	L 0-2
8 Feb	FL	A	Sunderland	D 1-1
15 Feb	F	H	Notts Co	W 3-1
22 Feb	FL	A	Preston NE	L 0-6
27 Feb	F	H	Grimsby T	W 4-2
29 Feb	F	A	Clyde	L 3-5
7 Mar	FL	H	Burnley	W 2-1
16 Mar	KCC	A	Kettering	L 0-1
18 Mar	F	A	Mansfield T	W 4-1
21 Mar	FL	A	Stoke	L 0-1
24 Mar	FL	A	Bury	L 0-1
28 Mar	FL	A	Wolves	L 1-6
2 Apr	FL	H	Aston Villa	L 0-2
4 Apr	FL	H	Wolves	W 3-2
6 Apr	F	*	Dundee	W 2-0
7 Apr	FL	H	Sheff Wed	W 1-0
11 Apr	F	A	St Bernards	D 2-2
18 Apr	F	A	Luton T	L 1-3
20 Apr	F	A	Bulwell U	W 7-3
22 Apr	F	A	Sutton T	W 2-0
27 Apr	F	A	Langley Mill Rangers	W 7-0
28 Apr	F	A	Gresley Rovers	D 1-1

Position in League Table

	P	W	D	L	F	A	Pts
1st A Villa	30	20	5	5	78	45	45
13th Forest	30	11	3	16	42	57	25

* at Crystal Palace

1896-97 Division One

Date	Comp	Venue	Opponent	Result
3 Sep	F	H	Burton W	W 8-0
5 Sep	FL	A	Derby Co	D 1-1
12 Sep	FL	H	Stoke	W 4-0
19 Sep	FL	A	Burnley	D 2-2
24 Sep	F	A	Grimsby T	L 2-5
26 Sep	FL	H	Sheff Utd	D 2-2
3 Oct	FL	H	Derby Co	Abnd
10 Oct	FL	A	Liverpool	L 0-3
17 Oct	FL	A	Stoke	L 0-3
24 Oct	FL	H	Burnley	W 4-1
31 Oct	FL	H	Sheff Wed	D 2-2
7 Nov	FL	A	Preston NE	L 2-3
14 Nov	FL	A	Blackburn R	D 0-0
18 Nov	FL	H	Derby Co	L 1-2
21 Nov	FL	H	Sunderland	W 2-1
28 Nov	FL	H	Liverpool	W 2-0
5 Dec	FL	A	Wolves	L 1-4
12 Dec	FL	H	Blackburn R	W 2-1
19 Dec	FL	A	Aston Villa	L 2-3
25 Dec	FL	A	Bury	L 0-2
26 Dec	F	A	Notts Co	W 2-1
28 Dec	FL	H	Bury	W 3-0
2 Jan	FL	H	WBA	L 0-1
9 Jan	FL	A	Everton	L 1-8
16 Jan	FL	H	Bolton W	W 2-0
23 Jan	FL	A	WBA	L 0-4
30 Jan	FAC1	A	Sheff Wed	W 1-0
13 Feb	FAC2	A	Sunderland	W 3-1
20 Feb	FL	A	Sheff Utd	W 3-0
27 Feb	FAC3	A	Liverpool	D 1-1
3 Mar	FAC3r	H	Liverpool	L 0-1
6 Mar	FL	H	Aston Villa	L 2-4
10 Mar	FL	H	Everton	W 3-0
13 Mar	FL	A	Sunderland	D 2-2
20 Mar	FL	A	Bolton W	D 0-0
25 Mar	BurC1	H	Grimsby T	W 3-0
27 Mar	F	A	Woolwich Arsenal	L 0-1
3 Apr	BurCsf	A	Leicester Fosse	L 0-3
5 Apr	FL	A	Sheff Wed	L 0-3
8 Apr	FL	H	Preston NE	D 0-0
10 Apr	FL	H	Wolves	L 1-2
16 Apr	F	A	Tottenham H	D 1-1
19 Apr	F	*	Dundee	W 2-1
24 Apr	F	A	Lincoln C	D 2-2
28 Apr	F	A	Mansfield T	W 3-0

Position in League Table

	P	W	D	L	F	A	Pts
1 A Villa	30	21	5	4	73	38	47
11 Forest	30	9	8	13	44	49	26

* at Crystal Palace

1897-98 Division One

Date	Comp	Venue	Opponent	Result
2 Sep	F	H	Gainsborough Trinity	W 5-0
4 Sep	FL	H	Notts Co	D 1-1
8 Sep	F	A	Loughborough	W 5-1
11 Sep	FL	A	WBA	L 0-2
13 Sep	F	A	Langley Mill Rangers	W 2-0
18 Sep	FL	H	Sheff Utd	D 1-1
20 Sep	F	A	Leicester Fosse	L 0-4
25 Sep	FL	A	Wolves	D 0-0
2 Oct	FL	H	Sunderland	D 1-1
9 Oct	FL	A	Notts Co	W 3-1
16 Oct	FL	H	Blackburn R	W 3-1
23 Oct	FL	A	Bolton W	L 0-2
27 Oct	F	A	Gainsborough Trinity	W 6-2
30 Oct	FL	H	Derby Co	L 3-4
6 Nov	FL	A	Liverpool	W 2-1
13 Nov	FL	H	Preston NE	W 4-1
20 Nov	FL	A	Stoke	W 2-1
27 Nov	FL	H	Liverpool	L 2-3
4 Dec	FL	A	Sheff Utd	D 1-1
11 Dec	FL	H	WBA	L 0-1
18 Dec	F	A	Derby Co	W 4-2
25 Dec	FL	A	Preston NE	L 0-3
27 Dec	F	A	Notts Co	W 1-0
1 Jan	FL	A	Sheff Wed	W 6-3
8 Jan	FL	H	Bolton W	W 2-0
15 Jan	FL	A	Blackburn R	D 1-1
22 Jan	FL	H	Sheff Wed	W 1-0
29 Jan	FAC1	H	Grimsby T	W 4-0
12 Feb	FAC2	H	Gainsborough Trinity	W 4-0
19 Feb	FL	H	Stoke	W 3-1
26 Feb	FAC3	A	WBA	W 3-2
12 Mar	FL	H	Everton	D 2-2
19 Mar	FACsf	*	Southampton	D 1-1
24 Mar	FACsfr	**	Southampton	W 2-0
26 Mar	FL	H	Aston Villa	W 3-1
2 Apr	FL	A	Everton	L 0-2
4 Apr	FL	A	Bury	D 2-2
8 Apr	FL	H	Wolves	D 1-1
9 Apr	FL	H	Bury	W 3-1
11 Apr	FL	A	Derby Co	L 0-5
16 Apr	FACf	**	Derby Co	W 3-1
23 Apr	FL	A	Sunderland	L 0-4
26 Apr	F	A	Newark	W 5-0
27 Apr	F	A	Worksop	W 4-1
28 Apr	BurCf	H	Leicester Fosse	W 1-0
30 Apr	FL	A	Aston Villa	L 0-2

Position in League Table

	P	W	D	L	F	A	Pts
1 Sheff U	30	17	8	5	56	31	42
8 Forest	30	11	9	10	47	49	31

* at Bramall Lane
** at Crystal Palace

1898-99 Division One

Date	Comp	Venue	Opponent	Result
3 Sep	FL	H	Blackburn R	L 0-1
10 Sep	FL	A	Sheff Wed	L 1-2
17 Sep	FL	H	Sunderland	D 1-1
22 Sep	F	A	Grimsby T	W 1-0
24 Sep	FL	A	Wolves	W 2-0
1 Oct	FL	H	Everton	D 0-0
6 Oct	FL	H	Preston NE	D 2-2
8 Oct	FL	A	Notts Co	D 2-2
15 Oct	FL	H	Stoke	W 2-1
22 Oct	FL	A	Aston Villa	L 0-3
29 Oct	FL	H	Burnley	L 0-1
5 Nov	FL	A	Sheff Utd	D 2-2
12 Nov	FL	H	Newcastle U	W 2-0
19 Nov	FL	A	Preston NE	L 0-1
26 Nov	FL	H	Liverpool	L 0-3
3 Dec	FL	A	Bury	L 0-2
10 Dec	FL	A	Bolton W	W 2-0
17 Dec	FL	H	Derby Co	D 3-3
24 Dec	FL	A	WBA	L 0-2
26 Dec	FL	A	Stoke	L 1-2
31 Dec	FL	A	Blackburn R	D 3-3
2 Jan	FL	A	Everton	W 3-1
7 Jan	FL	H	Sheff Wed	D 1-1
14 Jan	FL	A	Sunderland	D 1-1
21 Jan	FL	H	Wolves	W 3-0
28 Jan	FAC1	H	Aston Villa	W 2-1
4 Feb	FL	H	Notts Co	D 0-0
11 Feb	FAC2	A	Everton	W 1-0
18 Feb	FL	H	Aston Villa	W 1-0
25 Feb	FAC3	H	Sheff Utd	L 0-1
4 Mar	FL	H	Sheff Utd	W 2-1
6 Mar	FL	A	Burnley	D 1-1
11 Mar	FL	A	Newcastle U	W 1-0
15 Mar	F	A	Suffolk County	W 3-2
16 Mar	F	A	Kirkley & Lowestoft	W 3-0
25 Mar	FL	A	Liverpool	W 1-0
31 Mar	F	H	Notts Co	L 1-5
1 Apr	FL	H	Bury	L 1-2
3 Apr	F	*	Corinthians	L 2-3
4 Apr	F	A	Coventry C	W 1-0
6 Apr	BasCsf	A	Leicester Fosse	D 1-1
8 Apr	FL	H	Bolton W	L 1-2
15 Apr	F	A	Millwall Ath	W 5-2
17 Apr	BasCsfr	**	Leicester Fosse	W 7-1
20 Apr	FL	A	Derby Co	L 0-2
22 Apr	FL	H	WBA	W 3-0
26 Apr	BasCf	A	Burton Swifts	W 2-1
27 Apr	F	A	Swindon	L 0-1

Position in League Table

	P	W	D	L	F	A	Pts
1 A Villa	34	19	7	8	71	30	45
11 Forest	34	11	11	12	42	42	33

* at Crystal Palace
** at Burton

1894-95 League Appearances (Goals)
Abbott H 3; Allsopp D 27; Carnelly A 29 (16); Collins J 11 (4); Forman, Frank 4; Forman, Fred 13 (3); Geary G 6 (1); Hancock J 1; Jeacock T 1; McCracken P 28; McInnes T 17 (6); McPherson J 28 (3); Murray J 2; Pike, Horace 29 (10); Ritchie A 30; Rose T 22 (6); Scott A 30 (1); Severn W 2; Shaw A 17; Shrewsbury T 4; Stewart A 24; Walker T 2

1895-96 League Appearances (Goals)
Abbott J 1; Allsopp D 29; Carnelly A 23 (8); Forman, Frank 21 (1); Forman, Fred 22 (3); Hunt J 1; Iremonger J 3; Kerr N 1; McCracken P 19; McInnes 30 (10); McPherson J 24 (1); Pike, Horace 18 (4); Richards C 11 (5); Ritchie A 30; Rose T 6 (3); Scott A 26; Shaw A 20 (4); Smellie R 16 (3); Spencer F 1; Stewart A 26; Tebbutt T 1; Walker T 1.

1896-97 League Appearances (Goals)
Abbott J 1; Allsopp D 28; Capes, Adrian 29 (7); Capes, Arthur 30 (6); Dewey J 1; Forman, Frank 28 (3); Forman, Fred 20 (6); Goodchild G 3; Hollis J 1 (1); Iremonger J 19; McCracken P 4; McInnes T 28 (4); McPherson J 28 (2); Martin T 2; Richards W 26 (8); Ritchie A 20; Scott A 20; Shaw A 2 (2); Spencer F 9 (5); Stewart A 18; Walker T 1; Wragg W 12.

1897-98 League Appearances (Goals)
Allsopp D 26; Benbow J 2; Benbow L 24 (10); Bradshaw T 6; Capes, Adrian 1; Capes, Arthur 27 (9); Iremonger J 16; Forman, Frank 27 (6); Forman, Fred 7; Goodchild G 1; McInnes T 23 (4); McCracken P 9; McPherson J 27 (3); Martin T 4; Radford A 1; Richards W 25 (6); Richardson G 1; Ritchie A 19; Scott A 25; Shaw A 1; Spencer F 10 (2); Spouncer A 23 (6); Thornley J 1; Wragg W 24 (1)

1898-99 League Appearances (Goals)
Allsopp D 34; Benbow L 24 (7); Bradshaw T 12; Capes, Arthur 28 (4); Charlton A 3; Forman, Frank 27 (3); Forman, Fred 11 (3); Iremonger J 32; Kent T 2; McCracken P 8; McInnes T 12 (1); McPherson J 30 (1); Morris G 17 (6); Norris R 28 (2); Parkinson R 2; Radford A 3; Richards W 12 (2); Ritchie A 6; Robinson G 3; Scott A 19; Spencer F 16 (9); Spouncer A 13; Suddick J 14 (4); Thornley J 5; Wragg W 13.

1899-1900 Division One

2 Sep	FL	H	Preston NE	W 3-1
4 Sep	F	H	Leicester Fosse	W 4-1
9 Sep	FL	A	Wolves	D 2-2
16 Sep	FL	A	Glossop	L 0-3
23 Sep	FL	H	Stoke	W 1-0
30 Sep	FL	A	Sunderland	L 0-1
7 Oct	FL	H	WBA	W 6-1
12 Oct	F	H	Kaffirs	W 6-3
14 Oct	FL	A	Everton	L 1-2
21 Oct	FL	H	Blackburn R	W 3-2
28 Oct	FL	A	Derby Co	D 2-2
4 Nov	FL	H	Bury	D 2-2
11 Nov	FL	A	Notts Co	W 2-1
25 Nov	FL	A	Sheff Utd	L 0-3
2 Dec	FL	H	Newcastle U	W 1-0
9 Dec	FL	A	Aston Villa	D 2-2
16 Dec	FL	H	Liverpool	W 1-0
23 Dec	FL	A	Burnley	D 2-2
25 Dec	FL	A	Bury	L 1-2
26 Dec	F	A	Notts Co	W 4-2
27 Dec	FL	H	Man City	W 2-0
30 Dec	FL	A	Preston NE	L 0-3
6 Jan	FL	H	Wolves	D 0-0
13 Jan	FL	H	Glossop	W 5-0
20 Jan	FL	A	Stoke	D 0-0
27 Jan	FAC1	H	Grimsby T	W 3-0
10 Feb	FAC2	H	Sunderland	W 3-0
17 Feb	FL	H	Everton	W 4-2
24 Feb	FAC3	A	Preston NE	D 0-0
28 Feb	FAC3r	H	Preston NE	W 1-0
3 Mar	FL	H	Derby Co	W 4-1
5 Mar	FL	A	Blackburn R	L 1-2
10 Mar	F	A	Corinthians	D 2-2
17 Mar	FL	H	Notts Co	L 0-3
24 Mar	FACsf	*	Bury	D 1-1
29 Mar	FACsfr	**	Bury	L 2-3
31 Mar	FL	H	Sheff Utd	W 4-0
7 Apr	FL	A	Newcastle U	L 1-3
9 Apr	FL	A	Man City	L 0-2
14 Apr	FL	H	Aston Villa	D 1-1
16 Apr	FL	A	WBA	L 0-8
17 Apr	FL	H	Sunderland	L 1-3
21 Apr	FL	A	Liverpool	L 0-1
28 Apr	FL	H	Burnley	W 4-0

League Appearances (Goals)
Allsopp D 26; Benbow L 7 (1); Beveridge R 26 (5); Brentnall H 1; Calvey J 30 (16); Capes, Arthur 26 (5); Coles F 1; Forman, Frank 25 (4); Forman, Fred 24 (6); Iremonger J 34; Linacre H 7; Lockyer W 1; McPherson J 28 (2); Morris G 29 (11); Murray P 1; Norris R 31 (1); Peers E 33; Robinson G 13; Scott A 1; Spencer F 7 (2); Spouncer A 23 (2); Own Goals 1.

Position in League Table

		P	W	D	L	F	A	Pts
1st	A Villa	34	22	6	6	77	35	50
8th	Forest	34	13	8	13	56	55	34

*at Stoke ** at Bramall Lane

1900-01 Division One

1 Sep	FL	A	Newcastle U	D 0-0
8 Sep	FL	H	Sheff Utd	W 2-0
15 Sep	FL	A	Man City	L 0-1
22 Sep	FL	H	Bury	D 1-1
29 Sep	FL	H	Sheff Wed	W 1-0
4 Oct	FL	H	Preston NE	W 4-1
6 Oct	FL	A	Blackburn R	W 3-1
13 Oct	FL	H	Stoke	D 1-1
20 Oct	FL	A	WBA	W 6-1
27 Oct	FL	H	Everton	W 2-1
3 Nov	FL	A	Sunderland	W 1-0
10 Nov	FL	H	Derby Co	W 1-0
17 Nov	F	A	Gainsborough Trinity	W 4-2
24 Nov	FL	H	Notts Co	W 5-0
1 Dec	FL	A	Preston NE	D 1-1
8 Dec	FL	H	Wolves	W 2-1
15 Dec	FL	A	Aston Villa	L 1-2
22 Dec	FL	H	Liverpool	D 0-0
25 Dec	FL	H	Bolton W	W 3-0
26 Dec	FL	A	Notts Co	L 0-1
29 Dec	FL	H	Newcastle U	L 1-2
1 Jan	FL	A	Bolton W	L 2-4
5 Jan	FL	A	Sheff Utd	W 1-0
12 Jan	FL	H	Man City	W 4-2
19 Jan	FL	A	Bury	Abnd
9 Feb	FAC1	H	Leicester Fosse	W 5-1
16 Feb	FL	A	Stoke	W 3-0
23 Feb	FAC2	A	Aston Villa	D 0-0
27 Feb	FAC2r	H	Aston Villa	L 1-3
2 Mar	FL	A	Everton	L 1-4
9 Mar	FL	H	Sunderland	D 0-0
13 Mar	FL	H	WBA	L 2-3
16 Mar	FL	A	Derby Co	D 0-0
27 Mar	FL	A	Bury	W 1-0
5 Apr	F	A	Woolwich Arsenal	D 1-1
6 Apr	F	A	Corinthians	L 1-2
8 Apr	FL	H	Blackburn R	L 0-1
9 Apr	FL	A	Sheff Wed	L 1-4
13 Apr	FL	A	Wolves	L 0-1
20 Apr	FL	H	Aston Villa	W 3-1
27 Apr	FL	A	Liverpool	L 0-2
30 Apr	F	A	Small Heath	L 1-3

League Appearances (Goals)
Barnett T 1; Beveridge R 1; Calvey J 27 (13); Capes, Arthur 32 (8); Dean A 7; Forman, Frank 27 (1); Forman, Fred 27 (6); Forman T 2; Iremonger J 34; Linacre H 34; McCurdie W 7; McDiarmid G 4; McPherson J 11 (1); Morgan-Owen M 1; Morris G 31 (14); Murray P 13 (2); Norris R 22 (2); Peers E 24; Robinson G 33; Spouncer A 28 (6); Timmins S 8.

Position in League Table

		P	W	D	L	F	A	Pts
1st	Liverpool	34	19	7	8	59	35	45
4th	Forest	34	16	7	11	53	36	39

1901-02 Division One

2 Sep	FL	A	Wolves	L 0-2
7 Sep	FL	H	Sheff Utd	W 2-1
14 Sep	FL	A	Grimsby T	L 0-1
21 Sep	FL	A	Bury	D 1-1
28 Sep	FL	H	Blackburn R	W 3-0
5 Oct	FL	A	Stoke	D 1-1
12 Oct	FL	H	Everton	W 4-0
19 Oct	FL	A	Sunderland	L 0-4
26 Oct	FL	H	Small Heath	D 1-1
2 Nov	FL	A	Derby Co	D 1-1
9 Nov	FL	H	Sheff Wed	D 1-1
16 Nov	FL	A	Notts Co	L 0-3
23 Nov	FL	H	Bolton W	W 4-1
30 Nov	FL	A	Man City	L 1-3
7 Dec	FL	H	Wolves	W 2-0
14 Dec	FL	A	Liverpool	W 2-0
26 Dec	FL	H	Notts Co	W 1-0
28 Dec	FL	A	Aston Villa	L 0-3
1 Jan	FL	A	Blackburn R	L 0-1
2 Jan	FL	A	Bolton W	L 0-3
4 Jan	FL	A	Sheff Utd	D 2-2
11 Jan	FL	H	Grimsby T	L 0-1
18 Jan	FL	H	Bury	W 2-1
25 Jan	FAC1	A	Glossop	W 3-1
1 Feb	FL	H	Stoke	W 2-0
8 Feb	FAC2	A	Man City	W 2-0
15 Feb	FL	H	Sunderland	W 2-1
22 Feb	FAC3	H	Stoke	W 2-0
1 Mar	FL	H	Derby Co	W 3-1
8 Mar	FL	A	Sheff Wed	W 2-0
15 Mar	FACsf	*	Southampton	L 1-3
19 Mar	FL	H	Newcastle U	L 0-2
29 Mar	FL	H	Man City	W 3-1
31 Mar	FL	A	Everton	L 0-1
1 Apr	FL	H	Aston Villa	D 1-1
5 Apr	FL	A	Small Heath	D 1-1
12 Apr	FL	H	Liverpool	D 1-1
19 Apr	FL	A	Newcastle U	L 0-3
26 Apr	F	A	Plymouth A	W10-1

League Appearances (Goals)
Barnett T 1; Broughton M 16 (4); Calvey J 34 (12); Capes, Arther 25 (1); Forman, Frank 28 (2); Forman, Fred 15 (4); Forman T 2; Henderson G 23 (2); Hitch A 13 (2); Iremonger J 32; Linacre H 31; McCordie W 4; Morris G 27 (7); Murray P 14; Newbigging A 4; Norris R 4; Roberts T 2; Robinson G 23 (1); Saxton A 1; Spouncer A 32 (7); Timmins S 22; White J 21; Own Goals 1.

Position in League Table

		P	W	D	L	F	A	Pts
1st	S'land	34	19	6	9	50	35	44
5th	Forest	34	13	9	12	43	43	35

* at White Hart Lane

1902-03 Division One

1 Sep	FL	A	Sunderland	W 1-0
6 Sep	F	A	Barrow	W 2-0
8 Sep	F	A	Blackpool	W 1-0
9 Sep	FL	A	Grimsby T	W 1-0
13 Sep	FL	H	Aston Villa	W 2-0
20 Sep	FL	H	Derby Co	L 2-3
27 Sep	FL	A	Bury	L 1-3
2 Oct	FL	H	Everton	D 2-2
4 Oct	FL	H	Blackburn R	W 2-0
13 Oct	FL	A	Sheff Utd	L 0-2
18 Oct	FL	H	Stoke	L 1-3
25 Oct	FL	A	Everton	D 1-1
1 Nov	FL	H	Sheff Wed	L 1-4
8 Nov	FL	A	WBA	L 0-2
15 Nov	FL	H	Notts Co	D 0-0
22 Nov	FL	A	Bolton W	D 1-1
29 Nov	FL	H	Middlesbrough	W 1-0
6 Dec	FL	A	Newcastle U	W 2-0
13 Dec	FL	H	Wolves	W 2-0
20 Dec	FL	A	Liverpool	L 1-2
26 Dec	FL	A	Notts Co	D 1-1
27 Dec	FL	H	Sheff Utd	D 2-2
3 Jan	FL	H	Grimsby T	D 2-1
10 Jan	FL	A	Aston Villa	L 1-3
17 Jan	FL	A	Derby Co	W 1-0
24 Jan	FL	H	Bury	W 3-0
31 Jan	FL	A	Blackburn R	D 2-2
7 Feb	FAC1	H	Reading	D 0-0
11 Feb	FAC1r	A	Reading	W 6-3
14 Feb	FL	A	Stoke	L 2-3
21 Feb	FAC2	H	Stoke	D 0-0
26 Feb	FAC2r	A	Stoke	L 0-2
28 Feb	FL	A	Sheff Wed	L 0-1
7 Mar	FL	H	WBA	W 3-1
14 Mar	F	A	Cliftonville	W 4-0
21 Mar	FL	H	Bolton W	L 1-2
28 Mar	FL	A	Middlesbrough	L 0-2
4 Apr	FL	H	Newcastle U	W 3-2
11 Apr	FL	A	Wolves	L 1-2
13 Apr	FL	H	Sunderland	W 5-2
18 Apr	FL	H	Liverpool	W 1-0
29 Apr	F	A	Tottenham H	L 1-2
30 Apr	F	A	Ilford	W 4-2

League Appearances (Goals)
Broughton M 11 (1); Calvey J 29 (4); Craig C 31; Crawford J 3; Dudley W 1; Fielding R 10; Forman, Frank 26 (2); Forman, Fred 18 (3); Forman T 1; Gara A 6 (1); Henderson G 23; Iremonger J 34 (1); Linacre H 33; Morris G 33 (24); Newbigging A 1; Norris R 23; Roberts T 4; Robinson G 12; Spouncer A 26 (4); Stevenson J 6; Sugden S 8 (3); Timmins S 18 (3); Turner A 6; Warren F 8 (1); White J 3; Own Goals 1.

Position in League Table

		P	W	D	L	F	A	Pts
1st	Sheff W	34	19	4	11	54	36	42
10th	Forest	34	14	7	13	49	47	35

1903-04 Division One

5 Sep	FL	H	Liverpool	W 2-1
7 Sep	FL	A	Small Heath	D 3-3
12 Sep	FL	A	Bury	D 2-2
14 Sep	F	A	Blackpool	W 2-1
16 Sep	F	A	Swindon T	W 3-1
19 Sep	FL	H	Blackburn R	L 0-1
26 Sep	FL	A	Wolves	L 2-3
3 Oct	FL	A	Sheff Wed	L 1-2
10 Oct	FL	H	Sunderland	W 3-0
17 Oct	FL	A	WBA	D 1-1
24 Oct	FL	H	Small Heath	L 0-1
31 Oct	FL	A	Everton	W 2-0
14 Nov	FL	A	Derby Co	W 6-2
21 Nov	FL	H	Man City	L 0-3
25 Nov	FL	H	Stoke	W 4-2
28 Nov	FL	A	Notts Co	W 3-1
5 Dec	FL	H	Sheff Utd	D 1-1
12 Dec	FL	A	Newcastle U	L 1-3
19 Dec	FL	H	Aston Villa	L 3-7
25 Dec	FL	H	Notts Co	L 0-1
26 Dec	FL	A	Middlesbrough	D 1-1
1 Jan	FL	A	Blackburn R	L 1-3
2 Jan	FL	A	Liverpool	D 0-0
9 Jan	FL	H	Bury	D 2-2
23 Jan	FL	H	Wolves	W 5-0
30 Jan	FL	H	Sheff Wed	L 0-1
10 Feb	FAC1	A	WBA	D 1-1
13 Feb	FAC1r	H	WBA	W 3-1
20 Feb	FAC2	A	Blackburn R	L 1-3
27 Feb	FL	H	Everton	L 0-4
5 Mar	FL	A	Stoke	W 3-2
12 Mar	FL	H	Derby Co	W 5-1
17 Mar	F	A	Shepherds Bush	W 2-0
19 Mar	F	A	Bradford C	D 1-1
24 Mar	F	A	Barrow	D 0-0
26 Mar	F	A	Belfast Distillery	W 4-0
30 Mar	FL	H	WBA	W 2-0
2 Apr	FL	A	Sheff Utd	L 0-2
4 Apr	FL	A	Sunderland	L 1-3
5 Apr	F	A	Darlington	W 3-1
9 Apr	FL	H	Newcastle U	W 1-0
13 Apr	FL	A	Man City	D 0-0
16 Apr	FL	A	Aston Villa	L 1-3
23 Apr	FL	H	Middlesbrough	D 1-1

League Appearances (Goals)
Anthony W 1; Barnsdale J 5; Calvey J 11 (2); Comery H 1; Craig C 33 (2); Crawford J 7; Davies T 26 (1); Dudley W 2; Forman, Frank 3 (1); Griffiths H 8 (1); Henderson G 15 (1); Innes R 13; Iremonger J 26; Jones A 7; Jones T 2; Linacre H 34; Morris G 24 (12); Norris R 22 (1); Shearman W 24 (12); Spouncer A 33 (9); Sugden H 27 (13); Timmins S 27 (1); Turner A 3; Warren F 16 (1); Wright E 4.

Position in League Table

		P	W	D	L	F	A	Pts
1st	Sheff W	34	20	7	7	48	28	47
9th	Forest	34	11	9	14	57	57	31

1904-05 Division One

3 Sep	FL	A	Wolves	L 2-3
10 Sep	FL	H	Bury	W 5-1
17 Sep	FL	A	Aston Villa	L 0-2
24 Sep	FL	H	Blackburn R	W 5-2
1 Oct	FL	H	Stoke	L 0-1
6 Oct	FL	H	Preston NE	L 0-1
8 Oct	FL	A	Sheff Wed	L 0-2
15 Oct	FL	H	Sunderland	L 2-3
22 Oct	FL	A	Woolwich Arsenal	W 3-0
24 Oct	F	A	Fulham	D 1-1
29 Oct	FL	H	Derby Co	L 0-1
5 Nov	FL	A	Everton	L 1-5
12 Nov	FL	H	Small Heath	L 0-2
19 Nov	FL	A	Man City	D 1-1
26 Nov	FL	H	Notts Co	W 2-1
3 Dec	FL	A	Sheff Utd	L 0-4
10 Dec	FL	H	Newcastle U	L 1-3
17 Dec	FL	A	Preston NE	W 1-0
24 Dec	FL	H	Middlesbrough	D 1-1
26 Dec	FL	H	Sheff Wed	W 2-1
27 Dec	FL	H	Woolwich Arsenal	L 0-3
31 Dec	FL	H	Wolves	D 2-2
2 Jan	FL	A	Sunderland	L 0-1
7 Jan	FL	A	Bury	L 1-5
14 Jan	FL	H	Aston Villa	D 1-1
21 Jan	FL	A	Blackburn R	D 0-0
28 Jan	FL	A	Stoke	D 0-0
4 Feb	FAC1	H	Sheff Utd	W 2-0
18 Feb	FAC2	A	Fulham	L 0-1
25 Feb	FL	A	Derby Co	L 2-3
4 Mar	FL	A	Middlesbrough	D 0-0
11 Mar	FL	A	Small Heath	W 2-1
18 Mar	FL	H	Man City	W 2-1
25 Mar	FL	A	Notts Co	W 2-1
1 Apr	FL	H	Sheff Utd	L 1-2
8 Apr	FL	A	Newcastle U	L 1-5
24 Apr	FL	H	Everton	L 0-2
25 Apr	F	A	Leicester Fosse	W 2-1
11 Jun	F	A	Penarol	W 6-1
16 Jun	F	A	Rosario	W 5-0
18 Jun	F	A	Belgrano	W 7-0
22 Jun	F	A	Britanicos	W 13-1
24 Jun	F	A	Rosario	W 6-0
25 Jun	F	A	Alumni	W 6-1
29 Jun	F	A	Argentinos	W 5-0
2 Jul	F	A	Liga Argentina	W 9-1

League Appearances (Goals)
Anthony W 6; Barnsdale J 20; Chapman F 1; Craig C 31; Craggs J 8; Crawford J 3; Davies T 12; Dudley W 17; Forman, Frank 4 (1); Hardstaff J 3; Henderson G 21 (1); Holdstock H 1; Innes R 13; Iremonger J 18 (1); Jones A 5; Jones T 1; Lessons F 16 (3); Linacre H 32; Morris G 26 (11); Newbigging A 2; Niblo T 29 (7); Page W 1; Powell F (1); Robertson P 7; Shearman W 29 (13); Spouncer A 24 (2); Sugden S 12; Timmins S 31 (1).

Position in League Table

		P	W	D	L	F	A	Pts
1st	Newcastle	34	23	2	9	72	33	48
16th	Forest	34	9	7	18	40	61	25

1905-06 Division One

2 Sep	FL	H	Wolves	W 3-1
4 Sep	FL	A	Preston NE	L 1-3
9 Sep	FL	A	Man City	L 0-5
16 Sep	FL	H	Bury	W 3-2
23 Sep	FL	A	Middlesbrough	L 0-2
30 Sep	FL	H	Preston NE	W 1-0
7 Oct	FL	A	Newcastle U	L 2-3
14 Oct	FL	H	Aston Villa	D 2-2
21 Oct	FL	A	Liverpool	L 1-4
28 Oct	FL	H	Sheff Utd	W 4-1
4 Nov	FL	A	Notts Co	D 1-1
11 Nov	FL	H	Stoke	W 3-1
18 Nov	FL	A	Bolton W	L 0-6
25 Nov	FL	H	Woolwich Arsenal	W 3-1
2 Dec	FL	A	Blackburn R	D 1-1
9 Dec	FL	H	Sunderland	L 1-2
16 Dec	FL	A	Birmingham	L 0-5
23 Dec	FL	H	Everton	W 4-3
25 Dec	FL	H	Notts Co	L 1-2
26 Dec	FL	A	Derby Co	D 2-2
27 Dec	FL	A	Sheff Wed	L 0-1
30 Dec	FL	A	Wolves	L 1-2
6 Jan	FL	H	Man City	L 0-1
13 Jan	FAC1	A	Bury	D 1-1
17 Jan	FAC1r	H	Bury	W 6-2
20 Jan	FL	A	Bury	L 1-2
27 Jan	FL	H	Middlesbrough	W 2-1
3 Feb	FAC2	A	Fulham	W 3-1
10 Feb	FL	H	Newcastle U	W 2-1
17 Feb	FL	A	Aston Villa	L 1-3
24 Feb	FAC3	A	Sheff Wed	L 1-4
3 Mar	FL	A	Sheff Utd	W 4-1
14 Mar	FL	H	Liverpool	L 1-2
17 Mar	FL	A	Stoke	L 0-4
24 Mar	FL	H	Bolton W	W 4-0
2 Apr	FL	A	Woolwich Arsenal	L 1-3
7 Apr	FL	H	Blackburn R	L 1-2
14 Apr	FL	A	Sunderland	W 1-0
16 Apr	FL	H	Sheff Wed	L 3-4
17 Apr	FL	H	Derby Co	D 0-0
21 Apr	FL	H	Birmingham	W 2-1
28 Apr	FL	A	Everton	L 1-4

League Appearances (Goals)
Armstrong J 18; Chapman F 1; Craggs J 36 (7); Craig C 33; Davies T 2; Dudley W 38; Fullarton W 20; Hadley H 7; Hardstaff J 9 (1); Henderson G 21 (2); Holmes J 5; Hughes E 2; Iremonger J 5; Lessons F 14 (5); Linacre H 38; Morris G 32 (20); Needham G 1; Niblo T 17 (2); Rothery H 1; Shearman W 11 (5); Spouncer A 25 (2); Timmins S 19; West E 35 (14); Whitchurch W 1; Wolfe G 27.

Position in League Table

		P	W	D	L	F	A	Pts
1st	Liverpool	38	23	5	10	79	46	51
19th	Forest	38	13	5	20	58	79	31

1906-07 Division Two

1 Sep	FL	A	Grimsby T	L 1-3
8 Sep	FL	H	Burslem PV	D 2-2
15 Sep	FL	A	Burnley	L 1-2
22 Sep	FL	H	Leeds C	W 3-0
29 Sep	FL	A	Barnsley	W 1-0
4 Oct	FL	H	Chesterfield	W 3-1
6 Oct	FL	H	Chelsea	W 3-1
13 Oct	FL	A	Wolves	L 0-2
20 Oct	FL	H	Clapton Orient	W 4-0
27 Oct	FL	A	Gainsborough Trinity	W 3-2
3 Nov	FL	H	Stockport Co	W 2-1
10 Nov	FL	A	Hull C	W 2-1
17 Nov	FL	H	Glossop	W 2-0
24 Nov	FL	A	Blackpool	W 2-1
1 Dec	FL	H	Bradford C	W 3-0
8 Dec	FL	A	WBA	L 1-3
15 Dec	FL	H	Leicester Fosse	W 2-1
22 Dec	FL	A	Chesterfield	D 1-1
25 Dec	FL	H	Burton U	W 2-0
29 Dec	FL	H	Grimsby T	L 0-3
5 Jan	FL	A	Burslem PV	L 2-4
12 Jan	FAC1	H	Barnsley	D 1-1
17 Jan	FAC1r	A	Barnsley	L 1-2
19 Jan	FL	H	Burnley	W 2-0
26 Jan	FL	A	Leeds C	W 4-1
2 Feb	F	A	Northampton T	W 4-3
9 Feb	FL	A	Chelsea	W 2-0
16 Feb	FL	H	Wolves	W 1-0
23 Feb	FL	A	Clapton Orient	W 1-0
2 Mar	FL	H	Gainsborough Trinity	W 3-1
9 Mar	FL	A	Stockport Co	D 0-0
16 Mar	FL	H	Hull C	W 2-1
23 Mar	FL	A	Glossop	W 2-0
29 Mar	FL	A	Lincoln C	W 2-1
30 Mar	FL	H	Blackpool	W 3-0
1 Apr	FL	A	Burton U	W 2-0
2 Apr	FL	H	Barnsley	D 0-0
6 Apr	FL	A	Bradford C	W 2-1
13 Apr	FL	H	WBA	W 3-1
20 Apr	FL	A	Leicester Fosse	W 2-1
24 Apr	FL	H	Lincoln C	W 3-1

League Appearances (Goals)
Armstrong J 38 (2); Butler B 1; Chapman F 1; Craggs J 8; Craig C 8; Dudley W 38; Green A 13 (6); Hadley G 5 (1); Hooper W 13 (2); Hughes E 36; Iremonger J 5; Lessons F 1; Linacre H 32; Maltby G 29; Marrison T 25 (6); Morris G 36 (21); Needham G 22; Radnell C 1; Rothery H 4; Shearman W 23 (8); Spouncer A 21 (7); West E 33 (14); Whitchurch J 7 (5); Wolfe G 15; Woodland T 3 (1); Own Goals 1.

Position in League Table

		P	W	D	L	F	A	Pts
1st	Forest	38	28	4	6	74	36	60

1907-08 Division One

2 Sep	FL	H	Liverpool	W 3-1
7 Sep	FL	H	Middlesbrough	L 0-3
14 Sep	FL	A	Sheff Utd	D 2-2
21 Sep	FL	H	Chelsea	W 6-0
28 Sep	FL	A	Newcastle U	L 0-3
5 Oct	FL	A	Man Utd	L 0-4
12 Oct	FL	H	Blackburn R	W 3-2
19 Oct	FL	A	Bolton W	L 0-1
26 Oct	FL	H	Birmingham	D 1-1
2 Nov	FL	A	Everton	L 0-1
9 Nov	FL	H	Sunderland	W 4-1
16 Nov	FL	A	Woolwich Arsenal	L 1-3
23 Nov	FL	H	Sheff Wed	D 2-2
30 Nov	FL	A	Bristol C	L 0-3
7 Dec	FL	H	Notts Co	W 2-0
14 Dec	FL	A	Man City	L 2-4
21 Dec	FL	H	Preston NE	D 2-2
25 Dec	FL	A	Aston Villa	L 0-4
26 Dec	FL	H	Aston Villa	D 2-2
28 Dec	FL	A	Bury	D 0-0
1 Jan	FL	A	Liverpool	D 0-0
4 Jan	FL	A	Middlesbrough	D 1-1
11 Jan	FAC1	A	Newcastle U	L 0-2
18 Jan	FL	A	Chelsea	W 4-0
25 Jan	FL	H	Newcastle U	D 0-0
8 Feb	FL	A	Blackburn R	D 3-3
15 Feb	FL	H	Bolton W	W 1-0
22 Feb	FL	A	Birmingham	Abnd
29 Feb	FL	H	Everton	W 5-2
7 Mar	FL	A	Sunderland	L 2-7
14 Mar	FL	H	Woolwich Arsenal	W 1-0
21 Mar	FL	A	Sheff Wed	L 1-2
28 Mar	FL	H	Bristol C	W 3-1
30 Mar	FL	A	Birmingham	L 0-1
4 Apr	FL	A	Notts Co	L 0-2
11 Apr	FL	H	Man City	W 3-1
17 Apr	FL	H	Man Utd	W 2-0
18 Apr	FL	A	Preston NE	W 1-0
20 Apr	FL	H	Sheff Utd	D 1-1
25 Apr	FL	H	Bury	L 1-2

League Appearances (Goals)
Armstrong J 38; Dudley W 30; Gibson T 10; Green A 20 (7); Hooper W 19 (1); Hughes E 36 (1); Iremonger J 4; Linacre H 35; Maltby G 35; Marrison T 36 (6); Morris G 23 (7); Needham G 22 (1); Shearman W 21 (1); Spouncer A 27 (2); Stanley F 1; West E 35 (28); Whitchurch J 7 (3); Wolfe G 17; Woodland T 2 (1); Own Goals 1.

Position in League Table

		P	W	D	L	F	A	Pts
1st	Man Utd	38	23	6	9	81	48	52
9th	Forest	38	13	11	14	59	62	37

1908-09 Division One

5 Sep	FL	A	Sheff Utd	W 2-1
12 Sep	FL	H	Aston Villa	L 1-2
15 Sep	F	A	Bradford PA	W 2-1
19 Sep	FL	H	Sheff Wed	L 1-2
21 Sep	FL	A	Chelsea	L 1-2
26 Sep	FL	A	Sunderland	L 1-2
1 Oct	FL	H	Liverpool	W 5-1
3 Oct	FL	H	Chelsea	W 2-1
10 Oct	FL	A	Blackburn R	W 3-0
17 Oct	FL	H	Bradford C	W 2-1
24 Oct	FL	A	Man Utd	D 2-2
31 Oct	FL	H	Everton	L 1-2
7 Nov	FL	A	Leicester Fosse	W 3-0
14 Nov	FL	H	Woolwich Arsenal	L 0-1
21 Nov	FL	A	Notts Co	L 0-3
28 Nov	FL	H	Newcastle U	L 0-4
5 Dec	FL	A	Bristol C	L 1-2
12 Dec	FL	H	Preston NE	D 1-1
19 Dec	FL	A	Middlesbrough	L 0-4
25 Dec	FL	A	Bury	L 2-3
26 Dec	FL	A	Liverpool	D 1-1
28 Dec	FL	H	Man City	L 0-2
2 Jan	FL	H	Sheff Utd	L 0-2
9 Jan	FL	A	Aston Villa	W 2-1
16 Jan	FAC1	H	Aston Villa	W 2-0
23 Jan	FL	A	Sheff Wed	L 0-3
30 Jan	FL	H	Sunderland	W 4-0
6 Feb	FAC2	H	Brentford	W 1-0
13 Feb	FL	H	Blackburn R	W 2-1
20 Feb	FAC3	H	Millwall Ath	W 3-1
27 Feb	FL	H	Man Utd	W 2-0
13 Mar	FAC4	A	Derby Co	L 0-3
20 Mar	FL	A	Woolwich Arsenal	W 2-1
24 Mar	FL	A	Everton	D 3-3
27 Mar	FL	H	Notts Co	W 1-0
30 Mar	FL	A	Bradford C	D 1-1
3 Apr	FL	A	Newcastle U	D 1-1
10 Apr	FL	H	Bristol C	D 1-1
12 Apr	FL	H	Bury	L 0-2
13 Apr	FL	A	Man City	L 1-2
17 Apr	FL	A	Preston NE	D 1-1
21 Apr	FL	H	Leicester Fosse	W12-0
24 Apr	FL	H	Middlesbrough	W 4-1

League Appearances (Goals)
Armstrong J 37; Birch W 14 (2); Butler R 1; Dudley W 38; Gibson T 6; Green A 6 (3); Hooper W 37 (8); Hughes E 37 (3); Iremonger J 8; Linacre H 30; Maltby G 33; Marrison T 36 (10); Morris G 33 (11); Needham G 15 (1); Rowan F 1; Shearman W 2; Spouncer A 19 (3); West E 34 (22); Whitchurch J 8 (2); Wolfe G 23; Own Goals 1.

Position in League Table

		P	W	D	L	F	A	Pts
1st	Newcastle	38	24	5	9	65	41	53
14th	Forest	38	14	8	16	66	57	36

1909-10 Division One

1 Sep	FL	A	Preston NE	W 1-0
4 Sep	FL	H	Notts Co	W 2-1
11 Sep	FL	A	Newcastle U	W 2-1
18 Sep	FL	H	Liverpool	L 1-4
25 Sep	FL	A	Aston Villa	D 0-0
2 Oct	FL	H	Sheff Utd	L 2-3
9 Oct	FL	A	Woolwich Arsenal	W 1-0
16 Oct	FL	H	Bolton W	W 2-0
23 Oct	FL	A	Chelsea	W 1-0
30 Oct	FL	H	Blackburn R	L 0-4
3 Nov	FL	H	Bury	D 3-3
6 Nov	FL	A	Middlesbrough	L 1-2
13 Nov	FL	A	Sunderland	L 1-2
20 Nov	FL	H	Everton	W 1-0
27 Nov	FL	A	Man Utd	W 6-2
4 Dec	FL	H	Bradford C	D 1-1
11 Dec	FL	A	Sheff Wed	L 3-4
18 Dec	FL	H	Bristol C	D 0-0
25 Dec	FL	A	Tottenham H	D 2-2
27 Dec	FL	H	Tottenham H	D 2-2
1 Jan	FL	H	Aston Villa	L 1-4
3 Jan	FL	A	Bury	L 1-4
8 Jan	FL	A	Notts Co	L 1-4
15 Jan	FAC1	H	Sheff Utd	W 3-2
22 Jan	FL	H	Newcastle U	L 0-1
5 Feb	FAC2	A	Northampton T	D 0-0
9 Feb	FAC2r	H	Northampton T	W 1-0
12 Feb	FL	A	Sheff Utd	W 4-1
19 Feb	FAC3	A	Coventry C	L 1-3
26 Feb	FL	A	Bolton W	L 1-2
2 Mar	FL	H	Woolwich Arsenal	D 1-1
5 Mar	FL	H	Chelsea	D 0-0
12 Mar	FL	A	Blackburn R	D 2-2
19 Mar	FL	H	Middlesbrough	L 0-1
25 Mar	FL	H	Preston NE	D 0-0
26 Mar	FL	H	Sunderland	L 1-3
28 Mar	F	A	Merthyr T	D 0-0
29 Mar	F	A	Chesterfield	L 0-1
2 Apr	FL	A	Everton	W 4-0
9 Apr	FL	H	Man Utd	W 2-0
16 Apr	FL	A	Bradford C	D 1-1
20 Apr	FL	A	Liverpool	L 3-7
23 Apr	FL	H	Sheff Wed	L 0-6
30 Apr	FL	A	Bristol C	L 0-4

League Appearances (Goals)
Armstrong J 25 (2); Badger H 2; Butler R 1; Derrick J 5 (4); Dudley W 33; Fisher A 2; Gibson T 3; Hasell A 15; Hooper W 29 (4); Horrocks J 18; Hughes E 36; Iremonger J 6; Maltby G 38 (1); Marrison T 36 (6); Marsden J 2; Morris G 30 (19); Needham G 32; Palmer W 12 (1); Rowan F 1; Ryalls J 9; Smith JW 17; Spouncer A 5; Vaughan H 4; West E 32 (17); Whitchurch J 2; Wolfe G 23.

Position in League Table

		P	W	D	L	F	A	Pts
1st	A Villa	38	23	7	8	84	42	53
14th	Forest	38	11	11	16	54	72	33

1910-11 Division One

1 Sep	FL	A	Preston NE	W 2-0
3 Sep	FL	A	Notts Co	D 1-1
10 Sep	FL	H	Man Utd	W 2-1
17 Sep	FL	A	Liverpool	W 3-2
24 Sep	FL	H	Bury	L 1-2
26 Sep	NHC	A	Northampton T	L 0-1
1 Oct	FL	A	Sheff Utd	W 1-0
6 Oct	FL	H	Preston NE	L 1-3
8 Oct	FL	H	Aston Villa	W 3-1
15 Oct	FL	A	Sunderland	D 2-2
22 Oct	FL	H	Woolwich Arsenal	L 2-3
29 Oct	FL	A	Bradford C	L 1-2
5 Nov	FL	H	Blackburn R	W 5-2
12 Nov	FL	H	Oldham A	W 4-1
19 Nov	FL	A	Man City	L 0-1
26 Nov	FL	H	Everton	D 1-1
3 Dec	FL	A	Sheff Wed	L 2-5
10 Dec	FL	H	Bristol C	D 3-3
17 Dec	FL	A	Newcastle U	L 1-4
24 Dec	FL	H	Tottenham H	L 1-2
26 Dec	FL	A	Tottenham H	W 4-1
27 Dec	FL	H	Middlesbrough	D 1-1
31 Dec	FL	H	Notts Co	L 0-2
2 Jan	FL	A	Middlesbrough	D 2-2
7 Jan	FL	A	Man Utd	L 2-4
14 Jan	FAC1	A	West Ham U	L 1-2
21 Jan	FL	H	Liverpool	W 2-0
28 Jan	FL	A	Bury	L 0-1
4 Feb	FL	H	Sheff Utd	L 1-2
11 Feb	FL	A	Aston Villa	L 1-3
18 Feb	FL	H	Sunderland	L 1-3
25 Feb	FL	A	Woolwich Arsenal	L 2-3
4 Mar	FL	H	Bradford C	L 0-2
18 Mar	FL	A	Oldham A	L 0-2
25 Mar	FL	H	Man City	D 0-0
27 Mar	FL	A	Blackburn R	L 1-4
5 Apr	FL	H	Newcastle U	L 0-1
8 Apr	FL	H	Sheff Wed	L 0-1
14 Apr	FL	A	Everton	L 1-2
15 Apr	FL	A	Bristol C	L 1-5
17 Apr	F	H	Queens Park	L 1-2

League Appearances (Goals)
Armstrong J 37 (2); Bailey W 4 (1); Derrick J 19 (6); Drabble F 8; Dudley W 24; Fisher A 7 (1); Ford J 22 (5); Gibson T 18; Hasell A 18; Hooper W 37 (6); Horrocks J 4; Hughes E 16 (1); Lockett J 23 (5); Maltby G 36 (2); Marrison T 30 (10); Mercer J 13; Morris G 26 (11); Needham G 31 (2); Ripley J 4 (1); Rowlands A 1; Slater H 2; Smith J 3 (1); Smith JW 12; Wolfe G 23 (1).

Position in League Table

		P	W	D	L	F	A	Pts
1	Man Utd	38	22	8	8	72	40	52
20	Forest	38	9	7	22	55	75	25

1911-12 Division Two

2 Sep	FL	H	Leeds C	W 2-1
9 Sep	FL	A	Wolves	L 0-1
16 Sep	FL	H	Leicester Fosse	W 4-1
23 Sep	FL	A	Gainsborough Trinity	W 2-1
30 Sep	FL	H	Grimsby T	W 1-0
7 Oct	FL	A	Burnley	L 0-2
12 Oct	F	H	Hillhurst Ath	W 4-1
14 Oct	FL	A	Chelsea	L 0-2
21 Oct	FL	H	Clapton Orient	W 3-0
28 Oct	FL	A	Bristol C	D 2-2
4 Nov	FL	H	Birmingham	L 0-1
11 Nov	FL	A	Huddersfield T	W 2-1
18 Nov	FL	H	Blackpool	W 2-1
25 Nov	FL	A	Glossop	D 0-0
2 Dec	FL	H	Hull C	D 0-0
9 Dec	FL	A	Barnsley	L 0-1
16 Dec	FL	H	Bradford PA	W 2-1
23 Dec	FL	A	Fulham	L 0-2
25 Dec	FL	A	Stockport Co	D 2-2
26 Dec	FL	H	Derby Co	L 1-3
30 Dec	FL	A	Leeds C	L 1-3
1 Jan	F	A	Linfield Ath	L 1-2
6 Jan	FL	H	Wolves	D 0-0
13 Jan	FAC1	H	Bradford PA	L 0-1
27 Jan	FL	H	Gainsborough Trinity	W 2-0
10 Feb	FL	H	Burnley	L 0-1
17 Feb	FL	H	Chelsea	L 2-3
24 Feb	FL	A	Clapton Orient	W 2-0
29 Feb	FL	A	Leicester Fosse	D 1-1
2 Mar	FL	H	Bristol C	W 2-0
9 Mar	FL	A	Birmingham	L 2-4
16 Mar	FL	H	Huddersfield T	W 3-0
21 Mar	FL	A	Grimsby T	W 4-1
23 Mar	FL	A	Blackpool	L 0-2
30 Mar	FL	H	Glossop	L 0-1
6 Apr	FL	A	Hull C	L 1-2
8 Apr	FL	H	Stockport Co	L 1-2
9 Apr	FL	A	Derby Co	L 0-1
13 Apr	FL	H	Barnsley	L 0-2
20 Apr	FL	A	Bradford PA	L 1-2
27 Apr	FL	H	Fulham	D 1-1

League Appearances (Goals)
Armstrong J 23 (1); Banks F 17 (3); Blythe J 1; Condrey J 7(2); Derrick J 37 (6); Dodson A 1; Dudley W 27; Firth R 31 (4); Fisher A 21; Ford J 24 (4); Gibson T 36 (3); Hamilton A 6; Hanna J 32; Hooper W 11 (2); Langham F 2; McCann D 1; Machin P 1; Maltby G 13; Mercer J 36 (3); Morris G 19 (10); Needham G 38 (1); Poole H 1; Saunders F 27 (6); Stanway R 1; Walker W 1; Williams J 4 (1).

Position in League Table

		P	W	D	L	F	A	Pts
1st	Derby Co	38	23	8	7	74	28	54
15th	Forest	38	13	7	18	46	48	33

1912-13 Division Two

7 Sep	FL	A	Leicester Fosse	L 1-3
14 Sep	FL	H	Stockport Co	W 2-1
16 Sep	FL	A	Wolves	W 3-2
21 Sep	FL	A	Preston NE	D 1-1
28 Sep	FL	H	Burnley	W 2-1
3 Oct	FL	H	Barnsley	W 2-0
5 Oct	FL	A	Hull C	L 1-2
12 Oct	FL	H	Glossop	W 3-2
19 Oct	FL	A	Clapton Orient	D 2-2
26 Oct	FL	H	Lincoln C	L 1-2
2 Nov	FL	H	Blackpool	D 1-1
9 Nov	FL	A	Bristol C	W 2-1
16 Nov	FL	H	Birmingham	W 3-1
23 Nov	FL	A	Huddersfield T	D 1-1
30 Nov	FL	H	Leeds C	L 1-2
7 Dec	FL	A	Grimsby T	D 0-0
14 Dec	FL	H	Bury	D 1-1
21 Dec	FL	A	Fulham	D 0-0
25 Dec	FL	H	Wolves	W 2-0
26 Dec	F	A	Coventry C	D 2-2
28 Dec	FL	H	Leicester Fosse	W 4-2
1 Jan	FL	A	Barnsley	L 0-1
4 Jan	FL	A	Stockport Co	L 1-2
18 Jan	FAC1	A	Chesterfield	W 4-1
25 Jan	FL	A	Burnley	W 5-3
1 Feb	FAC2	A	Oldham A	L 1-5
5 Feb	FL	H	Preston NE	L 0-2
8 Feb	FL	H	Hull C	W 5-0
15 Feb	FL	A	Glossop	L 3-4
22 Feb	FL	H	Clapton Orient	D 0-0
1 Mar	FL	A	Lincoln C	L 1-2
8 Mar	FL	A	Blackpool	L 1-2
15 Mar	FL	H	Bristol C	W 4-1
21 Mar	FL	H	Bradford PA	L 1-2
22 Mar	FL	A	Birmingham	L 0-2
24 Mar	FL	A	Bradford PA	L 1-3
29 Mar	FL	H	Huddersfield T	L 0-1
5 Apr	FL	A	Leeds C	L 0-1
12 Apr	FL	H	Grimsby T	L 1-2
19 Apr	FL	A	Bury	L 0-2
26 Apr	FL	H	Fulham	L 2-4

League Appearances (Goals)
Allan J 16 (2); Armstrong J 34; Banks F 26 (1); Derrick J 25 (10); Dudley W 22; Firth R 24 (1); Fisher A 11; Ford J 35 (2); Gibson T 31 (17); Hamilton A 1; Hanna J 32; Jones H 11; Lemoine H 5; Maltby G 28; Mercer J 37; Morris G 34 (16); Needham G 38 (4); Reid R 9 (2); Own Goals 3.

Position in League Table

		P	W	D	L	F	A	Pts
1st	Preston	38	19	15	4	56	33	53
17th	Forest	38	12	8	18	49	68	32

1913-14 Division Two

3 Sep	FL	H	Leicester Fosse	L 1-3
6 Sep	FL	H	Wolves	L 1-3
11 Sep	FL	A	Leicester Fosse	L 1-5
13 Sep	FL	A	Hull C	L 0-1
20 Sep	FL	H	Barnsley	L 0-2
27 Sep	FL	A	Bury	L 0-1
4 Oct	FL	H	Huddersfield T	D 1-1
11 Oct	FL	A	Lincoln C	L 0-1
18 Oct	FL	H	Blackpool	W 3-0
25 Oct	FL	A	Fulham	L 0-2
1 Nov	FL	A	Woolwich Arsenal	L 2-3
8 Nov	FL	H	Grimsby T	W 4-1
15 Nov	FL	A	Birmingham	L 0-2
22 Nov	FL	H	Bristol C	D 1-1
29 Nov	FL	A	Leeds C	L 0-8
6 Dec	FL	H	Clapton Orient	D 1-1
16 Dec	FL	A	Glossop	L 0-3
20 Dec	FL	H	Stockport Co	D 2-2
25 Dec	FL	A	Notts Co	D 2-2
26 Dec	FL	H	Notts Co	W 1-0
27 Dec	FL	A	Wolves	L 1-4
3 Jan	FL	H	Hull C	L 1-2
10 Jan	FAC1	A	Clapton Orient	D 2-2
14 Jan	FAC1r	H	Clapton Orient	L 0-1
17 Jan	FL	A	Barnsley	L 0-5
24 Jan	FL	H	Bury	D 1-1
31 Jan	NSC	A	Notts Co	W 5-0
7 Feb	FL	A	Huddersfield T	D 1-1
14 Feb	FL	H	Lincoln C	W 2-1
21 Feb	FL	A	Blackpool	L 1-2
28 Feb	FL	H	Fulham	D 1-1
7 Mar	FL	H	Woolwich Arsenal	D 0-0
14 Mar	FL	A	Grimsby T	L 0-3
21 Mar	FL	H	Birmingham	W 3-1
28 Mar	FL	A	Bristol C	L 0-1
4 Apr	FL	H	Leeds C	W 2-1
10 Apr	FL	A	Bradford PA	L 0-4
11 Apr	FL	A	Clapton Orient	L 1-3
13 Apr	FL	H	Bradford PA	W 1-0
18 Apr	FL	H	Glossop	L 1-2
25 Apr	FL	A	Stockport Co	L 1-2

League Appearances (Goals)
Allan J 6 (1); Armstrong J 25; Banks F 15 (1); Bell J 30 (4); Derrick J 24 (8); Dudley W 8; Firth R 37 (6); Fisher A 27; Ford J 21 (1); Gibson T 36 (5); Hanna J 33; Harris F 14 (5); Iremonger H 1; Jones H 18; Lemoine H 4; Lockton J 12 (1); McKnight J 9; Maltby G 5; Mercer J 35 (2); Needham G 38 (1); Ritchie S 7; Simms W 3; Yates L 10 (1); Own Gls 1.

Position in League Table

		P	W	D	L	F	A	Pts
1st	Notts Co	38	23	7	8	77	36	53
20th	Forest	38	7	9	22	37	76	23

Election to Football League (2 places)
Forest 34, Lincoln C 24 (both re-elected), Stoke 16, Darlington 2, Chesterfield 1, South Shields 1, Gainsborough Trinity 0, South Liverpool 0 (all not elected).

1914-15 Division Two

2 Sep	FL	H	Birmingham	D 1-1
5 Sep	FL	H	Grimsby T	W 4-2
12 Sep	FL	A	Huddersfield T	L 0-4
19 Sep	FL	H	Bristol C	L 0-1
26 Sep	FL	A	Bury	L 2-4
1 Oct	FL	H	Lincoln C	W 3-2
3 Oct	FL	H	Preston NE	D 1-1
10 Oct	FL	A	Blackpool	L 0-3
17 Oct	FL	A	Leicester Fosse	L 1-3
24 Oct	FL	H	Barnsley	W 2-1
31 Oct	FL	A	Glossop	L 0-1
7 Nov	FL	H	Wolves	W 3-1
14 Nov	FL	A	Fulham	L 1-2
18 Nov	FL	H	Arsenal	D 1-1
21 Nov	FL	H	Stockport Co	D 1-1
28 Nov	FL	A	Hull C	L 1-3
5 Dec	FL	H	Leeds C	W 3-1
12 Dec	FL	A	Clapton Orient	D 0-0
19 Dec	FACq6	H	Shrewsbury T	W 6-1
25 Dec	FL	H	Derby Co	D 2-2
26 Dec	FL	A	Derby Co	L 0-1
28 Dec	FL	A	Birmingham	L 0-3
2 Jan	FL	A	Grimsby T	L 0-4
9 Jan	FAC1	H	Norwich C	L 1-4
16 Jan	FL	H	Huddersfield T	W 3-2
23 Jan	FL	A	Bristol C	W 2-1
4 Feb	FL	H	Bury	D 1-1
6 Feb	FL	A	Preston NE	D 2-2
13 Feb	FL	H	Blackpool	W 2-1
20 Feb	FL	H	Leicester Fosse	L 1-3
27 Feb	FL	A	Barnsley	L 0-3
6 Mar	FL	H	Glossop	W 1-0
13 Mar	FL	A	Wolves	L 1-5
20 Mar	FL	H	Fulham	D 2-2
27 Mar	FL	A	Stockport Co	L 0-1
3 Apr	FL	H	Hull C	W 1-0
5 Apr	FL	A	Lincoln C	L 1-2
10 Apr	FL	A	Leeds C	L 0-4
17 Apr	FL	H	Clapton Orient	L 0-1
24 Apr	FL	A	Arsenal	L 0-7

League Appearances (Goals)
Armstrong J 36; Bell J 24 (2); Belton J 24 (7); Coleman J 38 (14); Derrick J 22 (2); Fisher A 32 (2); Fiske W 4; Fletcher S 1; Gibson T 36 (5); Harris F 34 (7); Iremonger H 10; Jones H 23 (1); Lockton J 8 (1); Mercer J 29 (1); Needham G 38; Neve E 35 (3); Powell J 24.

Position in League Table

		P	W	D	L	F	A	Pts
1st	Derby Co	38	23	7	8	71	33	53
18th	Forest	38	10	9	19	43	77	29

1915-16 War League

MIDLAND SECTION
Principal (P) and Subsidiary (S) Tournaments

4 Sep	WLP	A	Grimsby T	D 1-1
11 Sep	WLP	H	Notts Co	L 3-5
18 Sep	WLP	A	Derby Co	W 4-3
2 Oct	WLP	A	Bradford PA	L 0-1
9 Oct	WLP	H	Leeds C	W 2-0
16 Oct	WLP	A	Hull C	W 3-1
23 Oct	WLP	H	Lincoln C	W 3-2
30 Oct	WLP	H	Barnsley	W 5-0
6 Nov	WLP	A	Leicester Fosse	W 3-1
13 Nov	WLP	H	Sheff Utd	W 2-0
20 Nov	WLP	A	Bradford C	D 0-0
27 Nov	WLP	H	Huddersfield T	W 2-0
4 Dec	WLP	H	Grimsby T	W 2-0
11 Dec	WLP	A	Notts Co	D 0-0
18 Dec	WLP	H	Derby Co	W 5-0
25 Dec	WLP	A	Sheff Wed	W 1-0
27 Dec	WLP	H	Sheff Wed	W 1-0
1 Jan	WLP	H	Bradford PA	D 0-0
8 Jan	WLP	A	Leeds C	L 0-1
15 Jan	WLP	H	Hull C	W 4-1
22 Jan	WLP	A	Lincoln C	W 4-1
29 Jan	WLP	A	Barnsley	D 1-1
5 Feb	WLP	H	Leicester Fosse	W 1-0
12 Feb	WLP	A	Sheff Utd	L 1-3
19 Feb	WLP	H	Bradford C	L 0-2
4 Mar	WLS	H	Derby Co	W 3-0
11 Mar	WLS	A	Stoke	W 1-0
18 Mar	WLS	A	Chesterfield	L 1-2
25 Mar	WLS	H	Leicester Fosse	W 4-0
1 Apr	WLS	A	Notts Co	L 0-2
8 Apr	WLS	A	Derby Co	L 1-4
15 Apr	WLS	H	Stoke	W 3-1
21 Apr	WLS	H	Chesterfield	W 8-1
22 Apr	F	A	Cardiff C	L 1-2
24 Apr	WLS	H	Notts Co	W 4-2
25 Apr	WLP	A	Huddersfield T	L 0-2
29 Apr	WLS	A	Leicester Fosse	W 3-1

Position in Principal Tournament

		P	W	D	L	F	A	Pts
1st	Forest	26	15	5	6	48	25	35

Position in Subsidiary Tournament

		P	W	D	L	F	A	Pts
1st	Forest	10	7	0	3	28	12	14

1916-17 War League

MIDLAND SECTION
Principal (P) and Subsidiary (S) Tournaments

2 Sep	WLP	H	Notts Co	W 4-3
9 Sep	WLP	A	Rotherham Co	L 1-2
16 Sep	WLP	H	Huddersfield T	L 0-1
23 Sep	WLP	A	Lincoln C	W 2-1
30 Sep	WLP	H	Sheff Wed	W 5-1
7 Oct	WLP	A	Bradford PA	L 0-1
14 Oct	WLP	H	Birmingham	L 0-4
21 Oct	WLP	A	Hull C	L 1-3
28 Oct	WLP	A	Chesterfield	W 3-0
4 Nov	WLP	H	Barnsley	W 3-0
11 Nov	WLP	A	Leeds C	L 1-3
18 Nov	WLP	H	Sheff Utd	D 0-0
25 Nov	WLP	A	Bradford C	L 2-3
2 Dec	WLP	H	Leicester Fosse	W 2-0
9 Dec	WLP	A	Notts Co	D 2-2
16 Dec	WLP	H	Rotherham Co	L 2-3
23 Dec	WLP	A	Huddersfield T	W 2-1
25 Dec	WLP	H	Grimsby T	W 5-1
26 Dec	WLP	A	Grimsby T	D 1-1
30 Dec	WLP	H	Lincoln C	W 2-0
6 Jan	WLP	A	Sheff Wed	W 4-1
13 Jan	WLP	H	Bradford PA	L 0-1
20 Jan	WLP	A	Birmingham	L 0-1
27 Jan	WLP	H	Hull C	W 3-0
3 Feb	WLP	H	Chesterfield	W 3-0
10 Feb	WLP	A	Barnsley	W 1-0
17 Feb	WLP	H	Leeds C	D 3-3
24 Feb	WLP	A	Sheff Utd	W 4-1
3 Mar	WLP	H	Bradford C	L 0-1
10 Mar	WLP	A	Leicester Fosse	D 1-1
24 Mar	WLS	A	Notts Co	D 2-2
31 Mar	WLS	H	Leicester Fosse	W 1-0
6 Apr	WLS	H	Birmingham	D 3-3
9 Apr	WLS	A	Birmingham	L 3-4
14 Apr	WLS	H	Notts Co	L 2-3
21 Apr	WLS	A	Leicester Fosse	L 1-2

Position in Principal Tournament

		P	W	D	L	F	A	Pts
1st	Leeds C	30	18	10	2	68	29	46
6th	Forest	30	14	5	11	57	39	33

Position in Subsidiary Tournament

		P	W	D	L	F	A	Pts
1st	Br'd'fd PA	6	3	2	1	10	5	8
14th	Forest	6	1	2	3	12	14	4

1917-18 War League

MIDLAND SECTION
Principal (P) and Subsidiary (S) Tournaments

1 Sep	WLP	A	Huddersfield T	L 1-2
8 Sep	WLP	H	Huddersfield T	W 3-0
15 Sep	WLP	A	Sheff Wed	W 3-0
22 Sep	WLP	H	Sheff Wed	W 3-1
29 Sep	WLP	A	Bradford C	W 3-0
6 Oct	WLP	H	Bradford C	W 2-0
13 Oct	WLP	H	Rotherham Co	L 1-3
20 Oct	WLP	A	Rotherham Co	W 3-1
27 Oct	WLP	H	Lincoln C	L 0-1
3 Nov	WLP	A	Lincoln C	L 1-3
10 Nov	WLP	H	Grimsby T	W 5-0
17 Nov	WLP	A	Grimsby T	D 1-1
24 Nov	WLP	H	Birmingham	W 2-1
1 Dec	WLP	A	Birmingham	D 1-1
8 Dec	F	A	Manton Colliery	W 5-2
15 Dec	F	A	Bolsover	W 4-0
22 Dec	WLP	A	Hull C	L 2-3
25 Dec	WLP	A	Notts Co	W 1-0
26 Dec	WLP	H	Notts Co	D 0-0
29 Dec	WLP	H	Hul C	W 5-1
5 Jan	WLP	A	Leicester Fosse	L 0-2
12 Jan	WLP	H	Leicester Fosse	W 2-0
19 Jan	WLP	A	Bradford PA	Abnd
26 Jan	WLP	H	Bradford PA	D 0-0
2 Feb	WLP	A	Leeds C	L 0-2
9 Feb	WLP	H	Leeds C	L 0-1
16 Feb	WLP	A	Sheff Utd	W 1-0
23 Feb	WLP	H	Sheff Utd	L 0-1
2 Mar	WLP	A	Barnsley	L 0-1
9 Mar	WLP	H	Barnsley	W 1-0
16 Mar	WLS	A	Birmingham	D 0-0
23 Mar	WLS	H	Birmingham	W 1-0
29 Mar	WLS	A	Notts Co	L 1-3
30 Mar	WLS	A	Leicester Fosse	L 0-1
1 Apr	WLS	H	Notts Co	L 0-3
2 Apr	WLP	A	Bradford PA	L 0-3
6 Apr	WLS	H	Leicester Fosse	W 2-0

Position in Principal Tournament

	P	W	D	L	F	A	Pts
1st Leeds C	28	23	1	4	75	23	47
5th Forest	28	13	4	11	41	28	30

Position in Subsidiary Tournament

	P	W	D	L	F	A	Pts
1st Grimsby	6	4	1	1	13	3	9
13th Forest	6	2	1	3	4	7	5

1918-19 War League

MIDLAND SECTION
Principal (P) and Subsidiary (S) Tournaments

7 Sep	WLP	H	Birmingham	W 1-0
14 Sep	WLP	A	Birmingham	W 3-2
21 Sep	WLP	H	Rotherham Co	W 3-1
28 Sep	WLP	A	Rotherham Co	D 1-1
5 Oct	WLP	H	Lincoln C	D 1-1
12 Oct	WLP	A	Lincoln C	W 3-1
19 Oct	WLP	A	Grimsby T	W 2-0
26 Oct	WLP	H	Grimsby T	W 6-1
2 Nov	WLP	A	Bradford C	L 0-1
9 Nov	WLP	H	Bradford C	W 6-1
16 Nov	WLP	A	Sheff Wed	W 2-1
23 Nov	WLP	H	Sheff Wed	W 3-1
30 Nov	WLP	A	Huddersfield T	D 0-0
7 Dec	WLP	H	Huddersfield T	W 1-0
14 Dec	WLP	H	Coventry C	L 0-1
21 Dec	WLP	A	Coventry C	W 5-2
25 Dec	WLP	H	Notts Co	W 2-0
26 Dec	WLP	A	Notts Co	D 1-1
28 Dec	WLP	H	Barnsley	W 2-0
11 Jan	WLP	H	Leicester Fosse	D 1-1
18 Jan	WLP	A	Leicester Fosse	W 1-0
25 Jan	WLP	H	Bradford PA	W 3-0
1 Feb	WLP	A	Bradford PA	L 0-2
8 Feb	WLP	H	Leeds C	L 0-2
15 Feb	WLP	A	Leeds C	W 4-0
22 Feb	WLP	H	Sheff Utd	W 3-1
1 Mar	WLP	A	Sheff Utd	D 1-1
8 Mar	WLP	H	Hull C	W 2-1
15 Mar	WLP	A	Hull C	L 0-5
22 Mar	WLS	H	Birmingham	L 1-3
29 Mar	WLS	A	Birmingham	L 0-1
5 Apr	WLS	H	Leicester Fosse	L 0-2
12 Apr	WLS	A	Leicester Fosse	L 0-1
18 Apr	WLS	H	Notts Co	W 3-2
19 Apr	F	A	West Ham U	D 0-0
21 Apr	WLS	A	Notts Co	W 3-1
22 Apr	WLP	A	Barnsley	L 2-3
26 Apr	F	A	South Shields	L 0-2
10 May	WLC f/1	H	Everton	D 0-0
17 May	WLC f/2	A	Everton	W 1-0

Position in Principal Tournament

	P	W	D	L	F	A	Pts
1st Forest	30	18	6	6	59	31	42

Position in Subsidiary Tournament

	P	W	D	L	F	A	Pts
1st Birm'ham	6	5	0	1	13	7	10
4th Forest	6	2	0	4	7	10	4

Football League competition resumed with both divisions extended to 22 clubs.

Election to Division One (2 places)
Chelsea re-elected without going to the vote, Arsenal 18 (elected), Tottenham H 8, Barnsley 5, Wolves 4, Forest 3, Birmingham 2, Hull C 1 (all not elected).

1919-20 Division Two

30 Aug	FL	A	Rotherham Co	L 0-2
1 Sep	FL	H	Bristol C	L 1-2
6 Sep	FL	H	Rotherham Co	W 4-1
8 Sep	FL	A	Bristol C	D 0-0
9 Sep	F	A	Mid-Rhondda	L 1-3
13 Sep	FL	H	Barnsley	L 0-1
15 Sep	F	A	Sutton T	W 3-2
20 Sep	FL	A	Barnsley	D 2-2
27 Sep	FL	H	Stockport Co	D 1-1
3 Oct	FL	H	Blackpool	W 2-0
4 Oct	FL	A	Stockport Co	D 0-0
11 Oct	FL	H	Hull C	L 0-2
18 Oct	FL	A	Hull C	L 0-2
25 Oct	FL	H	Wolves	W 1-0
1 Nov	FL	A	Wolves	L 0-4
8 Nov	FL	H	South Shields	D 0-0
15 Nov	FL	A	South Shields	L 2-5
22 Nov	FL	H	Tottenham H	D 1-1
29 Nov	FL	A	Tottenham H	L 2-5
6 Dec	FL	H	Clapton Orient	W 2-1
13 Dec	FL	A	Clapton Orient	L 0-1
25 Dec	FL	A	Lincoln C	W 4-1
26 Dec	FL	H	Lincoln C	W 2-1
3 Jan	FL	H	Bury	W 1-0
10 Jan	FAC1	A	Bradford PA	L 0-3
17 Jan	FL	A	Bury	D 1-1
24 Jan	FL	A	Stoke	W 2-0
28 Jan	FL	H	Stoke	L 0-2
31 Jan	FL	A	Port Vale	L 1-4
7 Feb	FL	A	Grimsby T	L 0-1
14 Feb	FL	H	Grimsby T	W 2-0
18 Feb	FL	H	Port Vale	L 0-1
28 Feb	FL	H	Birmingham	L 1-2
6 Mar	FL	H	Leicester C	D 0-0
10 Mar	FL	A	Birmingham	L 0-8
13 Mar	FL	A	Leicester C	D 0-0
20 Mar	FL	H	Fulham	L 0-3
27 Mar	FL	A	Fulham	L 0-1
2 Apr	FL	A	West Ham U	L 1-5
3 Apr	FL	H	Coventry C	W 2-1
5 Apr	FL	H	West Ham U	W 2-1
10 Apr	FL	A	Coventry C	L 2-4
17 Apr	FL	H	Huddersfield T	L 1-2
28 Apr	FL	A	Huddersfield T	L 1-2
1 May	FL	A	Blackpool	L 2-3
8 May	F	A	Notts Co	W 2-0

League Appearances (Goals)
Armstrong J 42 (1); Banks F 15; Barratt P 21; Bedford H 5 (3); Belton J 30 (6); Bulling H 20; Davis B 14 (7); Derrick J 7 (1); Firth R 30 (6); Gibson T 9 (1); Hart H 6 (1); Johnson J 36; Jones H 36 (3); Kirrage F 1; Lawton J 3; Lowe H 9; Lythgoe J 40 (12); Martindale H 1; Mills J 27; Newbigging H 9 (1); Orme J 5; Parker F 35 (1); Parker J 5; Shearman B 31 (1); Spaven J 13 (3); Stapleton L 10; Wagstaff G 1; Waplington S 1.

Position in League Table

	P	W	D	L	F	A	Pts
1st Spurs	42	32	6	4	102	32	70
18th Forest	42	11	9	22	43	73	31

1920-21 Division Two

28 Aug	FL	H	Stoke	D 2-2
30 Aug	FL	A	Sheff Wed	D 0-0
4 Sep	FL	A	Stoke	L 0-4
11 Sep	FL	H	Notts Co	W 1-0
18 Sep	FL	A	Notts Co	L 0-2
25 Sep	FL	H	Clapton Orient	D 1-1
2 Oct	FL	A	Clapton Orient	L 1-2
7 Oct	FL	H	Sheff Wed	W 4-2
9 Oct	FL	H	Port Vale	L 1-4
16 Oct	FL	A	Port Vale	W 1-0
23 Oct	FL	A	Bury	D 2-2
30 Oct	FL	H	Bury	W 4-2
6 Nov	FL	A	South Shields	W 1-0
13 Nov	FL	H	South Shields	L 1-2
20 Nov	FL	A	Bristol C	L 0-1
27 Nov	FL	H	Bristol C	L 0-1
4 Dec	FL	A	Hull C	W 3-0
11 Dec	FL	H	Hull C	W 2-0
18 Dec	FL	H	Barnsley	D 0-0
25 Dec	FL	H	Rotherham Co	W 6-1
27 Dec	FL	A	Rotherham Co	D 0-0
1 Jan	FL	A	Barnsley	D 0-0
8 Jan	FAC1	H*	Newcastle U	D 1-1
12 Jan	FAC1r	A	Newcastle U	L 0-2
15 Jan	FL	H	Blackpool	W 3-1
22 Jan	FL	A	Blackpool	L 0-1
5 Feb	FL	H	Wolves	D 1-1
12 Feb	FL	H	Leicester C	L 1-2
14 Feb	FL	A	Wolves	L 1-2
19 Feb	FL	A	Leicester C	L 0-2
26 Feb	FL	H	Cardiff C	L 1-2
5 Mar	F	A	Arsenal	L 1-2
12 Mar	FL	H	Fulham	W 5-1
19 Mar	FL	A	Fulham	L 1-2
25 Mar	FL	H	Stockport Co	D 1-1
26 Mar	FL	A	West Ham U	L 0-3
28 Mar	FL	A	Stockport Co	L 0-1
2 Apr	FL	H	West Ham U	W 1-0
4 Apr	FL	A	Cardiff C	L 0-3
9 Apr	FL	A	Birmingham	L 0-3
16 Apr	FL	H	Birmingham	D 1-1
23 Apr	FL	A	Leeds U	D 1-1
30 Apr	FL	H	Leeds U	W 1-0
2 May	FL	A	Coventry C	D 0-0
7 May	FL	H	Coventry C	L 0-2
14 May	F	H	H Bulling's XI	W 4-3

League Appearances (Goals)
Armstrong J 38 (1); Ashmore R 10 (1); Barratt P 5; Bedford H 13 (5); Bell J 1; Belton J 39 (1); Bennett A 19; Bulling H 39; Davis B 6; Dennis G 14 (1); Donoven A 3; Elliott T 28 (7); Firth R 18 (1); Harrold S 37 (8); Higgins A 33 (7); Johnson J 17; Jones G 8; Jones H 41 (2); Lyall T 1; Lythgoe J 21 (2); Mills J 4; Orme J 6; Parker F 32 (1); Spaven J 28 (11); Stapleton L 1.

Position in League Table

	P	W	D	L	F	A	Pts
1st Birm'ham	42	24	10	8	79	38	58
18th Forest	42	12	12	18	48	55	36

* Forest drawn at home, but tie switched to Newcastle

1921-22 Division Two

27 Aug	FL	A	Crystal P	L 1-4
29 Aug	FL	H	Hull C	W 3-2
3 Sep	FL	H	Crystal P	W 2-1
5 Sep	FL	A	Hull C	W 1-0
10 Sep	FL	A	Coventry C	W 1-0
12 Sep	F	A	Aberdare	L 1-3
17 Sep	FL	H	Coventry C	W 1-0
24 Sep	FL	A	Derby Co	W 2-1
1 Oct	FL	H	Derby Co	W 3-0
8 Oct	FL	A	Leicester C	D 2-2
15 Oct	FL	H	Leicester C	D 0-0
22 Oct	FL	A	West Ham U	L 0-1
29 Oct	FL	H	West Ham U	W 2-0
5 Nov	FL	A	Notts Co	D 1-1
14 Nov	FL	H	Notts Co	D 0-0
19 Nov	FL	H	Port Vale	D 1-1
26 Nov	FL	A	Port Vale	W 2-0
3 Dec	FL	A	South Shields	D 0-0
10 Dec	FL	H	South Shields	W 1-0
17 Dec	FL	H	Bristol C	W 1-0
24 Dec	FL	A	Bristol C	W 1-0
26 Dec	FL	H	Wolves	D 0-0
27 Dec	FL	A	Wolves	L 0-2
31 Dec	FL	A	Bury	W 2-1
7 Jan	FAC1	A	Bristol C	D 0-0
11 Jan	FAC1r	H	Bristol C	W 3-1
14 Jan	FL	H	Bury	L 1-2
21 Jan	FL	A	Rotherham Co	W 1-0
28 Jan	FAC2	H	Hull C	W 3-0
4 Feb	FL	A	Sheff Wed	W 4-0
8 Feb	FL	H	Rotherham Co	W 1-0
11 Feb	FL	H	Sheff Wed	W 2-0
18 Feb	FAC3	A	Cardiff C	L 1-4
25 Feb	FL	H	Fulham	D 0-0
28 Feb	FL	A	Fulham	L 0-2
4 Mar	FL	A	Blackpool	L 1-2
11 Mar	FL	H	Blackpool	D 0-0
18 Mar	FL	H	Bradford PA	W 4-1
25 Mar	FL	A	Bradford PA	L 0-1
1 Apr	FL	H	Clapton Orient	W 2-0
8 Apr	FL	A	Clapton Orient	W 2-1
14 Apr	FL	A	Barnsley	L 0-2
15 Apr	FL	A	Stoke	D 1-1
17 Apr	FL	H	Barnsley	D 1-1
22 Apr	FL	H	Stoke	W 3-1
29 Apr	FL	H	Leeds U	W 1-0
5 May	F	A	Boston	W 4-2
6 May	FL	A	Leeds U	D 0-0

League Appearances (Goals)
Armstrong J 37; Ashmore R 1; Barratt P 2; Belton J 40; Bennett A 10; Boyman W 10 (3); Bulling H 42 (1); Burton N 41 (4); Dennis G 10 (2); Gibson S 27 (2); Green J 1; Hardy S 32; Harrold S 13; Jones H 40; Mills J 7; Nelis P 10 (6); Parker F 40 (1); Parker R 32 (8); Ronald P 3; Spaven J 42 (18); Tinsley W 22 (6).

Position in League Table

	P	W	D	L	F	A	Pts
1st Forest	42	22	12	8	51	30	56

1922-23 Division One

26 Aug	FL	H	Sunderland	W 1-0
28 Aug	FL	A	Huddersfield T	L 1-2
2 Sep	FL	A	Sunderland	D 0-0
4 Sep	FL	H	Huddersfield T	L 0-1
9 Sep	FL	A	Oldham A	L 0-2
16 Sep	FL	H	Oldham A	W 1-0
23 Sep	FL	H	Sheff Utd	W 1-0
30 Sep	FL	A	Sheff Utd	D 0-0
5 Oct	FL	H	Bolton W	D 1-1
7 Oct	FL	H	Preston NE	W 3-0
14 Oct	FL	A	Preston NE	D 2-2
21 Oct	FL	H	Everton	W 2-1
28 Oct	FL	A	Everton	L 2-4
4 Nov	FL	A	Burnley	L 2-8
11 Nov	FL	H	Burnley	W 1-0
18 Nov	FL	A	Birmingham	L 0-2
25 Nov	FL	H	Birmingham	D 1-1
2 Dec	FL	A	Tottenham H	L 1-2
9 Dec	FL	H	Tottenham H	L 0-1
13 Dec	NSC	A	Notts Co	W 2-0
16 Dec	FL	A	Liverpool	L 1-2
23 Dec	FL	H	Liverpool	L 1-3
25 Dec	FL	A	Chelsea	D 2-2
26 Dec	FL	H	Chelsea	L 0-4
30 Dec	FL	H	Newcastle U	L 0-1
2 Jan	FL	A	Bolton W	L 2-4
6 Jan	FL	A	Newcastle U	L 0-1
13 Jan	FAC1	H	Sheff Utd	D 0-0
18 Jan	FAC1r	A	Sheff Utd	D 0-0
20 Jan	FL	H	Aston Villa	W 3-1
22 Jan	FAC1r2	*	Sheff Utd	D 1-1
25 Jan	FAC1r3	**	Sheff Utd	L 0-1
27 Jan	FL	A	Aston Villa	L 0-4
3 Feb	FL	H	Arsenal	W 2-1
10 Feb	FL	A	Arsenal	L 0-2
17 Feb	FL	H	Cardiff C	W 3-2
24 Feb	F	H	Corinthians	L 1-2
3 Mar	FL	H	WBA	L 0-4
10 Mar	FL	A	WBA	D 0-0
17 Mar	FL	A	Blackburn R	L 0-2
24 Mar	FL	H	Blackburn R	W 1-0
30 Mar	FL	H	Middlesbrough	W 2-1
31 Mar	FL	A	Stoke	W 1-0
2 Apr	FL	A	Middlesbrough	L 0-4
7 Apr	FL	H	Stoke	L 0-1
14 Apr	FL	A	Man City	D 1-1
21 Apr	FL	H	Man City	W 2-0
25 Apr	FL	A	Cardiff C	L 1-3
30 Apr	F	A	Boston	W 3-1
4 May	LHC	A	Lincoln C	W 2-1

League Appearances (Goals)
Armstrong J 3; Barratt P 4; Belton J 28 (1); Bennett A 5; Boyman W 2; Bulling H 31 (1); Burton N 42 (2); Cox W 1; Dennis G 5; Flood C 14 (3); Gibson S 35 (4); Green J 10 (2); Hardy S 37; Jones H 39 (1); Martin H 36 (4); Mills J 3; Morgan F 28; Nelis P 32 (4); Parker F 28; Parker R 14 (3); Ronald P 1; Spaven J 32 (10); Thompson W 9; Tinsley W 23 (5); Own Goals 1.

Position in League Table

	P	W	D	L	F	A	Pts
1st Liverpool	42	26	8	8	70	31	60
20th Forest	42	13	8	21	41	70	34

* at Meadow Lane ** at Hillsborough

1923-24 Division One

25 Aug	FL	A	Everton	L 1-2
27 Aug	FL	H	WBA	D 1-1
1 Sep	FL	H	Everton	W 1-0
3 Sep	FL	A	WBA	L 2-3
8 Sep	FL	A	Burnley	W 4-2
15 Sep	FL	H	Burnley	D 0-0
22 Sep	FL	A	Notts Co	L 1-2
29 Sep	FL	H	Notts Co	W 1-0
6 Oct	FL	A	Middlesbrough	L 2-5
8 Oct	F	A	St Mirren	D 1-1
13 Oct	FL	H	Middlesbrough	W 3-1
20 Oct	FL	A	Liverpool	L 2-4
27 Oct	FL	H	Liverpool	L 0-1
3 Nov	FL	H	Tottenham H	D 0-0
10 Nov	FL	A	Tottenham H	L 0-3
17 Nov	FL	H	Sheff Utd	L 1-2
24 Nov	FL	A	Sheff Utd	D 0-0
1 Dec	FL	H	Cardiff C	L 0-1
8 Dec	FL	A	Cardiff C	L 1-4
15 Dec	FL	H	West Ham U	W 2-1
22 Dec	FL	A	West Ham U	L 2-3
25 Dec	FL	H	Chelsea	W 2-0
26 Dec	FL	A	Chelsea	D 1-1
29 Dec	FL	H	Newcastle U	D 0-0
5 Jan	FL	A	Newcastle U	L 0-4
12 Jan	FAC1	A	Man City	L 0-2
19 Jan	FL	A	Birmingham	W 2-0
26 Jan	FL	H	Birmingham	D 1-1
2 Feb	FL	A	Preston NE	L 1-3
9 Feb	FL	H	Man City	L 1-2
13 Feb	FL	A	Man City	W 3-1
16 Feb	FL	A	Bolton W	L 0-4
23 Feb	FL	H	Bolton W	W 1-0
1 Mar	FL	A	Sunderland	L 0-1
8 Mar	FL	H	Sunderland	L 1-2
15 Mar	FL	H	Arsenal	W 2-1
22 Mar	FL	A	Arsenal	L 0-1
29 Mar	FL	H	Blackburn R	D 0-0
5 Apr	FL	A	Blackburn R	D 1-1
12 Apr	FL	H	Aston Villa	D 0-0
19 Apr	FL	A	Aston Villa	L 0-2
21 Apr	FL	H	Preston NE	D 1-1
26 Apr	FL	H	Huddersfield T	D 1-1
3 May	FL	A	Huddersfield T	L 0-3

League Appearances (Goals)
Barratt P 7; Belton J 33; Bennett A 16; Bulling H 33; Burton N 7; Dennis G 1; Dexter A 2; Falconer F 2; Flood C 40 (7); Gibson S 37 (4); Hardy S 24; Jones H 16; Marshall W 7 (2); Martin H 40 (4); Mills J 2; Morgan F 32; Nelis P 6 (1); Parker F 12 (3); Ransford H 4 (1); Spaven J 19 (1); Thompson W 25; Tinsley W 16 (2); Walker D 39 (17); Wallace R 42.

Position in League Table

		P	W	D	L	F	A	Pts
1st	Hudd'fld	42	23	11	8	60	33	57
20th	Forest	42	10	12	20	42	64	32

1924-25 Division One

30 Aug	FL	H	Arsenal	L 0-2
2 Sep	FL	A	Huddersfield T	L 0-3
6 Sep	FL	A	Man City	L 2-4
8 Sep	FL	H	Huddersfield T	L 0-1
13 Sep	FL	H	Bury	W 2-0
20 Sep	FL	A	Notts Co	D 0-0
22 Sep	F	A	Newark T	W 5-0
27 Sep	FL	A	Liverpool	L 0-3
2 Oct	FL	H	Aston Villa	L 0-2
4 Oct	FL	H	Newcastle U	D 1-1
11 Oct	FL	A	Sheff Utd	W 2-1
18 Oct	FL	H	West Ham U	W 2-1
25 Oct	FL	H	Everton	L 0-1
1 Nov	FL	A	Sunderland	L 1-3
8 Nov	FL	H	Cardiff C	W 2-1
15 Nov	FL	A	Preston NE	L 1-3
22 Nov	FL	H	Burnley	D 0-0
29 Nov	FL	A	Leeds U	D 1-1
6 Dec	FL	H	Birmingham	D 1-1
13 Dec	FL	A	WBA	L 1-5
20 Dec	FL	H	Tottenham H	W 1-0
25 Dec	FL	A	Bolton W	L 0-1
26 Dec	FL	H	Bolton W	D 1-1
27 Dec	FL	A	Arsenal	L 1-2
3 Jan	FL	H	Man City	L 0-3
10 Jan	FAC1	H	Clapton Orient	W 1-0
17 Jan	FL	A	Bury	L 0-3
24 Jan	FL	H	Notts Co	D 0-0
31 Jan	FAC2	H	West Ham U	L 0-2
4 Feb	FL	H	Liverpool	L 0-1
7 Feb	FL	A	Newcastle U	L 1-4
14 Feb	FL	H	Sheff Utd	L 2-3
28 Feb	FL	A	Everton	L 1-3
7 Mar	FL	H	Sunderland	D 1-1
14 Mar	FL	A	Cardiff C	L 0-2
21 Mar	FL	H	Preston NE	L 0-1
28 Mar	FL	A	Burnley	D 0-0
2 Apr	FL	A	West Ham U	D 0-0
4 Apr	FL	H	Leeds U	W 4-0
10 Apr	FL	H	Blackburn R	L 0-2
11 Apr	FL	A	Birmingham	D 1-1
13 Apr	FL	A	Blackburn R	D 0-0
18 Apr	FL	H	WBA	L 0-1
25 Apr	FL	A	Tottenham H	L 0-1
2 May	FL	A	Aston Villa	L 0-2
4 May	NHC	A	Northampton T	W 2-1

League Appearances (Goals)
Barratt P 32; Belton J 28; Bennett A 31 (2); Bulling H 21; Burton N 29 (1); Flood C 24 (6); Galloway S 11; Gibson S 31 (1); Hardy S 9; Hewitt A 4; Langford L 2; Marshall W 9; Martin H 31 (5); Miller A 5; Morgan F 34 (3); Morris H 22 (1); Nelis P 11 (2); Parker F 6; Spaven J 13 (1); Stocks C 3; Thompson W 28; Tilford A 1; Walker D 35 (7); Wallace R 42.

Position in League Table

		P	W	D	L	F	A	Pts
1st	Hudd'fld	42	21	16	5	69	28	58
22nd	Forest	42	6	12	24	29	65	24

1925-26 Division Two

29 Aug	FL	A	Darlington	D 0-0
31 Aug	FL	H	Chelsea	L 1-5
5 Sep	FL	H	Blackpool	D 1-1
7 Sep	FL	A	Chelsea	D 0-0
12 Sep	FL	A	Southampton	L 0-2
19 Sep	FL	H	Wolves	L 1-4
26 Sep	FL	H	Derby Co	L 1-2
3 Oct	FL	A	Bradford C	W 1-0
10 Oct	FL	H	Port Vale	W 2-0
12 Oct	FL	A	Hull C	L 1-4
17 Oct	FL	A	Swansea T	L 0-3
24 Oct	FL	H	Sheff Wed	W 2-0
28 Oct	F	A	Notts Co	D 2-2
31 Oct	FL	A	Middlesbrough	L 0-1
7 Nov	FL	H	Portsmouth	W 3-1
14 Nov	FL	A	Stockport Co	L 0-3
21 Nov	FL	H	Fulham	D 2-2
28 Nov	FL	A	South Shields	L 1-3
5 Dec	FL	H	Preston NE	W 4-0
12 Dec	FL	A	Stoke C	D 1-1
19 Dec	FL	H	Oldham A	D 1-1
25 Dec	FL	H	Barnsley	W 4-2
28 Dec	FL	A	Barnsley	L 1-4
2 Jan	FL	H	Darlington	W 2-0
9 Jan	FAC3	H	Bradford C	W 1-0
16 Jan	FL	A	Blackpool	L 0-3
23 Jan	FL	H	Southampton	L 1-2
30 Jan	FAC4	H	Swindon T	W 2-0
6 Feb	FL	A	Derby Co	L 0-2
8 Feb	FL	A	Wolves	L 0-4
13 Feb	FL	H	Bradford C	D 0-0
20 Feb	FAC5	A	Southend U	W 1-0
27 Feb	FL	H	Swansea T	L 0-2
6 Mar	FAC6	H	Bolton W	D 2-2
10 Mar	FAC6r	A	Bolton W	D 0-0
13 Mar	FL	H	Middlesbrough	W 1-0
15 Mar	FAC6r2	*	Bolton W	L 0-1
20 Mar	FL	A	Portsmouth	L 1-5
22 Mar	FL	A	Sheff Wed	L 0-2
27 Mar	FL	H	Stockport Co	W 2-0
2 Apr	FL	A	Clapton Orient	W 1-0
3 Apr	FL	A	Fulham	W 2-0
5 Apr	FL	H	Clapton Orient	W 1-0
10 Apr	FL	H	South Shields	W 4-1
12 Apr	FL	A	Port Vale	D 1-1
17 Apr	FL	A	Preston NE	L 0-2
21 Apr	FL	H	Hull C	W 4-0
24 Apr	FL	H	Stoke C	L 1-2
1 May	FL	A	Oldham A	L 3-8
3 May	NHC	A	Northampton T	D 1-1

League Appearances (Goals)
Ashworth J 3; Barratt P 41 (4); Belton J 41; Bennett A 2; Burton N 26 (6); Flood C 19 (5); Galloway R 25 (5); Gibson S 40 (10); Hodgkinson V 9 (1); Jones C 32 (1); Langford L 40; Lynas R 19 (2); Marsden H 6; Marshall W 3 (1); Morgan F 37 (3); Parker F 4; Saxton J 3; Scott J 1; Spaven J 10 (2); Stocks C 18 (7); Taylor J 1; Thompson W 37; Tilford A 7; Walker D 6 (3); Wallace R 32; Own Goals 1.

Position in League Table

		P	W	D	L	F	A	Pts
1st	Sheff W	42	27	6	9	88	48	60
17th	Forest	42	14	8	20	51	73	36

* at Old Trafford

1926-27 Division Two

28 Aug	FL	H	Blackpool	W 2-0
30 Aug	FL	A	Fulham	L 1-2
4 Sep	FL	A	Reading	L 0-4
6 Sep	FL	H	Grimsby T	D 1-1
11 Sep	FL	H	Swansea T	D 2-2
18 Sep	FL	A	Notts Co	W 2-1
25 Sep	FL	A	Barnsley	W 2-0
2 Oct	FL	H	Man City	D 3-3
7 Oct	FL	H	Fulham	W 2-0
9 Oct	FL	A	Darlington	L 2-4
16 Oct	FL	H	Middlesbrough	W 4-2
23 Oct	FL	A	Clapton Orient	D 2-2
30 Oct	FL	H	Wolves	D 1-1
6 Nov	FL	A	Hull C	W 2-1
13 Nov	FL	H	South Shields	W 4-2
20 Nov	FL	A	Preston NE	L 0-1
27 Nov	FL	H	Chelsea	W 4-1
4 Dec	FL	A	Bradford C	D 1-1
11 Dec	FL	H	Southampton	W 3-1
18 Dec	FL	A	Port Vale	W 2-0
25 Dec	FL	A	Portsmouth	D 0-0
27 Dec	FL	H	Portsmouth	W 1-0
1 Jan	FL	A	Grimsby T	D 1-1
8 Jan	FAC3	A	Ashington	W 2-0
15 Jan	FL	A	Blackpool	D 2-2
22 Jan	FL	H	Reading	W 5-1
29 Jan	FAC4	A	Wolves	L 0-2
5 Feb	FL	H	Notts Co	W 2-0
12 Feb	FL	H	Barnsley	W 3-1
19 Feb	FL	A	Man City	D 1-1
26 Feb	FL	H	Darlington	W 5-1
5 Mar	FL	A	Middlesbrough	L 0-1
10 Mar	FL	A	Swansea T	L 1-2
12 Mar	FL	H	Clapton Orient	D 1-1
19 Mar	FL	A	Wolves	L 0-2
26 Mar	FL	H	Hull C	W 3-1
2 Apr	FL	A	South Shields	D 1-1
9 Apr	FL	H	Preston NE	W 7-0
15 Apr	FL	H	Oldham A	D 1-1
16 Apr	FL	A	Chelsea	L 0-2
18 Apr	FL	A	Oldham A	D 3-3
23 Apr	FL	H	Bradford C	W 3-0
30 Apr	FL	A	Southampton	L 0-1
7 May	FL	H	Port Vale	L 0-3
9 May	NHC	A	Northampton T	W 1-0

League Appearances (Goals)
Barratt P 42 (8); Belton J 34 (1); Burton N 33 (12); Galloway R 3 (1); Gibson S 40 (17); Jones C 31 (11); Langford L 42; Laws J 7 (1); Linley E 29 (5); Lynas R 1; Marsden H 2; Morgan F 42; Price C 15 (5); Reed E 5; Saxton J 8; Stocks C 38 (14); Taylor J 1; Thompson W 40; Townsend A 8 (1); Walker D 2 (2); Wallace R 39; Own Goals 2.

Position in League Table

		P	W	D	L	F	A	Pts
1st	Midd'bro	42	27	8	7	122	60	62
5th	Forest	42	18	14	10	80	55	50

1927-28 Division Two

27 Aug	FL	A	Port Vale	D 2-2
29 Aug	FL	H	Fulham	W 7-0
3 Sep	FL	H	South Shields	W 7-2
10 Sep	FL	A	Leeds U	L 0-4
15 Sep	FL	A	Fulham	L 0-2
17 Sep	FL	H	Notts Co	W 2-1
24 Sep	FL	H	Man City	L 4-5
1 Oct	FL	A	Hull C	L 0-2
8 Oct	FL	H	Preston NE	W 3-1
15 Oct	FL	A	Swansea T	L 0-2
22 Oct	FL	A	Reading	W 2-0
29 Oct	FL	H	Grimsby T	W 5-2
5 Nov	FL	A	Oldham A	L 1-4
12 Nov	FL	H	Blackpool	W 4-1
19 Nov	FL	A	Chelsea	L 1-2
26 Nov	FL	H	Bristol C	D 1-1
3 Dec	FL	A	WBA	W 3-2
10 Dec	FL	H	Clapton Orient	W 4-3
17 Dec	FL	A	Stoke C	W 3-1
24 Dec	FL	H	Southampton	D 1-1
26 Dec	FL	H	Wolves	W 3-2
27 Dec	FL	A	Wolves	L 0-1
7 Jan	FL	A	South Shields	W 4-3
14 Jan	FAC3	H	Tranmere R	W 1-0
21 Jan	FL	H	Leeds U	D 2-2
28 Jan	FAC4	A	Derby Co	D 0-0
1 Feb	FAC4r	H	Derby Co	W 2-0
4 Feb	FL	A	Man City	D 3-3
11 Feb	FL	H	Hull C	D 1-1
18 Feb	FAC5	H	Cardiff C	W 2-1
22 Feb	FL	A	Notts Co	W 2-1
25 Feb	FL	H	Swansea T	L 0-2
3 Mar	FAC6	A	Sheff Utd	L 0-3
5 Mar	FL	A	Preston NE	L 0-5
10 Mar	FL	A	Grimsby T	L 1-2
17 Mar	FL	H	Oldham A	W 2-1
24 Mar	FL	A	Blackpool	L 3-5
29 Mar	FL	H	Reading	W 5-3
31 Mar	FL	H	Chelsea	D 2-2
7 Apr	FL	A	Bristol C	D 0-0
9 Apr	FL	H	Barnsley	D 1-1
10 Apr	FL	A	Barnsley	L 1-2
14 Apr	FL	H	WBA	L 0-2
21 Apr	FL	A	Clapton Orient	D 2-2
26 Apr	FL	H	Port Vale	L 0-2
28 Apr	FL	H	Stoke C	L 0-2
3 May	F	*	Derby Co	D 1-1
5 May	FL	A	Southampton	L 1-2
7 May	NHC	A	Northampton T	L 2-3
8 May	KHC	A	Kettering T	L 1-7

League Appearances (Goals)
Barratt P 40 (5); Belton J 25; Boot L 2; Burton N 31 (15); Dexter A 28; German A 2 (2); Gibson S 37 (12); Gordon L 2; Graham T 2; Green H 4; Harrison A 37 (2); Hicks T 8; Jones C 37 (10); Langford L 12; McKennan H 1; McKinlay W 13; McLachlan E 8 (2); McMillan S 9; Marsden H 3; Morgan F 12; Price C 5; Roe T 9 (4); Stocks C 32 (13); Sturton T 1; Thompson N 1; Thompson W 33 (3); Townsend A 7 (3); Wadsworth H 30 (9); Wallace R 31 (1); Own Goals 2.

Position in League Table

		P	W	D	L	F	A	Pts
1st	Man City	42	25	9	8	100	59	59
10th	Forest	42	15	10	17	83	84	40

* at Heanor Town

1928-29 Division Two

25 Aug	FL	H	Stoke C	L 1-5
27 Aug	FL	A	Clapton Orient	W 4-1
1 Sep	FL	A	Grimsby T	D 2-2
5 Sep	FL	H	Clapton Orient	D 0-0
8 Sep	FL	H	Bradford PA	W 3-2
15 Sep	FL	A	Swansea T	W 5-3
22 Sep	FL	H	Blackpool	W 2-0
29 Sep	FL	A	Chelsea	L 0-3
6 Oct	FL	H	Barnsley	L 1-3
13 Oct	FL	A	Bristol C	W 5-2
20 Oct	FL	A	Notts Co	D 1-1
27 Oct	FL	H	Millwall	L 0-4
3 Nov	FL	A	Port Vale	L 2-4
10 Nov	FL	H	Southampton	D 1-1
14 Nov	F	A	Arsenal	W 1-0
17 Nov	FL	A	Tottenham H	L 1-2
24 Nov	FL	H	Reading	L 1-2
1 Dec	FL	A	Preston NE	L 2-3
8 Dec	FL	H	Middlesbrough	D 1-1
15 Dec	FL	A	Oldham A	Abnd
22 Dec	FL	H	Hull C	W 3-1
25 Dec	FL	A	Wolves	W 3-2
26 Dec	FL	H	Wolves	W 2-1
29 Dec	FL	A	Stoke C	D 1-1
1 Jan	FL	A	Oldham A	L 0-2
5 Jan	FL	H	Grimsby T	L 0-1
12 Jan	FAC3	H	Swansea T	L 1-2
19 Jan	FL	A	Bradford PA	D 1-1
2 Feb	FL	A	Blackpool	D 2-2
9 Feb	FL	H	Chelsea	W 3-0
16 Feb	FL	A	Barnsley	W 2-1
20 Feb	FL	H	Swansea T	W 2-1
23 Feb	FL	H	Bristol C	D 1-1
2 Mar	FL	H	Notts Co	L 1-2
9 Mar	FL	A	Millwall	D 1-1
16 Mar	FL	H	Port Vale	D 2-2
23 Mar	FL	A	Southampton	L 1-2
29 Mar	FL	H	WBA	L 1-2
30 Mar	FL	H	Tottenham H	D 2-2
1 Apr	FL	A	WBA	L 0-3
6 Apr	FL	A	Reading	W 3-0
13 Apr	FL	H	Preston NE	W 4-1
20 Apr	FL	A	Middlesbrough	L 0-1
22 Apr	CHC	A	Chesterfield	D 1-1
27 Apr	FL	H	Oldham A	W 3-1
4 May	FL	A	Hull C	W 1-0

League Appearances (Goals)
Barratt P 22; Brown W 4; Burton N 29 (10); Cameron D 10; Dexter A 14; Dickinson W 5 (5); Gibson S 5 (2); Goucher G 1; Graham T 40; Hague E 4; Hales H 3; Harrison A 24 (2); Heathcock B 16 (14); Heslop R 24 (3); Howie C 16 91); Jennings S 27 (15); Langford L 28; Lennox W 9 (1); McKinlay W 38; Marsden H 3; Morgan G 15; Morton R 27 (4); Stocks C 33 (10); Thompson N 8 (2); Thompson W 40 (1); Turner T 1; Wallace R 16 (1).

Position in League Table

		P	W	D	L	F	A	Pts
1st	Midd'bro	42	22	11	9	92	57	55
11th	Forest	42	15	12	15	71	70	42

1929-30 Division Two

31 Aug	FL	A	Chelsea	L 0-2
4 Sep	FL	A	Bradford PA	L 1-5
7 Sep	FL	H	Notts Co	D 1-1
9 Sep	FL	A	Blackpool	L 1-5
14 Sep	FL	H	Oldham A	L 1-2
19 Sep	F	A	Arsenal	L 0-4
21 Sep	FL	A	Millwall	D 2-2
28 Sep	FL	H	Southampton	L 0-5
3 Oct	FL	H	Bradford PA	D 1-1
5 Oct	FL	A	Tottenham H	D 1-1
12 Oct	FL	H	WBA	L 0-2
19 Oct	FL	A	Reading	W 1-0
26 Oct	FL	H	Charlton A	L 0-2
2 Nov	FL	A	Hull C	W 2-1
9 Nov	FL	H	Stoke C	W 2-1
16 Nov	FL	A	Wolves	L 1-2
23 Nov	FL	H	Bradford C	W 2-1
30 Nov	FL	A	Swansea T	D 1-1
7 Dec	FL	H	Cardiff C	W 3-1
14 Dec	FL	A	Preston NE	W 2-1
21 Dec	FL	H	Bristol C	W 5-2
25 Dec	FL	H	Barnsley	W 4-0
26 Dec	FL	A	Barnsley	D 1-1
28 Dec	FL	H	Chelsea	D 0-0
4 Jan	FL	A	Notts Co	D 0-0
11 Jan	FAC3	A	Rotherham U	W 5-0
18 Jan	FL	A	Oldham A	D 0-0
25 Jan	FAC4	H	Fulham	W 2-1
1 Feb	FL	A	Southampton	L 0-2
5 Feb	FL	H	Millwall	D 1-1
8 Feb	FL	H	Tottenham H	D 0-0
15 Feb	FAC5	A	Sunderland	D 2-2
19 Feb	FAC5r	H	Sunderland	W 3-1
22 Feb	FL	H	Reading	W 5-0
1 Mar	FAC6	H	Sheff Wed	D 2-2
5 Mar	FAC5r	A	Sheff Wed	L 1-3
8 Mar	FL	H	Hull C	W 2-1
10 Mar	FL	A	Charlton A	L 0-5
15 Mar	FL	A	Stoke C	L 0-6
19 Mar	FL	A	WBA	W 3-1
22 Mar	FL	H	Wolves	W 5-2
29 Mar	FL	A	Bradford C	D 1-1
5 Apr	FL	H	Swansea T	W 1-0
12 Apr	FL	A	Cardiff C	D 1-1
18 Apr	FL	A	Bury	D 0-0
19 Apr	FL	H	Preston NE	L 2-4
21 Apr	FL	H	Bury	L 1-2
26 Apr	FL	A	Bristol C	L 1-4
3 May	FL	H	Blackpool	D 0-0

League Appearances (Goals)
Armstrong R 1; Barratt P 1; Barrington J 36; Bromage E 1; Brown W 1; Burton N 35 (7); Cameron D 11 (1); Dent J 24 (15); Dexter A 30; Dickinson W 13 (5); German A 15 (7); Graham T 24; Harrison A 16 (1); Heathcock B 4 (1); Heslop R 15 (3); Howie C 6; Langford L 12; Loftus J 24 (6); McKinlay W 41 (1); Morton R 7; Oakes J 2; Robins R 1; Scott J 30; Simpson W 3; Smith H 2; Stocks C 24 (7); Thompson N 3 (1); Thompson W 40; Venters J 1; Wallace R 39.

Position in League Table

		P	W	D	L	F	A	Pts
1st	Blackpool	42	27	4	11	98	67	58
10th	Forest	42	13	15	14	55	69	41

1930-31 Division Two

30 Aug	FL	H	Wolves	L 3-4
1 Sep	FL	A	Southampton	D 0-0
6 Sep	FL	A	Bradford PA	L 1-4
8 Sep	FL	A	Burnley	L 2-5
13 Sep	FL	H	Stoke C	W 3-0
17 Sep	FL	H	Burnley	D 3-3
20 Sep	FL	A	Millwall	L 1-5
27 Sep	FL	H	Oldham A	W 4-1
4 Oct	FL	A	Bristol C	W 4-1
11 Oct	FL	A	Tottenham H	L 1-2
18 Oct	FL	H	Everton	D 2-2
25 Oct	FL	A	Cardiff C	D 1-1
1 Nov	FL	H	Bradford C	W 4-1
6 Nov	F	A	Oxford University	W 4-0
8 Nov	FL	A	Port Vale	L 2-3
15 Nov	FL	H	Plymouth A	D 1-1
22 Nov	FL	A	Swansea T	L 2-3
29 Nov	FL	H	WBA	L 1-6
6 Dec	FL	A	Bury	L 0-1
13 Dec	FL	H	Barnsley	D 3-3
20 Dec	FL	A	Charlton A	D 1-1
25 Dec	FL	H	Reading	D 1-1
26 Dec	FL	A	Reading	L 2-5
27 Dec	FL	A	Wolves	L 2-4
3 Jan	FL	H	Bradford PA	W 1-0
10 Jan	FAC3	A	Newcastle U	L 0-4
17 Jan	FL	A	Stoke C	L 0-1
24 Jan	FL	H	Millwall	W 2-1
31 Jan	FL	A	Oldham A	L 1-3
7 Feb	FL	H	Bristol C	W 6-1
14 Feb	FL	H	Tottenham H	D 2-2
21 Feb	FL	A	Everton	L 0-2
28 Feb	FL	H	Cardiff C	W 3-1
4 Mar	F	A	Netherlands XI	W 3-1
7 Mar	FL	A	Bradford C	L 0-1
14 Mar	FL	H	Port Vale	W 1-0
21 Mar	FL	A	Plymouth A	L 0-1
28 Mar	FL	H	Swansea T	W 3-0
3 Apr	FL	A	Preston NE	W 4-2
4 Apr	FL	A	WBA	L 1-2
6 Apr	FL	H	Preston NE	L 1-4
11 Apr	FL	H	Bury	W 3-0
18 Apr	FL	A	Barnsley	L 1-3
25 Apr	FL	H	Charlton A	W 4-3
2 May	FL	H	Southampton	W 3-1

League Appearances (Goals)
Armstrong R 7; Ashton P 2; Barrington J 42; Brown O 9 (6); Burton N 22; Dent J 37 (23); Dexter A 40; Dickinson W 24 (18); Farmer A 15; Forrest J 1; German A 8 (1); Graham T 40; Heslop R 6 (2); Howie C 1 (1); Lloyd C 4; Loftus J 18 (6); McKay T 2; McKinlay W 34 (2); Pugh R 8; Quantrill A 9 (2); Robins R 1; cott J 17 (3); Simpson W 32 (7); Smith H 23; Stocks C 20 (9); Thompson W 33; Wallace R 7.

Position in League Table

		P	W	D	L	F	A	Pts
1st	Everton	42	28	5	9	121	65	61
17th	Forest	42	14	9	19	80	85	37

1931-32 Division Two

29 Aug	FL	A	Charlton A	L 1-3
5 Sep	FL	H	Wolves	W 2-0
7 Sep	FL	A	Preston NE	D 1-1
12 Sep	FL	A	Bradford PA	L 1-4
16 Sep	FL	H	Preston NE	D 2-2
19 Sep	FL	H	Man Utd	W 2-1
26 Sep	FL	A	Tottenham H	W 3-1
1 Oct	FL	H	Burnley	L 1-2
3 Oct	FL	H	Notts Co	W 2-1
10 Oct	FL	H	Chesterfield	W 4-0
17 Oct	FL	A	Plymouth A	L 1-5
24 Oct	FL	H	Bristol C	W 3-1
31 Oct	FL	A	Oldham A	W 4-2
7 Nov	FL	H	Barnsley	L 1-2
14 Nov	FL	A	Port Vale	L 0-2
21 Nov	FL	H	Millwall	D 1-1
28 Nov	FL	A	Bradford C	D 2-2
5 Dec	FL	H	Leeds U	D 3-3
12 Dec	FL	A	Swansea T	L 1-4
19 Dec	FL	H	Bury	L 0-2
25 Dec	FL	A	Stoke C	L 1-2
26 Dec	FL	H	Stoke C	D 1-1
2 Jan	FL	H	Charlton A	W 3-2
9 Jan	FAC3	A	Chesterfield	L 2-5
16 Jan	FL	A	Wolves	D 0-0
27 Jan	FL	H	Bradford PA	W 6-1
30 Jan	FL	A	Man Utd	L 2-3
6 Feb	FL	H	Tottenham H	L 1-3
13 Feb	FL	A	Notts Co	W 6-2
20 Feb	FL	A	Chesterfield	L 0-1
27 Feb	FL	H	Plymouth A	W 3-2
5 Mar	FL	A	Bristol C	D 1-1
12 Mar	FL	H	Oldham A	W 2-0
19 Mar	FL	A	Barnsley	L 1-3
25 Mar	FL	H	Southampton	W 2-0
26 Mar	FL	H	Port Vale	W 2-1
28 Mar	FL	A	Southampton	L 0-4
2 Apr	FL	A	Millwall	L 0-1
9 Apr	FL	H	Bradford C	W 2-1
16 Apr	FL	A	Leeds U	D 1-1
20 Apr	BnkC	*	Peterboro' & Fletton U	W 2-1
23 Apr	FL	H	Swansea T	W 6-1
25 Apr	PHC	A	Peterboro' & Fletton U	W 2-1
27 Apr	THC	**	Wolves	W 3-1
30 Apr	FL	A	Bury	D 2-2
2 May	CHC	A	Chesterfield	W 4-2
7 May	FL	A	Burnley	L 0-1

League Appearances (Goals)
Armstrong R 4; Ashton P 1; Barrington J 30; Bell M 31; Burton J 1; Burton N 1; Chambers R 9 (1); Clark R 5 (2); Dent J 37 (19); Dexter A 41; Dickinson W 40 (21); Dulson J 1; Farmer A 1; Forrest J 11 (2); Graham T 31 (1); Heslop R 12 (3); Loftus J 12 (2); McKay T 2; McKinlay W 33; Porter W 2; Pugh R 31 (2); Quantrill A 6; Simpson W 34 (6); Smith H 31 (1); Stocks C 33 (13); Thompson W 22; Own Goals 2.

Position in League Table

		P	W	D	L	F	A	Pts
1st	Wolves	42	24	8	10	115	49	56
11th	Forest	42	16	10	16	77	72	42

* at Long Sutton ** at Trowbridge

1932-33 Division Two

27 Aug	FL	A	Grimsby T	D 1-1
29 Aug	FL	H	Tottenham H	W 3-1
3 Sep	FL	H	Oldham A	L 2-3
5 Sep	FL	A	Tottenham H	D 0-0
10 Sep	FL	A	Preston NE	L 1-2
17 Sep	FL	H	Burnley	D 1-1
24 Sep	FL	A	Bradford PA	L 1-3
1 Oct	FL	H	Plymouth A	D 1-1
8 Oct	FL	A	Notts Co	W 4-2
15 Oct	FL	A	Charlton A	L 0-3
22 Oct	FL	H	Swansea T	D 2-2
29 Oct	FL	A	Bradford C	D 2-2
5 Nov	FL	H	Chesterfield	L 2-3
12 Nov	FL	A	Port Vale	W 1-0
19 Nov	FL	H	Bury	L 0-2
26 Nov	FL	A	Lincoln C	D 1-1
3 Dec	FL	H	West Ham U	D 2-2
10 Dec	FL	A	Southampton	W 2-0
17 Dec	FL	H	Millwall	D 0-0
24 Dec	FL	A	Fulham	W 1-0
26 Dec	FL	A	Stoke C	W 1-0
27 Dec	FL	H	Stoke C	W 1-0
31 Dec	FL	H	Grimsby T	W 3-2
7 Jan	FL	A	Oldham A	W 2-1
14 Jan	FAC3	A	Bury	D 2-2
18 Jan	FAC3r	H	Bury	L 1-2
21 Jan	FL	H	Preston NE	W 2-1
31 Jan	FL	A	Burnley	D 3-3
4 Feb	FL	H	Bradford PA	D 1-1
11 Feb	FL	A	Plymouth A	D 1-1
18 Feb	FL	H	Notts Co	W 3-0
4 Mar	FL	A	Swansea T	W 1-0
11 Mar	FL	H	Bradford C	W 3-1
16 Mar	FL	H	Charlton A	L 0-1
18 Mar	FL	A	Chesterfield	W 1-0
25 Mar	FL	H	Port Vale	D 1-1
1 Apr	FL	A	Bury	L 2-5
8 Apr	FL	H	Lincoln C	D 2-2
14 Apr	FL	H	Man Utd	W 3-2
15 Apr	FL	A	West Ham U	W 3-2
17 Apr	FL	A	Man Utd	L 1-2
22 Apr	FL	H	Southampton	W 4-2
29 Apr	FL	A	Millwall	D 1-1
6 May	FL	H	Fulham	W 1-0

League Appearances (Goals)
Armstrong R 1; Ashton P 1; Barrington J 10; Bell M 34 (1); Burton J 1; Dent J 14 (6); Dexter A 41; Dickinson W 37 (14); Forrest J 2; Graham J 23 (11); Graham T 40; Heslop R 28 (11); Howlett H 1; Keeton W 5; Langley R 5 (1); McKinlay W 42 (2); Masters A 6 (2); Porter W 3; Pugh R 40 (5); Simpson W 39 (9); Smith H 7; Stocks C 33 (3); Thompson W 38; Vasey R 11; Own Goals 2.

Position in League Table

		P	W	D	L	F	A	Pts
1st	Stoke	42	25	6	11	78	39	56
5th	Forest	42	17	15	10	67	59	49

1933-34 Division Two

26 Aug	FL	H	Brentford	D 1-1
30 Aug	FL	A	Man Utd	W 1-0
2 Sep	FL	A	Burnley	L 0-1
7 Sep	FL	H	Man Utd	D 1-1
9 Sep	FL	H	Oldham A	L 1-3
16 Sep	FL	A	Preston NE	L 0-4
23 Sep	FL	H	Bradford PA	W 3-0
30 Sep	FL	A	Grimsby T	L 1-2
7 Oct	FL	H	Notts Co	W 2-0
14 Oct	FL	H	West Ham U	L 0-1
21 Oct	FL	A	Swansea T	D 1-1
28 Oct	FL	H	Millwall	W 2-0
4 Nov	FL	A	Lincoln C	D 0-0
11 Nov	FL	H	Bury	W 7-2
18 Nov	FL	A	Hull C	D 2-2
25 Nov	FL	H	Fulham	W 2-0
2 Dec	FL	A	Southampton	L 0-2
9 Dec	FL	H	Blackpool	D 0-0
16 Dec	FL	A	Bradford C	L 2-3
23 Dec	FL	H	Port Vale	W 6-1
25 Dec	FL	A	Plymouth A	L 3-4
26 Dec	FL	H	Plymouth A	W 2-1
30 Dec	FL	A	Brentford	L 1-2
6 Jan	FL	H	Burnley	L 0-2
13 Jan	FAC3	H	QPR	W 4-0
20 Jan	FL	A	Oldham A	L 1-4
27 Jan	FAC4	A	Chelsea	D 1-1
31 Jan	FAC4r	H	Chelsea	L 0-3
3 Feb	FL	A	Bradford PA	L 2-6
7 Feb	FL	H	Preston NE	L 2-3
10 Feb	FL	H	Grimsby T	W 4-2
17 Feb	FL	A	Notts Co	L 0-1
24 Feb	FL	A	West Ham U	L 1-2
3 Mar	FL	H	Swansea T	W 4-2
10 Mar	FL	A	Millwall	D 0-0
17 Mar	FL	H	Lincoln C	W 6-2
24 Mar	FL	A	Bury	L 2-4
30 Mar	FL	A	Bolton W	D 1-1
31 Mar	FL	H	Hull C	L 0-1
2 Apr	FL	H	Bolton W	D 2-2
7 Apr	FL	A	Fulham	L 1-3
14 Apr	FL	H	Southampton	W 4-1
21 Apr	FL	A	Blackpool	W 3-2
25 Apr	F	H	Grimsby T	W 2-1
28 Apr	FL	H	Bradford C	L 1-2
3 May	F	A	Gorleston	W 5-2
5 May	FL	A	Port Vale	L 1-3

League Appearances (Goals)
Armstrong R 3; Ashton P 25; Barrington J 24 (1); Barry L 17 (1); Bell M 20; Burton J 1; Dent J 35 (27); Dexter A 17; Dickinson W 17 (5); Graham J 8 (2); Graham T 39 (1); Heslop 7 (1); McKinlay W 42 (3); Masters A 37 (8); Peacock T 15 (7); Porter W 3; Pugh R 32 (4); Race H 33 (11); Simpson W 26 (2); Smith H 30; Stocks C 7; Thompson W 17; Vasey R 7.

Position in League Table

		P	W	D	L	F	A	Pts
1	Grimsby	42	27	5	10	103	59	59
17	Forest	42	13	9	20	73	74	35

1934-35 Division Two

25 Aug	FL	H	Newcastle U	W 5-1
1 Sep	FL	A	West Ham U	L 1-3
3 Sep	FL	A	Bradford PA	D 1-1
8 Sep	FL	H	Blackpool	D 0-0
15 Sep	FL	A	Bury	L 0-1
22 Sep	FL	H	Hull C	W 2-1
29 Sep	FL	A	Notts Co	W 5-3
4 Oct	FL	H	Bradford PA	D 2-2
6 Oct	FL	A	Brentford	D 1-1
13 Oct	FL	H	Fulham	D 1-1
20 Oct	FL	H	Southampton	W 3-1
27 Oct	FL	A	Bolton W	W 3-2
3 Nov	FL	H	Oldham A	W 4-0
10 Nov	FL	A	Burnley	L 1-2
17 Nov	FL	H	Swansea T	W 1-0
24 Nov	FL	A	Man Utd	L 2-3
1 Dec	FL	H	Port Vale	W 2-0
8 Dec	FL	A	Barnsley	W 2-1
15 Dec	FL	H	Sheff Utd	W 2-1
22 Dec	FL	A	Bradford C	L 0-4
25 Dec	FL	H	Norwich C	W 5-2
26 Dec	FL	A	Norwich C	D 3-3
29 Dec	FL	A	Newcastle U	L 0-2
5 Jan	FL	H	West Ham U	W 2-0
12 Jan	FAC3	A	Chester	W 4-0
19 Jan	FL	A	Blackpool	L 0-1
26 Jan	FAC4	H	Man Utd	D 0-0
30 Jan	FAC4r	A	Man Utd	W 3-0
2 Feb	FL	A	Hull C	L 0-5
6 Feb	FL	H	Bury	L 1-4
9 Feb	FL	H	Notts Co	L 2-3
16 Feb	FAC5	H	Burnley	D 0-0
19 Feb	FAC5r	A	Burnley	L 0-3
23 Feb	FL	A	Fulham	L 1-2
28 Feb	FL	H	Brentford	D 0-0
2 Mar	FL	A	Southampton	W 2-1
9 Mar	FL	H	Bolton W	L 0-1
16 Mar	FL	A	Oldham A	W 5-0
23 Mar	FL	H	Burnley	W 5-0
30 Mar	FL	A	Swansea T	L 0-3
6 Apr	FL	H	Man Utd	D 2-2
13 Apr	FL	A	Port Vale	L 0-2
19 Apr	FL	H	Plymouth A	L 1-3
20 Apr	FL	H	Barnsley	W 4-1
22 Apr	FL	A	Plymouth A	L 2-5
27 Apr	FL	A	Sheff Utd	L 1-2
4 May	FL	H	Bradford C	W 2-0
6 May	NSC	A	Notts Co	L 2-3

League Appearances (Goals)
Armstrong R 1; Ashton P 29; Barrington J 35; Burditt G 14 (9); Burton J 16; Cargill J 7 (1); Dennison R 15 (5); Dent J 18 (13); Dexter A 12; Graham J 1; Graham T 24 (3); Hood C 3; Hunt J 1; McKinlay W 37 (4); McNaughton J 11; Masters A 31 (6); Mawson J 2; Peacock T 36 (21); Porter W 6; Pugh R 39; Race H 41 (6); Saxton F 1; Simpson W 37 (6); Smith E 2 (1); Smith H 35; Thompson W 2; Vasey R 5; Wall T 1; Own Goals 1.

Position in League Table

		P	W	D	L	F	A	Pts
1	Brentford	42	26	9	7	93	48	61
9	Forest	42	17	8	17	76	70	42

1935-36 Division Two

31 Aug	FL	H	Bury	D 2-2
2 Sep	FL	A	Fulham	L 0-6
7 Sep	FL	A	West Ham U	L 2-5
11 Sep	FL	H	Fulham	D 1-1
14 Sep	FL	H	Swansea T	D 2-2
16 Sep	FL	A	Blackpool	W 4-1
21 Sep	FL	A	Leicester C	L 1-2
28 Sep	FL	H	Bradford PA	W 2-0
3 Oct	FL	H	Blackpool	D 2-2
5 Oct	FL	A	Sheff Utd	L 0-1
12 Oct	FL	H	Southampton	W 2-0
19 Oct	FL	A	Burnley	L 0-1
26 Oct	FL	H	Charlton A	D 0-0
2 Nov	FL	A	Hull C	L 1-2
9 Nov	FL	H	Barnsley	W 6-0
16 Nov	FL	A	Plymouth A	L 1-3
23 Nov	FL	H	Port Vale	W 9-2
30 Nov	FL	A	Newcastle U	L 1-5
7 Dec	FL	H	Tottenham H	W 4-1
14 Dec	FL	A	Man Utd	L 0-5
21 Dec	FL	H	Bradford C	W 1-0
25 Dec	FL	A	Doncaster R	D 0-0
26 Dec	FL	H	Doncaster R	W 6-2
28 Dec	FL	A	Bury	W 6-2
4 Jan	FL	H	West Ham U	L 0-2
11 Jan	FAC3	A	Doncaster R	W 2-1
18 Jan	FL	A	Swansea T	L 1-2
25 Jan	FAC4	A	Derby Co	L 0-2
30 Jan	FL	H	Leicester C	L 0-1
1 Feb	FL	A	Bradford PA	W 4-1
8 Feb	FL	H	Sheff Utd	L 0-1
15 Feb	FL	A	Southampton	L 2-7
22 Feb	FL	H	Burnley	W 2-0
4 Mar	FL	A	Tottenham H	D 1-1
7 Mar	FL	H	Plymouth A	L 0-1
14 Mar	FL	A	Barnsley	W 2-0
21 Mar	FL	H	Hull C	D 0-0
28 Mar	FL	A	Port Vale	L 0-2
4 Apr	FL	H	Newcastle U	L 1-2
10 Apr	FL	H	Norwich C	D 2-2
11 Apr	FL	A	Charlton A	L 0-4
13 Apr	FL	A	Norwich C	L 0-4
18 Apr	FL	H	Man Utd	D 1-1
25 Apr	FL	A	Bradford C	D 0-0

League Appearances (Goals)
Ashton P 31; Barrington J 32; Bowden O 10 (2); Brown A Richard 1; Burditt G 4 (1); Burton J 17; Cargill J 3; Dent J 27 (12); Dexter A 11; Edgar D 34; Gardiner A 10 (3); Graham T 38 (1); McCall R 2; McKinlay W 29 (1); McNaughton G 1; Masters A 30 (7); Peacock T 29 (20); Pugh R 36 (1); Race H 34 (9); Simpson W 33 (5); Smith H 22; Stubbs E 20 (6); Wallbanks F 8; Own Goals 1.

Position in League Table

		P	W	D	L	F	A	Pts
1st	Man Utd	42	22	12	8	85	43	56
19th	Forest	42	12	11	19	69	76	35

1936-37 Division Two

29 Aug	FL	A	Burnley	L 0-3
2 Sep	FL	H	Aston Villa	D 1-1
5 Sep	FL	H	Fulham	W 5-3
7 Sep	FL	A	Aston Villa	D 1-1
12 Sep	FL	A	Doncaster R	W 2-0
16 Sep	FL	H	Southampton	D 1-1
19 Sep	FL	H	Coventry C	D 1-1
26 Sep	FL	A	Plymouth A	L 1-4
3 Oct	FL	H	West Ham U	W 1-0
8 Oct	NCCsf	A	Newark T	W 3-1
10 Oct	FL	H	Chesterfield	D 2-2
17 Oct	FL	A	Norwich C	L 0-4
24 Oct	FL	H	Newcastle U	L 0-2
28 Oct	NCCf	A	Notts Co	L 0-1
31 Oct	FL	A	Bradford PA	L 2-3
7 Nov	FL	H	Barnsley	W 4-1
14 Nov	FL	A	Sheff Utd	L 1-4
28 Nov	FL	A	Blackpool	L 1-7
5 Dec	FL	H	Blackburn R	W 2-0
12 Dec	FL	A	Bury	D 1-1
19 Dec	FL	H	Leicester C	L 0-3
25 Dec	FL	H	Bradford C	W 2-1
26 Dec	FL	H	Burnley	L 1-2
28 Dec	FL	A	Bradford C	L 1-2
2 Jan	FL	A	Fulham	L 2-5
9 Jan	FL	H	Doncaster R	W 2-1
16 Jan	FAC3	H	Sheff Utd	L 2-4
23 Jan	FL	A	Coventry C	D 2-2
3 Feb	FL	H	Plymouth A	L 2-3
6 Feb	FL	A	West Ham U	D 2-2
13 Feb	FL	A	Chesterfield	L 2-4
20 Feb	FL	H	Norwich C	L 3-4
5 Mar	FL	H	Bradford PA	W 3-2
13 Mar	FL	A	Barnsley	L 0-1
17 Mar	FL	A	Newcastle U	L 2-3
20 Mar	FL	H	Sheff Utd	D 1-1
26 Mar	FL	A	Swansea T	L 0-1
27 Mar	FL	A	Tottenham H	L 1-2
29 Mar	FL	H	Swansea T	W 6-1
3 Apr	FL	H	Blackpool	D 1-1
10 Apr	FL	A	Blackburn R	L 1-9
17 Apr	FL	H	Bury	W 1-0
21 Apr	FL	H	Tottenham H	W 3-0
24 Apr	FL	A	Leicester C	L 1-2
1 May	FL	A	Southampton	W 3-0

League Appearances (Goals)
Alsford W 19; Ashton P 22; Barrington J 1; Betts A 13 (4); Bowden O 4 (1); Brown A Roy 7 (1); Brown A Richard 19 (2); Burgin M 7 (6); Davies R 5; Dent J 4 (3); Dexter A 20; Edgar D 42; Gardiner A 16 (2); Getty J 6; Graham T 33; Hardy W 1; McCall R 1; McKinlay W 25; McNaughton G 21 (3); Martin D 37 (29); Masters A 5 (1); Munro J 18; Peacock T 7 (3); Pugh R 35 (4); Race H 7; Simpson W 25 (1); Smith, Horace 1; Smith H 7; Stubbs E 2; Surtees J 31 (7); Wood A 21; Own Goals 1.

Position in League Table

		P	W	D	L	F	A	Pts
1st	Leicester	42	24	8	10	89	57	56
18th	Forest	42	12	10	20	68	90	34

1937-38 Division Two

28 Aug	FL	A	Sheff Utd	L 1-2
1 Sep	FL	H	Stockport Co	L 1-2
4 Sep	FL	H	Tottenham H	W 3-1
6 Sep	FL	A	Stockport Co	L 0-1
11 Sep	FL	A	Burnley	D 0-0
15 Sep	FL	H	Barnsley	W 2-1
18 Sep	FL	H	Bury	W 1-0
25 Sep	FL	A	Coventry C	D 1-1
2 Oct	FL	H	Swansea T	W 2-1
9 Oct	FL	H	Newcastle U	D 0-0
13 Oct	NCCsf	H	Notts Co	W 1-0
16 Oct	FL	A	Norwich C	L 0-2
23 Oct	FL	A	Aston Villa	L 0-2
30 Oct	FL	A	Bradford PA	D 2-2
3 Nov	NCCf	A	Mansfield T	L 1-2
6 Nov	FL	H	West Ham U	D 0-0
13 Nov	FL	A	Southampton	L 0-2
20 Nov	FL	H	Fulham	L 0-1
27 Nov	FL	A	Sheff Wed	W 2-0
4 Dec	FL	H	Blackburn R	W 3-1
11 Dec	FL	A	Plymouth A	L 0-1
18 Dec	FL	H	Chesterfield	W 4-2
27 Dec	FL	A	Man Utd	L 3-4
28 Dec	FL	H	Man Utd	L 2-3
1 Jan	FL	H	Sheff Utd	W 2-1
8 Jan	FAC3	H	Southampton	W 3-1
15 Jan	FL	A	Tottenham H	L 0-3
22 Jan	FAC4	H	Middlesbrough	L 1-3
26 Jan	FL	H	Burnley	D 1-1
29 Jan	FL	A	Bury	L 0-2
5 Feb	FL	H	Coventry C	W 2-1
12 Feb	FL	A	Swansea T	L 0-1
19 Feb	FL	A	Newcastle U	L 1-3
26 Feb	FL	H	Norwich C	L 1-2
9 Mar	FL	A	Aston Villa	W 2-1
12 Mar	FL	H	Bradford PA	W 1-0
19 Mar	FL	A	West Ham U	L 1-2
26 Mar	FL	H	Southampton	W 2-1
2 Apr	FL	A	Fulham	L 0-2
9 Apr	FL	H	Sheff Wed	L 0-1
15 Apr	FL	H	Luton T	W 1-0
16 Apr	FL	A	Blackburn R	L 1-5
18 Apr	FL	A	Luton T	D 2-2
23 Apr	FL	H	Plymouth A	W 1-0
30 Apr	FL	A	Chesterfield	L 0-1
7 May	FL	A	Barnsley	D 2-2

League Appearances (Goals)
Alsford W 11; Ashton P 37; Baxter W 7; Betts A 32 (1); Brown A Roy 25 (3); Burgin M 15 (5); Davies R 26; Dyson J 9; Edgar D 24 (1); Gardiner A 12 (3); Getty J 1; Graham T 35 (1); McCall R 9; McNaughton G 27 (7); Martin D 37 (12); Munro J 24; Oakton A 7 (1); Peacock T 8 (3); Pugh R 26 (3); Richards S 1; Roberts S 1; Surtees J 35 (7); Todd A 5; Trim R 38.

Position in League Table

		P	W	D	L	F	A	Pts
1st	A Villa	42	25	7	10	73	35	57
20th	Forest	42	14	8	20	47	60	36

1938-39 Division Two

20 Aug	JTF	H	Notts Co	W 4-1
27 Aug	FL	H	Sheff Utd	L 0-2
31 Aug	FL	A	Plymouth A	L 0-3
3 Sep	FL	A	Burnley	L 1-2
7 Sep	FL	H	Norwich C	W 1-0
10 Sep	FL	H	Tottenham H	W 2-1
17 Sep	FL	A	Southampton	D 2-2
24 Sep	FL	H	Coventry C	W 3-0
1 Oct	FL	A	Tranmere R	D 1-1
8 Oct	FL	A	Newcastle U	L 0-4
12 Oct	NCCsf	H	Newark T	W 6-3
15 Oct	FL	H	West Ham U	D 0-0
22 Oct	FL	A	Bury	L 1-2
29 Oct	FL	H	Swansea T	L 1-2
2 Nov	NCCf	H	Mansfield T	D 2-2
5 Nov	FL	A	Fulham	D 2-2
12 Nov	FL	H	Blackburn R	L 1-3
19 Nov	FL	A	Millwall	L 0-5
26 Nov	FL	H	Man City	L 3-4
3 Dec	FL	A	Bradford PA	W 2-1
10 Dec	FL	H	Sheff Wed	D 3-3
17 Dec	FL	A	Chesterfield	L 1-7
24 Dec	FL	A	Sheff Utd	W 1-0
26 Dec	FL	H	Luton T	L 2-4
27 Dec	FL	A	Luton T	L 0-1
31 Dec	FL	H	Burnley	D 2-2
11 Jan	FAC3	A	Huddersfield T	D 0-0
14 Jan	FL	A	Tottenham H	L 1-4
16 Jan	FAC3r	H	Huddersfield T	L 0-3
28 Jan	FL	A	Coventry C	L 1-5
4 Feb	FL	H	Tranmere R	D 2-2
8 Feb	FL	H	Southampton	L 0-2
15 Feb	FL	H	Newcastle U	W 2-0
18 Feb	FL	A	West Ham U	L 0-5
25 Feb	FL	H	Bury	D 1-1
4 Mar	FL	A	Swansea T	L 0-1
11 Mar	FL	H	Fulham	D 1-1
18 Mar	FL	A	Blackburn R	L 2-3
25 Mar	FL	H	Millwall	W 3-0
1 Apr	FL	A	Man City	L 0-3
7 Apr	FL	H	WBA	W 2-0
8 Apr	FL	H	Bradford PA	W 2-0
10 Apr	FL	A	WBA	D 0-0
15 Apr	FL	A	Sheff Wed	D 1-1
22 Apr	FL	H	Chesterfield	L 0-1
29 Apr	FL	H	Plymouth A	W 2-1
6 May	FL	A	Norwich C	L 0-1

League Appearances (Goals)
Ashton P 28; Baxter W 1; Beaumont L 34 (3); Betts A 20 (5); Brown A Roy 19 (3); Clark T 27; Crawshaw H 22 (9); Davies R 18; Dyson J 6; Fryer J 22 (8); Getty J 11 (2); Graham T 26; Hindley F 6 (3); Hunt A 2; McCall R 30 (1); McNaughton G 18 (2); Martin D 7; Munro J 41; Peacock T 14 (3); Pritty G 21; Pugh R 1; Richards S 1; Roberts S 5; Stoker L 11; Surtees J 27 (9); Todd A 12; Trim R 32; Own Goals 1.

Position in League Table

		P	W	D	L	F	A	Pts
1st	Blackburn	42	25	5	12	94	60	55
20th	Forest	42	10	11	21	49	82	31

1939-40 Division Two

19 Aug	JTF	A	Notts Co	D 1-1
26 Aug	FL	A	Barnsley	L 0-4
30 Aug	FL	H	Newcastle U	W 2-0
2 Sep	FL	H	Newport Co	W 2-1

Football League suspended due to outbreak of World War Two

WAR LEAGUE EAST MIDLANDS

16 Sep	F	A	Peterborough U	L 3-4
23 Sep	F	H	Grimsby T	L 1-2
30 Sep	F	A	Lincoln C	W 6-0
7 Oct	F	H	Sheff Wed	L 1-2
14 Oct	F	H	Notts Co	W 2-1
21 Oct	WL	A	Sheff Utd	L 0-3
28 Oct	WL	H	Doncaster R	D 1-1
4 Nov	F	A	Chelmsford C	W 4-1
11 Nov	WL	H	Mansfield T	W 6-2
18 Nov	F	A	Bristol C	W 9-3
25 Nov	WL	H	Lincoln C	L 0-1
2 Dec	WL	A	Rotherham U	L 0-1
9 Dec	WL	H	Sheff Wed	D 1-1
16 Dec	F	H	Stockport Co	W 6-0
26 Dec	F	H	Leicester C	W 3-1
30 Dec	F	A	Port Vale	W 3-1
6 Jan	WL	H	Chesterfield	D 2-2
13 Jan	F	H	Birmingham Int XI	L 0-1
24 Jan	WL	A	Doncaster R	L 3-4
2 Mar	WL	A	Notts Co	L 3-4
9 Mar	WL	A	Mansfield T	L 0-3
16 Mar	F	H	Army XI	W 3-0
22 Mar	WL	A	Barnsley	L 0-3
23 Mar	WL	A	Lincoln C	L 0-1
25 Mar	WL	H	Barnsley	W 1-0
26 Mar	WL	H	Sheff Utd	W 4-1
30 Mar	WL	H	Rotherham U	W 4-1
6 Apr	WL	A	Sheff Wed	L 1-2
13 Apr	F	H	Stoke C	L 2-3
20 Apr	WC1/1	H	Charlton A	W 1-0
27 Apr	WC1/2	A	Charlton A	W 3-1
4 May	WC2/1	H	Southend U	W 3-1
11 May	WC2/2	A	Southend U	W 1-0
13 May	WL	H	Grimsby T	D 1-1
18 May	WC3	A	Fulham	L 0-2
25 May	WL	H	Notts Co	W 6-2
29 May	WL	A	Chesterfield	L 1-6
8 Jun	WL	A	Grimsby T	L 3-4

Position in War League Table

		P	W	D	L	F	A	Pts
1st	Ches'fld	20	14	2	4	69	23	30
10th	Forest	20	5	4	11	37	43	14

1940-41 War League South

31 Aug	WL	H	Birmingham	L 2-3
7 Sep	WL	A	Birmingham	L 1-2
14 Sep	WL	H	Leicester C	W 6-3
21 Sep	WL	A	Leicester C	D 2-2
28 Sep	WL	H	Walsall	W 2-0
5 Oct	WL	A	Walsall	L 3-4
12 Oct	WL	H	Northampton T	W 1-0
19 Oct	F	A	Lincoln C	W 3-2
26 Oct	WL	H	Stoke C	D 3-3
2 Nov	WL	A	Stoke C	L 0-5
9 Nov	F	H	RAF XI	L 1-4
16 Nov	WL	A	Northampton T	L 0-7
30 Nov	F	A	RAF XI	W 4-1
7 Dec	WL	A	WBA	L 0-5
14 Dec	WL	A	Mansfield T	L 1-2
21 Dec	WL	H	Mansfield T	L 1-4
25 Dec	WL	H	Notts Co	L 2-4
29 Dec	WL	A	WBA	L 3-5
11 Jan	MC1/1	H	Lincoln C	W 4-2
18 Jan	MC1/2	A	Lincoln C	L 1-2
1 Feb	MC2	A	Leicester C	L 2-6
15 Feb	WC1/1	A	Walsall	L 2-3
22 Feb	WC1/2	H	Walsall	W 8-1
1 Mar	WC2/1	H	Leicester C	L 0-2
8 Mar	WC2/2	A	Leicester C	D 1-1
15 Mar	WL	A	Notts Co	W 4-0
29 Mar	WL	A	Stoke C	L 0-4
5 Apr	WL	H	Stoke C	W 3-2
12 Apr	WL	H	Notts Co	L 1-3
19 Apr	WL	A	Sheff Wed	D 1-1
26 Apr	WL	A	Walsall	W 7-6
2 Jun	WL	A	Leicester C	L 0-2

Position in War League Table

		P	W	D	L	F	A	Ave
1st	Palace	27	16	4	7	66	44	1.954
28th	Forest	25	7	3	15	50	77	0.649

1941-42 War League South

30 Aug	WL	A	Luton T	L 1-5
6 Sep	WL	H	Luton T	W 4-1
13 Sep	WL	H	Northampton T	L 2-3
20 Sep	WL	A	Northampton T	L 3-4
27 Sep	F	H	RAF XI	L 1-2
11 Oct	WL	A	Walsall	L 2-8
18 Oct	WL	H	Walsall	W 4-0
25 Oct	F	A	REVO Electric	L 1-5
1 Nov	F	H	RAF XI	W 3-1
8 Nov	WL	H	Norwich C	L 0-2
22 Nov	WL	A	Leicester C	L 0-3
29 Nov	WL	H	Leicester C	L 0-1
6 Dec	WL	H	Wolves	D 0-0
13 Dec	WL	A	Wolves	L 0-7
20 Dec	WL	H	Leicester C	L 2-3
25 Dec	F	H	Mansfield T	W 3-0
25 Dec	WL	A	Leicester C	L 0-2
27 Dec	WCq	H	Sheff Utd	D 3-3
3 Jan	WCq	A	Sheff Utd	L 1-2
10 Jan	WCq	H	Chesterfield	W 1-0
17 Jan	WCq	A	Chesterfield	L 0-1
14 Feb	WCq	A	Lincoln C	W 3-0
21 Feb	WCq	H	Stoke C	W 1-0
28 Feb	WCq	A	Stoke C	W 3-1
14 Mar	WCq	A	Mansfield T	W 3-1
21 Mar	WCq	H	Northampton T	L 0-1
28 Mar	WL	H	Luton T	W 3-1
4 Apr	WC1/1	A	Lincoln C	L 5-6
6 Apr	WC1/2	H	Lincoln C	W 4-2
11 Apr	WC2/1	A	Grimsby T	L 1-3
18 Apr	WC2/2	H	Grimsby T	L 1-5
25 Apr	F	H	RAF XI	W 4-0
2 May	WL	H	Sheff Wed	W 2-1
9 May	WL	A	Sheff Wed	L 1-3

Position in War League Table

		P	W	D	L	F	A	Ave
1st	Leicester	17	11	3	3	42	17	26.4
12th	Forest	13	2	1	10	18	39	6.9

1942-43 War League North

29 Aug	WL	A	Lincoln C	D 3-3
5 Sep	WL	H	Lincoln C	L 0-1
12 Sep	WL	H	Sheff Utd	L 0-3
19 Sep	WL	A	Sheff Utd	D 2-2
26 Sep	WL	A	Mansfield T	W 1-0
3 Oct	WL	H	Mansfield T	W 3-1
10 Oct	WL	H	Derby Co	W 5-1
17 Oct	WL	A	Derby Co	L 2-3
24 Oct	WL	A	Chesterfield	L 0-3
31 Oct	WL	H	Chesterfield	W 6-1
7 Nov	WL	H	Notts Co	L 3-5
14 Nov	WL	A	Notts Co	W 3-1
21 Nov	WL	A	Leicester C	L 1-2
28 Nov	WL	H	Leicester C	D 1-1
5 Dec	WL	H	Lincoln C	W 4-1
12 Dec	WL	A	Lincoln C	L 1-4
19 Dec	WL	A	Northampton T	L 2-5
25 Dec	WL	H	Northampton T	L 1-2
26 Dec	WCq	A	Mansfield T	W 3-1
2 Jan	WCq	H	Mansfield T	W 3-1
9 Jan	WCq	H	Sheff Wed	D 1-1
16 Jan	WCq	A	Sheff Wed	D 1-1
23 Jan	WCq	A	Leicester C	L 0-5
30 Jan	WCq	H	Leicester C	W 4-0
6 Feb	WCq	H	Derby Co	W 4-1
13 Feb	WCq	A	Derby Co	L 1-3
20 Feb	WCq	A	Lincoln C	L 0-4
27 Feb	WCq	H	Lincoln C	W 3-2
6 Mar	WC1/1	H	Leicester C	L 0-1
13 Mar	WC1/2	A	Leicester C	W 2-0
20 Mar	WC2/1	H	Sheff Wed	W 1-0
27 Mar	WC2/2	A	Sheff Wed	L 1-5
10 Apr	WL	H	Doncaster R	L 1-2
17 Apr	WL	H	Notts Co	D 1-1
24 Apr	WL	A	Notts Co	L 1-2
26 Apr	WL	H	Grimsby T	D 4-4
26 Apr	F	A	Doncaster R	D 3-3

Position in War League Table

(First championship to 25 December 1942)

		P	W	D	L	F	A	Pts
1st	Blackpool	18	16	1	1	93	28	33
31st	Forest	18	6	3	9	38	39	15

(Second championship from 26 December 1942)

		P	W	D	L	F	A	Pts
1st	Liverpool	20	15	2	3	64	32	32
29th	Forest	18	7	4	7	30	34	18

1943-44 War League North

28 Aug	WL	H	Chesterfield	L 1-2
4 Sep	WL	A	Chesterfield	L 1-3
11 Sep	WL	A	Lincoln C	L 0-3
18 Sep	WL	H	Lincoln C	W 8-1
25 Sep	WL	H	Mansfield T	L 1-2
2 Oct	WL	A	Mansfield T	W 1-0
9 Oct	WL	A	Sheff Utd	D 1-1
16 Oct	WL	H	Sheff Utd	W 4-0
23 Oct	WL	H	Derby Co	W 4-3
30 Oct	WL	A	Derby Co	L 1-3
6 Nov	WL	A	Notts Co	W 1-0
13 Nov	WL	H	Notts Co	L 0-4
20 Nov	WL	H	Leicester C	W 1-0
27 Nov	WL	A	Leicester C	D 3-3
4 Dec	WL	A	Lincoln C	D 2-2
11 Dec	WL	H	Lincoln C	D 1-1
18 Dec	WL	H	Northampton T	D 2-2
25 Dec	WL	A	Northampton T	L 1-9
26 Dec	WCq	A	Derby Co	L 1-2
1 Jan	WCq	H	Derby Co	D 1-1
8 Jan	WCq	A	Sheff Wed	D 0-0
22 Jan	WCq	H	Notts Co	L 0-2
29 Jan	WCq	A	Notts Co	W 3-0
5 Feb	WCq	A	Mansfield T	W 1-0
12 Feb	WCq	H	Mansfield T	L 0-1
19 Feb	WCq	H	Leicester C	W 1-0
26 Feb	WCq	A	Leicester C	D 1-1
4 Mar	WL	A	WBA	W 1-0
11 Mar	WL	H	WBA	W 3-2
18 Mar	WL	A	Walsall	D 0-0
25 Mar	WL	H	Walsall	W 2-0
1 Apr	WL	H	Coventry C	W 4-1
8 Apr	WL	A	Coventry C	L 1-3
10 Apr	WL	H	Notts Co	W 3-0
15 Apr	WL	H	Northampton T	W 5-0
22 Apr	WL	A	Northampton T	L 1-3
29 Apr	MCf/1	A	WBA	D 2-2
6 May	MCf/2	H	WBA	L 3-4

Position in War League Table

(First championship to 25 December 1943)

		P	W	D	L	F	A	Pts
1st	Blackpool	18	12	4	2	56	20	28
26th	Forest	18	6	5	7	33	39	17

(Second championship from 26 December 1943)

		P	W	D	L	F	A	Pts
1st	Bath	21	16	2	3	78	26	34
16th	Forest	20	9	6	5	31	20	24

1944-45 War League North

26 Aug	WL	H	Derby Co	D 0-0
2 Sep	WL	A	Derby Co	L 0-5
9 Sep	WL	A	Sheff Utd	L 0-2
16 Sep	WL	H	Sheff Utd	D 2-2
23 Sep	WL	H	Notts Co	W 2-1
30 Sep	WL	A	Notts Co	D 0-0
7 Oct	WL	A	Chesterfield	W 1-0
14 Oct	WL	H	Chesterfield	W 2-1
21 Oct	WL	H	Mansfield T	L 2-5
28 Oct	WL	A	Mansfield T	L 2-4
4 Nov	WL	A	Rotherham U	W 2-1
11 Nov	WL	H	Rotherham U	L 1-2
18 Nov	WL	H	Lincoln C	D 2-2
25 Nov	WL	A	Lincoln C	D 2-2
2 Dec	WL	A	Sheff Wed	L 1-2
9 Dec	WL	H	Sheff Wed	W 1-0
16 Dec	WL	A	Grimsby T	L 1-3
23 Dec	WL	H	Grimsby T	L 1-2
30 Dec	WCq	H	Leicester C	D 0-0
6 Jan	WCq	H	Derby Co	D 1-1
13 Jan	WCq	A	Derby Co	L 0-3
3 Feb	WCq	A	Chesterfield	W 1-0
10 Feb	WCq	H	Chesterfield	D 1-1
17 Feb	WCq	H	Notts Co	L 1-4
24 Feb	WCq	A	Notts Co	W 2-1
3 Mar	WCq	A	Leicester C	D 1-1
10 Mar	WCq	H	Mansfield T	W 2-1
17 Mar	WCq	A	Mansfield T	L 0-1
2 Apr	WL	H	Notts Co	W 6-0
7 Apr	WL	H	Coventry C	D 1-1
14 Apr	WL	A	Coventry C	D 1-1
21 Apr	WL	A	Notts Co	W 3-1
28 Apr	WL	H	Notts Co	L 2-5
5 May	F	H	Chelmsford C	W 3-0
9 May	F	A	Derby Co	D 2-2
19 May	WL	A	Birmingham	L 1-4
26 May	WL	H	Birmingham	D 0-0

Position in War League Table

(First championship to 25 December 1944)

		P	W	D	L	F	A	Pts
1st	Hudd'fld	18	14	3	1	50	22	31
40th	Forest	18	5	5	8	22	34	15

(Second championship from 26 December 1944)

		P	W	D	L	F	A	Pts
1st	Derby	26	19	3	4	78	28	41
42nd	Forest	17	5	7	5	23	25	17

1945-46 War League South

15 Aug	F	H	Notts Co	W 3-2
16 Aug	F	H	Derby Co	L 1-4
25 Aug	WL	A	Chelsea	W 4-0
1 Sep	WL	H	Chelsea	L 0-1
8 Sep	WL	H	Millwall	D 2-2
12 Sep	WL	H	Fulham	D 1-1
15 Sep	WL	A	Millwall	L 1-2
17 Sep	WL	H	Plymouth A	W 2-0
22 Sep	WL	A	Southampton	L 2-5
29 Sep	WL	H	Southampton	W 4-0
6 Oct	WL	H	Derby Co	D 1-1
13 Oct	WL	A	Derby Co	L 2-3
20 Oct	WL	A	Leicester C	D 0-0
24 Oct	F	A	Rhine Army XI	L 1-4
27 Oct	WL	H	Leicester C	D 1-1
3 Nov	WL	H	Coventry C	D 0-0
10 Nov	WL	A	Coventry C	W 4-1
17 Nov	WL	A	Luton T	W 4-1
24 Nov	WL	H	Luton T	L 0-2
1 Dec	WL	A	Aston Villa	L 1-3
8 Dec	WL	H	Aston Villa	L 1-3
15 Dec	WL	A	Arsenal	D 2-2
22 Dec	WL	H	Arsenal	W 3-2
25 Dec	WL	H	Charlton A	L 0-2
26 Dec	WL	A	Charlton A	L 0-2
29 Dec	WL	A	Fulham	D 3-3
5 Jan	FAC3/1	H	Watford	D 1-1
9 Jan	FAC3/2	A	Watford	D 1-1
12 Jan	WL	A	Portsmouth	D 2-2
16 Jan	FAC3r	*	Watford	L 0-1
19 Jan	WL	H	Portsmouth	W 3-0
26 Jan	WL	H	Swansea T	D 2-2
2 Feb	WL	A	Swansea T	D 3-3
16 Feb	WL	A	Newport Co	W 4-2
23 Feb	WL	A	Wolves	L 0-4
2 Mar	WL	H	Wolves	D 0-0
9 Mar	WL	H	West Ham U	D 1-1
16 Mar	WL	A	West Ham U	W 3-1
23 Mar	WL	A	WBA	L 0-1
30 Mar	WL	H	WBA	L 0-2
6 Apr	WL	H	Birmingham C	W 1-0
13 Apr	WL	A	Birmingham C	L 1-3
19 Apr	WL	A	Tottenham H	L 2-3
20 Apr	WL	H	Brentford	W 2-0
22 Apr	WL	H	Tottenham H	L 0-2
23 Apr	WL	H	Newport Co	W 7-3
27 Apr	WL	A	Brentford	L 1-5
4 May	WL	A	Plymouth A	L 2-3

Position in War League Table

		P	W	D	L	F	A	Pts
1st	Birm'ham	42	28	5	9	96	45	61
15th	Forest	42	12	13	17	72	73	37

* at Tottenham

1946-47 Division Two

31 Aug	FL	A	Barnsley	L 2-3
5 Sep	FL	H	Newcastle U	L 0-2
7 Sep	FL	H	Newport Co	W 6-1
9 Sep	FL	A	Swansea T	L 2-3
14 Sep	FL	A	Southampton	L 2-5
21 Sep	FL	H	Luton T	W 4-2
25 Sep	F	A	Lincoln C	W 3-0
28 Sep	FL	H	Coventry C	W 1-0
5 Oct	FL	A	Birmingham C	L 0-4
12 Oct	FL	H	WBA	D 1-1
19 Oct	FL	A	Plymouth A	L 0-2
26 Oct	FL	H	Leicester C	W 2-0
2 Nov	FL	A	Chesterfield	D 1-1
6 Nov	F	A	Combined Services	D 2-2
9 Nov	FL	H	Millwall	L 1-2
16 Nov	FL	A	Bradford PA	W 1-0
23 Nov	FL	H	Man City	L 0-1
30 Nov	FL	A	West Ham U	D 2-2
7 Dec	FL	H	Sheff Wed	D 2-2
14 Dec	FL	A	Fulham	Abnd
21 Dec	FL	H	Bury	W 2-0
25 Dec	FL	A	Burnley	L 0-3
26 Dec	FL	H	Burnley	W 1-0
28 Dec	FL	H	Barnsley	W 2-1
1 Jan	FL	A	Newcastle U	L 0-3
4 Jan	FL	A	Newport Co	W 5-2
11 Jan	FAC3	A	Lincoln C	W 1-0
18 Jan	FL	H	Southampton	W 6-0
25 Jan	FAC4	A	Man Utd	W 2-0
29 Jan	FL	A	Luton T	L 2-3
1 Feb	FL	A	Coventry C	D 1-1
8 Feb	FAC5	H	Middlesbrough	D 2-2
12 Feb	FAC5r	A	Middlesbrough	L 2-6
1 Mar	FL	A	Leicester C	D 1-1
15 Mar	FL	A	Millwall	L 0-4
29 Mar	FL	A	Man City	L 1-2
4 Apr	FL	A	Tottenham H	L 0-2
5 Apr	FL	H	West Ham U	W 4-3
7 Apr	FL	H	Tottenham H	D 1-1
12 Apr	FL	A	Sheff Wed	L 0-2
19 Apr	FL	H	Fulham	W 2-1
26 Apr	FL	A	Bury	L 0-5
3 May	FL	H	Swansea T	D 1-1
10 May	FL	H	Birmingham C	D 1-1
17 May	FL	A	WBA	L 1-5
26 May	FL	A	Fulham	D 1-1
27 May	FL	H	Chesterfield	W 1-0
31 May	FL	H	Plymouth A	W 5-1
14 Jun	FL	H	Bradford PA	W 4-0

League Appearances (Goals)

Barks E 34 (3); Baxter W 7; Blagg E 33; Brigham H 28 (2); Brown G 1; Brown R 40 (16); Davies R 6; Edwards J 24 (9); Gunn A 2; Hinchcliffe T 1; Hutchinson J 9; Johnston T 32 (12); Knight F 25 (1); Leverton R 4 (1); Lyman C 23 (9); McCall R 32; Mee G 9 (1); Morley W 1; North T 1; O'Donnell F 11 (5); Orgill H 7; Platts L 1; Pritty G 26 (1); Rawson C 1; Roberts G 9; Savage R 20; Scott F 39 (3); Shufflebottom F 2; Simpson N 17 (1); Thomas G 13; Walker G 4; Own Goals 2.

Position in League Table

		P	W	D	L	F	A	Pts
1st	Man City	42	26	10	6	78	35	62
11th	Forest	42	15	10	17	69	74	40

1947-48 Division Two

23 Aug	FL	H	Bury	W 2-1
27 Aug	FL	H	Bradford PA	L 1-2
30 Aug	FL	A	West Ham U	L 1-2
3 Sep	FL	A	Bradford PA	L 1-3
6 Sep	FL	H	Chesterfield	L 1-3
10 Sep	FL	A	Brentford	L 1-3
13 Sep	FL	A	Millwall	L 0-2
17 Sep	FL	H	Brentford	W 2-0
20 Sep	FL	H	Tottenham H	W 1-0
27 Sep	FL	A	Sheff Wed	L 1-2
4 Oct	FL	H	Cardiff C	L 1-2
11 Oct	FL	A	Leicester C	L 1-3
18 Oct	FL	H	Leeds U	W 1-0
25 Oct	FL	A	Fulham	D 0-0
1 Nov	FL	H	Coventry C	W 4-0
8 Nov	FL	A	Newcastle U	W 2-0
15 Nov	FL	H	Birmingham C	L 0-2
22 Nov	FL	A	WBA	L 2-3
29 Nov	FL	H	Barnsley	D 1-1
6 Dec	FL	A	Plymouth A	D 1-1
13 Dec	FL	H	Luton T	L 1-2
20 Dec	FL	A	Bury	L 0-1
26 Dec	FL	A	Doncaster R	L 0-2
27 Dec	FL	H	Doncaster R	W 4-2
3 Jan	FL	H	West Ham U	W 2-1
10 Jan	FAC3	A	Liverpool	L 1-4
17 Jan	FL	A	Chesterfield	D 0-0
24 Jan	F	H	Arsenal	L 2-3
31 Jan	FL	H	Millwall	W 5-2
7 Feb	F	A	Crystal Palace	L 0-1
14 Feb	FL	H	Sheff Wed	D 0-0
21 Feb	FL	A	Cardiff C	L 1-4
28 Feb	FL	H	Leicester C	W 1-0
6 Mar	FL	A	Leeds U	D 2-2
13 Mar	FL	H	Fulham	L 0-2
20 Mar	FL	A	Coventry C	D 1-1
26 Mar	FL	A	Southampton	L 1-2
27 Mar	FL	H	Newcastle U	D 0-0
29 Mar	FL	H	Southampton	D 1-1
3 Apr	FL	A	Birmingham C	L 1-2
10 Apr	FL	H	WBA	W 3-1
12 Apr	FL	A	Tottenham H	W 3-0
17 Apr	FL	A	Barnsley	D 2-2
24 Apr	FL	H	Plymouth A	D 1-1
1 May	FL	A	Luton T	L 1-2

League Appearances (Goals)
Allen H 1; Barks E 30 (1); Blagg E 21; Brigham H 7; Brown R 5 (1); Clarke J 2; Edwards J 33 (6); Elliott B 1; Gager H 12 (1); Hutchinson J 38; Johnson T 32 (12); Jones 7 (5); Kaile G 9; Knight F 12; Lee G 41 (10); Leverton R 6 (4); McCall R 26; Martin F 2; Morley W 15 (3); Morris E 4 (1); Platts L 2; Pritty G 2; Rawson C 2; Scott F 41 (5); Simpson N 30 (2); Thomas G 26; Walker G 39; Ward D 1; Wheatley R 4; Wilkins G 11 (3).

Position in League Table

		P	W	D	L	F	A	Pts
1st	Birm'ham	42	22	15	5	55	24	59
19th	Forest	42	12	11	19	54	60	35

1948-49 Division Two

21 Aug	FL	H	WBA	L 0-1
24 Aug	FL	A	Grimsby T	W 2-1
28 Aug	FL	A	Fulham	L 0-4
1 Sep	FL	H	Grimsby T	D 0-0
4 Sep	FL	H	Plymouth A	W 1-0
8 Sep	FL	A	Barnsley	L 0-4
11 Sep	FL	A	Blackburn R	L 1-2
15 Sep	FL	H	Barnsley	L 0-1
18 Sep	FL	H	Cardiff C	D 0-0
25 Sep	FL	A	QPR	L 1-2
2 Oct	FL	H	Luton T	W 2-0
9 Oct	FL	H	Chesterfield	L 0-1
16 Oct	FL	A	Lincoln C	W 3-1
23 Oct	FL	H	Sheff Wed	L 1-2
30 Oct	FL	A	Coventry C	W 2-1
6 Nov	FL	H	Leeds U	D 0-0
13 Nov	FL	A	Leicester C	L 2-4
20 Nov	FL	H	Brentford	L 1-2
27 Nov	FL	A	Tottenham H	Abnd
4 Dec	FL	H	West Ham U	W 3-0
11 Dec	FL	A	Bury	D 1-1
18 Dec	FL	A	WBA	L 1-2
25 Dec	FL	H	Southampton	W 2-1
27 Dec	FL	A	Southampton	L 1-2
1 Jan	FL	H	Fulham	L 0-2
8 Jan	FAC3	H	Liverpool	D 2-2
15 Jan	FAC3r	A	Liverpool	L 0-4
22 Jan	FL	H	Blackburn R	W 1-0
29 Jan	FL	A	Plymouth A	L 0-1
5 Feb	FL	A	Cardiff C	L 0-1
12 Feb	FL	A	Tottenham H	L 1-2
19 Feb	FL	H	QPR	D 0-0
26 Feb	FL	A	Luton T	L 3-4
5 Mar	FL	A	Chesterfield	L 1-2
12 Mar	FL	H	Lincoln C	D 1-1
19 Mar	FL	A	Sheff Wed	L 1-2
26 Mar	FL	H	Coventry C	W 3-0
2 Apr	FL	A	Leeds U	L 0-1
9 Apr	FL	H	Leicester C	W 2-1
15 Apr	FL	H	Bradford PA	W 2-0
16 Apr	FL	A	Brentford	L 1-2
18 Apr	FL	A	Bradford PA	W 2-1
23 Apr	FL	H	Tottenham H	D 2-2
30 Apr	FL	A	West Ham U	W 5-0
7 May	FL	H	Bury	W 1-0

League Appearances (Goals)
Ashman G 3 (1); Barks E 2; Burkitt J 28 (1); Clarke J 1; Edwards J 20 (5); Elliott B 9; Gager H 40; Hullett W 13 (2); Hutchinson J 20; Johnson T 21 (5); Kaile G 16 (2); Knight F 5; Lee G 35 (10); Leverton R 15 (6); Linaker J 13 (2); Love J 13 (7); McCall R 36; Martin F 3; Morley W 15; Ottewell S 31 (3); Platts L 1; Scott F 26 (2); Thomas G 39; Walker G 41; Whare W 1; Wheatley R 2; Wilkins G 13 (3); Own Goals 1.

Position in League Table

		P	W	D	L	F	A	Pts
1st	Fulham	42	24	9	9	77	37	57
21st	Forest	42	14	7	21	50	54	35

1949-50 Division Three South

20 Aug	FL	A	Brighton & HA	D 2-2
24 Aug	FL	H	Bristol C	W 3-0
27 Aug	FL	H	Walsall	W 1-0
30 Aug	FL	A	Bristol C	W 2-0
3 Sep	FL	A	Millwall	L 1-2
8 Sep	FL	A	Northampton T	D 0-0
10 Sep	FL	H	Swindon T	W 2-1
14 Sep	FL	H	Northampton T	L 0-1
17 Sep	FL	A	Torquay U	L 0-2
24 Sep	FL	H	Aldershot	W 3-0
1 Oct	FL	A	Ipswich T	W 2-1
8 Oct	FL	H	Exeter C	W 5-0
15 Oct	FL	A	Leyton Orient	D 1-1
22 Oct	FL	H	Reading	L 1-2
29 Oct	FL	A	Watford	L 0-1
5 Nov	FL	H	Crystal Palace	W 2-0
12 Nov	FL	A	Bournemouth & BA	W 2-1
19 Nov	FL	H	Bristol R	W 2-0
26 Nov	FAC1	H	Bristol C	W 1-0
3 Dec	FL	H	Notts Co	L 1-2
10 Dec	FAC2	H	Stockport Co	L 0-2
17 Dec	FL	H	Brighton & HA	L 0-1
24 Dec	FL	A	Walsall	W 3-1
26 Dec	FL	A	Norwich C	D 1-1
27 Dec	FL	H	Norwich C	L 0-1
31 Dec	FL	H	Millwall	W 3-1
14 Jan	FL	A	Swindon T	W 5-0
21 Jan	FL	H	Torquay U	L 1-2
28 Jan	FL	A	Southend U	W 3-2
4 Feb	FL	A	Aldershot	D 1-1
11 Feb	FL	A	Port Vale	D 1-1
18 Feb	FL	H	Ipswich T	W 2-0
25 Feb	FL	A	Exeter C	D 0-0
4 Mar	FL	H	Leyton Orient	W 2-1
11 Mar	FL	A	Reading	D 1-1
18 Mar	FL	H	Watford	L 0-1
25 Mar	FL	A	Crystal Palace	D 1-1
1 Apr	FL	H	Bournemouth & BA	W 3-0
7 Apr	FL	A	Newport Co	L 1-4
8 Apr	FL	A	Bristol R	W 3-0
10 Apr	FL	H	Newport Co	W 3-0
15 Apr	FL	H	Southend U	L 1-2
22 Apr	FL	A	Notts Co	L 0-2
25 Apr	F	H	Tilbury	D 1-1
29 Apr	FL	H	Port Vale	W 2-0
13 May	F	A	Gooi Hilversum	W 1-0
18 May	F	A	Sparta Rotterdam	W 1-0
21 May	F	A	Gottingen 05	D 2-2
23 May	F	A	SV Bremen	L 1-5
25 May	F	A	Osnabruck	D 2-2
28 May	F	A	RC Malines	L 0-6

League Appearances (Goals)
Anderson J 32 (1); Ardron W 41 (25); Ashman G 10 (2); Baker D 3; Burkitt J 30 (1); Capel T 24 (9); Gager H 35 (1); Hutchinson J 17; Johnson T 4 (2); Kaile G 40 (6); Knight F 6; Leverton R 8 (3); Linaker J 2; Lindley E 1; Love J 37 (11); McCall R 25; Morley W 16; Ottewell S 1; Platts L 2; Rawson J 4; Scott F 41 (4); Thomas G 20; Walker G 40; Whare W 23; Own Goals 2.

Position in League Table

		P	W	D	L	F	A	Pts
1st	Notts Co	42	25	8	9	95	50	58
4th	Forest	42	20	9	13	67	39	49

1950-51 Division Three South

19 Aug	FL	A	Newport Co	W 2-0
23 Aug	FL	H	Brighton & HA	W 4-0
26 Aug	FL	H	Norwich C	W 4-2
30 Aug	FL	A	Brighton & HA	W 2-1
2 Sep	FL	A	Northampton T	D 2-2
6 Sep	FL	H	Plymouth A	W 4-1
9 Sep	FL	H	Port Vale	W 2-1
13 Sep	FL	A	Plymouth A	W 2-0
16 Sep	FL	A	Reading	W 2-0
23 Sep	FL	A	Torquay U	L 2-3
30 Sep	FL	H	Aldershot	W 7-0
7 Oct	FL	H	Ipswich T	D 0-0
14 Oct	FL	A	Leyton Orient	W 4-0
21 Oct	FL	H	Walsall	W 4-0
28 Oct	FL	A	Watford	D 1-1
4 Nov	FL	H	Millwall	W 2-0
11 Nov	FL	A	Bristol C	W 3-0
18 Nov	FL	H	Gillingham	W 9-2
25 Nov	FAC1	H	Torquay U	W 6-1
2 Dec	FL	H	Exeter C	D 2-2
9 Dec	FAC2	A	Rotherham U	L 1-2
23 Dec	FL	A	Norwich C	L 0-2
25 Dec	FL	H	Colchester U	D 0-0
26 Dec	FL	A	Colchester U	W 2-0
6 Jan	FL	H	Crystal Palace	W 1-0
13 Jan	FL	A	Port Vale	D 1-1
20 Jan	FL	H	Reading	D 1-1
27 Jan	FL	A	Crystal Palace	W 6-1
3 Feb	FL	H	Torquay U	W 3-1
10 Feb	FL	A	Bournemouth & BA	L 2-3
17 Feb	FL	A	Aldershot	L 0-1
24 Feb	FL	A	Ipswich T	W 3-1
3 Mar	FL	H	Leyton Orient	L 0-1
10 Mar	FL	A	Walsall	W 2-0
17 Mar	FL	H	Watford	W 2-1
24 Mar	FL	A	Millwall	D 1-1
26 Mar	FL	H	Bristol R	W 2-1
31 Mar	FL	H	Bristol C	D 0-0
7 Apr	FL	A	Gillingham	W 4-1
10 Apr	FL	A	Southend U	L 2-3
14 Apr	FL	H	Bournemouth & BA	W 1-0
18 Apr	FL	H	Swindon T	W 2-1
21 Apr	FL	A	Exeter C	W 5-0
25 Apr	FL	H	Northampton T	D 2-2
28 Apr	FL	H	Southend U	W 3-0
2 May	FL	H	Newport Co	W 2-1
3 May	FL	A	Bristol R	W 2-0
5 May	FL	A	Swindon T	W 3-2
12 May	F	H	RC Malines	W 3-1

League Appearances (Goals)
Anderson J 8; Ardron W 45 (36); Burkitt J 42 (1); Capel T 35 (23); Clarke J 1; Collindridge C 46 (16); Gager H 46 (2); Hutchinson J 6; Johnson T 32 (15); Leverton R 22 (6); Love J 4 (1); Morley W 42; Scott F 46 (9); Thomas G 45; Walker G 46; Whare W 40; Own Goals 1.

Position in League Table

		P	W	D	L	F	A	Pts
1st	Forest	46	30	10	6	110	40	70

1951-52 Division Two

18 Aug	FL	A	Rotherham U	W 2-1
22 Aug	FL	H	Southampton	W 3-0
25 Aug	FL	H	Cardiff C	L 2-3
29 Aug	FL	A	Southampton	L 2-5
1 Sep	FL	A	Birmingham C	W 2-0
5 Sep	FL	A	Everton	L 0-1
8 Sep	FL	H	Leicester C	D 2-2
12 Sep	FL	H	Everton	W 2-0
15 Sep	FL	A	Notts Co	D 2-2
22 Sep	FL	A	Brentford	D 1-1
29 Sep	FL	H	Doncaster R	D 1-1
6 Oct	FL	H	Luton T	W 2-0
13 Oct	FL	A	Bury	L 0-2
20 Oct	FL	H	Swansea T	D 2-2
27 Oct	FL	A	Coventry C	D 3-3
3 Nov	FL	H	West Ham U	D 0-0
10 Nov	FL	A	Sheff Utd	W 4-1
17 Nov	FL	H	Barnsley	D 3-3
24 Nov	FL	A	Hull C	W 4-1
1 Dec	FL	H	Blackburn R	W 1-0
8 Dec	FL	A	QPR	L 3-4
15 Dec	FL	H	Rotherham U	W 4-2
22 Dec	FL	A	Cardiff C	L 1-4
25 Dec	FL	A	Sheff Wed	D 1-1
26 Dec	FL	H	Sheff Wed	W 2-1
29 Dec	FL	H	Birmingham C	L 0-1
5 Jan	FL	A	Leicester C	L 1-3
12 Jan	FAC3	H	Blackburn R	D 2-2
16 Jan	FAC3r	A	Blackburn R	L 0-2
19 Jan	FL	H	Notts Co	W 3-2
26 Jan	FL	H	Brentford	W 2-0
9 Feb	FL	A	Doncaster R	W 1-0
16 Feb	FL	A	Luton T	D 3-3
23 Feb	F	H	Bolton W	D 3-3
1 Mar	FL	H	Bury	W 1-0
8 Mar	FL	A	Swansea T	W 2-1
15 Mar	FL	H	Coventry C	W 3-1
22 Mar	FL	A	West Ham U	L 1-3
29 Mar	FL	H	Sheff Utd	L 0-2
5 Apr	FL	A	Barnsley	D 1-1
7 Apr	F	A	Bexhill-on-Sea	W 12-1
11 Apr	FL	H	Leeds U	D 1-1
12 Apr	FL	H	Hull C	W 4-0
14 Apr	FL	A	Leeds U	D 0-0
19 Apr	FL	A	Blackburn R	L 2-3
26 Apr	FL	H	QPR	W 3-1
2 May	F	A	Brighton & HA	L 4-5
14 May	F	A	Guernsey XI	W 5-2

League Appearances (Goals)
Ardron W 39 (29); Burkitt J 23; Canning L 5; Capel T 32 (10); Clarke J 1; Collindridge C 32 (10); Gager H 38; Hutchinson J 31; Johnson T 11 (5); Kelly N 17 (3); Leverton R 15 (5); Love J 5 (2); McCall R 1; McKinlay R 1; Moore A 15 (5); Morley W 40 (2); Orr A 24; Scott F 41 (4); Thomas G 31; Walker G 37; Whare W 21; Wilson T 2; Own Goals 2.

Position in League Table

		P	W	D	L	F	A	Pts
1st	Sheff W	42	21	11	10	100	66	53
4th	Forest	42	18	13	11	77	62	49

1952-53 Division Two

23 Aug	FL	H	Blackburn R	L 1-2
27 Aug	FL	A	Barnsley	W 2-0
30 Aug	FL	A	Notts Co	L 2-3
3 Sep	FL	H	Barnsley	W 3-0
6 Sep	FL	A	Everton	L 0-3
10 Sep	FL	A	Lincoln C	W 3-2
13 Sep	FL	H	Brentford	W 3-0
17 Sep	FL	H	Lincoln C	D 1-1
20 Sep	FL	A	Doncaster R	L 0-1
22 Sep	FL	A	Sheff Utd	L 0-2
27 Sep	FL	H	Swansea T	W 6-4
4 Oct	FL	A	Huddersfield T	W 2-1
11 Oct	FL	H	Leicester C	L 1-3
18 Oct	FL	A	West Ham U	L 2-3
25 Oct	FL	H	Fulham	L 0-1
1 Nov	FL	A	Rotherham U	W 3-2
8 Nov	FL	H	Plymouth A	W 3-1
15 Nov	FL	A	Leeds U	Abnd
22 Nov	FL	H	Luton T	W 4-3
29 Nov	FL	A	Birmingham C	W 5-0
6 Dec	FL	H	Bury	W 4-1
13 Dec	FL	A	Southampton	D 2-2
20 Dec	FL	A	Blackburn R	L 1-2
26 Dec	FL	H	Hull C	W 4-1
27 Dec	FL	A	Hull C	L 1-3
3 Jan	FL	H	Notts Co	W 1-0
10 Jan	FAC3	A	Mansfield T	W 1-0
17 Jan	FL	H	Everton	D 3-3
24 Jan	FL	A	Brentford	D 1-1
31 Jan	FL	A	Everton	L 1-4
7 Feb	FL	H	Doncaster R	D 2-2
14 Feb	FL	A	Swansea T	L 1-2
21 Feb	FL	H	Huddersfield T	W 1-0
28 Feb	FL	A	Leicester C	D 1-1
7 Mar	FL	H	West Ham U	D 0-0
14 Mar	FL	A	Fulham	W 1-0
21 Mar	FL	H	Rotherham U	W 4-3
28 Mar	FL	A	Plymouth A	W 3-0
4 Apr	FL	H	Leeds U	W 2-1
6 Apr	FL	H	Sheff Utd	D 1-1
11 Apr	FL	A	Luton T	L 0-3
15 Apr	F	H	Clyde	W 6-0
18 Apr	FL	H	Birmingham C	L 0-2
22 Apr	FL	A	Leeds U	L 1-2
25 Apr	FL	A	Bury	L 0-2
29 Apr	FL	H	Southampton	L 2-3
30 Apr	F	A	Mansfield T	D 1-1

League Appearances (Goals)
Ardron W 30 (21); Burkitt J 42 (4); Capel T 29 (9); Clarke J 10; Collindridge C 40 (12); French J 27 (1); Gager H 41 (1); Hutchinson J 30; Kelly N 5; Lemon A 3; Leverton R 22 (6); McKinlay R 3; Martin T 18 (3); Moore A 30 (11); Morley W 8; Orr A 3; Scott F 28 (6); Thomas G 19; Thompson S 2; Walker G 42; Whare W 25 (1); Wilson T 5; Own Goals 2.

Position in League Table

		P	W	D	L	F	A	Pts
1st	Sheff Utd	42	25	10	7	97	55	60
7th	Forest	42	18	8	16	77	67	44

1953-54 Division Two

19 Aug	FL	H	Everton	D 3-3
22 Aug	FL	H	Plymouth A	W 3-0
26 Aug	FL	A	Luton T	W 1-0
29 Aug	FL	A	Swansea T	L 1-2
2 Sep	FL	H	Luton T	W 2-1
5 Sep	FL	H	Rotherham U	W 4-1
7 Sep	FL	A	Hull C	L 0-3
12 Sep	FL	A	Leicester C	L 0-1
16 Sep	FL	H	Hull C	W 2-0
19 Sep	FL	H	Stoke C	W 5-4
26 Sep	FL	A	Fulham	L 1-3
3 Oct	FL	H	West Ham U	W 4-0
10 Oct	FL	H	Notts Co	W 5-0
17 Oct	FL	A	Lincoln C	D 2-2
24 Oct	FL	H	Bristol R	W 3-1
31 Oct	FL	A	Brentford	D 1-1
7 Nov	FL	H	Derby Co	W 4-2
14 Nov	FL	A	Blackburn R	L 0-2
21 Nov	FL	H	Doncaster R	D 2-2
28 Nov	FL	A	Bury	L 1-2
5 Dec	FL	H	Oldham A	D 1-1
12 Dec	FL	A	Everton	D 3-3
19 Dec	FL	A	Plymouth A	L 0-1
25 Dec	FL	H	Leeds U	W 5-2
26 Dec	FL	A	Leeds U	W 2-0
2 Jan	FL	H	Swansea T	W 2-1
9 Jan	FAC3	A	Plymouth A	L 0-2
16 Jan	FL	A	Rotherham U	L 0-3
23 Jan	FL	H	Leicester C	W 3-1
30 Jan	F	H	Aston Villa	L 0-2
6 Feb	FL	A	Stoke C	D 1-1
13 Feb	FL	H	Fulham	W 4-1
20 Feb	FL	A	West Ham U	D 1-1
27 Feb	FL	A	Notts Co	D 1-1
6 Mar	FL	H	Lincoln C	W 4-2
13 Mar	FL	A	Bristol R	L 0-1
20 Mar	FL	H	Brentford	W 2-1
27 Mar	FL	A	Doncaster R	W 3-1
3 Apr	FL	H	Bury	D 2-2
10 Apr	FL	A	Derby Co	W 2-1
16 Apr	FL	H	Birmingham C	D 1-1
17 Apr	FL	H	Blackburn R	L 0-1
19 Apr	FL	A	Birmingham C	D 2-2
24 Apr	FL	A	Oldham A	W 3-1
27 Apr	F	*	Wolves/Birm/WBA	W 7-1
28 Apr	F	A	Rushden T	W 5-2
29 Apr	F	A	Gainsborough Trinity	W 4-1

League Appearances (Goals)
Ardron W 14 (10); Burkitt J 39 (2); Capel T 34 (18); Clarke J 3; Collindridge C 33 (7); Farmer W 12; French J 27; Gager H 41 (6); Hutchinson J 29; Kelly N 13; Lemon A 19 (1); Leverton R 11 (5); McKinlay R 1; McLaren H 10 (6); Martin T 11 (1); Moore A 42 (19); Orr A 15; Scott F 9 (1); Thomas G 28; Thompson S 14 (7); Walker G 30; Whare W 24; Wilson T 3; Own Goals 3.

Position in League Table

		P	W	D	L	F	A	Pts
1st	Leicester	42	23	10	9	97	60	56
4th	Forest	42	20	12	10	86	59	52

* at Darlaston

1954-55 Division Two

21 Aug	FL	A	Luton T	L 0-3
25 Aug	FL	H	Stoke C	L 0-3
28 Aug	FL	H	Hull C	L 0-1
30 Aug	FL	A	Stoke C	L 0-2
4 Sep	FL	A	Lincoln C	L 1-2
8 Sep	FL	A	Middlesbrough	W 4-1
11 Sep	FL	H	Bury	L 2-3
15 Sep	FL	H	Middlesbrough	W 4-2
18 Sep	FL	A	Leeds U	D 1-1
25 Sep	FL	H	Notts Co	L 0-1
2 Oct	FL	H	Ipswich T	W 2-0
9 Oct	FL	A	West Ham U	L 0-2
16 Oct	FL	H	Blackburn R	L 1-2
23 Oct	FL	A	Plymouth A	W 2-1
30 Oct	FL	H	Port Vale	L 2-3
6 Nov	FL	A	Doncaster R	W 3-0
13 Nov	FL	H	Derby Co	W 3-0
20 Nov	FL	A	Liverpool	L 0-1
27 Nov	FL	H	Bristol R	W 1-0
4 Dec	FL	A	Fulham	D 1-1
11 Dec	FL	H	Swansea T	D 0-0
18 Dec	FL	H	Luton T	L 1-5
25 Dec	FL	A	Birmingham C	W 1-0
27 Dec	FL	H	Birmingham C	L 0-2
1 Jan	FL	A	Hull C	W 3-2
8 Jan	FAC3	A	Sheff Utd	W 3-1
15 Jan	FL	H	Lincoln C	D 1-1
29 Jan	FAC4	A	Hartlepools U	D 1-1
2 Feb	FAC4r	H	Hartlepools U	W 2-1
5 Feb	FL	H	Leeds U	D 1-1
12 Feb	FL	A	Notts Co	L 1-4
19 Feb	FAC5	H	Newcastle U	D 1-1
28 Feb	FAC5r	A	Newcastle U	D 2-2
2 Mar	FAC5r2	A	Newcastle U	L 1-2
5 Mar	FL	A	Blackburn R	W 1-0
9 Mar	FL	A	Ipswich T	L 1-2
12 Mar	FL	H	Plymouth A	W 2-0
19 Mar	FL	A	Port Vale	W 2-1
21 Mar	F	A	East Fife	W 5-1
26 Mar	FL	H	Doncaster R	W 3-1
2 Apr	FL	A	Derby Co	W 2-1
8 Apr	FL	H	Rotherham U	L 0-2
9 Apr	FL	H	Liverpool	W 3-1
11 Apr	FL	A	Rotherham U	L 2-3
16 Apr	FL	A	Bristol R	L 1-2
20 Apr	FL	A	Bury	D 1-1
23 Apr	FL	H	Fulham	W 2-0
30 Apr	FL	A	Swansea T	L 2-3
2 May	FL	H	West Ham U	D 1-1

League Appearances (Goals)
Ardron W 13 (2); Barrett J 19 (8); Blackman R 11 (3); Burkitt J 40; Burton B 1; Cluroe M 1; Farmer W 28; French J 13 (4); Gager H 5; Holder A 3; Hutchinson J 19; Kelly N 13 (8); Lay P 1; Lemon A 2; McKinlay R 37; McLaren H 23 (9); Martin T 19; Moore A 15 (4); Morley W 30; Orr A 4; Scott F 22 (3); Small P 30 (8); Thomas G 42; Thompson S 6 (1); Turner K 1; Walker G 14; Whare W 22; Wilson T 28 (8).

Position in League Table

		P	W	D	L	F	A	Pts
1st	Birm'ham	42	22	10	10	92	47	54
15th	Forest	42	16	7	19	58	62	39

1955-56 Division Two

20 Aug	FL	H	Liverpool	L 1-3
22 Aug	FL	A	Leicester C	L 2-5
27 Aug	FL	A	Plymouth A	W 2-1
31 Aug	FL	H	Leicester C	W 2-0
3 Sep	FL	H	Stoke C	L 2-3
10 Sep	FL	A	Bristol R	L 1-4
17 Sep	FL	H	Doncaster R	W 5-0
24 Sep	FL	A	Sheff Wed	W 2-1
1 Oct	FL	H	Notts Co	L 0-2
8 Oct	FL	A	Leeds U	L 0-3
15 Oct	FL	H	Fulham	W 1-0
22 Oct	FL	A	Rotherham U	L 1-2
29 Oct	FL	H	Barnsley	W 1-0
5 Nov	FL	A	Middlesbrough	L 2-3
12 Nov	FL	H	Bristol C	L 0-2
19 Nov	FL	A	West Ham U	W 2-1
22 Nov	F	A*	East Fife	L 2-3
26 Nov	FL	H	Port Vale	D 2-2
3 Dec	FL	A	Bury	W 2-1
10 Dec	FL	H	Swansea T	W 2-1
17 Dec	FL	A	Liverpool	L 2-5
24 Dec	FL	H	Plymouth A	W 3-1
26 Dec	FL	H	Hull C	W 2-1
27 Dec	FL	A	Hull C	W 3-0
31 Dec	FL	A	Stoke C	D 1-1
2 Jan	FL	A	Blackburn R	D 2-2
7 Jan	FAC3	A	Doncaster R	L 0-3
14 Jan	FL	H	Bristol R	D 1-1
21 Jan	FL	A	Doncaster R	W 3-1
4 Feb	FL	H	Sheff Wed	L 0-1
11 Feb	FL	A	Notts Co	W 3-1
3 Mar	FL	H	Rotherham U	W 1-0
10 Mar	FL	A	Swansea T	W 1-0
17 Mar	FL	H	Middlesbrough	L 2-4
24 Mar	FL	A	Bristol C	D 0-0
31 Mar	FL	H	Leeds U	W 2-0
2 Apr	FL	A	Lincoln C	W 3-1
3 Apr	FL	H	Lincoln C	D 2-2
7 Apr	FL	A	Port Vale	W 2-0
14 Apr	FL	H	Bury	L 0-2
18 Apr	FL	H	West Ham U	D 0-0
21 Apr	FL	A	Barnsley	D 1-1
25 Apr	F	H	Arsenal	D 1-1
28 Apr	FL	H	Blackburn R	D 1-1
2 May	FL	A	Fulham	L 3-4

League Appearances (Goals)
Alexander D 19 (3); Banham R 1; Barrett J 34 (17); Burkitt J 42 (1); Farmer W 4; French J 13 (3); Higham P 39 (16); Hutchinson J 4; Imlach S 37 (5); Jones E 14 (3); Langford J 4; Lishman D 11 (6); McKinlay R 39 (1); Morley W 34 (1); Nicholson G 38; Scott F 7 (1); Small P 33 (8); Thomas G 38 (1); Watson P 1; Whare W 42; Wilson T 8 (2).

Position in League Table

		P	W	D	L	F	A	Pts
1st	Sheff W	42	21	13	8	101	62	55
7th	Forest	42	19	9	14	68	63	47

1956-57 Division Two

18 Aug	FL	A	Leyton Orient	W 4-1
21 Aug	FL	A	Bristol C	W 5-1
25 Aug	FL	H	Fulham	W 3-1
30 Aug	FL	H	Bristol C	D 2-2
1 Sep	FL	A	Swansea T	W 4-1
6 Sep	FL	H	Blackburn R	W 2-1
8 Sep	FL	H	Lincoln C	D 1-1
15 Sep	FL	A	Rotherham U	L 2-3
22 Sep	FL	H	Port Vale	W 4-2
29 Sep	FL	A	Barnsley	D 1-1
6 Oct	FL	A	Huddersfield T	L 0-1
13 Oct	FL	H	Bury	W 5-1
15 Oct	F	A	Coventry C	L 2-3
20 Oct	FL	A	Notts Co	W 2-1
27 Oct	FL	H	Doncaster R	W 2-1
3 Nov	FL	A	Stoke C	L 1-2
10 Nov	FL	H	Middlesbrough	L 0-4
17 Nov	FL	A	Leicester C	D 0-0
24 Nov	FL	H	Bristol R	D 1-1
1 Dec	FL	A	Grimsby T	D 0-0
8 Dec	FL	H	Liverpool	W 1-0
15 Dec	FL	H	Leyton Orient	L 1-2
22 Dec	FL	A	Fulham	W 1-0
25 Dec	FL	A	West Ham U	L 1-2
29 Dec	FL	H	Swansea T	W 4-3
1 Jan	FL	A	Blackburn R	D 2-2
5 Jan	FAC3	H	Goole T	W 6-0
12 Jan	FL	A	Lincoln C	W 2-0
19 Jan	FL	H	Rotherham U	W 3-1
26 Jan	FAC4	A	Portsmouth	W 3-1
2 Feb	FL	A	Port Vale	W 7-1
9 Feb	FL	H	Barnsley	W 7-1
16 Feb	FAC5	A	Barnsley	W 2-1
21 Feb	FL	H	Huddersfield T	D 0-0
23 Feb	FL	A	Bury	W 2-1
2 Mar	FAC6	A	Birmingham C	D 0-0
7 Mar	FAC6r	H	Birmingham C	L 0-1
9 Mar	FL	A	Doncaster R	D 1-1
16 Mar	FL	H	Stoke C	W 4-0
23 Mar	FL	A	Middlesbrough	D 2-2
30 Mar	FL	H	Leicester C	L 1-2
6 Apr	FL	A	Bristol R	L 2-3
13 Apr	FL	H	Grimsby T	W 2-1
15 Apr	FL	H	West Ham U	W 3-0
20 Apr	FL	A	Liverpool	L 1-3
22 Apr	FL	H	Sheff Utd	W 2-1
27 Apr	FL	A	Sheff Utd	W 4-0
1 May	FL	H	Notts Co	L 2-4
8 May	NNHC	A	Norwich C	W 7-2

League Appearances (Goals)
Alexander D 1 (1); Baily E 27 (6); Banham R 1; Barrett J 32 (27); Burkitt J 42 (2); Farmer W 8; Higham P 20 (4); Huddlestone E 1; Hutchinson J 28; Imlach S 40 (12); Jones E 3; Lishman D 27 (16); McKinlay R 39 (1); Morley W 42 (4); Nicholson G 34; Scott F 1 (1); Small P 24 (4); Thomas G 41; Watson P 6; Whare W 13; Wilson T 32 (14); Own Goals 2.

Position in League Table

		P	W	D	L	F	A	Pts
1st	Leicester	42	25	11	6	109	67	61
2nd	Forest	42	22	10	10	94	55	54

1957-58 Division One

24 Aug	FL	H	Preston NE	W 2-1
28 Aug	FL	H	Birmingham C	D 1-1
31 Aug	FL	A	Sheff Wed	W 2-1
4 Sep	FL	A	Birmingham C	W 2-0
7 Sep	FL	H	Man City	W 2-1
9 Sep	FL	A	Burnley	L 1-3
14 Sep	FL	A	Leeds U	W 2-1
18 Sep	FL	H	Burnley	W 7-0
21 Sep	FL	A	Portsmouth	W 4-1
23 Sep	F	H	All Stars XI	W 4-0
28 Sep	FL	H	WBA	L 0-2
5 Oct	FL	A	Tottenham H	W 4-3
12 Oct	FL	H	Man Utd	L 1-2
19 Oct	FL	A	Leicester C	L 1-3
26 Oct	FL	H	Blackpool	L 1-2
2 Nov	FL	A	Wolves	L 0-2
9 Nov	FL	H	Arsenal	W 4-0
16 Nov	FL	A	Bolton W	L 0-2
23 Nov	FL	H	Aston Villa	W 4-1
30 Nov	FL	A	Luton T	L 1-3
7 Dec	FL	H	Sunderland	W 2-0
14 Dec	FL	A	Everton	D 1-1
21 Dec	FL	A	Preston NE	L 0-2
25 Dec	FL	A	Newcastle U	W 4-1
26 Dec	FL	H	Newcastle U	L 2-3
28 Dec	FL	H	Sheff Wed	W 5-2
4 Jan	FAC3	H	Gillingham	W 2-0
11 Jan	FL	A	Man City	D 1-1
18 Jan	FL	H	Leeds U	D 1-1
25 Jan	FAC4	A	WBA	D 3-3
29 Jan	FAC4r	H	WBA	L 1-5
1 Feb	FL	H	Portsmouth	W 2-0
8 Feb	FL	A	WBA	L 2-3
15 Feb	FL	H	Tottenham H	L 1-2
22 Feb	FL	A	Man Utd	D 1-1
1 Mar	FL	H	Leicester C	W 3-1
8 Mar	FL	A	Blackpool	L 0-3
15 Mar	FL	H	Wolves	L 1-4
19 Mar	F	A	Fiorentina	D 0-0
29 Mar	FL	H	Bolton W	D 0-0
4 Apr	FL	A	Chelsea	D 0-0
7 Apr	FL	H	Chelsea	D 1-1
12 Apr	FL	H	Luton T	W 1-0
19 Apr	FL	A	Sunderland	L 0-3
21 Apr	FL	A	Arsenal	D 1-1
26 Apr	FL	H	Everton	L 0-3
30 Apr	FL	A	Aston Villa	D 1-1
14 May	F	A	Berlin	W 4-3
17 May	F	A	R-W Oberhausen	W 3-1
18 May	F	*	Flamingo	D 2-2
21 May	F	A	Dutch XI	L 0-1
25 May	F	A	Bremerhaven	L **

League Appearances (Goals)
Baily E 37 (8); Barrett J 17 (12); Burkitt J 40; Coyle F 3; Farmer R 9; Gray W 35 (9); Higham P 2; Hutchinson J 9; Imlach S 41 (14); Jones E 1; Joyce C 10; Lightening A 2; McKinlay R 40 (1); Morley W 34; Quigley J 21 (3); Sharratt H 1; Simcoe K 2 (1); Thomas G 41; Thomson C 39; Watson P 1; Whare W 35 (1); Wilson T 40 (19); Own Goals 1.

Position in League Table

		P	W	D	L	F	A	Pts
1st	Wolves	42	28	8	6	103	47	64
10th	Forest	42	16	10	16	69	63	42

* at Liege ** score not known

1958-59 Division One

23 Aug	FL	A	Wolves	L 1-5
27 Aug	FL	H	Man Utd	L 0-3
30 Aug	FL	H	Portsmouth	W 5-0
3 Sep	FL	A	Man Utd	D 1-1
6 Sep	FL	A	Aston Villa	W 3-2
10 Sep	FL	H	Tottenham H	D 1-1
13 Sep	FL	H	West Ham U	W 4-0
17 Sep	FL	A	Tottenham H	L 0-1
20 Sep	FL	A	Bolton W	L 2-3
27 Sep	FL	A	Chelsea	L 1-4
4 Oct	FL	H	Blackpool	W 2-0
11 Oct	FL	H	Luton T	W 3-1
18 Oct	FL	A	Birmingham C	W 3-0
25 Oct	FL	H	Preston NE	L 0-1
1 Nov	FL	A	Burnley	W 2-0
8 Nov	FL	H	Man City	W 4-0
15 Nov	FL	A	Arsenal	L 1-3
22 Nov	FL	H	Everton	W 2-1
29 Nov	FL	A	Leicester C	W 3-0
6 Dec	FL	H	WBA	D 1-1
13 Dec	FL	A	Leeds U	L 0-1
20 Dec	FL	H	Wolves	L 1-3
26 Dec	FL	A	Newcastle U	W 3-1
27 Dec	FL	H	Newcastle U	W 3-0
3 Jan	FL	A	Portsmouth	W 1-0
10 Jan	FAC3	A	Tooting & Mitcham U	D 2-2
24 Jan	FAC3r	H	Tooting & Mitcham U	W 3-0
28 Jan	FAC4	H	Grimsby T	W 4-1
31 Jan	FL	A	West Ham U	L 3-5
7 Feb	FL	H	Bolton W	W 3-0
14 Feb	FAC5	A	Birmingham C	D 1-1
18 Feb	FACr	H	Birmingham C	D 1-1
21 Feb	FL	A	Blackpool	L 0-1
23 Feb	FAC5r2	*	Birmingham C	W 5-0
28 Feb	FAC6	H	Bolton W	W 2-1
7 Mar	FL	H	Birmingham C	L 1-7
14 Mar	FACsf	**	Aston Villa	W 1-0
16 Mar	FL	A	Preston NE	W 5-3
21 Mar	FL	H	Burnley	L 1-2
27 Mar	FL	A	Blackburn R	L 0-3
28 Mar	FL	A	Man City	D 1-1
31 Mar	FL	H	Blackburn R	D 1-1
4 Apr	FL	H	Arsenal	D 1-1
9 Apr	FL	A	Luton T	L 1-5
11 Apr	FL	A	Everton	W 3-1
15 Apr	FL	H	Chelsea	L 1-3
18 Apr	FL	H	Leicester C	L 1-4
20 Apr	FL	H	Aston Villa	W 2-0
22 Apr	FL	H	Leeds U	L 0-3
25 Apr	FL	A	WBA	L 0-2
2 May	FACf	***	Luton T	W 2-1
20 May	F	A	Sporting Lisbon	W 1-0
24 May	F	A	Oviedo	L 0-1
27 May	F	A	Valencia	W 1-0
28 May	F	A	Atletico Madrid	L 1-6
30 May	F	A	Athletic Bilbao	L 0-3

League Appearances (Goals)
Armstrong J 1; Baily E 4; Barrett J 3; Burkitt J 39 (1); Dwight R 41 (20); Fraser W 2; Gray W 40 (7); Hutchinson J 1; Imlach S 37 (8); Kelly B 2; Lightening A 4; McDonald J 35; McKinlay R 39; Martin J 1; Morley W 5; Morrison R 1; Palmer C 2; Quigley J 39 (12); Thomas G 10; Thomson C 35; Watson P 3; Whare W 38; Whitefoot J 38 (1); Wilson T 41 (21); Younger W 1; Own Goals 1.

Position in League Table

		P	W	D	L	F	A	Pts
1st	Wolves	42	28	5	9	110	49	61
13th	Forest	42	17	6	19	71	74	40

* at Leicester ** at Hillsborough *** at Wembley

1959-60 Division One

15 Aug	CS	A	Wolves	L 1-3
22 Aug	FL	A	Man City	L 1-2
26 Aug	FL	H	Arsenal	L 0-3
29 Aug	FL	H	Blackburn R	D 2-2
1 Sep	FL	A	Arsenal	D 1-1
5 Sep	FL	A	Blackpool	W 1-0
9 Sep	FL	H	Sheff Wed	W 2-1
12 Sep	FL	H	Everton	D 1-1
16 Sep	FL	A	Sheff Wed	W 1-0
19 Sep	FL	A	Luton T	L 0-1
23 Sep	F	H	St Mirren	L 2-3
26 Sep	FL	H	Bolton W	W 2-0
30 Sep	F	A	St Mirren	D 2-2
3 Oct	FL	A	Fulham	L 1-3
10 Oct	FL	A	Newcastle U	L 1-2
17 Oct	FL	H	Birmingham C	L 0-2
21 Oct	F	A	Norwich C	L 1-3
24 Oct	FL	A	Tottenham H	L 1-2
26 Oct	F	A	Notts Co	L 1-3
31 Oct	FL	H	Chelsea	W 3-1
7 Nov	FL	A	Preston NE	L 0-1
14 Nov	FL	H	Leicester C	W 1-0
21 Nov	FL	A	Burnley	L 0-8
28 Nov	FL	H	Leeds U	W 4-1
5 Dec	FL	A	West Ham U	L 1-4
12 Dec	FL	H	Man Utd	L 1-5
19 Dec	FL	H	Man City	L 1-2
26 Dec	FL	A	WBA	W 3-2
28 Dec	FL	H	WBA	L 1-2
2 Jan	FL	A	Blackburn R	W 2-1
9 Jan	FAC3	H	Reading	W 1-0
16 Jan	FL	H	Blackpool	D 0-0
23 Jan	FL	A	Everton	L 1-6
30 Jan	FAC4	A	Sheff Utd	L 0-3
6 Feb	FL	H	Luton T	W 2-0
13 Feb	FL	A	Bolton W	D 1-1
20 Feb	FL	H	Fulham	D 2-2
27 Feb	FL	H	West Ham U	W 3-1
5 Mar	FL	A	Birmingham C	L 1-4
12 Mar	FL	H	Tottenham H	L 1-3
19 Mar	FL	A	Man Utd	L 1-3
26 Mar	FL	H	Preston NE	D 1-1
2 Apr	FL	A	Leicester C	W 1-0
9 Apr	FL	H	Burnley	L 0-1
16 Apr	FL	A	Chelsea	D 1-1
18 Apr	FL	A	Wolves	L 1-3
19 Apr	FL	H	Wolves	D 0-0
23 Apr	FL	H	Newcastle U	W 3-0
30 Apr	FL	A	Leeds U	L 0-1
4 May	F	A	Kings Lynn	W 5-1

League Appearances (Goals)
Armstrong J 11; Barton A 13 (1); Booth C 24 (8); Burkitt J 35 (1); Dwight R 3 (1); Gray W 37 (7); Iley J 35 (4); Imlach S 29 (4); Kelly B 1; Knight P 4; McDonald J 36; McKinlay R 42; Palmer C 4 (1); Patrick R 23; Quigley J 26 (6); Thomas G 11; Thomson C 31; Vowden G 10 (2); Whare W 14; Whitefoot J 37 (1); Wilson T 31 (11); Younger W 6 (1); Own Goals 2.

Position in League Table

		P	W	D	L	F	A	Pts
1st	Burnley	42	24	7	11	85	61	55
20th	Forest	42	13	9	20	50	74	35

1960-61 Division One

20 Aug	FL	H	Man City	D 2-2
24 Aug	FL	A	Blackburn R	L 1-4
27 Aug	FL	A	Arsenal	L 0-3
31 Aug	FL	H	Blackburn R	D 1-1
3 Sep	FL	H	Newcastle U	L 0-2
10 Sep	FL	A	Cardiff C	W 3-1
13 Sep	FL	A	Fulham	L 0-1
17 Sep	FL	H	WBA	L 1-2
21 Sep	FL	H	Fulham	W 4-2
24 Sep	FL	A	Birmingham C	L 1-3
1 Oct	FL	H	Sheff Wed	L 1-2
6 Oct	FLC2	H	Halifax T	W 2-0
15 Oct	FL	H	Tottenham H	L 0-4
22 Oct	FL	A	Blackpool	L 0-4
24 Oct	FL	A	Man Utd	L 1-2
29 Oct	FL	H	Everton	L 1-2
5 Nov	FL	A	Wolves	L 3-5
12 Nov	FL	H	Bolton W	D 2-2
15 Nov	FLC3	H	Bristol C	W 2-1
19 Nov	FL	A	West Ham U	W 4-2
26 Nov	FL	H	Chelsea	W 2-1
3 Dec	FL	A	Leicester C	D 1-1
10 Dec	FL	H	Aston Villa	W 2-0
17 Dec	FL	A	Man City	W 2-1
24 Dec	FL	H	Preston NE	W 2-0
26 Dec	FL	A	Preston NE	W 1-0
31 Dec	FL	A	Arsenal	L 3-5
7 Jan	FAC3	H	Birmingham C	L 0-2
10 Jan	FLC4	A	Burnley	L 1-2
14 Jan	FL	A	Newcastle U	D 2-2
21 Jan	FL	H	Cardiff C	W 2-1
4 Feb	FL	A	WBA	W 2-1
11 Feb	FL	H	Birmingham C	W 1-0
21 Feb	FL	A	Sheff Wed	L 0-1
25 Feb	FL	H	Man Utd	W 3-2
2 Mar	F	A	Watford	D 1-1
11 Mar	FL	H	Blackpool	D 0-0
18 Mar	FL	A	Everton	L 0-1
20 Mar	F	A	Peterborough U	L 1-4
25 Mar	FL	H	Wolves	D 1-1
31 Mar	FL	A	Burnley	L 1-4
1 Apr	FL	A	Aston Villa	W 2-1
3 Apr	FL	H	Burnley	W 3-1
8 Apr	FL	H	West Ham U	D 1-1
10 Apr	F	A	Barrow	W 2-1
15 Apr	FL	A	Bolton W	L 1-3
22 Apr	FL	H	Leicester C	D 2-2
26 Apr	FL	A	Tottenham H	L 0-1
29 Apr	FL	A	Chelsea	L 3-4
5 May	NCCsf	H	Mansfield T	W 1-0
8 May	NCCf	H	Notts Co	W 4-3
13 May	F	A	Karlovy Vary	W 4-0
16 May	F	A	Spartak Prague	D 1-1
21 May	F	A	Sp Hradek Kralove	W 2-1
24 May	F	A	Dynamo Zilina	W 2-0

League Appearances (Goals)
Addison C 14 (7); Baird D 4; Barton A 7; Booth C 35 (19); Burkitt J 19; Cobb W 6 (1); Grant B 1; Gray W 30 (3); Grummitt P 26; Iley J 24; Julians L 7 (1); Le Flem R 37 (3); McDonald J 38; McKinlay R 42; Palmer C 27 (2); Patrick R 34; Quigley J 35 (11); Rowland J 12 (1); Thomson C 16; Vowden G 24 (13); Wealthall B 2; Whitefoot J 16; Wilson T 1; Younger 5 (1).

Position in League Table

		P	W	D	L	F	A	Pts
1st	Spurs	42	31	4	7	115	55	66
14th	Forest	42	14	9	19	62	78	37

1961-62 Division One

19 Aug	FL	A	Chelsea	D 2-2
22 Aug	FL	H	Birmingham C	W 2-1
26 Aug	FL	H	Sheff Utd	W 2-0
30 Aug	FL	A	Birmingham C	D 1-1
2 Sep	FL	A	West Ham U	L 2-3
9 Sep	FL	H	Blackburn R	L 1-2
11 Sep	FLC1	H	Gillingham	W 4-1
13 Sep	ICFC1/1	A	Valencia	L 0-2
16 Sep	FL	A	Blackpool	W 3-1
19 Sep	FL	H	Wolves	W 3-1
23 Sep	FL	H	Tottenham H	W 2-0
27 Sep	FL	A	Wolves	L 1-2
30 Sep	FL	A	Cardiff C	D 2-2
4 Oct	ICFC1/2	H	Valencia	L 1-5
7 Oct	FL	A	Everton	L 0-6
11 Oct	FLC2	A	QPR	W 2-1
14 Oct	FL	H	Fulham	D 1-1
21 Oct	FL	A	Man City	L 0-3
28 Oct	FL	H	WBA	D 4-4
4 Nov	FL	A	Ipswich T	L 0-1
6 Nov	F	H	Malmo	Abnd
11 Nov	FL	H	Burnley	W 3-2
14 Nov	FLC3	H	Blackburn R	L 1-2
18 Nov	FL	A	Arsenal	L 1-2
25 Nov	FL	H	Bolton W	L 0-1
27 Nov	F	A	Stockport Co	L 2-4
2 Dec	FL	A	Sheff Wed	L 0-3
9 Dec	FL	H	Leicester C	D 0-0
16 Dec	FL	H	Chelsea	W 3-0
22 Dec	FL	A	Sheff Utd	L 0-2
26 Dec	FL	A	Man Utd	L 3-6
6 Jan	FAC3	A	Workington	W 2-1
13 Jan	FL	H	West Ham U	W 3-0
20 Jan	FL	A	Blackburn R	L 1-2
27 Jan	FAC4	H	Sheff Wed	L 0-2
3 Feb	FL	H	Blackpool	L 3-4
10 Feb	FL	A	Tottenham H	L 2-4
17 Feb	FL	H	Cardiff C	W 2-1
24 Feb	FL	H	Everton	W 2-1
3 Mar	FL	A	Fulham	D 1-1
10 Mar	FL	H	Man City	L 1-2
17 Mar	FL	A	WBA	D 2-2
20 Mar	FL	H	Man Utd	W 1-0
24 Mar	FL	H	Ipswich T	D 1-1
3 Apr	FL	A	Burnley	D 0-0
7 Apr	FL	H	Arsenal	L 0-1
14 Apr	FL	A	Bolton W	L 1-6
21 Apr	FL	H	Sheff Wed	W 3-1
23 Apr	FL	A	Aston Villa	L 1-5
24 Apr	FL	H	Aston Villa	W 2-0
28 Apr	FL	A	Leicester C	L 1-2
8 May	NCCsf	A	Notts Co	W 2-1
11 May	NCCf	H	Mansfield T	W 3-2

League Appearances (Goals)
Addison C 18 (6); Baird D 13; Barton A 2; Booth C 28 (12); Burkitt J 2; Cobb W 8 (3); Grant B 8; Gray W 34 (2); Grummitt P 42; Hockey T 17 (2); Iley J 33; Julians L 18 (8); Le Flem R 35 (5); McKinlay R 42 (1); Palmer C 30 (2); Pleat D 1 (1); Quigley J 41 (5); Rowland J 14 (2); Vowden G 27 (11); Whitefoot J 25; Wilson J 10; Winfield J 14 (1); Own Goals 2.

Position in League Table

		P	W	D	L	F	A	Pts
1st	Ipswich	42	24	8	10	93	67	56
19th	Forest	42	13	10	19	63	79	36

1962-63 Division One

18 Aug	FL	H	Sheff Utd	W 2-1
20 Aug	FL	A	Blackburn R	W 5-2
25 Aug	FL	A	Leicester C	L 1-2
28 Aug	FL	H	Blackburn R	W 2-0
1 Sep	FL	A	Ipswich T	D 1-1
3 Sep	FL	A	Blackpool	L 1-2
8 Sep	FL	H	Liverpool	W 3-1
11 Sep	FL	H	Blackpool	W 2-0
15 Sep	FL	A	Wolves	D 1-1
22 Sep	FL	H	Aston Villa	W 3-1
29 Sep	FL	A	Tottenham H	L 2-9
6 Oct	FL	H	Fulham	W 3-1
- Oct	F	A	Kettering T	W 2-0
13 Oct	FL	A	Sheff Wed	D 2-2
22 Oct	F	A	Stockport Co	W 6-0
27 Oct	FL	A	Bolton W	L 0-1
3 Nov	FL	H	Leyton Orient	D 1-1
10 Nov	FL	A	Birmingham C	D 2-2
13 Nov	FL	H	Everton	L 3-4
17 Nov	FL	H	Arsenal	W 3-0
24 Nov	FL	A	WBA	W 4-1
1 Dec	FL	H	Burnley	W 2-1
8 Dec	FL	A	Man Utd	L 1-5
15 Dec	FL	A	Sheff Utd	L 1-3
29 Dec	FL	H	West Ham U	L 3-4
29 Jan	FAC3	H	Wolves	W 4-3
19 Feb	FL	H	Leicester C	L 0-2
23 Feb	FL	A	Fulham	L 1-3
2 Mar	FL	H	Sheff Wed	L 0-3
6 Mar	FAC4	A	WBA	D 0-0
9 Mar	FL	A	Everton	L 0-3
11 Mar	FAC4r	H	WBA	W 2-1
16 Mar	FL	H	Bolton W	W 1-0
19 Mar	FAC5	H	Leeds U	W 3-0
23 Mar	FL	A	Leyton Orient	W 1-0
30 Mar	FAC6	H	Southampton	D 1-1
3 Apr	FAC6r	A	Southampton	D 3-3
6 Apr	FL	A	Arsenal	D 0-0
8 Apr	FAC6r2	*	Southampton	L 0-5
12 Apr	FL	A	Man City	L 0-1
13 Apr	FL	H	Birmingham C	L 0-2
15 Apr	FL	H	Man City	D 1-1
18 Apr	FL	A	Liverpool	W 2-0
20 Apr	FL	A	Burnley	D 0-0
22 Apr	FL	A	West Ham U	L 1-4
30 Apr	FL	H	Wolves	W 2-0
4 May	FL	A	Aston Villa	W 2-0
10 May	FL	H	Ipswich T	W 2-1
14 May	FL	H	WBA	D 2-2
18 May	FL	H	Tottenham H	D 1-1
20 May	FL	H	Man Utd	W 3-2
27 May	NCCf	H	Notts Co	L 1-2

League Appearances (Goals)
Addison C 35 (16); Armstrong J 8; Baird D 15; Cobb W 16 (1); Grant B 3; Gray W 25 (1); Grummitt P 34; Hindley P 5; Hockey T 41 (4); Iley J 1; Julians L 29 (14); Le Flem R 37 (5); McKinlay R 42; Mochan D 15 (1); Palmer C 25 (8); Quigley J 30 (6); Storey-Moore I 1; Vowden G 19 (8); Whitefoot J 19; Wilson D 4; Wilson J 30; Winfield J 28 (1); Own Goals 2.

Position in League Table

		P	W	D	L	F	A	Pts
1st	Everton	42	25	11	6	84	42	61
9th	Forest	42	17	10	15	67	69	44

* at White Hart Lane

1963-64 Division One

24 Aug	FL	H	Aston Villa	L 0-1
28 Aug	FL	A	Liverpool	W 2-1
31 Aug	FL	A	Tottenham H	L 1-4
3 Sep	FL	H	Liverpool	D 0-0
7 Sep	FL	H	Wolves	W 3-0
9 Sep	FL	A	West Ham U	W 2-0
14 Sep	FL	A	Stoke C	W 1-0
17 Sep	FL	H	West Ham U	W 3-1
21 Sep	FL	H	Bolton W	W 3-1
28 Sep	FL	H	Blackburn R	D 1-1
5 Oct	FL	A	Blackpool	L 0-1
8 Oct	FL	H	Leicester C	W 2-0
12 Oct	FL	A	Fulham	D 0-0
19 Oct	FL	H	Man Utd	L 1-2
26 Oct	FL	A	Arsenal	L 2-4
2 Nov	FL	H	Ipswich T	W 3-1
9 Nov	FL	A	Sheff Wed	L 1-3
16 Nov	FL	H	Everton	D 2-2
23 Nov	FL	A	Birmingham C	D 3-3
30 Nov	FL	H	WBA	L 0-3
7 Dec	FL	A	Burnley	D 1-1
14 Dec	FL	A	Aston Villa	L 0-3
21 Dec	FL	H	Tottenham H	L 1-2
26 Dec	FL	H	Sheff Utd	D 3-3
28 Dec	FL	A	Sheff Utd	W 2-1
4 Jan	FAC3	H	Preston NE	D 0-0
11 Jan	FL	A	Wolves	W 3-2
13 Jan	FAC3r	A	Preston NE	L 0-1
18 Jan	FL	H	Stoke C	D 0-0
25 Jan	NCCsf	A	Mansfield T	W 3-1
1 Feb	FL	A	Bolton W	W 3-2
8 Feb	FL	A	Blackburn R	L 0-2
15 Feb	FL	H	Blackpool	L 0-1
22 Feb	FL	H	Fulham	W 2-0
29 Feb	FL	A	Leicester C	D 1-1
7 Mar	FL	H	Arsenal	W 2-0
14 Mar	FL	A	Everton	L 1-6
21 Mar	FL	H	Sheff Wed	W 3-2
28 Mar	FL	A	Ipswich T	L 3-4
30 Mar	FL	A	Chelsea	L 0-1
31 Mar	FL	H	Chelsea	L 0-1
4 Apr	FL	H	Birmingham C	W 4-0
11 Apr	FL	A	WBA	W 3-2
14 Apr	NCCf	A	Notts Co	W 5-1
18 Apr	FL	H	Burnley	L 1-3
20 Apr	F	H	New Zealand XI	W 8-0
25 Apr	FL	A	Man Utd	L 1-3
2 May	F	A	Hertha Berlin	W 3-0
6 May	F	A	Basle	W 6-0
7 May	F	A	Lucerne	W 4-0
9 May	F	A	Winterthur	W 5-1

League Appearances (Goals)
Addison C 26 (10); Barnwell J 8 (2); Chapman R 1; Grant B 2; Grummitt P 41; Hindley P 10; Hinton A 15 (2); Hockey T 15; Julians L 4 (1); Kear M 11; Le Flem R 23 (5); McKinlay R 42 (2); Mochan D 36; Newton H 26 (2); Palmer C 3 (1); Parr J 1; Pleat D 5; Quigley J 37 (7); Storey-Moore I 12 (6); Taylor W 3; Vowden G 9 (5); Whitefoot J 35 (3); Wignall F 40 (16); Wilson D 2; Wilson J 33; Winfield J 22 (1); Own Goals 1.

Position in League Table

		P	W	D	L	F	A	Pts
1st	Liverpool	42	26	5	11	92	45	57
13th	Forest	42	16	9	17	64	68	41

1964-65 Division One

15 Aug	F	A	Brentford	W 3-0
22 Aug	FL	H	Birmingham C	W 4-3
25 Aug	FL	A	Everton	L 0-1
28 Aug	FL	A	West Ham U	W 3-2
1 Sep	FL	H	Everton	W 3-1
5 Sep	FL	H	WBA	D 0-0
8 Sep	FL	A	Burnley	D 2-2
12 Sep	FL	A	Man Utd	L 0-3
15 Sep	FL	H	Burnley	W 3-1
19 Sep	FL	H	Fulham	L 2-3
26 Sep	FL	A	Leeds U	W 2-1
3 Oct	FL	A	Stoke C	D 1-1
6 Oct	FL	A	Arsenal	W 3-0
10 Oct	FL	H	Chelsea	D 2-2
17 Oct	FL	A	Leicester C	L 2-3
24 Oct	FL	H	Sunderland	W 5-2
31 Oct	FL	A	Wolves	W 2-1
7 Nov	FL	H	Aston Villa	W 4-2
14 Nov	FL	A	Liverpool	L 0-2
21 Nov	FL	H	Sheff Wed	D 2-2
28 Nov	FL	A	Blackpool	W 2-0
5 Dec	FL	H	Blackburn R	L 2-5
12 Dec	FL	A	Birmingham C	D 1-1
19 Dec	FL	H	West Ham U	W 3-2
26 Dec	FL	H	Tottenham H	L 1-2
28 Dec	FL	A	Tottenham H	L 0-4
2 Jan	FL	A	WBA	D 2-2
9 Jan	FAC3	H	Norwich C	W 1-0
16 Jan	FL	H	Man Utd	D 2-2
18 Jan	F	A	Combined XI	L 0-1
23 Jan	FL	A	Fulham	L 1-4
30 Jan	FAC4	A	Sunderland	W 3-1
6 Feb	FL	H	Leeds U	D 0-0
13 Feb	FL	H	Stoke C	W 3-1
20 Feb	FAC5	A	Crystal Palace	L 1-3
22 Feb	FL	A	Chelsea	W 1-0
27 Feb	FL	H	Leicester C	W 2-1
6 Mar	FL	A	Sunderland	L 0-4
13 Mar	FL	H	Arsenal	W 3-0
20 Mar	FL	A	Aston Villa	L 1-2
1 Apr	FL	H	Liverpool	D 2-2
3 Apr	FL	A	Sheff Wed	D 0-0
10 Apr	FL	H	Blackpool	W 2-0
12 Apr	F	H	Celtic	W 3-0
19 Apr	FL	H	Sheff Utd	D 0-0
20 Apr	FL	A	Sheff Utd	W 2-0
24 Apr	FL	H	Wolves	L 0-2
27 Apr	FL	A	Blackburn R	D 1-1
2 May	F	A	Rapid Vienna	W 2-0
8 May	NCCf	H	Mansfield T	W 5-0
14 May	F	A	Hartford SC	W 8-2
16 May	F	A	Ukrainian Nationals	W 3-2
19 May	F	A	Boston Metros	W 4-2
23 May	F	*	Hannover 96	L 1-3
27 May	F	A	CYC All Stars	W 6-1
30 May	F	*	Hannover 96	W 2-0
2 Jun	F	*	Hannover 96	W 6-2
5 Jun	F	*	Hannover 96	W 2-1
9 Jun	F	A	British Columbia AS	W 2-0
12 Jun	F	**	Hibernian	L 1-2
14 Jun	F	A	Toronto Select XI	W 1-0

League Appearances (Goals)
Addison C 36 (14); Ball G 2; Barnwell J 40 (12); Cargill J 1; Chapman R 2 (2); Crowe C 33 (5); Grant B 4; Grummitt P 41; Hindley P 29 (2); Hinton A 41 (13); Kear M 1; McKinlay R 42 (1); Mochan D 38; Newton H 42; Quigley J 7 (1); Storey-Moore I 13 (4); Vowden G 1 (1); Whitefoot J 40; Wignall F 35 (14); Wilson D 1; Wilson J 11 (1); Winfield J 2; Own Goals 1.

Position in League Table

		P	W	D	L	F	A	Pts
1st	Man Utd	42	26	9	7	89	39	61
5th	Forest	42	17	13	12	71	67	47

* in USA on tour ** in Canada on tour

1965-66 — Division One

Date	V	Comp	Opponent	Res	Score
14 Aug	A	F	Coventry C	L	3-4
21 Aug	A	F	Newcastle U	W	4-2
24 Aug	H	F	Man Utd	W	3-2
28 Aug	H	FL	Man Utd	D	0-0
1 Sep	H	FL	Leeds U	L	0-1
4 Sep	A	FL	Arsenal	L	0-1
7 Sep	A	FL	Sheff Wed	W	2-1
11 Sep	H	FL	Northampton T	D	1-1
13 Sep	H	FL	Stoke C	W	3-0
18 Sep	A	FL	Doncaster R	W	3-0
25 Sep	H	FL	West Ham U	W	5-0
2 Oct	A	FL	Sunderland	L	2-3
4 Oct	H	FL	Aston Villa	L	1-3
9 Oct	A	FL	Liverpool	L	0-4
16 Oct	H	FL	Nuneaton Borough	W	1-0
23 Oct	A	FL	Tottenham H	L	1-3
30 Oct	H	FL	Blackpool	W	2-0
1 Nov	A	FL	Blackburn R	W	3-0
6 Nov	H	FL	Leicester C	D	1-1
13 Nov	A	FL	Sunderland	W	3-1
20 Nov	H	FL	Everton	L	1-2
26 Nov	A	FL	Sheff Utd	L	1-3
27 Nov	H	FAC3	Aston Villa	L	0-5
3 Dec	A	FL	Northampton T	L	0-4
11 Dec	H	FL	WBA	W	2-1
18 Dec	H	FL	Leeds U	L	0-1
27 Dec	A	FL	Crystal Palace	D	3-3
1 Jan	H	FL	Burnley	W	3-0
8 Jan	H	FAC4	Everton	W	3-0
15 Jan	A	FL	Stoke C	W	4-3
22 Jan	H	FL	Burnley	L	1-2
5 Feb	H	FL	Leicester C	L	0-1
12 Feb	A	FL	Blackpool	L	0-3
19 Feb	H	FL	Blackburn R	W	2-0
22 Feb	H	FL	Fulham	L	1-2
5 Mar	H	FL	Aston Villa	W	3-2
11 Mar	A	FL	Chelsea	L	0-1
15 Mar	H	FL	Blackpool	L	1-2
26 Mar	A	FL	Fulham	W	2-0
29 Mar	H	FL	Liverpool	L	1-2
2 Apr	A	FL	Standard Liege	L	1-4
11 Apr	A	FL	Valenciennes	W	3-1
15 Apr	A	F	SCO Angers	W	3-1

League Appearances (Goals)
Addison C 28 (9); Baker J 14 (5); Ball G 1;
Barnwell J 32 (2); Brindley J 4+1; Cargill J 1;
Chapman R 8+1 (2); Crowe C 33 (4); Grummitt P
41; Hennessey T 22 (1); Hindley P 38 (2);
Hinton A 33 (6); Kear M 7 (2); McArthur B 7+1 (4);
McKinlay R 41; Mochan D 3; Newton H 42 (2);
Stainwright D 3+1 (1); Storey-Moore J 39 (21);
Taylor W 1+1 (1); Whitefoot J 41; Wignall F 19 (6);
Wilson D 1+1.

Position in League Table
	P	W	D	L	F	A	Pts
1st Liverpool	42	26	9	7	79	34	61
18th Forest	42	14	8	20	56	72	36

1966-67 — Division One

Date	V	Comp	Opponent	Res	Score
6 Aug	A	F	Hibernian	L	2-3
7 Aug	A	F	Dundalk	W	4-1
13 Aug	A	F	Varna Select XI	L	0-1
20 Aug	H	FL	Stoke C	L	1-2
24 Aug	A	FL	Chelsea	W	2-1
27 Aug	A	FL	Sheff Utd	W	2-1
30 Aug	H	FL	Chelsea	W	2-1
3 Sep	H	FL	WBA	D	1-1
6 Sep	A	FL	Fulham	D	1-1
10 Sep	H	FL	Leeds U	W	3-0
13 Sep	H	FLC2	Birmingham C	W	3-0
17 Sep	A	FL	Newcastle U	D	1-1
20 Sep	A	FLC2r	Birmingham C	L	1-2
24 Sep	A	FL	Huddersfield T	L	1-2
1 Oct	H	FL	Tottenham H	W	4-1
8 Oct	H	FL	Chelsea	L	0-3
15 Oct	A	FL	Liverpool	L	1-3
22 Oct	H	FL	Blackpool	L	0-4
29 Oct	H	FL	Sunderland	W	2-0
5 Nov	A	FL	Liverpool	D	1-1
12 Nov	H	FL	Aston Villa	W	3-1
19 Nov	A	FL	Man City	L	1-2
26 Nov	A	FL	Sheff Wed	L	2-4
3 Dec	H	FL	Stoke C	D	1-1
10 Dec	H	FL	Everton	W	1-0
17 Dec	A	FL	Sheff Utd	D	0-0
26 Dec	H	FL	WBA	W	2-1
7 Jan	A	FL	Leeds U	D	0-0
14 Jan	A	FL	Newcastle U	W	2-0
21 Jan	H	FL	Plymouth A	W	4-1
28 Jan	A	FAC3	Tottenham H	D	1-1
4 Feb	H	FL	Newcastle U	W	2-0
11 Feb	H	FAC5	Blackpool	W	2-1
18 Feb	A	FL	Swindon T	W	3-0
25 Feb	H	FAC5r	Swindon T	W	2-0
4 Mar	A	FL	West Ham U	W	2-0
11 Mar	H	FAC6	Everton	W	3-2
14 Mar	H	FL	Sheff Wed	W	4-1
18 Mar	A	FL	Burnley	L	0-1
25 Mar	H	FL	Burnley	W	1-0
27 Mar	H	FL	Southampton	W	2-0
28 Mar	A	FL	Everton	W	1-0
1 Apr	H	FAC6	Aston Villa	W	2-0
8 Apr	A	FL	Sunderland	L	0-1
15 Apr	A	FL	Arsenal	L	1-2
19 Apr	H	FACsf	Tottenham H	L	1-2
22 Apr	A	FL	Man City	W	2-0
29 Apr	A	F	Southampton	W	2-0
2 May	H	FL	Notts Co	W	2-0
6 May	H	FL	Fulham	D	1-1
9 May	A	F	Barcelona	W	3-2
17 May	A	F	Valencia	W	3-1

* at Villa Park   ** at Hillsborough

League Appearances (Goals)
Baker J 39 (16); Barnwell J 17 (1); Baxter R 22 (2);
Bridgett R 1+2; Brindley J 1+1; Chapman R 24+2
(2); Grummitt P 27; Hall C 3+1; Harby M 3;
Hennessey T 36; Hilley D 16+4 (3); Hindley P 40;
Hinton A 2+2 (2); Lyons B 36+1 (6); McKinlay R 42;
Newton H 38 (3); Richardson P 11+6 (1); Sherratt B 1;
Storey-Moore J 26 (17); Taylor W 1-4;
Williamson B 7; Winfield J 42.

Position in League Table
	P	W	D	L	F	A	Pts
1st Man Utd	42	24	12	6	84	45	60
2nd Forest	42	23	10	9	64	41	56

1967-68 — Division One

Date	V	Comp	Opponent	Res	Score
5 Aug	A	F	Raith R	W	5-1
7 Aug	A	F	Partick Thistle	W	3-1
12 Aug	A	F	Derby Co	W	3-1
19 Aug	A	FL	Sheff Utd	D	3-3
22 Aug	H	FL	Coventry C	W	2-0
26 Aug	H	FL	Arsenal	L	0-2
29 Aug	A	FL	Coventry C	L	0-1
2 Sep	A	FL	Man City	W	4-0
5 Sep	H	FL	Liverpool	L	0-1
9 Sep	H	FLC2	Newcastle U	W	4-0
13 Sep	H	FL	Scunthorpe U	W	1-0
16 Sep	A	FL	WBA	L	1-2
20 Sep	H	ICFC1/1	Eintracht Frankfurt	W	1-0
23 Sep	H	FL	Chelsea	L	0-3
30 Sep	A	FL	Southampton	L	1-3
7 Oct	H	FL	Burnley	W	1-0
10 Oct	A	FL	Burnley	L	0-1
14 Oct	A	FL	Eintracht Frankfurt	W	4-0
17 Oct	H	ICFC1/2	Tottenham H	D	3-1
21 Oct	H	FL	Man Utd	L	1-3
25 Oct	H	ICFC2/1	Zurich	W	2-1
28 Oct	A	FL	Sunderland	D	1-1
4 Nov	A	FL	Leicester C	W	3-1
11 Nov	A	FL	Wolves	W	3-1
14 Nov	H	ICFC2/2	Zurich	L	0-1
18 Nov	A	FL	Leeds U	L	0-2
25 Nov	H	FL	Fulham	D	0-0
2 Dec	A	FL	Leicester C	D	2-2
16 Dec	H	FL	Everton	W	1-0
23 Dec	H	FL	Stoke C	W	3-0
26 Dec	A	FL	Sheff Utd	L	1-2
30 Dec	A	FL	Newcastle U	W	2-0
6 Jan	H	FAC3	Leeds U	D	0-0
13 Jan	A	FL	Chelsea	W	3-1
18 Jan	H	FL	Leeds U	L	1-2
25 Jan	H	FAC4	Tottenham H	W	2-1
1 Feb	A	FL	Man Utd	L	1-2
3 Feb	H	FL	Sunderland	W	2-0
17 Feb	A	FL	West Ham U	L	1-2
24 Feb	H	FL	Southampton	W	2-1
31 Mar	A	FL	Burnley	W	1-0
6 Apr	A	FL	Derby Co	W	1-0
13 Apr	H	FL	Tottenham H	D	2-2
16 Apr	H	FL	Man Utd	L	1-3
19 Apr	A	FL	Sunderland	D	0-0
22 Apr	H	FL	Leicester C	L	1-2
11 May	H	NCCf	Notts Co	W	3-0

League Appearances (Goals)
Baker J 39 (16); Barnwell J 17 (1); Baxter R 22 (2);
Bridgett R 1+2; Brindley J 1+1; Chapman R 24+2
(2); Grummitt P 42; Hall C 3+1; Harby M 3;
Hennessey T 36; Hilley D 37 (8); Hindley P 41 (2);
Hollins D 9; Ingram A 16 (3); Lyons B 36 (5);
McCaffrey J 2+6 (1); McKenzie D 5-3;
5+1; Newton H 41 (7); O'Kane W 24+3; Rees R 32
(8); Richardson P 27+2 (2); Storey-Moore 30
(11); Winfield J 41; Own Goals 1.

Position in League Table
	P	W	D	L	F	A	Pts
1st Leeds	42	27	13	2	66	26	67
18th Forest	42	14	11	17	52	64	39

* lost on away goals

1968-69 — Division One

Date	V	Comp	Opponent	Res	Score
1 Aug	A	F	Werder Bremen	W	1-0
4 Aug	A	F	SV Alsenborn	W	3-1
10 Aug	H	FL	Burnley	D	2-2
14 Aug	A	FL	Chelsea	L	0-1
17 Aug	A	FL	West Ham U	L	1-4
20 Aug	H	FL	Sheff Wed	D	1-1
24 Aug	H	FL	Leeds U	L	0-2
28 Aug	A	FL	Newcastle U	W	1-0
31 Aug	H	FL	Everton	D	1-1
3 Sep	A	FL	WBA	W	2-1
7 Sep	H*	FL	Coventry C	D	1-1
14 Sep	A	FL	Tottenham H	W	5-2
16 Sep	H	FL	Chelsea	L	0-0
21 Sep	H*	FL	Southampton	L	1-2
25 Sep	H	FLC2	Southampton	W	6-2
28 Sep	A	FL	Bristol XI	D	3-3
5 Oct	H*	FL	Stoke C	L	1-3
8 Oct	H	FL	Sunderland	L	1-3
12 Oct	A	FL	Ipswich T	D	1-1
19 Oct	A	FL	Everton	L	0-3
26 Oct	H*	FL	Man City	D	2-2
2 Nov	A	FL	Wolves	L	1-2
9 Nov	H*	FL	Leicester C	L	0-1
16 Nov	A	FL	Arsenal	D	0-0
23 Nov	A	FL	QPR	W	3-1
30 Nov	H	FL	Liverpool	L	0-1
7 Dec	A	FL	Southampton	D	1-1
14 Dec	H	FL	Ipswich T	L	0-1
21 Dec	A	FL	Stoke C	W	1-0
28 Dec	H	FL	Wolves	W	3-0
4 Jan	A	FAC3	Preston NE	W	2-1
11 Jan	A	FL	Leicester C	L	0-1
18 Jan	H	FL	Arsenal	L	0-2
25 Jan	H	FAC3	Norwich C	W	1-1
1 Feb	H	FL	Liverpool	L	0-2
8 Mar	H	FL	West Ham U	W	1-0
11 Mar	A	FL	Man City	L	1-3
22 Mar	A	FL	Man Utd	L	1-3
24 Mar	H	FL	Chelsea	D	1-1
31 Mar	A	FL	Sheff Wed	D	1-1
5 Apr	H	FL	Newcastle U	L	1-2
7 Apr	A	FL	Coventry C	D	0-1
12 Apr	A	FL	Everton	W	1-0
30 Apr	H	NCCf	Notts Co	W	2-1

League Appearances (Goals)
Baker J 30+1 (4); Barnwell J 24+3 (1); Baxter J
25+1 (2); Brindley J 2; Chapman R 27+2 (3);
Grummitt P 17; Hall C 15+4 (2); Harris L 1;
Hennessey T 38 (2); Hill A 10; Hilley D 17+9 (3);
Hindley P 36; Lyons B 41 (8); McKinlay R 30+2
(2); Marshall G 7; Newton H 42 (2); O'Kane W 1;
Rees R 11 (1); Richardson P 11+6 (1); Sherratt B 1;
Storey-Moore I 26 (17); Taylor W 1-4;
Williamson B 7; Winfield J 42.

Position in League Table
	P	W	D	L	F	A	Pts
1st Leeds	42	27	13	2	66	26	67
18th Forest	42	14	11	17	52	64	39

* home matches played at Meadow Lane during
rebuilding of Main Stand, following fire at City Ground

1969-70 — Division One

Date	V	Comp	Opponent	Res	Score
30 Jul	A	F	Maastricht	L	0-1
2 Aug	A	F	Rot Weiss Essen	L	0-2
9 Aug	A	FL	Ipswich T	D	0-0
12 Aug	A	FL	Stoke C	L	1-4
16 Aug	H	FL	Leeds U	L	0-1
20 Aug	A	FL	Stoke C	D	1-1
22 Aug	A	FL	Arsenal	W	1-0
26 Aug	A	FL	WBA	W	2-0
30 Aug	H	FL	West Ham U	W	2-1
3 Sep	H	FL	Barrow	D	0-0
6 Sep	A	FL	Wolves	D	3-3
13 Sep	H	FL	Southampton	W	2-1
16 Sep	A	FL	Coventry C	L	0-1
20 Sep	H	FL	Sunderland	W	2-1
27 Sep	A	FLC3	Crystal Palace	L	0-1
4 Oct	H	FL	Liverpool	D	0-0
11 Oct	A	FL	Man City	L	1-2
15 Oct	A	FLC4	Oxford U	L	0-1
18 Oct	H	FL	Man Utd	D	1-1
25 Oct	A	FL	Burnley	L	1-6
29 Oct	H	FL	Leeds U	D	2-2
1 Nov	A	FL	Tottenham H	D	1-3
8 Nov	H	FL	Newcastle U	D	1-1
15 Nov	A	FL	Rot Weiss Essen	W	2-0
17 Nov	H	FL	Sunderland	W	1-0
22 Nov	A	FL	Chelsea	W	2-1
6 Dec	H	FL	Derby Co	L	0-3
13 Dec	A	FL	Southampton	D	1-1
20 Dec	H	FL	Wolves	W	3-0
26 Dec	A	FL	Arsenal	L	0-1
27 Dec	H	FL	Everton	L	1-3
6 Jan	A	FAC3	Carlisle U	D	1-1
17 Jan	A	FL	Crystal Palace	D	1-1
24 Jan	A	FL	Sunderland	W	1-0
31 Jan	A	FL	Liverpool	L	0-1
7 Feb	H	FL	Man City	W	2-1
21 Feb	A	FL	Man Utd	L	1-2
28 Feb	H	FL	Sheff Wed	W	3-1
14 Mar	H	FL	Newcastle U	D	2-2
21 Mar	A	FL	Tottenham H	L	1-4
28 Mar	A	FL	WBA	L	1-4
4 Apr	H	FL	Coventry C	D	1-1
7 Apr	H	FL	Ipswich T	L	2-4
14 Apr	A	NCCf	ADO Den Haag	L	2-4
28 Apr	U	F	ADO Den Haag	W	2-3
12 May	A	F	ADO Den Haag	W	2-1

League Appearances (Goals)
Barnwell J 13+6; Bridgett R 1; Brindley J 0+3;
Chapman R 35 (2); Collier G 6 (1); Cormack P 1;
Grummitt P 2; Hall C 9+4; Harris L 1; Hennessey T
21; Hill A 31; Hilley D 37 (8); Hindley P 41 (2);
Hollins D 9; Ingram A 16 (3); Lyons B 36 (5);
McCaffrey J 2+6 (1); McKenzie D 5-3;
5+1; Newton H 41 (7); O'Kane W 24+3; Rees R 32
(8); Richardson P 27+2 (2); Storey-Moore 30
(11); Winfield J 41; Own Goals 1.

Position in League Table
	P	W	D	L	F	A	Pts
1st Everton	42	29	8	5	72	34	66
15th Forest	42	10	18	14	50	71	38

1970-71 — Division One

Date	V	Comp	Opponent	Res	Score
24 Jul	A	F	Halmia	W	3-0
26 Jul	A	F	Landskrona	W	4-2
28 Jul	A	F	Jonkoping Soedra	W	1-0
1 Aug	A	F	Hamburg SV	W	1-0
7 Aug	H	F	Coventry C	D	3-3
15 Aug	A	FL	WBA	D	0-0
18 Aug	A	FL	Ipswich T	D	0-1
22 Aug	H	FL	Newcastle U	W	1-0
26 Aug	H	FL	Wolves	W	4-1
29 Aug	A	FL	Crystal Palace	D	0-0
9 Sep	H	FL	Stoke C	L	0-2
12 Sep	A	FL	Man City	D	2-2
15 Sep	H	TC1/1	Airdrie	W	2-0
19 Sep	H	FL	Huddersfield T	L	0-3
21 Sep	A	FLC2	Huddersfield T	L	0-3
26 Sep	A	FL	Leeds U	L	0-0
28 Sep	A	TC1/2	Airdrie	D	0-2
3 Oct	A	FL	Arsenal	L	0-4
6 Oct	H	FL	Birmingham C	W	3-1
10 Oct	H	FL	Blackpool	D	0-0
17 Oct	A	FL	Coventry C	L	0-1
24 Oct	A	FL	Huddersfield T	L	1-2
31 Oct	H	FL	Tottenham H	D	1-1
14 Nov	H	FL	Everton	W	1-0
21 Nov	A	FL	Man Utd	L	1-2
28 Nov	A	FL	Derby Co	L	2-4
5 Dec	H	FL	Ipswich T	D	2-1
19 Dec	H	FL	Chelsea	L	0-2
11 Jan	A	FAC3	Luton T	D	1-1
16 Jan	A	FAC3r	Luton T	L	1-4
23 Jan	A	FL	Man Utd	D	1-1
6 Feb	H	FAC4	Orient	D	1-1
13 Feb	A	FAC4r	Orient	L	0-1
20 Feb	H	FAC5	Chelsea	L	1-2
24 Feb	H	FL	Burnley	W	1-0
27 Feb	H	FL	West Ham U	D	2-2
10 Mar	A	FL	Huddersfield T	L	0-4
13 Mar	H	FL	Man Utd	W	2-1
20 Mar	A	FL	Everton	L	0-3
27 Mar	H	FL	Crystal Palace	W	3-1
31 Mar	A	FL	Derby Co	L	2-0
3 Apr	A	FL	Wolves	W	1-0
10 Apr	H	FL	Man City	W	3-1
13 Apr	H	FL	West Ham U	D	0-0
17 Apr	A	FL	Arsenal	L	0-3
24 Apr	H	FL	Blackpool	W	3-0
27 Apr	U	FL	Liverpool	L	0-1
4 May	A	NCCf	Mansfield T	L	0-1
10 May	H	F	Notts Co	W	3-1

League Appearances (Goals)
Barron J 42; Chapman R 42 (1); Collier G 7 (1);
Cormack P 41 (9); Cottam J 0+2; Fraser D 19; Hilley D
2+3; Hindley P 42 (2); Ingram A 12; Jackson T 22;
Lyons B 33+1 (3); McIntosh D 5-3; McKenzie D 5-3
(2); Martin N 12; Newton H 12 (1); O'Kane W 42; Rees
R 26+1 (3); Richardson P 25+4 (1); Robertson J 1+1;
Storey-Moore I 33 (18); Winfield J 42.

Position in League Table
	P	W	D	L	F	A	Pts
1st Arsenal	42	29	7	6	71	29	65
16th Forest	42	14	8	20	42	61	36

* lost 2-5 on pens

1971-72 League Appearances (Goals)

Barron J 37; Buckley A 9+1; Chapman R 34; Cormack P 32 (7); Cottam J 17; Fraser D 36; Gemmell T 18 (5); Hindley P 40; Hulme E 5; Jackson T 12+3 (1); Lyons B 19+1 (1); McIntosh J 11+3 (1); McKenzie D 31+2 (7); Martin N 23+2 (5); O'Kane W 22; O'Neill M 10+7 (2); Rees R 7; Richardson P 32+2 (5); Robertson J 12+1; Serella D 8; Storey-Moore I 30 (13); Winfield J 17.

1972-73 League Appearances (Goals)

Baines S 2; Barron J 41; Buckley A 7+1 (1); Chapman R 32+2 (1); Cottam J 19 (1); Dennehy J 3 (1); Fraser D 30 (3); Galley J 18 (6); Gemmell T 21 (1); Hindley P 35 (2); Jackson T 6+1; Lyall G 26+5 (4); Lyons B 10 (1); McIntosh J 23+1 (1); McKenzie D 27+1 (6); Martin N 19 (6); O'Neill M 31+4 (6); Peacock D 1; Richardson P 20+2 (3); Robertson J 28+4 (4); Serella D 34; Winfield J 23.

1973-74 League Appearances (Goals)

Barron J 35; Bowyer I 28 (6); Chapman R 38; Cottam J 34 (1); Dennehy J 8+3 (1); Galley J 10+5; Hindley P 8; Jackson T 19+2 (3); Lyall G 41 (11); McIntosh J 5+1; McKenzie D 41 (26); Martin N 36 (6); O'Kane W 2; O'Neill M 42 (9); Peacock D 7; Peplow S 3; Richardson P 22+3 (2); Robertson J 5; Serella D 15+1; Winfield J 38 (1); Woodcock A 2.

1974-75 League Appearances (Goals)

Anderson V 14+2; Bowyer I 30+2 (6); Butlin B 29+1 (7); Chapman R 31; Cottam J 14+1 (1); Dennehy J 26+1 (3); Galley J 3+1; Greenwood P 15; Jackson T 14+2 (1); Jones D 36 (1); Lyall G 36+1 (7); McCann J 1; McGovern J 8; McIntosh J 1+1; Martin N 26+1 (10); Middleton J 28; O'Hare J 10 (2); O'Kane W 41; O'Neill M 16 (1); Peacock D 14; Richardson P 37+1 (4); Robertson J 17+3; Serella D 8+2; Woodcock A 5+4.

1975-76 League Appearances (Goals)

Anderson V 21; Barrett C 10; Bowery B 1; Bowyer I 40 (13); Butlin B 32 (7); Chapman R 37; Clark F 42; Cottam J 8 (1); Curran T 33 (6); Gunn B 11; Lyall G 5+2 (2); McCann J 14+1 (1); McGovern J 41; McIntosh J 1+1; Middleton J 19; O'Hare J 39+1 (9); O'Kane W 8; O'Neill M 29+1 (5); Richardson P 23+1 (1); Robertson J 37+2 (5); Sunley D 1; Wells P 23; Own Goals 3.

1971-72 — Division One

Date	Venue	Comp	Opponent	Result
3 Aug	A	F	Kaiserslautern	L 0-1
5 Aug	A	F	Hannover 96	W 2-1
7 Aug	H	F	Hannover 96	W 3-2
14 Aug	H	FL	Liverpool	L 1-3
18 Aug	A	FL	Leicester C	W 1-0
21 Aug	A	FL	West Ham U	L 2-3
24 Aug	H	FL	Southampton	D 1-1
28 Aug	A	FL	Crystal Palace	D 0-0
31 Aug	H	FL	Stoke C	L 2-3
4 Sep	H	FL	Sheff Utd	W 5-1
7 Sep	H	FLC2	Aldershot	D 1-1
11 Sep	A	FL	Coventry C	L 2-3
18 Sep	H	FL	Man City	L 2-4
25 Sep	A	FL	Wolves	L 1-2
2 Oct	H	FL	Huddersfield T	L 1-2
6 Oct	H	FLC3	Chelsea	L 1-2
9 Oct	A	FL	Chelsea	L 1-2
16 Oct	H	FLC3r	Huddersfield T	L 2-3
23 Oct	A	FL	Huddersfield T	L 1-2
30 Oct	H	FL	Derby Co	L 0-2
6 Nov	A	FL	Chelsea	L 0-2
13 Nov	H	FL	Notts Co	W 4-1
20 Nov	H	FL	WBA	L 1-2
27 Nov	A	FL	Newcastle U	L 0-2
4 Dec	H	FL	Leeds U	L 0-4
11 Dec	A	FL	Man Utd	L 0-2
18 Dec	H	FL	Ipswich T	L 1-2
27 Dec	A	FL	Chelsea	L 2-3
1 Jan	H	FL	Man City	L 2-4
8 Jan	A	FL	Crystal Palace	L 1-6
15 Jan	H	FAC3	Millwall	L 0-2
22 Jan	H	FL	Leicester C	L 0-1
29 Jan	A	FL	Southampton	L 1-3
12 Feb	A	FL	Derby Co	L 1-4
19 Feb	H	FL	Tottenham H	D 1-1
4 Mar	A	FL	WBA	W 4-1
11 Mar	H	FL	Chelsea	L 1-2
14 Mar	A	FL	West Ham U	L 2-4
25 Mar	H	FL	Coventry C	W 4-0
1 Apr	A	FL	Leeds U	L 0-3
8 Apr	H	FL	Arsenal	L 0-3
10 May	A	FL	Notts Co	L 0-3

Position in League Table

	P	W	D	L	F	A	Pts
1st Derby	42	24	10	8	69	33	58
21st Forest	42	8	9	25	47	81	25

1972-73 — Division Two

Date	Venue	Comp	Opponent	Result
31 Jul	A	F	Watford	W 2-1
7 Aug	H	F	Kaiserslautern	D 2-2
12 Aug	H	FL	Portsmouth	D 0-0
19 Aug	H	FL	Hull C	W 2-1
26 Aug	A	FL	Oxford U	W 1-0
29 Aug	H	FL	Brighton & HA	W 2-1
2 Sep	A	FL	Carlisle U	L 0-1
5 Sep	H	FLC2	Aston Villa	L 0-3
9 Sep	A	FL	Luton T	L 2-3
16 Sep	H	FL	QPR	W 5-1
19 Sep	H	FL	Cardiff C	W 2-1
23 Sep	H	FL	Aston Villa	D 1-1
25 Sep	A	FL	Millwall	L 1-2
30 Sep	H	FL	Sunderland	L 1-4
7 Oct	A	FL	Huddersfield T	L 1-2
14 Oct	H	FL	Bristol C	D 1-1
21 Oct	H	FL	Swindon T	D 2-2
28 Oct	A	FL	Sheff Wed	W 2-1
4 Nov	H	FL	Millwall	L 1-2
11 Nov	A	FL	Cardiff C	L 2-3
18 Nov	H	FL	Preston NE	W 4-0
25 Nov	H	FL	Burnley	L 1-2
2 Dec	H	FL	Orient	W 2-1
9 Dec	A	FL	Middlesbrough	D 0-0
16 Dec	A	FL	Fulham	D 0-0
23 Dec	H	FL	Blackpool	L 1-3
6 Jan	A	FL	Aston Villa	W 4-0
13 Jan	H	FAC3	Bristol C	D 2-2
16 Jan	A	FAC3r	Bristol C	W 2-3
22 Jan	H	FAC3r	Oxford U	W 2-1
27 Jan	H	FAC3r2	WBA	L 0-2
10 Feb	A	FL	QPR	D 0-0
17 Feb	H	FL	Portsmouth	L 0-2
24 Feb	A	FL	Fulham	W 2-1
3 Mar	H	FL	Huddersfield T	D 1-1
10 Mar	A	FL	Hull C	W 3-0
13 Mar	H	FL	Swindon T	W 3-0
17 Mar	H	FL	Sheff Wed	W 3-0
31 Mar	A	FL	Burnley	L 1-3
7 Apr	H	FL	Orient	L 1-2
14 Apr	A	FL	Preston NE	W 2-1
21 Apr	A	FL	Blackpool	D 2-2
23 Apr	H	FL	Sunderland	L 0-1
28 Apr	A	FL	Brighton & HA	W 1-0
2 May	H	NCCsf	Mansfield T	L 1-3
5 May	A	NCCf	Benfica	L 0-3
20 Jun	F		Benfica	L 1-1
23 Jun	F	A	Oporto	L 0-3

* at Leicester ** lost 3-4 on pens

Position in League Table

	P	W	D	L	F	A	Pts
1st Burnley	42	24	14	4	72	35	62
14th Forest	42	14	12	16	47	52	40

1973-74 — Division Two

Date	Venue	Comp	Opponent	Result
4 Aug	A	F	Rhyl	W 9-0
11 Aug	A	F	Port Vale	W 2-0
14 Aug	A	F	Limerick	W 3-0
15 Aug	A	F	Cork Hibs	W 2-0
17 Aug	A	F	Waterford	W 2-1
18 Aug	A	FL	Walsall	L 0-2
20 Aug	A	FL	Lincoln C	W 1-0
25 Aug	H	FL	Luton T	W 2-1
1 Sep	A	FL	Oxford U	L 0-1
8 Sep	H	FL	Sheff Wed	W 4-0
11 Sep	A	FL	Hull C	W 2-1
15 Sep	H	FL	WBA	L 0-1
18 Sep	A	FL	Swindon T	D 0-0
22 Sep	H	FL	Preston NE	W 2-0
26 Sep	A	FL	Derby Co	D 0-0
2 Oct	A	FL	Bolton W	W 3-0
6 Oct	H	FLC2	Bristol C	D 0-0
10 Oct	A	FLC2	Swindon T	L 0-1
13 Oct	A	FL	Millwall	D 2-2
16 Oct	H	FLC2r	Orient	L 1-3
20 Oct	H	FL	Millwall	W 2-1
23 Oct	H	FL	Orient	W 3-2
27 Oct	A	FL	Aston Villa	L 1-2
3 Nov	H	FL	Crystal Palace	L 0-1
10 Nov	H	FL	Fulham	W 2-0
17 Nov	A	FL	Carlisle U	L 1-3
8 Dec	H	FL	Cardiff C	W 4-0
15 Dec	A	FL	Middlesbrough	D 2-2
21 Dec	H	FL	Bolton W	L 0-1
26 Dec	H	FL	Notts Co	D 1-1
29 Dec	A	FL	Sheff Wed	W 3-1
1 Jan	H	FL	Bristol R	L 0-1
6 Jan	A	FAC3	WBA	D 1-1
12 Jan	H	FL	Luton T	L 1-4
19 Jan	A	FAC4	Man City	L 1-4
27 Jan	A	FL	Middlesbrough	L 0-2
2 Feb	H	FL	Preston NE	W 4-1
10 Feb	A	FL	Portsmouth	W 5-1
17 Feb	H	FAC5	Millwall	L 1-2
23 Feb	H	FL	Notts Co	W 2-1
3 Mar	H	FAC6	Newcastle U	W 4-3
6 Mar	A	FAC6	Newcastle U	D 0-0
16 Mar	A	FAC6	Newcastle U	W 1-0
18 Mar	H	FAC6r	Newcastle U	L 0-1
23 Mar	H	FL	Portsmouth	W 3-0
26 Mar	H	FL	Crystal Palace	W 3-0
30 Mar	A	FL	Bristol C	L 1-3
12 Apr	A	FL	Cardiff C	W 1-2
13 Apr	H	FL	Carlisle U	W 2-1
16 Apr	A	FL	Cardiff C	W 1-0
20 Apr	A	FL	Aston Villa	L 0-3
27 Apr	A	FL	Notts Co	D 1-3
6 May	H	NCCsf	Leicester C	L 0-3
13 May	H			D 1-1

* at Goodison Park

Position in League Table

	P	W	D	L	F	A	Pts
1st Midd'bro	42	27	11	4	77	30	65
7th Forest	42	15	15	12	57	43	45

1974-75 — Division Two

Date	Venue	Comp	Opponent	Result
3 Aug	A	F	Port Vale	W 3-1
6 Aug	A	F	Walsall	D 1-1
10 Aug	H	F	Leicester C	L 1-3
17 Aug	A	FL	Bristol C	D 0-3
19 Aug	A	FL	Millwall	L 0-3
24 Aug	H	FL	Portsmouth	L 0-2
27 Aug	H	FL	Millwall	D 2-2
31 Aug	A	FL	Oxford U	W 4-0
7 Sep	H	FL	Man Utd	D 2-2
10 Sep	H	FLC2	Hull C	D 1-1
14 Sep	A	FL	Sheff Wed	L 0-1
17 Sep	H	FLC2r	Hull C	W 2-1
21 Sep	H	FL	Sunderland	L 1-2
25 Sep	H	FL	Aston Villa	W 1-0
28 Sep	A	FL	Southampton	L 1-3
2 Oct	A	FL	Norwich C	D 0-3
5 Oct	H	FL	WBA	D 0-0
12 Oct	A	FL	Bristol R	L 2-3
19 Oct	H	FL	Coventry C	W 3-1
29 Oct	A	FL	Bolton W	D 2-2
2 Nov	H	FL	Oldham A	D 0-2
9 Nov	A	FL	Cardiff C	W 4-3
16 Nov	H	FL	York C	D 1-1
23 Nov	A	FL	Orient	L 1-4
30 Nov	H	FL	Fulham	D 0-2
14 Dec	A	FL	Bristol C	D 0-2
21 Dec	H	FL	Blackpool	D 2-2
26 Dec	H	FL	Notts Co	D 1-1
4 Jan	H	FAC3	Tottenham H	W 1-1
8 Jan	A	FAC3r	Tottenham H	L 0-1
11 Jan	A	FL	Fulham	D 0-0
18 Jan	A	FL	Orient	D 1-1
1 Feb	H	FL	Oldham A	D 0-2
3 Feb	A	FL	Fulham	D 0-1
8 Feb	H	FL	Bolton W	L 2-3
15 Feb	A	FL	York C	W 4-1
22 Feb	H	FL	Corby T	D 0-0
28 Feb	H	FL	Blackpool	D 0-0
8 Mar	A	FL	Charlton A	D 0-0
15 Mar	A	FL	Oldham A	L 0-1
22 Mar	H	FL	Sunderland	D 2-2
29 Mar	A	FL	Notts Co	D 2-2
1 Apr	A	FL	Blackpool	L 0-1
5 Apr	A	FL	Sheff Wed	L 2-4
12 Apr	H	FL	Bristol R	W 2-1
14 Apr	H	FL	Southampton	D 0-3
19 Apr	A	FL	Norwich C	L 2-1
21 Apr	H	FL	Grantham	W 2-1
26 Apr	F		Biggleswade A	W 6-1
8 May	A	NCCf	Notts Co	L 0-1

Position in League Table

	P	W	D	L	F	A	Pts
1st Man Utd	42	26	9	7	66	30	61
16th Forest	42	12	14	16	43	55	38

1975-76 — Division Two

Date	Venue	Comp	Opponent	Result
29 Jul	A	F	TSV Geingen	W 2-0
31 Jul	A	F	SV Kaufbeuren	D 1-1
1 Aug	A	F	BC Aichach	W 9-0
3 Aug	A	F	TSV Gamersheim	W 9-0
5 Aug	A	F	Stuttgart Kickers	L 0-1
9 Aug	A	F	Ballymena	W 3-0
11 Aug	A	F	Coleraine	W 3-2
16 Aug	H	FL	Plymouth A	W 2-0
19 Aug	A	FLC1/1	Rotherham U	D 1-1
23 Aug	A	FL	Portsmouth	W 2-0
27 Aug	H	FLC1/2	Rotherham U	D 1-1
30 Aug	H	FL	Notts Co	L 0-1
6 Sep	H	FL	Chelsea	W 1-0
10 Sep	A	FLC2	Plymouth A	L 1-2
13 Sep	A	FL	Hull C	W 1-0
20 Sep	H	FL	Oxford U	L 1-2
27 Sep	A	FL	Charlton A	L 2-4
4 Oct	H	FL	Bristol R	L 1-2
8 Oct	A	FLC3	Bristol C	L 1-2
11 Oct	A	FL	Fulham	D 0-0
18 Oct	H	FL	Southampton	W 3-0
25 Oct	A	FL	Luton T	L 1-0
1 Nov	H	FL	Carlisle U	W 4-0
4 Nov	H	FL	Sunderland	L 1-0
8 Nov	A	FL	Bristol C	L 1-3
15 Nov	H	FL	Hartlepool U	W 2-1
22 Nov	A	FL	Southampton	L 0-1
29 Nov	H	FL	York C	W 2-1
6 Dec	F		Qatar National XI	L 2-3
13 Dec	H	FL	Portsmouth	W 2-0
26 Dec	H	FL	WBA	L 0-2
27 Dec	H	FL	Orient	W 4-1
1 Jan	H	FAC3	Peterborough U	L 0-1
7 Jan	A	FAC3r	Peterborough U	L 0-1
10 Jan	H	FL	Hull C	L 1-3
23 Jan	H	NCCsf	Mansfield T	W 2-1
31 Jan	A	FL	Luton T	D 1-1
7 Feb	H	FL	Blackpool	W 2-0
21 Feb	H	FL	Charlton A	D 2-2
24 Feb	A	FL	Oldham A	W 4-3
28 Feb	A	FL	Fulham	D 1-1
6 Mar	A	FL	Sunderland	W 2-1
13 Mar	H	FL	Orient	L 1-2
17 Mar	A	FL	Bolton W	L 0-0
20 Mar	H	FL	Oxford U	W 4-0
3 Apr	A	FL	Notts Co	L 0-0
6 Apr	A	FL	WBA	L 1-0
13 Apr	H	FL	Bristol R	W 2-1
17 Apr	A	FL	Blackburn R	W 3-2
20 Apr	H	FL	Don Revie's All Stars	W 10-0
24 Apr	H		CD Serverence	
30 Apr	A			

Position in League Table

	P	W	D	L	F	A	Pts
1st S'land	42	24	8	10	67	36	56
8th Forest	42	17	12	13	55	40	46

1976-77 — Division Two

Date	Comp	V	Opponent	Res	1	2	3	4	5	6	7	8	9	10	11	Substitutes used
27 Jul	F	A	SV Furth	L 2-3												
28 Jul	F	A	Jahn Regensburg	W 5-0												
30 Jul	F	A	Augsburg	W 1-0												
1 Aug	F	A	Furstenfeldbruck	W 4-2												
3 Aug	F	A	HSB Heidenheim	W 3-1												
7 Aug	ASCq	A	Notts C	D 0-0	Wells	Saunders	Clark	McGovern	Chapman	Bowyer	Curran 1	Haslegrave *	O'Hare 1	Butlin	Robertson	Richardson (8)
14 Aug	ASCq	H	WBA	W 3-2	Wells	Saunders	Clark	McGovern	Chapman	Bowyer	Curran 1p	Richardson *	O'Hare	Butlin	Robertson	O'Neill (8)
21 Aug	ASCq	A	Bristol C	W 4-2	Wells	Saunders	Clark	McGovern *	Chapman	Bowyer	Curran	Barrett *	O'Hare	Butlin	Robertson	O'Neill (8)
25 Aug	FL	H	Fulham	D 2-2	Middleton	Barrett 1	Clark	McGovern *	Chapman	Bowyer	Curran 1	O'Neill 2	O'Hare	Butlin	Robertson 1	Anderson (4)
28 Aug	FL	A	Charlton A	D 1-1	Wells	Barrett	Clark	McGovern	Chapman	Bowyer	Curran	O'Neill	O'Hare	Butlin	Robertson	Anderson (4)
31 Aug	FLC2	H	Wolves	L 1-3 §	Middleton	Barrett	Clark	Anderson	Chapman	Bowyer	Curran	O'Neill	O'Hare	Butlin 1	Robertson	
4 Sep	FL	H	Walsall	W 4-2	Wells	Barrett 1	Clark	McGovern	Lloyd	Bowyer 2	Curran 1	O'Neill	O'Hare *	Withe 1	Robertson 1	Anderson (9)
11 Sep	FL	A	Hereford U	W 4-3	Middleton	Barrett	Clark	McGovern	Lloyd	Bowyer 1	Curran	O'Neill	O'Hare *	Butlin 1	Robertson	
14 Sep	FL	H	Southampton	W 2-1	Wells	Barrett 1	Clark	McGovern	Lloyd	Bowyer 2	Curran	O'Neill	O'Hare 1	Withe	Robertson	
18 Sep	FL	A	Coventry C	L 0-3	Middleton	Barrett	Clark	Anderson	Chapman	Bowyer	Curran	O'Neill	Withe	Butlin	Robertson	
21 Sep	FLC3	A	Carlisle U	W 5-1	Middleton	Barrett 1	Clark	McGovern	Lloyd	Bowyer 2	Curran 1	O'Neill	Withe 1	Butlin 1	Robertson	
25 Sep	ASC1/2	H	Kilmarnock	D 2-2	Middleton	Anderson 1	Clark	McGovern	Lloyd	Bowyer 2	Curran 1	O'Neill	O'Hare *	Withe	Robertson	
28 Sep	FL	A	Hull C	L 0-1	Middleton	Barrett	Clark	McGovern	Lloyd	Bowyer	Curran	O'Neill	O'Hare *	Withe	Robertson	Anderson (9)
2 Oct	FL	H	Sheffield U	W 6-1	Middleton	Anderson 1	Clark	McGovern	Lloyd	Bowyer 2	Curran 1	O'Neill 2	Withe 1	Butlin	Robertson	
9 Oct	F	A	Grantham	W 3-0	Middleton	Anderson	Clark	McGovern	Lloyd	Bowyer	Curran *	Haslegrave	Withe	Butlin 1	Robertson	
13 Oct	FL	H	Blackpool	D 0-1	Middleton	Anderson	Clark	McGovern	Lloyd	Bowyer	Curran 1	O'Neill	Withe	Butlin	Robertson	Barrett (7)
16 Oct	ASC2/1	H	Burnley	W 5-2	Middleton	Saunders	Clark	McGovern	Lloyd	Bowyer	Curran 1	O'Neill 2	Withe	Butlin	Robertson 1	Haslegrave (7)
20 Oct	FL	A	Notts Co	W 2-1	Middleton	Anderson	Clark	McGovern	Chapman	Bowyer 1	Haslegrave 1	O'Neill 1	Withe	Woodcock	Robertson	
23 Oct	NCCf	A	Oldham A	L 0-1	Middleton	Anderson	Clark	McGovern	Chapman	Bowyer	Haslegrave	O'Neill	Withe	Woodcock 1	Robertson	
26 Oct	FL	A	Ayr U	W 2-0	Middleton	Anderson	Clark	McGovern	Chapman 1	Bowyer 1	Haslegrave	O'Neill 1	Withe 1	Woodcock 1	Robertson 2 (1p)	
30 Oct	ASC2/2	A	Blackburn R	W 3-0	Middleton	Anderson	Clark	McGovern	Lloyd	Bowyer 1	O'Hare	O'Neill 1	Withe 1	Woodcock 1	Robertson	
6 Nov	FL	H	Orient	D 1-1	Middleton	Anderson	Clark	McGovern	Lloyd	Bowyer 1	O'Hare	O'Neill	Withe	Woodcock	Robertson	
13 Nov	FL	A	Chelsea	W 3-0	Middleton	Anderson	Clark	Chapman	Lloyd *	Bowyer 1	O'Hare	O'Neill 1	Withe	Woodcock 2	Robertson	
20 Nov	FL	H	Bristol R	W 4-2	Middleton	Anderson 1	Clark	McGovern	Lloyd 1	Bowyer 1	O'Hare	O'Neill	Withe	Woodcock 2	Robertson 2 (1p)	
27 Nov	FL	A	Millwall	D 1-1	Middleton	Anderson	Clark	McGovern	Lloyd	Bowyer	O'Hare	O'Neill	Withe	Woodcock 1	Robertson	
4 Dec	FL	H	Orient	W 4-0	Middleton	Anderson	Clark	McGovern	Lloyd	Bowyer	O'Hare	O'Neill *	Withe	Woodcock	Robertson	
11 Dec	ASCf/1	A	Orient	D 1-1	Middleton	Anderson	Clark	McGovern	Lloyd	Bowyer	Chapman	Haslegrave	O'Hare	Woodcock	Robertson	Chapman (8) 1
13 Dec	ASCf/2	H	Plymouth A	D 1-1	Middleton	Anderson	Clark	Chapman	Lloyd	Bowyer	O'Neill	O'Neill	Withe 1	Woodcock	Woodcock	
15 Dec	FL	A	Bolton W	D 1-1	Middleton	Anderson	Clark	McGovern	Lloyd	Bowyer 1	O'Neill	O'Neill	Withe 1	Woodcock	Robertson	
27 Dec	FL	H	Blackburn R	W 3-1	Middleton	Anderson	Clark	McGovern	Lloyd	Bowyer	O'Neill	O'Neill	Withe	Woodcock 1	Robertson 1p	O'Hare (7)
1 Jan	FL	H	Bristol R	D 1-1	Middleton	Anderson	Clark	Chapman	Lloyd	Bowyer	O'Hare	O'Neill	Withe	Woodcock	Robertson	Withe (7)
5 Feb	FL	A	Charlton A	D 1-2	Middleton	Anderson	Clark	McGovern	Chapman	Barrett	O'Hare	O'Neill	Curran	Woodcock	Robertson	
8 Jan	FAC3	H	Bristol R	D 1-1	Middleton	Anderson	Clark	McGovern	Chapman	Bowyer	Birtles	O'Neill	Withe 1	Woodcock 1	Robertson	
11 Jan	FAC3r	A	Bristol R	W 6-0	Middleton	Anderson	Clark	Chapman	Lloyd	Bowyer 1	McGovern	O'Neill 1	Withe	Woodcock	Robertson	
14 Jan	FAC3r2	A	Fulham	W 3-0	Middleton	Anderson	Clark	Chapman	Lloyd	Bowyer	McGovern	O'Neill	Withe 2	Woodcock 1	Robertson	McGovern
18 Jan	FAC4	A	Southampton	D 3-3	Middleton	Anderson	Clark	Chapman	Lloyd	Bowyer	McGovern	O'Neill 1	Withe 2*	Woodcock 1	Robertson 1p	
22 Jan	FL	H	Wolves	L 1-2	Middleton	Anderson	Clark	Chapman	Lloyd 1	Bowyer 1	McGovern	O'Neill	Withe 1	Woodcock 1	Robertson	McGovern
26 Jan	FAC4r	H	Southampton	D 1-2	Middleton	Barrett 1	Clark	McGovern	Lloyd	Bowyer	McGovern	O'Neill 1	Withe 1	Woodcock 1	Robertson 2 (1p)	O'Hare (10)
29 Jan	FL	A	Southampton	D 1-1	Middleton	Anderson	Clark	McGovern	Lloyd	Bowyer	McGovern	Haslegrave	O'Hare	Woodcock	Robertson	
1 Feb	FL	H	Hereford U	W 1-0	Middleton	Anderson	Clark	Chapman	Lloyd	Bowyer 1	Chapman	O'Neill 1	O'Hare	Woodcock	Robertson	
5 Feb	FL	A	Notts Co	D 1-1	Middleton	Anderson	Clark	Chapman	Chapman	Bowyer	Curran 1*	O'Neill	Withe	Woodcock	Robertson 1p	O'Hare (7)
8 Feb	FL	H	Hull C	W 3-1	Middleton	Anderson	Clark	Chapman	Chapman	Bowyer	O'Hare	O'Neill	Withe 1	Woodcock	Robertson	Withe (7)
11 Feb	FL	A	Grantham	D 1-1	Middleton	Anderson	Clark	Chapman	Lloyd	Bowyer	O'Hare	O'Neill	Withe 1	Woodcock	Robertson	
12 Feb	FL	H	Sheffield U	W 3-1	Middleton	Anderson	Clark	Chapman	Lloyd	Bowyer	McGovern	O'Neill 1	Withe 2	McGovern	Robertson 1p	Butlin (9)
16 Feb	FL	A	Blackpool	D 1-1	Middleton	Anderson	Clark	Chapman	Lloyd 1	Bowyer	McGovern	O'Neill	Withe 2*	McGovern	Robertson	Barrett (9)
5 Mar	FL	H	Orient	L 1-2	Middleton	Anderson	Clark	Chapman	Lloyd	Bowyer	McGovern	O'Neill 1	Withe 1	McGovern *	Robertson	Butlin (9)
12 Mar	FL	A	Bolton W	W 2-0	Middleton	Anderson	Clark	Chapman	Lloyd	Bowyer 1	McGovern	O'Neill 1	Withe 1	McGovern *	Robertson	Barrett (7)
16 Mar	FL	H	Notts Co	L 0-2	Middleton	Anderson	Clark	Chapman	Lloyd	Bowyer	Chapman	O'Neill	Withe *	Woodcock *	Robertson	
19 Mar	FL	H	Chelsea	W 2-1	Middleton	Anderson	Clark	Chapman	Lloyd	Bowyer	McGovern	O'Neill	Withe	Woodcock 1	Robertson 1	Butlin (9)
26 Mar	FL	A	Cardiff C	W 3-0	Middleton	Anderson	Clark	Chapman	Lloyd	Bowyer	McGovern	O'Neill	Withe	Woodcock	Robertson	Curran (3)
29 Mar	FL	A	Oldham A	L 0-1	Middleton	Anderson	Clark	Chapman	Lloyd	Bowyer	Chapman	O'Neill	Withe *	Woodcock	Robertson	Curran (4)
30 Mar	FL	H	Bristol R	D 1-2	Middleton	Anderson	Clark *	Chapman	Lloyd	Bowyer	McGovern	O'Neill	Withe	Woodcock 1	Robertson	
2 Apr	FL	H	Millwall	W 3-0	Middleton	Anderson	Clark	Chapman	Lloyd	Bowyer 1	McGovern	O'Neill 1	Withe 1	Woodcock 1	Robertson 1	
6 Apr	FL	A	Derby Co	D 1-1	Middleton	Anderson	Clark	Chapman	Lloyd	Bowyer	McGovern	O'Neill	Withe	Woodcock	Robertson	
9 Apr	FL	H	Mansfield T	W 2-1	Middleton	Anderson	Clark	Chapman	Lloyd	Bowyer	McGovern	O'Neill	Withe	Woodcock	Robertson	
10 May	NCCsf	A	Peterborough U	W 1-0 §	Middleton	Anderson	Clark	Chapman	Lloyd	Bowyer	McGovern	O'Neill	Withe 1	Woodcock 1	Robertson	
12 May	F			W 5-2	Middleton	Anderson	Clark	Chapman	Lloyd	Bowyer	McGovern	O'Neill	Withe	Woodcock	Robertson	

League Appearances (Goals)

Anderson V 35+3 (1); Barrett C 10+3 (2); Birtles G 1; Bowery H 1; Bowyer I 41 (12); Butlin B 10+2 (3); Chapman R 31+1 (2); Clark F 42; Curran T 13+2 (6); Haslegrave S 5+2 (1); Lloyd L 26 (3); McGovern J 39; Middleton J 38; O'Hare J 19+3 (3); O'Neill M 38+2 (9); Richardson P 1+1; Robertson J 41 (16); Saunders G 4; Wells P 4; Withe P 33+1 (16); Woodcock A 30 (11); Own goals 2.

Position in League Table

	P	W	D	L	F	A	Pts
1st Wolves	42	22	13	7	84	45	57
3rd Forest	42	21	10	11	77	43	52

Notes

§ denotes own goals

Oct 26, 1975-76 County Cup Final, held over from previous season

Jan 18, at Villa Park

1977-78 — Division One

Date	Comp	V	Opponent	Result	1	2	3	4	5	6	7	8	9	10	11	Substitutes used
1 Aug	F	A	St Gallen	W 3-2												
3 Aug	F	A	Wacker Innsbruck	W 2-0												
5 Aug	F	A	SV Plattling	W 5-1												
6 Aug	F	A	Neuburg	W 5-1												
9 Aug	F	A	SW Bregenz	W 3-0												
13 Aug	F	A	Skegness T	W 4-0												
15 Aug	NCC†	H	Notts Co	D 1-1												
20 Aug	FL	A	Everton	W 3-1	Middleton	Anderson	Clark	McGovern	Lloyd	Burns	O'Neill 1	Bowyer	Withe 1	Woodcock	Robertson 1	
23 Aug	FL	H	Bristol C	W 1-0	Middleton	Anderson	Clark	McGovern	Lloyd	Burns	O'Neill	Bowyer	Withe 1	Woodcock	Robertson	
27 Aug	FL	H	Derby Co	W 3-0	Middleton	Anderson	Clark	McGovern	Lloyd	Burns	O'Neill	Gemmill	Withe 2	Woodcock 1	Robertson	
30 Aug	FLC2	A	West Ham U	W 5-0	Middleton	Anderson	Clark *	McGovern	Lloyd	Burns	O'Neill 1	Bowyer 2	Withe 1	Woodcock 1	Robertson	Barrett (3)
3 Sep	FL	A	Arsenal	L 0-3	Middleton	Anderson	Barrett	McGovern	Lloyd	Burns	O'Neill	Bowyer	Withe	Woodcock	Robertson	
10 Sep	FL	A	Wolves	W 3-2	Shilton	Anderson	Barrett	McGovern	Lloyd	Burns	O'Neill	Bowyer	Withe 1	Woodcock	Robertson	
12 Sep	F	H	Leicester C	D 0-0												
17 Sep	FL	H	Aston Villa	W 2-0	Shilton	Anderson	Barrett	McGovern	Lloyd	Burns	O'Neill 1	Gemmill	O'Hare	Woodcock	Robertson	
24 Sep	FL	A	Leicester C	W 3-0	Shilton	Anderson	Barrett	Bowyer	Lloyd	Burns 1	O'Neill	Gemmill	Withe	Woodcock	Robertson	
1 Oct	FL	H	Norwich C	D 1-1	Shilton	Anderson	Barrett	McGovern	Lloyd	Burns	O'Neill	Bowyer *	Withe *	Woodcock	Robertson	
4 Oct	FL	A	Ipswich T	W 4-0	Shilton	Anderson	Barrett	McGovern	Lloyd	Burns	O'Neill *	Bowyer 1	Withe 1	Woodcock 1	Robertson	Gemmill (8)
8 Oct	FL	A	West Ham U	D 0-0	Shilton	Anderson	Barrett	Gemmill	Lloyd	Burns	O'Neill	Bowyer	Withe	Woodcock	Robertson	
15 Oct	FL	H	Man City	W 2-1	Shilton	Anderson	Barrett	McGovern 1	Lloyd	Burns	O'Neill	Bowyer	Withe	Woodcock 1	Robertson	Gemmill (7)
17 Oct	F	H	Sheffield U	W 6-1												
22 Oct	FL	H	QPR	W 2-0	Shilton	Anderson	Barrett	McGovern	Lloyd	Burns 1	O'Neill	Bowyer 1	Withe	Woodcock	Robertson 1p	O'Neill (7)
25 Oct	FLC3	H	Notts Co	W 4-0	Woods	Anderson 2	Barrett	McGovern 1	Lloyd *	Burns	Gemmill	Bowyer *	Withe	Woodcock	Robertson	O'Neill (8)
29 Oct	FL	A	Middlesbrough	L 0-1	Shilton	Anderson	Barrett	McGovern	Lloyd	Burns	Gemmill	Bowyer	Withe	Woodcock	Robertson	
5 Nov	FL	H	Chelsea	D 1-1	Shilton	Anderson	Barrett	McGovern	Lloyd	Burns 1	Gemmill 1	Bowyer *	Withe	Woodcock	Robertson	
12 Nov	FL	A	Man Utd	W 2-1	Shilton	Anderson	Barrett	McGovern	Lloyd	Burns	Gemmill	Bowyer	Withe	Woodcock 1	Robertson	
14 Nov	F	A	Hartlepool U	D 2-2												
19 Nov	FL	A	Leeds U	L 0-1	Shilton	Anderson	Barrett	McGovern	Lloyd	Burns	Gemmill	Bowyer	Withe	Woodcock	Robertson	Bowyer (9)
26 Nov	F	A	Maccabi Tel Aviv	W 6-1												
29 Nov	FLC4	H	Aston Villa	D 0-0	Woods	Anderson	Barrett	McGovern	Lloyd	Burns	O'Neill	Gemmill	Withe	Woodcock	Robertson	O'Hare (9)
3 Dec	FL	H	Birmingham C	W 4-2	Shilton	Anderson	Barrett	McGovern	Needham	Burns	O'Neill 1	Gemmill 1	Withe 1	Woodcock 1	Robertson	
10 Dec	FL	A	Coventry C	D 3-3	Shilton	Anderson	Barrett	McGovern	Needham	Burns	O'Neill 1	Gemmill	Withe	Woodcock 1	Robertson 1p	
17 Dec	FL	A	Man Utd	W 4-0 §	Shilton	Anderson	Barrett	McGovern 1	Needham 1	Burns	O'Neill	Gemmill	Withe *	Woodcock	Robertson 1p	
26 Dec	FL	H	Liverpool	D 1-1	Shilton	Anderson	Barrett	McGovern	Needham 1	Burns	O'Neill 1	Gemmill	Withe	Woodcock	Robertson 1p	
28 Dec	FL	A	Bristol C	W 3-1	Shilton	Anderson	Barrett	McGovern	Needham	Burns	O'Neill	Gemmill	Withe	Woodcock 1	Robertson 1p	
31 Dec	FL	A	Everton	W 4-1	Shilton	Anderson	Barrett	McGovern	Barrett	Burns	O'Neill	Gemmill	Withe 1	Woodcock	Robertson 1p	
2 Jan	FL	H	WBA	—	Shilton	Anderson	Clark	McGovern	Needham	Burns	O'Neill	Gemmill 1	Withe	Woodcock 2	Robertson 1p	
7 Jan	FAC3	A	Aston Villa	—	Woods	Anderson	Clark	McGovern	Needham	Burns	O'Neill 1	Gemmill	Withe 1*	Woodcock	Robertson	
14 Jan	FL	H	Bury	—	Shilton	Anderson	Clark	McGovern	Needham	Burns	O'Neill	Gemmill	Withe	Woodcock 1	Robertson 1p	
18 Jan	FLC5	H	Arsenal	—	Woods	Anderson	Clark	McGovern	Lloyd	Burns	O'Neill	Gemmill	Withe 2	Woodcock 2	Robertson 1p	
21 Jan	FL	A	Man City	—	Shilton	Anderson	Clark	McGovern	Lloyd	Burns	O'Neill	Gemmill	Withe	Woodcock 1	Robertson 1p	
24 Jan	FAC4	A	Wolves	—	Woods	Anderson	Barrett 1	Needham	Lloyd	Burns	O'Neill 1	Bowyer 1	Withe 1	Woodcock 2	Robertson 1p	
4 Feb	FL	H	Leeds U	—	Woods	Anderson	Clark	Needham	Lloyd	Burns	O'Neill	Gemmill	Withe	Woodcock	Robertson	
8 Feb	FLCsf/1	A	QPR	—	Woods	Anderson	Clark	O'Hare	Lloyd	Burns	O'Neill	Bowyer	Withe	Woodcock	Robertson	
18 Feb	FAC5	H	QPR	—	Shilton	Anderson	Clark	McGovern *	Lloyd	Burns	O'Neill	Gemmill	Withe	Woodcock	Robertson	
25 Feb	FLCsf/2	H	West Ham U	—	Woods	Anderson	Clark	O'Hare	Lloyd	Burns	O'Neill	Gemmill	Withe	Woodcock 2	Robertson 1p	
27 Feb	FAC5r	A	WBA	—	Shilton	Anderson	Clark	McGovern *	Lloyd	Burns	O'Neill	Bowyer	Withe	Woodcock	Robertson 1p	
2 Mar	FL	H	Leicester C	—	Shilton	Anderson	Clark	McGovern	Lloyd	Burns	O'Neill	Gemmill	Withe 1	Woodcock	Robertson 1p	
4 Mar	FAC5r2	H	Liverpool	—	Shilton	Bowyer	Clark	O'Hare	Needham 1	Burns	O'Neill	Gemmill	Withe	Woodcock	Robertson 1p	
11 Mar	FL	A	Liverpool	—	Woods	Anderson	Clark	O'Hare	Needham	Burns	O'Neill	Bowyer	Withe	Woodcock	Robertson 1p	
14 Mar	FAC6	A	Newcastle U	—	Shilton	Anderson 1*	Clark	McGovern *	Lloyd	Burns	O'Neill 1	Gemmill 1	Withe	Woodcock	Robertson 1p	O'Hare (4)
18 Mar	FLCf	H	Middlesbrough	—	Woods	Bowyer	Clark	O'Hare	Needham	Burns	O'Neill	Bowyer	Withe	Woodcock	Robertson	Bowyer (2)
22 Mar	FL	H	Chelsea	—	Shilton	Anderson	Barrett	O'Hare	Lloyd	Burns	O'Neill	Bowyer	Withe	Woodcock	Robertson 1p	
25 Mar	FL	A	Derby Co	—	Shilton	Anderson	Clark	O'Hare	Needham	Burns 1	O'Neill	Gemmill 1	Withe	Woodcock	Robertson 1p	
29 Mar	FL	H	Man City	—	Shilton	Anderson	Clark	O'Hare	Lloyd	Burns	O'Neill	Gemmill *	Withe	Woodcock 1	Robertson	
31 Mar	FL	A	Notts Co	—	Shilton	Anderson	Clark	O'Hare	Needham	Burns	O'Neill	Gemmill	Withe	Woodcock	Robertson 1p	
3 Apr	FL	A	Leeds U	—	Shilton	Anderson	Barrett	McGovern	Lloyd	Burns	O'Neill	Gemmill	Withe 1	Woodcock 1	Robertson	
5 Apr	FL	H	Derby Co	—	Shilton	Anderson	Barrett	McGovern	Lloyd	Burns	O'Neill	Gemmill	Withe	Woodcock	Robertson	
11 Apr	FL	A	Man City	—	Shilton	Barrett	Clark	McGovern	Lloyd	Burns	O'Neill	Gemmill	Withe 1	Bowyer	Robertson	
15 Apr	FL	H	QPR	—	Shilton	Barrett	Clark	McGovern	Lloyd	Burns	O'Neill	Gemmill	Withe	Bowyer	Robertson 1p	
18 Apr	FL	A	Coventry C	—	Shilton	Anderson	Barrett	O'Hare	Needham	Burns	O'Neill	Bowyer	Withe	Gemmill	Robertson	
22 Apr	FL	H	Ipswich T	—	Shilton	Anderson	Barrett	O'Hare	Needham	Burns	O'Neill	Bowyer	Withe *	Gemmill	Robertson	
25 Apr	FL	H	Birmingham C	—	Shilton	Anderson	Barrett	McGovern	Needham	Burns	O'Neill	Gemmill	Withe *	Woodcock *	Robertson	Clark (9) 1
29 Apr	FL	A	Derby Co	—	Shilton	Anderson	Clark	McGovern	Lloyd	Burns	O'Neill	Gemmill	Withe	Bowyer 1	Robertson 1p	Bowyer (10)
2 May	FL	H	WBA	D 2-2	Shilton	Anderson	Barrett	McGovern	Lloyd	Burns	O'Neill	Gemmill	Withe	Bowyer	Robertson 1p	
4 May	FL	A	Liverpool	D 0-0	Shilton	Anderson	Barrett	McGovern	Needham	Clark	O'Neill	Gemmill	Withe	Bowyer	Robertson	

League Appearances (Goals)

Anderson V 37 (3); Barrett C 33+2 (1); Burns K 41 (4); Clark F 12+1 (1); Gemmill A 32+2 (3); Lloyd L 26; McGovern J 31 (4); Middleton J 5; Needham D 16 (4); O'Hare J 10; O'Neill M 38+2 (8); Robertson J 42 (12); Shilton P 37; Withe P 40 (12); Woodcock A 36 (11); Own goals 2.

Position in League Table

	P	W	D	L	F	A	Pts
1st Forest	42	25	14	3	69	24	64

Notes

§ denotes own goals

Aug 15, 1976-77 County Cup Final, held over from previous season, Forest won 3-2 on penalties

Mar 18, at Wembley

Mar 22, at Old Trafford

217

1978-79 — Division One

Date	Comp	Vn	Opponent	Result	1	2	3	4	5	6	7	8	9	10	11	Substitutes used
25 Jul	F	A	Red Star Belgrade	L 2-3												
27 Jul	F	A	Dynamo Zagreb	D 1-1												
30 Jul	F	A	SK Osijek	D 1-1												
2 Aug	F	A	AEK Athens	W 1-0												
12 Aug	CS		Ipswich T	L 0-1	Shilton	Anderson	Barrett	McGovern	**Lloyd 1**	Burns	**O'Neill 2***	Gemmill	**Withe 1**	Woodcock	**Robertson 1**	Needham (7)
14 Aug	F	A	RC Celta Vigo	D 0-1												
16 Aug	F		FC Porto	D 0-1												
19 Aug	FL	H	Tottenham H	D 1-1	Shilton	Anderson	Barrett	McGovern	Needham	Burns	**O'Neill 1**	Gemmill	Elliott	Woodcock	Robertson	
22 Aug	FL	A	Coventry C	D 0-0	Shilton	Anderson	Barrett	McGovern	Needham	Burns	O'Neill	Gemmill	Elliott	Woodcock	Robertson	
26 Aug	FL	A	QPR	D 0-0	Shilton	Anderson	Barrett	McGovern	Needham	Burns	O'Neill	Gemmill	Elliott	Woodcock	Robertson	
29 Aug	FLC2	H	Oldham A	W 2-0	Shilton	Anderson	Barrett	McGovern	Needham	Burns	O'Neill	Gemmill	Elliott	Woodcock	Robertson	
2 Sep	FL	H	WBA	D 0-0	Shilton	Anderson	Barrett	McGovern	Needham	Burns	O'Neill	Gemmill	Elliott	Woodcock	Robertson	
4 Sep	FL	A	Mansfield T	W 6-1	Shilton	Anderson	Barrett	McGovern	**Needham 1**	**Burns 1**	O'Neill	Gemmill	Elliott	Woodcock	**Robertson 1p**	
6 Sep	FLC2r	H	Oldham A	W 4-2	Shilton	Anderson	**Barrett 1**	McGovern	Lloyd	Burns	Mills*	**Bowyer 1**	Birtles	Woodcock	**Robertson 1p**	
9 Sep	FL	H	Arsenal	W 2-1	Shilton	Anderson	Barrett	McGovern	Lloyd	Burns	Gemmill	**Bowyer 1**	**Birtles 1**	Woodcock	Robertson	
13 Sep	EC1/1	A	Liverpool	W 2-0	Shilton	Anderson	Barrett*	McGovern	Lloyd	Burns	**O'Neill 1**	Bowyer	**Birtles 1**	Woodcock	Robertson	O'Hare (3)
16 Sep	FL	H	Liverpool	W 4-0	Shilton	Anderson	Clark	McGovern	Lloyd	Burns	Gemmill	Bowyer	Birtles	Woodcock	Robertson	
19 Sep	NCC1	H	Mansfield T	D 2-2	Shilton	**Anderson 1**	Bowyer	**McGovern 1**	Lloyd	Burns	**O'Neill 1**	Gemmill	**Birtles 2**	Woodcock	**Robertson 1p**	O'Hare (10)
23 Sep	FL	A	Middlesbrough	D 0-0	Shilton	Anderson	Clark	McGovern	Lloyd	Burns	O'Neill	Gemmill	**Birtles 2**	**Woodcock**	Robertson	Bowyer (10)
27 Sep	EC1/2	H	Liverpool	D 0-0	Shilton	Anderson	Clark	McGovern	Lloyd	Burns	**O'Neill 1**	Gemmill	**Birtles 1**	Woodcock	Robertson	
30 Sep	FL	A	Aston Villa	W 2-1	Shilton	**Anderson 1**	Clark	**McGovern 1**	Lloyd	Burns	O'Neill	Gemmill	**Birtles 2**	Woodcock	**Robertson 2**	Needham (4) Mills (3)
4 Oct	FLC3	A	Oxford U	W 5-0	Shilton	Anderson	Clark	McGovern	Lloyd	Burns	Gemmill	Bowyer	**Birtles 1**	Woodcock*	Robertson	Mills (6)
7 Oct	FL	H	Wolves	W 3-1	Shilton	Anderson	Bowyer	O'Hare	Lloyd	**Needham 1**	Gemmill	O'Hare	**Birtles 1**	Woodcock	**Robertson 1**	
14 Oct	FL	A	Bristol C	W 2-1	Shilton	**Anderson 1**	Clark*	O'Hare	Lloyd	**Burns 1**	Gemmill	Gemmill	Birtles	Woodcock	Robertson	
18 Oct	EC2/1	H	AEK Athens	W 2-0	Shilton	**Anderson 1**	Bowyer	O'Hare	**Lloyd 1**	Needham	Gemmill	Bowyer	Birtles	**Woodcock 1**	Robertson	O'Hare (5)
21 Oct	FL	A	Ipswich T	W 2-0	Shilton	**Anderson 1**	Bowyer	Needham	Lloyd*	O'Hare	O'Neill	Needham	Birtles	Woodcock	**Robertson 1**	
28 Oct	FL	H	Southampton	D 0-0	Shilton	Anderson	Clark	Needham	Lloyd	Bowyer	O'Neill	Gemmill	Birtles	Woodcock	**Robertson 1**	
1 Nov	EC2/2	A	AEK Athens	W 5-1	Shilton	Anderson	Clark	McGovern	Lloyd	Bowyer	Gemmill	Bowyer	Birtles	**Woodcock 1**	**Robertson 1**	Bowyer (9)
4 Nov	FL	H	Everton	D 0-0	Shilton	Anderson	Clark	McGovern	Lloyd	Needham	Bowyer	Gemmill	**Birtles 1**	Woodcock	**Robertson 1**	
11 Nov	FLC4	H	QPR	W 3-2	Shilton	Anderson	Clark	McGovern	**Lloyd 1**	Needham	O'Neill	Bowyer	**Birtles 2**	**Woodcock 1**	**Robertson 1**	
18 Nov	FL	A	Tottenham H	W 3-1	Shilton	Anderson	Bowyer	McGovern	Lloyd	Burns	O'Neill	Gemmill	**Birtles 2**	Woodcock	**Robertson 1p**	
25 Nov	FL	H	Bolton W	W 1-0	Shilton	Anderson	Clark	Needham	Lloyd*	Bowyer	O'Neill	Gemmill	Birtles	Woodcock	Robertson	
5 Dec	F	A	Dynamo Zagreb	L 0-2												
9 Dec	FL	A	Liverpool	D 0-2	Shilton	Anderson	Clark	McGovern	Lloyd	Bowyer	Gemmill	McGovern	Elliott	Birtles	Robertson	
13 Dec	FLC5	H	Brighton & HA	W 3-1	Shilton	Anderson	Clark	McGovern	Lloyd	Needham	Bowyer	**Gemmill 1**	**Birtles 1**	Woodcock	Robertson	
16 Dec	FL	H	Birmingham C	W 1-0	Shilton	Anderson	Clark	McGovern	Lloyd	Needham	Bowyer	Gemmill	Birtles*	**Woodcock***	Robertson	
23 Dec	FL	A	Man City	D 0-0	Shilton	Anderson	Clark	McGovern	Lloyd	Needham	Francis	Gemmill	Birtles	Woodcock	Robertson	
26 Dec	FL	H	Derby Co	W 4-1	Shilton	Anderson	Clark	McGovern	Lloyd	Needham	Francis	Gemmill	Birtles	Woodcock	Robertson	Francis (7)
13 Jan	FAC3	A	Arsenal	L 1-2	Shilton	Anderson	Bowyer	McGovern	Lloyd	Needham	O'Hare	Francis	**Birtles 2**	Francis	**Robertson 1p**	
20 Jan	FL	H	Aston Villa	W 3-2	Shilton	Anderson	Clark	McGovern	Lloyd	Needham	O'Neill	Gemmill	Birtles	**Woodcock 2**	Robertson	
27 Jan	FACsf/1	A	Watford	W 3-0	Shilton	Anderson	Barrett	McGovern	Lloyd	Needham	**O'Neill 3**	Francis	**Birtles 1**	**Woodcock 2**	Robertson	
30 Jan	FAC4	A	York C	W 6-0	Shilton	Anderson	Bowyer	McGovern	Lloyd	Needham	**O'Neill 1**	Bowyer	**Birtles 1**	**Woodcock 2**	Robertson	
3 Feb	FL	H	Middlesbrough	D 1-1	Shilton	Anderson	Bowyer	McGovern	Lloyd	Burns	**O'Neill 1**	Gemmill	Birtles	**Bowyer 1**	Robertson	
10 Feb	FLCsf/2	A	Watford	W 4-0 §	Shilton	Anderson	Gunn	McGovern	Needham	Burns	O'Neill	Gemmill	**Birtles 2**	Woodcock	**Robertson 1p**	O'Hare (8)
21 Feb	F	H	Exeter C	D 3-3												
24 Feb	FL	A	Bristol C	D 0-0	Shilton	Barrett	Clark	McGovern	Lloyd	Needham	**O'Neill 1**	Gemmill	**Birtles 1**	Woodcock	**Robertson 1**	
26 Feb	FAC5	H	Arsenal	L 0-1	Shilton	Anderson	Clark	McGovern	Lloyd	Needham	O'Neill	Gemmill	Birtles	Woodcock	Robertson	
3 Mar	FL	A	Ipswich T	W 1-0	Shilton	Anderson	Barrett	Bowyer	Lloyd	Needham	Francis	Francis	Birtles	Francis	Robertson	
7 Mar	EC3/1	H	Grasshopper Zurich	W 4-1	Shilton	Anderson	Bowyer	McGovern	**Lloyd 1**	Needham	O'Neill	Francis	**Birtles 2**	**Woodcock**	**Robertson 1p**	
10 Mar	FL	A	Everton	D 1-1	Shilton	Anderson	Clark	McGovern	Lloyd	Needham	O'Hare	O'Hare	Birtles	Woodcock	Robertson	
17 Mar	FLCf		Norwich C	W 3-2	Shilton	Anderson	Clark	McGovern	Lloyd	Needham	**O'Neill 1**	Gemmill	**Birtles 2**	**Woodcock 2**	Robertson	
21 Mar	EC3/2	A	Grasshopper Zurich	W 3-0	Shilton	Barrett	Barrett	McGovern	Lloyd	Needham	**O'Neill 1**	Francis	**Birtles 1**	**Woodcock 2**	Robertson	
24 Mar	FL	H	Southampton	W 6-0	Shilton	Anderson	Bowyer	McGovern	Lloyd	Needham	**O'Neill 1**	Francis	Birtles	**Woodcock 2**	Robertson	
28 Mar	FL	H	Coventry C	D 3-3	Shilton	Anderson	Bowyer	McGovern	Lloyd	Needham	**O'Neill 3**	Francis	**Birtles 1**	**Woodcock 2**	Robertson	
31 Mar	FL	A	Chelsea	W 6-0	Shilton	Anderson	Bowyer	McGovern	Lloyd	Needham	**O'Neill 1**	**Francis 1**	Birtles	**Woodcock 2**	Robertson	
4 Apr	FL	H	Bolton W	W 4-0 §	Shilton	Anderson	Bowyer	McGovern	Lloyd	Needham	**O'Neill 1**	Gemmill	**Birtles 2**	**Bowyer 1**	**Robertson 1p**	
7 Apr	FL	A	Aston Villa	D 3-3	Shilton	Anderson	Gunn	Bowyer	Needham	Burns	O'Neill	Gemmill	Birtles	Woodcock	Robertson	
11 Apr	ECsf/1	H	Cologne	D 3-3	Shilton	Barrett	Clark*	Bowyer	Lloyd	Burns	**O'Neill 1**	Gemmill	**Birtles 1**	**Francis 1**	**Robertson 1**	
14 Apr	FL	A	Derby Co	D 2-1	Shilton	Anderson	Clark	McGovern	Lloyd	Burns	**O'Neill 1**	Bowyer	**Birtles 1**	Bowyer	Robertson	O'Hare (8)
18 Apr	FL	A	Man Utd	W 1-0	Shilton	Anderson	Barrett	McGovern	Lloyd	Burns	O'Neill	Francis	**Birtles 1**	Francis	Robertson	
21 Apr	FL	H	Birmingham C	W 1-0	Shilton	Anderson	Bowyer	McGovern	Lloyd	Burns	O'Neill	Bowyer	**Birtles 1**	Woodcock	Robertson	
25 Apr	ECsf/2	A	Cologne	W 1-0	Shilton	Anderson	Clark	McGovern	Lloyd	Burns	O'Neill	Francis	**Birtles 1**	Woodcock	Robertson	
28 Apr	FL	A	Liverpool	L 0-1	Shilton	Anderson	Clark	McGovern	Lloyd	Burns	O'Hare	Bowyer	Birtles	Woodcock	Robertson	
2 May	FL	H	Wolves	W 1-0	Shilton	Anderson	Bowyer	McGovern	Lloyd	Burns	Francis	Bowyer	**Birtles 1**	Bowyer	**Robertson 1**	
5 May	FL	H	Southampton	W 2-1	Shilton	Anderson	Clark	McGovern	Lloyd	Burns	O'Neill*	Francis	Birtles	**Woodcock 1**	Robertson	
9 May	FL	A	Norwich C	W 1-0	Shilton	Anderson	Clark	McGovern	Lloyd	Burns	O'Neill	Bowyer	Birtles	**Woodcock 1**	Robertson	
11 May	FL	H	Man City	W 1-0	Shilton	Anderson	Clark	McGovern	Lloyd	Burns	O'Neill	Bowyer	Birtles	**Woodcock 1**	Robertson	Bowyer (7) 1
15 May	F	H	Southampton	W 4-0												
18 May	NCC1	A	Leeds U	W 2-1 §	Shilton	Anderson	Clark*	O'Hare	Lloyd	Burns	**Mills 1**	Francis	Birtles	Bowyer	Robertson	Needham (3)
23 May	EC1	A	WBA	W 1-0	Shilton	Anderson	Bowyer	McGovern	Lloyd	Burns	O'Hare	Bowyer	Birtles	Woodcock	Robertson	
30 May	ECf	H	Malmo	W 1-0	Shilton	Anderson	Clark	McGovern	Lloyd	Burns	**Francis 1**	Francis	Birtles	Woodcock	Robertson	

League Appearances (Goals)
Anderson V 40 (1); Barrett C 11 (1); Birtles G 35 (14); Bowyer I 26+3 (4); Burns K 25; Clark F 20; Elliott S 4; Francis I 19+1 (6); Gemmill A 24 (1); Gunn B 1; Lloyd L 36; McGovern J 36; Mills G 4 (1); Needham D 23+3 (2); O'Hare J 9+3; O'Neill M 28 (10); Robertson J 42 (9); Shilton P 42; Withe P 1; Woodcock A 36 (10); Own goals 2.

Position in League Table

	P	W	D	L	F	A	Pts
1st Liverpool	42	30	8	4	85	16	68
2nd Forest	42	21	18	3	61	26	60

Notes
§ denotes own goals
Aug 12, at Wembley
Aug 16, in Vigo (four team tournament)
Sep 19, 1977-78 County Cup Final, held over from previous season
Feb 21, at Witney
Mar 17, at Wembley
May 30, in Munich

1979-80 Division One

Date	Comp	Venue	Opponent	Result	1	2	3	4	5	6	7	8	9	10	11	Substitutes used
30 Jul	F	A	Holsterbro BK	W 5-1												
1 Aug	F	A	Bayern Munich	L 0-5												
9 Aug	F		Botafogo	W 2-1												
10 Aug	F		Dynamo Bucharest	W 2-1												
14 Aug	F	A	Montpellier	W 1-0												
18 Aug	FL	A	Ipswich T	W 1-0	Shilton	Anderson	Gray	McGovern	Lloyd	Needham	O'Neill	Hartford	Birtles	**Woodcock 1**	Robertson	
22 Aug	FL	H	Stoke C	W 1-0	Shilton	Anderson	Gray	McGovern	Lloyd	Needham	**O'Neill 1**	Hartford *	Birtles	Woodcock	Robertson	Bowyer (8)
25 Aug	FL	H	Coventry C	W 4-1	Shilton	Anderson	Gray	**McGovern 2**	Lloyd	Burns	O'Neill	Hartford	Birtles	**Woodcock 1**	**Robertson 1p**	
29 Aug	FLC2/1	A	Blackburn R	D 1-1	Shilton	Anderson	Gray	McGovern	**Lloyd 1**	Burns	Mills	O'Neill	Bowyer	Woodcock	Robertson	
1 Sep	FL	A	WBA	W 5-1	Shilton	Anderson	**Gray 1**	McGovern	**Lloyd 1**	Burns	O'Neill	Bowyer	**Birtles 3**	Woodcock	Robertson	
5 Sep	FLC2/2	H	Blackburn R	W 6-1	Shilton	Anderson	**Gray 1**	McGovern	Lloyd	Burns	O'Neill	**Bowyer 2**	Birtles	**Woodcock 1**	**Robertson 2(1p)**	
8 Sep	FL	H	Leeds U	D 0-0	Shilton	Anderson	Gray	McGovern	Lloyd	Burns	O'Neill	Bowyer	Birtles	Woodcock	Robertson	
15 Sep	FL	A	Norwich C	L 1-3	Shilton	Anderson	Gray	McGovern	Lloyd	Burns	O'Neill	Bowyer	Birtles	**Woodcock 1**	Robertson	
19 Sep	EC1/1	H	Oesters Vaxjo	W 2-0	Shilton	Anderson	Gray	McGovern	Lloyd	Burns	O'Neill	**Bowyer 2**	Birtles	Woodcock	Robertson	
22 Sep	FL	A	Bristol C	D 1-1	Shilton	Anderson	Gray	McGovern	Lloyd	Burns	**Mills 1**	O'Hare	Birtles	Woodcock	Robertson	
25 Sep	FLC3	A	Middlesbrough	W 3-1	Shilton	Anderson	Gray	McGovern	Lloyd	Burns	Mills *	O'Hare	Birtles	**Woodcock 3**	Robertson	O'Neill (7)
29 Sep	FL	H	Liverpool	W 1-0	Shilton	Anderson	Gray	McGovern	Lloyd	Burns	O'Neill	O'Hare	**Birtles 1**	Woodcock	Robertson	
3 Oct	EC1/2	A	Oesters Vaxjo	D 1-1	Shilton	Anderson	Gray	McGovern	Lloyd	Burns	O'Neill *	Mills	Birtles	**Woodcock 1**	Robertson	Bowyer (7)
6 Oct	FL	H	Wolves	W 3-1	Shilton	Anderson	Gray	McGovern	Lloyd	Burns	**Francis 1**	O'Hare	**Birtles 1**	Woodcock	**Robertson 1p**	
10 Oct	FL	A	Stoke C	D 1-1	Shilton	Anderson	Gray	McGovern	Lloyd	Burns	Francis	Mills	**Birtles 1**	Woodcock	Robertson	
13 Oct	FL	A	Man City	L 0-1	Shilton	Anderson	Gray	McGovern	Lloyd	Burns	Francis	Mills	Birtles	Woodcock	Robertson	
20 Oct	FL	H	Bolton W	W 5-2	Shilton	**Anderson 1**	Gray	McGovern	**Lloyd 1**	Burns	**Francis 1**	Mills *	Birtles	**Woodcock 1**	**Robertson 1p**	Bowyer (8)
24 Oct	EC2/1	H	Arges Pitesti	W 2-0	Shilton	Anderson	Gray	McGovern	Lloyd	Burns	Mills	Bowyer	**Birtles 1**	**Woodcock 1**	Robertson	
27 Oct	FL	A	Tottenham H	L 0-1	Shilton	Anderson	Gray	McGovern	Lloyd	Burns	Mills	Francis	Birtles	Woodcock	Robertson	
30 Oct	FLC4	A	Bristol C	D 1-1	Shilton	Anderson	Gray	McGovern	Lloyd	Burns	**O'Hare 1**	Francis	Birtles	Woodcock	Robertson	
3 Nov	FL	H	Ipswich T	W 2-0	Shilton	Anderson	Gray	McGovern	Lloyd	Burns	**Francis 2**	O'Hare	Birtles *	Woodcock	Robertson	Mills (9)
7 Nov	EC2/2	A	Arges Pitesti	W 2-1	Shilton	Anderson	Gray *	McGovern	Lloyd	Burns	O'Hare *	**Bowyer 1**	**Birtles 1**	Woodcock	Robertson	Gunn (3), Mills (7)
10 Nov	FL	A	Southampton	L 1-4	Shilton	Anderson	Gray	McGovern	Lloyd	Burns *	Francis	Bowyer	**Birtles 1**	Woodcock	Robertson	Needham (6)
12 Nov	F	A	Plymouth A	W 2-1												
14 Nov	FLC4r	H	Bristol C	W 3-0	Shilton	**Anderson 1**	Gray	McGovern	Lloyd	Needham	**O'Neill 1**	Francis	Birtles	**Woodcock 1**	Robertson	
17 Nov	FL	H	Brighton & H A	L 0-1	Shilton	Anderson	Gray	McGovern	Lloyd	Needham	O'Neill	Francis	Birtles	Woodcock *	Robertson	Bowyer (10)
24 Nov	FL	A	Derby Co	L 1-4	Shilton	Anderson	Gray	McGovern	Lloyd	Needham	O'Neill	O'Hare	Birtles	Francis	**Robertson 1p**	
27 Nov	F	A	Cairo Select XI	W 3-1												
1 Dec	FL	H	Arsenal	D 1-1	Shilton	Anderson	Gray	McGovern	Lloyd	Burns	O'Neill	O'Hare	**Birtles 1**	Francis	Robertson	
4 Dec	FLC5	A	West Ham U	D 0-0	Shilton	Anderson	Gray	Bowyer	Lloyd	Burns	O'Neill	O'Hare	Birtles	Francis	Robertson	
8 Dec	FL	A	Crystal Palace	L 0-1	Shilton	Anderson	Gray	Bowyer	Lloyd	Burns	O'Neill	O'Hare	Birtles	Francis	Robertson	
12 Dec	FLC5r	H	West Ham U	W 3-0	Shilton	Anderson	Gray	Bowyer	Lloyd	Burns	**O'Neill 1**	**O'Hare 1**	**Birtles 1**	Francis	Robertson	
18 Dec	F	A	Cologne	D 1-1												
22 Dec	FL	A	Man Utd	L 0-3	Shilton	Anderson	Gray	McGovern	Lloyd	Burns	O'Neill	Bowles	Birtles	Francis	Robertson	
26 Dec	FL	H	Aston Villa	W 2-1	Shilton	Anderson	Gray	McGovern	Lloyd	Burns	Bowyer	**Bowles 1**	Birtles	Francis	**Robertson 1p**	
29 Dec	FL	A	Coventry C	W 3-0	Shilton	Anderson	Gray	McGovern	Lloyd	Burns	Francis	**Bowles 1**	Birtles	Bowyer	**Robertson 2(1p)**	
1 Jan	FL	A	Everton	L 0-1	Shilton	Anderson	Gray	McGovern	Lloyd	Burns	Francis	Bowles	Birtles	Bowyer	Robertson	
5 Jan	FAC3	A	Leeds U	W 4-1	Shilton	Anderson	**Gray 1**	McGovern	Lloyd	Burns	Francis	Bowles	**Birtles 1**	**Bowyer 1**	**Robertson 1**	
8 Jan	F	A	Gravesend	W 6-1												
12 Jan	FL	H	WBA	W 3-1	Shilton	**Anderson 1**	Gray	McGovern	Lloyd	**Needham 1**	O'Neill	Bowles	Birtles	**Francis 1***	Robertson	Mills (10)
19 Jan	FL	A	Leeds U	W 2-1	Shilton	Anderson	Gray	McGovern	Lloyd	Needham	**Francis 1**	George	**Birtles 1**	Bowles	Robertson	
22 Jan	FLCsf/1	H	Liverpool	W 1-0	Shilton	Anderson	Gray	McGovern	Lloyd	Needham	O'Neill	Bowyer	Birtles	Francis	**Robertson 1p**	
26 Jan	FAC4	H	Liverpool	L 0-2	Shilton	Anderson	Gray	McGovern	Lloyd *	Needham	O'Neill	Bowyer	Birtles	Francis	Robertson	Burns (5)
30 Jan	ESC/1	H	Barcelona	W 1-0	Shilton	Anderson	Gray	O'Neill	Lloyd	Burns	Francis	Bowyer	Birtles	**George 1**	Robertson	
5 Feb	ESC/2	A	Barcelona	D 1-1	Shilton	Anderson	Gray	McGovern	Lloyd	**Burns 1**	Francis *	Bowles	Birtles	George	Robertson	
9 Feb	FL	H	Bristol C	D 0-0	Shilton	Anderson	Gunn	McGovern	Lloyd	Burns	O'Neill	Bowles	Birtles	George	Robertson	
12 Feb	FLCsf/2	A	Liverpool	D 1-1	Shilton	Anderson	Gray	McGovern	Lloyd	Burns	O'Neill	Mills	Birtles	Bowyer	**Robertson 1p**	
16 Feb	FL	H	Middlesbrough	D 2-2	Shilton	Anderson	Gray	McGovern	Lloyd	Burns	**O'Neill 1**	Bowles *	Birtles	Francis	**Robertson 1p**	Bowyer (8)
19 Feb	FL	A	Liverpool	L 0-2	Shilton	Anderson	Gray	McGovern	Lloyd	Burns	O'Neill	Bowyer	Birtles	Francis	Robertson	
23 Feb	FL	H	Man City	W 4-0	Shilton	Anderson	Gray	McGovern	Lloyd	**Burns 1**	O'Neill	Bowles	Birtles	**Francis 3**	Robertson	
1 Mar	FL	A	Bolton W	L 0-1	Shilton	Gunn	Gray	McGovern	Lloyd	Burns	O'Neill	Bowles	Birtles	Francis	Robertson	
5 Mar	EC3/1	H	Dynamo Berlin	L 0-1	Shilton	Gunn	Gray	McGovern	Lloyd	Burns	O'Neill	Bowles	Birtles	Francis	Robertson	
11 Mar	FL	H	Tottenham H	W 4-0	Shilton	Anderson	Gray	McGovern	Lloyd	**Burns 2**	**Francis 2**	Bowles *	Birtles	O'Neill	Robertson	Bowyer (8)
15 Mar	FLCf		Wolves	L 0-1	Shilton	Anderson	Gray	McGovern	Needham	Burns	O'Neill	Bowyer	Birtles	Francis	Robertson	
19 Mar	ECsf/2	A	Dynamo Berlin	W 3-1	Shilton	Anderson	Gray	McGovern	Lloyd	Needham	O'Neill	Bowyer	Birtles	**Francis 2**	**Robertson 1p**	
22 Mar	FL	H	Southampton	W 2-0	Shilton	Anderson	Gray	McGovern	Lloyd	Burns	O'Neill	Bowles	**Birtles 1**	Francis	**Robertson 1p**	
29 Mar	FL	A	Brighton & H A	L 0-1	Shilton	Anderson	Gray	McGovern	Lloyd	Burns	O'Neill	Bowles	Birtles	Francis	Robertson	
2 Apr	FL	H	Man Utd	W 2-0	Shilton	Anderson	Gray	McGovern	Lloyd	Burns	O'Neill	Bowles	**Birtles 1**	Francis	**Robertson 1p**	
5 Apr	FL	A	Aston Villa	L 2-3	Shilton	Anderson	Gray	McGovern	Lloyd	Burns	O'Neill	Bowles *	**Birtles 1**	Francis	Robertson	**Bowyer** (8) **1**
9 Apr	ECsf/1	H	Ajax Amsterdam	W 2-0	Shilton	Anderson	Gray	McGovern	Lloyd	Burns	O'Neill	Bowles	Birtles	**Francis 1**	**Robertson 1p**	
11 Apr	F	A	Emirates SC	W 4-0												
13 Apr	F	A	Murrahaq SC	W 8-2												
16 Apr	F	A	Lincoln C	L 1-2												
19 Apr	FL	H	Derby Co	W 1-0	Shilton	Anderson	**Gray 1**	McGovern	Lloyd	Needham	O'Neill	Bowles	Birtles	Francis	Robertson	
23 Apr	ECsf/2	A	Ajax Amsterdam	L 0-1	Shilton	Anderson	Gray	McGovern	Lloyd	Burns	O'Neill	Bowyer	Birtles	Francis	Robertson	
26 Apr	FL	A	Middlesbrough	D 0-0	Shilton	Anderson	Gray	McGovern	Lloyd	Needham	Mills	Bowyer	Birtles	Francis	Robertson	
30 Apr	FL	H	Norwich C	W 2-0 §	Shilton	Anderson	Gray *	McGovern	Lloyd	Burns	Mills	Bowles	Birtles	**Francis 1**	Robertson	
3 May	FL	H	Crystal Palace	W 4-0	Shilton	Anderson	Gray *	McGovern	**Lloyd 1**	Burns	O'Neill	Bowles	Birtles	**Francis 2**	**Robertson 1**	Mills (3)
5 May	FL	A	Arsenal	D 0-0	Shilton	Anderson	Gray	McGovern	Lloyd	Burns	O'Neill	Bowyer	Birtles	Mills	Robertson	
6 May	NCCf	A	Notts Co	W 2-1												
9 May	FL	H	Everton	W 1-0	Shilton	Anderson 1	Gray	McGovern	Lloyd	Burns	O'Neill	Bowles	Birtles *	Mills	Robertson	Bowyer (9)
10 May	F	A	Stade Brestois	W 1-0												
12 May	FL	A	Wolves	L 1-3	Shilton	Anderson	Gray	McGovern	Lloyd	Burns *	**O'Neill 1**	Bowyer	Birtles	O'Hare	Robertson	Needham (6)
16 May	F	H	Leicester C	D 0-0												
28 May	ECf		Hamburg SV	W 1-0	Shilton	Anderson	Gray *	McGovern	Lloyd	Burns	O'Neill	Bowyer	Birtles	Mills *	**Robertson 1**	Gunn (3), O'Hare (10)

League Appearances (Goals)
Anderson V 41 (3);Birtles G 42 (12); Bowles S 19 (2); Bowyer I 12+7 (1); Burns K 34 (3); Francis T 30 (14); George C 2; Gray F 41 (2); Gunn B 2; Hartford A 3; Lloyd L 42 (3); McGovern J 41 (2); Mills G 10+3 (1); Needham D 8+2 (1); O'Hare J 7 (1); O'Neill M 28 (3); Robertson J 42 (11); Shilton P 42; Woodcock A 16 (4); Own goals 1.

Position in League Table

		P	W	D	L	F	A	Pts
1st	Liverpool	42	25	10	7	81	30	60
5th	Forest	42	20	8	14	63	43	48

Notes

§ denotes own goals

Aug 9, Aug 10, in Bilbao (four team tournament)

Mar 15, at Wembley

May 28, in Madrid

1980-81 — Division One

Date	Comp	V	Opponent	Result	1	2	3	4	5	6	7	8	9	10	11	Substitutes used
23 Jul	F	A	Vancouver W'caps	D 1-1												
25 Jul	F	A	Tampa Bay Rowdies	D 0-0												
27 Jul	F	A	Colombia XI	L 0-5												
31 Jul	F	A	Toronto Blizzard	W 3-1												
5 Aug	F	A	P Mulligan XI	W 3-2												
8 Aug	F	A	Alkmaar AZ67	L 1-2												
10 Aug	F	A	Bayern Munich	D 0-0												
11 Aug	F	A	Grasshopper Zurich	D 0-0												
16 Aug	FL	H	Tottenham H	W 2-0	Shilton	Gunn	Gray F	McGovern	Needham	Burns	Ponte	Bowyer	Birtles	Wallace	Robertson	
20 Aug	FL	A	Birmingham C	W 2-1	Shilton	Anderson	Gray F*	McGovern	Needham	Burns	O'Neill	**Ponte**	**Birtles 1**	Wallace	Robertson	**Bowyer (3)**
23 Aug	FL	A	Everton	W 3-0	Shilton	Anderson	**Gray F 1**	O'Hare	Lloyd	Needham	Ponte	Bowyer	Birtles	Wallace	Robertson	
27 Aug	FLC2/1	H	Peterborough U	W 5-0	Shilton	Anderson	Gray F	McGovern	Lloyd	Needham	O'Neill	Bowyer	**Birtles 2**	**Wallace 2**	**Robertson 1**	
30 Aug	FLC2/2	A	Peterborough U	W 0-0	Shilton	Anderson	Gray F	McGovern	Needham	Burns	O'Neill	Bowyer	Birtles	**Mills 1**	**Robertson 1p**	
3 Sep	FL	H	Stoke C	W 5-0	Shilton	Anderson	Gray F	McGovern	Needham	Burns	O'Neill	Bowyer	Birtles	Wallace	Robertson	
6 Sep	FL	A	Middlesbrough	D 0-0	Shilton	Anderson	Gray F	McGovern	Needham	Needham	O'Neill	**Bowyer 1**	**Birtles 1**	**Wallace 1**	Robertson	**Ponte (8)**
8 Sep	FL	H	Notts Co	W 3-2	Shilton	Anderson	Gray F	McGovern	Lloyd	Needham	O'Neill	Bowyer*	Birtles	Wallace*	**Robertson 1p**	**Mills (10) 1**
13 Sep	FL	H	Man City	W 2-0	Shilton	**Anderson 1**	Gray F	McGovern	Needham	Burns	O'Neill	**Ponte 3**	**Birtles 2**	**Mills 1**	Robertson	
17 Sep	EC1/1	H	CSKA Sofia	L 0-1	Shilton	Anderson*	Gray F	McGovern	Lloyd	Burns*	O'Neill	Ponte*	Birtles	Wallace	Robertson	**Bowyer (8); Lloyd (6)**
20 Sep	FL	A	Leicester C	W 5-0	Shilton	Anderson	Gray F	McGovern	Lloyd	Needham	O'Neill	Bowyer	Birtles	**Wallace 1**	Robertson	**Mills (2)**
23 Sep	FLC3	H	Bury	W 7-0	Shilton	Gunn	Gray F	McGovern	Lloyd	Needham	O'Neill	**Bowyer 1**	Birtles	**Wallace 1**	Robertson	
2 Oct	EC1/2	A	CSKA Sofia	L 0-1	Shilton	Gunn	Gray F	McGovern	Lloyd	Burns	O'Neill	Bowyer	**Mills 1**	Mills	Robertson	
4 Oct	FL	H	Man Utd	W 2-1	Shilton	Gunn	Gray F	Ponte	Lloyd	Burns	O'Neill	**Bowyer 1**	**Mills 1**	**Wallace 1**	**Robertson 1**	**Mills (7)**
8 Oct	FL	A	Arsenal	L 0-1	Sutton	Gunn	Gray F	Ponte	Lloyd	Burns	O'Neill	Bowyer	Ward	Wallace	Robertson	
11 Oct	FL	H	Sunderland	D 1-1	Sutton	Gunn	Gray F	McGovern	Lloyd	Burns	O'Neill	Bowyer	Ward	Wallace	**Robertson 1p**	
13 Oct	F	H	Brighton & HA		Sutton	Anderson	Gray F	Ponte	Lloyd	Burns	O'Neill	Bowyer	Ward	Wallace	Robertson	
18 Oct	FL	A	Tampa Bay Rowdies		Shilton	Anderson	Gray F	McGovern	Lloyd	Burns	O'Neill	**Bowyer 1**	**Ward 1**	Wallace	Robertson	**O'Neill (8)**
22 Oct	FL	H	WBA		Shilton	Anderson	Gray F	McGovern	Lloyd	Burns	O'Neill	Bowyer	Birtles	Wallace	Robertson	
25 Oct	FL	A	Leeds U		Shilton	Anderson	Gray F	McGovern	Lloyd	Burns	O'Neill	Bowyer*	**Mills 1**	Mills	Robertson	**Ponte (9)**
28 Oct	FL	H	Norwich C		Shilton	Anderson	Gray F	Gunn	Lloyd	Burns	Mills	**Bowyer 2**	Mills	**Wallace 1**	Robertson*	**Walsh (11)**
1 Nov	FL	A	Watford		Shilton	Anderson	Gray F	McGovern	Needham	Ponte	Mills	Bowyer*	**Ward 1**	**Wallace 1**	**Walsh 1**	**O'Neill (8)**
8 Nov	FL	H	Southampton		Shilton	Anderson	Gray F	Leeds U	Lloyd	Gunn	Mills*	O'Neill	Ward	Walsh	Walsh	
11 Nov	FL	A	Liverpool		Shilton	Anderson	Gunn	McGovern	Lloyd	Burns	O'Neill	Ponte	**Francis 1**	Wallace	Walsh	**Ponte (7)**
15 Nov	FL	H	Birmingham C		Shilton	Anderson	**Gray F 1p**	McGovern	Lloyd	Gunn	O'Neill	**Ponte 1**	**Francis 1**	Walsh	Walsh	
22 Nov	FL	A	Tottenham H		Shilton	Anderson	Gray F	McGovern	Lloyd	Gunn	Mills	**Ponte 1**	**Francis 2**	Walsh	Robertson	
25 Nov	ESC/1	H	Valencia		Shilton	Anderson	Gray F	McGovern	Lloyd	Gunn	Mills	Ponte	Francis	Walsh	Robertson	
29 Nov	FL	A	Coventry C		Shilton	Anderson	Gray F	McGovern	Needham	Burns	Mills	Bowyer	**Francis 1**	Ward	Robertson	**Mills (9)**
6 Dec	F		Grantham													
10 Dec	FL	A	Leeds U		Shilton	Anderson	Gray F	McGovern	Lloyd	Gunn	Mills	Wallace	Francis	Walsh	Robertson	
13 Dec	FL	A	Valencia		Shilton	Anderson	Gunn	McGovern	Lloyd	Burns	O'Neill	Ponte*	Francis	Wallace	Robertson	**Ward (8)**
17 Dec	ESC/2	A	Sunderland	§§	Shilton	Anderson	**Gray F 1p**	Gray S	Lloyd	Gunn	Mills	**Wallace 1**	Francis	Walsh*	**Robertson 1p**	**O'Neill (10)**
20 Dec	FL	H	Wolves		Shilton	Anderson	Gray F	Gray S	Lloyd	Gunn	Mills	Wallace	Francis	**O'Neill 2**	Robertson	**Ponte (7)**
26 Dec	FL	A	Aston Villa		Shilton	Anderson	Gray F	Gray S	Burns	Gunn	Mills	Wallace	Francis	**Walsh 1**	**Robertson 1p**	**Ponte (2)**
27 Dec	FL	H	Bolton W		Shilton	Anderson	Gray F	Gray S	Burns	Gunn	Mills	Wallace	Francis	**Walsh 1**	**Robertson 1p**	**Ward (9)**
1 Jan	FL	A	Bolton W		Shilton	Anderson*	Gray S	Gray S	Burns	Gunn	Mills	Wallace	Francis*	Walsh	Robertson	**Ward (4)**
6 Jan	FL	A	Ipswich T		Shilton	Gunn	Gray F	Gray S	Needham	**Burns 1**	Ponte	**Wallace 1**	**Mills 1**	Walsh	**Robertson 1p**	**Ward (7)**
10 Jan	F	A	Paris St Germain		Shilton	Gunn	Gray F	Gray S	Needham	Burns	Ponte	Wallace*	Mills	Walsh*	**Robertson 1p**	**Ponte (10)**
24 Jan	FL	A	Man Utd		Shilton	Gunn	Gray F	Gray S	Needham	Burns	Mills*	Wallace*	**Mills 1**	Walsh*	Robertson	
31 Jan	FL	H	Everton		Shilton	Anderson	Gray F	Gray S	Needham	Burns	Ponte	Wallace	Francis	Walsh*	Robertson	**Aas (5)**
4 Feb	F	H	Red Star Belgrade		Shilton	Anderson	Gray F	Gray S	Aas	Burns	Ponte	Wallace	Francis	Walsh	Robertson	
7 Feb	WCC	A	Man City		Shilton	Anderson	Gray F	McGovern	Burns	Aas	Mills	Wallace	Francis	Walsh	Robertson	
11 Feb	FAC5		Nacional Montevideo		Shilton	Anderson	Gray S	McGovern	Lloyd	Gunn	O'Neill	Ponte*	Francis	Wallace	Robertson	
18 Feb	FL	H	Bristol C	§	Shilton	Anderson	Gray S	Gray S	Burns	Burns	Mills	**Wallace 1**	Francis	Walsh	**Robertson 1p**	
21 Feb	FL	A	Stoke C		Shilton	Anderson	Gray S	Gray S	**Burns 1**	Gunn	Mills	Wallace	Francis	**Walsh 1**	Robertson	
24 Feb	FL	H	Arsenal		Shilton	Anderson	Gray S	Gray S	**Burns 1**	Gunn	Mills	Wallace	Francis	**O'Neill 1**	Robertson	
28 Feb	FL	A	Leicester C		Shilton	Anderson	Gray F	Gray S	Burns	Gunn	Mills	Wallace	Francis	**Walsh 1**	**Robertson 1p**	
3 Mar	FL	H	Middlesbrough		Shilton	Anderson*	Gray F	Gray S*	Burns	Gunn	Mills	Wallace	**Francis*	Walsh	**Robertson 1p**	
7 Mar	FL	A	Ipswich T		Shilton	Gunn	Gray S	Gray S	Needham	**Burns 1**	Ponte	**Wallace 1**	**Mills 1**	Walsh	**Robertson 1p**	
10 Mar	FAC6r	H	Brighton & HA		Shilton	Gunn	Gray F	Gray S	Needham	Burns	Ponte	Wallace	Mills	Walsh*	**Robertson 1p**	
14 Mar	FL	H	Man Utd		Shilton	Gunn	Gray F	Gray S*	Needham	**Burns 1**	Ponte*	**Wallace 1**	**Mills 1**	Walsh	Robertson	
21 Mar	FL	H	WBA		Smelt	Anderson	Gray F	Gray S	Needham	Burns	**Mills 1**	Wallace	Mills	Walsh*	Robertson	
28 Mar	FL	A	Norwich C		Shilton	Anderson	Gray F	Gray S	Needham*	Burns	Ponte	Wallace*	**Francis 2**	Walsh*	Robertson	
4 Apr	FL	H	Southampton		Shilton	Gunn	Gray F	Gray S	Aas	Burns	Mills	Wallace	Francis	Walsh	Robertson	
11 Apr	F	A	Kettering T		Shilton	Anderson	Gray F	McGovern	Needham	Aas	Mills	Gray S	Francis	Ward	Robertson	
18 Apr	FL		Cardiff C													
20 Apr	FL	H	Aston Villa		Shilton	Gunn	Gunn	McGovern	Needham	Aas	Mills	Ward	**Francis 1**	Gray S	Robertson	
25 Apr	FL	A	Wolves		Shilton	Gray F	Gray F	McGovern	Aas	Gunn	Mills	Ward	Francis	Walsh	Robertson	
4 May	FL	H	Crystal Palace		Shilton	Anderson	Gunn	McGovern	Burns	**Aas 1**	Mills	**Wallace 1**	Francis	**Gray S 1**	Robertson	
10 May	F	A	Real Madrid													
19 May	F	A	Real Mallorca													

League Appearances (Goals)

Aas E 6+1 (1); Anderson V 31; Birtles G 9 (6); Bowyer I 19+2 (3); Burns K 30 (5); Francis T 18 (6); Gray F 40 (3); Gray S 14 (1); Gunn B 26; Lloyd D 17; McGovern J 27; Mills G 23-4 (5); Needham D 17, O'Neill M 21+3 (3); Ponte R 17+4 (3); Robertson J 38 (6); Shilton P (40); Smelt L 1; Sutton S 1; Wallace I 37 (11); Walsh C 15-1 (4); Ward P 14+2 (2); Own goals 3.

Position in League Table

	P	W	D	L	F	A	Pts
1st A Villa	42	26	8	8	72	30	60
7th Forest	42	19	12	11	62	44	50

Notes

§ denotes own goals
Dec 17, lost on away goals
Feb 11, in Tokyo

1981-82 Division One

Date	Venue	Comp	Opponent	Result	1	2	3	4	5	6	7	8	9	10	11	Substitutes used
11 Aug	A	F	Linfield	W 5-1												
20 Aug	A	F	Osasuna Pamplona	W 2-1												
21 Aug	A	F	Real Zaragoza	D 1-1												
25 Aug	A	F	Naples	D 0-0												
29 Aug	A	FL	Southampton	W 2-1	Shilton	Anderson	Gray	McGovern	Burns	Aas	Francis 2	Ward	Fashanu	Proctor	Robertson	
31 Aug	A	FL	Man Utd	D 0-0	Shilton	Anderson	Gray	McGovern	Burns	Aas	Francis	Ward	Fashanu	Proctor	Robertson	
5 Sep	A	FL	Birmingham C	L 3-4	Shilton	Anderson	Gray	McGovern	Burns*	Aas	Mills	Wallace 3	Fashanu	Proctor	Robertson	Gunn (5)
12 Sep	H	FL	WBA	D 0-0	Shilton	Anderson	Gray	McGovern	Burns	Aas	Proctor	Wallace	Fashanu	Mills*	Robertson	Walsh (10)
19 Sep	A	FL	Stoke C	W 2-1	Shilton	Anderson	Gray	McGovern	Burns	Aas	Mills 1	Wallace 1	Fashanu	Proctor	Walsh 1	
23 Sep	A	FL	Sunderland	W 2-0	Shilton	Anderson	Gray	McGovern	Aas	Gunn	Mills	Wallace 1	Fashanu	Proctor	Robertson	
26 Sep	H	FL	Brighton & HA	W 2-1	Shilton	Anderson	Gray	McGovern	Burns 1	Gunn*	Mills	Wallace 2	Fashanu	Proctor	Robertson*	Walsh (11)
3 Oct	H	FL	Tottenham H	L 0-3	Shilton	Anderson	Gray	McGovern	Burns	Gunn*	Proctor 1	Wallace	Fashanu	Walsh	Robertson	Mills (6)
6 Oct	A	FLC2/1	Birmingham C	W 3-2	Shilton	Anderson	Gray	Aas	Aas	Gunn	Proctor	Wallace	Fashanu 1	Walsh*	Robertson	McGovern (10)
10 Oct	A	FL	Middlesbrough	D 1-1	Shilton	Anderson	Gray	Mills	Aas	Gunn	Proctor	Wallace	Fashanu	Walsh*	Robertson	
11 Oct	H	F	Vancouver W'caps	D 2-2												
13 Oct	H	F	Valerengen	W 2-1												
17 Oct	H	FL	Coventry C	W 2-1	Shilton	Anderson	Gunn	McGovern	Needham	Aas	Gray	Wallace 2	Fashanu	Proctor	Robertson*	Walsh (4)
24 Oct	H	FL	Man City	D 0-0	Shilton	Anderson	Gunn	McGovern	Needham	Aas	Proctor	Wallace	Fashanu	Gray	Robertson*	Walsh (11)
28 Oct	H	FLC2/2	Birmingham C	W 2-1	Shilton	Anderson	Gunn	McGovern	Needham 1	Aas	Gray*	Wallace	Fashanu	Proctor	Robertson 1	Walsh (7)
31 Oct	H	FL	Leeds U	W 2-1	Shilton	Anderson	Gunn	McGovern	Needham	Aas	Gray	Ward 1	Fashanu	Proctor	Robertson 1p	
4 Nov	H	F	Grantham	W 5-2												
7 Nov	A	FL	West Ham U	D 0-0	Shilton	Anderson	Gunn	McGovern	Needham	Aas*	Gray	Wallace	Ward	Proctor	Robertson	Walsh (6)
11 Nov	H	FLC3	Blackburn R	W 1-0	Shilton	Anderson	Gunn	McGovern	Needham	Aas	Gray	Ward	Ward	Proctor*	Robertson	Walsh (10)
21 Nov	H	FL	Arsenal	L 1-2	Shilton	Anderson	Gunn	McGovern	Needham	Aas*	Gray	Ward	Fashanu	Proctor	Robertson	Mills (6)
25 Nov	A	FL	Sunderland	W 3-2	Shilton	Anderson	Gunn	Gray	Needham 1	Gunn	Walsh 1	Ward	Fashanu 1	Walsh 1	Robertson*	Proctor (5)
28 Nov	A	FL	Aston Villa	L 1-3	Shilton	Anderson	Gray	Proctor	Fairclough	Gunn	Roeber 1*	Wallace 1	Fashanu	Walsh	Robertson*	Mills (7)
2 Dec	H	FLC4	Tranmere R	W 2-0	Shilton	Mills	Gray	Proctor	Anderson	Gunn	Roeber	Wallace	Fashanu	Walsh	Robertson	
5 Dec	H	FL	Liverpool	L 0-2	Shilton	Anderson	Gunn	Needham	Young 1	Gray	Roeber	Wallace	Fashanu	Proctor	Robertson 1p	
12 Dec	A	FL	Swansea C	W 2-1	Shilton	Anderson	Gunn	Needham	Young	Walsh	Roeber*	Wallace	Ward	Proctor	Robertson	McGovern (7)
29 Dec	A	F	Rotherham U	L 0-2												
2 Jan	H	FAC3	Wrexham	L 1-3	Shilton	Anderson	Gunn	Needham	Young	Walsh*	McGovern	McGovern	Ward 1	Gray	Robertson	McGovern (7)
4 Jan	H	F	Luton T	W 5-1												
9 Jan	A	FL	Birmingham C	W 2-1	Shilton	Anderson	Gray*	Gunn	Young	Roeber	McGovern	Wallace	Ward	Proctor	Robertson	Bowyer (6)
15 Jan	A	F	Torquay U	L 1-2												
18 Jan	H	FLC5	Tottenham H	L 0-1	Shilton	Proctor	Gray*	McGovern	Walsh	Roeber	Gray	Wallace	Ward	Proctor	Robertson	Roeber (3)
23 Jan	H	FL	Notts Co	L 0-2	Shilton	Gunn	Gray*	McGovern	Walsh*	Young	Gray	Wallace	Ward	Bowyer	Robertson	
26 Jan	A	F	Scunthorpe U	W 2-0												
30 Jan	H	FL	Stoke C	D 0-0	Shilton	Anderson	Bowyer	Gunn	Young	McGovern	Roeber	Wallace	Fashanu	Proctor	Robertson	Ward (8) 1
6 Feb	A	FL	Norwich C	L 1-2	Shilton	Anderson	Gray	Gunn	Young	McGovern	Roeber	Wallace*	Fashanu	Bowyer	Robertson	Gray (8)
13 Feb	A	FL	WBA	D 0-0	Shilton	Anderson	Gunn	Needham	Young	Bowyer	Mills	Roeber*	Ward	Ward	Robertson	
16 Feb	A	FL	Coventry C	W 1-0	Shilton	Anderson	Gunn	Gray	Young	Needham	Mills	Wallace	Ward	Bowyer	Robertson	
20 Feb	H	FL	Brighton & HA	L 0-1	Shilton	Anderson	Gunn	McGovern	Young	Needham	Proctor	Plummer	Ward 1	Bowyer	Walsh*	Wallace (11)
27 Feb	H	FL	Middlesbrough	D 1-1	Shilton	Anderson	Bowyer	McGovern	Young	Gunn	Roeber	Plummer	Ward	Bowyer	Walsh*	
5 Mar	A	FL	Norwich C	W 1-0	Shilton	Anderson	Bowyer	McGovern	Young	Gunn	Roeber	Wallace	Fashanu	Proctor	Gray	
9 Mar	A	FL	Coventry C	L 0-1	Shilton	Anderson	Bowyer	McGovern	Young	Gunn	Mills	Wallace	Fashanu	Proctor	Gray*	Fashanu (11)
13 Mar	H	FL	Man City	D 1-1	Shilton	Anderson	Bowyer	McGovern	Young	Gunn	Plummer*	Wallace	Ward	Proctor	Roeber	
17 Mar	H	FL	Ipswich T	L 0-1	Shilton	Anderson	Bowyer	McGovern	Young	Gunn	Roeber 1	Roeber 1	Ward 1p	Plummer	Plummer	
27 Mar	H	FL	West Ham U	W 1-0	Shilton	Anderson	Bowyer	Gunn	Young	Gray	Roeber	Wallace 1	Fashanu*	Proctor	Robertson*	Wallace (11)
3 Apr	A	FL	Everton	L 0-1	Shilton	Gunn	Bowyer	McGovern	Young	Gray	Roeber	Wallace	Fashanu	Proctor	Robertson	
10 Apr	H	FL	Wolves	W 2-0	Shilton	Kendal	Bowyer	Gunn	Young	Gray	Roeber	Plummer 1	Plummer 1	Proctor	Robertson*	
12 Apr	A	FL	Notts Co	L 1-2	Shilton	Anderson	Gray	Gunn	Young	Bowyer 1	Roeber	Plummer	Fashanu	Proctor	Robertson	Plummer (9)
17 Apr	H	FL	Arsenal	D 1-1	Shilton	Anderson	Gunn	Needham	Young	Bowyer	Roeber 1	Plummer*	Fashanu	Proctor	Robertson	Plummer (10)
20 Apr	H	FL	Everton	L 0-2	Shilton	Anderson	Gunn	Needham	Young	Bowyer	Roeber	Proctor	Fashanu	Proctor	Robertson*	McGovern (3)
24 Apr	A	FL	Aston Villa	L 0-1	Shilton	Anderson	Gunn	Needham	Young*	Bowyer	Roeber	Proctor	Fashanu	Wallace	Robertson	McGovern (8)
1 May	H	FL	Liverpool	L 0-2	Sutton	Anderson	Gunn	Needham	Young	Bowyer	Roeber	Proctor*	Davenport	Wallace	Robertson	McGovern (5)
5 May	A	FL	Swansea C	L 0-2	Shilton	Anderson	Gunn	Needham	Young	Bowyer	Roeber	Proctor*	Davenport	Wallace	Robertson	Walsh (8)
8 May	H	FL	Tottenham H	L 1-2	Shilton	Anderson	Gray	Gunn	Young	Gray 1	Proctor	Roeber	Fashanu*	Davenport 1	Robertson	Walsh (8)
12 May	H	FL	Ipswich T	W 3-1	Shilton	Bowyer	Bowyer	Gunn	Young	Gray	Roeber	McGovern	Hodge*	Davenport 3	Robertson	Proctor (9)
15 May	H	NCCf	Notts Co	W 7-0												
18 May	A	F	Burton A	W 7-1												
19 May	A	F	Kuwait XI	W 7-0												
22 May		F		D 1-1												

League Appearances (Goals)
Aas E 14; Anderson V 39; Bowyer J 23+1 (1); Burns K 7 (1); Davenport P 5 (4); Fashanu J 31+1 (3); Francis T 2 (2); Gray S 32+1 (2); Gunn B 36+1; Hodge S 1; Kendal S 1; McGovern J 26+4; Mills G 13+1 (1); Needham D 17 (2); Plummer C 7+2 (2); Proctor M 35+2 (1); Roeber H 21+1 (3); Robertson J 36 (2); Shilton P 41; Sutton S 1; Wallace I 28+1 (9); Walsh P 14+1 (5); Young W 25 (1).

Position in League Table

	P	W	D	L	F	A	Pts
1st Liverpool	42	26	9	7	80	32	87
12th Forest	42	15	12	15	42	48	57

Three points awarded for a win

Notes
Dec 29, in Guernsey
May 22, in Morocco

1982-83 — Division One

Date	Comp	Venue	Opponent	Result	1	2	3	4	5	6	7	8	9	10	11	Substitutes used
31 Jul	F	A	Malaysia Select	W 3-0												
7 Aug	F	A	Athletic Bilbao	L 1-3												
8 Aug	F	A	Vojvodina Novi Sad	L 1-2												
13 Aug	F	A	Dukla Prague	W 2-0												
14 Aug	F	A	Nuremburg	W 4-2												
21 Aug	F	A	Athletic Bilbao	W 3-1												
22 Aug	F	A	Recreat de Huelva	W 1-0												
28 Aug	FL	A	West Ham U	W 2-1	Sutton	Anderson	Bowyer	Proctor*	Young	Todd	Hodge	Wallace	Plummer	Walsh 1	Robertson 1p	Gunn (4)
1 Sep	FL	H	Man Utd	W 3-0	Sutton	Anderson	Bowyer	Proctor	Young	Todd	Hodge	Wallace	Plummer	Walsh	Robertson 1p	Hodge (9)
4 Sep	FL	A	Liverpool	L 0-3	Van Breukelen	Anderson	Bowyer	Proctor	Fairclough	Todd	Plummer	Wallace	Birtles*	Walsh 1	Robertson 1p	Proctor (6)
7 Sep	FL	A	Aston Villa	L 3-4	Van Breukelen	Anderson	Bowyer	Todd	Young	Fairclough*	Hodge	Hodge	Davenport 1	Walsh	Robertson 1p	Ward (6)
11 Sep	FL	H	Watford	W 1-4	Van Breukelen	Anderson	Gunn	Fairclough	Young	Gray*	Bowyer	Wallace*	Birtles 1	Wallace	Robertson	Ward (8)
18 Sep	FL	H	Tottenham H	W 1-0	Van Breukelen	Anderson	Gunn	Fairclough	Fairclough	Todd	Proctor	Wallace 2	Birtles 1	Walsh	Bowyer 1	Bowyer (7)
25 Sep	FL	H	Stoke C	W 1-4	Van Breukelen	Anderson	Gunn	Proctor	Fairclough	Todd	Hodge 1*	Wallace 1	Birtles 1	Walsh*	Robertson 2p	Bowyer (5)
2 Oct	FL	A	WBA	L 1-4	Van Breukelen	Swain	Gunn	Proctor	Fairclough	Todd	Hodge 1	Wallace 2	Birtles	Walsh	Robertson	Proctor (5)
6 Oct	FLC2/1	H	WBA	W 6-1	Van Breukelen	Anderson	Gunn	Bowyer	Fairclough	Todd	Hodge 1	Wallace 1	Birtles	Walsh*	Robertson	Bowyer (10)
9 Oct	FL	H	Birmingham C	W 1-2	Van Breukelen	Swain	Gunn	Proctor	Fairclough	Todd	Hodge 1	Wallace	Birtles	Walsh*	Robertson	Wigley (10)
16 Oct	FL	A	Leicester C	D 1-1	Van Breukelen	Swain	Gunn	Proctor	Young	Todd	Hodge	Wallace 1	Birtles	Walsh*	Robertson	Plummer (7)
20 Oct	F	A	WBA	L 2-1												
23 Oct	FL	A	Luton T	D 2-0	Van Breukelen	Swain	Gunn	Todd	Fairclough	Bowyer	Proctor 1	Wallace 1	Birtles 1	Walsh 1*	Robertson	Wigley (10)
27 Oct	FLC2/2	A	A1-Qadsiya	W 3-0	Van Breukelen	Swain	Gunn	Todd	Fairclough	Bowyer	Proctor*	Wallace	Birtles 1	Wigley	Robertson	Walsh (4)
30 Oct	FL	A	Al-Hilal	L 1-3	Van Breukelen	Swain	Gunn 1	Todd	Young	Bowyer	Proctor	Wallace 1	Birtles	Hodge	Robertson	Fairclough (6)
3 Nov	F	H	Arsenal	W 2-0												
6 Nov	FL	A	Ipswich T	D 1-1	Van Breukelen	Swain	Gunn	Todd*	Young 1	Bowyer 1	Proctor 2	Wallace 1	Birtles 2	Hodge	Robertson 1p	Fairclough (6)
10 Nov	FLC3	H	Watford	W 8-0	Van Breukelen	Swain	Gunn	Gunn	Young	Walsh*	Proctor	Wallace	Birtles	Hodge	Robertson	Walsh (7)
13 Nov	FL	A	Southampton	W 2-1 §	Van Breukelen	Swain	Bowyer	Gunn	Young	Bowyer	Proctor	Wallace 1	Birtles 2	Hodge	Robertson	Walsh (7)
15 Nov	F	H	Poole T	W 7-3												
20 Nov	FL	A	Sunderland	D 1-1	Van Breukelen	Swain	Bowyer	Gunn	Young 1	Walsh*	Proctor	Wallace 1	Birtles 1	Hodge	Robertson	Davenport (11)
27 Nov	FL	H	Man City	W 4-3	Van Breukelen	Swain	Gunn	Todd	Young 1	Bowyer	Proctor*	Wallace 1	Birtles	Hodge	Robertson	
1 Dec	FLC4	H	Brentford	W 1-0	Sutton	Swain	Bowyer	Gunn	Young 1	Walsh 1	Proctor	Wallace 1	Birtles 2	Hodge	Robertson	Davenport (11)
4 Dec	FL	A	Notts Co	W 3-0	Van Breukelen	Swain	Gunn	Gunn	Young	Bowyer	Proctor*	Wallace	Birtles	Hodge	Robertson	
6 Dec	F	A	Stamford	W 2-0												
11 Dec	FL	H	Swansea C	L 2-3	Sutton	Swain	Bowyer	Gunn	Young	Walsh 1	Proctor 1	Wallace 1	Birtles	Hodge	Robertson*	Gray (7)
13 Dec	F	A	Malta XI	W 8-2												
18 Dec	FL	H	Norwich C	W 2-1	Sutton	Swain	Bowyer	Gunn	Young	Bowyer	Proctor	Wallace	Birtles*	Hodge	Robertson*	Fairclough (7)
27 Dec	FL	A	Coventry C	L 1-3	Sutton	Swain	Gunn	Todd*	Young	Walsh	Proctor*	Wallace	Davenport	Hodge	Walsh	
28 Dec	FL	H	Everton	D 1-1	Sutton	Swain	Gunn	Todd*	Young	Bowyer	Proctor*	Wallace	Davenport	Hodge	Robertson*	Wilson (6)
1 Jan	FL	H	Sunderland	D 0-0	Sutton	Swain	Gunn	Gunn	Young	Walsh	Robertson*	Wallace	Davenport	Hodge	Walsh	Davenport (9) 1
3 Jan	FL	A	Brighton & HA	L 0-1	Sutton	Swain	Bowyer	Todd	Young	Bowyer	Wilson 1	Wallace	Birtles	Proctor	Walsh	Davenport (9)
8 Jan	FAC3	A	Derby Co	L 0-1	Sutton	Swain	Gunn	Anderson	Young	Bowyer	Proctor	Wallace	Birtles	Hodge	Walsh	
15 Jan	FL	H	West Ham U	L 0-2	Sutton	Swain	Swain	Todd	Young	Wilson	Wilson	Wallace	Birtles	Hodge	Walsh	Davenport (11)
19 Jan	FLC5	A	Man Utd	W 1-2	Sutton	Anderson	Swain	Todd	Young	Bowyer	Wilson	Wallace	Birtles	Hodge	Walsh	Robertson (11)
22 Jan	FL	A	Palma Mallorca	L 0-2	Sutton	Anderson	Swain	Stoke	Young	Bowyer	Wilson*	Wallace	Birtles*	Hodge	Walsh	Smalley (3)
2 Feb	F	H	Aston Villa	W 1-2												
5 Feb	FL	H	WBA	D 0-0	Sutton	Swain	Gunn	Todd	Young	Bowyer	Proctor	Wallace	Birtles	Proctor	Walsh	Wigley (7)
19 Feb	FL	H	Birmingham C	D 1-1	Sutton	Swain	Gunn	Anderson	Young	Bowyer	Wilson	Wallace	Birtles	Hodge	Walsh	Walsh (7)
26 Feb	FL	A	Arsenal	D 0-0	Sutton	Anderson	Swain	Todd	Young	Bowyer	Wilson	Wallace	Birtles*	Hodge	Walsh	
5 Mar	FL	H	Algeria XI	L 0-1	Sutton	Anderson	Swain	Todd	Young	Bowyer	Wilson	Wallace	Birtles	Hodge	Walsh	
8 Mar	F	A	Luton T	L 0-1	Sutton	Anderson	Swain	Todd	Young	Bowyer	Proctor	Wallace	Davenport	Proctor	Walsh*	
12 Mar	FL	H	Stoke C	L 0-2	Van Breukelen	Anderson	Swain*	Gunn	Fairclough	Bowyer	Wilson	Wallace	Birtles	Hodge	Walsh*	
16 Mar	FL	A	Ipswich T	W 1-2	Sutton	Anderson	Swain	Stoke	Fairclough	Bowyer	Wilson	Hodge	Birtles	Davenport	Robertson	Davenport (11)
19 Mar	FL	A	Southampton	L 1-2	Van Breukelen	Anderson	Bowyer	Gunn	Fairclough	Walsh	Wilson*	Wallace	Davenport	Davenport	Robertson	Smalley (3)
26 Mar	FL	H	Everton	D 2-2	Van Breukelen	Anderson	Swain	Todd	Young	Bowyer	Fairclough	Wallace	Davenport	Davenport	Robertson	Wigley (7)
2 Apr	FL	H	Coventry C	W 2-1	Van Breukelen	Anderson	Swain	Gunn	Young	Bowyer	Walsh	Wallace 1	Davenport 1	Hodge 1	Robertson 1p	Wigley (7)
5 Apr	FL	A	Tottenham H	D 3-1	Van Breukelen	Anderson	Swain	Gunn	Young	Bowyer 1	Walsh	Wallace	Davenport	Hodge	Robertson	Walsh (7)
9 Apr	FL	H	Watford	D 0-0	Van Breukelen	Anderson	Swain	Gunn	Young	Bowyer 1	Walsh	Wallace	Davenport 1	Hodge 1	Robertson	
19 Apr	FL	A	Grimsby T	W 1-2	Van Breukelen	Anderson	Swain 1	Gunn	Young	Bowyer	Proctor 1	Wallace	Davenport 1	Proctor	Robertson	
23 Apr	FL	H	Notts Co	W 2-1	Van Breukelen	Anderson	Swain	Gunn	Young	Bowyer	Hodge	Wallace 1	Davenport 1	Hodge	Robertson	
24 Apr	F	A	Darlington	W 3-1	Van Breukelen	Anderson	Swain	Gunn	Young	Bowyer 1	Hodge	Wallace	Davenport 1	Walsh	Robertson	
25 Apr	F	H	Gateshead	W 2-1	Van Breukelen	Anderson	Swain	Gunn	Young	Bowyer 1	Hodge	Wallace	Davenport	Walsh	Robertson	
30 Apr	FL	A	Huddersfield T	W 1-0	Van Breukelen	Anderson 1	Swain	Gunn	Young	Bowyer	Proctor 1	Wallace 2	Davenport	Walsh 1	Robertson	
2 May	FL	H	Man City	W 2-2	Van Breukelen	Anderson	Swain	Gunn	Young	Bowyer	Hodge	Wallace	Davenport	Walsh	Robertson	
7 May	FL	A	Liverpool	W 5-1	Van Breukelen	Anderson	Swain	Gunn	Young	Bowyer 1	Hodge	Wallace 1	Davenport 1	Walsh	Robertson	
10 May	FL	H	Norwich C	D 2-2	Van Breukelen	Anderson	Swain	Gunn	Young	Bowyer	Hodge	Wallace	Davenport	Walsh 1	Robertson	
14 May	F	A	Kettering T	W 3-0	Van Breukelen	Anderson	Swain	Gunn	Young	Bowyer	Hodge	Wallace 2	Davenport	Walsh	Robertson	Wigley (9)
18 May	NCCf	H	Swansea C	W 4-3												
27 May	F	A	Manic de Montreal	W 4-3												
29 May	F	A	Toronto Blizzard	L 1-2												

League Appearances (Goals)
Anderson V 25 (1); Birtles G 25 (7); Bowyer I 39+1 (4); Davenport P 15+3 (6); Fairclough C 12-3; Gray S 2; Gunn B 32+1 (1); Hodge S 38+1 (8); Plummer C 3; Proctor M 25+2 (4); Robertson J 33+1 (6); Smalley M 0+1; Sutton S 17; Swain K 32 (1); Todd C 23; Van Breukelen H 25; Wallace I 41 (13); Walsh C 32+5 (5); Ward P 0+2; Wigley S 0+4; Wilson D 9+1 (1); Young W 34 (4); Own goals 1.

Position in League Table

	P	W	D	L	F	A	Pts
1st Liverpool	42	24	10	8	87	37	82
5th Forest	42	20	9	13	62	50	69

Notes
§ denotes own goal
Aug 7, Aug 8, in La Linea
Aug 13, in Nuremburg
Aug 21, in Huelva

1983-84 — Division One

Date	Comp	V	Opponent	R	Score	1	2	3	4	5	6	7	8	9	10	11	Substitutes used
5 Aug	F	A	Utrecht	L	0-1												
7 Aug	F	A	Romania XI	W	2-0												
10 Aug	F	A	Groningen	L	1-2												
12 Aug	F	A	Club Brugge	D	1-1												
14 Aug	F	A	Real Zaragoza	L	1-2												
20 Aug	F	A	Swansea C	W	3-1 §												
23 Aug	F	A	Barcelona	L	0-2												
24 Aug	F	A	Anderlecht	L	2-4												
27 Aug	FL	H	Southampton	L	0-1	Van Breukelen	Anderson	Swain	Todd	Hart	Bowyer	Walsh *	Wallace	Birtles	Hodge	Davenport	Wigley (7)
29 Aug	FL	A	Liverpool	W	2-1	Van Breukelen	Anderson 1	Swain	Todd	Hart	Bowyer	Walsh	Wallace	Birtles	Hodge	Davenport 1	
3 Sep	FL	H	Aston Villa	L	1-2	Van Breukelen	Anderson	Swain	Todd	Hart	Bowyer	Walsh	Wallace	Birtles	Hodge	Davenport	
7 Sep	FL	H	QPR	D	2-2	Van Breukelen	Anderson	Swain	Todd	Fairclough	Bowyer	Walsh	Wallace	Birtles 1	Hodge 1	Wigley	Wigley (7)
10 Sep	FL	A	Sunderland	W	3-2 §	Van Breukelen	Anderson	Swain	Todd	Hart	Bowyer	Walsh *	Wallace 1	Davenport *	Hodge 1	Wigley	Gunn (9)
14 Sep	UC1/1	H	Vorwaerts	W	2-0	Van Breukelen	Anderson	Swain *	Todd	Fairclough	Bowyer	Walsh 3 *	Wallace 1	Birtles	Wigley	Walsh	Smalley (7)
17 Sep	FL	H	Norwich C	W	3-2	Van Breukelen	Anderson	Swain	Todd	Hart	Bowyer 1	Wigley	Wallace	Birtles	Hodge	Walsh *	
24 Sep	FL	A	Luton T	W	1-0	Van Breukelen	Anderson	Swain *	Todd	Hart	Bowyer	Wigley	Wallace	Birtles	Hodge	Walsh 1	
28 Sep	UC1/2	A	Vorwaerts	W	1-0	Van Breukelen	Anderson	Swain	Todd	Hart	Bowyer	Wigley	Davenport	Birtles	Hodge	Walsh	Gunn (3), Wilson (11)
2 Oct	FL	A	Tottenham H	L	1-2	Van Breukelen	Anderson	Swain	Todd	Hart	Bowyer 1	Wigley	Wallace	Birtles	Thijssen	Hodge	Fairclough (11)
4 Oct	FLC2/1	H	Wimbledon	W	2-0	Van Breukelen	Anderson	Swain	Todd	Hart	Bowyer	Wigley	Wallace	Davenport 1	Walsh 1p	Thijssen 1p	Walsh (10)
11 Oct	F	H	Derby Co		1-4	Sutton	Anderson	Swain	Todd	Hart	Bowyer	Wigley	Wallace	Davenport 1	Thijssen 1	Thijssen *	Fairclough (7), Birtles (8)
16 Oct	FL	H	Notts Co	W	3-1	Sutton	Anderson	Swain	Todd	Fairclough	Bowyer	Wigley *	Davenport	Davenport 1p	Walsh	Hodge	Walsh (10)
19 Oct	UC2/1	A	PSV Eindhoven		1-1	Sutton	Anderson	Swain	Todd	Hart	Bowyer	Wigley *	Davenport 1	Davenport	Thijssen *	Hodge	Walsh (10)
22 Oct	FL	H	Arsenal	W	5-0	Sutton	Anderson	Swain	Fairclough	Hart	Bowyer	Wigley	Davenport 1	Birtles 1	Walsh	Hodge 2	Wallace (8)
26 Oct	FLC2/2	A	Wimbledon		0-1	Sutton	Anderson	Swain	Fairclough	Hart *	Bowyer	Wigley	Davenport	Birtles	Thijssen	Hodge	
29 Oct	FL	H	Sunderland		2-1	Sutton	Anderson	Swain 1	Fairclough	Hart	Bowyer 1	Wigley	Thijssen 1	Birtles 1	Thijssen	Walsh	
2 Nov	UC2/2	H	PSV Eindhoven		1-1	Van Breukelen	Anderson	Swain	Fairclough	Hart	Bowyer	Wigley	Davenport	Birtles	Davenport	Walsh 1p	Wallace (5)
5 Nov	FL	A	Wolves		5-0	Van Breukelen	Anderson	Swain	Fairclough	Hart	Bowyer	Wigley *	Davenport	Birtles 2	Davenport	Walsh 1p	Wallace (7)
9 Nov	FL	H	Everton		0-1	Van Breukelen	Anderson	Swain	Fairclough	Hart	Bowyer	Wigley	Hodge	Birtles 1	Walsh	Hodge 1	Wallace (7)
19 Nov	FL	H	Ipswich T		2-1	Van Breukelen	Anderson	Swain	Fairclough	Hart	Bowyer 1	Wigley	Hodge 1	Birtles	Davenport 1	Walsh 1p	Wallace (7)
23 Nov	UC3/1	A	Celtic		0-0	Van Breukelen	Anderson	Swain	Fairclough	Hart *	Bowyer	Wigley	Davenport	Birtles	Davenport	Walsh 1	Wallace (7)
26 Nov	FL	H	Stoke C		1-1	Van Breukelen	Anderson	Swain	Fairclough	Fairclough	Bowyer	Wigley	Davenport	Birtles 2	Walsh	Walsh	Wigley (9)
4 Dec	FL	A	Leicester C		3-2	Van Breukelen	Anderson	Swain	Fairclough	Hart	Bowyer 1	Wigley	Hodge	Birtles 1 *	Hodge 1	Walsh 1	Wigley (9)
10 Dec	UC3/2	H	Celtic		2-1	Van Breukelen	Anderson	Swain	Fairclough	Hart *	Bowyer	Wigley *	Hodge	Birtles 1 *	Hodge	Hodge	
17 Dec	FL	A	Watford		3-0	Van Breukelen	Anderson	Swain	Fairclough	Hart	Bowyer	Thijssen 1	Wallace	Birtles 1 *	Walsh	Walsh	Davenport (9)
26 Dec	FL	A	West Ham U		3-0	Van Breukelen	Anderson	Swain	Fairclough	Hart	Bowyer	Thijssen	Wallace	Birtles	Hodge 1	Walsh	Wigley (7)
28 Dec	FL	H	Birmingham C		3-0	Van Breukelen	Anderson 1	Swain	Fairclough	Hart	Bowyer 1	Thijssen *	Wallace	Birtles	Hodge	Walsh	Wigley (7)
31 Dec	FL	H	Coventry C		3-2	Van Breukelen	Anderson 1	Swain	Fairclough	Hart	Bowyer	Thijssen * *	Wallace	Birtles	Hodge	Walsh	Wigley (8)
2 Jan	FL	A	Liverpool		1-2	Van Breukelen	Anderson	Swain	Fairclough	Hart 1	Bowyer	Thijssen	Wallace	Birtles	Hodge	Walsh	
7 Jan	FAC3	A	Luton T		1-0	Van Breukelen	Anderson	Swain	Fairclough	Hart	Bowyer	Wigley	Davenport	Birtles	Hodge	Walsh *	Wallace (7)
21 Jan	FL	A	Southampton		3-0	Van Breukelen	Anderson	Swain	Fairclough	Hart	Bowyer	Wigley	Davenport	Birtles	Davenport	Walsh	
23 Jan	FL	A	Norwich C		5-0	Van Breukelen	Anderson	Swain	Fairclough	Hart	Bowyer	Wigley	Davenport	Birtles	Davenport	Walsh 1p	Walker (9)
29 Jan	F	A	Oman Select XI		5-0	Van Breukelen	Anderson	Swain	Fairclough	Hart	Bowyer	Wigley	Hodge	Davenport	Hodge	Hodge	
31 Jan	F	A	Oman Select XI		5-0												
4 Feb	FL	H	Tottenham H		2-0 §	Van Breukelen	Anderson	Swain	Fairclough	Hart	Bowyer 1	Thijssen	Wallace	Birtles 1	Hodge 1	Walsh 1p	Davenport (9)
8 Feb	FL	A	QPR		5-0	Van Breukelen	Anderson 1	Swain	Fairclough	Hart	Bowyer	Thijssen *	Wallace	Birtles 1	Hodge 1	Walsh	Wigley (7)
11 Feb	FL	H	Sunderland		0-1	Van Breukelen	Anderson	Swain	Fairclough	Hart	Bowyer	Thijssen * *	Wallace	Birtles	Hodge	Walsh	
18 Feb	FL	A	Arsenal		0-1	Van Breukelen	Anderson	Swain	Fairclough	Hart	Bowyer	Thijssen	Wallace	Birtles	Hodge	Walsh	
25 Feb	FL	H	Wolves		1-0	Walker	Anderson *	Swain	Fairclough	Hart	Bowyer	Wigley	Wallace *	Birtles	Hodge	Walsh *	
3 Mar	UC4/1	A	Raika Sturm Graz		1-0	Van Breukelen	Walker	Swain	Fairclough	Hart	Bowyer	Wigley	Davenport	Birtles	Hodge	Walsh *	Gunn (2), Davenport (11)
14 Mar	FL	A	Everton		0-1	Van Breukelen	Walker	Swain	Fairclough	Hart	Bowyer	Wigley	Davenport	Birtles	Hodge	Walsh *	Wallace (11)
17 Mar	UC4/2	H	Raika Sturm Graz		0-0	Van Breukelen	Anderson	Swain	Fairclough	Hart	Bowyer	Thijssen	Wallace	Birtles	Hodge	Walsh 1p	
21 Mar	FL	A	Aston Villa		3-1	Van Breukelen	Anderson 1	Swain	Fairclough	Hart	Bowyer 1	Wigley	Mills	Davenport	Hodge	Walsh 1p	Walker (9)
24 Mar	FL	A	Notts Co		0-0	Van Breukelen	Anderson	Swain	Fairclough	Hart	Bowyer	Wigley	Mills	Birtles	Hodge 2	Walsh 1p	Riley (8)
31 Mar	FL	H	WBA		2-0	Van Breukelen	Anderson	Swain	Fairclough	Hart	Bowyer	Wigley 1	Mills	Davenport	Hodge	Walsh	
4 Apr	FL	A	Anderlecht		2-2	Van Breukelen	Anderson	Gunn	Walker	Hart	Bowyer	Wigley 1	Wallace 1	Davenport 1	Thijssen	Walsh 1	Mills (10)
11 Apr	UCsf/1	H	Ipswich T		1-1	Van Breukelen	Anderson	Swain	Fairclough	Hart	Bowyer 1	Wigley	Davenport	Davenport 2	Hodge	Walsh 1	Birtles (10)
14 Apr	FL	A	Birmingham C		2-2	Van Breukelen	Anderson	Swain	Fairclough	Hart	Bowyer	Wigley	Davenport	Davenport 1	Thijssen *	Walsh 1	Birtles (10)
21 Apr	UCsf/2	A	Coventry C		5-1	Van Breukelen	Anderson 1	Swain	Fairclough	Hart	Bowyer	Wigley	Wallace	Davenport	Mills *	Walsh	
25 Apr	F	H	Stoke C		0-3	Van Breukelen	Anderson	Swain	Fairclough	Hart	Bowyer	Wigley	Hodge	Davenport	Mills *	Davenport	
28 Apr	F	A	Trakia Plovdiv		1-2	Van Breukelen	Anderson	Swain	Fairclough	Hart	Bowyer	Wigley	Davenport 1	Birtles	Hodge	Mills	Mills (9)
1 May	FL	A	Leicester C		5-1 §	Van Breukelen	Anderson	Swain	Fairclough	Hart	Bowyer 1	Wigley	Davenport 2	Birtles *	Hodge	Walsh	
5 May	FL	A	Watford		2-0	Van Breukelen	Anderson	Swain	Fairclough	Hart	Bowyer	Wigley	Davenport 1	Birtles 1	Hodge	Walsh	
9 May	FL	H	West Ham U		2-0	Van Breukelen	Anderson 1	Swain	Gunn	Hart	Bowyer	Wigley	Wallace	Birtles 1	Davenport	Walsh	
12 May	FL	A	Man Utd		4-1												
16 May	FL	H	Mansfield T		3-0												
18 May	NCCt	H	Western Australia		1-1												
27 May	F	A	Australia A		0-1												
30 May	F	A	Man Utd		2-2												
3 Jun	F	A	Australia A		2-2												
7 Jun	F	A	Australia B		0-0												
11 Jun	F	A	Australia B		0-0												

1984-85 — Division One

Date	Comp	V	Opponents	Result	1	2	3	4	5	6	7	8	9	10	11	Substitutes used
29 Jul	F	A	Keyworth U	W 2-0												
3 Aug	F	A	FK Moss	W 1-0												
5 Aug	F	A	Fredrikstad	W 3-1												
7 Aug	F	A	Celtic	D 0-0												
8 Aug	F	A	Dundee U	L 0-2												
11 Aug	F	A	Lierse	W 1-0												
15 Aug	F	A	Den Bosch	W 1-0												
17 Aug	F	A	Volendam	W 5-1												
18 Aug	F	A	Derby Co	L 0-2												
20 Aug	F	A	Panathinaikos	D 2-2												
25 Aug	FL	H	Sheff Wed	L 1-3	Sutton	Swain	Bowyer	Fairclough	Hart	Metgod	Wigley	Hodge	Christie	Davenport 1	Walsh*	Mills (11)
29 Aug	FL	A	Arsenal	W 2-0	Sutton	Gunn	Swain	Fairclough	Hart	Bowyer	Wigley	Metgod	Christie	Davenport 1	Hodge	
1 Sep	FL	H	Sunderland	W 3-1	Sutton	Gunn	Swain	Fairclough	Hart	Bowyer	Wigley	Metgod	Christie	Davenport 3	Hodge	Mills (8)
5 Sep	FL	A	Aston Villa	W 5-0	Sutton	Gunn	Swain	Fairclough	Hart	Bowyer	Wigley	Metgod	Christie 3	Davenport	Hodge	Mills (9)
8 Sep	FL	H	QPR	L 0-3	Sutton	Gunn	Swain	Fairclough	Hart	Bowyer	Wigley	Metgod	Christie*	Davenport 1	Hodge	Mills (9)
15 Sep	FL	A	Luton T	W 3-1	Sutton	Gunn	Swain	Fairclough	Smalley	Bowyer	Wigley	Metgod	Christie 1	Davenport	Walsh	Mills (5)
19 Sep	UC1/1	H	Club Brugge	W 1-0	Sutton	Gunn	Swain	Fairclough	Smalley*	Bowyer	Wigley	Metgod	Hodge	Davenport	Walsh	Mills (7)
22 Sep	FL	H	West Ham U	D 0-0	Sutton	McInally	Swain	Gunn	Fairclough	Bowyer	Wigley*	Metgod	Christie	Davenport	Hodge	Walsh (9)
25 Sep	FLC2/1	H	Portsmouth	D 0-0	Sutton	Gunn	Swain	Fairclough	Hart	Bowyer	Mills	Metgod	Christie 1	Davenport 1p	Hodge	
29 Sep	FL	A	Norwich C	W 3-1 §	Sutton	Gunn	Swain	Fairclough	Hart	Bowyer	Wigley 1	Metgod	Christie	Davenport	Hodge	
3 Oct	UC1/2	A	Club Brugge	L 0-1	Sutton	Gunn 1	Swain	Fairclough	Hart	Bowyer 1	Wigley	Metgod	Christie*	Davenport*	Walsh	Walsh (9)
6 Oct	FL	H	Stoke C	W 3-0	Sutton	Gunn	Swain	Fairclough	Hart	Bowyer	Wigley	Metgod	Christie	Davenport 1	Walsh	Mills (10)
10 Oct	FLC2/2	A	Portsmouth	D 1-1	Sutton	Gunn*	Swain	Metgod	Fairclough	Bowyer	Mills	Hodge	Christie 1	Davenport	Walsh	Mills (9)
13 Oct	FL	H	WBA	L 1-4	Sutton	Mills	Swain	Metgod	Fairclough	Bowyer	Mills	Hodge	Christie	Davenport	Walsh	
20 Oct	FL	A	Liverpool	D 1-1	Sutton	Mills	Swain	Metgod	Fairclough	Bowyer	Mills	Hodge	Christie 1	Raynor	Walsh	Wigley (2)
28 Oct	FL	A	Newcastle U	L 0-2	Segers	Mills	Swain	Metgod	Fairclough	Bowyer	Wigley	Hodge	Raynor	Riley	Walsh	
31 Oct	FLC3	H	Sunderland	D 1-1	Segers	Davidson	Swain	Fairclough	Hart	Bowyer	Wigley	Metgod	Riley	Davenport 2(1p)	Walsh	Riley (9) 1
3 Nov	FL	A	Southampton	L 0-1	Segers	Davidson	Swain	Fairclough	Hart	Gunn	Mills	Metgod	Davenport	Bowyer	Walsh	
6 Nov	FLC3r	A	Sunderland	L 0-1	Segers	Mills	Swain	Fairclough	Hart	Bowyer	Wigley	Metgod	Riley	Davenport	Walsh	Walsh (2)
10 Nov	FL	H	Tottenham H	W 2-0	Segers	McInally	Swain	Fairclough	Hart	Bowyer	Wigley	Metgod	Christie	Davenport	Hodge	
17 Nov	FL	A	Coventry C	L 0-1	Segers	McInally	Swain	Fairclough	Hart	Bowyer	Wigley	Metgod	Christie	Davenport	Hodge	
18 Nov	F		Australia													
25 Nov	FL	H	Leicester C	W 3-0	Segers	McInally	Swain	Fairclough	Hart	Bowyer	Wigley	Metgod 1	Christie 1	Davenport	Hodge	
1 Dec	FL	A	Watford	L 0-2	Segers	McInally	Swain	Fairclough	Hart	Bowyer	Wigley	Metgod	Clough	Davenport	Hodge	Walsh (6)
8 Dec	FL	H	Man Utd	W 3-2	Segers	McInally	Swain	Fairclough	Hart	Bowyer	Wigley	Metgod	Christie	Davenport 2	Hodge	
10 Dec	F		Al Hilal													
12 Dec	F		Itthiad													
15 Dec	FL	A	Everton	L 0-5	Segers	McInally	Swain	Fairclough	Hart	Bowyer	Wigley	Metgod	Christie	Davenport	Hodge	
22 Dec	FL	H	Sunderland	W 2-0	Segers	McInally	Swain	Fairclough	Hart	Bowyer*	Wigley	Metgod	Christie 1	Davenport 1p	Hodge	
26 Dec	FL	A	Ipswich T	W 2-1	Segers	McInally	Swain	Fairclough	Hart	Bowyer 1	Wigley	Metgod	Birtles	Davenport 1	Hodge	Riley (9)
29 Dec	FL	H	Aston Villa	D 0-0	Segers	McInally	Swain	Fairclough	Hart	Bowyer 1	Wigley	Metgod	Birtles	Davenport	Hodge	Riley (9)
1 Jan	FL	A	Chelsea	L 0-1	Segers	McInally	Swain	Fairclough	Hart	Bowyer*	Wigley	Metgod	Birtles	Davenport 1p	Hodge	
6 Jan	FAC3	H	Newcastle U	W 1-0	Segers	McInally	Swain	Fairclough	Hart	Walsh	Wigley	Metgod	Clough	Davenport	Hodge	
9 Jan	FAC3r	A	Newcastle U	D 1-1	Segers	McInally	Swain	Fairclough	Hart	Walsh	Wigley	Metgod 1	Clough	Davenport 1	Hodge 1	Mills (4)
25 Jan	FAC4	H	Wimbledon	W 1-0	Segers	McInally	Swain	Fairclough	Hart	Bowyer	Wigley	Hodge	Birtles	Davenport	Hodge	Campbell (5)
30 Jan	FAC4r	A	Wimbledon	D 0-0	Segers	McInally	Swain	Fairclough	Hart	Bowyer	Wigley	Metgod	Birtles	Davenport	Hodge	Mills (9)
2 Feb	FL	H	Norwich C	W 1-0	Segers	McInally	Swain	Fairclough	Hart	Bowyer	Wigley	Hodge	Birtles	Davenport	Mills	
9 Feb	FL	H	QPR	W 2-0	Segers	McInally	Swain	Fairclough	Hart	Bowyer	Wigley	Metgod	Clough	Hodge*	Mills 1	Clough (10)
11 Feb	F		Iraq Select XI	D 1-1												
13 Feb	F		Iraq Select XI	W 2-0 §												
23 Feb	FL	A	Southampton	L 0-1	Segers	McInally	Swain	Gunn	Hart	Bowyer*	Mills	Metgod	Davenport	Birtles	Hodge	Birtles (3)
26 Feb	F		Notts Co	W 6-1												
2 Mar	FL	A	Liverpool	L 0-1	Segers	McInally	Swain	Gunn	Hart	Bowyer	Mills	Metgod*	Birtles	Birtles	Hodge	Walsh (6)
9 Mar	FL	H	Sunderland	D 1-1	Segers	McInally	Swain	Walker	Hart	Bowyer	Wigley	Mills	Clough	Clough	Hodge	
16 Mar	FL	A	Newcastle U	W 1-0	Segers	McInally	Swain	Walker	Hart	Bowyer	Mills	Metgod	Clough	Clough	Hodge	
20 Mar	FL	H	WBA	L 0-2	Segers	McInally	Swain	Walker	Hart	Bowyer	Mills	Metgod	Birtles	Davenport	Hodge	Wigley (8)

League Appearances (Goals)

Birtles G 12+1 (2); Bowyer I 39 (2); Campbell D 0+1; Christie T 14 (5); Clough N 8+1 (1); Davenport P 35 (16); Davidson A 3; Fairclough C 35; Fleming G 2; Gunn B 17; Hart P 34 (1); Hodge S 42 (12); Mills G 18+8 (4); McInally J 24; Metgod J 40 (6); Raynor P 3; Riley D 7+3 (2); Segers J 28; Smalley M 1; Sutton S 14; Swain K 39; Walker D 3; Walsh C 10+3 (1); Wigley S 34+1 (1); Own goals 3.

Position in League Table

		P	W	D	L	F	A	Pts
1st	Everton	42	28	6	8	88	43	90
9th	Forest	42	19	7	16	56	48	64

Notes

§ denotes own goals

1985-86 — Division One

Date	V	Comp	Opponent	Result	1	2	3	4	5	6	7	8	9	10	11	Substitutes used
3 Aug	A	F	Bournemouth	D 3-3												
5 Aug	A	F	Weymouth	W 5-2												
7 Aug	A	F	Portsmouth	W 3-1												
9 Aug	A	F	Brighton & H A	L 2-5												
12 Aug	A	F	Barnsley	W 2-1												
17 Aug	H	FL	Luton T	D 1-1	Segers	McInally	Pearce	Butterworth	Walker	Hodge	Mills	Webb 1	Birtles	Davenport	Robertson	
21 Aug	A	FL	Sheff Wed	L 0-1	Segers	McInally	Pearce	Butterworth	Walker	Hodge	Wigley	Webb	Birtles	Davenport	Robertson	
24 Aug	A	FL	Southampton	W 2-1 §	Segers	McInally	Pearce	Butterworth	Walker	Metgod 1	Wigley	Webb	Birtles	Davenport	Robertson*	Mills (11)
27 Aug	A	FL	QPR	L 1-2	Segers	McInally*	Pearce	Butterworth	Walker	Webb 1	Wigley	Metgod	Clough	Birtles	Davenport	Bowyer (2)
31 Aug	H	FL	Man Utd	L 1-3	Segers	Butterworth	Pearce	Walker	Metgod	Bowyer	Wigley	Webb	Birtles*	Davenport 1	Rice	Clough (9)
3 Sep	A	FL	Liverpool	L 0-2	Segers	Butterworth	Pearce	Walker	Metgod	Bowyer	Wigley	Webb	Birtles*	Davenport	Rice	Clough (9)
7 Sep	A	FL	Leicester C	W 3-0	Segers	Walker	Pearce	Butterworth	Metgod	Bowyer*	Wigley	Webb	Clough 1	Davenport	Rice 1	Campbell (6) 1
8 Sep		NCCf	Notts Co	L 1-2	Segers*	Walker	Pearce	Butterworth	Metgod	Campbell 2	Wigley	Webb	Clough 1	Davenport	Rice	Carr (2)
14 Sep	H	FL	Tottenham H	L 0-1	Sutton	Walker*	Pearce	Butterworth	Metgod	Bowyer*	Wigley	Webb	Clough	Davenport	Rice	Walsh (1)
21 Sep	H	FL	Watford	W 3-2	Sutton	Walker	Pearce	Butterworth	Walker	Bowyer*	Wigley	Webb	Clough 1	Davenport	Rice 1	Birtles (8)
25 Sep		FLC2/1	Bolton W	W 4-0	Sutton	McInally	Pearce	Butterworth	Metgod 1	Campbell*	Mills	Campbell	Clough 1	Davenport 1	Rice 1	Walsh (1)
28 Sep	A	FL	West Ham U	L 2-4	Sutton	Mills	Pearce	Butterworth	Walker	Bowyer 2	Metgod	Metgod*	Clough	Davenport	Robertson	Birtles (8)
5 Oct	H	FL	Ipswich T	W 3-1	Sutton	Mills	Pearce 1	Butterworth	Birtles	Webb	Wigley	Metgod*	Clough 1	Davenport 1	Rice 1	Walsh (8)
8 Oct		FLC2/2	Bolton W	W 3-0	Sutton	Mills	Pearce	Butterworth	Birtles	Webb	Carr	Metgod	Clough	Davenport	Rice 1	Walsh (8)
12 Oct	H	FL	Aston Villa	W 2-0 §	Sutton	Mills	Pearce	Butterworth	Birtles	Webb	Carr	Metgod	Clough	Davenport	Rice 1	
14 Oct	A	F	Bristol R	D 1-1												
19 Oct	H	FL	Newcastle U	W 3-0	Sutton	Mills	Pearce	Butterworth	Birtles	Webb	Carr	Metgod	Clough	Davenport	Rice 1	Walker (8)
22 Oct	A	F	Borrowash Victoria	W 3-1												
26 Oct	A	FL	Arsenal	W 3-2	Sutton	Mills	Pearce	Butterworth	Birtles	Webb	Carr 1	Metgod	Clough	Davenport 3	Rice	Walker (8)
30 Oct		FLC3	Derby Co	W 2-1	Sutton	Mills	Pearce	Butterworth	Birtles	Webb 1	Carr	Metgod	Clough 1	Davenport 1p	Rice*	Walker (11)
2 Nov	A	FL	WBA	L 2-4	Sutton	Mills	Pearce	Butterworth	Birtles*	Webb	Carr	Metgod	Clough	Davenport	Rice	Walker (5)
9 Nov	H	FL	Chelsea	L 0-2	Sutton	McInally	Pearce	Walker	Butterworth	Webb	Mills	Metgod	Clough	Davenport	Walsh	Walsh (8)
16 Nov	H	FL	Man City	W 3-1	Sutton	McInally	Pearce	Walker	Birtles	Webb	Mills	Metgod	Clough 1	Davenport 1p	Walsh	Metgod (3)
23 Nov	A	FL	Everton	L 1-3	Sutton	McInally	Pearce	Walker	Birtles	Bowyer	Carr	Webb 1	Clough	Davenport	Walsh	Walsh (2)
25 Nov		FLC4	QPR	L 1-2	Sutton	Mills	Pearce	Walker	Butterworth	Bowyer	Carr	Metgod*	Clough	Davenport	Walsh	
1 Dec	H	FL	Oxford U	D 1-1	Sutton	McInally	Pearce	Walker	Butterworth	Bowyer	Carr 1	Webb 1	Clough 1	Webb 1	Robertson	Walsh (8)
7 Dec	A	FL	Sheff Wed	L 1-2	Sutton	McInally	Pearce	Walker	Butterworth	Bowyer	Metgod	Webb 1	Clough	Walsh	Robertson	Metgod (3)
14 Dec	A	FL	Luton T	W 2-0	Sutton	McInally*	Pearce	Walker	Birtles	Bowyer	Metgod 1	Webb 3	Clough	Davenport 1	Robertson	Walsh (2)
20 Dec		FL	Southampton	L 1-3	Sutton	Mills	Birtles*	Walker	Birtles	Bowyer*	Metgod	Webb	Clough*	Davenport 2	Robertson	
26 Dec	A	FL	Birmingham C	W 1-0	Sutton	Mills	Williams	Walker	Birtles	Bowyer	Metgod	Webb	Clough	Davenport	Robertson	
28 Dec	H	FL	Liverpool	D 1-1	Sutton	Butterworth	Williams	Walker	Metgod	Bowyer	Carr	Webb	Clough	Webb	Robertson	
1 Jan	H	FL	Coventry C	W 5-2	Sutton	Butterworth	Williams	Walker	Metgod	Bowyer	Carr	Webb 1	Clough	Davenport	Robertson	
4 Jan		FAC3	Blackburn R	D 1-1	Sutton	Butterworth	Williams	Walker	Metgod	Bowyer	Carr	Campbell	Clough 1p	Walsh*	Walsh*	Walsh (6)
11 Jan	A	FL	Tottenham H	L 2-3	Sutton	Butterworth	Williams	Walker	Metgod	Bowyer*	Carr 1	Campbell	Clough 2	Campbell	Rice	Robertson (9)
13 Jan		FAC3r	Blackburn R	L 0-4	Sutton	Butterworth	Williams	Walker	Metgod	Bowyer	Carr	Campbell 1	Clough 1p	Webb	Rice 1	
18 Jan	H	F	PSV Eindhoven	D 3-2												
24 Jan		F	Newcastle U	W 3-0												
1 Feb	H	FL	QPR	W 4-0	Sutton	Fleming	Williams	Walker	Metgod	Bowyer	Carr 1*	Webb 1	Clough	Davenport	Walsh 2	Campbell (7)
8 Feb	H	FL	Newcastle U	L 1-2	Sutton	Fleming	Williams	Walker	Metgod 1	Bowyer	Carr 1*	Webb	Clough	Davenport	Walsh 1	Campbell (7)
4 Mar	A	F	Stoke C	L 1-2												
8 Mar	A	FL	Ipswich T	L 0-1	Sutton	Fleming	Williams	Walker	Metgod	Bowyer	Carr	Webb	Clough	Davenport	Rice*	Campbell (11)
15 Mar	A	F	Aston Villa	D 1-1												
19 Mar	A	F	Real Sociedad u21	W 4-3												
22 Mar	A	F	Ottery St Mary	W 5-0												
24 Mar	A	FL	Coventry C	D 0-0	Sutton	Fleming	Williams	Walker	Metgod	Bowyer	Carr	Campbell	Clough 1	Webb	Rice	Walsh*
29 Mar	H	FL	Birmingham C	W 3-0	Sutton	Fleming	Williams	Walker	Metgod	Bowyer	Campbell	Campbell	Clough	Birtles	Rice	
31 Mar	A	FL	WBA	W 2-1	Segers	Fleming	Pearce	Walker	Metgod 1	Bowyer	Carr	Webb 1	Clough 1p	Birtles	Rice 1	Walsh (10)
2 Apr	H	FL	Arsenal	D 1-1	Sutton	Fleming	Pearce	Walker	Butterworth	Walsh	Carr	Campbell 1	Clough	Campbell	Rice	
5 Apr	A	FL	Oxford U	D 1-1	Sutton	Fleming	Pearce	Walker	Metgod	Bowyer	Carr	Webb	Clough	Webb	Rice	
12 Apr	H	FL	Chelsea	D 0-0	Sutton	Fleming	Pearce	Walker	Metgod	Bowyer	Carr	Campbell	Clough	Campbell	Walsh	
15 Apr	A	F	Real Sociedad	W 3-0												
19 Apr	H	FL	Man City	W 2-1	Sutton	Fleming	Pearce	Walker	Metgod	Bowyer*	Carr	Webb 1	Clough 1	Campbell 1	Walsh	Butterworth (6)
21 Apr	A	FL	Watford	D 1-1	Sutton	Fleming	Pearce	Walker	Metgod	Rice	Carr	Webb	Clough	Campbell	Walsh	
26 Apr	H	FL	Everton	D 0-0	Sutton	Fleming	Pearce	Walker	Metgod	Walsh	Carr	Webb	Clough	Campbell	Rice	
3 May	A	FL	Derby C	W 2-1	Sutton	Fleming	Pearce	Walker	Metgod	Walsh	Carr	Webb	Clough 2	Campbell	Rice	
7 May		NCCsf	Mansfield T	W 1-0												
8 May		NCCf	Notts Co	W 2-0												

League Appearances (Goals)

Birtles G 24+1; Bowyer 25-1 (3); Butterworth I 33+1; Campbell D 14-4 (3); Carr F 23 (3); Clough N 37+2 (15); Davenport P 27 (13); Fleming G 16; Hodge S 2; McInally J 12; Metgod J 37+2 (6); Mills G 13+1; Pearce S 30 (1); Rice B 19 (3); Robertson J 10+1; Segers J 11; Sutton S 31; Walker D 36-3; Walsh C 16-4 (6); Webb N 38 (14); Wigley S 8; Williams B 11; Own goals 2.

Position in League Table

	P	W	D	L	F	A	Pts
1st Liverpool	42	26	10	6	89	37	88
8th Forest	42	19	11	12	69	53	68

Notes

§ denotes own goals
Sep 11, County Cup Final 1984-85, held over from previous season
Jan 24, in Bermuda

1986-87 — Division One

Date			Opponent	Result	1	2	3	4	5	6	7	8	9	10	11	Substitutes used
20 Jul	F	A	Brombella IF	W 3-0												
22 Jul	F	A	KB Copenhagen	L 0-2												
25 Jul	F	A	Myresjö IF	W 6-0												
27 Jul	F	A	Åhus IF	W 7-0												
29 Jul	F	A	Älmhult	W 8-0												
2 Aug	F	A	Valleivogels	W 6-1												
3 Aug	F	A	Stevo	W 4-2												
5 Aug	F	A	MSC	W 12-0												
6 Aug	F	A	Den Haag	W 2-0												
9 Aug	F	A	Utrecht	D 1-1												
10 Aug	F	A	Top	W 4-0												
12 Aug	F	A	Willem II	L 1-2												
13 Aug	F	A	DS79	W 1-0												
17 Aug	NCC†	H	Mansfield T	D 1-1												
20 Aug	F	A	Torpedo Moscow	L 0-1												
23 Aug	FL	A	Everton	L 0-2	Sutton	Fleming	Pearce	Walker	Metgod	Bowyer	Carr	Webb	Clough	Birtles	Campbell	
27 Aug	FL	A	Charlton A	W 4-0	Sutton	Fleming	Pearce	Walker	Metgod	Bowyer	Carr	**Webb 2**	**Clough 1***	**Birtles 1**	Campbell	
30 Aug	FL	H	Watford	D 1-1	Sutton	Fleming	Pearce	Walker	Metgod	Bowyer	Carr	Webb	**Clough 1**	Birtles	Campbell	Mills (9)
2 Sep	FL	A	West Ham U	W 2-1	Sutton	Fleming	Pearce	Walker	Metgod	Bowyer	**Carr 1**	**Webb 1**	Clough	**Birtles 1**	Campbell*	
6 Sep	FL	H	Southampton	W 3-1	Sutton	Fleming	Pearce	Walker	Metgod	Bowyer*	Carr	**Webb 2**	**Clough 1**	**Birtles 1**	Campbell	Mills (6)
13 Sep	FL	A	Aston Villa	W 6-0	Sutton	Fleming	Pearce	Walker	Metgod	Bowyer	**Carr 1**	**Webb 3**	Clough	**Birtles 2**	Campbell	Mills (11)
20 Sep	FL	H	Chelsea	W 6-2	Sutton	Fleming	Pearce	Fairclough	Metgod	Bowyer	**Carr 2**	Webb	**Clough 1**	**Birtles 3**	Campbell*	
24 Sep	FLC2/1	A	Brighton & HA	D 0-0	Sutton	Fleming	Pearce	Walker	Metgod	Bowyer	Carr	Campbell	Clough	Birtles	Campbell	Andrews (5), Rice (11)
27 Sep	FL	H	Arsenal	W 1-0	Sutton	Fleming	**Pearce 1p**	Walker	Metgod*	Bowyer	Carr	Webb	Clough	Birtles	Campbell	
4 Oct	FL	A	Man Utd	D 1-1	Sutton*	Fleming	Pearce	Walker	Metgod	Bowyer	Carr	Webb	Clough	**Birtles 1**	Campbell	Mills (1)
8 Oct	FLC2/2	H	Brighton & HA	W 3-0	Segers	Butterworth	**Pearce 1p**	Walker	Metgod	Bowyer	**Carr 1**	**Webb 1**	**Clough 1**	**Birtles 1**	Campbell*	
11 Oct	FL	A	Leicester C	L 1-3	Segers	Butterworth	**Pearce 1p**	Walker	Fairclough	Bowyer*	Carr	Webb	**Clough 1**	Birtles	Mills	
14 Oct	FL	H	Notts Co	W 5-2	Segers	Butterworth	Pearce	Walker	Metgod	Bowyer	Carr	Webb	**Clough 1**	**Birtles 1**	Campbell*	
18 Oct	F	H	QPR	L 0-1												
25 Oct	FLC3	A	Crystal Palace	W 1-2	Segers	Butterworth	**Pearce 1p**	Walker	Metgod	Campbell	Carr	Webb	**Clough 1**	**Birtles 1**	Campbell*	Fairclough (11)
29 Oct	FL	A	Crystal Palace	D 2-2	Segers	Butterworth	**Pearce 1p**	Walker	Metgod	Bowyer	Carr	Webb	Clough	**Birtles 1**	Metgod	Mills (6)
1 Nov	FL	H	Sheff Wed	W 3-2	Segers	Butterworth	**Pearce 1p**	Walker	Metgod	Campbell	Carr	Webb	Clough	**Birtles 1**	Mills	
5 Nov	FLC3r	H	Crystal Palace	W 1-0	Segers	Butterworth	Pearce	Walker	Metgod	Bowyer	Carr	Webb	**Clough 1**	Birtles	Mills	
8 Nov	FL	A	Coventry C	W 1-0	Segers	Butterworth	Pearce	Walker	Metgod	Bowyer	**Carr 1**	Webb	**Clough 1**	Birtles	Mills	
15 Nov	FL	H	Luton T	L 2-4	Segers	Fleming	Pearce	Walker	**Metgod 1**	Bowyer	**Carr 1**	Webb	**Clough 1p**	**Birtles 1**	Mills	
19 Nov	FLC4	H	Bradford C	W 5-0	Segers	Fleming	Williams	Walker	**Metgod 1**	**Bowyer 1**	Carr	**Webb 1**	**Clough 1**	Birtles*	**Mills 1**	Fairclough (6), Glover (10)
22 Nov	FL	H	Wimbledon	D 0-0	Segers	Fleming	Williams	Walker	**Fairclough 1**	Bowyer*	Carr	Webb	Clough	Birtles	Mills	
25 Nov	F	A	Plymouth A	L 1-6												
29 Nov	FL	A	Tottenham H	D 3-2 §	Segers	Fleming	**Pearce 1p**	Walker	**Metgod 1**	Bowyer	Carr	**Webb 1**	Clough	Birtles	Mills	**Fairclough (6), 1. Glover (10)**
2 Dec	F	A	Doncaster R	D 2-2												
6 Dec	FL	H	Man City	W 2-0	Segers	Fleming	Pearce	Walker	Metgod	Metgod	**Carr 1**	Webb	**Clough 1**	**Birtles 1**	Webb	
13 Dec	FL	A	Newcastle U	L 2-3	Segers	Fleming	Pearce	Walker	Fairclough	Metgod	**Carr 1**	Metgod	Clough	Starbuck	Mills	
20 Dec	FL	A	Southampton	D 0-0	Segers	Fleming	**Pearce 1**	Walker	Fairclough	Webb	Carr	Metgod	Clough	Starbuck	Webb	
26 Dec	FL	H	Norwich C	D 1-2	Segers	Fleming	Pearce	Walker	Fairclough	Bowyer	Carr	Metgod	Clough	Campbell	Webb	
28 Dec	FL	H	Luton T	D 2-2	Segers	Fleming	Pearce	Walker	Fairclough	Bowyer	Carr	Webb	**Clough 1**	Campbell	Mills	
1 Jan	FL	A	Liverpool	L 0-1	Sutton	Fleming	Pearce	Walker	Fairclough	Bowyer	Carr	Webb	Clough	Starbuck	Mills	
3 Jan	FL	H	Aston Villa	D 0-0	Sutton	Fleming	Pearce	Walker	Fairclough	Bowyer	Carr	Webb	Clough	Starbuck*	Mills	Campbell (10)
11 Jan	FAC3	A	Arsenal	L 0-2	Sutton	Fleming	Pearce	Walker	Fairclough	Bowyer	Metgod	Webb	Clough	Metgod	Mills	
21 Jan	FLC5	H	Arsenal	W 2-0	Sutton	Fleming	Pearce	Walker	Fairclough	Bowyer	Carr	Webb	**Clough 2**	Starbuck	Mills	
31 Jan	FL	A	Charlton A	W 1-0	Sutton	Fleming	Williams	Walker	Fairclough	Bowyer	Carr	Webb	Clough	**Birtles 1**	Mills	Metgod (8)
7 Feb	FL	H	Watford	W 1-0	Sutton	Fleming	Pearce	Walker	Fairclough	Bowyer	Carr	**Webb 1**	**Clough 1**	Birtles	Mills	Starbuck (11)
14 Feb	FL	A	West Ham U	L 0-2	Sutton	Fleming	Williams	Walker	Fairclough	**Bowyer 1**	Carr	Webb	Clough	**Birtles 1p**	Mills*	Foster (8)
28 Feb	FL	H	Chelsea	D 1-1	Sutton	Fleming	Pearce	Walker	Fairclough	Bowyer	Carr	Webb	Clough	Birtles	Mills	
7 Mar	FL	A	Oxford U	L 0-2	Sutton	Fleming	Williams	Walker	Fairclough	Bowyer	Carr	Metgod	**Clough 1**	Birtles	Mills*	
14 Mar	FL	H	QPR	W 1-0	Sutton	Fleming	Pearce	Walker	Fairclough	Bowyer	Carr	Webb*	Clough	Birtles*	Mills	Foster (10)
17 Mar	F	H	Arsenal	D 1-2												
22 Mar	FL	A	Leicester C	L 1-3	Sutton	Fleming	Pearce	Walker	Fairclough	Bowyer	**Carr 1**	**Metgod 1**	Clough	Birtles*	Mills*	
28 Mar	FL	H	Man Utd	W 2-0	Sutton	Walker	Pearce	Metgod	Fairclough	Bowyer	Carr	Webb*	**Clough 2**	Birtles	Mills	
31 Mar	F	A	VF Frölunda	W 2-0												
4 Apr	FL	H	Coventry C	D 0-0	Sutton	Fleming	**Pearce 1p**	Walker	Fairclough	Bowyer	Carr*	Webb	Clough	Birtles	Mills*	Mills (10)
14 Apr	FL	A	Sheff Wed	W 3-2	Sutton	Fleming	Pearce	Walker	Foster	Bowyer	Mills	Metgod	**Clough 1**	Wilkinson*	Rice	Fairclough (7)
18 Apr	FL	H	Liverpool	L 0-3	Sutton	Fleming	**Pearce 1p**	Foster	Foster	Bowyer	Mills	Metgod	Clough	Wilkinson*	**Rice 1**	Starbuck (10)
20 Apr	FL	A	Norwich C	W 2-0	Sutton	Walker	Pearce	Foster	Metgod	Bowyer	Mills	Metgod	**Clough 2**	Wilkinson*	Rice	
25 Apr	FL	A	Wimbledon	L 1-2	Sutton	Walker	Pearce	**Foster 1**	Fairclough	Bowyer	Carr*	Metgod	Clough	Wilkinson	Osvold	Riley (10)
2 May	FL	H	Tottenham H	D 1-1	Sutton	Fleming	Pearce	Walker	Fairclough	**Metgod 1**	Mills	Webb	Clough	Wilkinson	Osvold	
4 May	FL	H	Man City	W 2-0	Sutton	Walker	Pearce	Walker	Metgod	Metgod	Mills	Webb	Clough	Wilkinson	Osvold	
9 May	F	A	Varna Select XI	W 2-1												
11 May	FL	A	Newcastle U	W 2-1	Sutton	Walker	Pearce	Walker	Metgod	Metgod	Mills	Webb	Clough	Wilkinson	Osvold	
15 May	F	H	Derby Co	D 1-1												

League Appearances (Goals)

Birtles G 28 (14); Bowyer I 35 (3); Butterworth I 4; Campbell D 14; Carr F 36 (4); Clough N 42 (14); Fairclough C 24+2 (1); Fleming G 34; Foster C 7+2 (1); Metgod J 36+1 (3); Mills G 27+5; Osvold K 4; Pearce S 39 (6); Rice B 3 (1); Riley D 0+1; Segers J 14; Starbuck P 3+2 (2); Sutton S 28; Walker D 41; Webb N 32 (14); Wilkinson P 8; Williams B 3; Own goals 1.

Position in League Table

	P	W	D	L	F	A	Pts
1st Everton	42	26	8	8	76	31	86
8th Forest	42	18	11	13	64	51	65

Notes

§ denotes own goals
Aug 17, lost 3-4 on penalties
Mar 31, in Malta

1987-88 — Division One

Date	Comp	Venue	Opponent	Result	1	2	3	4	5	6	7	8	9	10	11	Substitutes used
27 Jul	F	A	Halmstad	W 3-2												
29 Jul	F	A	BK Copenhagen	W 4-1												
31 Jul	F	A	Waggeryds IK	W 7-1												
2 Aug	F	A	Hoeganas BK	W 6-0												
4 Aug	F	A	Malmo FF	L 0-2												
9 Aug	NCCsf	A	Notts Co	D 4-4												
15 Aug	FL	A	Charlton A	W 2-1	Sutton	Fleming	Pearce	Walker	Foster	Campbell	Carr	Webb	Clough 1	Wilkinson	Glover 1	
19 Aug	FL	H	Watford	W 1-0	Sutton	Fleming	Pearce 1p	Walker	Foster	Campbell	Carr	Webb	Clough	Wilkinson	Glover	
22 Aug	FL	H	Everton	D 0-0	Segers	Fleming	Pearce	Walker	Foster	Campbell	Carr	Webb	Clough	Wilkinson	Glover	
29 Aug	FL	A	Newcastle U	W 1-0	Segers	Fleming	Pearce	Walker	Foster	Campbell	Carr	Webb 1	Clough 1	Wilkinson	Glover	Wilson (2)
2 Sep	FL	H	Southampton	D 3-3	Segers	Fleming *	Pearce 1	Walker	Foster 1	Campbell *	Carr	Webb 1	Clough 1	Wilkinson	Glover *	Wilson (6), Chettle (14)
5 Sep	FL	A	Chelsea	L 3-4	Segers	Fleming	Pearce	Walker	Foster	Campbell *	Carr	Webb	Clough	Wilkinson	Glover	Wilson (6), Starbuck (10)
12 Sep	FL	H	Arsenal	L 0-1	Segers	Fleming *	Pearce 1p	Walker	Foster	Campbell *	Carr	Webb	Clough	Wilkinson	Glover *	Campbell (2)
19 Sep	FL	A	Coventry C	W 3-0	Sutton	Chettle	Pearce	Walker	Foster	Wilson 1	Carr 1	Webb 2	Clough 1	Wilkinson 1	Rice	Chettle (2), Glover (6)
23 Sep	FLC2/1	H	Hereford U	W 5-0	Sutton	Chettle	Pearce	Walker	Foster	Wilson *	Carr 1	Webb 2	Clough	Wilkinson	Rice	Glover (11)
26 Sep	FL	A	Norwich C	W 2-0	Sutton	Chettle	Pearce	Walker	Foster	Wilson	Carr	Webb	Clough 1	Wilkinson	Rice *	
7 Oct	FLC2/2	A	Hereford U	D 1-1	Sutton	Chettle	Pearce	Walker	Foster	Wilson	Carr	Webb	Clough	Wilkinson 1	Rice	Osvold (6)
10 Oct	FL	A	Derby Co	W 1-0	Sutton	Chettle	Pearce	Walker	Foster	Wilson	Carr	Webb	Clough 1	Wilkinson 1	Rice	Osvold (6)
17 Oct	FL	H	Sheff Wed	W 3-0	Sutton	Chettle	Pearce	Walker	Foster	Wilson *	Carr 1	Webb 1	Clough 1	Wilkinson 1	Rice	Starbuck (5), Osvold (10)
24 Oct	FL	H	Tottenham H	W 3-0	Sutton	Chettle	Pearce	Walker	Foster *	Wilson *	Carr 1	Webb	Clough 1	Wilkinson	Rice	
27 Oct	FLC3	A	Man City	L 0-3	Sutton	Chettle	Pearce	Walker	Foster	Wilson	Carr	Webb	Clough	Wilkinson	Rice	Starbuck (6), Glover (11)
31 Oct	FL	A	Man Utd	D 2-2	Sutton	Chettle	Pearce 1	Walker	Foster	Wilson 1 *	Carr	Webb 1	Clough 1	Wilkinson 1	Rice 1 *	Starbuck (7), Gaynor (10)
14 Nov	FL	H	Portsmouth	W 5-0	Sutton	Chettle	Pearce	Walker	Foster	Wilson	Carr *	Webb 1	Clough 1	Wilkinson *	Rice	
21 Nov	FL	A	West Ham U	L 2-3	Sutton	Chettle	Pearce	Walker	Foster	Wilson	Carr	Webb	Clough 1	Wilkinson *	Rice	
23 Nov	F	A	Saudi Arabia XI	W 1-0												
30 Nov	F	A	Celtic	W 3-1												
5 Dec	FL	A	Wimbledon	D 1-1	Sutton	Chettle	Pearce	Walker	Foster	Wilson	Plummer	Webb	Clough 1	Gaynor	Rice	Starbuck (6)
13 Dec	FMC3	H	QPR	W 4-0	Sutton	Fleming	Pearce 1p	Walker	Foster	Wilson *	Plummer	Webb	Clough 3(1p)	Gaynor 1	Rice 1	Starbuck (7)
19 Dec	FL	A	Oxford U	W 2-0	Sutton	Chettle	Pearce	Walker	Foster	Wilson 1	Plummer 1 *	Webb	Clough *	Gaynor	Rice	Starbuck (7)
26 Dec	FL	A	Arsenal	W 2-0	Sutton	Chettle *	Pearce	Walker	Foster *	Wilson	Plummer *	Webb	Glover	Gaynor 2	Rice	Fleming (2), Starbuck (7)
28 Dec	FL	H	Coventry C	W 4-1 §	Sutton	Chettle	Pearce	Walker	Foster	Wilson	Plummer	Webb	Starbuck	Gaynor	Rice	Fleming (9), Starbuck (10)
1 Jan	FL	A	Newcastle U	L 0-2	Sutton	Chettle	Pearce	Walker	Foster	Wilson	Carr *	Webb	Glover *	Gaynor *	Rice *	Fleming (7)
3 Jan	FL	A	Everton	L 0-1	Sutton	Chettle	Pearce 1	Walker	Foster	Wilson	Plummer 1 *	Webb 1	Glover *	Gaynor *	Rice *	Fleming (7), Wilkinson (10) 1
9 Jan	FAC3	A	Halifax T	W 4-0	Sutton	Chettle	Pearce	Walker	Foster	Wilson	Plummer 1	Webb	Glover *	Gaynor *	Rice	Crosby (9), Wilkinson (10)
16 Jan	FL	A	Charlton A	D 2-2	Sutton	Chettle	Pearce	Walker	Foster	Wilson	Plummer	Webb	Glover	Wilkinson	Rice	
23 Jan	FL	A	Watford	D 0-0	Sutton	Chettle	Pearce	Walker	Foster	Wilson	Plummer 1	Webb 1	Glover 1	Wilkinson	Gaynor	
30 Jan	FAC4	A	Leyton Orient	W 2-1	Sutton	Chettle	Pearce	Walker	Foster	Wilson	Plummer *	Webb	Glover	Wilkinson *	Rice *	Fleming (7), Starbuck (10)
3 Feb	FMC	A	Reading	L 1-2	Sutton	Fleming	Pearce	Walker	Foster 1 *	Wilson	Crosby 1	Webb	Clough 1p	Gaynor	Osvold	Chettle (5), Starbuck (11)
6 Feb	FL	H	Chelsea	W 3-2	Sutton	Fleming	Pearce	Walker	Foster	Wilson	Crosby	Webb	Clough 1	Wilkinson	Rice	
13 Feb	FL	A	Southampton	D 1-1	Sutton	Chettle	Pearce	Walker	Wassall	Wilson	Crosby 1	Webb	Clough	Wilkinson	Rice	
20 Feb	FAC5	A	Birmingham C	W 1-0	Sutton	Chettle	Pearce	Wassall	Foster	Wilson	Crosby *	Webb	Clough	Wilkinson 1	Rice	Gaynor (7)
5 Mar	FL	H	Sheff Wed	W 1-0	Sutton	Fleming	Pearce	Walker	Foster	Wilson	Crosby	Webb	Clough	Wilkinson	Rice	
12 Mar	FAC6	A	Arsenal	W 2-1	Sutton	Fleming	Pearce	Walker	Foster	Wilson	Crosby	Webb	Clough 1	Wilkinson	Rice	
16 Mar	FL	A	QPR	L 1-2 §	Sutton	Chettle	Pearce	Walker	Foster	Wilson	Crosby	Webb	Clough	Wilkinson	Rice	
19 Mar	FL	H	Man Utd	D 0-0	Sutton	Fleming	Pearce	Walker	Foster	Wilson	Crosby	Webb	Clough 2	Wilkinson	Rice	
26 Mar	FL	H	Tottenham H	D 1-1	Sutton	Fleming	Chettle	Walker	Foster	Wilson	Crosby	Webb 1	Clough	Wilkinson	Rice	
2 Apr	FL	A	Portsmouth	W 1-0	Sutton	Chettle	Pearce	Wassall	Foster	Wilson 1	Crosby	Webb	Clough	Wilkinson	Glover	Wassall (4)
4 Apr	FL	H	Liverpool	L 1-2	Sutton	Chettle	Pearce	Walker	Foster	Wilson	Crosby	Webb	Clough 1	Wilkinson	Glover	
9 Apr	FACsf	A	Liverpool	L 0-5	Sutton	Fleming	Pearce	Walker	Foster	Wilson	Crosby	Webb	Clough	Glover	Rice	
20 Apr	FL	H	West Ham U	W 1-0	Sutton	Fleming	Williams	Walker	Foster	Wilson	Carr	Webb 1	Gaynor	Carr	Rice	Glover (8)
30 Apr	FL	H	Wimbledon	W 2-0	Sutton	Fleming	Williams	Chettle	Foster	Wilson	Carr 1	Webb 2	Clough *	Parker	Rice	Parker (6), Wilkinson (9)
4 May	FL	H	Norwich C	W 5-3	Sutton	Fleming	Williams	Chettle	Foster	Wilson	Gaynor	Webb	Gaynor	Glover 1	Rice	
7 May	FL	A	Oxford U	D 2-2	Sutton	Fleming	Williams *	Chettle	Foster	Wilson *	Carr 1	Webb 1	Clough *	Glover 1	Rice	
8 May	F	A	Lincoln C	D 1-1	Sutton	Fleming	Chettle	Walker	Chettle	Wilson	Carr	Webb	Clough 2	Glover	Glover	Foster (3)
13 May	F	A	Luton T	D 1-1	Sutton	Fleming	Williams *	Walker	Chettle	Wilson	Carr	Webb	Clough	Glover	Crosby	Crosby (7)
15 May	F	H	Luton T	D 1-1	Sutton	Chettle	Chettle	Walker	Foster	Wilson	Carr *	Webb 1	Clough	Glover	Rice	

1988-89 — Division One

Date	Comp	Venue	Opponent	Result	1	2	3	4	5	6	7	8	9	10	11	Substitutes used
24 Jul	F	A	Keyworth	W 8-0												
28 Jul	F	A	IK Brage	L 0-1												
30 Jul	F	A	Helsingfors Vastra	W 2-0												
31 Jul	F	A	Sandvikens IF	W 2-0												
2 Aug	F	A	Vasteras	D 0-0												
3 Aug	F	A	Brommapojkarna	W 4-0												
11 Aug	F	A	Pescara	W 3-2												
13 Aug	F	A	Cologne	L 0-2												
17 Aug	F	A	Lincoln U	W 4-0												
21 Aug	NCCsf	A	Notts Co	D 1-1	Sutton	**Chettle 1**	Pearce	Walker	Foster	Wilson	Crosby	Webb	Clough	Hodge	Rice*	Carr (11)
27 Aug	FL	A	Norwich C	L 1-2	Sutton	Chettle	Pearce	Walker	Foster	Wilson	Crosby	**Webb 1**	Clough	Hodge	Rice*	Carr (11)
29 Aug	MCT	A	Liverpool	L 1-4	Sutton	Chettle	Pearce	Walker	Foster	Wilson	Crosby	**Webb 1**	Clough	Gaynor	Rice	Carr (7)
3 Sep	FL	H	Sheff Wed	D 1-1 §	Sutton	Chettle	Pearce	Walker	**Foster**	Hodge	Crosby*	**Webb 1**	Clough	Gaynor	Rice	**Carr (10) 1**
10 Sep	FL	A	Everton	D 1-1	Sutton	Chettle*	Pearce	Walker	Foster	**Hodge 1**	Crosby	Webb	Clough	**Gaynor 1**	Rice	Fleming (2)
12 Sep	F	A	Hearts	W 3-0												
17 Sep	FL	H	Derby Co	D 1-1	Sutton	Chettle	Pearce	Walker	Foster	Hodge	Crosby	Webb	**Clough 1**	Gaynor	Rice	Carr (10)
24 Sep	FL	A	Aston Villa	D 1-1	Sutton	Fleming	Pearce	Walker	Foster	Hodge	Carr	Webb	Clough	Gaynor	Crosby	
28 Sep	FLC2/1	H	Chester C	W 6-0	Sutton	Chettle	Pearce	Walker	Foster	**Hodge 2**	Crosby	Webb*	**Clough 1p**	**Gaynor 3***	Crosby	Parker (8), Laws (10)
1 Oct	FL	H	Luton T	D 0-0	Sutton	Chettle	Pearce	Walker	Foster	Hodge	Crosby	**Webb 1**	**Clough 1**	**Chapman**	Rice	
8 Oct	FL	A	QPR	W 2-1	Crossley	Chettle	Pearce	Walker	Foster	Hodge	Crosby	Webb*	Clough	Chapman	Gaynor	Wilson (8)
12 Oct	FLC2/2	A	Chester C	W 4-0	Crossley	Chettle	Pearce	Walker	**Foster 1**	**Hodge 1**	Charles	Wilson	Clough	**Chapman 1**	Rice	
22 Oct	FL	A	Millwall	D 2-2	Crossley	Chettle	Pearce	Walker	Foster	Hodge	Charles	Wilson	**Clough 2**	Chapman	Rice	Starbuck (7), Crosby (10)
26 Oct	FL	H	Liverpool	W 2-1	Sutton	Chettle	Pearce*	Walker	**Foster 1**	**Hodge 1**	Starbuck*	Webb	Clough	Chapman	Rice	Wilson (7)
29 Oct	FLC3	H	Newcastle U	W 1-0	Sutton	Chettle	Pearce*	Walker	Foster	Hodge	Crosby*	Webb	Clough	Chapman*	Rice	
2 Nov	FL	H	Coventry C	W 3-2	Sutton	**Chettle 1**	**Pearce 1**	Walker	Foster	Hodge	Starbuck	Webb	**Clough 1**	Chapman	Rice	Wilson (10)
6 Nov	FL	A	Arsenal	L 1-4	Sutton	Laws	Pearce	Leicester	Wassall	Hodge	Starbuck*	Webb	Clough	**Chapman 2**	Rice	Wilson (7), Carr (10)
12 Nov	FL	A	West Ham U	W 3-2	Sutton	Laws	Pearce	Chettle	Foster	Hodge	Carr	Webb	Clough	**Chapman 1***	Rice	
19 Nov	FL	H	Coventry C	D 3-3	Sutton	Williams	Williams	Chettle	Foster	Parker	Carr*	Webb	**Clough 1**	Chapman	Rice	Hodge (10)
21 Nov	F	A	Grantham T	W 4-1												
26 Nov	FL	A	Charlton A	D 0-0	Sutton	Williams	Williams	Walker*	Parker	Hodge*	Carr*	Webb	Clough	Chapman	Rice	Laws (2), Hodge (6)
30 Nov	FLC4	H	Leicester C	D 2-2	Sutton	Laws	Pearce	Walker	Wilson	Hodge	Carr*	Webb	**Gaynor 1**	Chapman	Parker	Starbuck (9), Gaynor (10)
3 Dec	FL	A	Middlesbrough	D 2-2	Sutton	Laws	Pearce	Walker	Wilson	**Hodge 1**	Carr*	**Webb 1**	**Gaynor 1**	**Chapman 1**	Parker	Starbuck (7)
10 Dec	FL	A	Southampton	D 1-1	Sutton	Laws	Pearce 1p	Walker*	Wilson	Hodge*	Carr*	Webb	**Clough 1**	Chapman	**Parker 1**	Starbuck (7)
14 Dec	FLC4r	H	Leicester C	W 2-0	Sutton	Laws	Pearce	Chettle	Foster	Parker*	Carr*	Webb	Clough	Chapman	**Parker 1**	
18 Dec	FL	H	Wimbledon	L 0-1	Sutton	**Laws 1**	**Pearce 1**	Chettle	Foster	Parker	Carr*	Webb	Clough	**Chapman 1***	**Parker 1**	Clough (6), Starbuck (7)
26 Dec	FL	H	Leeds U	W 3-0	Sutton	Laws	Pearce	Chettle	Wilson	Hodge	Carr	Webb	Clough	**Chapman 1**	Parker*	Chettle (4)
31 Dec	FL	A	Man Utd	W 2-0	Sutton	Laws	**Pearce 1**	Chettle	Wilson	**Hodge 1**	Carr*	Webb	Clough	Chapman	**Parker 1**	Crosby (11)
1 Jan	FL	H	Ipswich T	W 2-0	Sutton	Laws	Pearce	Chettle	Wilson	Hodge*	Carr*	Webb	**Clough 2(1p)**	**Chapman 1***	Parker	**Crosby (10) 1**
7 Jan	FAC3	H	Chelsea	W 2-0	Sutton	Laws	Pearce	Walker	Wilson	Hodge	Carr	Webb	**Clough 1**	Chapman	Parker	Starbuck (6)
10 Jan	FMCf	A	Tottenham H		Sutton	Laws	Pearce	Walker	Wilson	Hodge*	Carr	Webb	Clough	Chapman	Parker	
14 Jan	FL	H	QPR	W 1-0	Sutton	Laws	**Pearce 1**	Chettle	Wilson	**Hodge 1**	Carr*	Webb	Clough	Chapman	**Parker 1**	Starbuck (10)
18 Jan	FLC5	H	Aston Villa		Sutton	Laws	**Pearce 1**	Chettle	Wilson	**Hodge 1**	Carr*	Webb	Clough	Chapman	**Parker 1**	
21 Jan	FL	H	Ipswich T		Sutton	Laws	Pearce	Walker	Wilson	Hodge	Carr	Webb	Clough	**Chapman 4**	Parker*	
24 Jan	FMC4	A	Luton T		Sutton	Laws	**Pearce 1**	Chettle	Wilson	Hodge	Carr*	Webb	**Clough 1**	**Chapman 1***	Parker	
28 Jan	FAC4	H	Bristol C		Sutton	Laws	Pearce	Chettle	Wilson	Hodge	Carr	Webb	Clough	Chapman	**Parker 1**	
4 Feb	FL	H	Watford		Sutton	Laws	**Pearce 1**	Chettle	Wilson	Hodge	Carr	**Webb 1**	Clough	Chapman	**Parker 1**	
11 Feb	FLCsf/1	H	Crystal Palace		Sutton	Laws	Pearce	Walker	Wilson	Hodge	Carr	**Webb 2**	Clough	Chapman	**Parker 1**	
15 Feb	FAC5	A	Bristol C		Sutton	Laws	Pearce	Walker	Wilson	Hodge	Carr	Webb	Clough	Chapman	**Parker 1**	
19 Feb	FMCsf	H	Arsenal		Sutton	Laws	**Pearce 1**	Walker	Wilson	Hodge	Carr	Webb	**Clough 1**	Chapman	**Parker 1**	
26 Feb	FLCsf/2	A	Crystal Palace		Sutton	Laws	**Pearce 1**	Walker	Wilson	Hodge	Carr	Webb	Clough	Chapman	**Parker 1**	
11 Mar	FAC6	H	Man Utd		Sutton	Laws	**Pearce 1**	Chettle	Wilson	Hodge	Gaynor	Webb	Clough	Chapman	Parker*	
18 Mar	FL	A	Tottenham H		Sutton	Laws	Pearce	Walker	Wilson	Hodge	Gaynor	Webb	Clough	**Chapman 1**	Parker*	Chettle (7)
22 Mar	FL	H	Newcastle U		Sutton	Chettle	Pearce	Walker	Wilson	Hodge	Carr*	Webb	Clough	**Chapman 1**	Parker	Chettle (3)
25 Mar	FL	A	Man Utd		Sutton	Chettle	Pearce	Walker	Wilson	Hodge	Carr 1	Webb	Clough	Chapman	Parker	Foster (10)
27 Mar	FL	H	Norwich C		Sutton	Laws	**Pearce 1***	Walker	Wilson	Hodge	Gaynor	Webb	Clough	**Chapman 1**	Parker	
1 Apr	FL	A	Luton T		Sutton	Laws	**Pearce 1**	Walker	Wilson	Hodge	Gaynor	Webb	Clough	**Gaynor 1**	**Parker 1**	Rice (9)
5 Apr	FL	H	Southampton		Sutton	Chettle	Pearce	Walker	Wilson	Hodge	Carr*	Webb	Clough	Chapman	**Parker 1**	Chettle (7), Carr (7)
9 Apr	FLCf		Luton T		Sutton	Chettle	Pearce	Walker	Wilson	Rice	Carr*	Webb	Clough	Chapman	Parker	
15 Apr	FACsf		Liverpool	Abnd	Sutton	Laws	Pearce	Walker	Wilson	Rice	Carr 1	Webb	**Clough 1**	Chapman	Parker	Starbuck (7), Glover (11)
22 Apr	FL	H	Middlesbrough		Sutton	Laws	Pearce	Walker	Wilson	Hodge	Gaynor*	Webb	Clough	**Chapman 2**	Parker	Gaynor (7)
30 Apr	FMCf	A	Everton		Sutton	Laws	Pearce	Walker	Wilson	Hodge*	Gaynor*	Webb	Clough	**Gaynor 1**	Parker	Gaynor (10), Chettle (11)
3 May	FL	H	Millwall		Sutton	Laws	Pearce	Walker	Wilson	**Hodge 1**	Carr*	**Webb 1**	Clough	Chapman	Parker	
7 May	FACsf		Liverpool		Sutton	Laws	Pearce	Walker	Wilson	Rice	Carr 1	Webb	Clough	Chapman	Parker	
10 May	FL	A	Liverpool		Sutton	Laws	Pearce	Walker	Wilson	Rice	Carr*	**Webb 1**	Clough	Gaynor	Parker	
13 May	FL	H	Charlton A		Sutton	Laws	Pearce	Walker	**Wilson 1**	Rice	Carr	**Webb 1**	**Clough 1**	Chapman	Parker	
15 May	FL	A	Coventry C		Sutton	Laws	Pearce	Walker	Wilson	Hodge	Carr	Webb	Clough	Chapman	Parker	
18 May	FL	H	West Ham U		Sutton	Chettle	Pearce	Walker	Chettle	Hodge	Gaynor	Webb	Clough	**Chapman 1**	Parker	

League Appearances (Goals)

Carr F 18+5 (3); Chapman L 30 (8); Charles G 1; Chettle S 23+5 (2); Clough N 36 (14); Crosby G 11+2; Crossley M 2; Foster C 17+1 (2); Gaynor T 16+3 (4); Hodge S 33+1 (7); Laws B 20+2 (1); Parker G 22 (7); Pearce S 36 (6); Rice B 19+1 (1); Starbuck P 2-5; Sutton S 36; Walker D 34; Webb N 36 (6); Williams B 2; Wilson T 24+3 (1); Own goals 2.

Position in League Table

	P	W	D	L	F	A	Pts
1st Arsenal	38	22	10	6	73	36	76
3rd Forest	38	17	13	8	64	43	64

Notes

§ denotes own goals
Aug 13, in Pescara
Aug 21, lost 2-4 on penalties
Apr 9, Apr 30, at Wembley
Apr 15, at Hillsborough
May 7, at Old Trafford

1989-90 Division One

Date	Comp	Venue	Opponent	Result	1	2	3	4	5	6	7	8	9	10	11	Substitutes used
30 Jul	F	A	Bordeaux XI	W 4-3												
3 Aug	F	A	Villenave D'Ornan	W 3-1												
5 Aug	F	A	Angouleme	D 1-1												
8 Aug	F	A	La Roche Sur Yon	D 2-2												
13 Aug	NCCsf	H	Notts Co	W 3-1												
15 Aug	F	A	Leicester C	D 2-2	Sutton	Laws	Pearce	Walker	Foster	Hodge	Carr	Parker 1	Clough	Chapman	Crosby	
19 Aug	FL	H	Aston Villa	D 1-1	Sutton	Laws	Pearce	Walker	Foster	Hodge	Carr	Parker	Clough	Chapman 1	Crosby	
23 Aug	FL	A	Norwich C	D 1-1	Sutton	Laws	Pearce	Walker	Foster	Hodge	Carr*	Parker	Clough	Chapman	Crosby	Rice (7)
26 Aug	FL	A	Millwall	L 0-1	Sutton	Laws	Pearce	Walker	Foster	Hodge*	Crosby	Parker	Clough	Chapman	Rice	Wilson (6)
30 Aug	FL	H	Derby Co	W 2-1	Sutton	Laws	Pearce	Walker	Foster	Hodge*	Crosby 1	Parker	Clough	Chapman 2	Rice	Starbuck (8), Gaynor (10)
9 Sep	FL	H	Chelsea	D 2-2	Sutton	Laws	Pearce	Walker	Foster	Hodge	Crosby	Wilson*	Clough	Chapman*	Parker	Gaynor (11)
16 Sep	FL	H	Arsenal	L 1-2	Sutton	Laws	Pearce	Walker	Foster	Hodge	Crosby	Sheridan	Clough	Chapman	Parker	Gaynor (11)
20 Sep	FLC2/1	H	Huddersfield T	D 1-1	Sutton	Laws	Chettle	Walker	Wilson	Hodge	Crosby	Parker	Clough	Chapman 1	Rice*	Wilson (8)
23 Sep	FL	A	Crystal Palace	L 0-1	Sutton	Laws 1	Chettle	Walker	Wassall	Hodge	Carr	Parker	Clough	Chapman	Crosby*	
30 Sep	FL	H	Charlton A	W 2-0	Sutton	Laws	Pearce	Walker	Wassall	Hodge	Crosby 1	Parker*	Clough	Chapman 1	Gaynor 1	Starbuck (9)
3 Oct	FLC2/2	A	Huddersfield T	D 3-3	Sutton	Laws	Pearce	Walker	Wilson	Hodge	Crosby 1	Parker	Clough	Chapman	Chettle	
9 Oct	F	H	King's Lynn	W 5-0	Sutton	Laws	Pearce	Walker	Wilson	Hodge	Crosby 1	Parker 1	Clough*	Chapman 1	Crosby	Rice (8)
14 Oct	FL	A	Coventry C	W 2-0	Sutton	Laws	Pearce	Walker	Wilson	Hodge	Crosby	Parker	Clough*	Chapman 1	Chettle	Chettle (5), Rice (7)
21 Oct	FL	H	Wimbledon	W 3-1	Sutton	Laws	Pearce 1p	Walker	Wilson*	Hodge	Crosby	Parker*	Clough 1	Chapman	Gaynor*	Carr (11)
24 Oct	FLC3	A	Crystal Palace	D 0-0	Sutton	Laws	Pearce	Walker	Wilson*	Hodge	Crosby	Parker	Clough	Chapman	Gaynor*	Chettle (5)
28 Oct	FL	H	QPR	D 2-2	Sutton	Laws	Pearce	Walker	Chettle	Hodge	Crosby	Parker	Clough	Chapman	Rice	
1 Nov	FLC3r	H	Crystal Palace	W 5-0 §	Sutton	Laws*	Pearce 1	Walker	Chettle	Hodge 2	Crosby 1	Parker 1	Clough 1	Chapman	Rice 1	
4 Nov	FL	A	Sheff Wed	L 0-1	Sutton	Laws	Pearce	Walker	Chettle	Hodge	Crosby	Parker	Clough	Chapman	Rice	
12 Nov	FL	A	Man Utd	W 3-0	Crossley	Laws	Pearce	Walker	Chettle	Hodge 1	Crosby	Parker	Clough 2(1p)	Chapman	Rice 1	Rice (9), Clough (10)
18 Nov	FL	A	Man City	W 1-0	Crossley	Laws	Pearce	Walker	Chettle	Hodge	Crosby	Parker	Clough 1p	Chapman	Rice	
22 Nov	FLC4	H	Everton	W 1-0	Crossley	Laws	Pearce 1	Walker	Chettle	Hodge	Crosby	Parker	Gaynor	Chapman*	Rice	
25 Nov	FL	A	Everton	W 3-2	Crossley	Laws	Pearce 1	Walker	Chettle	Hodge	Crosby	Parker	Clough	Chapman 1	Carr 1	
29 Nov	FMC2	H	Man City	L 1-2	Crossley	Laws	Pearce	Walker	Chettle	Hodge 1	Crosby	Parker	Clough	Chapman 1	Rice	Charles (2), Orlygsson (11)
2 Dec	FL	A	Aston Villa	L 0-1	Sutton	Laws	Pearce	Walker	Chettle	Hodge 1	Crosby	Parker	Clough 1	Chapman 1	Rice	Charles (7)
9 Dec	FL	H	Norwich C	W 2-0	Sutton	Laws	Pearce	Walker	Chettle	Hodge	Crosby	Orlygsson	Clough	Chapman	Rice	
17 Dec	FL	A	Southampton	L 1-2	Sutton	Laws*	Pearce	Walker	Chettle	Hodge	Crosby	Parker 1	Clough	Chapman	Rice*	Charles (2), Wilson (11)
22 Dec	FMC3	A	Aston Villa	L 0-1	Sutton	Laws	Pearce	Walker	Chettle	Hodge	Crosby	Parker	Clough	Jemson	Orlygsson	
26 Dec	FL	A	Luton T	D 1-1	Sutton	Laws	Pearce 1	Walker	Chettle	Hodge	Crosby 1*	Parker 1	Clough 1	Jemson	Orlygsson	Wilson (6)
30 Dec	FL	H	Tottenham H	W 3-2	Sutton	Laws*	Pearce	Walker	Chettle	Hodge 1	Crosby	Parker	Clough 1p	Jemson	Orlygsson	Rice (11)
1 Jan	FL	H	Liverpool	D 2-2	Sutton	Laws*	Pearce	Walker	Chettle	Hodge	Crosby	Parker	Clough	Jemson	Orlygsson*	Currie (10)
7 Jan	FAC3	H	Man Utd	L 0-1	Sutton	Laws 1	Pearce	Walker	Chettle	Hodge 1*	Crosby 1	Parker 1	Clough	Jemson	Orlygsson*	Wilson (6)
9 Jan	F	F	Auxerre	D 2-2	Sutton	Laws	Pearce	Walker	Chettle	Hodge 1	Crosby 1	Parker	Clough	Jemson	Orlygsson	Rice (11)
13 Jan	FL	A	Millwall	W 3-1	Sutton	Laws 1	Pearce	Walker	Chettle	Hodge 1	Crosby	Parker 1	Clough	Jemson	Orlygsson	
17 Jan	FLC5	H	Tottenham H	D 2-2	Sutton	Laws	Pearce	Walker	Chettle	Hodge	Crosby	Parker	Clough	Jemson 1*	Orlygsson	Currie (10)
20 Jan	FL	A	Derby Co	W 3-2	Sutton	Laws	Pearce	Walker	Chettle	Hodge 2	Crosby	Parker	Clough 1	Jemson 1	Orlygsson	Orlygsson (2), Currie (8)
24 Jan	FLC5r	H	Tottenham H	W 3-1	Sutton	Laws*	Pearce	Walker	Chettle	Hodge 1	Crosby	Parker	Clough 1p	Jemson	Orlygsson*	Currie (11)
3 Feb	FLCsf/1	A	Crystal Palace	W 2-1	Sutton	Laws*	Pearce 1	Walker	Wilson	Hodge	Crosby	Parker	Clough	Jemson	Orlygsson 1	Starbuck (11)
11 Feb	FL	H	Coventry C	D 1-1	Sutton	Laws	Pearce	Walker	Chettle	Hodge	Crosby	Parker	Clough	Jemson	Wilson	
17 Feb	FL	A	Chelsea	D 0-0	Sutton	Laws	Pearce	Walker	Wilson	Hodge	Crosby	Parker	Clough	Jemson	Orlygsson	
25 Feb	FLCsf/2	H	Coventry C	W 2-1	Sutton	Laws	Pearce	Walker	Wilson	Rice	Crosby	Parker	Clough	Jemson	Orlygsson	
3 Mar	FL	A	Man City	L 0-3	Sutton	Laws 1	Pearce	Walker	Wilson	Orlygsson*	Crosby	Parker*	Clough	Currie 1	Rice	Wilson (5)
7 Mar	FL	H	Arsenal	L 2-4	Sutton	Laws*	Pearce	Walker	Wilson	Hodge 1	Crosby	Parker*	Clough	Currie*	Jemson	Jemson (6), Gaynor (8)
10 Mar	FL	H	Coventry C	D 1-1	Sutton	Laws	Pearce	Walker	Wilson	Rice	Carr	Parker*	Clough	Currie	Gaynor	Rice (8), Gaynor (10)
17 Mar	FL	H	Charlton A	L 0-2	Sutton	Laws	Pearce	Walker	Wilson	Rice	Crosby	Parker*	Clough	Currie	Carr	Orlygsson (2), Currie (8)
24 Mar	FL	A	Wimbledon	L 0-1	Crossley	Laws*	Pearce	Walker	Chettle	Hodge	Crosby	Wilson	Clough	Currie*	Rice	
31 Mar	FL	H	Everton	L 0-4	Crossley	Laws	Williams	Walker	Chettle	Hodge 1	Crosby	Wilson	Clough	Currie*	Carr	Parker (8), Carr (10)
4 Apr	FL	H	Tottenham H	L 1-3	Sutton	Laws	Chettle	Walker	Chettle	Hodge 1	Carr	Wilson	Clough	Jemson	Parker	
7 Apr	FL	H	Liverpool	D 2-2	Crossley	Laws	Pearce	Walker	Chettle	Hodge*	Carr 1	Wilson	Clough	Jemson	Parker 1	Currie (6), Gaynor (8)
14 Apr	FL	A	Luton T	W 3-0	Sutton	Laws	Pearce	Walker	Chettle	Hodge	Carr	Parker	Clough	Jemson	Parker	
16 Apr	FL	H	Southampton	L 0-2	Crossley	Laws	Pearce	Walker	Chettle 1*	Chettle 1*	Crosby	Parker 1	Clough 1	Jemson	Parker 1	Wassall (5), Carr (10)
21 Apr	FLCf	H	Oldham A	W 1-0	Sutton	Laws	Pearce 1	Walker	Chettle	Hodge	Crosby	Parker	Clough 1	Jemson*	Gaynor*	
2 May	FL	A	Man Utd	W 4-0	Crossley	Laws	Pearce 2	Walker	Wassall	Hodge	Crosby	Parker	Clough 1	Jemson 1	Gaynor*	Carr (11)
5 May	FL	A	Sheff Wed	W 3-0	Sutton	Laws	Pearce	Walker	Wassall	Hodge	Crosby	Parker	Clough	Jemson	Gaynor	
8 May	NCCf	A	Mansfield T	W 4-0	Sutton	Laws	Pearce	Walker	Wassall	Hodge	Crosby	Parker	Clough	Jemson 1	Gaynor	

League Appearances (Goals)

Carr F 10+4 (1); Chapman L 18 (7); Charles G 0+1; Chettle S 21+1 (1); Clough N 38 (9); Crosby G 34 (5); Crossley M 8; Currie D 4+4 (1); Foster C 6; Gaynor T 5+6; Hodge S 34 (10); Jemson N 17+1 (4); Laws B 38 (3); Orlygsson T 11+1 (1); Parker G 36+1 (6); Pearce S 34 (5); Rice B 15+3 (2); Starbuck P 0+2; Sutton S 30; Walker D 38; Wassall D 2+1; Williams B 1; Wilson T 18+3.

Position in League Table

	P	W	D	L	F	A	Pts
1st Liverpool	38	23	10	5	78	37	79
9th Forest	38	15	9	14	55	47	54

Notes

§ denotes own goals
Oct 3, won on away goals
Apr 29, at Wembley

1990-91 Division One

Date		Comp	V	Opponent	Result	1	2	3	4	5	6	7	8	9	10	11	Substitutes used
29 Jul	F		A	Bengtsfors	W 5-1												
30 Jul	F		A	Norrstrands	W 4-0												
1 Aug	F		A	Mariestads	W 2-0												
5 Aug	F		A	Kongshalla	W 3-0												
7 Aug	F		A	Karlsunds	W 7-1												
9 Aug	F		A	Wycombe W	D 1-1												
13 Aug	F		A	Salernitana	D 0-0												
15 Aug	F		A	Avellino	W 1-0												
17 Aug	F		A	Foggia	D 2-2												
25 Aug	NCC1		H	Mansfield T	W 5-0	Crossley	Laws	Williams	Walker	Chettle*	Hodge	Crosby	Parker	Clough	Jemson 1p	Carr	Wassall (5)
25 Aug	FL		A	QPR	D 1-1	Crossley	Laws	Williams	Walker	Chettle	Keane	Crosby	Parker	Clough	Jemson	Starbuck	
28 Aug	FL		A	Liverpool	L 0-2	Crossley	Laws	Williams	Walker	Chettle	Hodge*	Keane	Parker	Clough	Jemson	Keane	
1 Sep	FL		H	Coventry C	D 2-2	Crossley	Laws*	Pearce 2	Walker	Chettle	Wilson 1	Carr	Parker	Clough	Jemson 2(1p)	Gaynor	Wilson (6)
8 Sep	FL		H	Southampton	W 3-1	Crossley	Laws	Pearce	Walker	Chettle 1	Keane	Crosby	Parker	Clough	Jemson 2	Gaynor	Wassall (2), Gaynor (11)
15 Sep	FL		A	Crystal Palace	D 2-2	Crossley	Laws	Pearce	Walker	Chettle	Keane	Crosby	Parker	Clough	Jemson	Gaynor	Rice (11)
22 Sep	FL		A	Arsenal	L 0-2	Crossley	Laws	Pearce 1	Walker	Chettle	Hodge 2	Crosby	Parker	Clough*	Jemson 1	Keane	
26 Sep	FLC2/1		A	Burnley	W 4-1	Crossley	Laws	Pearce	Walker	Chettle	Hodge*	Crosby	Parker	Gaynor	Jemson	Keane	
29 Sep	FL		H	Man Utd	W 1-0	Crossley	Laws	Pearce	Walker	Chettle	Hodge	Crosby	Parker	Crosby	Jemson 1	Keane	Gaynor (9)
6 Oct	FL		A	Everton	W 3-1	Crossley	Laws	Pearce	Walker	Chettle	Hodge	Crosby 1	Parker	Clough 1	Jemson	Keane	Lyne (6)
10 Oct	FLC2/2		H	Burnley	W 1-0	Crossley	Laws	Pearce	Walker	Chettle	Keane	Crosby	Wilson	Clough	Jemson	Gaynor	Parker (8)
20 Oct	FL		A	Chelsea	D 0-0	Crossley	Laws	Pearce	Walker	Chettle	Keane	Carr	Parker	Clough	Jemson	Gaynor*	
24 Oct	FL		H	Tottenham H	L 1-2	Crossley	Laws	Pearce	Walker	Chettle	Carr	Crosby	Parker	Clough	Jemson*	Carr 1	Wassall (4), Starbuck (10)
30 Oct	FLC3		A	Plymouth A	W 2-1	Crossley	Laws	Pearce	Walker	Chettle 1	Hodge*	Crosby	Parker	Clough 1	Jemson 1	Parker	Starbuck (8), Charles (11)
3 Nov	FL		A	Leeds U	L 1-3	Crossley	Laws	Pearce	Walker	Chettle	Hodge	Crosby	Parker	Clough	Jemson 1*	Parker	
10 Nov	FL		H	Aston Villa	D 1-1	Crossley	Laws	Wassall	Walker	Chettle	Keane	Carr 1	Parker	Clough	Jemson	Parker 1	Wassall (4), Starbuck (10)
17 Nov	FL		H	Sunderland	W 2-0	Crossley	Laws	Pearce	Walker	Chettle	Keane	Carr	Parker	Clough 3	Jemson 1	Crosby	Starbuck (6)
21 Nov	FMC2		H	Newcastle U	W 2-1	Crossley	Laws	Pearce	Walker	Chettle	Hodge 1	Carr	Keane	Clough 1	Jemson 1	Crosby	Starbuck (8)
24 Nov	FL		A	Derby Co	L 1-2	Crossley	Laws	Pearce	Walker	Chettle	Hodge*	Carr	Keane	Clough 1	Jemson	Parker	Starbuck (6)
28 Nov	FLC4		H	Coventry C	L 4-5	Crossley	Laws	Pearce	Walker	Chettle	Keane	Carr	Parker	Clough	Jemson*	Parker*	
1 Dec	FL		H	Luton T	D 2-2	Crossley	Laws	Pearce 1	Walker	Chettle 1	Keane	Carr	Parker	Clough 1	Jemson	Crosby 1	Starbuck (10)
15 Dec	FL		A	QPR	W 2-1	Crossley	Laws	Pearce 1	Walker	Chettle	Keane	Carr	Keane	Clough 1	Jemson	Parker	
22 Dec	FL		A	Sheff Utd	L 2-3	Crossley	Laws	Pearce	Walker	Chettle	Wilson	Carr	Keane	Clough	Jemson*	Parker	Starbuck (10)
26 Dec	FL		H	Wimbledon	W 2-1	Crossley	Laws	Pearce	Walker	Chettle	Wilson 1*	Starbuck	Parker	Clough	Jemson	Parker	Wilson (6), Starbuck (10)
31 Dec	FL		H	Man City	L 1-3	Crossley	Laws	Pearce	Walker	Chettle	Keane	Carr*	Parker	Gaynor 1	Parker	Woan*	Starbuck (8), Crosby (11)
2 Jan	FAC3		A	Norwich C	W 6-2 §	Crossley	Laws	Pearce 1	Walker	Chettle	Keane	Carr*	Starbuck	Crosby	Gaynor*	Parker 2	Woan (6)
6 Jan	FL		A	Crystal Palace	D 0-0	Crossley	Laws	Pearce	Walker	Chettle	Keane	Crosby	Keane	Clough	Crosby	Keane	
12 Jan	FL		H	Coventry C	W 3-0	Crossley	Laws	Pearce	Walker	Chettle	Hodge 1	Crosby	Starbuck	Clough 1	Crosby 1	Keane	Wassall (10)
19 Jan	FL		A	Southampton	D 1-1	Crossley	Charles	Williams	Walker	Chettle	Hodge*	Crosby	Keane	Clough 1	Wilson 1*	Keane	Starbuck (7), Wassall (8)
21 Jan	FAC3r		H	Crystal Palace	D 2-2	Crossley	Charles	Pearce	Walker	Chettle 1	Hodge	Crosby 1	Keane	Clough*	Keane*	Parker	Hodge (7)
28 Jan	FAC3r2		A	Crystal Palace	W 3-0	Crossley	Charles	Pearce	Walker	Chettle	Keane 1	Crosby	Wilson	Clough	Parker 2	Woan*	Starbuck (10)
30 Jan	FMC3		H	Barnsley	D 2-2	Crossley	Laws	Pearce 1	Walker	Chettle	Keane	Crosby	Wilson	Clough 1	Keane	Parker	Gaynor (9), Starbuck (10)
13 Feb	FAC4		A	Newcastle U	L 1-2	Crossley	Laws	Pearce	Walker	Chettle	Keane 1	Starbuck*	Wilson	Clough	Keane	Keane	Gaynor (10), Starbuck (11)
16 Feb	FL		A	Sunderland	D 2-2	Crossley	Laws	Pearce	Walker	Chettle	Keane	Crosby	Wilson	Clough	Keane	Keane	
20 Feb	FL		H	Newcastle U	L 0-1	Crossley	Charles	Pearce	Walker	Chettle	Gaynor*	Crosby	Wilson	Clough 1	Keane	Parker	
23 Feb	FL		H	Aston Villa	D 2-2	Crossley	Charles	Pearce	Walker	Chettle	Hodge 1	Starbuck	Wilson	Clough 1	Keane	Parker	Hodge (6), Crosby (7)
25 Feb	FAC5		H	Southampton	D 1-1	Crossley	Laws	Pearce 1	Walker	Chettle	Hodge 1*	Crosby	Wilson	Clough	Keane*	Parker*	Starbuck (10)
2 Mar	FL		A	Luton T	L 0-1	Crossley	Laws	Pearce	Walker	Chettle	Keane	Crosby	Wilson	Clough	Keane	Parker 1	Woan (11)
4 Mar	FAC5r		H	Southampton	W 3-1	Crossley	Charles	Pearce	Walker	Chettle	Keane 1	Loughlan 1	Wilson	Clough	Jemson 3(1p)	Parker	Jemson (6)
9 Mar	FAC6		A	Norwich C	W 1-0	Crossley	Charles	Pearce	Walker	Chettle	Keane	Loughlan	Wilson	Clough	Jemson	Woan	
16 Mar	FL		A	Man Utd	D 1-1	Crossley	Laws	Pearce	Walker	Chettle	Parker	Gaynor	Gemmill	Clough	Jemson	Parker	
20 Mar	FL		A	Arsenal	D 1-1	Crossley	Laws	Pearce	Walker	Chettle	Keane	Gaynor*	Gemmill	Clough	Jemson 1	Parker	Starbuck (8)
23 Mar	FL		A	Everton	D 0-0	Crossley	Charles	Pearce	Walker	Chettle	Keane 1	Crosby 1	Parker	Clough	Jemson	Parker	Woan (3), Gemmill (8)
30 Mar	FL		H	Wimbledon	L 1-3	Crossley	Charles	Pearce	Walker	Chettle	Keane	Crosby 1	Keane 2	Clough 1	Gaynor 2	Woan	
1 Apr	FL		A	Sheff Utd	W 2-0	Crossley	Laws	Pearce 1	Walker	Chettle	Keane 1	Crosby 1	Parker 1	Clough 1	Glover	Parker	Laws (7)
6 Apr	FL		H	Man City	L 1-3	Crossley	Charles 1	Pearce*	Walker	Chettle	Keane*	Crosby 1	Keane*	Clough 1	Glover	Woan 1	Laws (8)
10 Apr	FL		A	Derby Co	W 4-0	Crossley	Charles*	Pearce 1	Walker	Chettle	Hodge	Crosby	Parker 1	Clough 1	Glover 1	Woan 1	
14 Apr	FACsf			West Ham U	W 4-0	Crossley	Charles	Pearce 2	Walker	Chettle	Keane	Crosby	Parker 1	Clough 1	Glover	Woan 1	Laws (8)
20 Apr	FL		H	Chelsea	W 7-0	Crossley	Laws	Pearce 1	Walker	Chettle	Keane*	Crosby 1	Parker 1	Clough 1*	Glover 1	Woan	
24 Apr	FL		H	Norwich C	W 5-0	Crossley	Laws	Pearce*	Walker	Chettle	Hodge	Crosby 1	Parker	Clough 1p	Glover 1	Woan 1	Laws (2), Gemmill (9)
1 May	FL		A	Tottenham H	D 1-1	Crossley	Charles	Pearce 1	Walker	Chettle	Hodge	Crosby	Parker 2	Clough 2	Glover	Woan	Wassall (6)
6 May	FL		A	Liverpool	W 2-1	Crossley	Charles	Pearce	Walker	Chettle	Keane	Crosby	Parker	Clough	Glover	Woan	
11 May	FL		H	Leeds U	W 4-3	Crossley	Laws	Pearce*	Walker	Chettle	Hodge	Crosby	Parker	Clough	Glover	Woan	Jemson (3)
13 May	F		A	Notts Co	L 1-2												
18 May	FACf		H	Tottenham H	L 1-2	Crossley	Charles	Pearce 1	Walker	Chettle	Keane	Crosby	Parker	Clough	Glover	Woan*	Laws (10), Hodge (11)

League Appearances (Goals)

Carr F 13 (2); Charles G 9+1; Chettle S 37 (2); Clough N 37 (14); Gaynor T 9+2 (3); Gemmill S 2+2; Glover L 8 (1); Hodge S 12+2 (3); Jemson N 22+1 (8); Keane R 35 (8); Laws B 30+2; Loughlan A 2 (1); Parker G 35+1 (3); Pearce S 33 (11); Rice B 0+1; Starbuck P 3+9; Walker D 37; Wassall D 3+4; Williams B 4; Wilson T 13+2 (3); Woan I 9+3 (3); Own goals 1.

Position in League Table

	P	W	D	L	F	A	Pts
1st Arsenal**	38	24	13	1	74	18	83
8th Forest	38	14	12	12	65	50	54

Notes

§ denotes own goals
** Arsenal 2 points deducted
Apr 14, at Villa Park
May 18, at Wembley

1991-92 — Division One

Date	Comp		Opponent	Result	1	2	3	4	5	6	7	8	9	10	11	Substitutes used
3 Aug	F	A	Cobh Ramblers	W 5-0												
5 Aug	F	A	Shelbourne	W 2-0												
6 Aug	F	A	Alta IF	W 6-0												
7 Aug	F	A	Enebyberg	W 13-0												
8 Aug	F	A	Tosi	W 3-1												
8 Aug	F	H	Vasalunds	D 2-2												
11 Aug	NCCf	H	Notts Co	W 2-1												
17 Aug	FL	A	Everton	W 2-1	Crossley	Charles	Pearce	Walker*	Tiler	Keane	Crosby	Gemmill	Clough 1	Sheringham	Jemson 1	Chettle (4)
20 Aug	FL	A	Leeds U	L 0-1	Crossley	Charles	Pearce	Chettle	Tiler	Keane 1	Crosby 1	Gemmill	Clough	Sheringham	Jemson*	Laws (11)
24 Aug	FL	A	Notts Co	L 1-3	Crossley	Charles 1	Pearce	Chettle	Tiler	Keane	Crosby	Gemmill 1	Clough 1	Sheringham	Jemson	
28 Aug	FL	H	Tottenham H	W 3-1	Crossley	Charles	Pearce 1	Chettle	Tiler	Keane 1	Crosby	Gemmill 1	Clough	Sheringham 1	Jemson	
31 Aug	FL	A	Oldham A	L 1-2	Crossley	Charles	Pearce	Chettle	Tiler	Keane	Crosby	Gemmill	Clough	Sheringham	Jemson	
4 Sep	FL	A	Man City	W 2-1	Crossley	Charles	Pearce	Chettle	Tiler	Keane	Crosby	Gemmill	Clough	Sheringham	Black	
7 Sep	FL	H	Sheff Wed	W 4-2 §	Williams	Charles	Williams	Chettle	Tiler	Keane 2	Crosby	Gemmill	Clough	Sheringham	Black 1	Parker (8), Laws (9)
14 Sep	FL	A	Wimbledon	L 1-3	Crossley	Charles	Pearce	Chettle	Tiler	Keane	Crosby	Gemmill*	Clough	Sheringham	Black	Laws (2), Boardman (6)
21 Sep	FLC2/1	H	Aston Villa	W 4-0	Crossley	Charles*	Pearce	Chettle	Tiler	Keane 1*	Crosby	Parker	Clough*	Sheringham 1	Woan	Walker (9)
25 Sep	FL	H	Bolton W	D 2-2	Crossley	Charles	Pearce	Chettle	Tiler	Keane	Black 1	Parker	Gaynor 2	Sheringham 1	Woan 1	Chettle (9)
28 Sep	FL	A	QPR	W 2-0	Crossley	Charles	Pearce	Walker	Tiler	Keane	Black	Parker	Gaynor*	Sheringham 2	Black	Chettle (2), Gemmill (8)
5 Oct	FLC2/2	H	Bolton W	W 5-2	Crossley	Charles	Pearce	Walker	Tiler	Keane 2	Crosby	Parker 1	Gaynor 1	Sheringham 1	Black 1	Chettle (6) 1, Woan (11)
8 Oct	FL	A	Sheff Utd	L 2-4	Crossley	Charles	Pearce	Walker	Tiler	Keane	Crosby	Parker*	Gaynor	Sheringham	Black*	Gaynor (9), Laws (11)
19 Oct	FMC2	H	Leeds U	W 3-1	Crossley	Chettle	Pearce	Walker	Chettle	Wassall	Crosby	Gemmill	Sheringham 2(1p)*	Black	Parker*	Laws (4)
22 Oct	FL	A	Bristol R	D 0-0	Crossley	Chettle	Pearce	Walker	Chettle	Gemmill	Crosby	Parker	Sheringham*	Sheringham	Black 1	Woan (9)
26 Oct	FL	A	Norwich C	L 0-1	Crossley	Charles	Pearce	Walker	Chettle	Keane	Crosby	Parker	Glover	Sheringham	Black	
30 Oct	FMC3	H	Coventry C	W 2-0	Crossley	Charles	Pearce	Walker	Chettle	Keane	Glover	Gemmill 1	Sheringham 1	Sheringham 1	Black	
2 Nov	FL	H	Aston Villa	W 5-1	Crossley	Charles	Pearce	Walker	Chettle	Wassall	Crosby	Gemmill	Sheringham 1	Sheringham	Woan	
9 Nov	FL	A	Crystal Palace	L 0-1	Crossley	Charles	Pearce	Walker	Chettle	Keane 2*	Crosby	Gemmill 1	Glover	Sheringham 2(1p)	Woan 1	Wassall (6), Clough (11)
19 Nov	FMC4	H	Chelsea	D 0-0	Crossley	Charles*	Pearce	Walker	Chettle*	Keane	Crosby	Gemmill 1	Glover	Sheringham	Woan 1	Wassall (6), Clough (7)
23 Nov	FL	A	Southampton	W 3-2	Crossley	Charles	Pearce	Walker	Chettle	Keane	Crosby	Gemmill	Glover	Sheringham	Woan	Wassall (6)
30 Nov	FL	H	Arsenal	W 2-0	Crossley	Charles	Pearce	Walker*	Tiler	Keane	Black	Gemmill	Clough	Sheringham 1	Woan	Tiler (5)
4 Dec	FLC4	A	Tranmere R	L 0-2	Crossley	Charles	Pearce	Walker	Chettle	Keane	Black	Gemmill	Clough	Sheringham	Woan 1	
8 Dec	FL	H	Liverpool	W 1-0	Crossley	Charles	Pearce	Walker	Tiler	Keane	Crosby	Gemmill	Clough	Sheringham	Woan	
10 Dec	FLC4r	H	Southampton	D 0-0	Crossley	Charles	Pearce	Walker	Tiler	Keane	Crosby	Gemmill	Clough	Sheringham	Woan	Wassall (4), Black (6)
14 Dec	FL	A	Leeds U	W 2-1	Crossley	Charles	Pearce	Walker	Tiler	Keane	Crosby	Gemmill	Clough	Sheringham	Woan*	Tiler (10)
17 Dec	FL	H	Tottenham H	L 1-2	Crossley	Charles	Pearce	Walker	Tiler	Keane	Crosby	Gemmill	Clough	Sheringham	Woan	Wassall (2), Glover (4)
22 Dec	FL	A	Oldham A	D 1-1	Crossley	Charles	Pearce	Walker	Tiler	Keane	Crosby	Gemmill 1	Clough	Sheringham	Woan	Glover (7)
26 Dec	FL	H	Luton T	W 1-0	Crossley	Charles	Pearce 1	Walker	Tiler	Keane	Black 1	Gemmill	Clough	Sheringham	Black	Wassall (6)
28 Dec	FL	H	Wolves	D 1-1	Crossley	Charles	Pearce 1	Walker	Tiler	Keane	Black	Gemmill	Clough	Sheringham	Black	Glover (10)
1 Jan	FL	A	Crystal Palace	D 1-1	Crossley	Charles	Pearce	Walker	Tiler	Keane	Crosby	Gemmill	Glover	Sheringham	Black	
4 Jan	FAC3	A	Notts Co	W 2-0	Crossley	Charles	Pearce	Walker 1	Tiler	Keane	Crosby	Gemmill	Clough 1	Sheringham	Black	
8 Jan	FLC5	H	Everton	D 1-1	Crossley	Charles	Pearce	Walker	Tiler	Keane	Crosby	Gemmill	Clough 1	Sheringham	Black	
11 Jan	FL	H	Hereford U	W 2-5	Crossley	Charles*	Pearce 1	Walker	Tiler*	Keane	Crosby	Gemmill 1	Glover	Sheringham 1	Woan	Glover (10)
19 Jan	FAC4	A	Sheff Utd	W 4-2	Crossley	Laws	Pearce 1p	Walker	Tiler	Keane	Crosby	Gemmill	Glover	Sheringham	Woan	Crosby (2), Wassall (5)
1 Feb	FL	H	Crystal Palace	D 1-1	Crossley	Charles	Pearce 1	Walker	Wassall	Keane 1	Crosby 1*	Gemmill 1	Clough	Sheringham 3(1p)	Black	Chettle (5)
5 Feb	FLC5r	H	Tottenham H	W 2-0	Crossley	Laws	Pearce	Walker	Tiler	Keane	Crosby	Gemmill	Clough 1*	Sheringham 1	Black	Crosby (2)
9 Feb	FL	A	Leicester C	D 1-1	Crossley	Laws	Glover	Walker	Wassall	Keane	Crosby	Gemmill	Clough	Sheringham 1	Black	Crosby (7)
12 Feb	FMCN/1	H	Bristol C	W 2-0	Crossley	Laws	Pearce	Walker	Wassall	Keane	Crosby	Gemmill	Clough	Sheringham 1	Black	
15 Feb	FMCN/1A	A	Chelsea	W 2-1	Crossley	Laws	Pearce	Walker	Wassall 1	Keane	Black	Gemmill	Clough	Glover	Black	Charles (9), Glover (10)
22 Feb	FMC5	H	Leicester C	D 0-0	Crossley	Laws	Pearce	Walker	Wassall 1	Keane	Wassall	Gemmill 1	Clough	Sheringham 1	Glover 1	
26 Feb	FL	A	Tottenham H	W 2-0	Crossley	Charles	Pearce	Walker	Tiler	Keane 1	Crosby 1	Gemmill	Clough	Sheringham	Glover	Glover (7), Charles (11)
1 Mar	FLCsf/1	A	Crystal Palace	L 0-1	Crossley	Laws	Pearce	Walker	Wassall	Keane	Crosby	Gemmill	Clough 1	Sheringham	Glover	
3 Mar	FLCsf/2	H	Portsmouth	L 0-1 §	Crossley	Charles	Pearce	Walker	Tiler	Keane	Crosby	Gemmill	Glover	Sheringham 1	Glover 1	Chettle (10)
7 Mar	FAC6	A	Coventry C	W 2-0	Marriott	Charles	Pearce	Walker	Wassall	Keane	Wassall	Gemmill	Glover	Glover	Black	
11 Mar	FL	H	Norwich C	W 1-0	Marriott	Charles	Pearce*	Walker	Tiler	Keane 1	Crosby	Gemmill 1	Glover	Glover	Black 1	Chettle (2)
14 Mar	FL	A	Man City	D 3-3	Marriott	Charles*	Pearce*	Walker	Wassall	Keane 1	Black	Gemmill 1	Clough	Sheringham	Woan	Chettle (3)
18 Mar	FL	A	Southampton	L 0-3	Marriott	Charles	Chettle	Walker	Wassall	Keane	Black	Gemmill	Clough	Sheringham	Black 1	
21 Mar	FL	H	Arsenal	L 0-2	Marriott	Charles	Chettle	Walker	Wassall	Keane	Black	Gemmill	Clough	Sheringham	Black 1	
29 Mar	FMCf		Southampton	W 3-2	Marriott	Chettle	Williams	Walker	Tiler	Keane 1	Black	Gemmill 2	Clough 1	Sheringham	Woan	Chettle (2)
31 Mar	FL	A	Wimbledon	L 0-1	Crossley	Chettle	Williams	Walker*	Tiler	Keane	Black	Gemmill	Clough 1	Sheringham	Woan	Chettle (3)
4 Apr	FL	H	Sheff Wed	W 2-0	Crossley	Williams	Williams	Walker	Wassall	Keane	Crosby	Gemmill 1	Glover	Glover	Glover 1	Tiler (2), Laws (3)
7 Apr	FL	H	Southampton	W 1-0	Crossley	Williams	Williams	Walker*	Wassall	Keane	Crosby	Gemmill 1	Glover	Sheringham	Tiler 1	Glover (4)
8 Apr	FL	A	Man Utd	L 0-1	Crossley	Charles*	Crossley	Walker	Glover	Keane	Crosby	Gemmill	Clough	Sheringham	Black 1	
12 Apr	FLCf		Man Utd	L 0-1	Crossley	Orlygsson	Williams	Orlygsson	Crosby	Keane	Crosby	Gemmill	Clough	Sheringham	Woan	Glover (4)
14 Apr	FL	A	Luton T	W 2-1	Crossley	Laws	Crossley	Walker	Crossley	Keane	Crosby	Gemmill	Clough	Sheringham	Woan 1	Laws (2)
18 Apr	FL	A	Aston Villa	D 1-1	Crossley	Laws	Crossley	Walker	Crossley	Keane	Black	Gemmill 1	Clough	Sheringham 1	Black 1	Kaminsky (4)
20 Apr	FL	H	Liverpool	L 0-3	Crossley	Laws	Woan	Walker	Crossley	Keane	Orlygsson	Gemmill 1	Clough	Sheringham 1p	Gemmill 1	
25 Apr	FL	H	QPR	D 1-1	Crossley	Woan	Laws	Walker	Crossley	Wilson*	Orlygsson	Gemmill	Clough	Sheringham	Black	Gaynor (7)
2 May	FL	A	West Ham U	L 0-3	Crossley	Laws	Williams	Walker	Crossley	Crosby	Black	Gemmill 1	Clough	Sheringham	Woan*	Stone (6), Glover (11)
7 May	F	A	Glenavon	W 5-0												

League Appearances (Goals)

Black K 25 (4); Charles G 30 (1); Chettle S 17+5 (1); Clough N 33+1 (5); Crosby G 31+2 (3); Crossley M 36; Gaynor T 3+1; Gemmill S 39 (8); Glover L 12+4; Jemson N 6(1); Kaminsky J 0+1; Keane R 39 (8); Laws B 10+5; Marriott A 6; Orlygsson T 5; Parker G 5+1 (1); Pearce S 30 (5); Sheringham E 39 (13); Stone S 0+1; Tiler C 24+2 (1); Walker D 32+1 (1); Wassall D 10+4; Williams B 9; Wilson T 1; Woan I 20+1 (5); Own goals 3.

Position in League Table

	P	W	D	L	F	A	Pts
1st Leeds	42	22	16	4	74	37	82
8th Forest	42	16	11	15	60	58	59

Notes

§ denotes own goals
Mar 29, Apr 12, at Wembley

1992-93	FA Premier League			1	2	3	4	5	6	7	8	9	10	11	Substitutes used
27 Jul	F	A	Dundalk	W 4-0												
29 Jul	F	A	Shamrock Rovers	D 0-0												
1 Aug	F		Sampdoria	L 0-2												
2 Aug	F		Stuttgart	L 0-1												
7 Aug	F	A	Ards	W 6-1												
9 Aug	F	A	Derry City	D 2-2												
16 Aug	PL	H	Liverpool	W 1-0	Crossley	Laws	Pearce	Wilson	Chettle	Keane	Crosby*	Gemmill	Clough	Sheringham 1	Woan	Black (7)
19 Aug	PL	A	Sheff Wed	L 0-2	Crossley	Laws	Pearce	Wilson	Chettle	Keane	Crosby	Gemmill	Clough	Sheringham	Woan	Black (4), **Bannister** (10) **2**
22 Aug	PL	A	Oldham A	L 3-5	Crossley	Laws	**Pearce 1p**	Wilson*	Chettle	Keane	Crosby	Gemmill	Clough	Sheringham*	Woan	
29 Aug	PL	H	Man Utd	L 0-2	Crossley	Laws	Pearce	Wilson	Chettle	Keane	Crosby	Gemmill	**Clough 1**	Bannister	Woan	
31 Aug	PL	A	Norwich C	L 1-3	Crossley	Laws	Pearce	Tiler	Chettle	Keane	Orlygsson	Gemmill	Clough	**Bannister 1**	Black	McKinnon (6)
5 Sep	PL	A	Blackburn R	L 1-4	Crossley	Laws	Pearce	Tiler	Chettle	Keane*	Orlygsson	Gemmill	Clough	**Bannister 1**	Crosby	
12 Sep	PL	H	Sheff Wed	L 1-2	Crossley	Laws	Pearce		Chettle		Crosby	Gemmill	Clough	Bannister	Black	
14 Sep	F	H	Derby County	L 0-2												
21 Sep	PL	H	Coventry C	D 1-1	Crossley	Laws	Pearce	McKinnon	Tiler	Keane	Crosby	Gemmill	**Clough 1**	**Bannister 1**	Orlygsson	Black (6)
23 Sep	FLC2/1	A	Stockport Co	W 3-2	Crossley	Laws	Pearce	McKinnon	Tiler	Keane	Crosby	Gemmill	**Clough 1**	**Bannister 1**	**Orlygsson 1**	Glover (10)
26 Sep	PL	A	Chelsea	D 0-0	Crossley	Laws	Pearce	McKinnon	Tiler	Keane	Crosby	Gemmill	Clough	Bannister	Orlygsson	Chettle (2)
3 Oct	PL	H	Man City	D 2-2	Crossley	Laws	**Pearce 1**	**McKinnon 1**	Tiler	Keane	Crosby	Gemmill	Clough	Bannister	Orlygsson	Bannister (6)
6 Oct	FLC2/2	H	Stockport Co	W 2-1 §	Crossley	Laws	Pearce	Chettle	Tiler	Keane	Crosby	Gemmill	Clough	Bannister	Black	
17 Oct	PL	A	Arsenal	L 0-1	Crossley	Charles	Pearce	Keane	Tiler	McKinnon*	Crosby	Gemmill	Clough	Bannister*	**Black 1**	
21 Oct	PL	H	Middlesbrough	W 1-0	Crossley	Charles	Pearce	Keane	Tiler	Orlygsson	Crosby	Gemmill	Clough	Glover	Orlygsson	Glover (7)
24 Oct	PL	A	Sheff Utd	D 0-0	Crossley	Charles	Pearce	Keane	Tiler	Orlygsson	Crosby	Gemmill	Clough	Glover	**Black 1**	
28 Oct	FLC3	H	Crewe Alex	W 1-0	Crossley	Charles*	Pearce	Keane	Tiler	**Orlygsson 1**	Crosby	Gemmill	Clough	Glover	Black	
31 Oct	PL	H	Ipswich T	L 0-1	Crossley	Laws	Pearce	Keane	Tiler	Orlygsson*	Crosby	Gemmill	Clough	Glover	Black	
7 Nov	PL	A	Everton	L 0-1	Crossley	Laws	Pearce	Chettle	Tiler	Keane	Orlygsson	Gemmill	Clough	Glover	Woan	Glover (7)
21 Nov	PL	H	Crystal Palace	D 1-1	Crossley	Laws	Pearce	Chettle	Tiler	Keane	**Bannister 1**	**Gemmill 1**	Clough	Webb	Woan	Bannister (11)
28 Nov	PL	H	Southampton	L 1-2	Crossley	Laws	Pearce	Chettle	Tiler	Keane	Bannister*	Gemmill	Clough	Glover	Woan	Bannister (10), **Black** (11) **1**
2 Dec	FLC4	H	Tottenham H	W 2-0	Crossley	Laws	Pearce	Chettle	Tiler	**Keane 1**	Black	Gemmill	**Clough 1**	Glover*	**Woan 1***	Orlygsson (10)
5 Dec	PL	A	Leeds U	W 4-1	Crossley	Laws	Pearce	Chettle	Tiler	**Keane 2**	Webb	Gemmill	Clough	Glover*	**Woan 1***	Bannister (11), **Black** (11) **1**
12 Dec	PL	A	Aston Villa	L 1-2	Crossley	Laws	Pearce	Chettle	Tiler	**Keane 1**	Webb	Gemmill	**Clough 1**	Webb	Black	Orlygsson (10)
20 Dec	PL	H	Wimbledon	D 1-1	Crossley	Laws	Pearce	Chettle	Tiler	Keane	Crosby	**Gemmill 1**	Clough	Webb	Black*	Woan (11)
26 Dec	PL	A	Tottenham H	L 1-2	Crossley	Laws	Pearce	Chettle	Tiler	Keane	Crosby	Gemmill	**Clough 1**	Black*	Woan	
9 Jan	FAC3	H	Southampton	W 2-1	Crossley	Laws	Pearce	Chettle	Tiler	**Keane 1**	Crosby	Gemmill	Clough	Webb	**Woan 1**	Stone (7), Orlygsson (10)
12 Jan	FLC5	H	Arsenal	L 0-2	Crossley	Laws	Pearce	Chettle	Tiler	Keane	Bannister	Gemmill	Clough	**Webb 1**	Woan	**Orlygsson** (8) **1**
16 Jan	PL	A	Chelsea	W 3-0	Crossley	Laws	Pearce	Chettle	Tiler	Keane	Black*	Gemmill	**Clough 1**	Wilson*	**Woan 1**	
23 Jan	FAC4	H	Middlesbrough	D 1-1	Crossley	Laws	Pearce	Chettle	Tiler	Keane	**Bannister 2**	Gemmill	Clough	Webb	Woan	
27 Jan	PL	A	Man Utd	L 0-2	Crossley	Laws	Williams	Chettle	Tiler	Keane	Bannister	Gemmill	Clough	**Webb 1**	Woan	
30 Jan	PL	A	Oldham A	W 2-0	Crossley	Laws	Williams	**Stone 1**	Tiler	Keane*	Bannister	Gemmill	Clough	Webb	**Woan 2**	Orlygsson (6), Crosby (11)
3 Feb	FAC4r	A	Middlesbrough	W 3-0	Crossley	Laws	Williams	Stone	Tiler	Keane	**Bannister 1**	Gemmill	**Clough 1**	Webb	**Woan 1**	
6 Feb	PL	H	Liverpool	D 0-0	Crossley	Laws	Pearce	Chettle	Tiler	**Keane 1**	Crosby	Orlygsson	Clough	Orlygsson	Woan	
13 Feb	FAC5	A	Arsenal	L 0-2	Crossley	Laws	Chettle	Chettle	Tiler	Keane	Bannister	Black	**Clough 1**	Webb*	Woan	Crosby (10)
20 Feb	PL	A	Middlesbrough	W 2-1	Crossley	Charles	Chettle	Chettle	Tiler	Keane	Orlygsson	Gemmill	Clough	Bannister	Woan	
24 Feb	PL	H	QPR	W 1-0	Crossley	Charles	Chettle	Stone	Tiler	Orlygsson	**Crosby 1**	Gemmill	Clough	Bannister	Woan	Laws (4)
27 Feb	PL	H	Man City	L 0-2	Crossley	Charles*	Laws	Stone	Tiler	Keane	Crosby	Black	Clough	Glover	Woan	Bannister (8)
7 Mar	F	A	Portugese (Jersey)	W 10-0												
13 Mar	PL	A	Everton	L 0-3	Crossley	Charles	Laws	Chettle	Tiler	Orlygsson	Crosby*	McKinnon	Clough	Orlygsson	Woan	Glover (7)
17 Mar	PL	H	Norwich C	L 0-3	Crossley	Charles	Chettle	Stone	Tiler	Orlygsson	Crosby*	Stone	Clough	Bannister*	Woan	Black (7), Glover (10)
24 Mar	PL	A	Southampton	W 2-1	Crossley	Charles	Laws	Stone	Tiler	**Keane 1**	Black	Bannister	**Clough 1p**	Rosario	Woan	Crosby (2)
4 Apr	PL	A	Aston Villa	L 0-1	Marriott	Charles	Chettle	Stone	Tiler	Keane	Black	Bannister	Clough	Rosario	Black	Crosby (10)
7 Apr	PL	A	Blackburn R	L 3-4	Marriott	Charles	Chettle	Stone	Tiler	Keane	Bannister	Bannister	**Clough 1p**	Rosario	Black	Orlygsson (10)
10 Apr	PL	A	QPR	L 1-3	Marriott	Laws	Williams	Stone	Tiler	Keane	Bannister	**Bannister 1**	Clough	**Rosario 1***	Black	Glover (10)
12 Apr	PL	H	Tottenham H	W 2-1	Marriott	Laws	Williams	Stone	Tiler	Keane	**Black 1**	Bannister	**Clough 1p**	Rosario	Gemmill	Stone (10)
17 Apr	PL	A	Wimbledon	L 0-1	Marriott	Laws	Williams	Glover	Tiler	**Keane 1**	Black*	Bannister	Clough	Rosario*	Woan	Orlygsson (10)
21 Apr	PL	A	Arsenal	L 0-1	Marriott	Laws	Williams	Chettle	Tiler	Keane	Black	Gemmill	Clough	Rosario	Woan	Glover (7)
1 May	PL	A	Sheff Utd	L 1-2	Marriott	Laws	Williams	Chettle	Tiler	Keane	Black*	Gemmill	**Clough 1p**	Rosario	Woan	Orlygsson (7)
8 May	NCC1	H	Notts Co	W 3-0	Marriott	Laws	Williams	Chettle	Tiler	Keane	Black*	Gemmill	Clough	Glover	Woan	

League Appearances (Goals)
Bannister G 27+4 (8); Black K 19+5 (5);
Charles G 14; Chettle S 30; Clough N 42 (10);
Crosby G 20+3 (1); Crossley M 37; Gemmill
S 33 (1); Glover L 9+5; Keane R 40 (6); Laws
B 32+1; McKinnon R 5+1 (1); Marriott A 5;
Orlygsson T 15+5 (1); Pearce S 23 (2);
Rosario R 10 (1); Sheringham E 3 (1); Stone
S 11+1 (1); Tiler C 37; Webb N 9; Williams B
9; Wilson T 5; Woan I 27+1 (3).

Position in League Table

	P	W	D	L	F	A	Pts
1st Man Utd	42	24	12	6	67	31	84
22nd Forest	42	10	10	22	41	62	40

Notes
§ denotes own goals
Aug 1, Aug 2, at Elland Road

1993-94 · Division One

Date			Opponents	Result	1	2	3	4	5	6	7	8	9	10	11	Substitutes used
23 Jul	F		Napoli	W 2-0												
26 Jul	F		Atalanta	L 0-1												
29 Jul	F		Butzano	W 3-0												
1 Aug	F		Slovan Bratislava	W 1-0												
4 Aug	F	A	Lincoln City	W 5-1												
7 Aug	F	A	Cambridge U	L 2-3												
15 Aug	FL	A	Southend U	W 2-0	Crossley	Lyttle	Pearce **1**	Cooper	Chettle	Stone	Black	Webb	Rosario	Glover*	Woan*	Laws (10), Harvey (11)
18 Aug	FL	H	Derby Co	D 1-1	Crossley	Lyttle	Pearce	Cooper	Chettle	Stone	Black	Webb	Rosario	Glover*	Woan **1**	Harvey (10)
21 Aug	FL	H	Grimsby T	W 5-3 §	Crossley	Lyttle	Pearce	Cooper	Chettle	Stone	Black **1**	Webb	Rosario **1**	Glover **1**	Woan **1***	Phillips (11)
24 Aug	FL	A	Crystal Palace	L 0-2	Crossley	Lyttle	Pearce	Warner	Chettle	Stone*	Black **1***	Webb	Rosario	Glover	Woan **1**	Phillips (6), Glover (10)
28 Aug	FL	A	Luton T	W 2-1	Crossley	Lyttle	Laws	Blatherwick	Chettle	Stone	Phillips	Glover **1***	Rosario	Collymore	Woan	Phillips (7)
8 Sep	AICp	A	Derby Co	L 2-3	Crossley	Laws	Pearce	Blatherwick	Chettle	Stone	Phillips	Webb	Rosario	Collymore	Woan	McGregor (8)
11 Sep	FL	A	Barnsley	L 0-1	Crossley	Lyttle	Pearce	Blatherwick	Chettle	Stone	Black	Webb*	Rosario	Collymore **1**	Woan	Glover (7)
15 Sep	AICp	H	Notts Co	D 1-1	Crossley	Lyttle	Pearce **1**	Warner*	Chettle	Phillips **1**	Phillips	Glover	Rosario **1**	Collymore	Woan	Black (8)
19 Sep	FL	H	Stoke C	L 2-3	Crossley	Lyttle	Pearce	Blatherwick	Chettle	Stone **1**	Phillips	Gemmill	Rosario	Collymore **3**	Woan*	Gemmill (9)
21 Sep	FLC2/1	A	Wrexham	D 3-3	Wright	Lyttle	Laws	Crosby	Chettle	Stone	Phillips	Gemmill	Howe	Collymore	Black	Laws (4)
26 Sep	FL	A	Bolton W	D 3-4	Wright	Laws	Lyttle	Crosby	Chettle	Stone	Phillips	Gemmill	Howe	Collymore **1**	Black **1**	Kilford (9), Howe (11)
2 Oct	FL	H	Portsmouth	D 1-1	Wright	Laws	Wright	Crosby	Chettle	Stone	Phillips	Gemmill **1**	Rosario	Collymore **1**	Black	Harvey (4)
6 Oct	FLC2/2	H	Wrexham	W 3-1	Wright	Laws	Lyttle	Cooper*	Chettle	Stone	Phillips	Gemmill	Rosario*	Howe*	Black	Howe (9)
16 Oct	FL	A	Tranmere R	W 2-1	Wright	Laws	Pearce	Crosby	Chettle	Stone	Phillips	Gemmill	Glover*	Collymore	Black	Cooper (10)
20 Oct	FL	A	Oxford U	D 0-0	Wright	Laws	Pearce	Cooper	Chettle	Stone	Phillips	Gemmill	Glover **1**	Collymore	Black	Crosby (4), Webb (9)
24 Oct	FL	A	Leicester C	L 0-1	Wright	Laws	Pearce	Cooper	Chettle	Stone	Phillips	Gemmill	Glover **2**	Glover	Black **1**	Webb (9)
27 Oct	FLC3	H	West Ham U	W 2-1	Wright	Laws	Pearce	Cooper	Chettle	Stone	Phillips	Gemmill	Glover	Collymore **1**	Black	
30 Oct	FL	H	Notts Co	D 1-1	Wright	Laws	Pearce	Cooper	Chettle	Stone	Phillips	Gemmill	Glover	Collymore	Black	Webb (8)
3 Nov	FL	A	Millwall	L 1-3	Crossley	Lyttle	Bohinen*	Cooper	Chettle	Stone	Phillips	Gemmill	Bohinen	Collymore **1**	Black	Webb (3)
6 Nov	FL	A	Birmingham C	W 3-0	Wright*	Lyttle	Pearce	Cooper **1**	Chettle	Stone	Phillips	Gemmill	Bohinen	Collymore **1**	Black	
10 Nov	FL	H	Wolves	D 1-1	Crossley	Lyttle	Pearce	Cooper **1**	Chettle	Stone	Phillips	Gemmill	Bohinen	Collymore **2**	Black	Crossley (1)
21 Nov	FL	A	WBA	W 2-0	Crossley	Lyttle	Pearce	Cooper **1**	Chettle	Stone	Phillips	Gemmill **1**	Bohinen	Collymore **1**	Black	Glover (1)
27 Nov	FL	A	Sunderland	W 3-2	Crossley	Lyttle	Pearce	Cooper	Chettle	Stone	Phillips	Gemmill	Bohinen	Collymore **2**	Black	Glover (2)
1 Dec	FLC4	H	Man City	W 0-0	Crossley	Bull*	Webb **1**	Cooper	Chettle	Webb	Phillips	Gemmill	Bull*	Bull*	Black	
4 Dec	FL	H	Birmingham C	W 1-0 §	Crossley	Lyttle	Pearce	Cooper	Chettle	Stone	Phillips	Gemmill*	Bohinen	Collymore	Black	Webb (8) **1**
15 Dec	FLC4r	A	Man City	W 2-1	Crossley	Lyttle	Pearce	Cooper	Chettle	Stone	Phillips	Gemmill	Bohinen	Collymore	Crosby	
19 Dec	FL	A	Southend U	W 2-0	Crossley	Lyttle	Pearce	Cooper	Chettle	Black	Phillips	Gemmill	Black*	Collymore	Black	
28 Dec	FL	A	Bristol C	W 4-1	Crossley	Lyttle	Pearce	Haaland	Chettle	Stone	Phillips	Gemmill	Bohinen	Collymore	Black	
1 Jan	FL	A	Charlton A	D 1-1	Crossley	Lyttle	Pearce	Cooper	Chettle	Stone	Phillips	Webb	Bull*	Collymore **1**	Woan **1**	Black (6)
3 Jan	FL	H	Watford	W 2-1	Crossley	Lyttle	Pearce	Cooper	Chettle	Stone	Phillips **1**	Gemmill **1**	Bohinen	Collymore	Woan	Bull (10), Black (11)
8 Jan	FAC3	A	Sheff Wed	D 1-1	Crossley	Gemmill	Pearce	Cooper	Chettle	Stone	Phillips	Webb*	Bohinen	Collymore	Woan	Bull (8)
16 Jan	FLC5	H	Tranmere R	W 2-1	Crossley	Lyttle	Pearce	Cooper	Chettle	Stone	Phillips	Webb	Bohinen	Collymore **2**	Woan **1**	Bull (6), Black (11)
19 Jan	FAC3r	H	Sheff Wed	L 0-2	Crossley	Lyttle	Pearce	Cooper	Chettle	Stone	Phillips	Gemmill **1**	Webb	Glover **1**	Woan	Crosby (6), Bull (9)
23 Jan	FLC5r	A	Tranmere R	D 0-0	Crossley	Lyttle	Pearce	Cooper	Chettle	Stone	Phillips	Gemmill	Bohinen	Collymore*	Glover	Bull (9)
26 Jan	FL	H	Birmingham C	W 2-1	Crossley	Lyttle	Pearce **1**	Cooper **1**	Chettle	Stone	Phillips	Gemmill	Bohinen	Glover	Glover	Black (6), Webb (9)
29 Jan	FL	A	Southend U	W 2-0	Crossley	Lyttle	Pearce	Cooper **1**	Chettle	Stone	Phillips	Gemmill **2**	Bohinen	Glover	Glover	Bohinen (9), Glover (10)
5 Feb	FL	A	Leicester C	L 1-2	Crossley	Lyttle	Pearce	Cooper	Chettle	Stone	Phillips	Gemmill	Bohinen	Glover	Glover	
12 Feb	FL	H	Notts Co	D 1-1	Crossley	Lyttle	Pearce	Cooper	Chettle	Stone	Phillips	Gemmill	Bohinen	Bull	Bull	Bull (6)
19 Feb	FL	A	Crystal Palace	L 0-1	Crossley	Lyttle	Pearce	Tiler	Chettle	Stone	Phillips	Gemmill	Lee	Lee	Black	Bull (11)
26 Feb	FL	A	Oxford U	W 2-0	Crossley	Lyttle	Pearce **1**	Cooper **1**	Chettle	Stone	Phillips	Bohinen	Bohinen	Lee*	Black	Bull (11)
2 Mar	FL	H	Peterborough U	W 2-0	Crossley	Lyttle	Pearce	Cooper **1**	Chettle	Stone	Phillips	Webb	Bohinen	Lee*	Black	
5 Mar	FL	A	Luton T	W 1-0	Crossley	Lyttle	Pearce **1**	Cooper	Chettle	Stone	Phillips	Webb	Webb	Webb **1**	Black	Webb (9)
16 Mar	FL	H	Stoke C	W 2-1	Crossley	Lyttle	Pearce	Cooper	Chettle	Stone **1**	Phillips	Webb **1**	Bull*	Lee*	Black	
19 Mar	FL	H	Barnsley	W 3-2	Crossley	Haaland	Pearce **1**	Cooper	Chettle **1**	Stone	Phillips	Webb*	Bohinen	Collymore **1**	Black	Bull (10)
26 Mar	FL	A	Portsmouth	L 1-2	Crossley	Lyttle	Pearce	Cooper	Chettle	Stone **1**	Phillips	Bohinen	Lee	Lee **1**	Black	
30 Mar	FL	H	Watford	W 2-1	Crossley	Lyttle	Pearce*	Cooper	Chettle	Stone **1**	Phillips	Woan	Lee	Lee	Black	Crosby (6), Collymore (9) **1**
2 Apr	FL	A	Middlesbrough	D 2-2	Crossley	Lyttle	Pearce **1**	Cooper	Chettle	Stone **1**	Phillips	Gemmill	Rosario	Lee **1**	Black	Rosario (2), Lee (9)
4 Apr	FL	H	Bristol C	D 0-0	Crossley	Lyttle*	Pearce **1**	Cooper	Chettle	Stone	Phillips	Gemmill	Rosario*	Collymore	Black	
9 Apr	FL	A	Charlton A	W 1-0	Crossley	Lyttle*	Pearce	Cooper	Chettle	Stone	Phillips	Gemmill	Lee	Collymore	Black	Bull (8)
17 Apr	FL	H	Millwall	D 2-2	Crossley	Lyttle*	Pearce	Cooper	Chettle	Stone	Phillips	Gemmill	Lee	Collymore	Black	Woan (8)
27 Apr	FL	A	Derby Co	W 2-0	Crossley	Lyttle	Pearce **1**	Cooper **1**	Chettle	Stone	Phillips	Gemmill	Bohinen	Collymore **2**	Woan	Bohinen (9)
30 Apr	FL	A	Peterborough U	W 3-2	Crossley	Tiler	Pearce	Cooper	Chettle	Stone	Phillips	Gemmill	Rosario	Collymore	Woan	
3 May	FL	H	Grimsby T	D 0-0	Crossley	Tiler	Pearce **1**	Cooper	Chettle	Stone	Phillips	Gemmill	Bohinen	Collymore	Woan	Black (3)
8 May	FL	H	Sunderland	D 2-2	Crossley	Tiler	Pearce	Cooper	Chettle	Stone	Phillips	Gemmill	Bohinen	Collymore **1**	Woan	Black (2), Lee (9)
10 May	F	A	Mansfield T	D 3-3	Crossley	Tiler	Pearce **1**	Cooper	Chettle	Stone	Phillips	Gemmill	Woan	Collymore **1**	Woan	Black (9)

League Appearances (Goals)
Black K 30+7 (3); Blatherwick S 3; Bohinen L 22+1 (1); Bull G 3-8; Chettle S 46 (1); Collymore S 27+1 (19); Cooper C 36+1 (7); Crosby G 4+2; Crossley M 36+1; Gemmill S 30+1 (8); Glover L 15+3 (5); Haaland A 3; Harvey L 0-2; Howe S 2+2; Kilford I 0+1; Laws B 6+1; Lee J 10+3 (2); Lyttle D 37 (1); Pearce S 42 (6); Phillips D 40+3 (4); Rosario R 15+1 (2); Stone S 45 (5); Tiler C 3; Warner V 1; Webb N 17-4 (3); Woan I 23+1 (5); Wright T 10; Own goals 2.

Position in League Table

	P	W	D	L	F	A	Pts
1st C Palace	46	27	9	10	73	46	90
2nd Forest	46	23	14	9	74	49	83

Notes
§ denotes own goals
Jul 23, Jul 26, Jul 29, Aug 1, Pre-Season
Tournament in Italy

1994-95 — FA Premier League

Numbers 1-11 used for consistency only, players actually wore squad numbers

Date	Comp	Venue	Opponent	Result	1	2	3	4	5	6	7	8	9	10	11	Substitutes used
26 Jul	F	A	IF Silvia	L 0-1												
28 Jul	F	A	Vaesteraas	W 2-1												
30 Jul	F	A	Krylbo IF/Avesta	W 4-0												
31 Jul	F	A	Ludvika FK	D 0-0												
3 Aug	F	H	Taby IS	W 8-1												
8 Aug	F	A	Leyton Orient	W 2-1												
11 Aug	F	A	Olympiakos	D 2-2												
20 Aug	PL	A	Ipswich T	W 1-0	Crossley	Lyttle	Pearce	Cooper	Chettle	Stone *	Phillips	Gemmill	Roy 1 *	Lee	Woan	Bohinen (6), Rosario (9)
27 Aug	PL	H	Man Utd	D 1-1	Crossley	Lyttle	Pearce	Cooper	Chettle	Stone	Phillips	Gemmill	Roy	Collymore 1	Woan	Bohinen (9)
30 Aug	PL	H	Leicester C	W 1-0	Crossley	Lyttle	Pearce	Cooper	Chettle	Stone	Phillips	Gemmill *	Roy	Collymore 1	Woan	Bohinen (8)
3 Sep	PL	A	Everton	W 2-1 §	Crossley	Lyttle	Pearce 1	Cooper 1	Chettle	Stone	Phillips	Bohinen 1	Roy 1	Collymore	Black 1	Woan (9)
10 Sep	PL	H	Sheff Wed	W 4-1	Crossley	Lyttle	Pearce	Cooper	Haaland	Stone	Phillips	Bohinen	Roy 1	Collymore 1	Black	Haaland (8)
17 Sep	PL	A	Southampton	D 1-1	Crossley	Lyttle	Pearce	Cooper	Chettle	Stone	Phillips	Bohinen	Roy *	Collymore 2	Black	
21 Sep	FLC2/1	H	Hereford U	W 2-1	Crossley	Lyttle	Pearce	Cooper	Chettle	Stone 1	Phillips	Bohinen 1	Roy 2	Collymore	Black 1	Lee (9), **Woan** (11) **1**
24 Sep	PL	H	Tottenham H	W 4-1	Crossley	Lyttle	Pearce	Cooper	Chettle	Stone	Phillips	Bohinen	Roy 1	Collymore	Black *	Lee (9)
2 Oct	FLC2/2	A	Hereford U	W 3-2	Crossley	Haaland	Pearce	Cooper	Chettle	Stone	Phillips	Bohinen	Roy	Collymore 1	Black	Lee (10)
4 Oct	PL	A	QPR	D 0-0	Crossley	Haaland	Pearce	Cooper	Chettle	Stone	Phillips	Bohinen	Gemmill	Collymore 1	Black *	Black (11)
8 Oct	PL	H	Man City	W 3-1	Crossley	Lyttle	Pearce	Cooper	Chettle	Stone 1	Phillips	Bohinen	Roy *	Collymore 1	**Woan** 1	Black (11)
22 Oct	PL	A	Aston Villa	W 2-0	Crossley	Lyttle	Pearce 1	Cooper	Chettle	Stone	Phillips	Bohinen	Roy *	Collymore	Woan	Lee (9)
26 Oct	PL	H	Wolves	W 3-1	Crossley	Lyttle	Pearce 2	Cooper	Chettle	Stone	Phillips	Bohinen	Roy 1	Collymore *	Woan *	Lee (10)
29 Oct	PL	A	Blackburn R	L 0-2	Crossley	Lyttle	Pearce	Cooper	Chettle	Stone	Phillips	Bohinen	Roy	Lee	Woan *	Black (11)
5 Nov	PL	H	Liverpool	L 0-1	Crossley	Lyttle	Pearce	Cooper	Chettle	Stone	Phillips	Bohinen	Roy	Lee	Woan *	Black (11)
7 Nov	PL	A	Newcastle U	D 0-0	Crossley	Lyttle	Pearce	Cooper	Chettle	Stone	Phillips	Bohinen	Roy	Collymore	Woan *	Black (8)
15 Nov	F	H	Northampton T	L 1-2												
19 Nov	PL	H	Chelsea	L 0-1	Crossley	Lyttle	Pearce	Cooper	Chettle	Stone	Phillips	Bohinen 1	Roy	Collymore	Woan	Lee (8)
23 Nov	NCCf	A	Leeds U	W 3-1	Crossley	Lyttle	Pearce	Cooper	Chettle	Stone	Phillips	Bohinen *	Roy	Collymore	Woan	Lee (9)
26 Nov	PL	H	Millwall	L 0-1	Crossley	Lyttle	Gemmill	Cooper *	Chettle	Stone	Phillips	Bohinen *	Roy	Collymore	Woan	Haaland (4), Lee (8)
30 Nov	FLC4	H	Arsenal	L 0-2	Crossley	Lyttle	Pearce 1	Haaland	Chettle	Gemmill	Gemmill 1	Bohinen 1	Roy 1	Collymore 1	Woan	Black (8)
3 Dec	PL	A	Ipswich T	W 2-1	Crossley	Lyttle	Pearce 1	Haaland	Chettle	Stone	Phillips *	Gemmill	Roy *	Collymore 1	Woan	McGregor (8), Lee (9)
10 Dec	PL	A	Coventry C	D 0-0	Crossley	Lyttle	Pearce	Cooper	Chettle	Stone	Haaland	Gemmill	Gemmill	Collymore	Woan	Bohinen (9)
17 Dec	PL	H	Norwich C	D 0-0	Crossley	Lyttle	Pearce	Cooper *	Chettle	Stone	Haaland	Bohinen 1	Roy	Collymore	Woan *	Haaland (7), McGregor (9)
26 Dec	PL	A	West Ham U	L 1-3	Crossley	Lyttle	Pearce	Warner	Chettle	Stone	Haaland	Bohinen 1	Roy	Collymore	Woan	Black (11)
27 Dec	PL	H	Crystal Palace	W 1-0	Crossley	Lyttle	Tiler	Haaland	Chettle	Stone	Phillips	Gemmill 1	Roy *	Collymore	Woan	**McGregor** (4) **1**, Black (8)
31 Dec	FAC3	H	Plymouth A	W 2-0	Crossley	Lyttle	Tiler	Haaland	Chettle	Stone	Phillips	Gemmill 1	Roy *	Collymore 1	Woan	McGregor (8)
2 Jan	PL	A	Blackburn R	L 0-3	Crossley	Lyttle	Tiler	Haaland	Chettle	Stone	Phillips	Bohinen	Roy	Bull 1	Woan	Webb (9)
7 Jan	PL	H	Aston Villa	L 1-2	Crossley	Lyttle	Haaland	Cooper	Chettle	Stone	Phillips	Gemmill	Roy	Collymore 1	Woan	McGregor (8)
14 Jan	PL	A	Chelsea	W 2-0	Crossley	Lyttle	Tiler	Cooper	Chettle	Stone	Phillips	Bohinen	Roy *	Collymore	Woan	McGregor (9)
21 Jan	PL	A	Crystal Palace	L 1-2	Crossley	Lyttle	Pearce	Haaland	Chettle	Stone	Phillips	Gemmill	Roy *	Collymore 2	Woan	Bull (11)
25 Jan	PL	H	Liverpool	L 1-2	Crossley	Lyttle	Haaland	Cooper	Chettle	Stone	Phillips	Gemmill	Roy *	Collymore	Gemmill	Lee (9) 1
28 Jan	FAC4	H	Crystal Palace	W 2-0	Crossley	Lyttle	Pearce	Cooper	Chettle	Stone	Phillips	Gemmill	Haaland *	Collymore	Gemmill	McGregor (11)
4 Feb	PL	H	Newcastle U	L 0-1	Crossley	Lyttle	Pearce	Cooper	Chettle	Stone	Phillips	Bohinen	Gemmill	Lee	Woan *	McGregor (11)
11 Feb	PL	A	Arsenal	D 1-1	Crossley	Lyttle	Haaland	Cooper	Chettle	Stone	Phillips	Gemmill	Roy	Collymore	Gemmill	Woan (11) 1
15 Feb	F	A	Dynamo Croatia	D 2-2												
21 Feb	PL	A	QPR	W 2-1	Crossley	Lyttle	Pearce 1	Cooper	Chettle	Stone	Phillips	Bohinen 1	Roy *	Collymore 1	Woan	Lee (9) 1
26 Feb	PL	H	Tottenham H	D 1-1	Crossley	Lyttle	Pearce 1	Cooper	Chettle	Stone	Phillips	Bohinen	Roy 2 *	Collymore 1	Woan 1 *	Lee (9) 1
4 Mar	PL	H	Everton	D 2-2	Crossley	Lyttle	Haaland	Cooper	Chettle	Stone	Phillips	Bohinen	Roy 2	Collymore 1	Woan	Lee (9)
8 Mar	PL	A	Leicester C	W 4-2	Crossley	Lyttle	Pearce 1	Cooper	Chettle	Stone	Phillips	Bohinen 1	Roy *	Collymore 1	Woan *	McGregor (2), Lee (10)
11 Mar	PL	H	Southampton	W 3-0	Crossley	Lyttle	Pearce	Cooper	Chettle	Stone	Phillips	Bohinen	Roy 2	Collymore 1	Woan 1 *	McGregor (11)
18 Mar	PL	A	Sheff Wed	W 7-1	Crossley	Haaland	Pearce 1	Cooper	Chettle	Stone	Phillips	Bohinen 1	Roy	Collymore 1	Woan *	Lee (8), McGregor (11)
22 Mar	PL	H	West Ham U	D 1-1	Crossley	Lyttle	Pearce	Cooper	Chettle	Stone 1	Phillips	Bohinen *	Roy	Collymore 1	Woan *	Lee (9), McGregor (11)
1 Apr	PL	A	Norwich C	W 2-0	Crossley	Lyttle	Pearce	Cooper	Chettle	Stone	Phillips	Bohinen	Roy	Collymore	Woan *	Lee (9), McGregor (11)
8 Apr	PL	H	Coventry C	W 2-1	Crossley	Lyttle	Pearce	Cooper	Chettle	Stone 1	Phillips	Bohinen	Roy *	Collymore 1	Woan	Lee (9)
12 Apr	PL	A	Crystal Palace	W 1-0	Crossley	Lyttle	Pearce	Cooper	Chettle	Stone	Phillips	Gemmill	Roy 1 *	Collymore 1	Woan	Lee (9)
17 Apr	F	H	Crusaders	D 2-2												
17 Apr	PL	A	Man City	W 2-1	Crossley	Lyttle	Pearce	Cooper	Chettle	Stone	Phillips 1	Gemmill	Roy *	Collymore	Woan	
19 Apr	PL	H	Wimbledon	W 1-0												
29 Apr	PL	A	Birmingham C	D 2-2												
6 May	F	H	Man City	W 4-1												
13 May	F	A	Wimbledon	W 3-1												
21 May	F	A	Singapore XI	W 1-0												
24 May	F	A	Adelaide City	D 2-2												
27 May	F	A	W. Australia	L 1-2												

League Appearances (Goals)

Black K 5+5 (2); Bohinen L 30+4 (6); Bull G 1 (1); Chettle S 41; Collymore S 37 (22); Cooper C 35 (1); Gemmill S 19 (1); Haaland A 18+2 (1); Lee J 5+17 (3); Lyttle D 38; McGregor P 0+11 (1); Pearce S 36 (8); Phillips D 38 (1); Rosario R 0+1; Roy B 37 (13); Stone S 41 (5); Tiler C 3; Warner V 1; Woan I 35+2 (5); Own goals 2.

Position in League Table

	P	W	D	L	F	A	Pts
1st Blackburn	42	27	8	7	80	39	89
3rd Forest	42	22	11	9	72	43	77

Notes

§ denotes own goals
Nov 11, County Cup Final 1993-94, held over from previous season

The Official Handbook for Nottingham Forest 1998/99, Volume Ten

Available end September, price £4.95

Following on from the great success over the past nine seasons of our official handbook, Nottingham Forest Football Club are once again, publishing a handbook for our supporters for the 1998/99 season.

This attractive, and now very collectable, A5 handbook contains photographs, statistics, fixtures, reviews, pen-pictures, features and up-to-date club records. It will be available at the end of September.

Polar Publishing of Leicester have produced this popular publication for the past nine years and will be pleased to send you a copy direct; alternatively it will be on sale in the Forest Club Shop and in branches of W H Smith in Nottingham.

Complete the form below in BLOCK CAPITALS and SEND to:
Polar Print Group Ltd **FREEPOST 5731** Leicester LE4 7ZA

Name:

Address (including postcode)

I would like to order   copy(ies) of Nottingham Forest Handbook Vol Ten @ £5.45 each (incl 50p P & P within the UK)
For overseas add £1 per book. Please make cheques payable to Polar Print Group Ltd.

1995-96 — FA Premier League

Numbers 1-11 used for consistency only, players actually wore squad numbers

Date	Comp	Venue	Opponent	Res	1	2	3	4	5	6	7	8	9	10	11	Substitutes used
25 Jul	F	A	Vang FK	W 7-0												
27 Jul	F	A	Tistedalen Turn	W 3-0												
29 Jul	F	A	Foerde IL	W 3-0												
31 Jul	F	H	Skjetten	W 4-2												
1 Aug	F	A	Stabekk IF	W 3-0												
5 Aug	F	A	Lincoln City	W 3-1												
12 Aug	F	A	Riccioni	W 3-0												
12 Aug	F	A	Rimini	D 0-0												
	F	A	Torino	L 2-1												
	F	A	Genoa	L 0-1												
19 Aug	PL	A	Southampton	W 4-3	Crossley	Lyttle	Pearce	Cooper 1	Chettle	Phillips	Stone	Bohinen	Roy 2*	Campbell*	Woan	Lee (9), Gemmill (10)
23 Aug	PL	H	Chelsea	D 0-0	Crossley	Lyttle	Pearce	Cooper	Chettle	Phillips	Stone	Bohinen	Roy*	Campbell*	Woan	Lee (10)
26 Aug	PL	H	West Ham U	D 1-1	Crossley	Lyttle	Pearce 1	Cooper	Chettle	Phillips	Stone	Bohinen*	Roy*	Campbell	Woan	Gemmill (8), Lee (9)
29 Aug	PL	A	Arsenal	D 1-1	Crossley	Lyttle	Pearce	Cooper	Chettle	Phillips	Stone	Bohinen	Roy	Campbell 1*	Woan 1	Lee (9)
9 Sep	PL	A	Coventry C	D 1-1	Crossley	Lyttle	Pearce*	Cooper	Chettle	Phillips	Stone	Bohinen	Roy	Campbell 1*	Woan 1	Gemmill (8), Silenzi (10)
12 Sep	UC1/1	A	Malmo	L 1-2 §	Crossley	Lyttle	Pearce*	Cooper	Chettle	Bart-Williams	Stone	Bohinen	Roy	Campbell*	Woan 1	Bart-Williams (3), Lee (10)
17 Sep	PL	H	Everton	W 3-2	Crossley	Lyttle	Bart-Williams	Cooper	Chettle	Bart-Williams	Stone	Bohinen 2	Roy	Lee 1	Woan	Gemmill (9)
19 Sep	FLC2/1	A	Bradford C	L 2-3	Crossley	Lyttle	Haaland	Cooper	Chettle	Bart-Williams	Stone	Bohinen	Roy 1	Lee	Woan	
23 Sep	PL	H	Aston Villa	D 1-1	Crossley	Lyttle	Pearce 1	Cooper	Chettle	Bart-Williams	Stone	Bohinen	Roy*	Lee	Woan	Gemmill (8), Silenzi (9)
26 Sep	UC1/2	H	Malmo	D 2-2	Crossley	Lyttle	Pearce	Cooper	Chettle	Bart-Williams	Stone 1	Gemmill	Silenzi 1	Lee 2	Woan	Gemmill (8), Silenzi (9)
30 Sep	PL	H	Man City	W 3-0	Crossley	Lyttle	Pearce 1	Cooper	Chettle	Bart-Williams	Stone 1	Gemmill	Roy*	Lee	Woan	McGregor (9)
4 Oct	FLC2/2	H	Bradford C	D 2-2	Crossley	Lyttle	Pearce	Cooper	Chettle	Bart-Williams	Stone 1	Gemmill	Haaland	Lee*	Woan	Silenzi (10)
14 Oct	PL	A	Tottenham H	W 1-0	Crossley	Lyttle	Pearce	Cooper	Chettle	Bart-Williams	Stone	Gemmill 1	Roy 1	Lee	Woan	Haaland (8), McGregor (9)
17 Oct	UC2/1	A	Auxerre	D 1-1	Crossley	Lyttle	Pearce	Cooper	Chettle	Bart-Williams	Stone	Gemmill	Roy*	Lee 1	Woan	Silenzi (10)
21 Oct	PL	A	QPR	W 1-0	Crossley	Lyttle	Pearce 1	Cooper 1	Chettle	Bart-Williams	Stone	Gemmill 1	Roy 1	Lee 1*	Woan	Phillips (4), Silenzi (10)
28 Oct	UC2/2	H	Auxerre	D 0-0	Crossley	Lyttle	Pearce	Cooper*	Chettle	Bart-Williams	Stone	Gemmill	Haaland	Silenzi*	Woan	McGregor (9) 1, Howe (10)
31 Oct	PL	H	Wimbledon	W 4-1	Crossley	Lyttle	Pearce	Cooper	Chettle	Bart-Williams	Stone	Gemmill	Roy*	McGregor 1*	Woan	Irving (9), Haaland (10)
6 Nov	PL	A	Blackburn R	L 0-7	Crossley	Lyttle	Pearce	Cooper	Chettle	Bart-Williams	Stone	Gemmill	Howe	Silenzi	Woan	Howe (2)
18 Nov	PL	A	Lyon	L 0-1	Crossley	Lyttle	Pearce	Cooper	Chettle	Bart-Williams	Stone	McGregor	McGregor	Lee*	Woan	Haaland (8), Silenzi (10)
21 Nov	UC3/1	H	Bolton W	D 1-1	Crossley	Lyttle	Pearce	Haaland	Chettle	Bart-Williams	Stone	Gemmill	Howe	Lee	Woan	Haaland (8)
27 Nov	PL	A	Lyon	W 1-0	Crossley	Lyttle	Pearce	Cooper	Chettle	Bart-Williams	Stone	Gemmill	Howe	Lee	Haaland	
2 Dec	UC3/2	H	Aston Villa	D 0-0	Crossley	Lyttle	Pearce	Cooper	Chettle	Bart-Williams	Stone	Gemmill	McGregor	Lee*	Woan	Silenzi (9)
5 Dec	PL	A	Man City	D 1-1	Crossley	Lyttle	Pearce	Cooper	Chettle	Bart-Williams	Stone	Gemmill 1	Campbell 1*	Lee 1	Woan	Silenzi (9)
10 Dec	PL	H	Newcastle U	L 1-3	Crossley	Phillips	Pearce	Cooper	Chettle	Bart-Williams	Stone	Phillips	Campbell	Lee 1	Woan	McGregor (9)
18 Dec	PL	A	Sheff Wed	W 1-0	Crossley	Lyttle	Pearce	Cooper	Chettle	Bart-Williams	Stone	Gemmill	Campbell	Lee	Woan	Roy (9)
23 Dec	PL	A	Middlesbrough	L 1-3	Crossley	Lyttle	Pearce 1	Cooper	Chettle	Bart-Williams	Stone	Gemmill	Campbell	Lee*	Woan	Roy (10)
26 Dec	PL	H	Liverpool	L 1-4	Crossley	Lyttle	Pearce 1	Cooper	Chettle	Bart-Williams	Stone	Haaland	Campbell	McGregor	Woan	Roy (10)
30 Dec	PL	A	Stoke C	D 1-1	Crossley	Lyttle	Pearce 1	Cooper	Chettle	Bart-Williams	Stone	Gemmill	Campbell*	Campbell	Woan*	Lee (9), Lee (10)
6 Jan	FAC3	A	Southampton	D 1-1	Crossley	Lyttle	Pearce 1	Cooper	Chettle	Bart-Williams	Stone 1	Gemmill	Roy*	Lee*	Woan	Lee (9), Lee (10)
13 Jan	FAC3r	H	Stoke C	W 2-0	Crossley	Lyttle	Pearce 1	Cooper 1	Chettle	Bart-Williams	Stone	Gemmill	Roy	McGregor	Woan*	Lee (8)
20 Jan	PL	A	Chelsea	L 0-1	Crossley	Lyttle	Pearce	Cooper	Chettle	Bart-Williams	Stone	Gemmill	Roy	Campbell	Woan	Phillips (9), Lee (10)
31 Jan	PL	A	Leeds U	D 1-1	Crossley	Lyttle	Phillips	Cooper	Chettle	Bart-Williams	Silenzi	Gemmill	Roy	Campbell 1	Woan*	Lee (10)
7 Feb	PL	H	West Ham U	L 0-1	Crossley	Lyttle	Phillips	Cooper	Chettle	Bart-Williams	Silenzi	Gemmill	Roy	Campbell	Woan	Haaland (2), Howe (7)
10 Feb	FAC4	A	Oxford U	W 1-0	Crossley	Lyttle*	Phillips	Cooper	Chettle	Bart-Williams	Silenzi	Gemmill	Silenzi 1	Campbell 1	Woan	Haaland (8)
13 Feb	FAC4r	H	Oxford U	D 1-1	Crossley	Lyttle	Phillips	Cooper 1	Chettle	Bart-Williams	Stone 1	Gemmill 1	Campbell 1*	Campbell 1	Woan 1	McGregor (8), Lee (11)
17 Feb	PL	H	Arsenal		Crossley	Lyttle	Pearce 1	Cooper 1	Chettle	Bart-Williams	Stone	Gemmill	Campbell	Campbell	Woan	
21 Feb	FAC5	A	Oxford U		Crossley	Lyttle	Pearce 1	Cooper	Chettle	Bart-Williams	Stone	Gemmill	Roy	Campbell	Black 1	
24 Feb	PL	H	Tottenham H		Crossley	Lyttle	Phillips	Cooper	Chettle	Bart-Williams	Stone	Gemmill	Roy	Campbell	Woan*	Haaland (11)
28 Feb	PL	A	Everton	L 0-3	Crossley	Lyttle	Phillips	Cooper	Chettle	Bart-Williams	Stone	Gemmill	Roy	Campbell	Woan 2	Haaland (4), Silenzi (7)
2 Mar	PL	A	Tottenham H	D 2-2	Crossley	Lyttle	Pearce	Cooper	Chettle 1	Bart-Williams	McGregor 1*	Gemmill 1*	Roy	Campbell	Howe 1*	Allen (7), Black (11)
5 Mar	UC4/1	A	Sheff Wed	W 3-1	Crossley	Lyttle	Pearce	Cooper	Chettle	Bart-Williams	Stone	Gemmill	Roy 1	Campbell	Woan	Phillips (4), McGregor (7), Lee (10)
9 Mar	FAC5	H	Tottenham H		Crossley	Lyttle	Pearce	Cooper	Chettle	Bart-Williams	Stone*	Gemmill	Roy	Campbell	Woan	McGregor (9), Lee (11)
13 Mar	FAC6	H	Aston Villa		Crossley	Lyttle	Pearce	Cooper	Chettle	Bart-Williams	Phillips	Gemmill	McGregor	Campbell	Allen 1	Howe (8)
16 Mar	PL	A	Bayern Munich		Crossley	Lyttle*	Pearce	Cooper	Chettle	Bart-Williams	Stone 1	Gemmill	Roy	Campbell	Woan	Haaland (8), McGregor (6), Lee (10)
19 Mar	UC4/2	A	Bayern Munich		Crossley	Lyttle*	Pearce	Cooper	Chettle	Bart-Williams*	Stone 1	Phillips	McGregor	Phillips	Woan	Phillips (8), Allen (9)
30 Mar	PL	H	Wimbledon		Crossley	Lyttle	Pearce	Cooper	Chettle	Bart-Williams	Stone 1	Gemmill	Roy	Lee	Guinan 1	McGregor (11)
6 Apr	PL	A	Tottenham H		Crossley	Haaland	Pearce	Cooper	Chettle	Bart-Williams	Stone	McGregor	Roy	Lee	Woan	Guinan (8), Haaland (9)
8 Apr	PL	A	Blackburn R		Crossley	Lyttle*	Pearce	Cooper	Chettle	Bart-Williams	Stone	Haaland	Campbell	Lee 1	Woan 1	McGregor (9)
13 Apr	PL	H	Coventry C		Crossley	Haaland	Pearce	Cooper 1	Chettle	Bart-Williams	Stone 1	Gemmill	Campbell	Lee	Woan 1	McGregor (2)
17 Apr	PL	A	Man Utd		Crossley	Lyttle*	Pearce	Cooper	Chettle	Bart-Williams	Stone	Gemmill	Campbell	Lee	Woan 1	
28 Apr	PL	A	Leeds U		Crossley	Haaland	Pearce	Cooper	Chettle	Bart-Williams	Stone	Gemmill	Roy	Lee	Woan	McGregor (8), Howe (9)
2 May	PL	H	QPR	W 3-0	Crossley	Haaland	Pearce	Cooper	Chettle	Bart-Williams	Stone	Gemmill	Roy	Lee	Woan	Phillips (8), Howe (9)
5 May	PL	A	Newcastle U		Crossley	Haaland	Pearce	Cooper	Chettle	Bart-Williams	Stone	Howe 1	Howe 1	McGregor	Woan	Lyttle (2), Phillips (7), Silenzi (10)
8 May	F	H	Newcastle U	W 6-5												

League Appearances (Goals)

Allen C 1+2 (1); Bart-Williams C 33;
Black K 1+1; Bohinen L 7; Campbell K 21 (3);
Chettle S 37; Cooper C 37 (5); Crossley M
38; Gemmill S 26+5 (1); Guinan S 1+1;
Haaland A 12+5; Howe S 4+5 (2);
Irving R 0+1; Lee J 21+7 (8); Lyttle D 32+1
(1); McGregor P 7+7 (2); Pearce S 31 (3);
Phillips D 14+4; Roy B 25+3 (8);
Silenzi A 3+7; Stone S 34 (7); Woan I 33 (8);
Own goals 1.

Position in League Table

		P	W	D	L	F	A	Pts
1st	Man Utd	38	25	7	6	73	35	82
9th	Forest	38	15	13	10	50	54	58

Notes

§ denotes own goals
Sep 26, won on away goals
Mar 9, won 3-1 on penalties

1996-97 — FA Premier League

Numbers 1-11 used for consistency only, players actually wore squad numbers

Date	Comp	Ven	Opponents	Res	1	2	3	4	5	6	7	8	9	10	11	Substitutes used
24 Jul	F	A	Chesterfield	L 1-2												
27 Jul	F	A	Gillingham	W 3-0												
30 Jul	F	A	Hastings Town	D 0-0												
1 Aug	F	A	Hull City	W 4-0												
3 Aug	F	H	Chelsea	D 0-0												
4 Aug	F	H	Man Utd	L 1-3												
7 Aug	NCCf	H	Notts County	D 1-1												
10 Aug	F	H	Shelbourne	W 9-0												
17 Aug	PL	H	Coventry C	W 3-0	Crossley	Cooper	Pearce	Jerkan	Chettle	Bart-Williams	Stone *	Haaland	Saunders *	Campbell 3	Woan	Gemmill (7), McGregor (9)
21 Aug	PL	A	Sunderland	L 1-4	Crossley	Cooper	Pearce	Jerkan	Chettle	Bart-Williams	Stone	Haaland 1	Saunders	Campbell	Woan *	Allen (11)
24 Aug	PL	H	Middlesbrough	D 1-1	Crossley	Cooper	Pearce 1	Jerkan	Allen *	Bart-Williams	Stone	Haaland	Saunders	Campbell	Woan	Roy (5)
4 Sep	PL	A	Southampton	D 2-2	Crossley	Cooper	Pearce	Jerkan	Chettle	Bart-Williams	Stone	Haaland	Saunders 1	Campbell 1*	Woan	Silenzi (10)
7 Sep	PL	A	Leicester C	D 0-0	Crossley	Cooper	Pearce	Jerkan	Chettle	Bart-Williams	Stone *	Haaland	Saunders	Silenzi *	Woan	Gemmill (7), Lee (10)
14 Sep	PL	A	Man Utd	L 1-4	Crossley	Lyttle	Pearce	Cooper	Chettle	Bart-Williams	Phillips	Haaland 1	Saunders	Lee	Woan *	Roy (9), Allen (11)
18 Sep	FLC2/1	H	Wycombe W	W 1-0	Crossley	Lyttle	Pearce	Cooper	Chettle	Bart-Williams	Phillips	Haaland *	Saunders	Roy 1	Woan *	Lee (8), Gemmill (11)
21 Sep	PL	A	West Ham U	L 0-2	Crossley	Lyttle	Pearce	Cooper	Jerkan *	Allen	Phillips	Haaland	Saunders	Roy	Woan *	Lee (5)
24 Sep	FLC2/2	A	Wycombe W	D 1-1	Crossley	Lyttle	Pearce	Cooper	Blatherwick	Bart-Williams	Phillips	Gemmill	Saunders *	Lee 1	Woan	Haaland (8), Roy (9)
28 Sep	PL	A	Chelsea	D 1-1	Crossley	Lyttle *	Pearce	Cooper	Jerkan	Bart-Williams *	Phillips	Haaland	Saunders	Roy *	Woan	McGregor (2), Allen (6), Lee (9) 1
12 Oct	PL	A	Leeds U	D 1-1	Crossley	Lyttle *	Pearce *	Cooper	Blatherwick	Bart-Williams	Allen	Gemmill *	Saunders	Lee 1	Woan	Haaland (2), Roy (8)
19 Oct	PL	H	Derby Co	L 0-2	Crossley	Lyttle *	Pearce *	Cooper	Blatherwick	Bart-Williams	Allen	Gemmill *	Saunders 1	Roy *	Woan	Chettle (3), Roy (8)
23 Oct	FLC3	A	West Ham U	L 1-4	Crossley	Haaland	Phillips	Cooper 1	Blatherwick	Bart-Williams	Roy	Gemmill *	Saunders 1	Lee	Woan	Allen (7)
28 Oct	PL	H	Everton	L 0-1	Crossley	Lyttle	Pearce	Cooper	Chettle	Phillips	Haaland	Gemmill	Saunders	Lee	Woan	Roy (6)
2 Nov	PL	A	Aston Villa	L 0-2	Crossley	Lyttle	Pearce	Cooper	Chettle	Phillips	Haaland	Gemmill	Saunders	Lee	Woan	Gemmill (8), Allen (11)
18 Nov	PL	A	Sheff Wed	L 0-2	Crossley	Lyttle	Pearce *	Cooper	Chettle	Phillips	Haaland	Gemmill	Saunders	Lee	Woan	Lee (5), Roy (9)
25 Nov	PL	H	Blackburn R	D 2-2	Crossley	Lyttle *	Pearce	Cooper	Chettle	Phillips *	Haaland	Gemmill *	Saunders *	Campbell	Allen	Lee (2)
30 Nov	PL	A	Wimbledon	L 0-1	Crossley	Lyttle	Pearce	Cooper	Chettle	Phillips	Haaland	Gemmill	Saunders	Campbell	Allen	Howe (9)
9 Dec	PL	H	Newcastle U	D 0-0	Crossley	Lyttle	Pearce	Cooper	Chettle	Phillips	Haaland	Gemmill	Saunders *	Campbell	Allen	Lyttle (2), Clough (6)
17 Dec	PL	A	Liverpool	L 2-4	Crossley	Lyttle	Pearce	Cooper	Warner	Roy *	Haaland	Woan	Saunders *	Campbell	Allen	Lee (6), Gemmill (9)
21 Dec	PL	H	Arsenal	W 2-1	Crossley	Jerkan *	Pearce 1	Cooper	Chettle	Clough *	Haaland 2	Woan	Saunders *	Campbell	Woan *	Lyttle (8), Allen (11)
26 Dec	PL	H	Man Utd	L 0-4	Crossley	Jerkan *	Pearce	Cooper	Chettle	Clough 1	Haaland	Woan	Saunders	Campbell	Woan	Phillips (8), Gemmill (10)
28 Dec	PL	A	Leicester C	D 2-2	Crossley	Blatherwick	Pearce	Cooper	Chettle	Phillips	Haaland	Gemmill *	Saunders 2	Campbell 1	Woan	Gemmill (8), Roy (10)
1 Jan	PL	A	West Ham U	W 1-0	Crossley	Lyttle	Pearce	Cooper	Chettle	Phillips	Haaland	Blatherwick *	Saunders *	Campbell	Woan	Allen (9)
4 Jan	FAC3	H	Ipswich T	W 3-0	Crossley	Lyttle	Pearce 1	Cooper	Chettle	Phillips	Haaland	Allen 1*	Saunders *	Campbell 1*	Woan	Gemmill (6), Lee (9)
11 Jan	PL	A	Chelsea	W 2-0	Crossley	Lyttle	Pearce	Cooper	Chettle	Phillips	Haaland	Bart-Williams 1	Roy 2*	Clough	Woan 2	Lee (9)
19 Jan	PL	H	Tottenham H	W 2-1	Crossley	Lyttle	Pearce	Cooper	Chettle	Phillips	Haaland	Bart-Williams	Roy *	Campbell	Woan	Guinan (6), Lee (9)
26 Jan	FAC4	A	Newcastle U	L 0-1	Crossley	Lyttle	Pearce	Cooper	Chettle	Phillips	Haaland	Bart-Williams	Clough *	Campbell	Woan	McGregor (9)
29 Jan	PL	H	Coventry C	L 0-1	Crossley	Lyttle	Pearce	Cooper	Chettle	Roy *	Haaland	Bart-Williams	Allen *	Allen *	Woan	McGregor (3), Fettis (6), Gemmill (11)
1 Feb	PL	A	Everton	L 0-2	Crossley	Lyttle	Pearce	Cooper	Chettle	Roy *	Haaland	Bart-Williams	Saunders	Campbell	Woan	Woan (6)
15 Feb	FAC5	A	Chesterfield	L 0-1	Crossley	Lyttle	Blatherwick *	Cooper	Chettle	Phillips	Haaland	Bart-Williams	Saunders 1*	Campbell 1*	Woan *	McGregor (9), Phillips (11)
22 Feb	PL	H	Aston Villa	D 0-0	Crossley	Lyttle	Phillips	Cooper	Chettle	Jerkan	Haaland	Gemmill	Saunders	Clough	Gemmill	Roy (11)
1 Mar	PL	H	Tottenham H	W 1-0	Crossley	Lyttle	Pearce	Cooper	Chettle	Jerkan	Haaland	Gemmill	Saunders 1*	Clough	Allen *	Guinan (6), Roy (10)
5 Mar	PL	A	Sheff Wed	L 0-3	Wright	Lyttle	Pearce	Cooper	Chettle	Jerkan *	Haaland	Gemmill	Saunders	Clough	Allen *	Clough (6), Woan (7), McGregor (10)
8 Mar	PL	A	Arsenal	L 0-2	Crossley	Lyttle	Pearce 1	Cooper	Chettle	Jerkan *	Haaland	Gemmill	Saunders	Clough	Phillips	Clough (7)
11 Mar	PL	A	Blackburn R	L 0-1	Crossley	Lyttle	Pearce	Cooper	Chettle	Roy *	Haaland	Gemmill	Saunders	Clough *	Phillips	Moore (9), Roy (11)
15 Mar	PL	H	Liverpool	D 1-1	Crossley	Lyttle 1	Pearce	Jerkan	Chettle	Phillips	Haaland 1*	Gemmill	Saunders *	Hoojidonk	Woan	O'Neil (7), Roy (9), Moore (11)
22 Mar	PL	A	Sunderland	D 1-1	Crossley	Lyttle	Pearce	Cooper	Chettle	Phillips	Haaland *	Gemmill	Saunders	Hoojidonk	Woan *	Roy (11)
24 Mar	PL	A	Middlesbrough	L 1-3	Crossley	Lyttle	Pearce 1	Cooper	Chettle	Phillips	Haaland 1*	Gemmill	Saunders	Hoojidonk	Woan *	Warner (4), Woan (6), Moore (9)
5 Apr	PL	A	Southampton	W 5-2	Crossley	Lyttle	Pearce	Cooper	Chettle	Phillips	Haaland	Gemmill	Saunders	Hoojidonk	Woan *	Haaland (6), Moore (8)
15 Apr	NCCsf	A	Mansfield T	D 1-1	Fettis	Lyttle	Phillips	Cooper *	Chettle	Bart-Williams *	O'Neil	Gemmill	Roy *	Hoojidonk	Allen	Phillips (3), Roy (7) 1, Campbell (9)
19 Apr	PL	H	Leeds U	D 1-1	Fettis	Lyttle	Phillips	Warner	Chettle	Woan *	O'Neil	Gemmill *	Saunders	Hoojidonk	Allen	Saunders (6), Allen (8)
23 Apr	PL	A	Derby Co	D 0-0	Fettis	Lyttle	Pearce *	Cooper	Chettle	O'Neil *	Haaland *	Gemmill *	Saunders	Hoojidonk	Allen	
3 May	PL	H	Wimbledon	D 1-1	Fettis	Lyttle	Pearce *	Cooper	Chettle	O'Neil *	Haaland *	Gemmill	Saunders *	Hoojidonk 1	Woan	
11 May	PL	A	Newcastle U	L 0-5	Fettis	Lyttle	Phillips	Cooper	Chettle	Bart-Williams	Gemmill	Bart-Williams	Campbell	Moore		

League Appearances (Goals)

Allen C 16+8; Bart-Williams C 16 (1); Blatherwick S 7; Campbell K 16+1 (6); Chettle S 31+1; Clough N 10+3 (1); Cooper C 36 (2); Crossley M 33; Fettis A 4; Gemmill S 18+6; Guinan S 0+2; Haaland A 33+2 (6); Howe S 0+1; Jerkan N 14; Lee J 5+8 (1); Lyttle D 30+2 (1); McGregor P 0+5; Moore I 1+4; O'Neil B 4+1; Pearce S 33 (5); Phillips D 24+3; Roy B 8+12 (3); Saunders D 33+1 (3); Silenzi A 1+1; Stone S 5; Van Hooijdonk 8 (1); Warner V 2+1; Woan I 29+3 (1); Wright T 1.

Position in League Table

	P	W	D	L	F	A	Pts
1st Man Utd	38	21	12	5	76	44	75
20th Forest	38	6	16	16	31	59	34

Notes

§ denotes own goals

Aug 3, lost 3-4 on penalties

Aug 7, County Cup Final 1995-96, held over from previous season, lost 1-3 on penalties

1997-98 — Division One

Date	C	V	Opponent	Res	1	2	3	4	5	6	7	8	9	10	11	Substitutes used
19 Jul	F	A	Lincoln C	D 1-1												
24 Jul	F	A	Pallo-Ilrol	W 5-0												
26 Jul	F	A	Valkeakoski Haka	W 2-1												
28 Jul	F	A	Finnpa	D 4-4												
2 Aug	F	H	Leeds U	W 1-0												
4 Aug	NCC†	A	Notts Co	W 6-1												
9 Aug	FL	A	Port Vale	W 1-0	Pascolo	Lyttle	Rogers	Hjelde	Chettle	Thomas	Stone*	Johnson A	Hooijdonk	Campbell 1	Bonalair*	Saunders (7), Gemmill (11)
13 Aug	FLC1/1	A	Doncaster R	W 8-0	Pascolo	Lyttle*	Rogers*	Hjelde 2	Chettle	Thomas 1*	Bonalair*	Gemmill	Hooijdonk 2	Saunders 2	Allen 1	Armstrong (3), Phillips (6), Moore (7)
16 Aug	FL	A	Norwich C	W 4-1	Pascolo	Lyttle	Rogers	Hjelde	Chettle	Thomas 2*	Stone*	Gemmill	Hooijdonk 1	Campbell 1	Bonalair*	Saunders (6), Johnson A (7)
24 Aug	FL	A	Oxford U	W 1-0	Beasant	Lyttle	Rogers	Hjelde	Chettle	Thomas	Gemmill	Johnson A*	Hooijdonk	Allen*	Bonalair*	Guinan (10), Bart-Williams (11) 1
27 Aug	FLC1/2	H	Doncaster R	W 2-1	Fettis	Lyttle	Rogers	Armstrong	Thom	Bart-Williams*	Howe	Johnson A*	Hooijdonk 1*	Guinan 1	Allen	Moore (6), Warner (8), Woan (9)
30 Aug	FL	A	QPR	W 4-0	Pascolo	Lyttle*	Rogers	Hjelde	Chettle	Thomas	Bonalair*	Gemmill	Saunders	Campbell 1	Bart-Williams	Moore (2), Johnson A (7)
3 Sep	FL	A	Man City	L 1-3	Beasant	Lyttle	Rogers*	Hjelde	Chettle	Thomas	Johnson A	Gemmill	Saunders*	Campbell 1	Bart-Williams	Armstrong (3), Hooijdonk (9)
7 Sep	FL	A	Swindon T	D 0-0	Beasant	Lyttle*	Rogers	Hjelde	Chettle	Thomas*	Johnson A	Gemmill	Hooijdonk	Campbell	Bart-Williams	Saunders (2), Bonalair (6)
13 Sep	FL	A	Sheffield U	L 0-1	Beasant	Lyttle*	Rogers	Hjelde	Chettle	Thomas*	Johnson A*	Gemmill	Hooijdonk	Campbell	Bart-Williams	Saunders (6), Armstrong (8)
17 Sep	FLC2/1	H	Walsall	L 0-1	Beasant	Lyttle	Rogers	Hjelde	Chettle	Phillips	Saunders	Gemmill	Hooijdonk	Campbell	Bart-Williams	Johnson A (6)
20 Sep	FL	H	Portsmouth	D 2-2	Beasant	Lyttle	Rogers	Cooper	Chettle	Hjelde*	Saunders*	Gemmill	Hooijdonk 1	Campbell 1	Bart-Williams	Johnson A (10)
24 Sep	FLC2/2	A	Walsall	W 1-0	Beasant	Lyttle	Rogers	Cooper	Chettle	Saunders	Saunders 1	Gemmill	Hooijdonk 1	Campbell	Bart-Williams	Johnson A (4)
27 Sep	FL	H	Stoke C	W 1-0	Beasant	Lyttle*	Rogers	Cooper 1	Chettle	Armstrong 1	Saunders	Gemmill	Hooijdonk 1	Campbell	Bart-Williams	Johnson A (3)
3 Oct	FL	A	Huddersfield T	D 2-2	Beasant	Lyttle	Rogers	Cooper	Chettle	Armstrong	Saunders 1	Gemmill 1	Hooijdonk	Campbell	Bart-Williams	Stone (11)
18 Oct	FL	A	Tranmere R	D 2-2	Beasant	Lyttle	Rogers	Cooper	Chettle	Hjelde	Bart-Williams*	Gemmill	Hooijdonk 1	Campbell	Woan*	Johnson A (6), Stone (7)
21 Oct	FL	H	WBA	W 1-0	Beasant	Lyttle	Rogers	Cooper	Chettle	Hjelde*	Woan*	Gemmill	Hooijdonk 2 (1p)	Campbell 1	Bart-Williams	
24 Oct	FL	A	Reading	D 3-3	Beasant	Lyttle	Rogers	Cooper	Chettle	Armstrong*	Stone	Gemmill	Hooijdonk 2	Campbell 1	Bart-Williams	Hjelde (6)
1 Nov	FL	A	Crewe Alex	W 3-1	Beasant	Lyttle	Rogers	Cooper	Chettle	Hjelde	Stone	Gemmill	Hooijdonk	Campbell	Bart-Williams	Woan (6)
4 Nov	FL	A	Bury	L 0-2	Beasant	Lyttle	Rogers	Cooper	Chettle	Hjelde 1	Stone	Gemmill	Hooijdonk	Campbell	Bart-Williams	
8 Nov	FL	A	Sunderland	D 1-1	Beasant	Lyttle	Rogers	Cooper	Chettle	Hjelde	Stone	Gemmill	Hooijdonk 3	Campbell 3	Woan 1*	Armstrong (3), Woan (11)
15 Nov	FL	H	Birmingham C	W 1-0	Beasant	Lyttle	Rogers	Cooper	Chettle	Hjelde	Stone	Gemmill	Hooijdonk 1	Campbell 1	Bart-Williams	Bart-Williams (11)
22 Nov	FL	A	Charlton A	W 5-2	Beasant	Lyttle	Rogers	Cooper	Chettle	Hjelde	Stone	Gemmill	Hooijdonk 1	Campbell 1	Woan*	
26 Nov	FL	A	Middlesbrough	D 0-0	Beasant	Lyttle	Rogers	Cooper	Chettle	Hjelde*	Stone	Gemmill	Hooijdonk	Campbell	Woan	Bonalair (2) 1, Armstrong (6)
29 Nov	FL	A	Ipswich T	W 1-0	Beasant	Lyttle*	Rogers*	Cooper	Chettle	Hjelde	Stone	Gemmill	Hooijdonk	Campbell	Woan	Johnson A (2) 1, Moore (3), Armstrong (6)
6 Dec	FL	H	Bradford C	D 2-2	Beasant	Lyttle*	Rogers*	Cooper 1	Chettle	Hjelde*	Bonalair	Gemmill	Hooijdonk 1p	Campbell	Woan	Bonalair (2), Armstrong (3), Moore (10)
14 Dec	FL	A	Wolves	L 1-2	Pascolo	Lyttle*	Rogers*	Cooper	Chettle	Johnson A	Stone 1	Gemmill	Hooijdonk 2(2p)	Campbell 2	Woan	Moore (7), Bonalair (8), Armstrong (11)
20 Dec	FL	H	Stockport Co	W 2-1	Beasant	Lyttle*	Rogers*	Cooper	Chettle	Johnson A	Stone*	Gemmill	Hooijdonk	Campbell 2	Woan	Armstrong (6), Bonalair (11)
26 Dec	FL	H	Swindon T	W 3-0	Beasant	Lyttle	Rogers*	Cooper	Chettle	Johnson A	Stone	Gemmill	Hooijdonk	Campbell 2	Bonalair	Hooijdonk (11) 1
28 Dec	FL	A	Man City	W 3-2	Beasant	Lyttle	Rogers	Cooper	Chettle	Johnson A	Bonalair	Gemmill	Hooijdonk 2	Campbell 1	Bonalair	Armstrong (5)
3 Jan	FAC3	A	Charlton A	L 1-4	Beasant	Lyttle	Rogers	Cooper	Chettle	Johnson A*	Johnson D*	Gemmill	Hooijdonk 1p	Guinan*	Woan*	Moore (7), Thomas (11)
10 Jan	FL	H	Port Vale	W 2-1	Beasant	Lyttle	Rogers	Cooper	Chettle	Johnson A	Johnson D	Gemmill	Moore	Campbell 2	Woan*	Moore (7), Armstrong (8), Thomas (11)
17 Jan	FL	A	Norwich C	L 0-1	Beasant	Lyttle	Rogers	Cooper	Chettle	Johnson A	Johnson D*	Gemmill	Hooijdonk 2*	Campbell 1	Woan*	Moore (7), Armstrong (11)
24 Jan	FL	A	QPR	W 1-0	Beasant	Lyttle*	Rogers	Cooper	Chettle	Johnson A*	Bonalair	Gemmill	Hooijdonk 1	Campbell	Armstrong*	
31 Jan	FL	A	Oxford U	W 1-0	Beasant	Lyttle	Rogers	Cooper	Chettle	Johnson A*	Johnson D*	Gemmill	Hooijdonk 1	Campbell	Woan	
7 Feb	FL	A	Portsmouth	L 1-3	Beasant	Lyttle	Rogers	Cooper	Chettle	Johnson A	Johnson D	Thomas	Hooijdonk 2*	Campbell	Woan*	Armstrong (3), Thomas (6), Moore (9)
17 Feb	FL	H	Huddersfield T	W 3-0	Beasant	Lyttle	Rogers	Cooper	Chettle	Johnson A	Johnson D	Thomas	Hooijdonk 1p	Bonalair	Woan*	Armstrong (5), Thomas (6), Bart-Williams (7)
21 Feb	FL	H	Stoke C	W 1-0	Beasant	Lyttle	Rogers	Cooper	Chettle	Johnson A	Bonalair	Gemmill	Hooijdonk 2*	Bonalair	Bart-Williams	Thomas (8)
24 Feb	FL	A	Tranmere R	D 0-0	Beasant	Bonalair	Rogers	Cooper	Chettle	Johnson A	Johnson D*	Gemmill	Hooijdonk 2	Campbell	Bart-Williams	Bonalair (7)
1 Mar	FL	H	Middlesbrough	W 4-0	Beasant	Bonalair	Rogers	Cooper	Chettle	Johnson A	Thomas 1*	Gemmill	Hooijdonk 2	Campbell	Bart-Williams	Bonalair (2), Thomas (7)
4 Mar	FL	H	Sunderland	L 0-3	Beasant	Bonalair	Rogers	Cooper	Chettle	Johnson D*	Stone*	Gemmill	Hooijdonk	Campbell	Woan*	Johnson A (8), Moore (10), Armstrong (11)
7 Mar	FL	A	Crewe Alex	W 3-0 §	Beasant	Bonalair	Rogers	Cooper	Chettle	Thomas	Stone*	Gemmill	Hooijdonk	Campbell 3*	Bart-Williams	Johnson D (7), Johnson A (8)
14 Mar	FL	H	Bury	W 2-1	Beasant	Bonalair	Rogers	Hjelde	Chettle	Thomas	Stone	Gemmill	Hooijdonk 1	Campbell	Bart-Williams	Thomas (6), Woan (8)
21 Mar	FL	A	Birmingham C	L 2-4	Beasant	Bonalair	Rogers 1	Hjelde	Chettle	Johnson A*	Stone	Gemmill	Hooijdonk 2	Campbell	Woan*	
28 Mar	FL	A	Charlton A	W 3-0	Beasant	Bonalair	Rogers	Cooper	Chettle	Johnson A	Stone	Gemmill	Hooijdonk 1	Campbell 3	Bart-Williams	Armstrong (3), Johnson A (6), Woan (11)
1 Apr	FL	H	Sheffield U	W 2-1	Beasant	Bonalair	Rogers	Cooper	Chettle	Johnson A	Stone	Gemmill	Hooijdonk	Campbell 2	Bart-Williams	Hjelde (6)
5 Apr	FL	H	Bradford C	W 3-0	Beasant	Bonalair	Rogers	Cooper 1	Chettle	Johnson A	Stone	Gemmill	Hooijdonk 2	Campbell*	Bart-Williams 1	Hjelde (4), Woan (10)
11 Apr	FL	A	Wolves	W 3-0	Beasant	Bonalair	Rogers	Cooper*	Chettle*	Johnson A	Stone	Gemmill 1	Hooijdonk	Campbell 1*	Bart-Williams	
13 Apr	FL	H	Stockport Co	D 2-2	Beasant	Bonalair	Rogers	Hjelde	Chettle	Johnson A 1	Stone	Gemmill	Hooijdonk 1	Campbell 1*	Woan*	Woan (10)
18 Apr	FL	A	Reading	W 1-0	Beasant	Bonalair	Rogers	Hjelde	Chettle	Johnson A 1	Stone	Gemmill	Hooijdonk 1	Campbell*	Bart-Williams	Hjelde (5), Woan (10)
25 Apr	FL	H	Shrewsbury T	L 1-4	Beasant	Bonalair	Rogers	Cooper	Chettle*	Johnson A	Stone	Gemmill	Hooijdonk	Campbell*	Bart-Williams 1	Hjelde (6), Woan (8)
27 Apr	F	A	WBA	D 1-1	Beasant	Bonalair	Rogers	Cooper	Chettle	Johnson A*	Stone 1	Gemmill 1	Hooijdonk	Harewood	Bart-Williams	
3 May	FL	H	Chelsea	D 3-3												
6 May	F	A	Middlesbrough	W 5-0												

Individual career records with Forest

The following are the individual career records for all Nottingham Forest players since the first FA Cup match on 16 November 1878 until 1 August 1998.

Key: 20/1 indicates 20 Apps + 1 substitute appearance. OTHERS refers to Full Members'/Simod/Zenith Data Systems Cups, European/UEFA/Fairs/Super/Anglo-Italian/Anglo-Scottish/Texaco Cups, Mercantile Challenge Trophy, World Club Championship and the FA Charity Shield.

The three League matches played at the beginning of the abandoned 1939-40 season are excluded.

Player	Played	LEAGUE App	Gls	FA CUP App	Gls	FL CUP App	Gls	OTHERS App	Gls	TOTAL App	Gls
AAS, E.J.	1980-81	20/1	1	-	-	3	-	-	-	23/1	1
ABBOTT, H.	1894-96	5	-	-	-	-	-	-	-	5	-
ADDISON, C.	1960-66	160	62	11	6	3	1	2	-	176	69
ALEXANDER, D. L.	1955-56	20	4	-	-	-	-	-	-	20	4
ALLAN, J.S.	1912-13	22	3	-	-	-	-	-	-	22	3
ALLEN, C.	1995-98	18/10	1	1	1	2	1	-	-	21/10	3
ALLEN, H.A.	1947-48	1	-	3	1	-	-	-	-	4	1
ALLSOPP, D.	1892-99	206	-	27	-	-	-	-	-	233	-
ALSFORD, W.J.	1936-37	30	-	-	-	-	-	-	-	30	-
ANDERSON, J.	1949-50	40	1	2	-	-	-	-	-	42	1
ANDERSON, Viv A.	1974-83	323/5	15	23	1	39	5	40	1	425/5	22
ANDREWS, G.	1986-87	-	-	-/1	-	-	-	-	-	-/1	-
ANTHONY, W.	1904-05	5	-	-	-	-	-	-	-	5	-
ARDRON, W.	1949-55	182	123	9	1	-	-	-	-	191	124
ARMSTRONG, C.	1997-98	4/14	-	1	-	2/2	1	-	-	7/16	1
ARMSTRONG, Jack	1905-22	432	8	28	1	-	-	-	-	460	9
ARMSTRONG, John	1958-62	20	-	1	-	1	-	-	-	22	-
ARMSTRONG, R.J.	1929-34	17	-	-	-	-	-	-	-	17	-
ASHMAN, G.A.	1948-50	13	3	-	-	-	-	-	-	13	3
ASHMORE, R.	1920-21	11	1	1	-	-	-	-	-	12	1
ASHTON, P.	1930-38	176	-	9	-	-	-	-	-	185	-
ASHWORTH, J.E.	1925-26	3	-	-	-	-	-	-	-	3	-
BADGER, H.O.	1909-10	2	-	-	-	-	-	-	-	2	-
BAILEY, W.G.	1910-11	4	1	-	-	-	-	-	-	4	1
BAILY, E. F.	1956-58	68	14	8	3	-	-	-	-	76	17
BAINES, S.J.	1972-73	2	-	-	-	-	-	-	-	2	-
BAIRD, D.H.	1960-62	32	-	1	-	3	-	1	-	37	-
BAKER, D.H.	1949-50	3	-	-	-	-	-	-	-	3	-
BAKER, J.H.	1965-68	117/1	41	8	5	5	-	4	3	134/1	49
BALL, G.A.	1964-65	3	-	-	-	-	-	-	-	3	-
BANHAM, R.	1955-56	2	-	-	-	-	-	-	-	2	-
BANKS, F.	1911-19	71	5	2	-	-	-	-	-	73	5
BANNISTER, G.	1992-93	27/4	8	3	1	2/1	1	-	-	32/5	10
BARBOUR, A.	1892-93	1	-	-	-	-	-	-	-	1	-
BARKS, E.	1946-49	66	5	7	2	-	-	-	-	73	7
BARLOW	1883-84	-	-	1	-	-	-	-	-	1	-
BARNETT, T.	1900-01	2	-	-	-	-	-	-	-	2	-
BARNSDALE, J.D.	1903-04	26	-	-	-	-	-	-	-	26	-
BARNWELL, J.	1963-69	172/8	22	12/1	2	5	1	3	-	192/9	25
BARRATT, P.	1919-29	216	17	13	-	-	-	-	-	229	17
BARRETT, C.	1975-78	64/5	4	3/2	-	10	1	9/1	3	86/8	8
BARRETT, J.G.	1954-58	105	64	12	5	-	-	-	-	117	69
BARRINGTON, J.	1929-36	211	1	18	-	-	-	-	-	229	1
BARRON, J.	1970-73	155	-	15	-	8	-	2	-	180	-
BARRY, L.J.	1933-34	17	1	-	-	-	-	-	-	17	1
BARTON, A.E.	1959-61	22	1	1	-	1	1	-	-	24	2
BART-WILLIAMS, C.	1995-98	79/3	5	2	-	6	-	7/1	-	94/4	4
BATES, A.J.	1878-79	-	-	7	-	-	-	-	-	7	-
BAXTER, J.C.	1967-68	47/1	3	-	-	-	-	-	-	49/1	3
BAXTER, W.E.	1937-46	15	-	-	-	-	-	-	-	15	-
BEARDSLEY, F.W.	1884-88	-	-	15	-	-	-	-	-	15	-
BEASANT, D.	1997-98	41	-	1	-	2	-	-	-	44	-
BEAUMONT, L.	1938-39	34	3	1	-	-	-	-	-	35	3
BEDFORD, H.	1919-20	18	8	2	1	-	-	-	-	20	9
BELL, James	1920-21	1	-	-	-	-	-	-	-	1	-
BELL, J.J.	1913-14	54	6	3	1	-	-	-	-	57	7
BELL, M.	1931-33	85	1	2	-	-	-	-	-	87	1
BELTON, J.	1914-27	321	17	26	-	-	-	-	-	347	17
BENBOW, J.A.	1897-98	2	-	-	-	-	-	-	-	2	-
BENBOW, L.	1897-99	54	20	8	2	-	-	-	-	62	22
BENNETT, A.	1920-25	83	-	6	-	-	-	-	-	89	-
BETTS, A.	1936-38	65	10	2	-	-	-	-	-	67	10
BEVERIDGE, R.	1899-1900	28	5	5	2	-	-	-	-	33	7
BILLYEALD, H.	1882-87	-	-	17	1	-	-	-	-	17	1
BIRCH, W.	1908-09	14	2	-	-	-	-	-	-	14	2
BIRTLES, G.	1976-80/82-86	209/3	70	11	3	31	15	27/2	8	278/5	96
BISHOP, J.	1878-79	-	-	1	1	-	-	-	-	1	1
BLACK, K.	1991-95	79/17	14	4	-	19/1	5	4/2	1	106/20	20
BLACKMAN, R.H.	1954-55	11	3	-	-	-	-	-	-	11	3
BLAGG, E.A.	1946-47	54	-	7	-	-	-	-	-	61	-
BLATHERWICK, S.	1993-97	10	-	1	-	2	-	2	-	15	-
BLYTHE, J.R.	1911-12	1	-	-	-	-	-	-	-	1	-
BOARDMAN, C.	1991-92	-	-	-	-	-/1	-	-	-	-/1	-
BOHINEN, L.	1993-96	59/5	7	2	1	7/1	2	1	-	69/6	10
BONALAIR, T.	1997-98	24/7	2	1	-	1	-	-	-	26/7	2
BONSER	1882-83	-	-	1	-	-	-	-	-	1	-
BOOT, L.G.W.	1927-28	2	-	-	-	-	-	-	-	2	-
BOOTH, C.	1959-61	87	39	5	1	4	1	2	-	98	41
BOWDEN, O.	1935-36	14	3	-	-	-	-	-	-	14	3
BOWERY, H.N.	1975-76	2	2	2	-	-	-	-	-	4	2
BOWLES, S.	1979-80	19	2	1	-	-	-	3	-	23	2
BOWYER, I.	1973-80/81-86	425/20	68	34	7	45/2	13	37/1	8	541/23	96
BOYMAN, W.R.	1921-22	12	3	1	-	-	-	-	-	13	3
BRADSHAW, T.D.	1897-98	18	-	3	-	-	-	-	-	21	-
BRENTNALL, A.A.	1899-1900	2	-	-	-	-	-	-	-	2	-
BRIDGETT, R.	1967-69	2/2	-	-	-	-	-	-	-	2/2	-
BRIGHAM, H.	1946-47	35	2	4	-	-	-	-	-	39	2
BRINDLEY, J.C.	1965-69	7/8	1	1	-	-	-	-	-	8/8	1
BRODIE, J.	1893-94	9	5	3	2	-	-	-	-	12	7
BROMAGE, E.	1929-30	1	-	-	-	-	-	-	-	1	-
BROUGHTON, M.	1901-02	27	5	1	-	-	-	-	-	28	5
BROWN, A.R.	1935-38	51	7	3	-	-	-	-	-	54	7
BROWN, O.M.	1930-31	9	6	-	-	-	-	-	-	9	6
BROWN, Richard	1936-37	19	2	1	-	-	-	-	-	20	2
BROWN, Robert A.J.	1946-47	46	17	4	-	-	-	-	-	50	17
BROWN, W.	1892-93	22	-	10	-	-	-	-	-	32	-
BROWN, William	1928-29	4	-	-	-	-	-	-	-	4	-
BROWN, William	1929-30	1	-	-	-	-	-	-	-	1	-
BUCKLEY, A.P.	1971-72	16/2	1	-	-	-/1	-	-	-	16/3	1
BULL, G.	1993-95	4/8	1	-/3	-	2	-	-	-	6/11	1
BULLING, H.	1919-24	186	2	13	-	-	-	-	-	199	2
BULLOCK, J.	1892-93	1	-	-	-	-	-	-	-	1	-
BURDITT, G.L.	1934-35	18	10	2	-	-	-	-	-	20	10
BURKE, S.J.	1976-77	-	-	-	-	-/1	-	-	-	-/1	-
BURGIN, M.	1936-37	22	11	-	-	-	-	-	-	22	11
BURKITT, J.O.	1948-61	464	14	37	1	2	-	-	-	503	15
BURNS, K.	1977-81	137	13	14	-	25	1	20	1	196	15
BURTON, B.B.	1954-55	1	-	2	-	-	-	-	-	3	-
BURTON, F.E.	1887-91	-	-	6	3	-	-	-	-	6	3
BURTON, J.W.	1931-35	36	-	4	-	-	-	-	-	40	-
BURTON, N.	1921-31	296	57	24	5	-	-	-	-	320	62
BUTLER	1906-07	1	-	1	-	-	-	-	-	2	-
BUTLIN, B.D.	1974-76	71/3	17	7	-	2	-	5	3	85/3	20
BUTTERWORTH, I.S.	1985-86	26/1	-	1	-	6	-	-	-	33/1	-

Player	Played	LEAGUE App	Gls	FA CUP App	Gls	FL CUP App	Gls	OTHERS App	Gls	TOTAL App	Gls
CABORN, C.J.	1878-87	-	-	32	-	-	-	-	-	32	-
CALVEY, J.	1899-1903	131	48	19	9	-	-	-	-	150	57
CAMERON, D.	1928-29	21	1	-	-	-	-	-	-	21	1
CAMPBELL, D.A.	1985-87	35/6	3	-/2	-	4	2	-	-	39/8	5
CAMPBELL, K.	1995-98	79/1	32	11	3	2	-	3	-	95/1	35
CANNING, L.D.	1951-52	5	-	-	-	-	-	-	-	5	-
CAPEL, T.A.	1949-53	154	69	8	3	-	-	-	-	162	72
CAPES, A.	1896-97	30	7	3	-	-	-	-	-	33	7
CAPES, A.J.	1896-1901	168	33	23	9	-	-	-	-	191	42
CARGILL, J.	1934-35	10	1	-	-	-	-	-	-	10	1
CARGILL, J.G.	1964-65	2	-	1	-	-	-	-	-	3	-
CARNELLY, A.F.	1894-95	52	24	4	1	-	-	-	-	56	25
CARR, F.A.	1985-91	122/9	17	4	-	16/2	5	5/1	1	147/12	23
CHAMBERS, J.	1931-32	9	1	-	-	-	-	-	-	9	1
CHAPMAN, F.W.S.	1904-06	3	-	-	-	-	-	-	-	3	-
CHAPMAN, L.R.	1988-89	48	15	5	3	12	6	6	3	71	27
CHAPMAN, R.D.	1963-76	347/12	17	30/2	2	19	1	11/1	3	407/15	23
CHARLES, G.A.	1988-93	54/2	1	8/2	1	9	-	4/2	-	75/6	2
CHARLTON, A.	1898-99	3	-	-	-	-	-	-	-	3	-
CHETTLE, S.	1987-98	356/14	8	34/1	-	42/3	1	21/2	2	453/20	11
CHRISTIE, T.	1984-85	14	5	2	1	2	1	2	-	20	7
CLARK, F.A.	1975-78	116/1	1	12	-	13	-	14/1	-	155/2	1
CLARK, T.G.	1938-39	27	2	2	-	-	-	-	-	29	2
CLARKE, J.	1947-53	18	-	2	-	-	-	-	-	20	-
CLOUGH, N.H.	1984-93	307/4	101	28	6	46	22	11/3	1	392/7	130
	1996-97	10/3	1	-	-	-	-	-	-	10/3	1
CLUROE, M.	1954-55	1	-	-	-	-	-	-	-	1	-
COBB, W.W.	1960-62	30	5	4	-	1	1	1	1	36	7
COLEMAN, J.G.	1914-15	38	14	2	2	-	-	-	-	40	16
COLES, F.G.	1899-1900	1	-	2	-	-	-	-	-	3	-
COLLIER, G.R.	1969-70	13/2	2	2/2	2	-	-	-	-	15/4	4
COLLINDRIDGE, C.	1950-53	151	45	5	2	-	-	-	-	156	47
COLLINS, J.	1893-94	40	15	4	-	-	-	-	-	44	15
COLLYMORE, S.	1993-95	64/1	41	2	1	9	7	2	1	77/1	50
COLMAN, J.	1889-90	-	-	1	-	-	-	-	-	1	-
COMERY, H.	1903-04	1	-	-	-	-	-	-	-	1	-
CONDREY, J.F.	1911-12	7	2	-	-	-	-	-	-	7	2
CONNOR, J.	1893-94	5	-	-	-	-	-	-	-	5	-
COOPER, C.	1993-98	179/1	20	12	1	14	2	7	-	212/1	23
CORMACK, P.B.	1969-71	74	15	6	1	4	2	2	2	86	20
COTTAM, J.E.	1970-75	92/3	4	7/1	-	5	-	-	-	104/4	4
COX, W.	1922-23	1	-	-	-	-	-	-	-	1	-
COYLE, F.	1957-58	3	-	-	-	-	-	-	-	3	-
CRAGGS, J.	1904-06	52	7	4	1	-	-	-	-	56	8
CRAIG, C.T.	1902-06	137	2	11	-	-	-	-	-	148	2
CRAWFORD, J.	1902-04	13	-	-	-	-	-	-	-	13	-
CRAWSHAW, H.	1938-39	22	9	-	-	-	-	-	-	22	9
CROSBY, G.	1987-94	139/13	12	18/3	3	29/1	6	10/1	4	196/18	25
CROSS, J.	1893-94	1	-	-	-	-	-	-	-	1	-
CROSSLEY, M.	1988-97	270/1	-	32	-	34	-	18	1	354/1	1
CROWE, C.	1964-66	73	12	3	2	2	1	-	-	78	15
CURRAN, E.(Terry)	1975-76	46/2	12	-	-	2	1	5	4	53/2	17
CURRIE, D.	1989-90	4/4	1	-	-	-	-	-	-	4/4	1
DAFT, H.B.	1892-93	4	1	-	-	-	-	-	-	4	1
DANKS, T.	1882-88	-	-	15	6	-	-	-	-	15	6
DAVENPORT, P.	1981-85	114/4	54	7/1	1	10	1	10/1	2	141/6	58
DAVIDSON, A.E.	1984-85	3	-	2	-	-	-	-	-	5	-
DAVIES, R.G.	1936-46	55	-	4	-	-	-	-	-	59	-
DAVIES, T.D.	1903-05	39	1	4	-	-	-	-	-	43	1
DAVIS, A.	1919-20	20	7	-	-	-	-	-	-	20	7
DEAN, A.	1900-01	7	-	-	-	-	-	-	-	7	-
DENNIS, G.T.	1920-23	30	3	3	1	-	-	-	-	33	4
DENNISON, R.S.	1934-35	15	5	1	1	-	-	-	-	16	6
DENNEHY, J.	1972-74	37/4	4	2/1	-	2	-	-	-	41/5	4
DENT, J.G.	1929-36	196	119	10	3	-	-	-	-	206	122
DERRICK, J.H.	1909-19	139	35	8	1	-	-	-	-	147	36
DEWEY, J.	1896-97	1	-	-	-	-	-	-	-	1	-
DEXTER, A.	1923-36	256	-	18	-	-	-	-	-	274	-
DICKINSON, W.	1928-33	136	68	7	5	-	-	-	-	143	73
DODSON, A.	1911-12	1	-	-	-	-	-	-	-	1	-
DONOVON, A.	1920-21	3	-	-	-	-	-	-	-	3	-
DRABBLE, F.	1910-11	8	-	-	-	-	-	-	-	8	-
DUDLEY, W.W.	1902-13	279	-	21	-	-	-	-	-	300	-
DUSLON, J.	1931-32	1	2	-	-	-	-	-	-	1	2
DWIGHT, R.E.	1958-59	44	21	9	6	-	-	-	-	53	27
DYSON, J.	1937-38	15	-	1	-	-	-	-	-	16	-
EARP, F.W.	1878-84	-	-	17	3	-	-	-	-	17	3
EARP, M.J.	1889-91	13	-	8	-	-	-	-	-	21	-
EDGAR, D.	1935-37	100	1	4	-	-	-	-	-	104	1
EDWARDS, J.(Jack)	1946-47	77	20	4	1	-	-	-	-	81	21
ELLIOTT, B.H.	1947-48	10	-	-	-	-	-	-	-	10	-
ELLIOTT, S.B.	1978-79	4	-	-	-	2	-	-	-	6	-
ELLIOTT, T.W.	1920-21	28	7	-	-	-	-	-	-	28	7
FAIRCLOUGH, C.H.	1982-86	102/5	1	6	-	9/1	1	9/2	-	126/8	2
FALCONER, F.	1923-24	2	-	-	-	-	-	-	-	2	-
FARMER, A.	1930-31	16	-	-	-	-	-	-	-	16	-
FARMER, R.J.	1957-58	9	-	1	-	-	-	-	-	10	-
FARMER, W.A.	1953-56	52	-	6	-	-	-	-	-	58	-
FASHANU, J.S.	1981-82	31/1	3	-	-	4	1	-	-	35/1	4
FETTIS, A.	1996-98	4	-	-/1	-	1	-	-	-	5/1	-
FIELDING, A.R.	1902-03	10	-	-	-	-	-	-	-	10	-
FIRTH, R.E.	1911-20	141	14	5	-	-	-	-	-	146	14
FISHER, A.	1909-14	100	1	5	-	-	-	-	-	105	1
FISKE, W.A.	1914-15	5	-	1	-	-	-	-	-	6	-
FLEMING, J.G.	1984-89	71/3	-	2/1	-	5/1	-	-/1	-	78/6	-
FLETCHER, S.E.	1914-15	1	-	-	-	-	-	-	-	1	-
FLETCHER, W.	1882-83	-	-	4	1	-	-	-	-	4	1
FLOOD, C.W.	1922-25	97	21	3	-	-	-	-	-	100	21
FORD, J.B.	1910-13	102	12	2	-	-	-	-	-	104	12
FORMAN, Francis	1894-1905	223	23	33	5	-	-	-	-	256	28
FORMAN, F.R.	1893-1902	158	34	23	6	-	-	-	-	181	40
FORMAN, T.	1900-02	5	-	-	-	-	-	-	-	5	-
FORREST, J.R.	1930-33	14	2	-	-	-	-	-	-	14	2
FOSTER, C.J.	1986-89	68/4	5	5	-	8	1	2	-	83/4	6
FOX, F.	1883-87	-	-	19	7	-	-	-	-	19	7
FRANCIS, T.J.	1978-81	69/1	28	8	5	6	-	9	4	92/1	37
FRASER, D.M.	1970-72	85	3	7	-	2	1	-	-	94	4
FRASER, W.A.	1958-59	2	-	-	-	-	-	-	-	2	-
FRENCH, J.W. (Jack)	1952-55	80	8	6	-	-	-	-	-	86	8
FRYER, J. (Jack)	1938-39	22	8	1	-	-	-	-	-	23	8
FULLARTON, W.M.	1905-06	20	-	1	-	-	-	-	-	21	-
GAGER, H.E.	1947-54	258	11	10	-	-	-	-	-	268	11
GALLEY, J.E.	1972-74	31/6	6	3	2	2/1	-	-	-	36/7	8
GALLOWAY, R.	1924-26	39	8	4	-	-	-	-	-	43	8
GARA, A.	1902-03	6	1	-	-	-	-	-	-	6	1
GARDINER, C.	1935-37	38	8	3	-	-	-	-	-	41	8
GAYNOR, T.	1987-92	43/14	10	5/1	1	10	7	3/2	1	61/17	19
GEARY, G.	1893-94	7	3	-	-	-	-	-	-	7	3
GEMMELL, T.	1971-72	39	6	1	-	1	-	-	-	41	6
GEMMILL, A.	1977-78	56/2	4	7	-	7	-	8	1	78/2	5
GEMMILL, S.	1990-98	210/15	21	18/2	1	27/2	3	13/1	4	268/20	29
GEORGE, C.F.	1979-80	2	-	-	-	-	-	2	1	4	1
GERMAN, A.C.J.	1927-30	25	10	7	-	-	-	-	-	32	10
GETTY, J.	1936-38	18	2	-	-	-	-	-	-	18	2
GIBSON, S.G.	1921-28	252	53	24	2	-	-	-	-	276	55
GIBSON, T.	1907-19	185	32	7	3	-	-	-	-	192	35
GLOVER, E.L.	1987-94	61/16	9	8	1	6/5	2	4/1	1	79/24	13
GOODCHILD, G.	1896-97	4	-	-	-	-	-	-	-	4	-
GOODYER, A.C.	1878-79	-	-	10	4	-	-	-	-	10	4
GORDON, L.W.	1927-28	2	-	-	-	-	-	-	-	2	-

Player	Played	LEAGUE App	Gls	FA CUP App	Gls	FL CUP App	Gls	OTHERS App	Gls	TOTAL App	Gls
GOUCHER, G.H.	1928-29	1	-	-	-	-	-	-	-	1	-
GOWTHORPE, C.G.	1881-82	-	-	1	-	-	-	-	-	1	-
GRAHAM, J.A.	1923-34	31	13	2	1	-	-	-	-	33	14
GRAHAM, T.	1927-38	372	7	18	-	-	-	-	-	390	7
GRANT B.P.	1961-64	18	-	1	-	3	-	-	-	22	-
GRAY, F.T.	1979-80	81	5	8	1	14	2	15	-	118	8
GRAY, S.	1980-82	48/1	3	3	-	5/1	-	1	-	57/2	3
GRAY, W.P.	1957-62	201	29	17	5	2	-	3	-	223	34
GREEN, A.W.	1906-08	40	19	-	-	-	-	-	-	40	19
GREEN, H.	1927-28	4	-	-	-	-	-	-	-	4	-
GREEN, J.	1921-22	10	2	3	1	-	-	-	-	13	3
GREENWOOD, P.G.	1974-75	15	-	4	-	-	-	-	-	19	-
GRIFFITHS, H.	1903-04	8	1	-	-	-	-	-	-	8	1
GRUMMITT, P.M.	1960-69	313	-	26	-	7	-	6	-	352	-
GUINAN, S.	1995-98	2/4	-	-	-	1	1	-	-	3/5	-
GUNN, A.H.	1946-47	2	-	-	-	-	-	-	-	2	-
GUNN, B.C.	1975-84	129/2	1	9	-	17	1	4/5	-	159/7	2
GUNN, W.	1881-82	-	-	1	-	-	-	-	-	1	-
GUTTERIDGE, F.	1889-90	-	-	1	-	-	-	-	-	1	-
HAALAND, A.I.	1993-97	66/9	7	5/1	-	2/2	-	2/3	-	75/15	7
HADLEY, H.	1905-06	12	1	-	-	-	-	-	-	12	1
HAGUE, E.M.	1928-29	4	-	-	-	-	-	-	-	4	-
HALES, H.	1928-29	3	-	-	-	-	-	-	-	3	-H
HALL, C.T.	1968-69	27/9	2	1	-	-/1	-	-	-	28/10	2
HAMILTON, A.	1911-12	7	-	-	-	-	-	-	-	7	-
HAMILTON, T.	1891-92	7	-	2	-	-	-	-	-	9	-
HANCOCK, W.T.	1881-88	-	-	26	-	-	-	-	-	26	-
HANCOCK, J.B.	1894-95	1	-	-	-	-	-	-	-	1	-
HANNA, A.J.	1911-13	97	-	5	-	-	-	-	-	102	-
HARBY, M.J.	1967-68	3	-	-	-	-	-	-	-	3	-
HARDSTAFF, J.	1904-05	11	1	1	-	-	-	-	-	12	1
HARDY, S.	1921-24	102	-	7	-	-	-	-	-	109	-
HARDY, W.H.	1936-37	1	-	-	-	-	-	-	-	1	-
HAREWOOD, M.	1997-98	1	-	-	-	-	-	-	-	1	-
HARRIS, F.M.	1913-14	47	12	1	-	-	-	-	-	48	12
HARRIS, L.J.	1968-69	2	-	-	-	-	-	-	-	2	-
HARRISON, A.	1927-29	77	3	4	-	-	-	-	-	81	3
HARROLD, S.	1920-21	50	8	2	-	-	-	-	-	52	8
HART, H.	1919-20	6	1	-	-	-	-	-	-	6	1
HART, P.A.	1983-84	70	1	3	1	3	-	11	1	87	3
HARTFORD, R.A.	1979-80	3	-	-	-	-	-	-	-	3	-
HARVEY, L.	1993-94	-/2	-	-	-	-/1	-	-	-	-/3	-
HASLEGRAVE, S.M.	1976-77	5/2	1	-	-	-	-	6	-	11/2	1
HASSELL, A.A.	1909-10	35	-	4	-	-	-	-	-	39	-
HEATHCOCK, J.B.	1928-29	20	15	-	-	-	-	-	-	20	15
HENDERSON, G.	1901-05	101	6	10	-	-	-	-	-	111	6
HENNESSEY, W.T.	1965-69	159	5	12	1	8	-	4	-	183	6
HENSON	1888-89	-	-	1	-	-	-	-	-	1	-
HESLOP, R.	1928-33	93	23	2	-	-	-	-	-	95	23
HEWITT, A.	1924-25	4	-	1	-	-	-	-	-	5	-
HICKS, T.G.	1927-28	8	-	-	-	-	-	-	-	8	-
HIGGINS, A.F.	1890-93	47	18	17	18	-	-	-	-	64	36
HIGGINS, A.	1920-21	33	7	2	-	-	-	-	-	35	7
HIGHAM, P.	1955-57	61	20	6	1	-	-	-	-	67	21
HILL, A.	1968-69	41	-	2	-	3	-	-	-	46	-
HILLEY, D.	1967-70	72/16	14	3	1	5	-	2	1	82/16	16
HINCHCLIFFE, T.	1946-47	1	-	-	-	-	-	-	-	1	-
HINDLEY, F.C.	1938-39	6	3	2	-	-	-	-	-	8	3
HINDLEY, P.	1962-73	366	10	30	1	14	-	6	-	416	11
HINTON, A.T.	1963-67	108/4	24	7/1	-	-/1	-	1	-	116/6	24
HITCH, A.	1901-02	13	2	-	-	-	-	-	-	13	2
HJELDE, J.	1997-98	23/5	1	1	-	2	2	-	-	26/5	3
HOCKEY, T.J.	1961-63	73	6	6	2	-	-	-	-	79	8
HODGE, S.B.	1981-85/88-91	201/4	50	17/1	2	30/1	8	19	6	267/6	66
HODGKINSON, V.A.	1925-26	9	1	-	-	-	-	-	-	9	1
HOLDER, A.M.	1954-55	3	-	1	-	-	-	-	-	4	-
HOLDSTOCK, H.	1904-05	1	-	-	-	-	-	-	-	1	-
HOLLAND, J.H.	1889-90	-	-	3	-	-	-	-	-	3	-
HOLLINS, D.M.	1969-70	9	-	-	-	-	-	-	-	9	-
HOLLIS, J.N.	1896-97	1	1	-	-	-	-	-	-	1	1
HOLMES, J.A.	1905-06	5	-	1	1	-	-	-	-	6	1
HOLROYD, A.M.	1878-80	-	-	11	-	-	-	-	-	11	-
HOOD, C.	1934-35	3	-	-	-	-	-	-	-	3	-
HOOPER, W.	1906-11	147	22	9	2	-	-	-	-	153	24
HORROCKS, J.	1909-10	20	-	-	-	-	-	-	-	20	-
HOWE, S.	1993-98	6/8	2	-	-	2	-	1/1	-	9/9	2
HOWIE, C.	1928-30	23	2	1	-	-	-	-	-	24	2
HOWLETT, H.	1932-33	1	-	-	-	-	-	-	-	1	-
HUDDLESTONE, E.	1956-57	1	-	-	-	-	-	-	-	1	-
HUGHES, E.	1905-10	165	5	12	1	-	-	-	-	177	6
HULLETT, W.A.	1948-49	13	2	2	-	-	-	-	-	15	2
HULME, E.M.	1971-72	5	-	-	-	1	-	-	-	6	-
HUNT	1895-96	1	-	-	-	-	-	-	-	1	-
HUNT, A.K.	1938-39	2	-	-	-	-	-	-	-	2	-
HUNT, J.F.	1934-35	1	-	-	-	-	-	-	-	1	-
HUTCHINSON, J.A.	1946-58	241	-	13	-	-	-	-	-	254	-
ILEY, J.	1959-62	93	4	4	1	3	-	3	-	103	5
IMLACH, J.J.S.	1956-59	184	43	19	5	-	-	1	-	204	48
INGRAM, A.	1969-70	28	3	-	-	2	-	1	-	31	3
INNES, R.	1903-04	23	-	-	-	-	-	-	-	23	-
IREMONGER, H.	1913-14	11	-	-	-	-	-	-	-	11	-
IREMONGER, J.	1895-1909	274	2	26	1	-	-	-	-	300	3
IRONS	1887-88	-	-	1	-	-	-	-	-	1	-
IRVING, R.	1995-96	-/1	-	-	-	-	-	-	-	-/1	-
JACKSON, T.A.	1970-74	73/8	6	8	-	6	-	-	-	87/8	6
JARDINE, E	1878-79	-	-	3	-	-	-	-	-	3	-
JEACOCK, T.W.	1888-94	1	-	8	-	-	-	-	-	9	-
JEMSON, N.	1989-92	45/2	13	4	3	9	4	1	-	59/2	20
JEFFRIES, T.	1886-87	-	-	4	-	-	-	-	-	4	-
JENNINGS, S.	1928-29	27	15	1	1	-	-	-	-	28	16
JERKAN, N.	1996-97	14	-	-	-	-	-	-	-	14	-
JOHNSON, A.	1997-98	24/10	4	-	-	2/1	-	-	-	26/11	4
JOHNSON, D.	1997-98	5/1	-	-	-	-	-	-	-	5/1	-
JOHNSON, J.	1919-20	53	-	1	-	-	-	-	-	54	-
JOHNSON, T.	1948-51	68	27	4	3	-	-	-	-	72	30
JOHNSTON, T.	1946-47	64	26	5	-	-	-	-	-	69	26
JONES, A.T.	1903-04	10	-	3	-	-	-	-	-	13	-
JONES, C.	1925-27	100	22	10	-	-	-	-	-	110	22
JONES, C.W.	1947-48	7	5	-	-	-	-	-	-	7	5
JONES, D.	1974-75	36	1	3	1	2	-	-	-	41	2
JONES, E.	1955-57	18	3	-	-	-	-	-	-	18	3
JONES, G.W.	1920-21	8	-	-	-	-	-	-	-	8	-
JONES, H.	1912-23	225	7	15	3	-	-	-	-	240	10
JONES, T.D.	1903-04	2	-	-	-	-	-	-	-	2	-
JOYCE, C.	1957-58	10	-	-	-	-	-	-	-	10	-
JULIANS, L.B.	1960-63	58	24	3	1	-	-	-	-	61	25
KAILE, G.	1947-49	65	8	2	1	-	-	-	-	67	9
KAMINSKY, J.	1991-92	-/1	-	-	-	-	-	-	-	-/1	-
KEANE, R.	1990-93	114	22	18	3	17	6	5	2	154	33
KEAR, M.	1963-66	26/1	5	-	-	-	-	-	-	26/1	25
KEETON, W.W.	1932-33	5	-	-	-	-	-	-	-	5	-
KELLY, B.	1958-59	2	-	-	-	-	-	1	-	3	-
KELLY, N.	1951-57	48	11	3	1	-	-	-	-	51	12
KENDAL, S.J.	1981-82	1	-	-	-	-	-	-	-	1	-
KENT, T.	1898-99	2	-	-	-	-	-	-	-	2	-
KERR, N.	1895-96	1	-	-	-	-	-	-	-	1	-
KILFORD, I.	1993-94	-/1	-	-	-	-	-	-	-	-/1	-
KIRRAGE, F.B.	1919-20	1	-	-	-	-	-	-	-	1	-
KNIGHT, F.	1946-49	48	1	5	-	-	-	-	-	53	1
KNIGHT, P.R.	1959-60	4	-	-	-	-	-	-/1	-	4/1	-

Player	Played	LEAGUE App	Gls	FA CUP App	Gls	FL CUP App	Gls	OTHERS App	Gls	TOTAL App	Gls
LANGFORD, J.W.	1955-56	4	-	-	-	-	-	-	-	4	-
LANGFORD, L.	1924-29	136	-	8	-	-	-	-	-	144	-
LANGHAM, F.	1911-12	2	-	-	-	-	-	-	-	2	-
LANGLEY, R.	1932-33	5	1	-	-	-	-	-	-	5	1
LAWS, B.	1988-94	136/11	4	16/2	1	28/4	-	11/1	-	191/18	5
LAWS, J.	1926-27	7	1	-	-	-	-	-	-	7	1
LAWTON, J.	1919-20	3	-	-	-	-	-	-	-	3	-
LAY, P.J.	1954-55	1	-	-	-	-	-	-	-	1	-
LEE, G.	1947-48	76	20	3	-	-	-	-	-	79	20
LEE, J.	1993-97	41/35	14	-/5	-	4/3	1	4/2	-	49/45	15
Le FLEM, R.P.	1960-64	132	18	7	1	5	-	2	-	146	19
LEIGHTON, E.J.	1884-87	-	-	16	6	-	-	-	-	16	6
LEMOINE, H.M.	1912-13	9	-	-	-	-	-	-	-	9	-
LEMON, A.	1952-53	23	1	-	-	-	-	-	-	23	1
LENNOX, W.	1928-29	9	1	-	-	-	-	-	-	9	1
LESSONS, G.F.	1904-06	31	8	3	-	-	-	-	-	34	8
LEVERTON, R.	1946-53	104	36	1	-	-	-	-	-	105	36
LIGHTENING, A.D.	1957-58	6	-	-	-	-	-	-	-	6	-
LINACRE, J.H.	1899-1908	308	-	27	-	-	-	-	-	335	-
LINDLEY, L.	1979-80	-	-	1	-	-	-	-	-	1	-
LINAKER, J.E.	1948-49	15	2	-	-	-	-	-	-	15	2
LINDLEY, E.	1949-50	1	-	-	-	-	-	-	-	1	-
LINDLEY, Dr. T.	1883-91	-	-	25	15	-	-	-	-	25	15
LINLEY, E.	1926-27	29	5	2	-	-	-	-	-	31	5
LISHMAN, D.J.	1955-56	38	22	-	-	-	-	-	-	38	22
LLOYD, C.	1930-31	4	-	-	-	-	-	-	-	4	-
LLOYD, L.V.	1976-80	148	6	14	1	23	3	28/1	3	213/1	13
LOCKETT, H.	1910-11	23	5	-	-	-	-	-	-	23	5
LOCKTON, J.H.	1913-14	21	2	2	1	-	-	-	-	23	3
LOCKYER, T.W.	1899-1900	1	-	-	-	-	-	-	-	1	-
LOFTUS, J.L.	1929-31	54	14	7	5	-	-	-	-	61	19
LOUGHLAN, A.S.	1991-92	2	1	-	-	-	-	-	-	2	1
LOVE, J.T.	1948-51	59	21	3	-	-	-	-	-	62	21
LOWE, H.C.	1919-20	9	-	-	-	-	-	-	-	9	-
LUNTLEY, E.	1878-83	-	-	14	-	-	-	-	-	14	-
LUNTLEY, J.	1883-86	-	-	6	-	-	-	-	-	6	-
LUNTLEY, W.	1878-83	-	-	14	-	-	-	-	-	14	-
LYALL, C.	1920-21	1	-	-	-	-	-	-	-	1	-
LYALL, G.	1972-75	108/8	24	11/2	3	7	2	-	-	126/10	29
LYMAN, C.C.	1946-47	23	9	4	1	-	-	-	-	27	10
LYNAS, R.J.H.	1925-26	20	2	2	-	-	-	-	-	22	2
LYNE, N.J.	1990-92	-	-	-	-	-/1	-	-	-	-/1	-
LYONS, B.	1966-72	201/2	28	19	2	12	2	5	1	237/2	33
LYTHGOE, J.	1919-20	61	13	3	-	-	-	-	-	64	13
LYTTLE, D.	1993-98	172/3	3	15	-	18	-	8	-	213/3	3
McARTHUR, B.	1965-66	7/1	4	2	-	-	-	-	-	9/1	4
McCAFFREY, J.	1969-70	2/6	1	-/2	1	-/1	-	-	-	2/9	2
McCALL, R.H.	1935-51	162	1	10	-	-	-	-	-	172	1
McCALLUM, C.J.	1892-93	37	13	5	2	-	-	-	-	42	15
McCANN, D.	1911-12	1	-	-	-	-	-	-	-	1	-
McCANN, J.	1974-75	2/4	1	-	-	-	-	-	-	2/4	1
McCRACKEN, P.	1892-98	113	-	10	-	-	-	-	-	123	-
McCURDY, W.	1900-01	11	-	-	-	-	-	-	-	11	-
McDIARMID, G.	1900-01	4	-	-	-	-	-	-	-	4	-
McDONALD, J.	1958-60	109	-	12	-	2	-	1	-	124	-
McGLINCHEY, C.	1961-62	-	-	-	-	1	-	-	-	1	-
McGOVERN, J.P.	1974-81	249/4	6	17/1	1	33	3	31	1	330/5	11
McGREGOR, P.	1993-97	7/23	3	-/3	-	-	-	-/4	1	7/30	5
MACHIN, P.U.	1911-12	1	-	-	-	-	-	-	-	1	-
McINALLY, J.E.	1984-85	36	-	4	-	1	-	-	-	41	-
McINNES, T.	1892-99	167	45	18	10	-	-	-	-	185	55
McINTOSH, J.W.	1970-75	45/7	2	8	1	1	-	-	-	54/7	3
MacJOHN	1888-89	-	-	1	-	-	-	-	-	1	-
McKAY, T.R.	1930-31	4	-	-	-	-	-	-	-	4	-
McKENNAN, H.	1927-28	1	-	-	-	-	-	-	-	1	-
McKENZIE, D.	1969-73	105/6	41	6	2	6/1	3	-	-	117/7	46

Player	Played	LEAGUE App	Gls	FA CUP App	Gls	FL CUP App	Gls	OTHERS App	Gls	TOTAL App	Gls
McKINLAY, R.	1951-69	611/3	9	53	1	11	-	7	-	682/3	10
McKINLAY, W.H.	1927-36	334	13	22	-	-	-	-	-	356	13
McKINNON, R.	1992-93	5/1	1	-	-	1	-	-	-	6/1	1
McKNIGHT, J.	1913-14	9	-	2	1	-	-	-	-	11	1
McLACHLAN, E.R.	1927-28	8	2	-	-	-	-	-	-	8	2
McLAREN, H.	1953-54	33	15	-	-	-	-	-	-	33	15
McMILLAN, S.T.	1927-28	9	-	1	-	-	-	-	-	10	-
McNAUGHTON, J.	1934-35	11	-	-	-	-	-	-	-	11	-
McNAUGHTON, G.M.	1936-38	66	12	4	1	-	-	-	-	70	13
MacPHERSON, J.	1892-1900	225	25	34	1	-	-	-	-	259	26
MALTBY, G.H.	1906-14	216	3	14	-	-	-	-	-	230	3
MARRIOTT, A.	1991-93	11	-	-	-	1	-	1	-	13	-
MARRISON, T.	1906-10	162	38	9	1	-	-	-	-	171	39
MARSDEN, J.W.	1909-10	2	-	-	-	-	-	-	-	2	-
MARSDEN, H.	1925-28	14	-	-	-	-	-	-	-	14	-
MARSHALL, G.	1968-69	7	-	-	-	-	-	-	-	7	-
MARSHALL, W.H.	1923-25	19	3	-	-	-	-	-	-	19	3
MARTIN, T.	1896-97	6	-	-	-	-	-	-	-	6	-
MARTIN, D.K. (Boy)	1936-38	81	41	3	5	-	-	-	-	84	46
MARTIN, F.A.	1947-48	5	-	2	-	-	-	-	-	7	-
MARTIN, H.	1922-24	107	13	7	-	-	-	-	-	114	13
MARTIN, J.P.	1958-59	1	-	-	-	-	-	-	-	1	-
MARTIN, N.	1970-74	116/3	28	14/1	4	5	2	-	-	135/4	34
MARTIN, T.	1952-54	48	4	1	-	-	-	-	-	49	4
MARTINDALE, S-Lt.H.	1919-20	1	-	-	-	-	-	-	-	1	-
MASON, W.	1891-92	5	-	-	-	-	-	-	-	5	-
MASTERS, A.	1932-36	109	24	9	2	-	-	-	-	118	26
MAWSON, J.S.	1934-35	2	-	2	1	-	-	-	-	4	1
MAY, E.E.	1890-91	-	-	2	-	-	-	-	-	2	-
MEE, G.E.	1946-47	9	1	3	-	-	-	-	-	12	1
MERCER, J.	1910-14	150	6	8	-	-	-	-	-	158	6
METGOD, J.A.B.	1984-86	113/3	15	7	-	14	2	2	-	136/3	17
MIDDLETON, J.	1974-77	90	-	11	-	6	-	5	-	112	-
MILLER, H.	1924-25	5	-	-	-	-	-	-	-	5	-
MILLS, G.R.	1978-86	113/23	12	5	-	16/5	2	8/2	-	142/30	14
MILLS, J.	1919-23	43	-	2	-	-	-	-	-	45	-
MOCHAN, D.	1962-64	108	1	11	-	-	-	-	-	119	1
MORGAN, F.G.	1922-28	200	6	19	-	-	-	-	-	219	6
MORGAN-OWEN, M.M.	1900-01	1	-	-	-	-	-	-	-	1	-
MORLEY, W.	1946-58	282	10	19	-	-	-	-	-	301	10
MOORE, A.	1951-54	102	38	2	-	-	-	-	-	104	38
MOORE, I.	1996-98	3/12	1	1	-	-/2	-	-	-	4/14	1
MORRIS, A.G.	1898-1912	423	199	37	18	-	-	-	-	460	217
MORRIS, E.	1947-48	4	1	-	-	-	-	-	-	4	1
MORRIS, H.	1924-25	22	1	1	-	-	-	-	-	23	1
MORRISON, R.	1958-59	1	-	-	-	-	-	-	-	1	-
MORTON, R.	1928-29	34	3	2	-	-	-	-	-	36	3
MUNRO, J.S.	1936-38	93	-	4	-	-	-	-	-	97	-
MURRAY, P.	1900-01	26	2	3	-	-	-	-	-	29	2
MURRAY, R.	1894-95	2	-	-	-	-	-	-	-	2	-
MURRAY, R.	1899-1900	1	-	-	-	-	-	-	-	1	-
NEEDHAM, D.W.	1977-81	81/5	9	10	1	15	2	6/1	1	112/6	13
NEEDHAM, G.	1905-15	274	10	16	-	-	-	-	-	290	10
NELIS, P.	1921-24	59	13	1	-	-	-	-	-	60	13
NEVE, E.	1914-15	35	3	2	1	-	-	-	-	37	4
NEWBIGGING, A.	1901-04	7	-	-	-	-	-	-	-	7	-
NEWBIGGING, H.	1919-20	9	1	-	-	-	-	-	-	9	1
NEWTON, H.A.	1963-70	282	17	18	-	10	1	5	-	315	19
NIBLO, T.D.	1904-05	46	9	2	-	-	-	-	-	48	9
NICHOLSON, G.H.	1955-56	72	-	6	-	-	-	-	-	78	-
NORMAN, S.	1881-88	-	-	27	5	-	-	-	-	27	5
NORRIS, R.	1898-1903	129	7	18	-	-	-	-	-	147	7
NORTH, T.W.	1946-47	1	-	2	-	-	-	-	-	3	-

Player	Played	LEAGUE App	Gls	FA CUP App	Gls	FL CUP App	Gls	OTHERS App	Gls	TOTAL App	Gls
OAKES, J.	1929-30	2	-	-	-	-	-	-	-	2	-
OAKTON, A.E.	1937-38	7	1	-	-	-	-	-	-	7	1
O'DONNELL, F.	1946-47	11	5	-	-	-	-	-	-	11	5
O'HARE, J.	1974-78	94/7	14	7/1	1	14/2	3	7/1	2	122/11	20
O'KANE, W.J.	1968-75	186/3	-	20	1	12/1	-	2	-	220/4	1
O'NEIL, B.	1996-97	4/1	-	-	-	-	-	-	-	4/1	-
O'NEILL, M.H.M.	1971-80	264/21	48	28	3	34/1	8	22/1	3	348/23	62
ORGILL, H.	1946-47	7	-	-	-	-	-	-	-	7	-
ORME, J.	1919-20	11	-	-	-	-	-	-	-	11	-
ORR, A.	1951-54	46	-	-	-	-	-	-	-	46	-
ORLYGSSON, T.	1989-93	31/6	2	1	-	5/1	2	-/1	-	37/8	4
OSVOLD, K.	1986-87	5/2	-	-	-	-/1	-	-	-	5/3	-
OTTEWELL, S.	1948-49	32	3	2	-	-	-	-	-	34	3
PAGE, W.	1904-05	1	-	-	-	-	-	-	-	1	-
PALMER, C.I.	1958-63	91	14	5	-	4	-	1	-	101	14
PALMER, W.	1909-10	12	1	4	-	-	-	-	-	16	1
PARKER, F.	1919-25	157	6	7	-	-	-	-	-	164	6
PARKER, G.S.	1987-92	99/4	17	16	5	22/1	4	9	3	146/5	29
PARKER, J.	1919-20	5	-	-	-	-	-	-	-	5	-
PARKER, R.	1921-22	46	11	5	1	-	-	-	-	51	12
PARKINSON, R.	1898-90	2	-	-	-	-	-	-	-	2	-
PARR	1880-82	-	-	5	2	-	-	-	-	5	2
PARR, J.B.	1963-64	1	-	-	-	-	-	-	-	1	-
PASCOLO, M.	1997-98	5	-	-	-	1	-	-	-	6	-
PATRICK, R.	1959-60	57	-	-	-	2	-	-	-	59	-
PEACOCK, D.	1972-74	22	-	-	-	2	-	-	-	24	-
PEACOCK, T.	1933-38	109	57	11	5	-	-	-	-	120	62
PEARCE, S.	1985-97	401	63	37	9	60	10	24	6	522	88
PEERS, E.	1899-1900	56	-	9	-	-	-	-	-	65	-
PEPLOW, S.T.	1973-74	3	-	-	-	2	-	-	-	5	-
PHILLIPS, D.	1993-98	116/10	5	10/2	-	16/1	-	4	-	146/13	5
PIKE, A.	1887-89	-	-	3	-	-	-	-	-	3	-
PIKE, Herbert	1886-88	-	-	11	-	-	-	-	-	11	-
PIKE, Horace	1888-95	91	23	19	4	-	-	-	-	110	27
PLATTS, L.	1946-49	7	-	1	-	-	-	-	-	8	-
PLEAT, D.J.	1961-63	6	1	-	-	-	-	-	-	6	1
PLUMMER, C.S.	1981-82/87-88	18/2	4	2	2	-/1	-	1	-	21/3	6
PONTE, R.	1980-81	17/4	3	2/2	1	3	3	2/2	-	24/8	7
POOLE, H.	1911-12	1	-	-	-	-	-	-	-	1	-
PORTER, W.C.	1931-34	14	-	-	-	-	-	-	-	14	-
POWELL, A.F.	1904-05	1	-	-	-	-	-	-	-	1	-
POWELL, J.	1914-15	23	-	1	-	-	-	-	-	24	-
PRICE, E.C.	1926-27	20	5	2	-	-	-	-	-	22	5
PRITTY, G.	1938-47	49	1	5	-	-	-	-	-	54	1
PROCTOR, M.A.	1981-82	60/4	5	2	1	10	3	-	-	72/4	9
PUGH, R.A.L.	1930-38	248	19	15	-	-	-	-	-	263	19
QUANTRILL, A.	1930-31	15	2	-	-	-	-	-	-	15	2
QUIGLEY, J.	1957-64	236	51	26	4	5	3	3	-	270	58
RACE, H.	1933-36	115	26	9	4	-	-	-	-	124	30
RADFORD, A.	1897-98	4	-	-	-	-	-	-	-	4	-
RADNALL, C.H.	1906-07	1	-	-	-	-	-	-	-	1	-
RANSFORD, H.	1923-24	4	1	-	-	-	-	-	-	4	1
RAWSON, C.	1946-47	1	-	1	1	-	-	-	-	2	1
RAWSON, J.K.	1947-49	6	-	-	-	-	-	-	-	6	-
RAYNOR, P.J.	1984-85	3	-	-	-	1	-	-	-	4	-
REED, E.	1926-27	5	-	-	-	-	-	-	-	5	-
REES, R.R.	1968-71	76/9	12	4/3	1	6/1	-	2	-	88/13	13
REID, R.T.	1912-13	9	1	1	-	-	-	-	-	10	1
RICE, B.	1985-91	86/5	9	4	1	12/3	2	3/1	-	105/9	12
RICHARDS, S.	1937-38	2	-	-	-	-	-	-	-	2	-
RICHARDS, W.C.	1895-98	72	18	10	6	-	-	-	-	82	24
RICHARDSON, J.	1897-98	1	-	-	-	-	-	-	-	1	-
RICHARDSON, P.	1967-76	199/23	18	16	1	9/1	2	-	-	224/24	21
RIDLEY, J.	1910-11	4	1	-	-	-	-	-	-	4	1
RILEY, D.S.	1983-86	7/5	2	-	-	1	-	-	-	8/5	2
RITCHIE, S.J.	1913-14	7	-	-	-	-	-	-	-	7	-
RITCHIE, A.	1891-98	157	-	21	-	-	-	-	-	178	-
ROBER, H.J.	1981-82	21/1	3	1	-	2	1	-	-	24/1	4
ROBERTS, S.G.	1937-38	6	-	-	-	-	-	-	-	6	-
ROBERTS, G.D.	1946-47	9	-	2	-	-	-	-	-	11	-
ROBERTS, E.T.	1901-02	6	-	1	-	-	-	-	-	7	-
ROBERTSON, JN.	1970-82/85-86	384/14	61	35/1	10	46	16	34	8	499/15	95
ROBERTSON, P.	1904-05	7	-	-	-	-	-	-	-	7	-
ROBERTSON, T.	1892-93	1	-	-	-	-	-	-	-	1	-
ROBINS, R.W.V.	1929-30	2	-	-	-	-	-	-	-	2	-
ROBINSON, G.H.	1898-1902	84	1	7	-	-	-	-	-	91	1
ROE, T.W.	1927-28	9	4	-	-	-	-	-	-	9	4
ROGERS, A.	1997-98	46	1	1	-	4	-	-	-	51	1
RONALD, P.M.	1921-22	4	-	-	-	-	-	-	-	4	-
ROSARIO, R.	1992-95	25/2	3	-	-	1	-	2	-	28/2	3
ROSE, T.	1893-96	30	9	2	2	-	-	-	-	32	11
ROTHERY, H.	1906-07	4	-	-	-	-	-	-	-	4	-
ROWAN, F.	1909-10	2	-	-	-	-	-	-	-	2	-
ROWLAND, J.D.	1960-61	26	3	-	-	3	-	-	-	29	3
ROWLANDS, A.S.	1910-11	1	-	-	-	-	-	-	-	1	-
ROY, B.	1994-97	70/15	24	10/1	1	7/1	2	6	1	93/17	28
RUSSELL	1890-91	-	-	10	-	-	-	-	-	10	-
RYALLS, J.	1909-10	8	-	-	-	-	-	-	-	8	-
SANDS, J.	1878-82	-	-	13	-	-	-	-	-	13	-
SAUNDERS, D.	1996-98	39/4	5	2	2	5/1	2	-	-	46/5	9
SAUNDERS, F.	1911-12	28	7	-	-	-	-	-	-	28	7
SAUNDERS, G.	1976-77	4	-	-	-	-	-	3	-	7	-
SAVAGE, R.	1946-47	20	-	5	-	-	-	-	-	25	-
SAXTON, G.	1901-02	1	-	-	-	-	-	-	-	1	-
SAXTON, F.	1934-35	1	-	-	-	-	-	-	-	1	-
SAXTON, J.	1925-26	11	-	1	-	-	-	-	-	12	-
SCOTT, A.	1890-99	179	4	31	-	-	-	-	-	210	4
SCOTT, F.H.	1946-56	301	40	21	6	-	-	-	-	322	46
SCOTT, J.	1925-26	1	-	-	-	-	-	-	-	1	-
SCOTT, J.	1929-30	46	3	7	2	-	-	-	-	53	5
SEGERS, H.	1984-88	58	-	5	-	4	-	-	-	67	-
SERELLA, D.E.	1971-74	65/3	-	6	-	2	-	-	-	73/3	-
SEVERN, W.	1894-95	2	-	-	-	-	-	-	-	2	-
SHARRATT, H.	1957-58	1	-	-	-	-	-	-	-	1	-
SHAW, A.F.	1889-97	79	11	19	4	-	-	-	-	98	15
SHEARMAN, B.	1919-20	31	1	1	-	-	-	-	-	32	1
SHEARMAN, W.J.	1903-08	113	39	7	6	-	-	-	-	120	45
SHERIDAN, J.	1989-90	-	-	-	-	1	-	-	-	1	-
SHERINGHAM, E.	1991-93	42	14	4	2	10	5	6	2	62	23
SHERRATT, B.	1968-69	1	-	-	-	-	-	-	-	1	-
SHILTON, P.L.	1977-81	202	-	18	-	26	-	26	-	272	-
SHREWSBURY, T.F.	1894-95	3	-	-	-	-	-	-	-	3	-
SHUFFLEBOTTOM, F.	1946-47	2	-	-	-	-	-	-	-	2	-
SILENZI, A.	1995-97	4/8	-	2/1	1	1	1	1/3	-	8/12	2
SIMCOE, K.E.	1957-58	2	1	-	-	-	-	-	-	2	1
SIMMS, W.	1913-14	3	-	-	-	-	-	-	-	3	-
SIMPKINS	1888-89	-	-	1	-	-	-	-	-	1	-
SIMPSON, N.H.	1946-47	47	3	3	-	-	-	-	-	50	3
SIMPSON, W.	1929-36	229	36	14	3	-	-	-	-	243	39
SLATER, H.	1910-11	2	-	-	-	-	-	-	-	2	-
SMALL, P.V.	1954-56	87	20	7	1	-	-	-	-	94	21
SMALLEY, M.A.	1982-84	1/2	-	-	-	1	-	1	-	3/2	-
SMELLIE, D.	1895-96	16	3	1	-	-	-	-	-	17	3
SMELT, L.A.	1980-81	1	-	-	-	-	-	-	-	1	-
SMITH, A.H.	1878-80	-	-	11	9	-	-	-	-	11	9
SMITH, A.W.	1889-93	23	1	17	-	-	-	-	-	40	1
SMITH, E.	1934-35	2	1	-	-	-	-	-	-	2	1
SMITH, H.	1936-37	1	-	-	-	-	-	-	-	1	-
SMITH, H.S.	1929-36	156	1	13	-	-	-	-	-	169	1
SMITH, J.	1909-10	27	-	1	-	-	-	-	-	28	-

Player	Played	LEAGUE App	Gls	FA CUP App	Gls	FL CUP App	Gls	OTHERS App	Gls	TOTAL App	Gls
SMITH, J.W.	1910-11	3	1	-	-	-	-	-	-	3	1
SMITH, W.	1889-93	39	5	15	5	-	-	-	-	54	10
SOUTHWARD, J.	1888-89	-	-	1	-	-	-	-	-	1	-
SPAVEN, J.R.	1919-25	157	46	13	4	-	-	-	-	170	50
SPENCER, F.	1895-99	44	19	1	-	-	-	-	-	45	19
SPOUNCER, W.A.	1897-1909	300	47	36	5	-	-	-	-	336	52
STAINWRIGHT, D.P.	1965-66	4/3	1	-	-	-	-	-	-	4/3	1
STANLEY, F.	1907-08	1	-	-	-	-	-	-	-	1	-
STANWAY, R.E.	1911-12	1	-	-	-	-	-	-	-	1	-
STAPLETON, L.	1919-20	10	-	-	-	-	-	-	-	10	-
STARBUCK, P.M.	1986-91	9/27	2	2/5	-	1/3	-	-/4	-	12/39	2
STEVENSON, J.	1902-03	6	1	-	-	-	-	-	-	6	1
STEVENSON, V.	1888-89	-	-	3	-	-	-	-	-	3	-
STEWART, A.	1893-96	97	1	8	1	-	-	-	-	105	2
STOCKS, C.W.	1924-33	242	76	15	4	-	-	-	-	257	80
STOKER, L.	1938-39	11	-	-	-	-	-	-	-	11	-
STONE, S.	1991-98	163/4	20	10	-	11/1	-	10	2	194/5	22
STOREY-MOORE, I.	1962-71	235/1	105	19	6	13	5	4	2	271/1	118
STUBBS, E.	1935-36	22	6	1	-	-	-	-	-	23	6
STURTON, W.T.	1927-28	1	-	-	-	-	-	-	-	1	-
SUDDICK, J.	1898-99	14	4	-	-	-	-	-	-	14	4
SUNLEY, D.	1975-76	1	-	-	-	-	-	-	-	1	-
SUGDEN, S.H.	1902-04	48	16	1	-	-	-	-	-	49	16
SURTEES, J.	1936-38	93	23	3	-	-	-	-	-	96	23
SUTTON, S.J.	1980-92	199	-	14	-	33	-	11	-	257	-
SWAIN, K.M.	1982-84	112	2	4	-	10	-	12	-	138	2
TAYLOR, J.	1925-26	2	-	-	-	-	-	-	-	2	-
TAYLOR, W.J.	1963-68	10/10	1	1	-	1	-	1/1	-	13/11	-
TEBBUTT, T.	1895-96	1	-	-	-	-	-	-	-	1	-
THIJSSEN, F.J.	1983-84	17	3	-	-	1	-	1	-	19	3
THOMAS, G.	1997-98	13/7	3	-	-	1	-	-	-	14/7	3
THOMAS, G.S.	1946-60	403	1	28	-	-	-	-	-	431	1
THOMPSON, F.	1892-93	1	-	-	-	-	-	-	-	1	-
THOMPSON, N.	1927-29	12	3	-	-	-	-	-	-	12	3
THOMPSON, S.	1952-54	22	8	-	-	-	-	-	-	22	8
THOMPSON, W.P.	1922-24	364	4	26	1	-	-	-	-	390	5
THOMSON, C.	1957-60	121	-	13	-	1	-	1	-	136	-
THORN, S.	1997-98	-	-	-	-	1	-	-	-	1	-
THORNHILL, J.	1892-93	3	-	-	-	-	-	-	-	3	-
THORNLEY, J.F.	1897-98	6	-	-	-	-	-	-	-	6	-
TILER, C.	1991-95	67/2	1	6	-	10/1	-	1	-	84/3	1
TILFORD, A.	1924-25	8	-	-	-	-	-	-	-	8	-
TIMMINS, S.	1900-05	125	5	12	-	-	-	-	-	137	5
TINSLEY, W.	1921-23	61	13	3	-	-	-	-	-	64	13
TODD, A.	1937-38	17	-	4	-	-	-	-	-	21	-
TODD, C.	1982-83	36	-	-	-	7	-	4	-	47	-
TOLLEY, O.	1888-89	-	-	4	1	-	-	-	-	4	1
TOWNSEND, A.H.	1926-27	15	4	-	-	-	-	-	-	15	4
TRIM, R.F.	1937-38	70	-	2	-	-	-	-	-	72	-
TURNER, A.D.	1902-03	9	-	-	-	-	-	-	-	9	-
TURNER, J.P.	1878-80	-	-	10	3	-	-	-	-	10	3
TURNER, K.J.	1954-55	1	-	-	-	-	-	-	-	1	-
TURNER, T.	1928-29	1	-	-	-	-	-	-	-	1	-
TUTIN, G.	1885-87	-	-	9	6	-	-	-	-	9	6
TUTIN, O.	1887-88	-	-	2	-	-	-	-	-	2	-
UNWIN, G.	1882-85	-	-	16	4	-	-	-	-	16	4
VASEY, R.H.	1932-34	23	-	-	-	-	-	-	-	23	-
VAN BREUKELEN, H.	1982-83	61	-	1	-	5	-	8	-	75	-
VAN HOOIJDONK, P.	1996-98	49/1	30	-/1	1	4	4	-	-	53/2	35
VAUGHAN, W.	1909-10	6	-	-	-	-	-	-	-	6	-
VENTERS, J.C.	1929-30	1	-	-	-	-	-	-	-	1	-
VOWDEN, G.A.	1959-64	90	40	10	2	4	2	1	-	105	45
WADSWORTH, H.	1927-28	30	6	5	1	-	-	-	-	35	7
WAGSTAFFE, J.	1919-20	1	-	-	-	-	-	-	-	1	-
WALKER, D.S.	1983-92	259/5	1	28	-	40	-	14	-	341/5	1
WALKER, D.	1923-26	82	29	6	4	-	-	-	-	88	33
WALKER, G.H.	1946-54	293	-	11	-	-	-	-	-	304	-
WALKER, T.T.	1894-96	4	-	-	-	-	-	-	-	4	-
WALKER, V.	1945-46	-	-	2	-	-	-	-	-	2	-
WALKER, W.W.	1911-12	1	-	-	-	-	-	-	-	1	-
WALL, T.H.	1934-35	1	-	-	-	-	-	-	-	1	-
WALLACE, I.A.	1980-83	128/6	36	7/1	1	12	9	10/1	1	157/8	47
WALLACE, R.S.	1923-29	248	2	21	-	-	-	-	-	269	2
WALLBANKS, F.	1935-36	8	-	-	-	-	-	-	-	8	-
WALSH, C.D.	1980-85	115/24	32	8/2	2	8/5	-	12	3	143/31	37
WAPPLINGTON, S.	1919-20	1	-	-	-	-	-	-	-	1	-
WARD, A.W.	1884-87	-	-	18	-	-	-	-	-	18	-
WARD, D.	1947-48	1	-	-	-	-	-	-	-	1	-
WARD, P.D.	1980-82	28/5	7	2	-	2	-	1/1	-	33/6	7
WARNER	1887-88	-	-	1	-	-	-	-	-	1	-
WARNER, V.	1993-98	4/1	-	-	-	1/1	-	-	-	5/2	-
WARREN, F.	1902-03	27	2	2	-	-	-	-	-	29	2
WASSALL, D.P.	1987-92	17/10	-	3/1	-	6/2	-	4/2	1	30/15	1
WATSON, P.F.	1955-58	13	-	-	-	-	-	-	-	13	-
WEALTHALL, B.A.	1960-61	2	-	1	-	1	-	-	-	4	-
WEBB, N.J.	1985-89/92-94	172/4	50	19/1	4	23/3	5	7	4	221/8	63
WELLS, P.A.	1975-76	27	-	2	-	1	-	4	-	34	-
WEST, E.J.	1905-09	168	93	15	7	-	-	-	-	183	100
WHARE, W.F.	1948-59	298	2	23	-	-	-	1	-	321	2
WHEATLEY, R.	1947-48	6	-	-	-	-	-	-	-	6	-
WHITCHURCH, J.H.	1905-09	23	8	4	-	-	-	-	-	27	8
WHITE, J.W.	1901-02	24	-	4	-	-	-	-	-	28	-
WHITE, T.	1971-72	-	-	-	-	-/1	-	-	-	-/1	-
WHITEFOOT, J.N.	1958-67	255	5	23	1	4	1	3	-	285	7
WIDDOWSON, S.	1878-84	-	-	23	19	-	-	-	-	23	19
WIDDOWSON, T.	1887-90	-	-	4	-	-	-	-	-	4	-
WIGLEY, S.	1982-85	69/13	2	5	-	8/1	1	10	-	92/14	3
WIGNALL, F.	1963-67	156/1	47	15	6	4	-	3	-	178/1	53
WILKINS, G.E.	1947-48	24	6	3	1	-	-	-	-	27	7
WILKINSON	1896-97	1	-	-	-	-	-	-	-	1	-
WILKINSON, P.	1986-87	32/2	5	4/1	2	3	1	1	-	40/3	8
WILLIAMS, B.	1985-93	43	-	4	-	2	-	-	-	49	-
WILLIAMS, J.	1911-12	4	1	-	-	-	-	-	-	4	1
WILLIAMSON, B.W.	1967-68	19	-	-	-	1	-	-	-	20	-
WILSON, D.J.	1982-83	9/1	1	-	-	-	-	-/1	-	9/2	1
WILSON, D.E.J.	1962-65	8/1	1	1	-	-	-	-	-	9/1	1
WILSON, J.	1961-64	84	-	7	-	-	-	-	-	91	-
WILSON, Terry	1987-93	94/11	9	17/1	2	12/2	-	8	-	131/14	11
WILSON, Tom	1951-60	191	75	25	13	-	-	1	1	217	89
WINFIELD, B.J.	1961-73	353/2	4	33	1	16	-	6	-	408/2	5
WITHE, P.	1976-78	74/1	28	11	3	8	5	5	3	98/1	39
WOAN, I.S.	1990-98	159/17	30	17	4	12/3	1	13	2	201/20	37
WOLFE, G.	1905-10	128	1	10	-	-	-	-	-	138	1
WOOD, A.L.	1936-37	21	-	1	-	-	-	-	-	22	-
WOODCOCK, A.S.	1973-79	125/4	36	14	10	21	12	16	4	176/4	62
WOODLAND, T.	1906-07	5	2	-	-	-	-	-	-	5	2
WOODS, C.C.E.	1977-78	-	-	-	-	7	-	-	-	7	-
WOODS, N.	1961-62	-	-	-	-	1	-	-	-	1	-
WRAGG, W.	1896-98	48	1	10	-	-	-	-	-	58	1
WRIGHT, E.J.	1903-04	4	-	1	-	-	-	-	-	5	-
WRIGHT, T.	1993-97	11	-	-	-	2	-	-	-	13	-
WRIGHTMAN	1889-90	-	-	1	-	-	-	-	-	1	-
YATES, L.	1913-14	10	1	-	-	-	-	-	-	10	1
YOUNG, W.D.	1981-82	59	5	2	-	3	1	-	-	64	6
YOUNGER, W.	1958-60	12	-	-	-	1	2	-	-	13	2

BIBLIOGRAPHY

- Arnold, Peter and Davis, Christopher **The Hamlyn Book of World Soccer**. *Hamlyn, London, 1973*
- Clough, Brian, **Clough, An Autobiography**. *Dunk, Peter, Editor Panini's Football Yearbook 1989-90 Panini Publishing Ltd, London, 1989*
- Fabian, A.H. and Green, Geoffrey, editors **Association Football, volumes 1-4** *Caxton Publishing Co. Ltd, London, 1960*
- Francis, Tony **Clough, A Biography** *Stanley Paul, London, 1989*
- Horridge, Dave **Nottingham Forest Annual 1979** *Circle Publications, Ilford, 1979*
- Hugman, Barry J. **Football Players Records 1946-1984** *Newnes Books, Feltham 1984*
- Lawson, John **Forest 1865-1978** *Granada Publishing, London, 1979*
- Lawson, John **Forest, the 1979 Season** *Wensum Books, Norwich, 1979*
- Lawson, John **Forest, the 1980 Season** *Wensum Books, Norwich, 1980*
- Longmore, Andrew **Viv Anderson** *Heinemann Kingswood, London, 1988*
- Morrison, Ian **The World Cup, A Complete Record 1930-1990** *Breedon Books Sport, Derby, 1990*
- Motson, John and Rowlinson, John **The European Cup 1955-1980** *Queen Anne Press, London, 1980*
- Nawrat, Chris and Hutchings, Steve **The Sunday Times Illustrated History of Football** *Hamlyn, London, 1997*
- Signy, Dennis **A Pictorial History of Soccer** *Hamlyn, London, 1968*
- Smales, Ken **Forest, The First 125 Years** *Temple Printing, Nottingham, 1991*
- Soar, Phil **Hamlyn A-Z of British Football Records** *Hamlyn, London, 1981*
- Soar, Phil **Illustrated Encyclopedia of British Football** *W.H. Smith, London, 1989*
- Tyler, Martin and Soar, Phil **The Story of Football** *Marshall Cavendish, London, 1976*
- Turner, A.J., editor **Nottingham Forest Football Club, Centenary 1865-1965** *Nottingham Forest Football Club, Nottingham, 1965*

Periodicals, Yearbooks, etc.

- **Forest Official Handbooks** (compiled by Julian Baskcomb, John Lawson and Fraser Nicholson) *Polar Print Group, Leicester, 1989-90 to 1997-98*
- **Orbis Football Collection** (partwork) *Orbis Publishing Ltd, London, 1990-91 (40 parts)*
- **Rothmans Football Yearbook** (various editions) *Queen Anne Press, London (1970-71 to 1991-92), Headline, London (1992-93 to 1997-98)*
- **World Soccer** *IPC Magazines Ltd, London, monthly*

INDEX

Note: Pages in the statistical section (193-243) are not included within this index.

Page numbers in *italic* refer to photograph captions, page numbers in **bold** refer to photographs,
page numbers in ***bold italic*** refer to both photograph and caption.

SUBSCRIBERS

Key: (a) or (h) = League game FAC = FA Cup FLC = League Cup FMC = Full Members' Cup EC = European Champions' Cup UEFA = UEFA Cup
ICFC = Inter-Cities Fairs Cup ESC = European Super Cup CS = Charity Shield A-S = Anglo-Scottish Cup

	Subscriber name	Favourite Player	Favourite Match
1	PAUL BIDDULPH, Long Bennington, Newark	Ian Storey-Moore	v Everton (FAC 6) 1967
2	SIMON CLARKE, Great Yarmouth	John Robertson	v Arsenal (FAC 6) 1988
3	M.J. GASCOIGNE, Grimsby	Ian Storey-Moore	v Everton (FAC 6) 1967
4	TIM FARR, Kirklingon, Newark	Ian Storey-Moore	v Chelsea (a) 1986
5	TOM FARR, Kirklingon, Newark	Stuart Pearce	v Charlton 1997
6	WILL FARR, Kirklingon, Newark	Colin Cooper	
7	THOMAS ALBERT BEAVON (1903-1960)	Jack Spaven	v Man United 1957-8
8	JOHN STAPLEFORD, West Bridgford	Joe Baker	v Luton (FAC f) 1959
9	CHRIS MEAKIN, Sandiacre, Notts	John Robertson	v Cologne (EC s/f 1) 1979
10	JASON ANDREWS, Uxbridge, Middlesex	Stuart Pearce	v Malmo (EC f) 1979
11	GILES FARRAND, Chilwell, Nottm	Nigel Clough	v Malmo (EC f) 1979
12	NEIL STUART FRAZER, Kimberley, Nottm	Stuart Pearce	v Middlesbrough (h) 1998
13	NEIL HEPPENSTALL, Loughborough, Leics	Stuart Pearce	v Malmo (EC f) 1979
14	LINDSEY CARTER, Measham, Swadlincote	Stuart Pearce	v Celtic (UEFA 3 leg 2) 1984
15	T.G. BRADFIELD, North Runcton, Kings Lynn	Tony Woodcock	v Southampton (FLC f) 1979
16	STUART ASTILL, Sandiacre, Notts	John Robertson	v Man United (a) 1977
17	STEPHEN RAYMOND FORD, Halifax	Stuart Pearce	v Bristol City (FLC s/f 2) 1989
18	RICHARD, DAVID & CHRISTOPHER MERRIMAN, Long Eaton	Stuart Pearce	v Cologne (EC s/f 1) 1979
19	PHILIP OLIVER BOAM, Jacksdale, Notts	Stuart Pearce	v Chelsea (h) 1991
20	STEVEN P. WILLIAMS, Long Eaton, Nottm	John Robertson	v FC Cologne (EC s/f 1) 1979
21	SIMON COOPER, South Normanton, Alfreton	Stuart Pearce	v Sheffield Wed (a) 7-1
22	BRENDAN DALY, Maghera, Co Derry, N. Ireland	Stuart Pearce	v Hamburg (EC f) 1980
23	NIGEL WEBSTER, Bulwell, Nottm	Stuart Pearce	v Luton (FLC f) 1989
24	TRACY NEWTON, Chesterfield	Stuart Pearce	v Tottenham (FAC 5 rep) 1996
25	ROBIN M. MORRIS, West Bridgford	Bob McKinlay/Ian S-Moore/Calvin Palmer	v Leeds (FLC s/f 1) 1978
26	PAUL & GERALDINE ELLIS, West Bridgford	Joe Baker	v Malmo (EC f) 1979
27	ROBERT PAYNE, Leicester	John Robertson	v Man United (a) 1977
28	CHRISTOPHER CLEMENTS, Benington, Boston, Lincs	Stuart Pearce	v Man United 1994-5
29	GARETH LEE COOKE, Cotmanhay, Ilkeston, Derbys	Stuart Pearce	v Sheffield Wed (a) 7-1
30	WILLIAM DONGER, Stapenhill, Burton-on-Trent	Stuart Pearce	v Everton (FMC f) 1989
31	ALEX HACK, Glemsford, Nr Sudbury, Suffolk	Stuart Pearce	v Oldham Athletic 9FLC f) 1990
32	NORMAN ANDREW SIMPSON, Whetstone, Leicester	Ian Storey-Moore	v Hamburg (EC f) 1980
33	GARY SALT, Cheddleton, Nr Leek, Staffs	John Robertson	v Hamburg (EC f) 1980
34	MICHAEL LITMAN, Beeston, Nottm	Stuart Pearce/Pierre Van Hooijdonk	v Middlesbrough (h) 1998
35	DAVID JEFFORD, Arnold, Nottm	John Robertson	v Malmo (EC f) 1979
36	MAY TOWNSEND, Toton, Nottm	John Robertson	v Hamburg (EC f) 1980
37	M.F. HOLFORD, Mapperley, Nottm	John Robertson	v Man United 1977
38	PAUL RENNIE, Winterton, Scunthorpe	Stuart Pearce	v Sheffield Wed (a) 7-1
39	ROBERT H. BROWN, Hucknall, Nottm	Stuart Pearce	v Malmo (EC f) 1979
40	ANDREW P. CROFTS, Durkar, Wakefield	Stuart Pearce	Every game we win!
41	ALAN HEALEY, Gravesend, Kent	Joe Baker	v Man City (FAC 4) 1974
42	HUGH CARTER, Radford Semele, Leamington Spa	Jack Burkitt	v Man United 1957
43	TOM RAWLINGS, Tenbury Wells, Worcs	Stuart Pearce	v Luton (FLC f) 1989
44	MARTYN K. PING, Kirk Hallam, Ilkeston	Pierre Van Hooijdonk	v Arsenal (h) 1996
45	COLIN HENRY ILLSLEY, Sutton-in-Ashfield	Terry Hennessey	v Grasshoppers 1978
46	WILLIAM EDWARD KING, Ilkeston	John Robertson/Ian Storey-Moore	v Everton (FAC 6) 1967
47	SCOTT CHAMBERS, Forest Town, Mansfield	Pierre Van Hooijdonk	v Middlesbrough (h) 1998
48	JOHN BARRIE FELL, Heanor, Derbys	John Robertson	v Man United (a) 1977
49	JAMES YOUNG, Corby, Northamptonshire	Stuart Pearce	v Malmo (EC f) 1979
50	JULIE COOKE, Keyworth, Notts	Steve Chettle	v Man United (h) 1992
51	ANDY J. FINCH, Breaston, Derbys	Stuart Pearce	v Tottenham (a) 1991
52	NEIL SIMPSON, Amsterdam	Stuart Pearce/John Robertson	v Malmo (EC f) 1979
53	MAGNUS ERIKSSON, Mölndal, Sweden	Gary Parker	v Everton (FMC f) 1989
54	MIKE BISHOP, Sevenoaks, Kent	Ian Storey-Moore	v Man United (h) 1965
55	STEPHEN SAYER, Easton in Gordano, Bristol	Ian Storey-Moore	v Middlesbrough (h) 1998
56	STEPHEN PURDY, Hucknall, Nottm	Stuart Pearce	v Man United (a) 1977
57	DANIEL PARKER, Quorn, Leics	Franz Carr	v Malmo (EC f) 1979
58	NICK WINSTONE, Whittlesey, Peterborough	Stuart Pearce	v Man United (h) 1984
59	MARK OTTER, Folkingham, LIncs	Bob McKinlay	v Malmo (EC f) 1979
60	MICHAEL EWERS, Nottingham	Jim Baxter	v Everton (FAC 6) 1967
61	MARK & SOPHIE MILLER, Gloucester	Stuart Pearce	v Cologne (EC s/f 1) 1979
62	ANGELO SOLAZZO, Northampton	Colin Cooper	v Luton (FLC f) 1989
63	JOHN STORER, Arnold, Nottingham	Stuart Pearce	v Malmo (EC f) 1979
64	DAVID TURNER, Polebrook, Peterborough	Tony Woodcock	v Malmo (EC f) 1979
65	RONALD PETER COOKE, Heronbridge, Nottm	Garry Birtles	
66	RUPERT BELLAMY, Littleover, Derby	Stuart Pearce	v Peterborough (a) 1994
67	ANDREW & JOHN BRODIE, Sutton Bonington, Leics		
68	ROBERT J MEE, Guilden Sutton, Chester	John Robertson	v Everton (FAC 6) 1967
69	SIMON WINFIELD, Risley, Derby	Trevor Francis	v Tottenham (FLC 5 rep) 1989
70	STEVE HARPER, Grantham, Lincs	Stuart Pearce	v Malmo (EC f) 1979
71	MARK GOSLING, Brookwood, Woking	Stuart Pearce	v Man United (a) 1994
72	STAN & EDWARD KERRY, Sneinton, Nottm	Peter Withe/John McGovern	v Malmo (EC f) 1979
73	CHRIS KERRY, Lenton, Nottm	Joe Baker/Stuart Pearce	v Everton (FAC 6) 1967
74	ALAN EAMES, West Bridgford, Nottm	John Robertson	v Liverpool (EC 1.1) 1978
75	FLYNN ANTHONY HARDING, Carlton, Nottm	Stuart Pearce	v Middlesbrough (h) 1998
76	STEPHEN JOHN DAWSON, Mapperley, Nottm	Stuart Pearce	v Everton (FAC 6) 1967
77	ANDREW ROBINSON, East Leake, Leics	Steve Stone	v Middlesbrough (h) 1998
78	M.D. FLETCHER, Ollerton, Notts	Ian Storey-Moore	v Everton (FAC 6) 1967
79	CHRIS WELLARD, Barnby-in-the-Willows, Newark	Steve Stone	V Man United (a) 1994
80	CHRISTOPHER WATERS, Bulwell, Nottm	John Robertson	v Peterborough (a) 1994
81	GORDON EADY, Dunkirk, Nottm	Ian Storey-Moore	v Everton (FAC 6) 1967
82	R.E. NOLAN, Eastwood, Nottm	Ian Storey-Moore	v Luton (FAC f) 1959
83	DEBBIE PEARSON, Bulwell, Nottm	John Robertson	v Hamburg (EC f) 1980
84	TONY BLACKBOURN, Giltbrook, Notts	John Robertson	v Liverpool (EC 1.1) 1978
85	F.G. WILLIAMSON, Sherwood, Nottm	John Robertson	v Man United (h) 1957
86	TREVOR GRICE, Grantham, Lincs	Ian STorey-Moore	v Everton (FMC f) 1989
87	KENNETH ERIC HANRAHAN, Shepperton Green, Middx	Tommy Capel	v Luton (FAC f) 1959
88	NICHOLAS SHAUN HOULDSWORTH, Tiverton, Devon	Stuart Pearce	v Malmo (EC f) 1979
89	ANTHONY SMITH, Horsham, W. Sussex	Henry Newton	v West Ham (FAC s/f) 1991
90	WARREN STARK, Ruskington, Sleaford, Lincs	Stuart Pearce	v Man United (a) 1990
91	K.D. BELSEY, Bretton, Peterborough	Trevor Francis	v Ajax (EC s/f 1) 1980
92	SHANE ROSS, Knighton, Leicester	Johnny Metgod	v Chelsea (h) 1991
93	DAVID WILKINS, Radcliffe-on-Trent, Nottm	Terry Hennessey	v Everton (FAC 6) 1967
94	LUC LEGENTIL, Glons, Province de Liege, Belgium	Stuart Pearce	v Everton (FAC 6) 1967
95	MARK ALSOP, Forest Town, Mansfield	John Robertson	v Hamburg (EC f) 1980
96	EDDIE WALKER, Ashby-de-la-Zouch, Leics	Roy Keane	v Chelsea (h) 1991
97	ANDY BODDINGTON, Ashby-de-la-Zouch, Leics	Stuart Pearce	v Chelsea (h) 1991
98	IAN COLLINDRIDGE, Blythe Bridge, Staffs	John Robertson	v Malmo (EC f) 1979
99	JAMIE COLLINDRIDGE, Blythe Bridge, Staffs	Pierre Van Hooijdonk	v Middlesbrough (h) 1998
100	BARRIE WARD, Vernham Dean, Andover, Hants	Steve Stone/Stuart Pearce	v WBA (h) '81 & v Arsenal (FAC 6) '88
101	PAUL EDWARD WIDDOWSON, Bramcote, Nottm	Ian Storey-Moore	v Malmo (EC f) 1979
102	STEPHEN MICHAEL CHARLES, Carlton, Nottm	John Robertson	v Man City (FAC 4) (h) 1974
103	RAYMOND T.F. PYKE, Wexham, Slough	Stuart Pearce	v Norwich City (a) 1995
104	MEL HART, Beeston, Nottm	Joe Baker	v Derby County (a) 1994
105	JON SINGLETON, Barkestone-le-Vale, Nottm	Steve Stone	v Man United (h) 1984
106	ROGER PETER TOWLE, Beeston, Nottm	John Robertson	v Malmo (EC f) 1979
107	CHRISTOPHER MELL, Sutton-in-Ashfield	Stuart Pearce	v Auxerre (UEFA 2 leg 1) 1995
108	ROLAND B. CARLISH, Deanshanger, Northants	Martin O'Neill	v Leeds (FLC s/f 2) 1978
109	ANDREW WEAVER, Quorn, Leics	Duncan McKenzie	
110	JASON YOUNG, Stretton, Burton-upon-Trent	Stuart Pearce	v Man United (FAC 6) (a) 1989
111	IVAN ROCKLEY, Kimberley, Notts	John Robertson	v Liverpool (FLC f 2) 1978
112	JOHN P. EVANS, Brundall, Norwich	Bob McKinlay	v Luton (FAC f) 1959
113	ROBERT P. EVANS, Norwich		
114	PETER M. EVANS, Robin Hills, Transvaal, R.S.A.		
115	MIKE JEPSON, Chilwell, Notts	Tony Woodcock	v Man United (a) 1977
116	HOWARD MAKEMSON, Whatton, Notts	John Robertson	v Malmo (EC f) 1979
117	JAMES D. HULL, Boston, Lincs	Stuart Pearce	v Everton (FAC 6) 1967
118	RICHARD DANBURY, Bladon, Woodstock, Oxon	Ian Storey-Moore	v Malmo (EC f) 1979
119	T.P. BLAKE, Boston, Lincs	Stuart Pearce	v Liverpool (EC 1.1) 1978
120	S.J. CAUNT, Oakwood, Derby	John Robertson	v Malmo (EC f) 1979
121	CLIVE SAMUEL SIMKISS, Great Barr, Birmingham	Stuart Pearce	v Everton (FAC 6) 1967
122	HOWARD P. MATTHEWS, Loughborough, Leics	Stan Collymore	v Man United (FAC 6) 1989
123	CHRIS CLIFFORD, Lyddington, Oakham, Rutland	Ian Storey-Moore	v Everton (FAC 6) 1967
124	ROBERT PALETHORPE, Auborn, Lincs	Des Walker	v Everton (FAC 6) 1967
125	ALASTAIR GUNN, Epperstone, Nottm	Stuart Pearce	v Hereford United (FAC 4) 1992
126	DAVID M. HARRISON, Toton, Nottm	John Robertson	v Man City (FAC 4) 1974
127	LARAYNE DAVIES, Portchester, Fareham, Hants	Steve Hodge	v Tottenham (FLC 5 rep) 1990
128	GEOFFREY WOODS, Ravenshead, Nottm	John Robertson	v Southampton (FLC f) 1979
129	PAM BENNETT, Bolborough, Nottm	John Robertson	v Everton (FMC f) 1989
130	J.G. PERFECT, Attenborough, Beeston, Nottm	John Robertson	v Luton (FAC f) 1959
131	MICHAEL FORSTER, Radcliffe-on-Trent	Stuart Pearce	v Luton (FLC f) 1989
132	JOAN M. BAKEWELL, Gedling, Nottm	Bob McKinlay	
133	Dr J.G. TELFORD, Moresby, Whitehaven, Cumbria	John Robertson	v Luton (FLC f) 1989
134	SEAN KIERON SMITH, Long Eaton, Nottm	Stuart Pearce	v Tottenham (FLC s/f 2) 1992
135	ANTHONY BEECROFT, Ruddington, Nottm	John Robertson	v Liverpool (EC 1.1) 1978
136	P.A. ELLIOTT, Wellesbourne, Warwickshire	Steve Stone	v Tottenham (h) 1993
137	CHRIS PARKES, Trowell Park, Nottm	Stuart Pearce	v Hamburg (EC f) 1980
138	NAOMI STRACHAN & ANDREW WHITAKER, W. Bridgford	Des Walker	v Peterborough United (a) 1994
139	MARK DILLOWAY, Grantham, Lincs	Duncan McKenzie	v West Ham (FLC 2) 1977
140	DONALD S.J. WESTBURY, Carlton, Nottm	Stuart Pearce	v Everton (FAC 6) 1967
141	ANDREW PARKES, Rowley Regis, West Midlands	Joe Baker	v Cologne (EC s/f 2) 1979
142	ANDREW HARTSHORN, Burton-upon-Trent, Staffs	John Robertson	v Newcastle (FAC 4) 1991
143	MURRAY WHITTAKER, Heanor, Derbys	Ian Storey-Moore	v Man United 1957/8
144	ALAN FREEDMAN, Hendon, London	John Robertson	v Leeds (FLC s/f 1) 1978
145	D.F. BROWN, Hucknall, Nottm	Stuart Pearce	v Malmo (EC f) 1979
146	DAVID HERBERT, Newport, Gwent	John Robertson	v Malmo (EC f) 1979
147	MICHAEL HURST, Long Eaton, Nottm	John Robertson	v Malmo (EC f) 1979
148	PHILIP BARKER, West Bridgford, Nottm	Stuart Pearce	v Liverpool (EC 1.1) 1978
149	LEE WALKER, Sunderland	Des Walker	v Tottenham (FLC s/f 2) 1992
150	JOHN SHEFFIELD, Stanley Common, Ilkeston	Ian Storey-Moore	v Everton (FAC 6) 1967
151	ANDREW WEBBER. Creech-St-Michael, Taunton	Stan Collymore	v Luton (FLC f) 1989
152	Dr DOMENICO LEONE, Ancona, Italy	Trevor Francis	v D.Berlin (EC 3 leg 2)1980
153	MALCOLM JONES, Ainsley Estate, Nottingham	Joe Baker	v Everton (FAC 6) 1967
154	CRAIG MAWBY, Stutensee, Germany	Stuart Pearce	v Ipswich Town (FAC 3) 1997
155	MARTIN THORNBER, Loughborough, Leics	Stuart Pearce	v Cologne (EC s/f 2) 1979
156	JOSH SHINNER, Blyth, Worksop	Pierre Van Hooijdonk	v Sheffield Wed (1-7)
157	MICHAEL BEARDSMORE, Newthorpe, Notts	Stuart Pearce	v Coventry City (a) 1978
158	IAN TREMBIRTH, Long Eaton, Nottm	Des Walker	Stuart Pearce's Testimonial
159	RAY SCOTT, South Harrow, Middlesex	Peter Shilton	v Tottenham (FLC 5 rep) 1990
160	RODNEY DAVIES, Aldercar, Langley Mill, Notts	Ian Storey-Moore	v Hamburg (EC f) 1980
161	ROGER BRUMPTON, Maidenhead, Berks	Bob McKinlay	v Valencia (ICFC) 1961/62
162	J.P. THOMAS, Deeping St James, Peterborough	Stuart Pearce	v Tottenham (FLC s/f 2) 1992
163	RICHARD PAUL DARWIN, Warton, Tamworth, Staffs		
164	PAUL BRINDLEY, Weddington, Nuneaton	Stuart Pearce	v Coventry (FLC 4) 1990
165	JANE ANN WRIGHT, Arnold, Nottingham	Stuart Pearce	v Peterborough (a) 1994
166	BILL BARNES, East Bridgford, Notts	John Robertson	v Liverpool (FLC f rep) 1978
167	P.J. BRAMLEY, Kirkby-in-Ashfield, Notts	Stuart Pearce	v Sheffield Wed (a) 1995
168	J.W. BRAMLEY, Gedling, Notts	Bob McKinlay	v Luton (FAC f) 1959
169	STUART CAMERON, St Johns, Woking, Surrey		
170	LYNNE CAMERON, St Johns, Woking, Surrey		
171	RICHARD WOOD, Belvoir, Lincs	Stuart Pearce	v Luton (FLC f) 1989
172	MARK EVANS, Ockbrook, Derby	Stuart Pearce	v Southampton (FLC f) 1979
173	COLIN McGRORY, Melton Mowbray, Leics	Stuart Pearce	v Auxerre (UEFA 2 leg 1) 1996
174	Mrs P.M. GREENWOOD, West Bridgford, Nottm	Stuart Pearce	v Celtic (UEFA 3) 1983
175	DARREN GALBRAITH, Moss Pit, Stafford	John Robertson	v Malmo (EC f) 1979
176	JAMES NEWBURY, Oldbrook, Milton Keynes	Stuart Pearce	v Southampton (FLC f) 1979
177	HANNAH DEXTER, Brickhill, Bedford	Pierre Van Hooijdonk	v Middlesbrough (h) 1998
178	P.J. HARDESTY, Calcot, Reading	Stuart Pearce	v Everton (FMC f) 1989
179	MICHAEL COOMBES, Malkins Bank, Sandbach, Cheshire	John Robertson	v Everton (FAC 6) 1967
180	MARK LYSENKO, Newark, Notts	Stuart Pearce	v Cheslea (h) 1991
181	CHRISTOPHER JOHN BROUGHTON, Acocks Green, B'ham	Ian Storey-Moore	v Southampton (FLC f) 1979
182	GRENVILL WILLIAM SISSON, Underwood, Notts	Ian Storey-Moore	v Liverpool (EC 1-1) 1978

	Subscriber name	Favourite Player	Favourite Match
183	DAVID WATSON, West Bridgford, Nottm	Stuart Pearce	v Malmo (EC f) 1979
184	JAMES ALAN HOFTON, Aspley Hall, Nottm	Joe Baker	v Everton (FAC 6) 1967
185	STEVEN M. NAYLOR, Kirkby-in-Ashfield, Notts	John Robertson	v Cologne (EC s/f 1) 1979
186	NIGEL WARNER, Gedney Hill, Spalding, Lincs	Stuart Pearce	v Cologne (EC s/f 2) 1979
187	ALISTAIR PILLING, Kirkby-in-Ashfield, Notts	Stuart Pearce	v Luton (FLC f) 1989
188	THOMAS LAMBERT, Hucknall, Nottm	Stuart Pearce	v Everton (FAC 6) 1967
189	NEIL MARSHALL, West Bridgford, Nottm	Stuart Pearce	v Cologne (EC s/f 2) 1979
190	GLENN HAIGH, Huntington, York	Stuart Pearce	v West Ham (FAC s/f) 1991
191	DEBORAH SCARLE, Heanor, Derbyshire	Stuart Pearce	v Sunderland (h) 1994
192	GRAHAM CLARKSON, Calcot, Reading	Too many to choose from!	v Luton (FAC f) 1959
193	LOUISE MELBOURNE, Loughborough, Leics	Stuart Pearce	v West Ham (FAC s/f) 1991
194	DAVID S. HILL, Shepshed, Leics	Stuart Pearce	v Malmo (EC f) 1979
195	VIRGINIA BALL, Nottingham	Stuart Pearce/Eine Aas	
196	RUSSELL BALL, Nether Exe, Devon	Kenny Burns	v Man City (FAC 4) 1974
197	GORDON FRANCIS MORRISON, Calverton, Nottm	Bob McKinlay	v Luton (FAC f) 1959
198	ERIC ETHERINGTON, Mansfield Woodhouse	Bob McKinlay	v Luton (FAC f) 1959
199	DAVID CURRY, Newark	John Robertson	v Liverpool (EC 1-1) 1978
200	SCOTT DAY, Balderton, Newark	John Robertson	v Cologne (EC s/f 1) 1979
201	MARK BANKS, Darlington, Co Durham	Stuart Pearce	v Sheffield Wed (a) 1995
202	BILL WALKER, Stapleford, Nottm	Ian Storey-Moore	v Everton (FAC 6) 1967
203	SAMUEL NIGHTINGALE, Barrow upon Soar, Leics	Stuart Pearce	v Man City (FAC 4) 1974
204	LUCY AWCOCK, Witney, Oxfordshire	Pierre Van Hooijdonk	v Middlesbrough (h) 1998
205	ROY HARDSTAFF, Worksop, Notts	Robert McKinlay	v Southampton (FLC f) 1979
206	IAN SMITH, Thorne, nr Doncaster, S. Yorkshire	Stan Collymore/Colin Cooper	v Luton (FLC f) 1989
207	ANDREW ELKERTON, Cranleigh, Surrey	Stuart Pearce	v Hamburg (EC f) 1980
208	JOHN E. PICKERING, Southwell, Nottm	Walter Ardron	
209	PAUL JOHN ATHERTON, Grantham, Lincs	Stuart Pearce	v Man United (a) 1996
210	STEVE SMITH, Ilkeston, Derbyshire	Stuart Pearce	v Luton (FLC f) 1989
211	P. SMITH, Bilborough, Nottm	Stuart Pearce	v Bristol City (FLC s/f 2) 1989
212	DAVID IAN NICHOLS, Kiveton Park, Sheffield	Garry Birtles	v Sheffield Wed (a) 7-0 1995
213	JENNIFER LITTLEWOOD, Swadlincote, Derbyshire	Ian Storey-Moore	v Everton (FAC 6) 1967
214	MALCOLM CULPIN, Ilkley, West Yorkshire	Kenny Burns	v Sheffield Wed (a) 1995
215	ANDREW SCOTT, Childswickham, Nr Broadway, Worcs	Stuart Pearce	v Malmo (EC f) 1979
216	ADELE TURNER, Willerby, Hull	Stuart Pearce	v Tottenham (FAC f) 1991
217	PAUL NEEDHAM, Stepney, London	Peter Shilton	v Cologne (EC s/f 1) 1979
218	S. HANNON, Holmfirth, West Yorkshire	Pierre Van Hooijdonk	v Middlesbrough (h) 1998
219	IAN MURRAY, Reading, Berkshire	Stuart Pearce	v Hamburg (EC f) 1980
220	ARTHUR HOLT, Shepshed, Leics	Jack Burkitt	v Luton (FAC f) 1959
221	CHRIS MANNERS, Shirenewton, Nr Chepstow, Gwent	Joe Baker	v Everton (FAC 6) 1967
222	MARK COOPER, Los Angeles, USA	Archie Gemmill	
223	DAVID & FRANKIE BARNETT, Wilmslow, Cheshire	Stuart Pearce	v Everton (FAC 6) 1967
224	M.T. HAZELDINE, Mapperley, Nottm	John Robertson	v Southampton (FLC f) 1979
225	JAMES PATRICK BERRY, Nova Santa Ponsa, Mallorca	Stuart Pearce	v Malmo (EC f) 1979
226	CHARLES WHEELER, Cardiff	John Robertson	v Everton (FAC 6) 1967
227	GORDON ROWLAND, Portadown, Co. Armagh	John Robertson	v Cologne (EC s/f 1) 1979
228	SHANE COURTNEY, Foynes, Co. Limerick	Stuart Pearce	v Malmo (EC f) 1979
229	PHIL HOLLIDAY, Ashby-de-la-Zouch, Leics	Roy Keane	v Liverpool (h) 1978
230	STEVEN JOSEPH WILSON, Fullers Slade, Milton Keynes	Martin O'Neill	v Luton (FAC f) 1959
231	MARK SCRIMSHAW, Fenham, Newcastle upon Tyne	Ian Storey-Moore	v Hamburg (EC f) 1980
232	ALAN STEPHEN MARSHALL, Cinderhill, Nottm	Stuart Pearce	v Cologne (EC s/f 1) 1979
233	GARY HOPEWELL, Cramlington, Northumberland	Peter Shilton	v Cologne (EC s/f 1) 1979
234	MATTHEW DOBSON, Langworth, Lincoln	Stuart Pearce	v Luton (FLC f) 1989
235	JOSEPH DOBSON, Langworth, Lincoln	Stuart Pearce	v Luton (FLC f) 1989
236	NICK ADAMS, North Harrow, Middlesex	Pierre Van Hooijdonk	v Newcastle (FAC 4) 1997
237	ANTHONY JOHN BISSETT, Droitwich Spa, Worcs	John Robertson	v Tottenham (FLC s/f 2) 1992
238	BRIAN RORISON, Beeston, Nottm	Des Walker/Stuart Pearce	v Cologne (EC s/f 1) 1979
239	ADAM STEWART, South Park, Lytham, Lancs	Stuart Pearce	v Liverpool (h) 1992
240	RONALD P. STEWART, South Park, Lytham, Lancs	Joe Baker	v Hamburg (EC f) 1980
241	IAIN STEWART, South Park, Lytham, Lancs	Stuart Pearce	v Malmo (EC f) 1979
242	COLIN STEWART, South Shore, Blackpool	Stuart Pearce	v West Ham (FAC s/f) 1991
243	ANDY WALVIN, Oakwood, Derby	Tony Woodcock/John Robertson	v Malmo (EC f) 1979
244	CHRIS COLDWELL, West Bridgford, Nottm	John Robertson	v Malmo (EC f) 1979
245	STEVE & MICHAEL SMYTH, Calcot, Reading	Stuart Pearce	v Everton (FAC 6) 1967
246	BALRAJ JOHAL, Wollaton Park, Nottm	John Robertson	v Hamburg (EC f) 1980
247	DEREK HAWKE, Melton Mowbray, Leics	Kenny Burns	v Luton (FAC f) 1959
248	CHRIS INGLE, Radcliffe-on-Trent, Notts	Stuart Pearce	v Liverpool (EC 1-1) 1978
249	YVONNE LEE, Croxley Green, Herts	Stuart Pearce	v Sheffield Wed (a) 1995
250	JOHN ANDY FLEMING, Feltham, Middlesex	Stuart Pearce	All 42 unbeaten games in a row!
251	ROGER DRAPER, Western Boulevard, Nottm	John Robertson	v Everton (FAC 6) 1967
252	The GINGELL FAMILY, Mansfield Woodhouse, Notts	Duncan McKenzie	v Cologne (EC s/f 2) 1979
253	MICHAEL PAYNE, Bridgnorth, Shropshire	Stuart Pearce	v Chelsea (h) 1991
254	MARK SILLITOE, Beeston, Nottm	John Robertson	v Liverpool (EC 1-1) 1978
255	GERALD GREGORY, Clifton Grove, Nottm	Jack Burkitt	v Everton (FAC 6) 1967
256	DONALD I. MACKENZIE, Selkirk, Scotland	Archie Gemmill	v Hamburg (EC f) 1980
257	BRENDAN McCORRY, Belfast	Stuart Pearce	
258	KARPAL SINGH, Horfield, Bristol		v Middlesbrough (h) 1998
259	STEPHEN P. CHAMBERS, Heaton, Newcastle upon Tyne	John Robertson	v Man United (a) 1978
260	ANTHONY M. JAMES, Worthing, Sussex	Stuart Pearce	v Liverpool (FAC f rep) 1978
261	D. SKERMER, Annesley Woodhouse, Kirkby-in-Ashfield	Wally Ardron	v Luton (FAC f) 1959
262	MARK LEWIS, Driffield, East Yorkshire	Stuart Pearce	v Malmo (UEFA 1-2) 1995
263	PETER GILLOTT, Stanton-under-Bardon, Leics	Stuart Pearce	v Malmo (EC f) 1979
264	STEPHEN CARTER, Lincoln	John Robertson	v Ipswich Town (h) 1977
265	KY KIRK, Warsop, Mansfield	Stuart Pearce	
266	CHRIS WADE, West Bridgford, Nottm	Stuart Pearce	v Tottenham (FLC s/f 2) 1992
267	DERRICK WADE, Newark, Notts	Jack Burkitt	v Sheffield Wed (a) 1995
268	JOHN SHANLEY, Westport, Co. Mayo, Eire	Stuart Pearce	
269	JOHN MICHALSKI, Newthorpe, Nottingham	Pierre Van Hooijdonk	v Middlesbrough (h) 1998
270	DALLAS LIDDELL, Langford Village, Bicester	John Robertson	v Liverpool (EC 1-1) 1978
271	JOHN GLADSTONE BACON, Cheshunt, Herts	Stuart Pearce	v Tottenham (h) 1961
272	J.E.B. WHEATLEY, Blidworth, Notts	Peter Withe	v Man City (FAC 4) 1974
273	ROY ADKINS, Kirkby-in-Ashfield	Joe Baker	v Everton (FAC 6) 1967
274	COLIN ROOSKEY, Hillingdon, Uxbridge	Stuart Pearce	v Malmo (EC f) 1979
275	MAUREEN MORTON, New Houghton, Derbyshire	John Robertson	v Cologne (EC s/f 2) 1979
276	BELINDA A. PULVER, Bushey Heath, Herts	Ian Woan	v Auxerre (UEFA 2-2) 1995
277	TREVOR DRAPER, Heanor, Derbyshire	Ian Storey-Moore	v Everton (FAC 6) 1967
278	SEAN QUEALLY, Bulwell, Nottm	John Robertson	v Ipswich (FAC 6) 1981
279	GLORIA HAYES, West Bridgford, Nottm	Des Walker	v Malmo (EC f) 1979
280	CHARLES NICHOLAS CLIFFORD, Woodthorpe, Nottm		
281	JOHN D. CRANFIELD, Nuthall, Nottm	John Robertson	v Cologne (EC s/f 1) 1979
282	PATRICIA GARNESS, Clifton Estate, Nottm	John Robertson	v Liverpool (EC 1-1) 1978
283	GARY TAYLOR, Long Bennington, Newark	Stuart Pearce	v Everton (FMC f) 1989
284	IAN LLOYD, Stainton, Penrith, Cumbria	Ian Storey-Moore	v Liverpool (FAC f rep) 1978
285	MARTIN FLETCHER, Lighthorne, Warwickshire	Stuart Pearce	West Ham (FAC s/f) 1991
286	PRESTON SHAW, Sutton-in-Ashfield, Notts	John Robertson	v Malmo (EC f) 1979
287	MICHAEL S. HARROLD, Long Eaton, Nottm		
288	JUSTIN BEDINGFELD, Lower Earley, Reading	Steve Stone	v Luton (FLC f) 1989
289	LLOYD D.M. HAWTHORNE, Portadown, Craigavon, Co Armagh	Trevor Francis	v Malmo (EC f) 1979
290	JAMES TUBB, Retford, Notts	Stuart Pearce	v Southampton (FLC f) 1979
291	ANDREW JOHNSON, Diggle, Saddleworth, Lancs	Stuart Pearce	v Man United (a) 1977
292	STEVEN PRICE, Castle Donington, Derbyshire	Ian Storey-Moore	v Everton (FAC 6) 1967
293	STEPHEN CROSSLAND, Uphampton, Ombersley, Worcs	Bob McKinlay	v Luton (FAC f) 1959
294	MARK NIGHTALL, Hove, East Sussex	Stuart Pearce	v Hamburg (EC f) 1980
295	ALAN SPENCER, Holland-on-Sea, Essex	John Robertson	v Man United (a) 1977
296	PAUL A. HILLIER, Edwinstowe, Mansfield, Notts	Stuart Pearce	v Luton (FLC f) 1989
297	ANTHONY CURTIS, Wollaton Park, Nottm	Ian Storey-Moore	v Sheffield Wed (a) 1995
298	ISABELLE LOUISE STABLES, Lenton, Nottm	John Robertson	v Liverpool (EC 1-1) 1978
299	KEITH BAYLISS, Alvaston, Derbyshire	Ian Storey-Moore	v Everton (FAC 6) 1967
300	DAVID HOWARD, Newark, Notts	Stuart Pearce	v Everton (FAC 6) 1967
301	MICHAEL JOHN BAILEY, St Albans, Herts	Bob McKinlay	v Everton (FAC 6) 1967
302	RICHARD HOGG, East Leake, Loughborough, Leics	Stuart Pearce	v Middlesbrough (h) 1998
303	PHIL ASHMORE, Stretton, Burton-upon-Trent	Duncan McKenzie	v Liverpool (EC 1-1) 1978
304	JOHN LATHAM, Ilkeston, Derbyshire	Stuart Pearce	v Malmo (EC f) 1979
305	JEFFREY WALTERS, Mansfield, Notts	Ian Storey-Moore	Any Forest win!
306	G.M. CLARKE, Langley Mill, Notts	Stuart Pearce	v Luton (FLC f) 1989
307	WILLIAM A. SMITH, Kinoulton, Nottm	Steve Hodge	v Everton (FMC f) 1989
308	ALAN KING, Holme Pierrepont, Notts	Peter Shilton	v Malmo (EC f) 1979
309	GRAHAM LAMONT, Edinburgh	John Robertson	v Luton (FLC f) 1989
310	BOB DUCK-MANTON, Locks Heath, Hampshire	Stan Collymore	v Man United (a) 1977
311	KIM GOODMAN, Sandiacre, Notts	Ian Storey-Moore	Beating Derby.... any time!
312	ALAN KELLY, Blidworth, Mansfield	John Robertson	v Man City (FAC 4) 1974
313	ANTHONY CROSS, Granchester, Cambridge	Tommy Capel	v Luton (FAC f) 1959
314	ASHLEY EASTWOOD, Nelson, Lancashire	Stuart Pearce	v Luton (FLC f) 1989
315	GRAHAM McGREGOR GORDON, Sth Normanton, Derbyshire	Archie Gemmill	v Luton (FAC f) 1959
316	DENNIS ARTHUR SMITH, Mansfield, Notts	Peter Shilton	
317	I.A. WATT, North Queensferry, Fife		
318	KEITH EDWARDS, Goring by Sea, West Sussex	Martin O'Neill	v Man United (a) 1977
319	JASON HEAFORD, St Ives, Huntingdon, Cambs	Stuart Pearce	v Peterborough (a) 1994
320	DAVID KENNA, Kidwelly, Carmarthenshire	Ian Woan	v Middlesbrough (h) 1998
321	ANDREW M. DOVE, Kirkby-in-Ashfield, Notts	Stuart Pearce	England v Holland Euro '96
322	GRAHAM PAUL FOGELMAN, Mapperley Park, Nottm	Ian Storey-Moore	v Man United (a) 1977
323	ERNEST WORTHINGTON, Calverton, Notts	John Robertson	v Hamburg (EC f) 1980
324	PETER GIDDINGS, Solihull, West Midlands	John Robertson	v Everton (FAC 6) 1967
325	RICKY KOTECHA, Colwick, Nottm	Pierre Van Hooijdonk	v Middlesbrough (h) 1998
326	JOHN PATRICK HOLMES, Mapperley, Nottm	John Robertson	v Man City (FAC 4) 1974
327	Miss A.J. RIGLEY, Colne, Lancashire	Stuart Pearce	v Malmo (EC f) 1979
328	COLIN C. BALL, Greasley, Nottm	John Robertson	v Cologne (EC s/f 1) 1979
329	COLIN BUXTON, Chineham, Basingstoke, Hants	John Robertson	v Liverpool (FLC f rep) 1978
330	DAVID STONEBRIDGE, Balderton, Nr Newark, Notts	John Robertson	v Cologne (EC s/f 2) 1979
331	N.E. TINSLEY, Shrewsbury, Shropshire	Tommy Graham	v Luton (FAC f) 1959
332	Dr & Mrs M.A. PRICE, Wimbledon, London	John Robertson	both European Cup Finals
333	BECKY GAMESTER, Threshfield, Skipton, N. Yorkshire	Stuart Pearce	v Man United (a) 1994
334	FRANCIS EIZENS, Swallowcrest, Sheffield	Ian Storey-Moore	v Everton (FAC 6) 1967
335	EDWARD WINIARSKI, West Bridgford, Nottm	John Robertson	v Liverpool (EC 1-1) 1978
336	SIMON RICHARDS, Tunbridge Wells, Kent	Stuart Pearce	v Oldham (FLC f) 1990
337	STEVEN ANDREW VASSELIN, Vicars Cross, Chester	Stuart Pearce	v Man United (a) 1986
339	MICK DAWBER, Spring Bank, Hull	John Robertson	v Middlesbrough (h) 1998
340	CHRIS POOLE, Arnold, Nottm	Stuart Pearce	v Southampton (FLC f) 1979
341	D.A. NICHOLS, Meadows, Nottm	Jack Burkitt	v Luton (FAC f) 1959
342	KEVIN PAUL KIRK, Glossop, Derbyshire	Stuart Pearce	v Liverpool (EC 1-1) 1978
343	PAUL JAMES, Kew, Richmond, Surrey	Joe Baker	v Hamburg (EC f) 1980
344	S.G. TOMLINSON, Oakwood, Derby	Ian Storey-Moore	v Everton (FAC 6) 1967
345	PETER GIBSON, South Normanton, Alfreton	Stuart Pearce	v Sheffield Wed 1995
346	DONALD E. BARTON, Lincoln	Stuart Pearce	both European Cup Finals
347	PETER TAYLOR, Coningsby, Lincoln	Joe Baker	v Everton (FAC 6) 1967
348	PETER S. SMITH, Bothamsall, Nr Retford	Peter Shilton	both European Cup Finals
349	DAVID W. STAINSBY, Watnall, Nottm	Ian Storey-Moore	v Everton (FAC 6) 1967
350	JOE BONNICI, Heanor, Derbyshire	Stuart Pearce	v Man United (a) 1977
351	NICKY DEAN, Cotmanhay, Ilkeston	Stuart Pearce	v Oldham (FLC f) 1990
352	MARK JACKSON, West Bridgford, Nottm	John Robertson	v Liverpool (EC 1-1) 1978
353	ANDREW FOWLER, Ruddington, Nottm	Stuart Pearce	England v Spain (Euro '96)
354	SIMON RUSSELL, The Park, Nottm	Stuart Pearce	v Arsenal (h) 1997/98
355	LEE SARGENT, Boston, Lincs	Archie Gemmill	v Cologne (EC s/f 1) 1979
356	JOHN EDWARD PERRIN, Great Missenden, Bucks	John Robertson	v Middlesbrough (h) 1998
357	CRISPIN MORTON, Bridport, Dorset	John Robertson	v Liverpool (EC 1-1) 1978
358	NIGEL G. KIRK, Smalley, Ilkeston	Ian Storey-Moore	v Man City (FAC 4) 1974
359	DAVID HARRIS, Allestree, Derby	Stuart Pearce	v Liverpool (EC 1-1) 1978
360	PETER STORER, Selston, Nottm	Stuart Pearce	v Peterborough (a) 1994
361	C. NORMAN, Worksop, Notts	Joe Baker	v Everton (FAC 6) 1967
362	ISABELLA FLORENCE WALKER, Wilford, Nottm	Steve Stone	v Doncaster (a) 1997
363	ISAAC LUTHER WALKER, Wilford, Nottm	Pierre Van Hooijdonk	v Middlesbrough (h) 1998
364	JACOB SIMEON VICTOR WALKER, Wilford, Nottm	Stuart Pearce	v Norwich City (h) 1997
365	T.A. WALKER, Wilford, Nottm	John Robertson	v Man United (a) 1977
366	IAN LANKESTER, Cannington, Somerset	John Robertson	v Cologne (EC s/f 1) 1979
367	STEVEN LANKESTER, Chilwell, Nottm	John Robertson	v Peterborough (a) 1994
368	Mrs D. MILNES, Coalville, Leics	John McGovern	v Luton (FAC f) 1959
369	KEVIN DRYDEN, Spittal, Berwick-on-Tweed	Stuart Pearce	v Newcastle (FAC 4) 1997
370	KEVIN MILMOE, Broughton, Kettering, Northamptonshire	John Robertson	v Everton (FAC 6) 1967
371	PEER HEMPEL, Eisenhüttenstadt, Germany	Too many to choose from!	v Vorwärts (UEFA 1) 1983
372	BJÖRN BALLDIN, Falkenberg, Sweden	Stuart Pearce	v Luton (FLC f) 1989
373	LESLIE KINNEAR, Ballymena, Co Antrim, N. Ireland	Stuart Pearce	v Malmo (EC f) 1979
374	DANNY PHILLIPS, Rochford, Essex	John Robertson	v Cologne (EC s/f 1) 1979
375	TIM WOOD, West Bridgford, Nottm	John Robertson	v Hamburg (EC f) 1980
376	ALAN MAYOR, Bingham, Nottm	Stuart Pearce	v Hamburg (EC f) 1980
377	ALAN MAYOR		
378	ROBERT W.J. STICKNEY, The Park, Nottm	Ian Storey-Moore	v Everton (FAC 6) 1967
379	ALAN TOULSON, Nottingham	Tony Woodcock	v Man United (a) 1977
380	ROB RAYNHAM, Nottingham	John Robertson	v Man City (FAC 4) 1974
381	T.G. MORRIS, Chilwell, Beeston, Nottm	Ian Storey-Moore	v Everton (FAC 6) 1967

	Subscriber name	Favourite Player	Favourite Match
382	T.G. MORRIS, Chilwell, Beeston, Nottm		
383	DAVID J. SMITH, Peterborough	Peter Grummit	v Liverpool (FLC s/f 1) 1980
384	ANDREW F. SMITH, Peterborough	Peter Shilton	v Southampton (FLC f) 1979
385	MARTIN J. PULLON, Cowbridge, Cardiff	John Robertson	v Cologne (EC s/f 2) 1979
386	KEITH FREDERICK JOHN SHILLINGFORD, Gt. Bookham, Surrey	Archie Gemmill	v Liverpool (EC 1-1) 1978
387	DAVID WATSON, Newton-on-Trent, Lincs	Kenny Burns	v Malmo (EC f) 1979
388	HOWARD LEE PARKER, North Hykeham, Lincoln	Pierre Van Hooijdonk	v Middlesbrough (h) 1998
389	ANDREW JOHN FLOYD, West Bridgford, Nottm	Stuart Pearce	v Man United (FAC 6) 1989
390	PETER QUINCE, Sutton Coldfield, Birmingham	Stuart Pearce	v Peterborough (a) 1994
391	Communications Yeoman DAVE BROWN, Royal Navy	Kenny Burns/Stuart Pearce	v Malmo (EC f) 1979
392	MALCOLM ANCLIFF, Kirk Hallam, Ilkeston	Stuart Pearce	v Malmo (EC f) 1979
393	PAUL T. SPENCER, Kimberley, Nottm	Peter Grummit	v Everton (FAC 6) 1967
394	JOHN WHITE, Petersfield, Hampshire	Kenny Burns	v Southampton (FMC f) 1979
395	KARL THORNE, Radcliffe-on-Trent, Notts	Stuart Pearce	v Middlesbrough (h) 1998
396	ALLISON WHEELHOUSE, Ilkeston, Derbyshire	John Robertson	v Sheffield Wed (a) 1995
397	MICHAEL J. FARNSWORTH, Radcliffe-on-Trent, Notts	Stuart Pearce	v Luton (FAC f) 1959
398	MIKE JACKSON, Sandal, Wakefield	John Robertson	v Cologne (EC s/f 1) 1979
399	JOHN HOLLYHEAD, Aspley, Nottm	Stuart Pearce	v Luton (FAC f) 1959
400	KEITH G. MARSHALL, Kirkby-in-Ashfield, Notts	Stuart Pearce/John Robertson	v Cologne (EC s/f 1) 1979
401	PAUL SLOAN JENNINGS, Denton Burn, Newcastle upon Tyne	Stuart Pearce	v Peterborough (a) 1994
402	SIMON HOWSE, West Bridgford, Nottm	Nigel Clough	v Man United (h) 1984
403	IAN G. CHAPLIN, Wollaton, Nottm	Stuart Pearce	v Everton (FAC 6) 1967
404	IAN D. MARSHALL, Sutton-in-Ashfield, Notts	Stuart Pearce/John Robertson	v Arsenal (FAC 6) 1988
405	DIANA ANDERSON, Deeping St James, Peterborough	Stuart Pearce	v Chelsea (h) 1991
406	LYNNE MORGAN, Shepperton, Middlesex	Nigel Clough	All Wembley Finals!
407	KEVIN A. STORER, Lossiemouth, Morayshire	Stuart Pearce	v Ipswich Town (CS) 1979
408	ALAN D. STORER, Whittlesey, Peterborough	Stuart Pearce	v Tottenham (FAC f) 1991
409	R.Z. GORSKI, Hucknall, Nottm	John Robertson	
410	HOWARD DIXEY, Long Eaton, Nottm	Stuart Pearce	v Malmo (EC f) 1979
411	DAVID SHAW, Long Eaton, Nottm	John Robertson	v Liverpool (EC 1-1) 1978
412	MAX SMITH, Cranford Heath, Poole, Dorset	Stuart Pearce	v Hamburg (EC f) 1980
413	SIMON GUEST, Bridgwater, Somerset	Stuart Pearce	v Malmo (EC f) 1979
414	CHRISTINE BAILEY, Hoveringham, Notts	Stuart Pearce	v Malmo (EC f) 1979
415	ANDREW JOHN WEIGHTMAN, Sutton-in-Ashfield, Notts	Stuart Pearce	v Cologne (EC s/f 1) 1979
416	KEITH RIGG, Burton Joyce, Nottm	Ian Storey-Moore	v Middlesbrough (h) 1998
417	P. STENNETT, Sleaford, Lincs	Stuart Pearce	v Hamburg (EC f) 1980
418	PAUL SIMMONS, Forest Park, Bracknell, Berkshire	John McGovern	v Hamburg (EC f) 1980
419	WILLIAM STEPHEN YARDLEY, Redlynch, Salisbury, Wiltshire	John Robertson	v Oldham (FLC f) 1990
420	PHILIP TAYLOR, Shepshed, Leics	Stuart Pearce	v Malmo (EC f) 1979
421	ALEC CASTERTON, Arnold, Nottm	Jack Burkitt	v Everton (FAC 6) 1967
422	NEIL BERNARD STAFFORD, West Bridgford, Nottm	John Robertson	v Southampton (FLC f) 1979
423	JOHN WILLIAM DICKINSON, Nuthall, Nottm	Trevor Francis	v Man United (a) 1977
424	TIM KILBRIDE, Loughborough, Leics	Nigel Clough	v Man United (a) 1977
425	PATRICK SMITH, Arnold, Nottm	Brian Rice	v Liverpool (FLC f rep) 1978
426	A. METHERINGHAM, Long Eaton, Nottm	Stuart Pearce	v Sheffield Wed (a) 1995
427	KEVIN CARTER, Highworth, Swindon	Archie Gemmill	v Chelsea (a) 1986
428	JOSEPH FINIANOS, Parramatta, NSW, Australia	Stuart Pearce	v Malmo (EC f) 1979
429	PAUL J. McROBERT, Swanwick, Derbyshire	Joe Baker	v Everton (FAC 6) 1967
430	MARK JEFFREYS, Vale, Guernsey, C.I.	Peter Shilton	v Man Utd (h) 1984 & (a) 1986
431	MICHAEL H. PHILLIPS, Newquay, Cornwall	Jack Burkitt	v Luton (FAC f) 1959
432	PETER G. CLARK, Bridport, Dorset	Wally Ardron	v Portsmouth (FAC 4) 1957
433	MATTHEW GORE, Paston, Peterborough	Archie Gemmill	
434	JOHN BELTON, Loughborough, Leics	Kenny Burns	v Malmo (EC f) 1979
435	LEE COLSON, Codnor, Derbyshire	Stuart Pearce	v Tottenham (a)
436	PETER SICILIANO, Castle Bytham, Lincs	Peter Shilton	v Malmo (EC f) 1979
437	MARK CHAPMAN, The Gresley Red, Derbyshire	Stuart Pearce	v Derby County (a) 1994
438	A.L. THOMAS, Hucknall, Nottm	Ian Storey-Moore	v Everton (FAC 6) 1967
439	PETER GEORGE JACKSON, Chilwell, Nottm	John Robertson + many others!	v Man United (a) 1977
440	DAVID SMITH, Newark, Notts	Stuart Pearce	v Sheffield Wed (a) 1995
441	BRIAN E. LEIVERS, Felling, Gateshead	Stuart Pearce	v Everton (FAC 6) 1967
442	STEVE CLEWS, Solihull, West Midlands	Archie Gemmill	v Cologne (EC s/f 2) 1979
443	MICHAEL CHALLANDS, Thurmaston, Leicester	Ian Storey-Moore	v Southampton (FLC f) 1979
444	CHRISTOPHER JOHN SCOFFIELD, Gateford, Worksop, Notts	Steve Stone	v Swindon 26.12.1997
445	GARY INGLIS, Thundersley, Essex	Stuart Pearce	v Cologne (EC s/f 2) 1979
446	MICHAEL BROOKS, Clifton, Nottm	Stuart Pearce	England v Germany (EC s/f) 1996
447	DAVID WHEATLEY, Eggbuckland, Plymouth, Devon	John Robertson	v Cologne (EC s/f 1) 1979
448	DAVID LYNAM, Underwood, Nottm	Stuart Pearce	v Malmo (UEFA 1-2) 1995
449	NIGEL DOLEMAN, Newark, Notts	Stuart Pearce	v Luton (FLC f) 1989
450	TERENCE CHARLES ADCOCK, Chilwell, Nottm	John Robertson	v Everton (FAC 6) 1967
451	DAVID R. REAVILL, Tewin, Herts	Bob McKinlay	v Malmo (EC f) 1979
452	DAVID R. REAVILL, Tewin, Herts		
453	STEPHEN RILEY, Sutton Coldfield, West Midlands	John Robertson	v Luton (FAC f) 1959
454	RUSSELL JOHN HOME, Ash, Aldershot, Hants	Peter Shilton	v Celtic (UEFA 3-2) 1983
455	CLAIRE & PAUL O'HIGGINS, Melton Mowbray, Leics	Stuart Pearce	v Leicester City (h) 1994
456	JULIE SAUNDERS, Winslow, Buckingham	Stuart Pearce	v Luton (FLC f) 1989
457	ROGER GRAHAM, Breaston, Derby	Kenny Burns	v Hamburg (EC f) 1980
458	DOMINIC GRAHAM, Breaston, Derby	Stuart Pearce	v Hamburg (EC f) 1980
459	PETER GRAHAM, Melbourne, Australia		
460	DEBBIE PARKES, Ruskington, Sleaford, Lincs	Tony Woodcock	v Malmo (UEFA 1-2) 1995
461	ALAN JOHN HOLLIS, Toton, Notts	John Robertson	v Tottenham (FLC s/f 2) 1992
462	C.F. TEMPERTON, Colsterworth, Grantham, Lincs	Bob McKinlay	v Luton (FAC f) 1959
463	R.H. MARSH, Sleaford, Lincs	John Robertson	v Liverpool (EC 1-1) 1978
464	MICHAEL W. SMITH, Chilwell, Nottm	Stuart Pearce	v Luton (FAC f) 1959
465	ALAN SPRINGTHORPE, Anneseley, Notts	John Robertson	v Peterborough (a) 1994
466	JOHN THOMAS SIMPSON, Woodthorpe, Notts	Stuart Pearce	v Cologne (EC s/f 1) 1979
467	PAUL KEELING, Hyson Green, Nottm	Des Walker	
468	JAMES MERCER, Bristol	Stuart Pearce	v Malmo (EC f) 1979
469	JUSTIN SMITH, Chasetown, Walsall	Stuart Pearce	v Bayern Munich (UEFA 4) 1996
470	KETIL KRISTIANSEN, Oslo, Norway	Martin O'Neill	v Cologne (EC s/f 1) 1979
471	TOR K SCHULSTOCK, Lillestrøm, Norway	Steve Hodge	v Southampton (FLC f) 1979
472	BJØRN SUNDFAER, Oslo, Norway	Garry Birtles	v Southampton (FLC f) 1979
473	GARD PAULSEN, Drammen, Norway	Robert Rosario	v Tottenham (h) 1993
474	KIERAN O'KEEFFE, Shepshed, Leics	Stuart Pearce	v Newcastle (FAC 4 rep) 1991
475	RICHARD B. PIPE, Chelmsford, Essex	Stewart Imlach	v Malmo (EC f) 1979
476	JONATHAN BUTTERY, Cotgrave, Nottm	Stuart Pearce & John Robertson	v Cologne (EC s/f 1) 1979
477	FRANCIS TREVOR VINTER, Clacton-on-Sea, Essex	Trevor Francis	v Malmo (EC f) 1979
478	NICHOLAS PARKER, New Ollerton, Notts	Stuart Pearce	v Malmo (EC f) 1979
479	JOHNATHAN B. WARD, Hong Kong, Tokyo & Singapore!	Stuart Pearce	v Arsenal (FAC 6) 1988
480	MATTHEW ARCHER, Colwick, Nottm	Stuart Pearce	v Southampton (FLC f) 1979
481	MARK CHAMBERS, Bolsover, Derbyshire	Stuart Pearce	v Man United (a) 1990
482	ANDREW STANLEY, London N1	Stuart Pearce	v Cologne (EC s/f 1) 1979
483	MARTIN AUCKLAND, Ruddington, Nottm	John Robertson	v Cologne (EC s/f 1) 1979
484	GARETH AUCKLAND, Ruddington, Nottm	John Robertson	v Cologne (EC s/f 1) 1979
485	JAMES L. WHITE, Petersfield, Hampshire	Stuart Pearce & Steve Stone	v Lyon (UEFA 3-1) 1995
486	TONY HALLAM, Skegby, Sutton-in-Ashfield	Terry Hennessey	v Everton (FAC 6) 1967
487	ROWLAND W. BRAITHWAITE, Clifton, Nottm	Joe Baker	v Everton (FAC 6) 1967
488	JOHN & MICHAEL GOULDER, Woodthorpe, Nottm	Joe Baker	v Coventry City (a) 1978
489	DONALD MERRITT, Finchley, London	Tony Woodcock	v Malmo (EC f) 1979
490	R. MARSHALL, BFPO 808	Ian Storey-Moore	v Everton (FMC f) 1989
491	M.A. FOSTER, Blakesley, Northamptonshire	Stuart Pearce	v Sheffield Wed (a) 7-1
492	GARY ANDREWS, Ilkeston, Derbyshire	Viv Anderson	v Cologne (EC s/f 2) 1979
493	DAVID BRUCE, Willenhall, West Midlands	Nigel Clough & Stuart Pearce	v Tottenham (FLC s/f 2) 1992
494	PHILLIP ANTHONY ALDRIDGE, Upton-on-Severn, Worcs	Ian Storey-Moore	v Everton (FMC f) &Malmo (EC f)
495	GEOFFREY & JAMES SENTANCE, Bottesford, Nottm	Nigel Clough/Stuart Pearce	v Luton (FAC f) 1959
496	PAUL GREENSMITH, Pleasley, Mansfield	Martin O'Neill	v Liverpool (EC 1-1) 1978
497	Mrs M. TANNER, Mapperley, Nottm	Ian Storey-Moore	v Luton (FAC f) 1959
498	GEOFF READMAN, North Muskham, Newark, Notts	Stuart Pearce	v Luton (FMC f) 1989
499	ANDREW JAMES DALY, Bingley, West Yorkshire	Stan Collymore	v Man City (h) 1995
500	JOHN HARRIS, Southgate, London		
501	ANDREW JAMES KIRKHAM, St Ives, Cambridge	Peter Shilton	v Malmo (EC f) 1979
502	DOUGLAS ARTHUR MEAKIN, Maltby, South Yorkshire	Peter Shilton	v Luton (FAC f) 1959
503	A. SANDERS, West Bridgford, Nottm	Ian Storey-Moore	v Everton (FMC f) 1989
504	DAVE SAVAGE, Ruddington, Notts	John Robertson	v Man City (FAC 4) 1974
505	PAUL WANT, Loughborough, Leics	Kenny Burns	v Malmo (EC f) 1979
506	RICHARD HANNAY, Ramsey, Isle of Man	Stuart Pearce	v Chelsea (h) 1991
507	JAMES BATES, Madeley, Crewe, Cheshire	Stuart Pearce	v Tottenham (FAC f) 1991
508	CHRISTOPHER WINFIELD, Gedling, Nottm	John Robertson	v Everton (FAC 6) 1967
509	DAVID KEATS, Thornton Heath, Surrey		
510	MARTIN TAYLOR, Worcester Park, Surrey	John Robertson	v Norwich City (h) 1977
511	RICHARD KNOWLES, Chigwell, Essex	Stuart Pearce	v Swindon Town (h) 1997
512	RICHARD I. LIVESEY, Iver Heath, Bucks	Stuart Pearce	v Tottenham (h) 1993
513	PATRICK DAVENPORT, Inkersall, Chesterfield	Archie Gemmill	v Sheffield Wed (a) 1995
514	MARY JOSEPHINE COLLINS, Nottingham	Peter Shilton	
515	STEVE WILKINSON, Bingham, Nottm	Stuart Pearce	v Sheffield Wed (a) 1995
516	MICHAEL PENSON, Northolt, Middlesex	John Robertson	v Malmo (EC f) 1979
517	CHRISTINE LORRAINE EDWARDS, Beeston, Nottm	Peter Grummit/John Robertson	v Everton (FAC 6) 1967
518	JOHN NEIL PATRICK, Nuthall, Nottm	Stuart Pearce	v Cologne (EC s/f 1) 1979
519	KEVIN PAUL SHELDON, Clifton, Nottm	Stuart Pearce	v Luton (FLC f) 1989
520	NEIL ATTEWELL, Rowner, Gosport, Hants	John Robertson	v Hamburg (EC f) 1980
521	BRETT NEWTON, Elson, Gosport, Hants	Steve Chettle	v Sheffield United (a) 1995
522	JOHN R. STODDART, South Gosforth, Newcastle upon Tyne		
523	GEOFFREY WRIGHT, Ware, Herts		
524	DEREK WALLIS, Arnold, Nottingham	John Robertson	v Man United (a) 1977
525	ERNEST CLEMENTS, Nuthall, Nottm	Wally Ardron	v Man United (FAC 4) 1947
526	MICHAEL GRAYSON, Handsworth, Sheffield		
527	FRANK COOKE, Sandbach, Cheshire	Stuart Pearce	v Southampton (FLC f) 1979
528	PAUL HUMPHREY, Bakersfield, Nottm	Tony Woodcock	v Peterborough (a) 1994
529	JULIE STAINES, Brussels,Belgium	Peter Shilton	v Tottenham (h) 1978
530	ALAN MAPLETHORPE, Chaddesdon, Derby	Stuart Pearce	v Cologne (EC s/f 2) 1979
531	PAUL EMANUEL, Llanelli, Carmarthen	Stuart Pearce	v Malmo (EC f) 1979
532	DAVID TRICKEY, Radcliffe-on-Trent, Notts	Chris Allen	v Man United 1996
533	IAN J. MORRISON, Bournemouth	John Robertson	v Hamburg (EC f) 1980
534	PAUL MARTIN NEEVES, Bournemouth	Pierre Van Hooijdonk	v Huddersfield Town (h) 1998
535	ANDREW HASLAM, Codnor, Derbyshire	Stuart Pearce	v Tottenham (FLC s/f 2) 1992
536	JOE COVENTRY, Lincoln	Stuart Pearce	v Man United (a) 1994
537	DENNIS KEMP, Keyworth, Notts	Wally Ardron	v Luton (FAC f) 1959
538	JUSTIN HEATON, Codnor, Derbyshire	Stuart Pearce	v Derby County (a) 1994
539	'FOREST FOREVER' Fanzine	Jason Lee	v Derby County (a) 1994
540	ANDREW WILKINSON, Hinchley Woods, Esher, Surrey	Stuart Pearce	v Peterborough (a) 1994
541	DAVID W. PRESCOTT, Choppington, Northumberland	Stuart Pearce	v Luton (FLC f) 1989
542	WILLIAM JAMES EATON, Blaenau Ffestiniog, Gwynedd	Trevor Hockey	v Burnley (h) 1962
543	MATTHEW MAWSON, Spondon, Derby	Stuart Pearce	v Everton (FMC f) 1989
544	JAMES KIFER, Semilong, Northampton	Stuart Pearce	v Coventry City (FLC 4) 1991
545	R.C.A. GREY, Wimbledon, London	Nigel Clough	v Tottenham (FLC s/f 2) 1992
546	STEVE PLEWS, Knighton, Leicester	Stuart Pearce	v Liverpool (EC 1.1) 1978
547	KIERAN JAMES INGRAM, Berwick-upon-Tweed	At just 18 months old, too young to choose!	
548	D. BURROWS, Bletchley, Milton Keynes	Stuart Pearce	v Ajax (EC s/f 1) 1980
549	D. LOAT, Chelsea, London	Tommy Capel	
550	HAROLD & COLIN WHITE, The Park, Nottm	Tommy Graham/Bob McKinlay/Stuart Pearce	v Luton (FAC f) 1959
551	PHILIP BAMFORD, Ilkeston, Derbyshire	Trevor Francis	v Cologne (EC s/f 1) 1979
552	CLARE WALKER, Skegness, Lincs	Colin Cooper	
553	DAVID JOHN SWANWICK, Gresley, Nottm	Kenny Burns	v Cologne (EC s/f 1) 1979
554	GRAHAM HUNTER, West Bridgford, Nottm	Nigel Clough	v Auxerre (UEFA 2-2) 1995
555	RICHARD STOCKEN, Holmes Chapel, Crewe, Cheshire		
556	IAN FORSYTHE, Oakham, Rutland	Stuart Pearce	v Leicester City (h) 1994
557	RICHARD NAYLOR, Haddenham, Ely, Cambs	Peter Shilton	v Malmo (EC f) 1979
558	MIKE HARRIS, Bramhall, Stockport	Duncan McKenzie	v Man United (a) 1977
559	SEAN McAULIFFE, Glasheen, Cork, Eire	Garry Birtles	v Hamburg (EC f) 1980
560	NICK OPACIC, Gedling Village, Nottm	John Robertson	v Peterborough (a) 1994
561	P.H. JAMES, Wokingham, Berkshire	Joe Baker	v Luton (FAC f) 1959
562	TIM GOUGH, Sandiacre, Nottm	Joe Baker	v Tottenham (FLC s/f 2) 1992
563	DAVE WINDROSS, Barlby, Selby, Yorkshire	Fred Scott	
564	GAVIN FABLE, Lincoln	Stuart Pearce	v Sheffield Wed (a) 1995
565	KARL FABLE, Lincoln	Stuart Pearce	v Arsenal (FAC 6) 1988
566	K. ALLEN, Hurst Green, Halesowen	Kenny Burns	v Malmo (EC f) 1979
567	LINDSEY M. JESSOP, Oakwood, Hartlepool	John McGovern	v Luton (FLC f) 1989
568	BEN KILMISTER-BLAND,Shouldham, Norfolk	Stuart Pearce	v Malmo (EC f) 1979
569	DAVID WASS, Sutton-in-Ashfield, Notts	Jim Baxter	v Man United (a) 1977
570	RICHARD BEAL, Arnold, Nottm	John Robertson	v Luton (FAC f) 1959
571	PETER HOLLINGWORTH, Woodthorpe, Nottm	Bob McKinlay	v Everton (FAC 6) 1967
572	DARREN BALL, Norwich, Norfolk	Peter Shilton	v Norwich City (h) 1997
573	JONATHAN RYCROFT, Carlton, Nottm	Stuart Pearce	v Tottenham (FLC s/f 2) 1992
574	RICHARD J. ADCOCK, Corby Glen, Grantham	Kenny Burns	v Liverpool (EC 1.1) 1978
575	ANDY GETTINGS, Abbeydale, Gloucester	Stuart Pearce	v Man United (a) 1994
576	MICHAEL CARRETT, Grays, Essex	Stuart Pearce	v Middlesbrough (h) 1998
577	PHIL SHEPHERD, Castle Bromwich	Peter Shilton	v Malmo (EC f) 1979
578	LEE M. TOMBS, Kirton, Newark	Stuart Pearce	v Peterborough (a) 1994
579	MICHAEL PINTO, Friern Barnet, London	John Robertson	v Aston Villa (h) 1986

	Subscriber name	Favourite Player	Favourite Match
580	ROBERT PAUL MARTINSON, Aspley, Nottm	Sammy Chapman	v Leeds (FLC s/f 1) 1978
581	ADRIAN LOVE, West Bridgford, Nottm	Stuart Pearce	v Tottenham (FLC s/f 2) 1992
582	FRAZER MORRIS, Arnold, Nottm	Des Walker	v Hamburg (EC f) 1980
583	G.C. BOND, Burbage Manor, Southwell, Nottm	Stuart Pearce	v Tottenham (FLC s/f 2) 1992
584	SIMON R.R. CASAJUANA, Hounslow, Middlesex		
585	BRIAN ANTONY CASAJUANA, Grimsby, N.E. Lincs		
586	JAMES CROSBY, Cottingham, East Yorkshire	Stuart Pearce	v Man United (a) 1994
587	SIMON CROSBY, Cottingham, East Yorkshire	Stuart Pearce	v West Ham (FAC s/f) 1991
588	MARK S. COLLAR, Great Yarmouth, Norfolk	John Robertson	v Malmo (EC f) 1979
589	DENNIS HOBBS, Arnold, Nottm	Ian Storey-Moore	v Everton (FAC 6) 1967
590	STUART WILSON, Cromford, Matlock, Derbyshire	Duncan McKenzie	v Luton (FAC f) 1959
591	IAN MIDDUP, Underwood, Nottm	Stuart Pearce	v Malmo (UEFA 1-2) 1995
592	DAVID HENRY HENTON, Wilford Village, Nottm	John Robertson	v Liverpool (EC 1-1) 1978
593	JOHN BARRY WILSON, Mansfield Woodhouse, Notts	Stuart Pearce	v Malmo (EC f) 1979
594	SIMON HILL, Heckington, Sleaford, Lincs	Stuart Pearce	v Middlesbrough (h) 1998
595	CATHY COUPE, Castle Donington, Derbyshire	John Robertson	v Hamburg (EC f) 1980
596	BEN PARKES, Wordsley, West Midlands	Steve Stone	
597	ALAN BRYANT, Feltham, Middlesex	Garry Parker	v Luton (FLC f) 1989
598	R. FISHER, Eastwood, Nottm	Stuart Pearce	v Everton (FAC 6) 1967
599	BRYAN FAWCETT, Washinborough, Lincoln	Pierre Van Hooijdonk	
600	MYLES CARROLL, Carnew, Co Wicklow, Eire	John Robertson	v Hamburg (EC f) 1980
601	WILLIAM G.S. CASTLE, East Bridgford, Nottm	John Robertson	v Malmo (EC f) 1979
602	CHRISTOPHER DAVID BOWRON, Cotgrave, Notts	Roy Keane	v Tottenham (FLC s/f 2) 1992
603	MICHAEL JOHN ANDREW, Newark, Notts	Ian Bowyer	v Man City (FAC 4) 1974
604	ROB BROWN & DONNA GARRATT, Hucknall, Nottm	Stuart Pearce/Pierre Van Hooijdonk	v Middlesbrough (h) 1998
605	DAVID BATES, Mansfield, Notts	Pierre Van Hooijdonk	v Norwich City (h) 1997
606	MOIRA & FREDERICK FURNESS, North Shields, Tyne & Wear	Jackie Milburn	Newcastle v Ujpesti Dozsa (ICFC f 1) 1969
607	FRED LEE, Ford, Plymouth, Devon	Many players	Many games!
608	CHRIS TURNER, Islington, London	John Robertson	v Man City (FAC 4) 1974
609	ARTHUR JAMES DALE, Stapleford, Nottm	Bob McKinlay	v Everton (FAC 6) 1967
610	FRANK WELTON, Carlton, Nottm	Bob McKinlay	v Luton (FAC f) 1959
611	R.F. SCHILLER, Cuddington, Northwich, Cheshire	Ian Storey-Moore	v Man United (a) 1996
612	J. GOULD, Bulwell, Nottm	Stuart Pearce	v Cologne (EC s/f 1) 1979
613	Dr DAVID HUTCHINSON, Aldershot, Hants	Ian Storey-Moore/Stuart Pearce	v Everton (FAC 6) 1967
614	SIMON HUDSON, Ilkeston, Derbyshire	John Robertson	v Bristol City (FLC s/f 2) 1989
615	GRACE & GEOFF FYLES, West Bridgford, Nottm	Bob McKinlay	v Luton (FAC f) 1959
616	JOHN D. LAWRIE, Groby, Leicester	Stuart Pearce	v Southampton (FLC f) 1979
617	GEOFFREY GERALD GOOCH, Chilwell, Beeston, Nottm	Stuart Pearce	v Luton (FAC f) 1959
618	TONY BROWN, Beeston, Nottm	Ian Storey-Moore	v Luton (FAC f) 1959
619	LINDSAY BURRETT, Maidstone, Kent	Stuart Pearce	v Luton (FLC f) 1989
620	THOMAS G. ELDRED, Walkeringham, Doncaster	Pierre Van Hooijdonk	v Middlesbrough (h) 1998
621	LAWRENCE BARBER, Nottingham	Stuart Pearce	v Cologne (EC s/f 1) 1979
622	MATTHEW DEAVES, Woodsetts, Nr Worksop, Notts	Trevor Francis	v Man United (h) 1984
623	DENIS G. SUTTON, Ickenham, Middlesex	Stuart Pearce	v Malmo (EC f) 1979
624	DARREN STURGESS, Gedling, Nottm	Stuart Pearce	v Cologne (EC s/f 1) 1979
625	ATMAN MEHTA, Cheltenham, Glos		
626	P. BAXTER, Tilehurst, Reading		
627	AIDAN GRAEME-TURNER, Greatham, Hants	Stuart Pearce	v Southampton (FMC f) 1992
628	ADRIAN MARK CAFFERY, Droitwich Spa, Worcs	Stuart Pearce	v Auxerre (UEFA 2 leg 1) 1995
629	PETER SCOTT, Arnold, Nottm	Stuart Pearce	Football!
630	STEVE PEARCE, Gosport, Hants	Stuart Pearce	v Man United (a) 1994
631	CHRISTOPHER FRANCUZ, Newton, Alfreton, Derbys	Stuart Pearce	v Sheffield Wed (a) 1995
632	DANIEL TAYLOR, Sibthorpe, Nr Newark, Notts	Stuart Pearce	v Tottenham (FLC s/f 2) 1992
633	GRAHAM WARD, Beeston Rylands, Nottm	Stuart Pearce	v Man United (h) 1984
634	SIMON COCKS, Larkhall, Bath	Stuart Pearce	v Middlesbrough (h) 1998
635	DAVID DICKENS, Braunton, Devon		
636	RICHARD MARRIOTT, RAF Laarbruch	Stuart Pearce	v Southampton (FLC f) 1979
637	MICHAEL CLIFFORD, Stapleford, Nottm	Stuart Pearce	v Luton (FLC f) 1989
638	P. WILLIAMSON, Sandiacre, Nottm	John Robertson	v Everton (FAC 6) 1967
639	NICHOLAS YOUNG, West Bridgford, Nottm	Colin Cooper	v Leicester City (h) 1994
640	JOHN FRANK BAKER, Nuthall, Notts	Ian Storey-Moore	v Everton (FAC 6) 1967
641	ANDREW MEACHAM, Long Eaton, Nottm	Stuart Pearce	v Derby County (a) 1994
642	PHIL GULLEN, Uxbridge, Middlesex	Ian Storey-Moore	v Derby County (a) 1969
643	MATTHEW LYMN ROSE, Arnold, Nottm	Stuart Pearce	v Malmo (EC f) 1979
644	MARTIN STRICKSON, Spalding, Lincs	Stuart Pearce	v Sheffield Wed (a) 1995
645	MARTIN HOUSE, Church Crookham, Fleet, Hants	Stuart Pearce	v Hamburg (EC f) 1980
646	CHRIS B. CONWAY, Blackheath, London	Stuart Pearce	v Liverpool (EC 1-1) 1978
647	COLIN DOUGLAS MELVILLE, West Bridgford, Nottm	Stuart Pearce	v Cologne (EC s/f 1) 1979
648	NORMAN PINKNEY, Kimberley, Nottm	Joe Baker	v Everton (FAC 6) 1967
649	STEVE CODLING, Selly Oak, Birmingham	Stuart Pearce	v West Ham (FAC s/f) 1991
650	ALLAN CLARKE, Kirkby-in-Ashfield, Notts	Stuart Pearce	v Cologne (EC s/f 2) 1979
651	URBANE COOPER, Pierrefonds, Canada	Bob McCall	v Luton (FAC f) 1959
652	NICHOLAS H. SKINNER, Woodthorpe, Nottm	Trevor Francis	v Middlesbrough (h) 1998
653	WILLIAM A. YEOMANS, Breaston, Derby	John Robertson	v Cologne (EC s/f 1) 1979
654	MICHAEL A. GAN, Horsforth, Leeds	Ian Storey-Moore	v Everton (FAC 6) 1967
655	PAUL COLCOMB, Balderton, Newark	Stuart Pearce	v Peterborough (a) 1994
656	GARY LEIVERS, Arnold, Nottm	Joe Baker/Stuart Pearce	v Liverpool (EC 1-1) 1978
657	ALAN DANCE, Chilwell, Nottm	Duncan McKenzie	v Everton (FAC 6) 1967
658	T.C.GILBERTSON, Ilkeston, Derby	Stuart Pearce	v Tottenham (FLC s/f 2) 1992
659	T. FERMIE, Ruddington, Nottm	Stuart Pearce	v Luton (FAC f) 1959
660	J.E. TOMKINS, Higher Whipton, Exeter, Devon	Stuart Pearce	v Hamburg (EC f) 1980
661	KENNETH WILLIAM CONGREAVE, Stapleford, Nottm	Ian Storey-Moore	v Everton (FAC 6) 1967
662	GONZALO GANGOITI, Bilbao, Spain	Pitxitxi	Athletic Club Bilbao 12 v Barcelona 1 1931
663	RICHARD A. KINGSLAND, Wollaton Park, Nottm	Tommy Capel	v Luton (FAC f) 1959
664	PAUL BENTLEY, Keyworth, Notts	Stuart Pearce	v Cologne (EC s/f 1) 1979
665	RON MARSHALL, Rainworth, Notts	Joe Baker	v Everton (FAC 6) 1967
666	PAUL EDEN-SMITH, Ravenstone, Coalville, Leics	Des Walker	v Celtic (UEFA 3-1) 1983
667	THOMAS EDEN-SMITH, Ravenstone, Coalville, Leics	Stuart Pearce	v Birmingham City (a) 1998
668	IAN JAMES WILLIAM THORNHILL, Eastwood, Nottm	Stuart Pearce	v Man United (h) 1994
669	P. BARAN, Burnham-on-Sea, Somerset	John Robertson	v Cologne (EC s/f 1) 1979
670	KAREN BRAITHWAITE, Mountsorrel, Leics	Stuart Pearce	v Leicester City (h) 1994
671	GORDON MACEY, QPR Historian, Woking, Surrey	Steve Burke	v Queens Park Rangers (a) 1993
672	ROBERTO PIAZZA, Lakeside, Cardiff	Stuart Pearce	v Malmo (EC f) 1979
673	NIGEL SMALLWOOD, Church Gresley, Derbyshire	Stuart Pearce	v West Ham (h) 1986
674	STEPHEN RAWLINSON, Rayners Lane, Harrow, Middx	John Robertson	v Cologne (EC s/f 1) 1979
675	A.F. VOCKINS, Croxton Kerrial, Nr Grantham, Lincs	Kenny Burns	v Hamburg (EC f) 1980
676	PAUL COLLINDRIDGE, Edwalton, Nottm	Steve Hodge/Duncan McKenzie	v Arsenal (FAC 6) 1988
677	DAVID FLETCHER, Dulwich Wood Park, London	Kenny Burns	v Cologne (EC s/f 2) 1979
678	SIMON HOLBROOK, Borrowash, Derby	Pierre Van Hooijdonk/Stuart Pearce	v Malmo (UEFA 1-2) 1995

	Subscriber name	Favourite Player	Favourite Match
679	MARK K. MAXWELL, Brackley, Northamptonshire	Peter Shilton	v Ipswich Town (h) 1983
680	CHRIS WALKER, Ashby-de-la-Zouch, Leics		
681	ALISTAIR RAMSAY, London W4	Stuart Pearce	v Man United (a) 1977
682	GRAHAM W. MARSON, Arnold, Nottm	Peter Shilton	v Everton (FAC 6) 1967
683	SIMON GIDDENS, Burton Lazars, Leics	Stuart Pearce	v Liverpool (FLC f rep) 1978
684	PETE WASHINGTON, Ravenstone, Leics	John Robertson	v Hamburg (EC f) 1980
685	LESLIE WEBSTER, Wilford, Nottm	Stuart Pearce	v Everton (FAC 6) 1967
686	DENNIS & GLENIS PINKETT, Keyworth, Notts	Eddie Bailey/Jack Burkitt	v Luton (FAC f) 1959
687	ROBERT GRAHAM, Bulwell, Nottm	John Robertson	v Everton (FMC f) 1989
688	D. THORNLEY, Aspley, Nottm	Ian Storey-Moore	v Malmo (EC f) 1979
689	AMANDA GREGORY, Puckeridge, Herts	Archie Gemmill	v Southampton (FMC f) 1992
690	J. RINGROSE, Romford, Essex		
691	STEVE MOORE, Blaenplwyf, Aberystwyth	Peter Grummitt	v Liverpool (EC 1-1) 1978
692	CAROLINE THURSTON, Long Bennington, Newark	Stuart Pearce	v Middlesbrough (h) 1998
693	SUSAN PINKETT, Keyworth, Notts	Duncan McKenzie	All Wembley Finals!
694	BRIAN HAYWOOD, Kettering, Northamptonshire		
695	NICOLA MARIE SHELTON, Attenborough, Nottm	Steve Hodge	v Everton (FMC f) 1989
696	DARRAN, ALISON & CHRISTOPHER MURR, Bridgnorth	Stuart Pearce	
697	DAVID BREWSTER, Carlton, Nottm	Stuart Pearce	v Luton (FAC f) 1959
698	MICHAEL J. SPENCER, Par, Cornwall	John Robertson	v Cologne (EC s/f 1) 1979
699	MARTIN BRYAN TOTTERDALE, Pontllanfraith, Gwent	Peter Shilton	v Malmo (EC f) 1979
700	SARAH JANE STREET, York	Stuart Pearce	v Man United (h) 1990
701	MARK BOLTON, Coleraine, Northern Ireland	Stuart Pearce	v Malmo (EC f) 1979
702	ROAR GUVAAG, Hølen, Norway	Nigel Clough	v Malmo (EC f) 1979
703	DONALD WRIGHT, Southwell, Nottm	John Robertson	v Sheffield United (a) 1957
704	HELEN, NEIL & CLARE BROWN, Mansfield, Notts	Stuart Pearce	v Peterborough (a) 1994
705	R.B. TATTERSALL, Gotham, Nottm	Ian Storey-Moore	v Cologne (EC s/f 1) 1979
706	SAM HEATH, Wash Common, Newbury, Berkshire	Stuart Pearce	v Peterborough (a) 1994
707	DAVID R. FARROW, Newport, Nr Brough, E. Yorks	Des Walker	v Luton (FLC f) 1989
708	R.A. NORRIS, Radlett, Herts	John Robertson	v Hamburg (EC f) 1980
709	GERALD CONNOLLY, Raunds, Northamptonshire	Stuart Pearce	v Liverpool (EC 1-1) 1978
710	JOHN HARRISON, Clumber Park, Worksop	Stuart Pearce	v Man United (a) 1977
711	PETER JOHN BANKS, Bourne, Lincs	John Robertson	v Everton (FAC 6) 1967
712	Mrs S. LAMMIMAN, Lincoln	Stuart Pearce	v Bayern Munich (UEFA 4-1) 1996
713	NICOLA BARTON, Lincoln	Stuart Pearce	v Everton (FMC f) 1989
714	PETER DAWSON, Rainworth, Mansfield, Notts	Stuart Pearce	v Hamburg (EC f) 1980
715	ANDREW TAYLOR, Carlton, Nottm	John Robertson/Stuart Pearce	v Cologne (EC s/f 1) 1979
716	JOHN ALLAN MILLS, Arnold, Nottm	Joe Baker	v Cologne (EC s/f 1) 1979
717	SYLVIA ACKROYD, Barton-under-Needwood, Staffs	Stuart Pearce	v Tottenham (FAC 5 rep) 1996
718	PAULINE TROUT, Cossall, Nottm	John Robertson	v Bristol Rovers (FAC 3) 1974
719	P. THORSEN, Shirebrook, Mansfield	Stuart Pearce	v Hamburg (EC f) 1980
720	E. ANNE WALTERS, Ruddington, Nottm	Bob McKinlay	v Luton (FAC f) 1959
721	LEE URBANSKI, Eastwood, Nottm	Peter Shilton	v Liverpool (EC 1-1) 1978
722	PETER KEAL, Blairgowrie, Randburg, Jo'burg, S. Africa	Peter Shilton	v Man United (a) 1977
723	A.J. TURNER, Bingham, Nottm	Joe Baker	v Everton (FAC 6) 1967
724	MICHAEL MELLING, Pleasley, Mansfield, Notts		
725	DAVE ATKINS, Ockbrook, Derby	Joe Baker	v Bolton Wanderers (FAC 3) 1968
726	DAVID JACKSON, Irlam, Greater Manchester	John Robertson	v Leeds United (FLC s/f 1) 1978
727	RICHARD ROGERS, Maidenhead, Berkshire	Martin O'Neill	v Malmo (EC f) 1979
728	MARK ALLIN, Peterborough	Johnny Metgod	v Malmo (EC f) 1979
729	GEOFF A. NEWHOUSE, Dibden Purlieu, Hampshire	Trevor Francis	v Malmo (EC f) 1979
730	IAIN NEWHOUSE, Dibden Purlieu, Hampshire	Trevor Francis	v Malmo (EC f) 1979
731	DAVID H. SIMPSON, Gedling, Nottm	Bob McKinlay	v Middlesbrough (FAC 5 (h)) 1947
732	D. ROBINSON, Parkside, Stafford	Pierre Van Hooijdonk	v Luton (FAC f) 1959
733	PHILIP GEORGE PLUME, Eggington, Derby	Duncan McKenzie	v Man City (FAC 4) 1974
734	JIM HAWKER, Lincoln	Ian Storey-Moore	v Man United (a) 1977
735	S.J. RICHARDSON, Retford, Notts	John Robertson	v Man United (a) 1977
736	PAUL WAYMAN, Allestree, Derby	John Robertson	v Liverpool (EC 1-1) 1978
737	NIGEL BRYN JONES, Skellingthorpe, Lincoln	Des Walker	v Derby County (a) 1994
738	CHRIS BRADBURY, Loughborough, Leics	John Robertson	v West Ham (FAC s/f) 1991
739	CHRIS CARR, Ettington, Warwickshire	Des Walker	v Derby County (a) 1994
740	NATALIE LOUISE WEBSTER, Birmingham	Stuart Pearce	v Sheffield United (h) 1998
741	JOHN CARTER, Market Rasen, Lincs	Nigel Clough	v Man United (FAC 6) 1989
742	LORNA HARRISON, Chester	Tony Woodcock/Des Walker	v West Ham (FAC s/f) 1991
743	DAVID F. HARRISON, Benwick, March, Cambs	Stuart Pearce	v Luton (FAC f) 1959
744	CRAIG FREEMAN, Codnor, Derbyshire	Steve Stone	v Swindon Town (h) 1997
745	RICHARD & LAURA FREEMAN, Codnor, Derbyshire	Kevin Campbell	v Charlton (h) 1997
746	S.J. SHAW, Rainworth, Notts	Stuart Pearce	v Luton (FAC f) 1959
747	ALASTAIR D. GRIFFIN, Keelby, Grimsby	Stuart Pearce	v Liverpool (EC 1.1) 1978
748	STEVE BUTLER, Kimberley, Nottm	Stuart Pearce	v Hamburg (EC f) 1980
749	DORA COBBIN, Radcliffe-on-Trent, Nottm	Too many to mention!	
750	JOHAN BERGVALL, Ankarsrum, Sweden	Peter Shilton	v Malmo (EC f) 1979
751	ALBERT EDWARD PETER THOMPSON, Boughton, Notts	John Barnwell	v Everton (FAC 6) 1967
752	ANDREW C. SMITH, Shenstone, Lichfield, Staffs	Stuart Pearce	v Everton (FAC 6) 1967
753	STEVE J. BENNETT, Church Lawton, Stoke on Trent	Peter Withe	v Cologne (EC s/f 1) 1979
754	PAUL BRINDLEY, Stanton-on-the-Wolds, Notts	Colin Cooper	v Man United (h) 1995
755	ANDREW GRIEVE, Eggborough, Goole, E.Yorkshire	Steve Stone	v Peterborough (a) 1994
756	MARK HALL, Carlton, Nottm	Joe Baker	v Everton (FAC 6) 1967
757	ANDREW HILL, Brookwood, Surrey	Stuart Pearce	v Malmo (EC f) 1979
758	S.W. GREGORY, West Bridgford, Nottm	John Robertson	v Sheffield Wed (a) 1995
759	JORDAN LEEMING, Stanley Common, Ilkeston	Stuart Pearce	v Sheffield Wed (a) 1995
760	RICHARD ALLEN, Hundleby, Lincs	John Robertson	v Middlesbrough (h) 1998
761	STUART J. ANNABLE, Swanwick, Derbyshire	Stan Collymore	v Derby County (a) 1994
762	DAVID BISHOP, Basildon, Essex	Peter Shilton	v Cologne (EC s/f 2) 1979
763	DAVID BREWSTER Jnr, Carlton, Nottm	Stuart Pearce	v Malmo (EC f) 1979
764	BOB GRESHAM, Rankin Park, NSW, Australia	Ian Storey-Moore	v Swindon (FAC 5 rep) 1967
765	BRIAN COLIN REARDON, Beechwood Park, Worcester	Bob McKinlay	v Luton (FAC f) 1959
766	CLAIRE REARDON, Malvern, Worcs	Nigel Clough	v Arsenal (FAC 6) 1988
767	PAUL SMITH, Ilkeston, Derbyshire	Stuart Pearce	
768	STEPHEN SAVILLE, Sandiacre, Nottm	John Robertson	v Malmo (EC f) 1979
769	Dr CHRISTOPHER EDWARD LAWRENCE, Greenwich, London	Ian Storey-Moore	v Malmo (EC f) 1979
770	FRANK MORGAN, West Hallam, Derbyshire	Joe Baker	v Man United (a) 1977
771	JOHN FERNLEY, Rise Park, Nottm	John Robertson	v Cologne (EC s/f 1) 1979
772	PETER MYATT, Wollaton, Nottm	Bob McKinlay	v Luton (FAC f) 1959
773	ANDREW PETER FRITCHLEY, Long Eaton, Nottm	Stuart Pearce	v Hamburg (EC f) 1980
774	JOHN MICHAEL OSWIN, Calverton, Nottm	Stuart Pearce	v Cologne (EC s/f 2) 1979
775	KEN PEARSON, Hucknall, Nottm	John Robertson	v Everton (FAC 6) 1967
776	ANTHONY SCOTT, Huthwaite, Sutton-in-Ashfield	Stuart Pearce	v Luton (FLC f) 1989
777	ADRIAN RICHES, Bramcote View, Nottm	Stuart Pearce	v Middlesbrough (h) 1998

	Subscriber name	Favourite Player	Favourite Match
778	MALCOLM LEECH, Selston, Nottm	Stuart Pearce	v Malmo (EC f) 1979
779	DAVID JOHN WINCHCOMBE, Arnold, Nottm	John Robertson	v Malmo (EC f) 1979
780	JAMES WILLIAMS, Kirkby-in-Ashfield, Notts	Ian Storey-Moore	v Liverpool (FLC f rep) 1978
781	PAUL RAYSON, Lancaster	Stuart Pearce	v Malmo (EC f) 1979
782	PHILIP GEORGE BROWN, Copmanthorpe, York	John Robertson	v Malmo (EC f) 1979
783	REG GODBEHERE, Gainsborough, Lincs	Trevor Francis	v Malmo (EC f) 1979
784	IAN JONES, New Basford, Nottm	John Robertson	v Man City (FAC 4) 19974
785	JOHN BAILEY, Uxbridge, Middlesex	Stuart Pearce	v West Ham (FAC s/f) 1991
786	I.R. DITCHFIELD, Trent Bridge, Nottm	Peter Shilton	v Man United (a) 1977
787	ANDREW BANDURKA, Putney, London	Stan Collymore	v Tottenham (FAC f) 1991
788	PAUL DOBSON, Adlington, Chorley, Lancs	Stuart Pearce	v Malmo (EC f) 1979
789	MICHAEL DOBSON, Adlington, Chorley, Lancs	Bob McKinlay	v Malmo (EC f) 1979
790	GEORGE THOMAS HOPKIN, Nottingham	Ian Storey-Moore	v Everton (FAC 6) 1967
791	MARTIN & JAMES HALLAM, Aspley Park, Nottm	Trevor Francis	v Malmo (EC f) 1979
792	STEVE BUTT, Chilwell, Beeston, Notts	John Robertson	v Cologne (EC s/f 1) 1979
793	NICHOLAS SIGGS, Radcliffe-on-Trent, Notts	Stuart Pearce	v Sheffield Wed (a) 1995
794	STEPHEN BLOW, Cleethorpes, Lincs	Stuart Pearce	v Sheffield Wed (a) 1995
795	GEOFF ALLMAN, Essington, Wolverhampton	Doug Lishman	v Sheffield United (a) 1957
796	IAN & MAGGIE PEARCE, Hayes, Middlesex	Stuart Pearce	Stuart Pearce's Testimonial 1996
797	IAN McGLASHAN, Sedlescombe, Battle, East Sussex	John Robertson	v Hamburg (EC f) 1980
798	PARMAVIR SINGHA, Leamington Spa, Warwicks	Viv Anderson	v Hamburg (EC f) 1980
799	PAUL EDWARDS, Stoke Golding, Warwickshire	Steve Chettle	v Leicester City (h) 1994
800	PETER FROGSON, Wollaton, Nottm	Stuart Pearce	v Man United (h) 1984
801	STEVE BRAY, London NW6	Archie Gemmill	v Tottenham (h) 1978
802	PAUL HOLMES, Carlton, Nottm	Stuart Pearce	v Liverpool (FLC f rep) 1978
803	FRED LLEWELLYN HOPKIN, Nottm	Tommy Lawton	v Malmo (EC f) 1979
804	RAY GREENWOOD, Brighton, E. Sussex	Bob McKinlay	v Cologne (EC s/f 2) 1979
805	STANLEY M. LEES, Radmanthwaite, Pleasley, Notts	John Robertson	v Luton (FAC f) 1959
806	SHAYNE DORRIAN, Yeovil, Somerset	Stuart Pearce	v Man United (a) 1994
807	DAVID G. INGHAM, Worksop, Notts	Stuart Pearce	v Middlesbrough (h) 1998
808	ANDREW GORDON SEMPLE, Redcar, Cleveland	Stuart Pearce	v Middlesbrough (h) 1998
809	DAVID HOBSON, Hereford	John Robertson	v Everton (FAC 6) 1967
810	GRAHAM WOODWARD, Nuthall, Nottm	Bob McKinlay	v Luton (FAC f) 1959
811	GEOFFREY JOHN BUDD, Sherwood, Nottm	Ian Storey-Moore	v Southampton (FLC f) 1979
812	IAN ROBINSON, Ruddington, Nottm	Stuart Pearce	v Tottenham (FAC f) 1991
813	WILLIAM YATES, Rustington, W. Sussex	John McGovern	v Malmo (EC f) 1979
814	CYRIL GEORGE, Aberfan, Merthyr Tydfil, Mid-Glamorgan	Bob McKinlay	v Celtic (UEFA 3.1) 1983
815	DAVID JOHN STERRY, Slough, Berkshire	Ian Storey-Moore	v Blackpool (h) 1977
816	SIMON WRIGHT, Soham, Ely, Cambs	Trevor Francis	v Middlesbrough (h) 1998
817	NEIL (FOOTITT), The Park, Nottm	John Robertson	v Liverpool (EC 1.1) 1978
818	JONATHAN HALL, Henleaze, Bristol		
819	JOHN C. BALDWIN, New Eltham, London	Larry Lloyd	v Malmo (EC f) 1979
820	TOM TOMLINSON, Hillarys, Perth, Australia	Stuart Pearce	Every game Pearce played in!
821	STUART CHADWICK, Mansfield, Notts	Peter Shilton	v Liverpool (FLC f rep) 1978
822	ROBERT B. RICHARDSON, Forest Town, Mansfield, Notts	Stuart Pearce	
823	HARRY PITCHFORD, Biggar, Lanarkshire	Bob McKinlay	v Luton (FAC f) 1959
824	SIMON STEPANIAN, Chilwell, Notts	John Robertson	v Liverpool (EC 1.1) 1978
825	CARL HARRIS, Harrow, Middlesex	Stuart Pearce	v Everton (FMC f) 1989
826	CATHERINE HEMMINGS, Thornton Cleveleys, Lancs	Stuart Pearce	v Luton (FLC f) 1989
827	MIKE EYRES, Kumeu, New Zealand	Joe Baker	v Swindon (FAC 5 rep 2) 1967
828	COLIN MICHAEL GENT, Long Eaton, Nottm	Joe Baker	v Everton (FAC 6) 1967
829	PETER McEVOY, West Martham, Norfolk	Martin O'Neill	v Southampton (FLC f) 1979
830	ROBERT BENTLEY, Carlton, Nottm	John Robertson	v Malmo (EC f) 1979
831	GERARD MILANO, Bestwood Park, Nottm	Stuart Pearce	v Arsenal (FAC 6) 1988
832	SIDNEY GEORGE BARNES, Clifton, Beds	Viv Anderson	v Luton (FAC f) 1959
833	MATTHEW YOUNG-McLAREN, Lenton, Nottm	Pierre Van Hooijdonk	v Leeds United (h) 1991
834	MATT THOMAS, Balderton, Newark	Stuart Pearce	v Arsenal (h) 1996
835	JOHN CROSS, Sutton St. James, Lincs	Stuart Pearce	v Arsenal (FAC 6) 1988
836	EWAN FARR, Sherwood, Nottm		
837	ADAM EDWARDS, Ashgate, Chesterfield	Pierre Van Hooijdonk	v Derby County (a) 1994
838	J.A. GLYNN, Carlton-in-Lindrick, Notts	John Robertson	v Everton (FAC 6) 1967
839	ROBERT DAUCCIA, Radcliffe-on-Trent, Notts	John Robertson	v Malmo (EC f) 1979
840	CHARLES J. WHYTE, Woodthorpe, Nottm	John Robertson	v Luton (FAC f) 1959
841	DARREN IBELL, Woodthorpe, Nottm	Des Walker	v Peterborough (a) 1994
842	GAVIN ATKINSON, Somercotes, Alfreton, Derbys	John Robertson	v Everton (FMC f) 1989
843	M. BADDER, Ilkeston, Derbyshire	Duncan McKenzie	v Man City (FAC 4) 1974
844	B.A. DABELL, Whitemoor Estate, Nottm	Stuart Pearce	v Luton (FAC f) 1959
845	PETER WALLIS, Abinger Common, Surrey	Wally Ardron	v Luton (FAC f) 1959
846	PAUL NAYLOR, York	Stuart Pearce	v Middlesbrough (h) 1998
847	THERESA FURY, Kilcreggan, Dunbartonshire	John Robertson/Stuart Pearce	v Malmo (EC f) 1979
848	JOHN HAYES, Sheffield	Stuart Pearce	v Man United (a) 1978
849	In loving memory of DENIS WHAYMAN from Nottingham 18th September1923 - 14th March1998		
850	PAUL WHAYMAN, Seagrave, Leics & MATTHEW WRATE, Nottm	Stuart Pearce/Ian S.-Moore	v Lyon (UEFA) 1996 & Everton 1967
851	NEIL STRUTHERS, Truro, Cornwall	Stuart Pearce	v Malmo (EC f) 1979
852	TONY WILKINS, Ingham, Lincoln	John Robertson	v Cologne (EC s/f 1) 1979
853	DAVID LYON, Breaston, Notts	Garry Birtles	v Everton (FMC f) 1989
854	DAVID BLACKBURN, Thorpe, Newark, Notts	Kenny Burns	v Anderlecht (UEFA s/f 1) 1984
855	NICK HOULDSWORTH, Gatley, Cheadle, Cheshire	Des Walker	v Hamburg (EC f) 1980
856	CRAIG BARTRAM, Wollaton, Nottm	Stuart Pearce	v Luton (FLC f) 1989
857	MANDY DALY, Hamworthy, Poole, Dorset	John Robertson	v Malmo (EC f) 1979
858	IAN LYONS, Northampton	John Robertson	v Liverpool (EC 1.1) 1978
859	MARK SMITH, Spalding, Lincs	John Robertson	v Peterborough (a) 1994
860	A. ROLFE, Spalding, Lincs	Bob McKinlay	v Celtic (UEFA 3.2) 1984
861	ANTHONY FRANCIS DORAN, Newthorpe, Nottm	Bob McKinlay/Steve Stone	v Luton (FAC f) 1959
862	DAVE SIMKISS, Sandiacre, Nottm	Calvin Palmer	v Luton (FAC f) 1959
863	JAMES P. JONES, Hasland, Chesterfield	Nigel Clough	v Tottenham (FLC 5 rep) 1990
864	SIMON CROWSTON, Alkborough, Scunthorpe, Lincs	Stuart Pearce	v West Ham (FAC s/f) 1991
865	ROB ROY ANDREW KEELER, Birchwood, Lincoln	Stuart Pearce	v Tottenham (FLC 5 rep) 1990
866	MARTIN DALLAS, Thorne, Doncaster	Stuart Pearce	v Cologne (EC s/f 1) 1979
867	KEITH RANGASAMY, Croydon, Surrey	John Robertson	v Malmo (EC f) 1979
868	MICHAEL J. PHIPPS, Burnbridge, Harrogate	Barry Lyons	v West Ham (FAC s/f) 1991
869	DARREN LEE ABBOTT, Barnby Dun, Doncaster	Stuart Pearce	v Man United (h) 1984
870	KAREN, STAN, STEPH & STEPHEN CLARK, Eastwood, Notts	Ian Storey-Moore	v Everton (FAC 6) 1967
871	BARRIE WOOD, Bacup, Rossendale, Lancs	Johnny Metgod	v Cologne (EC s/f 1) 1979
872	LEE SHOOTER, Hucknall, Nottm	Stuart Pearce	v Tottenham (FLC s/f 2) 1992
873	ANDY WALDEN, Woodthorpe, Nottm		
874	KEVIN DAYBELL, Underwood, Notts	Stuart Pearce	v Hamburg (EC f) 1980
875	ANDREW & SUSANNE WHITMORE, Worksop, Notts	Stuart Pearce	
876	MARK VICKERSTAFF, Edwalton, Nottm	Des Walker	

	Subscriber name	Favourite Player	Favourite Match
877	CLIVE BARBER, Arnold, Nottm	Ian Bowyer	v Cologne (EC s/f 1) 1979
878	PIPPA EDWARDS, Bilbrook, Wolverhampton	Stuart Pearce	v Sheffield Wed (a) 1995
879	NEIL SMITH, Old Sawley, Long Eaton, Nottm	John Robertson	v Cologne (EC s/f 2) 1979
880	JOY FOWLER, Wollaton, Nottm	Stuart Pearce	v Sheffield Wed (a) 1995
881	WILLIAM CASHMORE, Islington, London	Bert Bowery	v Cologne (EC s/f 1) 1979
882	ANDY LOWE, West Bridgford, Nottm	Steve Stone	v Peterborough (a) 1994
883	ROBERT CLARK, Sutton in Ashfield	John Robertson	v Everton (FAC 6) 1967
884	KEVIN MALPASS, Hibaldstow, Brigg, Lincs	John Robertson	v Liverpool (EC 1.1) 1978
885	PAUL NEWMAN, Newbold, Chesterfield	Stuart Pearce	v Cologne (EC s/f 2) 1979
886	DARRELL BOWSER, Eastwood, Notts	John Robertson	v Man City (FAC 4) 1974
887	ROBIN GUYMER, Oakington, Cambridge	Stuart Pearce	v Cologne (EC s/f 1) 1979
888	BARRY SPENCER, Newthorpe, Notts	Peter Shilton	v Hamburg (EC f) 1980
889	GRAHAM THOMAS BOWDEN, Spalding, Lincs	Steve Hodge	v Peterborough (a) 1994
890	STEPHEN METCALFE, Bushey, Watford, Herts	Nigel Clough	v Malmo (EC f) 1979
891	M.H. BUTLER, Rickmansworth, Herts	Stuart Pearce	v Peterborough (a) 1994
892	MICHAEL ATKINSON, Kimberley, Nottm	Ian Storey-Moore/John Robertson	v Malmo (EC f) 1979
893	SIMON ANDREW FLINN, Melton, Mowbray, Leics	Stuart Pearce	v Peterborough (a) 1994
894	PAUL RAYMOND ARCHER, Gosport, Hampshire	Ian Storey-Moore	v Man United (a) 1977
895	MARTIN SIMONS, Bekkevoort, Belgium		
896	MICHAEL HOLLINGWORTH, Asfordby, Leics	Joe Baker	v Everton (FAC 6) 1967
897	TREVOR J. COUPE, Southwell, Nottm	John Robertson	v Celtic (UEFA 3.2) 1984
898	DAVID R. WOOLLEY, Mansfield, Notts	John Robertson	v Everton (FAC 6) 1967
899	PETER SHIRRA, Aspley, Nottm	John Robertson	v Everton (FAC 6) 1967
900	GRAHAM BARNES, Brockley, London	Roy Dwight	v Luton (FAC f) 1959
901	DANIEL BARNES, Blackheath, London	Stuart Pearce	v Luton (FLC f) 1989
902	DAVID WOODS, Redfield, Bristol	Jack Connor (Bristol City)	Bristol Casuals 13 Ranella Ran. 3 1968
903	BARRY CLARKE, Sutton in Ashfield, Notts	Stuart Pearce	v Everton (FMC f) 1989
904	SUE EXTON, Oakwood, Derby	Colin Cooper	v Man United (h) 1994
905	PAUL ANCELL, Macclesfield, Cheshire	Ian Storey-Moore	v Luton (FAC f) 1959
906	BRIAN CLARKE, Rainworth, Mansfield	Ian Storey-Moore	v Everton (FAC 6) 1967
907	NATHAN K. HARRISON, Benwick, Cambs	Pierre Van Hooijdonk	v Stoke City (h) 1997
908	PETER LOWE, New Marske, Redcar, Cleveland	Stuart Pearce	v Everton (FMC f) 1989
909	PHILIP MAGNESS, Willenhall, West Midlands		
910	NICK PAYNE, Grantham, Lincs	Des Walker	v Chelsea 7-0
911	BOB TAYLOR, Grantham, Lincs	Ian Bowyer	v Cologne (EC s/f 1) 1979
912	ANTHONY W. HUBBARD, Toton, Beeston, Nottm	Peter Shilton	v Liverpool (EC 1.1) 1978
913	MICHAEL GEISSLER, Nürnberg, Germany	Tommy Wilson	v Luton (FAC f) 1959
914	NICOLA MASON, Kirkby in Ashfield, Notts	Pierre Van Hooijdonk	v West Ham (h) 1997
915	ROBERT J. NADIN, Sutton Bonington, Notts	Duncan McKenzie	v Middlesbrough (h) 1998
916	MARTIN LEE, Beckenham, Kent	John Robertson	v Arsenal (FAC 6) 1988
917	RICHARD GLENN BOOTH, Oswaldwick, York	Stuart Pearce	v Luton (FLC f) 1989
918	PHIL NEWPORT, Sutton Coldfield, West Midlands		
919	GREG MEEK, Kingswinford, West Midlands	Steve Stone	v Middlesbrough (h) 1998
920	GARETH G. DAVIES, Tregadillet, Cornwall	John Robertson	v Hamburg (EC f) 1980
921	TIM TOPHAM, Nottingham	John Robertson	v Everton (FAC 6) 1967
922	JENNY RICHARDSON, Forest Fields, Nottm	Joe Baker	v Everton (FAC 6) 1967
923	C.A. FORMAN, West Bridgford, Nottm	Terry Hennessey	v Luton (FAC f) 1959
924	NORMAN LEATHERLAND, Arnold, Nottm	Wally Ardron/Doug Lishman	v Luton (FAC f)/v Hamburg 1980
925	DAVID LESLIE PRITCHETT, Wollaton Park, Nottm	Stuart Pearce	v Liverpool (FLC f rep) 1978
926	AMBER CHRISTIAN, Ravenshead, Nottm	Stuart Pearce	v Middlesbrough (h) 1998
927	KEVIN HURST, Woodthorpe, Nottm	John Robertson	v Cologne (EC s/f 1) 1979
928	RON GREATREX, Worksop, Notts	Stuart Pearce	v Hamburg (EC f) 1980
929	MATTHEW WILKINSON, Farnham, Surrey	Pierre Van Hooijdonk	'Swan Vesta'
930	ANDREA GREENWOOD, Putney, London	Steve Chettle	v Reading (h) 1998
931	TONY BALFE, Harlaxton, Grantham, Lincs	John Robertson	v Man City (FAC 4) 1974
932	MARK DAVIS, Meir Park, Stoke on Trent	Duncan McKenzie	v Man City (FAC 4) 1974
933	JONATHAN BULLOCK, Papplewick, Notts	Stuart Pearce	v Cologne (EC s/f 1) 1979
934	SHAUN RAWLINS, Chilmark, Wiltshire	Stuart Pearce	v Malmo (EC f) 1979
935	CHRISTOPHER JOHN LEWIS, Nuthall, Nottm	Joe Baker	
936	NICK SCOURFIELD, Sageston, Pembrokeshire	Stuart Pearce	v Man United (FAC 6) 1989
937	JOHN C. BARLOW, Radcliffe on Trent, Nottm	Stuart Pearce	v Crewe Alexandra (h) 1997
938	GARY TAYLOR, Chilwell, Nottm	Martin O'Neill	v Cologne (EC s/f 1) 1979
939	EDWARD JOHN WEBSTER-FEARN, Huthwaite, Notts	Stuart Pearce	v Sheffield Wed (a) 1995
940	ROB MEEK, Barnt Green, Birmingham	Stuart Pearce	v Everton (FAC 6) 1967
941	JASON COUPE, Mansfield, Notts		
942	JOE SARGISON, Maida Vale, London	Stuart Pearce	v Luton (FLC f) 1989
943	RICHARD BONSALL, Nottingham	Stuart Pearce	v Chelsea (h) 1991
944	SAMUEL ELLIOTT BRYAN, Mapperley, Nottm		
945	JAMES WELDON, Chalgrove, Oxon	Ian Storey-Moore	v Cologne (EC s/f 1) 1979
946	LYNDOM GRICE, Broxstowe		
947	STEPHEN WORRALL, Basford, Notts		
948	KEVIN & KAREN LOCKHART, Chilwell, Nottm	John Robertson	v Malmo (EC f) 1979
949	TERRY PERKINS, Springwood, NSW, Australia	Stuart Pearce	v Southampton (FLC f) 1979
950	RHYS MARK LESLIE HOPKINSON, Bolsover, Derbyshire	Stuart Pearce	v Malmo (EC f) 1979
951	KARL BIRKINSHAW, Spondon, Derby	Stuart Pearce	v Anderlecht (UEFA f) 1984
952	BEN SHELTON, Attenborough, Nottm	Stuart Pearce	v Everton (FAC 6) 1967
953	NORMAN S. ORAM, West Bridgford, Nottm	John Robertson	v Hamburg (EC f) 1980
954	MICHAEL SPENCER ORAM, West Bridgford, Nottm	Trevor Francis	v Luton (FLC f) 1989
955	LORRAINE HAMMOND, Langwith Junction, Mansfield	Stuart Pearce	v Hamburg (EC f) 1980
956	BRETT JEFFRIES-SHAW, Wimbledon, London	Stuart Pearce	v Liverpool (EC 1.1) 1978
957	FRANK MITCHELL, Romanby, Northallerton, N. Yorks	Stuart Pearce	v Malmo (EC f) 1979
958	GRAHAM HICKS, Newark, Notts	Ian Storey-Moore	v Leeds (FLC s/f 1) 1978
959	VICTOR PAIGE, Berkhamsted, Herts	Kenny Burns	v Everton (FAC 6) 1967
960	GILES GARNETT, Wooburn Green, High Wycombe, Bucks	John Robertson	v Malmo (EC f) 1979
961	TONY WILSON, Chilwell, Nottm	John Robertson	v Hamburg (EC f) 1980
962	JOHN SAXTON, Edwalton, Nottm	John Robertson	v Liverpool (EC 1.1) 1978
963	MARTYN ALLEN, Toton, Beeston, Nottm	Stuart Pearce	v Liverpool (EC 1.1) 1978
964	DAVID J. GODFREY, Raglan, New Zealand	Peter Shilton	v Malmo 1979 & v Hamburg 1980
965	JOHN LOMAX, Oadby, Leicester	Joe Baker	v Everton (FAC 6) 1967
966	TARA JANE LOMAX, Oadby, Leicester	Stuart Pearce	v Leicester City (h) 1994
967	RICHARD DURANCE, Southwell, Nottm	Stuart Pearce	v Malmo (EC f) 1979
968	ALAN DAVIES, Worcester		
969	THOMAS MORGAN, Shrewsbury, Shropshire	Stuart Pearce	v Queens Park Rangers (h) 1994
970	MALCOLM PARNELL, Leicester	Jack Burkitt	v Luton (FAC f) 1959
971	MARK ANDREW RUSHBY, Kidlington, Oxon		
972	ANDREW STOTT, Sudbury, Suffolk	Stan Collymore	v Peterborough (a) 1994
973	ANGUS STOTT, Mendlesham, Suffolk	Stuart Pearce	v Everton (FAC 6) 1967
974	NIGEL STOTT, Bottesford, Notts	Stuart Pearce	v Peterborough (a) 1994
975	NICHOLAS AYERS, Morton, Southwell, Nottm	Stuart Pearce	v Tottenham (FLC s/f 2) 1992

SUBSCRIBERS

#	Subscriber name	Favourite Player	Favourite Match
976	DEAN FLEMING, Braintree, Essex	Stuart Pearce	v Tottenham (FLC s/f 2) 1992
977	DAWN ASHFORD, Longbridge, Birmingham	Nigel Clough	
978	MICK WOODS, Mansfield Woodhouse, Notts	Kenny Burns	v Malmo (EC f) 1979
979	KEITH & STEVE MILLER, Torquay, Devon	Stuart Pearce	v Cologne (EC s/f 1) 1979
980	DENNIS W. WOODS, Allington, Grantham, Lincs	Stuart Pearce	v Ipswich Town
981	R. CAPP, Stewkley, Bedfordshire	Stuart Pearce	v Man United (a) 1994
982	ROBERT PARKIN, Sandal, Wakefield, W. Yorks	John Robertson	v Coventry City (a) 1978
983	F.A. BARBER, Dersingham, Norfolk	Ian Storey-Moore	v Southampton (FLC f) 1979
984	DAVID J. SHARPE, Sheffield	Stuart Pearce	v Sheffield Wed (a) 1995
985	ALEX CZOPOWYJ, Helpringham, Sleaford, Lincs	Steve Stone	v Middlesbrough (h) 1998
986	P.A. HILL, North Chingford, London	Tony Woodcock	v Hamburg (EC f) 1980
987	RICHARD MARTIN, Seagrave, Leics	Colin Cooper	v Leicester City (h) 1994
988	JOHN M. RICHARDSON, Greenwich, London	Stuart Pearce	v Liverpool (FLC f rep) 1978
989	KEN BURROWS, Walmley, Sutton Coldfield, W. Mids	Stuart Pearce	v Luton (FAC f) 1959
990	BARRY CHARLES WHITING, Farnsfield, Newark, Notts	John Robertson	v Everton (FAC 6) 1967
991	AARON BETTS, Higham Ferrers, Northamptonshire		
992	LES HOUGHTON, Cotgrave, Notts	Stuart Pearce	v FC Cologne (EC s/f 1) 1979
993	JENNY SNOW, Tunbridge Wells, Kent	Stuart Pearce	v Reading (a) 1997
994	JOHN DICKSON, Burlington, Ontario, Canada	Pele	Brazil 4 Italy 1 (World Cup f) 1970
995	JOHN ROWLAND, Borrowash, Derby	Duncan McKenzie	v Everton (FAC 6) 1967
996	JASON ROBERT STODDART PAGE, Swithland, Leics	Des Walker	v Man United (FAC 6) (a) 1989
997	RAY TAYLOR, Nottingham	Horace Gager	v Everton (FAC 6) 1967
998	SUZANNE UPTON, St Leonards on Sea, E. Sussex	Stuart Pearce	v Hamburg (EC f) 1980
999	JOE & KATIE PARLATT, Southwell, Nottm	Stuart Pearce	v Hamburg (EC f) 1980
1000	ALEX & DANIEL BENSON, Morton, Southwell, Nottm	Pierre Van Hooijdonk	v Swindon Town (h) 1998
1001	JOHN WHITTAKER, Washingborough, Lincoln		
1002	GRAHAM WHITTAKER, Washingborough, Lincoln	Jack Burkitt	v Luton (FAC f) 1959
1003	NEIL SAWBRIDGE, Southampton	John Robertson	v Cologne (EC s/f 2) 1979
1004	RICHARD BUXTON, Worle, Weston-super-Mare	Stuart Pearce	v West Ham (FAC s/f) 1991
1005	TONY MURPHY, Poppintree, Dublin	Stuart Pearce	v West Ham (FAC s/f) 1991
1006	ADAM PETER HILTON, Donington, Lincs	Kevin Campbell	v Middlesbrough (h) 1998
1007	JEREMY M. THOMPSON, Calverton, Notts	Tony Woodcock	v Cologne (EC s/f 1) 1979
1008	TIM McCARTHY, Nuthall, Nottm	John Robertson	v Everton (FAC 6) 1967
1009	HARRY DOOLEY, Cranfield, Bedfordshire	Pierre Van Hooijdonk	Any game we win!
1010	D. WATSON, Langley Mill, Notts	Tommy Wilson	v Malmo (EC f) 1979
1011	CHRIS WARREN, Sibthorpe, Notts	Stuart Pearce	v Tottenham (FAC f) 1991
1012	PAUL BRAMWELL, Holton Le Moor, Lincs	Pierre Van Hooijdonk	v Malmo (EC f) 1979
1013	ROGER GREAVES, Cape Town, South Africa	Colin Cooper	v Gillingham, Div 3 South (h) 1950
1014	CHRISTOPHER GREAVES, Putney, London	Stuart Pearce	v Middlesbrough (h) 1998
1015	RUSSELL LEECH, West Bridgford, Nottm	Stuart Pearce	v Leeds (FLC s/f 1) 1978
1016	ANDREW JOHNSON, Alton, Hampshire	John Robertson	v Chelsea (h) 1991
1017	Master A. MORLEY, Long Eaton, Nottm	Pierre Van Hooijdonk	v Wolves (h) 1998
1018	CORY TIDSWELL, Beeston, Nottm	Chris Bart-Williams	v Reading (h) 1998
1019	WADE ANDERSON, Clifton, Nottm	Stuart Pearce	v Aston Villa (h) 1986
1020	DAVID ROBERT COOK, South Normanton, Derbyshire	Neil Webb	v Derby County (a) 1989
1021	CHRISTOPHER HODGE, Bricket Wood, St Albans, Herts	Stuart Pearce	
1022	TERRY CHAPMAN, Beckingham, Doncaster	Ian Storey-Moore	v Everton (FAC 6) 1967
1023	ROBERT HOLLIS, Whatton, Notts	Joe Baker	v Everton (FAC 6) 1967
1024	GARY BOSWORTH, Warmington, Peterborough	Stuart Pearce	v Luton (FLC f) 1989
1025	IAVA PARAPA-FALVEY, Wollaton, Nottm	Stuart Pearce	
1026	GEOFFREY MACPHERSON, West Bridgford, Nottm	Bob McKinlay	
1027	NEIL MACPHERSON, Greensboro, North Carolina, USA	Joe Baker	v Burnley (a) 1967
1028	LEE ALAN FRETWELL, Ilkeston, Derbyshire	Stuart Pearce	v Luton (FLC f) 1989
1029	ANDY FROST, Stevington, Bedford	John Robertson	v Coventry City (a) 1978
1030	MIKE ALLWOOD, Broughton Astley, Leics	Stuart Pearce	v Malmo (EC f) 1979
1031	C. JONES, Stourport-on-Severn, Worcs		v Malmo (EC f) 1979
1032	DAVE HARRIS, Sherwood Rise, Nottm	Stuart Pearce	v Malmo (EC f) 1979
1033	JOHN BOWNS, Colwick, Nottm		
1034	STEVEN SWIFT, Arnold, Nottm	John Robertson	v Coventry City (a) 1978
1035	MARK BLAKE, Haxton, Salisbury	Colin Cooper	v Middlesbrough (h) 1998
1036	MICHAEL FORD, Halifax, W. Yorks	Andy Johnson	v Reading (h) 1998
1037	ANDREW FORD, Halifax, W. Yorks	Stan Collymore	v Reading (h) 1998
1038	DAVID & BEN FORD, Halifax, W. Yorks	Every Forest player!	v Reading (h) 1998
1039	TANIA WALKER, Oakwood, Derby	Pierre Van Hooijdonk	v West Bromwich A. (a) 1998
1040	LEON JENIEC, Severn Stoke, Worcester	Ian Storey-Moore	
1041	DAVID KUJAWA, Nagoya, Japan		
1042	GARY N. MASKELL, Portishead, Bristol	Stuart Pearce	v Wimbledon (a) 1995
1043	IAN DAVID MASON, Taunton, Somerset	Stuart Pearce/Garry Birtles	v Wimbledon (a) 1995
1044	DAVID DRAKE, Nuthall, Nottm	Stuart Pearce	v West Ham (FAC s/f) 1991
1045	HENRY A. HARRISON, Mapperley Park, Nottm	Ian Storey-Moore	v Man United (h) 1957
1046	RICHARD H. HARRISON, Cheltenham, Glos	Stuart Pearce	v Cologne (EC s/f 1) 1979
1047	MATTHEW EDWARDS, Crossgates, Leeds	John Robertson	v Cologne (EC s/f 1) 1979
1048	DAVID MEADS, Rowlands Castle, Hampshire	Joe Baker	v Everton (FAC 6) 1967
1049	PETER ROWSON, Wollaton Park, Nottm	Stuart Pearce	v Liverpool (h) 1996
1050	KEITH McLEAN, Torry, Aberdeen	John Robertson	v Malmo (EC f) 1979
1051	ANNE MARKS, Arnold, Nottm	Stuart Pearce	v Liverpool (EC 1.1) 1978
1052	S.W. HAYES, Loughborough, Leics	Stuart Pearce	v Everton (FAC 6) 1967
1053	TOM FREESTON, Spalding, Lincs	Steve Stone	
1054	GREG PICKETT, Belton Lane, Grantham	Stuart Pearce	v West Ham (FAC s/f) 1991
1055	DAVID JOHN GILLIAN, Grasscroft, Oldham	Stuart Pearce	v Everton (FMC f) 1989
1056	PETR ZAPLETAL, Uherske Hradiste, Czech Republic	Peter Shilton	v Everton (FMC f) 1989
1057	JOAN PAMELA ABBOTT, Radcliffe-on-Trent, Notts	Steve Chettle	v Hamburg (EC f) 1980
1058	IAN McCLEAN, Chilwell, Nottm	John Robertson	v Cologne (EC s/f 1) 1979
1059	G. GIBAS, Hoeilaart, Belgium		
1060	DAVID T. GODDARD, Whitchurch, Cardiff	Roy Dwight	v Luton (FAC f) 1959
1061	EDWIN (EDGAR) AUSTIN, Sneinton, Nottm	Archie Gemmill/John Robertson	v Liverpool (FLC f) 1978
1062	JOHN GODDARD, Swindon, Wilts	Steve Stone	v Sunderland (h) 1994
1063	RACHAEL BUCKLEY, Northfield, Birmingham	Stuart Pearce	v Malmo (UEFA 1.2) 1995
1064	PHILIP WELLS, South Croydon, Surrey	John Robertson	v Cologne (EC s/f 2) 1979
1065	MARK JOPLING, St Margarets, Middlesex	Stuart Pearce	v Liverpool (EC 1.1) 1978
1066	LESLIE ERIC VICTOR PERRY, Nottm	Sammy Chapman	v Malmo (EC f) 1979
1067	CHRISTOPHER BURTON, Grantham, Lincs		
1068	RAYMOND SHAW, Sutton-in-Ashfield, Notts	Duncan McKenzie	v Mansfield Town (a) 10/1/53
1069	IAN COPPING, West Bridgford, Nottm	Ian Storey-Moore	v Liverpool (EC 1.1) 1978
1070	R.A. NUTT, Rise Park, Nottm	Wally Ardron	v Luton (FAC f) 1959
1071	CHARLES DAYBELL, Blackmore End, Braintree, Essex	Ian Storey-Moore & many others!!	v Everton (FAC s/f) 1967
1072	CLARE DAYBELL, Hull	Stuart Pearce	v West Ham (FAC s/f) 1991
1073	KATIE DAYBELL, Ware, Herts	John Robertson	v Middlesbrough (h) 1998
1074	PETER BRIXTOFTE, Farum, Denmark	Stuart Pearce	v Queens Park Rangers (h) 1996
1075	A.R. & T.R. QUANTOCK, Bower Hinton, Somerset	Stuart Pearce	v Southampton (h) 1995
1076	DAVID JOHNSTON, Newtown Abbey, Co Antrim, N. Ireland	Stuart Pearce	v Notts County (h) 1993
1077	STUART GRIMSHAW, Calverton, Nottm	Stuart Pearce	v Bristol City (FLC s/f 2) 1989
1078	MARK ESSWOOD, Arnold, Nottm	Stuart Pearce	v Liverpool (EC 1.1) 1978
1079	STEVEN KEELING, Newthorpe, Notts	Stuart Pearce/Steve Stone	v Auxerre (UEFA 2.1) 1996
1080	IAN & PIERCE EVLEY, Devizes, Wilts	Stuart Pearce	v Cologne (EC s/f 1) 1979
1081	BARRIE EVLEY, Wollaton, Nottm	Wally Ardron	v Malmo (EC f) 1979
1082	RAYMOND MICHAEL SCOTT, St Helier, Jersey, C.I.	Peter Shilton	v Malmo (EC f) 1979
1083	ROB & JANE ARCHER, Greasbrough, S. Yorkshire	John Robertson	v Everton (FAC 6) 1967
1084	IAN CHRISTOPHER BARKER, Didcot, Oxon	Stuart Pearce	v Malmo (EC f) 1979
1085	ROBERT JOHN SMEDLEY, Ashford, Middlesex	John Robertson	v Sheffield Wed (a) 1995
1086	DAVID & KATIE ROWSON, South Hykeham, Loncoln	Stuart Pearce	v Hamburg (EC f) 1980
1087	DONALD NANNESTAD, Lincoln		
1088	PETER HIGGINBOTHAM, Lea, Lincs	Stuart Pearce	v Cologne (EC s/f 2) 1979
1089	JOHN & JANICE HEPWORTH, Retford, Notts	Joe Baker	v Man United (h) 1969
1090	GRAHAM J. PALING, Boston, Lincs	Stuart Pearce	v Everton (FAC 6) 1967
1091	MATTHEW MOORE, Newcastle-under-Lyme, Staffs	Stuart Pearce	v Peterborough (h) 1994
1092	P. WILLIAMS, Arnold, Nottm	John Robertson	v Everton (FAC 6) 1967
1093	MICK McCONKEY, Luton, Beds		v Luton (FAC 3 rep) 1971
1094	HENRY PARTA, Mantyharju, Finland	John Robertson	v Luton (FLC f) 1989
1095	ROBERT IAIN PHILLIPS, Harpenden, Herts	Stuart Pearce	v Sheffield Wed (a) 1995
1096	JAMES DILLON, Sandiacre, Notts	Des Walker	v Man City (h) 1990
1097	J.W. GIBSON, Northampton	John Robertson	v Tottenham (FAC 5 rep) 1996
1098	STEVEN HOLLAND, Nottingham	Stuart Pearce	v Malmo (EC f) 1979
1099	JOHN L. HUTCHINSON, Heanor, Derbyshire	Martin O'Neill	v Everton (FAC 6) 1967
1100	JAMES BYRON, Nuthall, Nottm	Peter Shilton	v Luton (FAC f) 1959
1101	RICHARD BLACKAMORE, Kirton, Boston, Lincs	Steve Stone	v Middlesbrough (h) 1998
1102	STEPHEN SPENCE, Beeston, Nottm	Des Walker	v Tottenham (FLC s/f 2) 1992
1103	ANDREW GRAHAM, Gosport, Hampshire	Pierre Van Hooijdonk	v Wolves (h) 1998
1104	DAVID WELLS, Newthorpe, Notts	Stuart Pearce	v Everton (FAC 6) 1967
1105	JEFFREY SIMS, Grovehill, Hemel Hempstead, Herts	Stuart Pearce	v Man United (a) 1994
1106	SILVANO TAYLOR, Mansfield, Notts	Joe Baker	v Everton (FAC 6) 1967
1107	DAVID BRINDLEY, Weddington, Nuneaton, Warwicks	Ian Storey-Moore	v Coventry City (h) 1970
1108	PETER PREECE, Southwell, Notts	Stuart Pearce	v Malmo (EC f) 1979
1109	MARTIN PREECE, Hallam, Notts	Trevor Francis	v Liverpool (EC 1.1) 1978
1110	RYSZARD IWANIAK, Woodley, Reading	John Robertson	v Liverpool (EC 1.1) 1978
1111	BARRY HUGHES, Bramcote, Nottm	Ian Storey-Moore	v Man City (FAC 4) 1974
1112	JIM LEDBETTER, West Bridgford, Nottm	Stuart Pearce	v Luton (FAC f) 1959
1113	RICHARD MILLER, London NW3	Stuart Pearce	v Tottenham (FAC f) 1991
1114	S. BURROWS, Eastwood, Notts		
1115	NEIL R. SMITH, Melbourne, Derbyshire	John Robertson	v Cologne (EC s/f 1) 1979
1116	ERIC UPTON, Hastings, East Sussex	Steve Hodge	v Southampton (FLC f) 1979
1117	NICHOLAS R. PERHAM, North Hill, Plymouth, Devon	Stuart Pearce	v Hamburg (EC f) 1980
1118	JOHN M. ROWLSTON, West Bridgford, Nottingham		
1119	CHRIS LEWIS, Guildford, Surrey	Peter Shilton	v Hamburg (EC f) 1980
1120	ROGER WASH, Newmarket		
1121	D. HAYLES, Cotgrave, Nottm		
1122	PETER R. MITCHELL, Mansfield Woodhouse, Notts	Stuart Pearce	v Liverpool (EC 1.1) 1978
1123	ROBERT GILLARD, Horndean, Hampshire	John Robertson	v Everton (FAC 6) 1967
1124	COLIN C. JOHNSON, Oxton Hill, Southwell, Notts	Stuart Pearce	v Malmo (EC f) 1979
1125	PAUL CLAYTON, White Court, Braintree, Essex	John Robertson	v Peterborough (a) 1994
1126	PETER A.J. DAVIS, Sleaford, Lincs	Stuart Pearce	v Hamburg (EC f) 1980
1127	PETER R. WARRINGTON, Gedling, Nottm	Ian Storey-Moore	v Everton (FAC 6) 1967
1128	DARREN J. BURLEY, Langley Mill, Notts	Stuart Pearce	v Man United (a) 1978
1129	MICK ELLIS, Hoton, Loughborough, Leics	Jack Burkitt	v Everton (FAC 6) 1967
1130	NEIL SYSON, Wandsworth, London	Ian Storey-Moore	v Man United (a) 1978
1131	VEGARD THONSTAD, Trondheim, Norway	Colin Cooper	v Newcastle (FAC 4) 1997
1132	ERIK AARSETH, Hamar, Norway	Stuart Pearce	v Luton (FAC f) 1959
1133	GRUNDE DALSØREN, Vennesla, Norway	Stuart Pearce	v Man United (a) 1994
1134	ROGER ANTHONSEN, Tananger, Norway	Steve Stone	v Newcastle (FAC 4) 1997
1135	ØYVIND MARCUSSEN, Gjoevik, Norway	Nigel Clough	v Man United (a) 1994
1136	INGE HAAGENSEN, Leknes, Norway	Archie Gemmill	v Derby (FAC 3) 1983
1137	HENRIK ANDERSSON, Vaargaarda, Sweden	Stuart Pearce	v Norwich City (h) 1997
1138	ARNE AMUNDSEN, Arendal, Norway	Stuart Pearce	v Hamburg (EC f) 1980
1139	HENRIK ROMCKE, Drammen, Norway	Nigel Clough	v Tottenham (h) 1993
1140	BJORN INGE BALLESTAD HAUG, Porsgrunn, Norway	Stuart Pearce	v Malmo (EC f) 1979
1141	STEINAR LERBREKK, Varhaug, Norway	Steve Stone	v Liverpool (h) 1996
1142	JOAR KOKKIN, Levanger, Norway	Stuart Pearce	v Sheffield Wed (a) 1995
1143	KRISTIAN GUNTVEDT, Lorenskog, Norway	Stuart Pearce	v Man United (a) 1994
1144	CARL ROBERTS, Bergen, Norway	Stuart Pearce	v Man United (a) 1994
1145	RONNY ROBERTS, Bergen, Norway	Stuart Pearce	v Man United (a) 1994
1146	KETIL KVAM, Fet, Norway	John Robertson	v Hamburg (EC f) 1980
1147	TROND ANDRÉ STORKSEN, Langesund, Norway	Stuart Pearce	v Sheffield Wed (a) 1995
1148	JAN CHR. HAUGLAND, Norway	Stuart Pearce	
1149	JANNE JOHANSSON, Nora, Sweden	Viv Anderson	v Malmo (EC f) 1979
1150	ALAN CARROLL, South Croydon, Surrey	Tommy Gaynor	v West Ham (FAC s/f) 1991
1151	STUART HILL, Gunthorpe, Notts	Stuart Pearce	v Norwich (h) 1997
1152	S.G. (GEOFF) PARKES, St Ives, Cornwall	Ian Storey-Moore	v Luton (FAC f) 1959
1153	STEVEN MARSH, Markham Moor, Notts	Stuart Pearce	v Malmo (EC f) 1979
1154	JASON SMART, Gleadless, Sheffield	Stuart Pearce	v Malmo (EC f) 1979
1155	KEVIN TAYLOR, Walesby, Newark, Notts	Stuart Pearce	v Liverpool (EC 1.1) 1978
1156	J.M. ADCOCK, Underwood, Nottm	Des Walker	v Hamburg (EC f) 1980
1157	NICHOLAS SHEPPARD, Norwich, Norfolk	John Robertson	v Man City (h) 1980
1158	KEITH WRIGHT, Linby, Nottm	Peter Shilton	The next one!
1159	RICHARD WATKINS, Old Marston, Oxford	John Robertson	v Hamburg (EC f) 1980
1160	NEIL SHOEBRIDGE, Beeston, Nottm	John Robertson	v Everton (FAC 6) 1967
1161	JOHN BUXTON, Radcliffe on Trent, Nottm	Stuart Pearce	v Everton (FAC 6) 1967
1162	HECTOR FREDERICK WOOD, Exmouth, Devon	Sam Hardy	v Luton (FAC f) 1959
1163	TREVOR BATES, Marehay, Ripley, Derbys	Stuart Pearce	v Leeds (FLC s/f) 1978
1164	A.G. BURROWS, Bestwood Park, Notts	John Robertson	v Tottenham (FLC s/f 2) 1992
1165	ANDREW LEACH, East Croydon, Surrey	Trevor Francis	v Everton (FMC f) 1989
1166	JOE DURANCE, Southwell, Nottm	Stuart Pearce	v Everton (FMC f) 1989
1167	AUSTIN FAIRLEY, Bothenhampton,Dorset	Mark Crossley	
1168	BENJAMIN T. WATKINSON, Hagwortham, Spilsby, Lincs	Pierre van Hooijdonk	v Cologne (EC s/f 1) 1979
1169	TREVOR JOHNSON, Lichfield, Staffs	Ian Storey-Moore	v Everton (FAC 6) 1967
1170	JOHN KERRY, Holbeach, Spalding, Lincs	Steve Stone	Stuart Pearce's Testimonial
1171	RICHARD HAMPSON-SMITH, Burton Joyce, Notts	John Robertson	v Man City (FAC 4) 1974
1172	TONY SPENCER, Screveton, Notts	Stuart Pearce	
1173	SIMON WESSON, Newark, Notts	Stuart Pearce	England v W. Germany 1966